ANCRENE WISSE

EARLY ENGLISH TEXT SOCIETY
No. 325
2005

ANCRENE WISSE
A CORRECTED EDITION OF THE TEXT IN CAMBRIDGE, CORPUS CHRISTI COLLEGE, MS 402, WITH VARIANTS FROM OTHER MANUSCRIPTS

BY

BELLA MILLETT

DRAWING ON THE UNCOMPLETED EDITION
BY
E. J. DOBSON

WITH A GLOSSARY AND ADDITIONAL NOTES
BY
RICHARD DANCE

Published for
THE EARLY ENGLISH TEXT SOCIETY
by the
OXFORD UNIVERSITY PRESS
2005

OXFORD
UNIVERSITY PRESS

Great Clarendon Street, Oxford OX2 6DP

Oxford University Press is a department of the University of Oxford.
It furthers the University's objective of excellence in research, scholarship,
and education by publishing worldwide in

Oxford New York

Auckland Cape Town Dar es Salaam Hong Kong Karachi
Kuala Lumpur Madrid Melbourne Mexico City Nairobi
New Delhi Shanghai Taipei Toronto

With offices in

Argentina Austria Brazil Chile Czech Republic France Greece
Guatemala Hungary Italy Japan Poland Portugal Singapore
South Korea Switzerland Thailand Turkey Ukraine Vietnam

Oxford is a registered trade mark of Oxford University Press
in the UK and in certain other countries

Published in the United States
by Oxford University Press Inc., New York

© Early English Text Society, 2005

The moral rights of the author have been asserted
Database right Oxford University Press (maker)

First published 2005

All rights reserved. No part of this publication may be reproduced,
stored in a retrieval system, or transmitted, in any form or by any means,
without the prior permission in writing of Oxford University Press,
or as expressly permitted by law, or under terms agreed with the appropriate
reprographics rights organisation. Enquiries concerning reproduction
outside the scope of the above should be sent to the Rights Department,
Oxford University Press, at the address above

You must not circulate this book in any other binding or cover
and you must impose this same condition on any acquirer

British Library Cataloguing in Publication Data
Data available

Library of Congress Cataloging in Publication Data
Data applied for

ISBN 0-19-722328-1   978-0-19-722328-4

1 3 5 7 9 10 8 6 4 2

Typeset by Anne Joshua, Oxford
Printed in Great Britain
on acid-free paper by
The Cromwell Press, Trowbridge, Wiltshire

PREFACE

The foundation of this edition is the edition of *Ancrene Wisse* which Eric Dobson left unfinished at his death in 1984; it also owes much to his published research on *Ancrene Wisse*.

His uncompleted edition included an Introduction, with a brief list of the manuscripts and versions, an account (summarizing his earlier research) of their relationship and contents, and a description of his principles and conventions of editing; an edited text with apparatus criticus (to 3. 417); and a Textual Commentary (to the end of Part 2), 'chiefly a discussion of the text and the reasons for my editorial decisions in forming it . . . and of its grammar and meaning'.

The first volume of the present edition includes a Textual Introduction, the edited text, and its apparatus criticus. The Textual Introduction follows the structure of Dobson's Introduction, and although it has sometimes been modified to incorporate later research, it is essentially a continuation of his work; the main departure from the original is that I have adopted rather different principles of editing. For overall consistency, the part of the text edited by Dobson has been re-collated and re-edited throughout, but his editorial decisions have been taken into account as part of the editing process. Volume 2 will include a General Introduction, a Textual Commentary, and Richard Dance's Glossary. The Textual Commentary will incorporate some of the material from Dobson's Commentary, with additional notes on the language by Richard Dance, but its scope has been extended to allow a fuller treatment of the content and sources of *Ancrene Wisse*. Since the volumes are not being published simultaneously, each has a separate bibliography.

I would like to thank the British Academy for the two-year research readership which helped me to complete this edition, and the AHRC for a semester's research leave to investigate the pastoral context of *Ancrene Wisse*; the Master and Fellows of Corpus Christi College, Cambridge, for a Visiting Fellowship and permission to use Cambridge, Corpus Christi College, MS 402; and the members of EETS Council (particularly the two readers of this edition, Ralph Hanna and Derek Pearsall) and its Editorial Secretary, Helen Spencer, for their advice and help. I also owe thanks to my present collaborator, Richard Dance, and my former collaborator, the late George Jack, for their expert and tactful advice, which has saved me from many errors and much improved the quality of the edited text; to Malcolm Parkes for his generosity with both palaeographical information and much-needed encouragement; to my fellow *Ancrene Wisse* scholars, particularly Nicholas Watson and Jocelyn Wogan-Browne, for sharing their unpublished research with me; and to my past and present medievalist colleagues at Southampton, John Swannell, Mishtooni Bose, and John McGavin, for their practical and moral support. But my greatest debt of gratitude is to my *Doktorvater* Eric Dobson, the kindest and most thorough of supervisors, meticulous in attention to detail but adventurous in breaking new ground, learned without arrogance and magnanimous in dispute. This edition is affectionately dedicated to his memory.

Bella Millett
University of Southampton

CONTENTS OF VOLUME 1

SIGLA OF MANUSCRIPTS AND VERSIONS ... ix

TEXTUAL INTRODUCTION ... xi
  Manuscripts and Versions ... xi
  The Relationship of the Manuscripts and Versions ... xxvii
  The Development of the Work ... xxxvii
  Editorial Aims and Principles ... xlv
  Editorial Procedures and Conventions ... lxii
  Bibliography ... lxvii

TEXT
  Preface ... 1
  Part 1 ... 7
  Part 2 ... 20
  Part 3 ... 48
  Part 4 ... 68
  Part 5 ... 114
  Part 6 ... 132
  Part 7 ... 145
  Part 8 ... 155

APPARATUS CRITICUS ... 167

SIGLA OF MANUSCRIPTS AND VERSIONS

A   Cambridge, Corpus Christi College, MS 402
Bd Oxford, Bodleian Library, MS Bodley 90
BN Paris, Bibliothèque Nationale de France, MS fonds français 6276
C   London, British Library, MS Cotton Cleopatra C. vi
C^2 'Scribe B', the earlier corrector of C
C^3 'Scribe D', the later corrector of C
F   London, British Library, MS Cotton Vitellius F. vii
G   Cambridge, Gonville and Caius College, MS 234/120
H   Oxford, Bodleian Library, MS Eng. th. c. 70 (the 'Lanhydrock fragment')
L   Latin translation of *Ancrene Wisse*
Ma Oxford, Magdalen College, MS Latin 67
Me Oxford, Merton College, MS C. 1. 5 (Coxe 44)
N   London, British Library, MS Cotton Nero A. xiv
P   Cambridge, Magdalene College, MS Pepys 2498
R   London, British Library, MS Royal 8 C. i
R^2 London, British Library, MS Royal 7 C. x[1]
S   later French translation of *Ancrene Wisse*
T   London, British Library, MS Cotton Titus D. xviii
Tr Cambridge, Trinity College, MS 883 (R. 14. 7)
V   Oxford, Bodleian Library, MS Eng. poet. a. 1 (the 'Vernon manuscript')
V^1 London, British Library, MS Cotton Vitellius E. vii

---

[1] D'Evelyn (1944) gives this manuscript the siglum R; it has been altered to R^2 to avoid confusion with BL Royal 8 C. 1 (R) above.

TEXTUAL INTRODUCTION

MANUSCRIPTS AND VERSIONS

A Cambridge, Corpus Christi College, MS 402

Description: Ker in Tolkien 1962, pp. ix–xviii. Diplomatic edition: Tolkien 1962. Bibliography: Millett 1996, pp. 49–50.

Text of the English version of *Ancrene Wisse* (ff. 1^r–117^v). Parchment, 117 folios (two missing between f. 14 and f. 15), page size 215 × 148 mm. (after rebinding); written space *c.*156 × 95 mm. (ff. 1–68), 156 × 100 mm. (ff. 69–117), ruled in a single column of 28 lines. Coloured initials and paragraph-marks (red and blue); on their use to mark divisions in the text, see Dahood 1988. In the bottom margin of f. 1^r, an *ex libris* inscription added towards the end of the thirteenth century records the gift of the manuscript by John Purcel, a Shropshire landowner, to the house of Victorine canons at Wigmore Abbey in Herefordshire, at the request of its precentor, Walter of Ludlow (see Ker in Tolkien 1962, pp. xvii–xviii). Carefully written in Textura semi-quadrata, dated by Ker (in Tolkien 1962, p. xv) to the first half of the thirteenth century; but Malcolm Parkes proposes a date later in the century, 'probably 1270s or early 1280s.'[1] Dialect localized by Jeremy Smith to northern Herefordshire or southern Shropshire (see Millett 1996, p. 11, fn. 7). The manuscript includes minor corrections, alterations, and marginalia in hands of the thirteenth and fourteenth centuries. In the sixteenth century, it was owned by Archbishop Parker; on Parker's death in 1575 it passed to Corpus Christi College, Cambridge, where it was further marked and annotated by the Anglo-Saxon scholar William Lisle (*c.*1569–1637), who transcribed some passages from it.[2]

The text is complete, apart from the two lost folios after f. 14 (2. 122–225). It is generally of high quality, although not free of errors, mainly of omission. It reflects the adaptation of *Ancrene Wisse* for a

---

[1] Private communication, September 2004.
[2] In Oxford, Bodleian Library, MSS Laud misc. 201 and Laud misc. 381; on these transcriptions, which archaize the language of their exemplar, see Napier 1909, and the articles by Pulsiano and Lee in Graham 2000.

larger and more geographically scattered group of anchoresses than the three sisters addressed in the original version. The A text includes most of the revisions and additions found elsewhere in the early manuscript tradition, sometimes developed further, and also some added material not found elsewhere. The main alterations to the text, much of which remains untouched, are in Parts 2, 4, and 8. Part 4 includes an expanded account of the offspring of the Seven Deadly Sins (apparently based on an earlier stage of revision) and some direct addresses to the larger group of anchoresses (found only in A); there are also three substantial additions (shared with F, and in one case V as well) in Part 2. The text of Part 8, the most thoroughly worked-over section, takes further the revisions to the 'Outer Rule' found in the C^2 annotations of C, probably again building on an intermediate stage of revision.

Bd Oxford, Bodleian Library, MS Bodley 90

Description: Madan and Craster 1922, no. 1887 (p. 98); see also Trethewey 1958, pp. xv–xvi.

Extracts from the 'Compilation' incorporating the later French translation of *Ancrene Wisse* (S) (ff. 1^r–77^r), followed by six short religious texts in Latin.

Parchment, 108 folios, page size 220 × 120 mm., written space 177 × 90 mm., ruled in a single column of 38 lines. Spaces left for coloured initials not filled; some capitals touched with red; coloured headings (red), and Latin quotations underlined in red. Neatly written in a small Anglicana formata hand. Dated by Ker to the late thirteenth or early fourteenth century (see Trethewey 1958, p. xv). Copied in England; given to the Bodleian Library in 1607 by Richard Worsley of Appledorecombe, Isle of Wight, a student at Magdalen.

The first extract, ff. 1^r–52^r/34, gives most of the *Compileisun des set pecchez morteus*; the second, ff. 52^r/35–77^r/17, an incomplete text of the *Compileisun de seinte penance*. Trethewey assesses the quality of the text as 'fairly good' but 'somewhat less reliable than that of Tr or Bn' (p. xvi).

BN Paris, Bibliothèque Nationale de France, MS fonds français 6276

Description: Trethewey 1958, pp. xiv–xv.

Text of the 'Compilation' incorporating the later French translation of *Ancrene Wisse* (S) (ff. 3ra–127ra/36), followed by a Latin text of the Creed with a French translation and commentary (as in Tr), and an exposition of the *Pater noster* by Adam of Exeter.

Parchment, 134 folios, page size 380 × 245 mm., written space 280 × 165 mm., ruled in two columns (each 75 mm. wide) of 57 lines. Spaces left for coloured initials not filled; coloured headings (red), and Latin quotations underlined in red. Most capitals faintly tinted with ochre. Written in Textura quadrata. Dated by Ker to the early fourteenth century, it includes on f. 132^v a fifteenth-century note (probably in an English hand) which specifies its price in English currency (*xls̄ monete Anglie*), perhaps indicating a sale to an overseas buyer; see Trethewey 1958, pp. xiv–xv.

Trethewey, who cites selected variants from BN, describes its text as 'not markedly inferior' to that of Tr (p. xvii).

C London, British Library, MS Cotton Cleopatra C. vi

Description: Dobson 1972, 'Introduction'. **Diplomatic edition:** Dobson 1972. **Bibliography:** Millett 1996, pp. 51–2.

English text of *Ancrene Wisse* (ff. 4^r–198^v); the conclusion to Part 7, lost after f. 190, is supplied from another manuscript by C^3 (f. 199^r).

Parchment, 203 folios (one missing between f. 190 and f. 191), page size 194 × 140 mm., written space 114–42 × 56–72 mm., ruled in a single column of 18–28 lines. Dobson (1972, pp. xxix–xlvi) explains the variations in written space and lineation by the initial influence of an exemplar in 'a smaller, more compact hand' than the scribe's own; their pattern, together with some irregularities in quiring and in the continuity of the copying, indicates that the scribe copied his exemplar in six sections, some out of sequence, suggesting that 'some form of the *pecia* system was in use' (p. xxxiv). Coloured initials and paragraph-marks (red and blue); on their use to mark divisions in the text, see Dahood 1988. Written in an informal and idiosyncratic small book hand with occasional cursive features, dated by Ker (1964, p. 29) to the first half of the thirteenth century, and by Parkes to the early 1230s.[3] The dialect of the main scribe has

---

[3] Private communication, September 2002.

been localized by Jeremy Smith to North Worcestershire.[4] An inscription (*c.*1300) on f. 3^r records the gift of the manuscript to the abbey of Canonsleigh in Devon (refounded as a house of Augustinian canonesses in 1284) by Matilda de Clare, Countess of Gloucester (d. before 10 March 1288/9); it was later owned by the antiquary Robert Talbot (d. 1558), prebendary and canon of Norwich Cathedral, before its acquisition by Sir Robert Cotton.

The text in C is flawed by errors, numerous small-scale omissions, and careless rephrasing, and has been extensively corrected and revised by two hands, C^2 and C^3 (Dobson's 'Scribe B' and 'Scribe D'). C^2, plausibly identified by Dobson with the original author of *Ancrene Wisse*,[5] appears to have worked on the manuscript before it was bound; Parkes dates his additions palaeographically as 'probably 1240s/50s'.[6] Most of his alterations are to the Preface and Parts 1 and 2, the account in Part 4 of the remedies against the seven deadly sins (4. 1398–1595), and Part 8. He corrects many of the misreadings and rewritings in C's text, provides clarifications of difficult passages, and adds a number of revisions, some of which are carried over into later manuscripts. C^3 adds further corrections and annotations, drawing on another manuscript of *Ancrene Wisse* which has not survived (see Dobson 1972, pp. cxl–clxxii). He also adds a vernacular sermon and some lyrics; most of these pieces are added in the same hand, together with the 'Atte wrastlinge' sermon and a rhymed version of the Ten Commandments, to Trinity College, Cambridge, MS B. 1. 45. Dobson argued that C^3 was an Augustinian canon working at Canonsleigh; but Parkes dates his textual interventions to the third quarter of the thirteenth century, before the manuscript was presented to Canonsleigh,[7] and both his apparent interest in preaching and the internal evidence of his annotations suggest that he may have been a Dominican friar.[8]

---

[4] See Laing 1993, pp. 74–5.

[5] See Dobson 1962, pp. 158–62, Dobson 1966, pp. 199–202, and Dobson 1972, pp. xciii–cxl; also pp. lvi–lviii below.

[6] Private communication, September 2002.

[7] Private communication, September 2002.

[8] On f. 198^v he copies out a Dominican prayer for preachers (see Dobson 1972, p. 316, fn. 1 on f. 198^v); and on f. 138^r he adds a twenty-eight-point list of 'conditions of confession' also found in the mid-thirteenth-century *Flos summarum*, attributed by one of its copyists to the Dominicans of Saint-Jacques in Paris (see Millett 1999, p. 201, fn. 40). His apparent familiarity with the Rule of St Augustine (see Dobson 1972, p. cxlviii) and the presence of an exposition of the Rule of St Augustine in the main text of Trinity B. 1. 45 do not necessarily indicate that he was an Augustinian canon; the Dominicans,

TEXTUAL INTRODUCTION

F London, British Library, MS Cotton Vitellius F. vii

Description: Herbert 1944, 'Introduction'. Diplomatic edition (text of *Ancrene Wisse*): Herbert 1944. Bibliography: Millett 1996, p. 54.

Text of the earlier French translation of *Ancrene Wisse* (ff. 2^r–70^r), followed by various devotional works in French: a treatise on the pains of Purgatory and Hell and the joys of Heaven, OF versions of the *Tractatus de tribulatione* and part of Gregory's *Regula Pastoralis*, and miscellaneous prayers and meditations translated from Augustine, Anselm, Bernard of Clairvaux, and the Scriptures.

Parchment, 164 folios, damaged at top and bottom by the Cottonian fire of 1731, page size *c*.220 × 165 mm. at most, ruled in double columns of 41–3 lines; coloured headings (red) and initials (red and blue). Written by a single scribe in Textura semi-quadrata, dated by Herbert to 'about the beginning of the fourteenth century' (p. ix); but Parkes has noted the similarity of the hand to that of the French text of the Douce Apocalypse (Oxford, Bodleian Library, MS Douce 180, made for Henry III's son Edward before 1272).[9] A fragmentary inscription on the last page suggests that the manuscript was given between 1433 and 1441 to Eleanor Cobham, second wife of Humphrey, Duke of Gloucester, by Joan, widow of the 8th Earl of Kent (see Herbert, pp. xi–xiii).

This is the only surviving copy of the earlier French translation. Although the manuscript is relatively late, and the scribe careless, the translation is a close rendering of what appears to have been a good early text of the English version. It shares three substantial additions in Part 2 with A (in one case, the *Quomodo obscuratum* addition at 2. 884–940, drawing on a better text than A's), and also includes a unique addition in Part 8 (see 8. 32 fn.), comparing the regulations of the different orders on abstinence. An extended omission (3. 648–4. 437) was probably caused by the loss of a quire in its exemplar.

---

following the requirements of Canon 13 of the Fourth Lateran Council, had adopted the rule and constitutions of an existing order, the Premonstratensian canons, for their newly-founded order, and hence followed the Rule of St Augustine.

[9] Private communication, September 2002.

G Cambridge, Gonville and Caius College, MS 234/120

Description: James 1907–8, 1. 278–80; Ker in Wilson 1954, pp. ix–xiii (*Ancrene Wisse* only). **Diplomatic edition** (text of *Ancrene Wisse*): Wilson 1954. **Bibliography:** Millett 1996, p. 50.

A composite manuscript: extracts from the English version of *Ancrene Wisse* (pp. 1–185) and the *Vitae Patrum* (pp. 185–96), bound together with an originally separate collection of pastoral material (pp. 197–368).

First section on parchment, page size $c.130 \times 92$ mm., written space $c.100 \times 70$ mm., ruled in a single column of 17–27 lines (normally 19–20). Spaces for coloured initials left unfilled; only a few coloured headings (red) in the *Ancrene Wisse* material. Written in 'a mixed hand with some cursive features and a distinctive personal idiom' (Malcolm Parkes),[10] dated by Ker 'probably in the second half of the thirteenth century or perhaps a little earlier' (Wilson 1954, p. ix), and by Parkes to the third quarter of the thirteenth century; the scribe's problems with the English 'special characters' suggest that he may have been of Continental origin.

The G text of *Ancrene Wisse* is a compilation drawn from different parts of the 'Inner Rule': extracts from Part 3 on remedies against wrath (3. 50–123) and the need to do good by stealth (3. 355–469); the whole of Part 5 and most of Part 6 (to 6. 417); extracts from Part 7 on Christ as the lover of the soul (7. 118–242), Part 2 on the soul as the bride of Christ (2. 735–824), and Part 3 on reasons for fleeing from the world (3. 615–743); and all but the first few pages and conclusion of Part 4 (4. 236–1702). The extracts include material suitable for both pastoral and contemplative use. They generally reproduce the original text accurately, but there is a tendency to omit or modify passages referring to the anchoresses (though the final section of Part 5 is retained almost unaltered). Feminine pronouns are sometimes replaced by masculine; *leoue sustren* is normally replaced by *leoue frend*, and *ancre(n) / recluse(s)* sometimes by *men of religiun* (6. 10) or *reli(gi)use* (3. 723, 724, 728 (for *ancre-hus*), 729, 6. 74, 87). A comment in the original on the shame of being sometimes obliged to beg for one's living 'as ȝe beoð, leoue sustren' (6. 133–6) is modified to address *breþren*, perhaps indicating adaptation for a mendicant community.

---

[10] Private communication, September 2002.

H Oxford, Bodleian Library, MS Eng. th. c. 70 (the 'Lanhydrock fragment')

Description: Zettersten in Mack and Zettersten 1963, pp. 163–5. **Diplomatic edition:** Zettersten in Mack and Zettersten 1963, pp. 166–71 (with reproduction of MS). **Bibliography:** Millett 1996, p. 58.

Fragment of the English version of *Ancrene Wisse* (3. 292–343), preserved from the seventeenth century in the library at Lanhydrock, Bodmin, Cornwall. Has also been called the 'Lord Robartes fragment' after its nineteenth-century owner, and the 'Napier fragment' after its first editor (see Napier 1898). Sometimes given the alternative siglum O.

Single parchment leaf (formerly used as the wrapper of a book), 198 × 135 mm. Written space, ruled as a single column of 34 lines, now 170 × 100 mm.; but Zettersten notes 'originally about 170 × 115 mm. . . . A written space of about 15 mm. has been cut off at the inner edge' (Mack and Zettersten 1963, p. 163). Wear caused by folding the leaf and severe rubbing on the verso have led to further loss of text. Written in an Anglicana hand dated by Ker to the first half of the fourteenth century (see Mack and Zettersten 1963, p. 163).

Dobson comments, 'At a number of points H has aberrant readings unparalleled in any other extant manuscript . . ., which suggests that its text, though reasonably good for a late manuscript, was not especially faithful.'[11]

L Latin translation

Edition: d'Evelyn 1944, from Me and (for Part 8) V^1, with variants from V^1, R^2, and Ma.

The Latin translation survives in four manuscripts, Ma, Me, R^2, and V^1; a fifth manuscript, now lost, was owned by the Augustinian canons of Leicester abbey (see below, p. xxvii).

There is an attribution (whether of the work or the translation is unclear, although the wording rather suggests the former) in the *incipit* of Ma to Simon of Ghent, Bishop of Salisbury (d. 1315): *Hic incipit prohemium uenerabilis patris magistri Simonis de Gandavo episcopi Sarum in librum de uita solitaria quem scripsit sororibus suis anachoritis apud Tarente* (i.e. Tarrant in Dorset). A version of this

---

[11] Dobson 1967, p. 191.

also appears in the catalogue entry for V¹ in Smith 1696, referring to *Ancrene Wisse* and the following item, the 'Dublin Rule': *Regulae vitae Anachoretarum utriusque sexus, scriptae per Simonem de Gandavo, Episcopum Sarum, in usum suarum sororum.* The Latin translation, however, shows evidence of adaptation for a wider audience of religious, including male and female regulars as well as recluses.[12]

It is a free but generally accurate translation, with a tendency to minor abridgement—often, as Dobson noted, at points of textual difficulty (Dobson 1962, p. 134). It retains from Part 1 only the passage on devotions during Mass (1. 207–44); and although it includes a translation of Part 8, this is largely or wholly omitted in all the manuscripts other than V¹. It provides chapter and verse references to Scriptural quotations, a feature shared with R; and incorporates revisions to Part 4 and Part 8 also found in PV and (in a later form) in A.

Ma Oxford, Magdalen College, MS Latin 67

Description: Coxe 1852, vol. 2, Magdalen manuscripts, pp. 39–40; see also d'Evelyn 1944, pp. xi–xiii.

A composite manuscript: text of the Latin translation (L) of *Ancrene Wisse* (ff. 1ʳ–95ʳ), bound together with a late-fourteenth-century collection of Latin hymns (ff. 96ʳ–120ᵛ). Its *incipit* gives an attribution to Simon of Ghent, Bishop of Salisbury (see the section on L above).

Ff. 1ʳ–95ʳ parchment, page size 218 mm. × 150 mm., written space 158 × 105 mm., ruled in a single column of 25 lines. First initial (unfinished) partly filled in and ornamented with gold, other coloured initials in blue ornamented with red, coloured headings (red), blue paragraph-marks, some capitals lightly touched with ochre. Written in Textura quadrata, probably *c.*1400 (see d'Evelyn 1944, p. xii).

The text lacks Part 8; the *explicit* to Part 7 concludes *Octauus omnino taceatur*. D'Evelyn, who cites selected variants, finds it a 'less reliable' text than Me (see d'Evelyn 1944, pp. xv–xix, for examples).

---

[12] At 2. 104 L adds *uel moniales* after *ancres*; at 2. 269, the instructions on the anchoress's reception of guests are modified to include religious of both sexes (*Cum ad locutorium accedit religiosus uel religiosa* . . .); at 2. 300 *3e*¹ (addressing the anchoresses) is replaced by the more general *homo religiosus*; and at 2. 880 enclosure in the religious life is described more specifically as *in claustro uel domo*.

Me Oxford, Merton College, MS C. 1. 5 (Coxe 44)

Description: Coxe 1852, vol. 1, Merton MSS, p. 30; see also d'Evelyn 1944, pp. ix–xi. **Edition** (text of *Ancrene Wisse*): d'Evelyn 1944. **Bibliography**: Millett 1996, p. 59.

A composite manuscript: text of the Latin translation (L) of *Ancrene Wisse* (ff. 90^r–165^v, corrected foliation; see d'Evelyn 1944, p. ix), bound together with other Latin religious works (see Coxe 1852 and Millett 1996).

Ff. 90^r–165^v parchment, page size 245 × 170 mm., written space 185 × 120 mm., ruled in a single column of 28 lines. Spaces left for coloured initials not filled; some capitals tinted with light brown. Neatly written in a mixed hand with some cursive features, dated by Herbert to the first half of the fourteenth century (see d'Evelyn 1944, p. x).

The text lacks the beginning of its table of contents (ff. 90^r–91^v), which does not mention Part 8; it has only the first few lines of Part 8, ending at 8. 13 (the same point as in R^2).

N London, British Library, MS Cotton Nero A. xiv

Description: Day 1952, 'Introduction'. **Diplomatic edition** (text of *Ancrene Wisse*): Day 1952. **Bibliography**: Millett 1996, pp. 52–3.

Text of the English version of *Ancrene Wisse* (ff. 1^r–120^v), followed (in a different hand) by an *Ureisun of ure Lefdi* in rhyming verse (ff. 120^v–123^v), three 'Wooing Group' works, *Ureisun of God Almihti* (ff. 123^v–126^v), '*Lofsong of ure Lefdi*' (ff. 126^v–128^r), and '*Lofsong of ure Louerde*' (ff. 128^r–131^r), the Apostles' Creed in English (f. 131^{r-v}), twelve lines of Latin verse on death, and a Latin prose meditation (f. 131^v); see Day 1952, pp. xxii–xxiv, and Thompson 1958, p. ix.

Parchment, 139 folios (foliated 1*–4*, 1–135), page size 144 × 107 mm., written space 122–30 × 77 mm., ruled in a single column of 28–30 lines. Coloured initials and paragraph-marks (mainly red); on their use to mark divisions in the text, see Dahood 1988. Written in a small book hand, dated by Day (1952, p. ix), advised by Ker, to the second quarter of the thirteenth century; Parkes suggests a dating in the 1240s.[13] Franzen (2003) notes the close similarity (though not identity) of the hand of the *Ancrene Wisse* text in appearance and orthography with that of the 'tremulous hand' which annotated

---

[13] Private communication, September 2004.

ninth- to twelfth-century manuscripts of Old English works in the cathedral library of Worcester. The dialect of the manuscript has been assigned to Worcestershire (see *LALME* 1. 25, and Laing 1993, p. 78; Laing has recently reassigned the dialect to Worcester or its immediate neighbourhood). Day suggests, from the evidence of fifteenth- and sixteenth-century annotations on the first flyleaf, that the manuscript may have been owned towards the end of the Middle Ages by the Benedictine house of Winchcombe Abbey in Gloucester, passing at the Dissolution to a local family, before it entered the Cotton collection in the early seventeenth century (Day 1952, pp. x–xvi).

Dobson's harsh criticism of N as 'an innovating manuscript, the most remote from the original of all the thirteenth-century English texts . . . written by a fussy and interfering scribe' (Dobson 1962, p. 133) has been contested by Scahill (2002), who explains its linguistic modifications by the 'desire to produce a readily intelligible text', and emphasises its 'value as a guide to the meaning' compared with the other early manuscripts C, G, and T (p. 76). It preserves a passage, abridged or cut in other manuscripts, on the circumstances of the initial audience of three anchoresses (see 4. 192 fn.), and includes an added passage possibly by the original author, not found elsewhere, recommending the lay brothers' Hours of the writer's order (see 1. 134 fn.).

P Cambridge, Magdalene College, MS Pepys 2498

Description: McKitterick and Beadle 1992, pp. 86–8. **Diplomatic edition** (text of *Ancrene Wisse*): Zettersten 1976. **Bibliography**: Millett 1996, pp. 50–1.

Collection of religious works in Middle English, including the fourteenth-century prose translation of Robert of Gretham's thirteenth-century *Miroir* (verse homilies in French addressed to a lay audience) and a number of Biblical translations; text of the English version of *Ancrene Wisse* (called on p. 449[a] 'þis good book Recluse') pp. 371[a]–449[a]. For a recent discussion of the manuscript and its probable audience, see Hanna 2003.

Parchment, 232 folios, page size $c.340 \times 240$ mm., ruled in two columns, each $c.290 \times 100$ mm., of 52–4 lines. Coloured headings (red), initials (red and blue), and paragraph-marks (blue). Written by a single scribe in Anglicana formata, dated by Hanna (2003) to *c.* 1365-75; Hanna notes that the text has been 'reformatted' in the manuscript to resemble a Biblical commentary, each Latin quotation beginning a new paragraph. Dialect localized in *LALME*, 1. 64, to the Waltham Abbey area of Essex.

P incorporates revisions to Parts 4 found in L and V and, in a later form, in A. Its text has been extensively abridged, rewritten, and interpolated; it addresses a general audience of both sexes, and sometimes works against the sense of the original, celebrating the active rather than the contemplative life and offering 'a rule for all Christians' (Watson 2003, p. 219). Colledge (1939) argued that it had been reworked by a Lollard reviser, probably at some point between 1381 and 1401; but Hanna's dating of the manuscript places it too early for its content to be categorized as 'Lollard'. Hudson (1988) postulated two layers of revision, the earlier orthodox, 'the second by a perfunctory and unorthodox redactor who endeavoured rather sporadically to convert the text to a secular purpose' (p. 28), a hypothesis explored more fully by von Nolcken (2003). The text in P is extraordinarily garbled, probably through a combination of its remoteness from the original and the scribe's inability to cope adequately either with Latin or with the *Ancrene Wisse* author's difficult Middle English; but the textual history of P, which links it particularly with V (see p. xxv below), is of some interest.

R London, British Library, MS Royal 8 C. i

Description: Warner and Gilson 1921, 1. 228; see also Baugh 1956, pp. ix–xi. **Diplomatic edition** (text of *Ancrene Wisse*): Baugh 1956. **Bibliography:** Millett 1996, p. 55.

Collection of theological tracts in Latin and English, including a reworking of Parts 2 and 3 of the English version of *Ancrene Wisse* for a lay audience (ff. 122^v–143^v), described in the table of contents as *optimus tract[at]us de quinque sensibus secundum Lichef(eld)*. 'Lichfield' was identified by Warner and Gilson with the preacher William Lichfield, rector of Allhallows the Great, London (d. 1448); but Doyle (1954, 1. 136–7) thinks the manuscript is too early, and suggests two other possible candidates, the anchorite who presented a *liber devotus* to Robert Wolveden (d. 1432), archdeacon of Norwich, and the hermit or anchorite William Lichfield of Highgate, Middlesex (*fl.* 1386).

Paper, 170 folios, page size 215 × 145 mm., written space of

Ancrene Wisse text 207 × 105 mm., ruled in a single column of 41 lines; coloured opening initial (red), some capitals tinted with faint red, no other decoration. Written in a cursive hand showing a mixture of Anglicana and Secretary features. Dated by Doyle (1954) to the early or mid-fifteenth century.

The textual adaptation of *Ancrene Wisse* in R is relatively free, both omitting and adding material; it modifies the concept of the solitary life in its original, outlining a form of detachment from the world open to the devout laity (see the discussion in Watson 2003, pp. 216–19).

R² London, British Library, MS Royal 7 C. x

Description: Warner and Gilson 1921, 1. 180; see also d'Evelyn 1944, pp. xiv–xv. **Bibliography:** Millett 1996, p. 54.

Early sixteenth-century manuscript, in a single hand, containing sermons by the Dominican St Vincent Ferrer (d. 1419) and a text of the Latin translation of *Ancrene Wisse* (L).

Paper, 124 folios, 310 × 213 mm., written space 230 × 150 mm., ruled in a single column of 32–5 lines (usually 34); no coloured initials or headings. Written in a cursive hand showing a mixture of Anglicana and Secretary features.

The text of *Ancrene Wisse* lacks a section of Part 4 (4. 909–1320) and all but the first few lines of Part 8 (up to 8. 13, as in Me, the end indicated by the scribe's addition of *Telos*). Selected variants are cited in d'Evelyn 1944.

S later French translation

Edition: Trethewey 1958, from Tr, with variants from BN and Bd.

Translations of material from *Ancrene Wisse*[14] (apparently independent of the earlier French translation in F) incorporated in a larger French manual on confession and the religious life, probably of Franciscan origin,[15] and compiled not later than the last quarter of the thirteenth century (see Trethewey 1958, p. xxiii). The borrowings from *Ancrene Wisse* were first identified by Allen (1936; see further Allen 1940). Trethewey calls this work 'The Trinity Compilation'; it is made up of four *compileisons*—on the seven

---

[14] For a detailed table of correspondences, see Trethewey 1958, pp. xxv–xxvi.

[15] See the compiler's claim that the work has been produced in honour of God, the Virgin Mary, and St Francis (Trethewey 1958, 157/28–9).

deadly sins (including extracts from Part 4), penance (using Parts 5–7), the pains of Purgatory, and the ten commandments—and a treatise on the *Vie de gent de religion* (based solely on *Ancrene Wisse*, using the Preface, Parts 2 and 3, and an extract from Part 4). Only the concluding passages of Parts 1 and 8 are used; Watson and Wogan-Browne argue from the evidence of a surviving table of contents preceding the *Vie* that the 'Compilation' was originally planned as 'an expanded rewriting' of *Ancrene Wisse* as a whole, but was subsequently modified to accommodate more general pastoral aims.[16] The translation in S addresses (often explicitly) a much wider audience than the original work: all kinds of religious, of either sex ('monie, ou chanoine, ou frere blanc ou bis ou noir, ou nonein, ou recluse, ou en autre manere de religion, vus homme ou vus femme'[17]) in the *Vie de gent de religion*, and a general audience including both religious and laity in the first two *compileisuns*. Although the content of those parts of *Ancrene Wisse* which are used remains more or less intact, their wording has sometimes been considerably expanded by the translator(s).

Complete copies of the 'Compilation' survive in Tr and BN, and extracts from the first two *compileisons* in Bd; Trethewey concludes that Tr and Bd share the same textual line of descent, from which BN is independent.

T London, British Library, MS Cotton Titus D. xviii

Description: Mack in Mack and Zettersten 1963, pp. ix–xvii; see also d'Ardenne and Dobson 1981, pp. xlix–liii. **Diplomatic edition** (text of *Ancrene Wisse*): Mack in Mack and Zettersten 1963, pp. 1–160. **Bibliography**: Millett 1996, p. 53.

A composite manuscript: ff. 1–12, in a fifteenth-century hand, contain a *liber alphabetarius* and other texts, ff. 14–147 a text of the English version of *Ancrene Wisse* (ff. 14^r–105^r) followed by other works from the *Ancrene Wisse* Group: *Sawles Warde* (ff. 105^v–112^v), *Epistel of Meidenhad* (ff. 112^v–127^r), *þe Wohunge of ure Lauerd* (ff. 127^r–133^r), and *Seinte Katerine* (ff. 133^v–147^v).

Parchment, 147 folios, page size 157 × 120 mm.; written space of text of *Ancrene Wisse* 112 × 88 mm., ruled in two columns of 24–30

---

[16] See Watson and Wogan-Browne 2004.
[17] Trethewey 1958, 267/4–6 (in a modification of the author's address to the original three anchoresses; see 4. 192 fn. and note).

lines. Coloured initials and paragraph-marks in red and green; on their use to mark divisions in the text, see Dahood 1988. Written in a small book hand, below top line, 'which suggests that the second quarter of the thirteenth century is a better date than *c.*1225' (Mack in Mack and Zettersten 1963, p. x); Parkes sees the 1240s as the most probable date.[18]

The text of *Ancrene Wisse* in T is physically incomplete; the Preface and most of Part 1 (to 1. 391) are missing, and two other lost leaves have left gaps at 3. 335–84 and 4. 1366–1423. Laing and McIntosh provisionally locate the non-original features of its dialect to the southern border of Cheshire; internal dialectal variation suggests that its exemplar was produced by two copyists, one (T2) a *literatim* copyist, the other (T1) more prepared to 'translate' the text into North-West Midland dialect (see Laing and McIntosh 1995). The text shows signs of modification for a male religious community (notably the recommendation, shared by P, of fifteen rather than four haircuts a year at 8. 204–5), but also of an apparent attempt to reverse it (although the T text includes numerous substitutions of masculine for feminine pronouns, at some points it has feminine pronouns against all the other manuscripts running).[19]

Tr Cambridge, Trinity College, MS 883 (R. 14. 7)

Description: James 1901, 2. 289–91, and Trethewey 1958, pp. xii–xiv. **Edition** (parts of text based on *Ancrene Wisse*): Trethewey 1958. **Bibliography:** Millett 1996, p. 51.

Collection of works in French from Norwich Cathedral Priory, dated by James (1901) to the thirteenth or early fourteenth century; an inscription of ownership names the monk Geoffrey of Wroxham (d. 1322). Includes a text of the 'Compilation' incorporating the later French translation of *Ancrene Wisse* (S) (ff. 1^r–154^v), a Latin text of the Creed with French translation and commentary, an extract from Edmund of Abingdon's *Mirour de seinte eglyse*, a piece on the *Merveilles de Engletere*, and a *Chronicon Anglie*.

Parchment, 216 folios, 270 × 170 mm. Written space of 'Compilation' 205 × 130 mm., ruled in two columns of 46–9 lines (normally 48); neatly written in a small book hand. Coloured initials in blue and

---

[18] Private communication, September 2004.
[19] e.g. 2. 357–8, 4. 873–4, 4. 1339–40, 4. 1352, 5.217, 5. 236, 6. 229, 7. 331.

red, with ornamentation running down the margins, and frequent coloured headings (red); Latin quotations underlined in red.

The text of the 'Compilation' in Tr has some minor abridgements and omissions (see Trethewey 1958, p. xiii).

V Oxford, Bodleian Library, MS Eng. poet. a. 1 (the 'Vernon manuscript')

Description: Doyle 1987, pp. 1–16. **Facsimile:** Doyle 1987. **Diplomatic edition** (text of *Ancrene Wisse*): Zettersten and Diensberg 2000. **Bibliography:** Millett 1996, p. 57.

Very large, handsomely-illuminated manuscript containing religious and moral literature, mainly in Middle English, produced in the West Midlands probably towards the end of the fourteenth century; its exact date, place of origin, patron(s) and intended audience are uncertain. Internal evidence places it after 1384; dialectal and other evidence links it with the area including South Staffordshire, North Worcestershire, and West Warwickshire. Doyle (1987) suggests tentatively that its production may have been initiated by the Cistercian abbey at Bordesley, North Worcestershire, for the house of nuns at Nuneaton, Shropshire, although an audience of pious laity cannot be ruled out. The text of *Ancrene Wisse* (called in the medieval list of contents *Roule of Reclous*) is on ff. 371vb–392ra, preceded by *A Talkyng of the Loue of God* (which draws on two *Ancrene Wisse* Group works, *þe Wohunge of ure Lauerd* and *Ureisun of ure Louerde*), and followed by 'The Pains of Sin and the Joys of Heaven', a Middle English work also found in P.[20]

Parchment, 350 folios (originally probably 422 or 426), page size 544 × 393 mm. Written space in Section IV (ff. 319–406) *c.*412–20 × 284–94 mm., ruled in two columns of 80 lines; illuminated initials and coloured paragraph-marks (red and blue). Text of *Ancrene Wisse* written by the second Vernon scribe, 'Scribe B', in Anglicana formata. In spite of its late date, the Vernon text of *Ancrene Wisse* is of relatively high quality, with only minor modifications (largely modernizations of vocabulary). It incorporates a number of the revisions found in A, including the earlier form of the revisions to Parts 4 and 8 also found in L and (in the case of Part 4) P.

Three folios (ff. 389–91) are missing from the manuscript, which lacks the latter part of Part 6 (from *heaued*, 6. 185), all of Part 7, and

---

[20] See Hanna 1997, pp. xiii, 8, and Doyle 1990, p. 7.

most of Part 8, from which only two sections survive, part of the expanded denunciation of wimples (from *werien* 8. 144 to *wiðuten* 8. 162) and the paragraph warning against idleness (8. 188–96); the *Quomodo obscuratum* addition (2. 884–940) which it shares with A and F is entered at the end of the text.

V¹ London, British Library, MS Cotton Vitellius E. vii

Description: d'Evelyn 1944, pp. xiii–xiv. **Diplomatic edition:** d'Evelyn 1944 (Part 8 of *Ancrene Wisse* only). **Bibliography:** Millett 1996, pp. 53–4.

Fragmentary manuscript, damaged in the Cottonian fire of 1731. According to the seventeenth-century catalogue of the Cottonian manuscripts (Smith 1696), it was presented by a former prior, Robert of Thornton, to the monks of Bardney, and included three saints' lives (of Ethelbert, David, and Patrick), Aelred's *De Institutione Inclusarum*, a service for the enclosure of anchoresses, and a text of the Latin translation of *Ancrene Wisse* (L) (ff. 61–113). A pre-1731 annotator of one of the British Library copies of Smith's catalogue noted two further items, another anchoritic rule (identified in Allen 1929 as a text of the 'Dublin Rule'; see Oliger 1928), and a treatise *De Oculo*. The surviving fragments show that the saints' lives were in an earlier hand than the rest of the manuscript, which is dated by Macaulay (1914) to the early fourteenth century.

34 parchment fragments include material from *Ancrene Wisse*. Ruled in two columns; coloured initials and paragraph-marks in red. Carefully written in a mixed hand with some cursive features.

Unlike the other manuscripts of L (Ma, Me, and R²), V¹ appears originally to have included a full text of Part 8; the surviving fragments of Part 8 are edited in d'Evelyn 1944, with selected variants cited from other parts of the text.

OTHER MANUSCRIPT AND PRINTED TEXTS

The manuscripts listed here are those which have been used for collation. I have not collated the *Tretyse of Loue* (ed. Fisher 1951), a retranslation into English of extracts from Parts 4 and 7 from the later French translation of *Ancrene Wisse* (S), combined with other material, printed by Wynkyn de Worde in 1493 or 1494. I have also not taken into account shorter borrowings from *Ancrene Wisse* in other works; for a good recent survey of its use by religious writers in the later Middle Ages, see Watson 2003.

What appears to be a lost manuscript of the Latin translation (L) is mentioned in the fifteenth- or sixteenth-century catalogue of the library of the Augustinian canons at Leicester Abbey (see Webber and Watson 1998). Item 452 is a collection of religious works of which the first is *Liber Anachoritarum diuisus in vii partes in papiro et quatern' cum alb. co.* The list of manuscript contents and the opening of the second folio (*et sic omnes*) confirm that it is not identical with R², the only surviving paper manuscript of the Latin translation; the mention of *vii partes* suggests that Part 8 was omitted.

Doyle (1954, 1. 234) notes the early fifteenth-century bequest by a London mason, John Clifford, to the Minoresses *iuxta Towrhill*, of a book called *Recti diligunt te* which 'can only have been some version (English, Latin, or French) of the *Riwle*' (see also Doyle 1954, 2. 304); it is not certain whether this was one of the surviving manuscripts of *Ancrene Wisse*.

THE RELATIONSHIP OF THE MANUSCRIPTS AND VERSIONS

The textual tradition of *Ancrene Wisse* raises considerable problems for the editor. The relationship of the manuscripts and versions is difficult to establish because of the complex and often contradictory pattern of textual agreements, which seems to reflect not only convergent variation but extensive cross-collation. Dobson argued that in spite of this difficulty it was possible to produce a stemma tracing the genetic relationships of the surviving manuscripts and versions; but he also noted that 'there is not a single manuscript [apart from A] . . . which has only the readings that might be expected to come to it by lineal descent.'[21] He explained this by the kind of cross-collation for which there is surviving evidence in the C³ annotations of C: 'Several of the lost manuscripts which must be assumed in the chain of descent must, like C, have been annotated manuscripts, with variant readings written in between the lines or in the margins, so that successor scribes were offered in effect a choice of readings, which they exercised in varying ways; and in the result manuscripts descended from a common original may often fail to

[21] Dobson 1962, p. 137.

show the expected agreements. One can plot the main lines of descent and the normal affiliations, but one can certainly not predict the behaviour even of closely related manuscripts'.[22] With a textual tradition of this kind, purely 'stemmatic' editing is not a practical possibility; although the editor still needs to take the genetic affiliation of the manuscripts into account, it is only one of the factors involved in determining the status of a particular reading.

The detailed discussion of the affiliations of the manuscripts of *Ancrene Wisse* in Dobson 1962 was supplemented, and in some respects modified, in Dobson's 1972 edition of C and his 1976 study, *The Origins of Ancrene Wisse*.[23] Dobson's stemma was based on a partial collation of *Ancrene Wisse*, covering about two-fifths of the work;[24] full collation has provided corroborative evidence for much of its structure, but has also suggested some readjustment of the manuscript groupings. In the following discussion, I have focused in citing evidence on those aspects of the manuscript tradition where full collation has modified his preliminary conclusions, and on areas which remain problematic.

I have followed Dobson in concentrating in the main discussion of manuscript relationships on what he called the 'basic text', the original form of the work, and dealing with later revisions separately. In reassessing the manuscript affiliations, I have used as evidence all shared errors (by which I mean mechanical errors and misunderstandings) and other substantive variants from the 'basic text'[25] (which, for the reasons given under 'Editorial Aims and Principles' below, is not identical with the edited text). Although variants must be weighed as well as counted, and some types of variation in the textual tradition of *Ancrene Wisse* are more likely to be convergent than others (e.g. modernization of vocabulary in the later Middle English texts, normalization and modernization of word-order in rewritten texts, and minor omissions shared by abridged texts), I have taken a high level of shared variants as *prima facie* evidence for a

[22] Dobson 1962, p. 148.
[23] See Dobson 1972, p. cxxii, fn. 1, and Dobson 1976, pp. 286–304 (revised stemma on p. 287).
[24] From the beginning of *Ancrene Wisse* to the end of Part 2, two sections of Part 4 (4. 236–602, 4. 1001–33), and most of Part 8 (8. 90–end).
[25] The category of 'other substantive variants from the "basic text"' includes minor textual modifications (e.g. alterations of vocabulary and word-order and small expansions) but not adaptations for other audiences or more substantial additions, which are dealt with separately below under 'The Development of the Work'. For a fuller discussion of the distinction made here between 'errors' and 'other variants', see pp. li–lii below.

textual relationship, whether by genetic descent or collation, and assumed that those manuscripts with an even distribution of shared variants are more likely to be genetically related than those which agree only intermittently (although this does not rule out the possibility of intermittent agreement caused by a temporary change of exemplar,[26] or of consistent agreement caused by systematic cross-collation). I have also assumed that agreement in error on difficult or nonsensical readings is a better indicator of genetic relationship than agreement on plausible errors.

The modified version of Dobson's stemma below represents the genetic groupings suggested by full collation.

ANCRENE WISSE: STEMMA CODICUM

```
                O (holograph)
                     |
                O¹ (archetype)
               /     |      \
              /      |       \
             A       |        \
                    / \        \
                   C   F        \
                      /|\        \
                     / | \        \
                    N  H  V  G     \
                              L     \
                             /|\     \
                            P R S     T
```

All the surviving manuscripts appear to be descended from a single archetype (O¹), which itself contained errors (though not very many);[27] it was probably not identical with the author's holograph (O).[28]

[26] There is a surviving example of this in BL MS Cotton Cleopatra C. vi, f. 199ʳ, where C³ supplies the missing conclusion of Part 7 from a different exemplar; see Dobson 1972, pp. 317–18, and the illustration facing p. 317.

[27] See notes on P. 76 *alle þe ten heastes*, P. 98 *openluker*, 2. 792 *to hinene hulen*, 3. 397 *uecordia*, 3. 494 *habes*, 3. 612 *ut . . . floc*, 4. 337 *horn*, 4. 1246 *Paralipomenon*, 4. 1304 *þet . . . biȝulet*, 5. 69 *schulen*, 5. 228–9 *he hit seide*, 5. 357 *ant*, 6. 69 *quem*, 6. 486 *pinene sarest*.

[28] Although the probably authorial corrections entered by C² in C suggest that the author of *Ancrene Wisse* was prone to slips of the pen (see p. li below), some of the erroneous readings noted in the previous footnote are misunderstandings for which he is unlikely to have been responsible.

Dobson's view that A had a separate line of descent has not been challenged by the full collation. It rarely shares variants with other manuscripts; its most frequent links with individual manuscripts are with L (14), P (13), V (13), N (9), C (8), S (8), and T (5).[29] Some of these shared variants are trivial (e.g. omission of minor words); of those that are not, some may reflect errors in the archetype O^1,[30] some may be convergent,[31] and most of the remainder are probably to be explained by cross-collation. Since L, P, and V include revisions also incorporated in A (see pp. 26–7), it is possible that the texts underlying them were collated with an A-type manuscript at other points; and double readings in some of the manuscripts also suggest cross-collation.[32]

Dobson argued further in his 1962 article that all manuscripts other than A descended from a common ancestor, β, with some (though not many) distinctive errors of its own. The evidence for this single hyparchetype, however, is inconclusive. A often retains rare or obsolescent words or expressions not retained in other manuscripts,[33] but although these are sometimes demonstrably original, the other manuscripts usually have a range of variants apparently derived from the original reading rather than from a single hyparchetypal variant. Where the agreement of the other manuscripts against A is unanimous, the direction of variation is

---

[29] These numbers, and the others cited below, are based on the apparatus criticus of this edition, and depend on the specific editorial decisions made in producing it. This means that the absolute numbers of shared variants cited (which might differ considerably in an edition by another editor) are less significant than the relative proportions of shared variation that they indicate.

[30] e.g. see notes on P. 76 *alle þe ten heastes* (*þe alde ten heastes* AC, sim. N), 4. 1218 *fatigemini* (AP *fatiget*, N *fatigetis*), 6. 486 *pinene sarest* (AT *wiuene sarest*).

[31] For shared errors and omissions probably caused by eyeskip, see 1. 150 *oðer sum oþer* (AV *oðer*), 1. 226 *Quid* (*quis* AN, eyeskip from *Quis* at beginning of previous sentence), 3. 344 after *tecto* (*Vigilaui* added in ANV, probably through eyeskip to following sentence), 3. 519 *anlich lif* (*anlich stude* AS, repeating same phrase in previous sentence), 4. 200–1 *wreaððe is . . . wreaððe* (om. AP, eyeskip from preceding *wreaððe*), 4. 861–2 *Nawt . . . penne* (om. AT, eyeskip from preceding *penne*), 6. 452–4 *ouerleapinde . . . dunes* (om. AL, eyeskip from preceding *dunes*). ALN *swetnesse* for 3. 434 *wetnesse* could be the result of convergent agreement on an easier reading; and the apparent shared error *flih* in AN for 5. 21 *fliðd* may only reflect N's idiosyncratic orthography (see note).

[32] See notes on 1. 198 *þe . . . þolieð* (double reading in V), 3. 519 *lif* (AS *stude*, C *stude* (. . .) *ant* (. . .) *lif*), and 5. 417–18 *eadiliche* (A *eadmodliche*, N *eadiliche* (. . .) *and edmodliche*). V *whelpes cundles* for 4. 308 *whelpes* (A only; other English MSS *cundles*) and L *cornu seu spinam* for 4. 337 *horn* (AC *þorn*) may also indicate collation with an A-type text.

[33] e.g. 1. 10 *apet*, 3. 486 *edeawde*, P. 58 *eðelich*, 4. 907 *ʒeide*, 7. 144 *ʒeiʒeð*, 1. 291 and 3. 249 *lanhure*, 7. 339 *leaskeð*, 2. 298 and 8. 43 *nurð*, 4. 143 *striken*, 2. 672 *weoret*, 8. 339 *Godd hit wite*.

often uncertain.[34] Dobson cited seven instances from his partial collation where he saw A as 'right against all the other manuscripts running',[35] but all but two have been questioned,[36] and it is hard to find unambiguous instances elsewhere.[37]

It is possible that we need not assume a 'bifid stemma' for *Ancrene Wisse*,[38] and that CF form a separate group, genetically independent both of A and of the remaining manuscripts. C and F are linked together by 68 shared errors and other non-original variants;[39] they do not share a significant number of errors with A, but agree with it at some points on original readings against the other manuscripts running.[40]

The relationship of G, N, and V has been modified in this stemma. I have followed Dobson in taking N and V as genetically related;[41] where V is running,[42] they share a high number of variants (192). Most are small additions and omissions, or minor modifications of vocabulary and word-order, but the consistency of agreement, even on less-than-obvious substitutions,[43] is notable, and the

[34] See notes on 2. 950 *froure*, 4. 616 *adiuuaret*, 4. 655 *irobbet*, 4. 929 *stuhen*, 4. 1286 *uuel*, 8. 294 *hehe*.

[35] See Dobson 1962, pp. 130–1.

[36] The readings were: 1) P. 165 *hwet* (CFNSV *wit*); 2) 2. 120 *herre* (FNSTV *ear*); 3) 2. 544 *ʒef he walde* (CNTV *ʒet walde he*, sim. FSP); 4) 2. 609 *feor* (CNRTV *feor from*); 5) 2. 1042 *willes lust* (CFNST *wittes luste(s)*); 6) 4. 390 *þeo þah* (G *peo þat*, P *ac þise*, CLNTV *þeo*); 7) 8. 127 *luðere* (*feole* CFNT). Stanley (1964) criticized 1) as a 'less good' reading in context, 2) as 'no better and no worse' than that of the other MSS, 4) as not substantiated by ME parallels, and 7) as giving inferior sense; Stanley (1964, p. 130) and Hasenfratz (2000, p. 485) suggested alternative palaeographical explanations for the reading *hwet* in 1); and Dobson in the unpublished notes to his *AW* edition accepted the majority reading of 3) as original. It is likely that both 3) and 7) were rewritings in A (see notes on 2. 544, 8. 127).

[37] For a possible example, see 1. 199 *ifeðeret* (a rarer word than *ifeteret*, giving good though less obvious sense); but even if *ifeðeret* was the original reading, the rarity of the verb and the contextual appropriateness of *ifeteret* could have encouraged convergent error in unrelated manuscripts.

[38] In his review of Davis and Wrenn 1962, Eric Stanley questioned the exclusively 'bifid' nature of Dobson's stemma (Stanley 1964, p. 131).

[39] 23 of the 68 variants are shared omissions, usually minor. Shared errors include P. 106 *religiuse* (CF *religiun*) and 1. 292 *iblisset* (CF *in blisse*), both corrected by C² in C; 1. 348 *hwile* (C *wil*, F *voluntee*); 1. 356–7 *buten ane imearket* (CF *imarked bute an*; see note); 3. 357 *wei* (CF *lif*); 3. 401 *haldeð* (CF *habbeð*); 4. 829 *trone* (CF *crune*); 5. 555 *unnet* (C *vnneð*, F *se adonne*). There is also a shared rewriting of 2. 829 *O Godes half*.

[40] See 2. 111 *þes*, 5. 106 *monne*, 6. 371 *sker*, 6. 462 *lanhure*, 7. 90 *þe . . . dead*, 7. 103 *efter monies wene*.

[41] Diensberg (1997) argued that V was more closely related to A than to N; but see the detailed criticism of Diensberg's arguments in Laing 1998.

[42] See pp. xxv–xxvi.

[43] e.g. 1. 395 and 8. 192 *iʒemen* (NV *ihwulen*); see note on 8. 192.

shared readings include some significant errors.[44] Dobson assigned G a separate branch on his stemma between CF and NV, a position consistent with the evidence of his partial collation; however, the full collation indicates that G, where it is running, has a significant number of variants shared with V (55) and N (35), and in some cases with both (27). The links are more numerous and striking with V than with N, but this may be because collation with a C-type text (see p. xxxv) eliminated some shared errors in N. I have accordingly postulated a GNV group, with NV as a sub-group.[45] The 'Lanhydrock fragment' (H) probably also belongs to this group. Although the shortness and poor physical condition of its text mean that the evidence is limited, its variants link it mainly with texts in the lower part of the stemma, N, P, T, and V; its closest affinities are with the NV group, particularly V, and its links with P and T could be accounted for by cross-collation or convergence.[46]

The relationship between the remaining manuscripts and versions, L (the Latin translation), P, R, S (the later French translation), and T, is more difficult to establish. All have been modified for different audiences, and Dobson refers to them collectively as the 'generalized text'; they are clearly interrelated, but the exact nature of their connection is less clear. Dobson's stemma assigned P to a separate branch of the stemma above LRST, LRS to a sub-group below T, and LR to a sub-group within LRS; the full collation, however, suggests some modifications to this configuration.

---

[44] See P. 41 *weote* (NV *wite*), 2. 107 *surquide sire* (NV *surquiderie*), 3. 267–8 *haueð þe feond strengðe*, where *feond* is the subject of *haueð* (NV *haueð þe feondes strengðe*), 3. 307 *hehschipe* (NV *heuischipe*), 4. 76 *hwilinde* (N *wilninde*, V *wilnynge*), 4. 1218 *fatigemini* (NV *fatigetis*), 4. 1219 *wergið*, translating *fatigemini* (NV *weorreð*), 4. 1661 *nim* (NV *nin*), 4. 1680 *strueð*, translating *destruunt* (NV *sturieð*).

[45] The existence of this group cannot be demonstrated from the full text, since G contains only selections from the 'Inner Rule', and V is not running (except for a couple of brief extracts from Part 8) from 6. 185. Shared errors in GN include 3. 118 *þe*¹ (GN *him*, losing track of the overall sense), 4. 1640 *cauernis* (GN *cauernas*), 7. 210 *Creasuse* (G *Cresoles*, N *Kresules*), and 4. 520 *euch wis mon* (G *þis euch mon*, N *euerich wis mon þis*, a double reading suggesting collation with another manuscript). Shared errors in GV include 3. 734 *fowr* (GV *fif*), 5. 306 *as on urn* (A; GV *to derfliche* for original *todreauetliche*), 5. 422 *teares* (GV *tittes*), 6. 15 *gode* (GV *Godes*), 6. 169 *simul* (GV *similes*). The shared GNV variants are generally minor (the most striking shared errors probably go back to an earlier point in the MS tradition; see apparatus criticus for 3. 654 *Apocalypsis* (GNV variants on *Apostol(ic)us*), and note on 5. 152 *muche deale* (GNV *unliche*)).

[46] H shares five variants with V, three with P (including the possible double reading for 3. 315 *mixne* (P *dunge hylle*, H *mixne 'id est dunchul'*: insertion by H scribe)), and one with N. There are also two shared variants with NV, and one each with NP, PTV, and TV. For fuller discussion of the textual affinities of H, see Dobson 1967 and Scahill 2000.

TEXTUAL INTRODUCTION xxxiii

Although L shares some variants with P, R, S, and T, individually or in various combinations, these are comparatively few,[47] and it often retains original readings against the other texts. Since L incorporates some revisions and additions from an A-type text, at least some of these correspondences with the original may be attributable to cross-collation; but sometimes the variation is not of a kind which would obviously have required correction.[48] Also, while L makes some modifications for a mixed audience of religious, it does not share all the modifications in this group, or incorporate the adaptations for male religious in P and T.[49] I have accordingly placed it above PRST on the stemma.

PST form a clear sub-group, with 69 shared variants.[50] Within this sub-group, P shares 105 variants with T,[51] 34 with S; but the strongest link is between S and T, which share a very high number of variants (169), including some significant errors.[52] R, which draws only on Parts 2 and 3 and adapts their material freely, is harder to place. Dobson noted that R and L are linked by their shared

---

[47] 24 agreements with P, 18 with S, 11 with T, 10 with PS, 8 with PST, 6 with ST, and 4 (excluding shared Scriptural references) with R.

[48] e.g. for 6. 359 *mearci* (L *misericordie*) PST have *mede*, and for 6. 373 *ennu* (L *tedio*) forms of *ende*, both variants which give plausible sense in context; and L does not share the omissions in PST at 5. 204, 6. 121–2, and 6. 195–6, although in all three cases the text in PST still makes acceptable sense. Correction of these errors would probably have involved more systematic collation than the relatively small number of shared AL variants suggests.

[49] At 2. 75 L retains the original reading *dehtren* (referring to the descendants of Eve) where PRST have 'sons and daughters'. At 8. 204–6 the recommendations that the anchoresses should have their hair cut *fowr siðen i þe ȝer* and be let blood *as ofte* are altered in PT to *fiftene siþes* and *foure siþes* respectively, but L retains the original advice; and at 8. 209 L has *ancillis* for *meidnes* but P substitutes *seruaunt*, T *seruanz*.

[50] P, although it is running in all parts, has been extensively rewritten and sometimes abridged (particularly in Part 8). T is not running before 1. 391, and has smaller gaps in Parts 3 (335–84) and 4 (1366–423); S is not running for parts of Part 4 (245–437, 554–866, 1704–end), and for all but the end of Parts 1 (449–51) and 8 (336–49).

[51] Most are minor; the most striking shared error is at 4. 490, where T has *luf*, P *loue* for *lust* 'hearing'.

[52] Shared errors in ST include 2. 1029 *wiðhuhe* (TS *wiðhuhe*), 3. 90 *eir* (N *eare*, TS *eares*; cf. P *flessche*), 4. 3 *se . . . þron* (om. ST), 4. 24 *sunegin* (T *ruine him*, S *li* (. . .) *greuer*), 4. 1365 *þe spec oþer þeo* (TS *þu spek oðer ȝer*; cf. G *þu speke þo*), 4. 1515 *grede* (T *grete*, S *ploure*), 4. 1587 *to fulle þe dede* (T *to þe fole dede*, S *a fere la folie*), 5. 159 *þear-as ha liuieð aa* (T *her as he liues aa*, S *tant com il uist en pecche*), 5. 298 *flatrunge* (TS *fluttunge*), 6. 208 *riche* (TS *rihte*), 7. 153 *in integrum* (ST *genus* [sic, for *gentes*] *integrum*; cf. P *gen's integre*); other shared variants include 2. 127–8 *þeo þet vnwrið þe put* (TS *þe vnwrihene put*), 2. 556 *gong-þurl* (TS *gange-hus oðer þe þurl*), 3. 49 (before *wuluene*) TS *ruhe*, 4. 1683 *bihinden strong* (TS *burðenstronge bihinde*), 5. 275 *as he offrede* added after *weouede*, 6. 307 *me neaure* (TS *neauer to mi bodi*). The figure given here for ST agreements does not include the numerous adaptations for a different audience which they also share.

Scriptural chapter- and verse-references (including one referring not to the actual saying quoted in *Ancrene Wisse*, Prov. 13: 3, but to its expansion in Prov. 21: 23); but otherwise their agreements are few and inconclusive,[53] and since Scriptural references would be a desirable addition to an existing text, it is possible that the references in R are the result of collation at some point with an L-type text. R's closest links, if the Scriptural references are discounted, are with P (26 shared variants, including a significant shared error),[54] and I have tentatively grouped it with P on the stemma.

The diagram of the stemma makes no attempt to indicate lost intermediate manuscripts, of which there were probably many more than have survived.[55] None of the surviving manuscripts appears to have influenced any of the others directly, and sometimes their readings imply the existence of intermediate texts.[56]

The genetic relationships indicated by the stemma give only a partial indication of the connections between the surviving texts, which are also linked non-genetically by extensive cross-collation. C (in the surviving annotations by C³) shows physical evidence of later collation with another manuscript, now lost,[57] and most of the surviving texts seem to have been produced in an environment in which cross-collation was the norm rather than the exception;

---

[53] See the instances cited in Dobson 1962, p. 136, fn. 3.

[54] 2. 578 *Let iwurðe, god-mon* (P *lete God yworþe*, R *let God alon, man*, misunderstanding *god* 'good' as 'God'). After P, R's closest links are with T (13 shared variants).

[55] D'Avray (2001), pp. 15–20, argues that 'we should think of a colossal loss rate where sermon manuscripts are concerned', emphasising the relatively low chances of survival for small utilitarian manuscripts used in pastoral care; similar arguments might apply to the manuscripts of *Ancrene Wisse*, whose anchoritic content and difficult Middle English could further have impaired their post-medieval prospects of survival.

[56] e.g. at P. 117 F's *vermail* for A *nempneð* can only be explained as a misunderstanding of a substituted verb, *read*, in its English original, suggesting at least one intermediate manuscript between F and the common ancestor of CF; similarly, at 1. 249 CN have *deorewurðe* for *derue*, suggesting an intermediate manuscript with *deore* between C and the common ancestor of CF. For 2. 945 *deð*, T has *dos*, a correct translation into a more northerly dialect, probably already in its exemplar (scribe T1; see Laing and McIntosh 1995), but S has *morz* 'death', a misunderstanding of the original *deð*, indicating that T must be at at least one further remove from their common ancestor; that S was similarly removed is suggested by the S reading *plaie* for 5. 375 *wune*, presumably from an intermediate Middle English text with *wunde*.

[57] The textual affiliations of this lost exemplar are discussed in detail in Dobson 1972, pp. clxv–clxxii; its closest textual affinities are with L, but there are also agreements with S, T, and P, and some with N and V (particularly V). Dobson concludes, 'it seems that scribe D's lost second manuscript, like all the surviving manuscripts of the Nero-Titus group, was characterized by extensive and complicated cross-agreements with the other members of the group' (p. clxx).

TEXTUAL INTRODUCTION

Dobson noted in particular double readings in F, G, L, N, P, and S, 'in which the inherited reading (either true or false) is blended with another belonging to a different tradition.'[58] The possible influence of a revised A-type text, particularly on L, P, and V, has been discussed above; and there are more numerous cross-agreements between manuscripts other than A. Dobson saw C as 'the most important manuscript' for the understanding of these cross-agreements, pointing out the 'very numerous and significant cross-agreements between C as originally written' and other manuscripts or versions lower on the stemma.[59] The text most clearly influenced by collation with a C-type manuscript is N. Although it corresponds most consistently with V, it also has a high number of variants (194) shared uniquely with C, occasionally with double readings at points of shared variation.[60] Other texts which share a significant number of variants with C are G,[61] P,[62] T,[63] and V.[64] In Dobson's 1972 edition of C he withdrew his 1962 suggestion that these cross-agreements showed the influence of a lost manuscript π, copied from β, with which C and the other manuscripts had been collated,[65] noting that the main scribe of C was dependent on the receipt of separate, non-consecutive quires to compile his manuscript,[66] and therefore cannot have had access when copying to more than one exemplar. He argued instead that C, because of the relatively authoritative status conferred on it by the C² modifications, had

---

[58] Dobson 1962, p. 137.   [59] Dobson 1962, p. 139.

[60] The distribution of agreements is uneven, with a much lower proportion in Parts 5–8 than in earlier parts of the work. Double readings in N incorporating C-type variants include 1. 107 *in aniuersaries* (C *ant 3ef hit bið ani munedai*, N *ine aniuersaries, þet is ine munedawes*); 1. 180 *best*, C *mest*, N *best and mest*; 1. 197 *gederið* (C *pencheð vpo* (corr. C²), N *pencheð and gedereð*); and 4. 1213 *Godes monhead* (C *monnes. God wat*, N *Godes monheade. God wot*).

[61] 34 shared variants, including a striking double reading (4. 437 *stingeð* (C *stinkeð*, G *stinkeð uel stingeð*)).

[62] 89 shared variants, mostly up to the end of Part 4; about a third, however, are shared omissions (unlikely to be significant in this case, since both texts tend to abridge). P's reading for 1. 93 *Non* 'Nones' (C *naut* (corr. C²), P *and elles nou3th. Onon*) may reflect a failed attempt to make sense both of the original reading and of the erroneous reading in C. The adoption in P of two significant errors in C, for P. 41 *inwit* (C *inwið* (corr., with gloss, by C²), P *inwiþ and wiþoute*) and 4. 740 *offearen* (C *offren*, P *enticen* (*þer-to*)), can be explained by the plausibility in context of *inwið* (a problem recognized by C² and further addressed in A; see note on P. 41), and the obsolescence of *offearen* (not recorded in *MED* after the mid-thirteenth century), which would have encouraged its confusion with *offren*.

[63] 84 shared variants, mostly in Parts 2–4 (T only running from 1. 391) and Part 8.

[64] 79 shared variants, mostly up to the end of Part 4 (just under a quarter, however, are minor shared omissions).

[65] See Dobson 1962, pp. 136–44.   [66] See Dobson 1972, pp. xxix–xxxvi.

exercised a direct influence on later tradition.[67] But the objections he raised in his 1962 article to this possibility still retain much of their force: why do later manuscripts with C-type readings only rarely include the C² modifications?[68] And why do their readings sometimes include errors corrected in C either by the main scribe or by C²?[69] The use of the *pecia* method of reproduction for C raises a third possibility: that at an early point in the textual tradition multiple C-type texts were produced, of which only C itself has survived.[70]

N also shares 58 variants with F;[71] and other cross-agreements at lower points of the stemma suggest extensive cross-collation with texts related to N and V, as well as C. N has 212 shared variants with P,[72] 158 with S,[73] and 117 with T;[74] V has 176 shared variants with P,[75] 89 with T,[76] and 35 with S. [77]

---

[67] Dobson 1972, p. cxxii, fn. 1.

[68] V incorporates a C² addition not carried over to A at P. 16 (see note); F shares the C² gloss on *inwit* at P. 41; L *Hoc ideo consulo* may reflect the C² addition at P. 67; N shares an added *rihte* at 1. 88, and NPR an added gloss, *þe unwreah þe put*, at 2. 125; C² *monnes* at 2. 5 may be reflected in R *of man*', and C² *of his hus* at 2. 187–8 in R *of hire hus*. The C² addition 'Inoh meaðful ... lutel' shared by N (see 8. 349–50 and note) is, as Dobson says, 'a special case' (Dobson 1962, p. 140, fn. 2), and may have reached N by a different route.

[69] For examples, see fns. 60 and 62 above; also 1. 89 *þis* (CP *þe*, corr. in C by C²) and 1. 113 *suffragies* (CP *suffrages*, corr. in C by the main scribe and glossed by C²).

[70] On the '*pecia* system' of manuscript copying and its historical antecedents, see Parkes 1991, pp. xix, 304–8, and the references given there.

[71] Most are minor, but there are three agreements on significant (though plausible) errors: misinterpretations of 5. 487 *to* as 'two', 6. 481 *þeh* 'thigh' as 'though', and 7. 217 *bodi* as *bode* 'offer'.

[72] The variants are fairly evenly distributed; they include smoothings and adjustments of word-order (about a fifth are additions of 'and'), modernizations of vocabulary, and some minor shared glosses and additions. There are a few significant shared errors: *luue* for 2. 653 *leome*, *imprudentem* for 3. 705 *inpudentem*, *cundles* for 4. 408 *fundles*, and *Ieremie* for 5. 453 *Ierome*.

[73] The shared variants occur wherever S is running, but there are more in Part 2 than Part 4, and in Part 6 than Part 5. Most are minor smoothings and expansions; about a third are additions of 'and'. There are seven double readings shared by N and S in Part 2 (see app. crit. for 2. 564, 2. 667, 2. 688, 2. 706, 2. 732, 2. 955, 2. 962), with a more doubtful one at 5. 27, and two in N only, at 2. 880 and 4. 1290.

[74] Most of the variants are minor rewritings and substitutions of commoner for rarer words; there are three double readings in N (at 2. 190, 3. 760, and 4. 226).

[75] The variants are fairly evenly distributed where P and V are running. Most of them are minor; about 60% are modernizations of vocabulary. There are three double readings in P (4. 77, 4. 995, and 4. 1011); the most notable shared errors are *hastilich* for 4. 383 *Esteliche* and *bellum* for 5. 186 *Belial*.

[76] Most of the variants are minor; about a quarter are modernizations of vocabulary.

[77] These include some S readings apparently derived from V-type errors, for P. 123 *hweðer* (V *wereþ*, S *userunt*), 3. 148 *iwurðeð* (V *iwordet*, S *paroles parolent*), and 4. 1313 *wis* (V *wiþ*, S *par*).

THE DEVELOPMENT OF THE WORK

Ian Doyle, writing on the dissemination of *Ancrene Wisse*, commented that the 'social changes of ownership and the geographical movement of copies and versions of the *Riwle*, as well as the adaptations of it, throughout its history, between one sex and the other, one class and another, one region and another, and back again, manifest its exceptionally dynamic character.'[78]

This 'dynamic' textual development reflects the success of *Ancrene Wisse* as a work of practical religious instruction; from a very early stage it began to be modified for different social and institutional contexts. The potential for textual evolution is present even in the original version, where the author emphasises that the detailed prescriptions of the 'Outer Rule' are no more than recommendations that can be modified according to the needs of its users. He also allows for the possibility of a more general audience; in the *Preface*, he notes that the 'Inner Rule' is relevant not just to anchoresses but to 'euch mon' (P. 79), and much of the pastoral material on the sins and confession in Parts 4 and 5 is not adapted exclusively for an anchoritic audience but applies, as he says in Part 5, 'to alle men iliche' (5. 595–6).[79] The author himself seems to have responded to changes in the numbers and circumstances of his immediate audience of anchoresses by a series of textual modifications, to the 'Inner Rule' as well as the 'Outer Rule'; and the 'multi-layered functionality'[80] of his work encouraged its adaptation for other kinds of user, including nuns, male religious, the secular clergy, and the laity.

For the editor of A, the most important textual developments are those connected with the expansion of the original group of anchoresses. The manuscript evidence suggests a cumulative process of change, with successive additions and revisions at various points in the textual tradition; and although these modifications are most fully represented in A, a few survive only in other manuscripts.

An early casualty of the process of change was an address to the three anchoresses for whom the work was first composed, preserved

---

[78] Doyle 1954, I. 234.
[79] See further Millett 1990, pp. 139–43.
[80] The phrase is borrowed from Schnell (1999), who speaks of the *vielschichtige Funktionalität* (p. 385) of vernacular sermons which might be used both by preachers and for private reading by the laity.

in full only in N (see 4. 192 fn. and note). This passage, since it is an integral component of the author's argument, must have been part of the original work, but its specific references to the number and circumstances of the anchoresses have been reduced or removed in other surviving texts, and in AV the entire passage is omitted.

More extensive changes can be found in the alterations to C by the earlier of its two thirteenth-century correctors, C², identified by Dobson with the original author.[81] These include a number of additions and revisions to the original text, particularly to the 'Outer Rule' in Part 8. The personal details of the original three anchoresses had already been cut in the C text,[82] indicating that the composition of the audience had changed by the time it was copied, and C²'s revisions to Part 8 suggest a corresponding change in their circumstances: the anchoresses are now geographically dispersed,[83] dependent on a variety of patrons, not necessarily known to them or trustworthy,[84] and forced to be more reliant on their own labour.[85] The general tendency of the C² revisions is to modify the rigour of the original prescriptions,[86] discouraging excessive austerity[87] and reasserting the value, within limits, of politeness and sociability[88] (although an extended tirade against wimples stresses the danger of too much contact with the outside world).[89]

Further layers of revision, again addressed to the expanding group of anchoresses, underlie the text in A. One of the most important is represented by two sets of revisions in separate *distinctiones*, Part 4 and Part 8; they seem also to have been wholly or partly incorporated, in an earlier form, in texts antecedent to L, P, and V, although the evidence is fuller for Part 4 than for Part 8.[90]

The first set consists mainly of expansions to the description of the

---

[81] See p. xiv above.
[82] See 4. 192 fn. and note.
[83] See 8. 73 and note.
[84] See 8. 84–9 and notes.
[85] See 8. 90–4 (on keeping animals), 8. 101–4 (on the sale of goods).
[86] See, for example, 8. 108–9 (on storing others' property), 8. 200–1 (on teaching), and 8. 204–6 (on haircutting); also the references in the previous footnote.
[87] See 8. 60, 8. 62 (the anchoress should live *meaðfulliche* rather than *gnedeliche*).
[88] See 8. 73–83 and fn. 6 (on the treatment of visitors), 8. 167–9 (on giving presents).
[89] See 8. 141–60.
[90] Part 8 is very imperfectly represented in LPV. The full text of Part 8 is preserved in only one manuscript of the Latin version, V¹, in a fragmentary form; V, which has three folios missing between 6. 185 and 8. 144, preserves only two short passages, the first of which is incomplete (8. 144–62, 8. 188–96; see Zettersten and Diensberg 2000, pp. 128/26–129/12); and P's text of Part 8 is drastically abridged. However, where L is running it shares the majority of the revisions in A; both passages included in V reflect them; and there is a possible, though faint, echo of one of them in P (see note on 8. 131–3).

offspring of the seven deadly sins, running from 4. 247 to 4. 368;[91] some of these have been further expanded or otherwise modified in A. It may also include a few minor additions elsewhere in Part 4.[92] The content of the added passages on the sins suggests that they are directed particularly at women religious,[93] and their style (where they are more than brief explanatory glosses) is consistent with that of the original work.

The second set either incorporates or adapts further most of the revisions to Part 8 made in C², and adds further revisions; as in Part 4, sometimes these revisions are expanded or otherwise modified in A. Some are further mitigations of the severity of the original prescriptions[94] or warnings against too much voluntary asceticism,[95] and one first-person addition emphasizes that inner disposition is more important than outward austerity ('Me is leouere þet ȝe þolien wel an heard word þen an heard here', 8. 138–9); but the anchoresses are also warned against over-attachment to their families and pride in their fine needlework,[96] and of the importance of observing the Outer Rule.[97]

Another significant group of revisions is the four substantial additions shared by A and F, the last also by V: 1. 359–90 (on devotions, beginning 'þus Ich biginne mine Auez oðerhwiles'), 2. 208–62 (on the need for the anchoresses to guard themselves from the gaze of visitors), 2. 311–26 (a recommendation of 'Vre Freres Prechurs ant ure Freres Meonurs' as trustworthy visitors, and advice on confession to them), and 2. 884–940 (a warning to the anchoresses against frivolous, arrogant, and malicious speech, opening with the text *Quomodo obscuratum est aurum*). All are consistent in style with the original version, and all use the first person;[98] it seems likely, as

---

[91] See app. crit. for 4. 247–50 (ALPV), 4. 257–9 (ALPV), 4. 260 (ALV), 4. 271–96 (ALPV), 4. 318–33 (ALV), 4. 339–42 (ALPV), 4. 344–9 (ALPV), 4. 351 (ALP(?)V), 4. 367–8 (ALV).

[92] See app. crit. for 4. 618–19 (APV), 4. 620–1 (ALV), 4. 891–3 (APV), 4. 1611 (AV).

[93] Most notably the warning against 'acointance i religiun', 4. 249–50. The linking of quarreling specifically to nuns at 4. 281 is a further addition in A; see note.

[94] See 8. 29–30 (fasting), 8. 120–3 (girdling), 8. 131–3 (footwear), 8. 164–5 (clothing).

[95] See 8. 125–7 (disciplines), 8. 134–5 (sleeping arrangements), 8. 218–19 (washing).

[96] See 8. 171–82.

[97] See 8. 225–6 'ah . . . wundre' (addition in AL to C² revision).

[98] The F version of the first replaces the opening sentence by the more impersonal 'Ici comence askunes Aueez.' The *we* of the last could be no more than a generic preacher's 'we', but the addition also includes an apparently personal address to the anchoresses: the writer comments on a saying by Solomon, 'þet hit limpe to ei of ow, Godd ne leue neuer' (2. 903).

with the ALPV revisions, that they were added by the original author for the expanding group of anchoresses. Dobson has argued convincingly that at least some of these additions were separately circulated on slips of parchment.[99] The first is placed a few lines later in F than in A, at a less appropriate point, after *awakenin* 1. 399; and although the fourth was clearly written to develop further the points made in 2. 866–83, it is copied immediately after the second addition in F (suggesting that the two additions had travelled together), and in V is added at the very end of the work. In A they are correctly placed; but the textual quality of the *Quomodo obscuratum* addition in A is unexpectedly poor.

Some material appears in A only. This includes the further expansions of the LPV revisions mentioned above and five longer additions, four in Part 4 and one in Part 8. The modifications of the LPV revisions sometimes involve no more than tidying-up or clarifying by expansion,[100] but sometimes extend their concessions or warnings further.[101] All but one of the longer additions (4. 414–18, a compliment to the audience on their sexual innocence) directly address the concerns of the expanded group of anchoresses, described in the addition beginning *Pax uobis* at 4. 1076–1101 as 'twenti nuðe oðer ma' (4. 1078): maintaining unity (the *Pax uobis* addition), dealing with malicious gossip (4. 1108–14), requesting and accepting donations (4. 1188–1209), and observing the proper boundaries with one's own and visiting maids (8. 320–35). Again, they are consistent in style with the original work; three of the five use the first person,[102] and it is likely that they are the responsibility of the original author.

The exact dating and chronological relationship of these revisions are uncertain. Those including references to visits from the friars (2. 311–26 (AF) and 8. 78–9 (A only, but possibly part of the ALPV group of revisions; see note)) certainly postdate their arrival in England (Dominicans in 1221, Franciscans in 1224), and probably also their settlement in the West Midlands (Franciscans in

[99] See Dobson 1962, pp. 152–5.
[100] See 4. 257–9, 8. 73–83, and the incomplete revisions at 4. 259–60 and 8. 204–6.
[101] See, e.g., 8. 104–5 (justification of manual labour), 8. 107–8 (more restrictions on storing possessions), 8. 182–5 (further warnings on fine needlework), 8. 199 (another concession on teaching), and 8. 217–8 (additional recommendation on washing). At 8. 211–12, however, the recommendations of the original version on relaxation during bloodletting are qualified by the comment in A, 'þah euch worltlich froure is unwurðe to ancre'; cf., in a longer A addition, 8. 331–5.
[102] 4. 414–18, 4. 1076–1101, 4. 1188–1209.

TEXTUAL INTRODUCTION   xli

Worcester, c.1227, and Hereford, before 1228; Dominicans in Shrewsbury, before 1232, and Chester, before 1236). It is also possible that the address to the larger group of anchoresses in 4. 1076–1101, in A only, refers to the Dominican priories at Shrewsbury and Chester (see note on 4. 1084–5). There is a clear line of development from the revisions of Part 8 by C² (whose hand has been dated as 'probably 1240s/50s'[103]) to the revisions in ALPV, and the A text in Parts 4 and 8 seems to represent a later stage of the revisions in LPV, but it is less clear how they are related chronologically to the other groups of revisions incorporated in A (though the addition in A at 4. 1188–1209 appears to reflect a rather earlier policy on requesting and accepting donations than the C² and AL revisions to the original version at 8. 84–9).

Dobson argued that the text in A was 'a close copy of the author's own final and definitive revision of his work';[104] but there is some internal evidence which suggests that it was the product of a less systematic and comprehensive process of 'rolling revision', responding as necessary to the increasing numbers and changing circumstances of its audience of anchoresses. The only identifiable 'definitive textual moment'[105] in the production of *Ancrene Wisse*— a specific point at which the author saw his work as complete— belongs to an earlier stage of its development; he tells his readers at the end of the original version, 'Me were leouere, Godd hit wite, do me toward Rome þen forte biginnen hit eft forte donne' (8. 339–40). The form of the work in A seems to be less a new version of *Ancrene Wisse, cohérente et harmonieuse* (to borrow a phrase from Bédier)[106] in its own right, than a modified and updated form of the original version, retaining distinct and sometimes incompatible elements from the different stages of its development. Although the major revisions preserved in the A text are almost certainly authorial, it is less certain that it reflects an overall authorial revision. Some problems in the original version, or arising in the earlier stages of its development, have been allowed to stand;[107] adjustments to the

[103] See p. xiv above. [104] Dobson 1962, p. 163.
[105] The phrase is Derek Pearsall's; see Pearsall 1985, p. 100.
[106] See Bédier 1928, p. 353.
[107] A discrepancy in the numbering of *exempla* in the original (4. 1015–53) has not been picked up in A (although it has in LPV; see note on 4. 1046); and early marginal annotations and additions have sometimes been awkwardly or wrongly incorporated in the main text (see notes on 2. 456, 2. 506–7, 2. 568–71, 3. 513, 3. 560, 3. 765, 3. 777–8, 4. 159–60, 4. 351, 5. 400–1).

text made necessary by the process of revision have not always been carried out;[108] and it is difficult to reconcile the hypothesis of hands-on authorial revision with the poor textual quality of the *Quomodo obscuratum* addition, apparently copied from a faulty exemplar at at least one remove from the original.[109]

Although A incorporates most of the revisions made for the expanding group of anchoresses, a few revisions for the same or a similar audience are found only in other manuscripts. A does not normally carry over the modifications made by C² to parts of the text other than Part 8—perhaps, as Dobson suggests, because they were seen as 'merely incidental to [the author's] work of correction' rather than purposeful revision[110]—and omits two of C²'s Part 8 revisions, on the adaptability of the 'Outer Rule' and on the maids' clothing.[111] A possibly authorial addition to Part 1 incorporated in N (see 1. 134 fn.) recommends the lay brothers' Hours of the writer's order as an alternative devotional routine ('3if ei of ow wule don þus, heo voleweð her, ase in oþre obseruances, muchel of vre ordre, and wel Ich hit reade'); and in F the recommendation in Part 8 to abstain from meat is replaced by a description of various monastic regulations on abstinence, including the less demanding customs of the Augustinian canons (see 8. 32 fn.).

In addition to the revisions described above, *Ancrene Wisse* was modified as it developed by the incorporation of a variety of minor additions and alterations. Some seem to have originated as marginal additions intended for integration in the text, others as marginal annotations; they may not appear in all manuscripts, and even when they do it may be at different points in the text. They include Latin source texts supplied for English quotations, supplementary Latin quotations, Scriptural and patristic references, additional cross-references, glosses on difficult Middle English words, explanatory expansion of difficult passages, and qualifications of statements which

---

[108] The damage to the argument in A caused by the cutting of the address to the original three sisters (see 4. 192 fn. and note) has not been repaired; a surviving reference to them at 2. 1027–30 remains undeleted; and the original numbering of the offspring of the seven deadly sins in Part 4 has not been adjusted in A to match the Part 4 revisions, although LPV have made the necessary alterations (see notes on 4. 308, 4. 338).

[109] See Dobson 1962, pp. 154–5. The text in A is linked by shared errors with V against F, and has further errors of its own (not necessarily the responsibility of the normally accurate A scribe).

[110] See Dobson 1972, pp. cix–cxx.

[111] The first (see 8. 25 fn.) may have been seen as duplicating material in another C² addition, incorporated at 8. 220–5; for the second, see 8. 249 fn.

might be seen as morally or theologically problematic.[112] A number of the additions by C² to C fall into this category, and some of the other modifications can probably be attributed to the original author (e.g. the qualification of the advice on frank confession at 5. 252–6, which appears in all manuscripts running, though not always in the same place); but often there is not enough evidence to determine their origin, and some of the minor alterations are unlikely to be authorial.[113]

Most of the textual developments described so far seem to reflect a specific historical and institutional context: a continuing, though evolving, connection between the original author of the work and a particular group of anchoresses, from the first three 'leoue sustren' described in N (see 4. 192 fn.) to the 'deore dehtren' addressed in a Part 8 addition found only in A (8. 106). From an early stage, however, the work began to be adapted for users other than the original anchoresses. In some cases, the change of audience was not accompanied by significant textual change. The earlier French translation (F) is a close rendering of the Middle English;[114] and the text in the Vernon manuscript (V), although late, seems to have been carefully copied from a good early exemplar, with no significant adaptation for its late-fourteenth-century readers other than modernization of vocabulary, and the omission of at least some material from Part 8.[115] The modifications in other surviving texts, however, show that at least some users regarded it as an 'open' work[116] which could be freely altered for different purposes. These modifications (described in detail in the section on 'Manuscripts and Versions' above) include not only minor textual adjustments to address new audiences, but in some cases more general rewriting, the addition of new—and sometimes radically different—content, the rearrangement or omission of sections of the work, and the incorporation of material from it in other works.

The earliest adaptations seem to have been intended primarily to extend the use of the work to a broader audience of religious. G may have been compiled for a mendicant community;[117] the Latin translation (L) takes into account nuns and male religious as well as

[112] For examples of the last category, see 4. 397, 4. 410, 5. 252–6, 5. 451–2, 7. 193–4.
[113] See notes on 6. 238, 6. 466–7, and pp. lviii–lix below.
[114] Even, occasionally, falling back on Middle English vocabulary: see notes on 2. 259 *itild*, 8. 50 *husewifschipe*, 8. 141 *cappen*.
[115] See fn. 90 above.
[116] For this concept, see Thompson 1991, p. 180.   [117] See p. xvi.

anchoresses;[118] and T is derived from a text adapted for a male religious community.[119] In G, L, and T the modifications to the original version are minor (mainly alteration of pronoun-forms for a mixed or male audience, generalization or omission of addresses to the original 'leoue sustren', and occasional adaptations of anchorite-specific references), and there are some indications in the text of T of an attempt to reverse them.[120] Both G and L, however, discard parts of the work inappropriate for their users. G draws only on the 'Inner Rule' for its compilation of selections; L deliberately omits all but a short extract from Part 1,[121] and its translation of Part 8 is wholly or mostly omitted in all but one of the manuscripts.[122]

The adaptations of *Ancrene Wisse* for a more general audience involve more extensive modifications of the original work. The later French translation (S) is addressed partly to a mixed audience of religious of all kinds, partly to a general audience of religious and laity. It could, in a sense, be seen as a different work, since its material from *Ancrene Wisse* constitutes less than half of a longer 'Compilation' incorporating other pastoral material. While it is possible that it was originally planned as an expansion of the full text of *Ancrene Wisse*, the 'Compilation' as it stands does not reflect its structure, rearranging and separating different parts of the 'Inner Rule', and omitting the 'Outer Rule' altogether. Although the content of the source text, where it is used, is generally preserved, it is sometimes augmented by additional Latin quotations, and the phrasing is often expanded.[123] The two later English adaptations, P and R, both of which address a lay audience, depart even further from the original version. R's *Tractatus de quinque sensibus*, which Dobson describes as 'really a new work',[124] draws only on Parts 2 and 3, rewriting freely, omitting some material from the original and adding further material from other sources; Watson (2003, p. 217) sees it as articulating, though in a 'less radical' way than P, 'the connection between the solitary ideal and the devout laity . . . [which] is the strongest thread in *Ancrene Wisse*'s later reception.'[125]

---

[118] See p. xviii. [119] See notes on 8. 204–5 and 8. 206.
[120] See p. xxiv.
[121] The extract begins: *Inter cetera que in prima parte continentur quoad officium divinum notandum quod in missa eleuato corpore Christi dicendum est* . . . (d'Evelyn 1944, 9/18–20).
[122] See pp. xviii–xix (Ma and Me), xxii (R²), xxvi (V¹), and xxvii.
[123] See further pp. xxii–xxiii.
[124] Introduction to unpublished edition of *Ancrene Wisse*.
[125] See further pp. xxi–xxii.

Although P retains the structure of the original work, it is heavily abridged and extensively rewritten, probably for a readership of London bourgeoisie.[126] It shows signs of multiple layers of adaptation, not only the traces of a thirteenth-century adaptation for male religious which it shares with T but at least two stages of revision in the fourteenth century, adding new and to some extent unorthodox content.[127] Some of the revisions it includes, emphasizing the merits of the active life, are in direct conflict with the values of the original version; and its often barely intelligible text illustrates (more than any other surviving text of *Ancrene Wisse*) the potentially destructive effects of a long chain of manuscript transmission.

The 'dynamic' textual history of *Ancrene Wisse* suggests a context in which its continuing functionality was sometimes seen as more important than its textual integrity. Although the high level of cross-collation in the manuscript tradition indicates that its users were concerned with the quality of their texts, its adaptations for new and different audiences might involve major changes to its language, style, content, and structure. This process of adaptation helped to extend the active life and influence of *Ancrene Wisse* to the end of the Middle Ages; but it also entailed a cumulative erosion of its original identity, and (as the example of P shows) there was a limit to the amount of variation that it could sustain. 'Nous retrouvons ici le facteur temps: la capacité d'étirement du texte a des limites, au-delà desquelles tout craque, et il n'y a plus de communication possible.'[128]

EDITORIAL AIMS AND PRINCIPLES

A long-standing need in *Ancrene Wisse* studies has been an edition of *Ancrene Wisse* which draws on the evidence of the manuscript tradition as a whole to provide an edited text suitable for general scholarly use. The earliest full-text edition, based on N with selected variants from C and T, and accompanied by an interleaved translation, was published by James Morton in 1853; in spite of the editorial limitations sharply pointed out by his successors,[129] its accessibility has kept it in use to the present day. Later full-text editions of *Ancrene Wisse* have been almost exclusively diplomatic. Between 1944 and 2000 the Early English Text Society published

---

[126] See Hanna 2003.   [127] See pp. xx–xxi.
[128] Zumthor 1972, p. 11.   [129] See Millett 1996, p. 34.

diplomatic editions of all the Middle English texts, and diplomatic or semi-diplomatic editions of the French and Latin versions.[130] These editions, intended (in Dobson's words) *in usum editorum philologorumque*,[131] offered mostly minimal, mainly palaeographical, commentary and annotation, as does the recent parallel-text edition (diplomatic transcripts of A, C, N, and V) by Kubouchi and Ikegami (2003, 2005). Some editions of individual parts of *Ancrene Wisse*, and the full-text TEAMS edition by Robert Hasenfratz, have offered more approachable corrected texts of single manuscripts, with substantial commentaries but without a full critical apparatus.[132]

I have followed Dobson (and most other recent editors, with the exception of Ackerman and Dahood, who preferred the earliest surviving manuscript, C) in choosing Cambridge, Corpus Christi College, MS 402 (A) as the base manuscript. In the first place, it offers an excellent copy-text, very consistently spelt and in a dialect which is probably not far removed from that of the original author.[133] In the second place, its text is relatively free from error in substantive readings; although it includes a number of omissions caused by eyeskip, and occasional clusters of errors apparently caused by temporary inattention, in general it requires very little emendation. In the third place, it contains substantial revisions and additions, some not found in any other manuscript, which are probably to be attributed to the original author.

Dobson's editorial principles have been modified, however, to take account both of recent developments in textual theory[134] and of the special problems raised by the textual transmission of the work itself. Although the edited text probably differs very little in practice from the text that Dobson himself would have produced, it is not, as his would have been, a 'critical edition' in the traditional sense; instead, it offers a corrected version of one historical form of the work, the text in A, set in the broader context of the textual evolution of the work as a whole.

[130] See Millett 1996, pp. 34–6.
[131] Dobson 1972, p. xix.
[132] See Shepherd 1959 (Parts 6 and 7, based on A), Ackerman and Dahood 1984 (*Preface* and Part 1, based on C), Millett and Wogan-Browne 1990 (Parts 7 and 8, based on A), and Hasenfratz 2000 (complete text, based on A).
[133] See Dobson's analysis of the language of C² ('Scribe B') in Dobson 1972, pp. cxxx–cxl.
[134] See Greetham 1995 and Greetham 1999 for an overview of recent developments in textual theory; and, on the textual criticism of Middle English works in particular, Pearsall 1994 and Moffat and McCarren in McCarren and Moffat 1998, pp. 25–57.

It is difficult even to discuss the problems of editing the A text of *Ancrene Wisse* in the language of traditional textual criticism. This terminology, originally developed to describe the post-classical transmission of classical works, carries with it implicit assumptions and value-judgements which are not necessarily appropriate to other kinds of textual transmission. In particular, it tends to set the terms 'author' and 'scribe' in binary opposition, a tendency encouraged by the wide chronological and cultural gap between classical authors and their post-classical copyists: 'instead of seeing manuscripts as embodiments or versions of the text, the classical editor regards them as imperfect carriers of an entity that is wholly independent from them and far superior to them in value'.[135] In a tradition which sees textual transmission primarily as a degenerative process, the progressive destruction of the form and sense of the author's original by repeated copying, this binary opposition can become a Manichaean dualism, in which the scribes are identified with the forces of darkness: they are responsible for the 'corruption' of their text by 'scribal error' (a term sometimes applied by editors to all non-authorial variants), and, if they draw on more than one exemplar, for its 'contamination'.[136]

Although the use of this terminology, in the textual criticism of both classical and medieval works, can coexist with much more complex and subtle analysis of the process of textual change—and even, in recent years, with quite radical questioning of traditional assumptions—it still carries with it the inherited assumption of the binary opposition of author and scribe, by which (as Jerome J. McGann puts it), 'the author's productive work and the institutions of reproduction are either divorced from each other ... or ... set in a negative relationship.'[137] For some Middle English works, this raises no major problems; Chaucer's address to his scribe Adam neatly exemplifies the traditional author-scribe opposition.[138] But, as Ralph Hanna has pointed out, Chaucer's attitude to textual transmission is wholly untypical of his time;[139] and with some types of work,

---

[135] Tarrant 1995, p. 96.
[136] A *locus classicus* for this approach is Maas 1927.
[137] McGann 1992, p. 119.
[138] 'Chaucers wordes unto Adam, his owne scriveyn', in Benson 1988, p. 650.
[139] Hanna 1996, p. 175: 'He knew that he was sui generis, that he made demands of a unique sort on contemporary transmission procedures. These forms of transmission were geared to other kinds of textual production—for example, the varieties of active redaction that typify surviving versions of Auchinleck romances ...'.

the assumption of an author-scribe opposition can be an impediment to thinking clearly about the actual or probable circumstances of their composition and transmission.

One problem with this opposition is the ambiguity of the term 'scribe'. Is the 'scribe' the copyist of a particular manuscript, someone whose primary occupation is the copying of manuscripts, or any agent of textual change other than the author? The binary opposition between scribe and author carries with it the implication that the two are different kinds of people, which is not always the case; and the identification of scribes as the agents of textual change does not allow sufficiently for other possibilities.

Although *Ancrene Wisse* has traditionally been treated by scholars as a self-contained literary work, 'das wichtigste prosadenkmal der frühmittelenglischen zeit',[140] it is also a work of practical pastoral instruction, and its function as *Gebrauchsprosa*[141] influenced the nature of its textual transmission. From an early stage it was revised and adapted for different purposes both by its original author and by others, a process entailing a significant overlap between production and reproduction. The problem of editing works of this kind has recently been addressed by David d'Avray in his study of thirteenth-century Paris marriage sermons.[142] The textual tradition of these sermons has some features in common with that of *Ancrene Wisse*, whose early transmission seems to have taken place in an an institutional context which, like the better-documented *milieu* described by d'Avray, included 'friars, other educated clerics, and professional scribes'.[143] The model sermons d'Avray edits are in Latin, and some of the surviving manuscripts reflect the relatively stable textual transmission characteristic of medieval Latin works; but others show a level of variation more common in vernacular sermons, ranging from casual substitution ('free variation by a confident copyist'[144]) through glosses and minor modifications of phrasing to quite extensive and skilful rewriting. D'Avray explains these different patterns of transmission by the different types of

---

[140] Heuser 1907, p. 104.
[141] For a discussion of the concept of *Gebrauchsprosa*, with a detailed case-study of later-medieval sermon transmission in Latin and the vernacular, see Schnell 1999.
[142] *Medieval Marriage Sermons: Mass Communication in a Culture without Print* (d'Avray 2001).
[143] D'Avray 2001, pp. 15–16. For a discussion of the probable social and institutional context of the *Ancrene Wisse* group, see Millett 2004.
[144] D'Avray 2001, p. 24.

copyist involved in the dissemination of the sermons. He argues (against current orthodoxy, but persuasively) that the contribution of the friars in particular to the copying of devotional literature has been considerably underestimated; points out that it is unlikely that commercial scribes would deliberately alter the texts they were paid to copy; and attributes the high level of textual variation in some manuscripts to preachers adapting the texts in the process of copying them for their personal use.[145]

A manuscript tradition of this kind is hard to accommodate within the conceptual framework of classical textual criticism. D'Avray comments on one modified sermon, 'As with some other nonconformist versions of other sermons edited here, the skill at play in abridging and adapting the standard text is remarkable. The scribe (or the scribe of some ancestor manuscript) is almost an author.'[146] In a *milieu* of the kind described by d'Avray, where there is no significant chronological gap between production and reproduction, where those who copy works may belong to the same educational and institutional context as their original authors, and where transmission may also involve recomposition, the assumption of a binary opposition between 'scribe' and 'author' becomes problematic.

Some scholars working with textual traditions of this kind have addressed the problem by adopting a modified terminology, setting up a third, intermediate category. Rüdiger Schnell, analysing the textual transmission of a group of Latin sermons and their late-medieval vernacular adaptations, distinguishes between *Schreiber* (who simply reproduce works, or modify them only in minor and local ways) and *Textproduzenten* (who rework them);[147] Eric H. Reiter sees textual change in late-medieval Latin devotional literature as driven by 'scribe-readers', clerics copying and adapting devotional works for their own use;[148] John Thompson, discussing textual instability in late Middle English religious literature, uses the term 'scribe-editors';[149] and d'Avray himself speaks of 'scribe-users' and 'copyist-adaptors'.[150]

But this terminology is still too inflexible to accommodate all the possible forms of textual change. In particular, the tendency to identify 'scribes' (however the term is qualified) as the agents of

[145] See d'Avray 2001, pp. 15–30.
[146] D'Avray 2001, p. 285.
[147] Schnell 1999, p. 391.
[148] See Reiter 1996.
[149] See Thompson 1991.
[150] D'Avray 2001, pp. 39, 237.

textual change implies that change takes place at the point of copying; this may be the point at which changes are incorporated into a text, but it is not necessarily the point at which they are made. Some types of textual change can be linked more or less directly with the copying process: mechanical errors and misunderstandings, the casual variation of vocabulary and word-order often found in the transmission of vernacular works, and, in some cases, more purposeful linguistic modification, like the consistent modernization of the original word-order of *Ancrene Wisse* in BL MS Cotton Nero A. xiv (N).[151] Other types of change, however, such as correction, collation with other manuscripts, annotation, revision, and adaptation for different audiences, might be carried out separately from the copying process, not necessarily by the copyist; and some, like the cutting or rearrangement of parts of a work, might not involve any physical involvement at all in its textual transmission, only the expressed wishes of the 'patron' commissioning a particular manuscript.[152] Once alterations to a work have been incorporated in the text by a copyist, it can be difficult to establish whether the copyist or a predecessor (whether 'the scribe of some ancestor manuscript' or another agent) was responsible for them; but the evidence of BL MS Cotton Cleopatra C. vi (C), which preserves extensive modifications to its text of *Ancrene Wisse* by two people other than the main scribe, illustrates how copying and textual alteration might be independent processes. The earlier modifier, C^2, corrects, glosses, annotates, expands, and revises the main text; the later, C^3, adds further annotations and corrections, collating it with another manuscript. C^2 is probably to be identified with the original author;[153] and neither C^2 nor C^3 could strictly be categorized as 'scribes' either by profession (it is likely that both were Dominican friars)[154] or by their function in this manuscript, where they are not reproducing a text but repairing and (in the case of C^2) updating it.

A complex textual situation of this kind requires a more flexible

[151] The modification in N of the author's original request that the reader should pray 'for him þet swonc her-abuten' to 'for him ðet makede þeos Riwle, and for him þet hire wrot and swonc her-abuten' (see 8. 349 and fn.) suggests that at least some of the textual alterations in N were made in the process of copying.

[152] See the case-study of the textual transmission of Higden's *Polychronicon* in Hanna 1996, ch. 4, 'Producing Manuscripts and Editions' (pp. 63–82).

[153] See pp. xiv, lvi–lviii.

[154] On the original author's institutional affiliations, see Millett 1992 and 2000; on C^3, see p. xiv above.

approach than the traditional terminology allows, allowing for the possibility that the same function might be carried out by different kinds of people, or different functions by the same person. The three-term systems described above address the limitations of the traditional binary categorization; but although they usefully draw attention to the often close cultural and institutional links between those who produced pastoral works and those who reproduced them, they still make insufficient allowance for functional overlap between categories, and for the possible disjunction between copying and other forms of textual intervention. Since the accumulated connotations of the term 'scribe' make it difficult to use precisely, its use has been limited in this edition—apart from a few references to 'commercial scribes'—to its functional sense, 'the copyist of a particular manuscript'.

Another problematic expression in the language of traditional textual criticism is 'scribal error', which is sometimes applied by editors to readings which are not, strictly speaking, either scribal or erroneous. Even when the phrase is used in its narrower sense, to describe the mechanical errors involved in copying, the ambiguity of the term 'scribal' makes it potentially misleading (the original author of *Ancrene Wisse*, if he is to be identified with C², seems to have been prone to mechanical error[155]). In its wider sense, it is sometimes used by editors of medieval works to cover all manuscript readings which cannot be attributed to the original author;[156] the taxonomy of variants developed by George Kane for his edition of the A text of *Piers Plowman* lists not only mechanical error but 'careless or unconscious substitution' and 'conscious variation' as sources of 'textual corruption.'[157]

In recent years this approach to non-authorial variation has increasingly been challenged by textual theorists and editors, partly because its concentration on the author has become theoretically unfashionable, but partly also because it is arguably inappropriate for

[155] See Dobson 1972, p. cxxv, fn. 2.

[156] See, for instance, the tacit equation of 'wrong' with 'scribal' readings and 'unoriginal' with 'erroneous' variation in Russell and Kane 1997, p. 19: 'the only evidence for genetic relation is agreement in wrong readings. Therefore classification depends for its feasibility before all else on the possibility of correctly differentiating between authorial and scribal readings in a sufficient number of instances to produce a significant quantity of valid data . . . no one kind of unoriginal variation is more reliable than any other as evidence of genetic relation: therefore persistence in agreement in all kinds of erroneous variation is the best evidence.'

[157] Kane 1960, p. 127.

certain types of medieval textual transmission.[158] How far those involved in the production and transmission of medieval works equated 'error' with divergence from an authorial original might depend both on the nature of the work[159] and on the purpose for which it was being used. In some textual traditions, a degree of textual variation seems to have been regarded as acceptable, and even as necessary to ensure the continuing effectiveness of the work; in this kind of context, there is a case for reinterpreting Kane's taxonomy of 'scribal error' more neutrally as a taxonomy of textual change in general, and restricting the term 'error' to mechanical error and misunderstanding.[160]

In the A text of *Ancrene Wisse*, for example, the word *nurð* 'uproar' appears six times;[161] both the rarity of the word and its capacity to account for the variants in the manuscripts indicate that it was the original reading. In four cases it is retained in C, but otherwise it is replaced in the surviving English manuscripts by various substitutes, *muð, mur(h)þe, noise,* and *dune.* From the point of view of traditional textual criticism all four readings could be categorized as 'erroneous', but there is a qualitative difference between them. The first two seem to be the product of mechanical error (misreading of minims), misunderstanding, or a combination of both. In the second two, however, *nurð* has been correctly understood and replaced (whether casually or purposefully) by a more generally recognizable equiva-

---

[158] For the broader theoretical European and North American context of this shift, with its increased emphasis on textual change and variation, see Greetham 1999; for some recent criticisms of Kane's editorial approach, see Patterson 1985, Brewer 1991, and Greetham 1997.

[159] The textual transmission of Latin works, and of works by named authors, tends to be more stable than that of vernacular and anonymous works. A noticeable feature of the textual transmission of *Ancrene Wisse* is the contrast between the high level of textual variation in the Middle English parts of the work and the relative textual stability of its quotations from the Scriptures and other Latin *auctoritates*. The Scriptural quotations in particular tend to converge rather than diverge textually in the later stages of the manuscript tradition, as the original author's tendency to quote from memory (and even, at times, to conflate different texts into a single 'portmanteau' quotation) is corrected by reference to the Vulgate; see Wada 2000, and the review of Imai and Watanabe 2000 by Millett (2002).

[160] Hanna and Lawton (2003, p. xci), see textual variation as testifying 'neither to the stupidity nor the malignity of scribes, but rather to a generally conscientious effort at recording what may often have appeared for various reasons inexplicable'; I have applied the term 'misunderstanding' in this edition to cases where it can reasonably be assumed that if the problem underlying a variant reading had been explained, the person responsible for the variant would have conceded that it was erroneous.

[161] 2. 298, 2. 648, 2. 649, 3. 193, 3. 593, 8. 43.

TEXTUAL INTRODUCTION   liii

lent. That even the original author of *Ancrene Wisse* found this kind of substitution acceptable is suggested by the fact that the substitution in C of *medlaseschipe* for *medlese nurð* (8. 42–3) is left uncorrected by C² in an otherwise heavily corrected passage. The textual transmission of *Ancrene Wisse* is marked by a relatively high level of both casual and conscious variation. Casual variation, located by Kane 'on the difficult borderline between mechanical and conscious variation', is characterized by small omissions and 'variants of dialect, construction, tense, mood or number, word order or vocabulary equivalents, which do not materially alter the substance of the communication in any way now determinable'.[162] Conscious variation is found not only in the substantive adaptations of content for different audiences described in the previous section but, at the lower level discussed by Kane, in the simplification and modernization of vocabulary and syntax, expansion or glossing of difficult words and constructions, corrections of real or perceived errors, added emphasis on key points, and the literalization of allegory and metaphor.[163] Both types of variation are at least partly to be explained (as Kane explains them in the textual tradition of Langland's work) as a response by later users to difficulties inherent in the *usus scribendi* of the original author; the style of the original version of *Ancrene Wisse* is characterized by an exceptionally wide vocabulary (including rare dialect words, colloquialism, archaism, and innovative borrowings from French and Latin), free word-order, a tendency to ellipsis, asyndeton, and anacoluthon, and frequent use of allegory and metaphor. But this does not necessarily mean either that the later modifications represent a exclusively 'scribal' response, or that they can be categorized simply as 'errors'; the C² corrections to C suggest an alternative interpretation of the evidence. Dobson's detailed analysis of C²'s working methods[164] concentrates on the evidence pointing towards his identity with the author of the original version; but it incidentally demonstrates an editorial approach to the text in C which differs strikingly from that of most modern editors, and also suggests that what Kane defines as distinctively 'scribal' types of textual modification may exemplify more general rules governing the process of textual change.

[162] See Kane 1960, pp. 125–6, on 'careless or unconscious substitution'.
[163] See Kane 1960, pp. 126–43. For examples of the last category, see notes on 5. 195–7, 6. 237–8, 6. 466–7.
[164] Dobson 1972, pp. xciii–cxxv.

It is clear that C² was as dissatisfied as any modern editor would be with the 'negligence and rape' of the main scribe of C; he corrects his mechanical errors and misunderstandings, even down to the fine detail of punctuation, orthography, morphology, and word-division, with some care (although not very comprehensively or systematically). However, he does not make his corrections by reference back to a better text of the original work, even though he appears to have had access to one (a 34-word omission in C is supplied almost verbatim).[165] Instead, he works directly from the manuscript; 'for this reason', Dobson comments, 'he often misses minor omissions or derangements of word-order that do not affect the sense, or leave it substantially unaffected, and his corrections are often designed to restore the sense (or occasionally an acceptable sense that varies from the original sense), not the original wording.' Dobson goes on to note that 'sometimes indeed the principle governing his correction seems to be to restore sense by the slightest change possible',[166] and it is likely that C² was reluctant to correct the manuscript unnecessarily at the expense of legibility; but even when this is allowed for, his method of correction suggests that he is less concerned with restoring the exact verbal form of the original work than with the effective communication of its meaning, and the further modification of its content where changing circumstances had made it necessary. Occasionally he introduces casual variation of his own.[167] Where the original text had caused difficulty to the C scribe—and even in a few cases where it had not—he makes it more 'foolproof' (to borrow Dobson's word); and this may involve the kind of textual alteration which Kane and Donaldson would have characterized as 'scribal', producing readings which are 'more explicit or more emphatic or easier.'[168] Dobson notes that 'In some cases there is an element of revision which is not clearly separable from the work of correction, as when words are added for clarification of the sense or easing of the syntactical construction, or words that were a source of difficulty or scribal corruption are omitted.'[169] C² adds glosses or expansions,

---

[165] C f. 13ᵛ/15 (1. 192–5); see Dobson 1972, p. 26, note h.
[166] Dobson 1972, pp. xcvi–xcvii.
[167] At C f. 5ᵛ/10–11, C² replaces C *stude-staðeluestninge* (AN *stude-steaðeluestnesse*) by *studeuestnesse*; at C f. 23ʳ/18, he repairs the omission of *leor* by adding *hude*; and at C f. 13ᵛ/15, supplying an omitted passage (see fn. 165 above), he replaces the original *feolahredden* by *feorredne*.
[168] Kane and Donaldson 1975, p. 130.
[169] Dobson 1972, pp. cxii–cxiii.

particularly in passages where the C scribe had had problems,[170] replaces ambiguous or difficult words or constructions with clearer ones,[171] smooths abrupt or elliptical readings,[172] and occasionally adds further emphasis.[173]

The evidence of the C² alterations suggests that in the textual tradition of *Ancrene Wisse* a qualitative distinction between authorial and non-authorial alterations cannot always be taken for granted; changes by the original author and by others may follow the same patterns and for the same reason, the continuing adjustment of a work of practical instruction to the needs and understanding of its users.[174] It also suggests that revisions by the original author of a work cannot always be disentangled from the broader process of textual change. Traditional textual criticism depends methodologically on the 'originality' of authorial revisions to determine the direction of variation, and hence their authenticity;[175] but in practice, revisions by the original author may be based on texts whose non-authorial variants are incorporated in new authorial readings, and whose mechanical errors and misunderstandings may provide both the incentive and the basis for further modification of the text.[176]

---

[170] C ff. 4ᵛ/21, 7ᵛ/1, 8ʳ/23, 11ʳ/4–5, 13ᵛ/1–2, 14ʳ/4, 16ᵛ/17–18, 19ᵛ/11, 26ʳ/1–3 (see Dobson 1972, pp. cix–cxiii). For longer elaborations, see Dobson 1972, pp. cxvi–cxviii.

[171] C ff. 20ᵛ/19–20 (*clað* supplied after the elliptical *þe parlures*), 24ʳ/4 (see note on 2. 124–6), 25ʳ/8 (*cuple* for *weie*; see Dobson 1972, p. cxi); perhaps also C f. 150ᵛ/3 (*nedeliche* for *medeliche*, orig. *meadlesliche*).

[172] C ff. 16ᵛ/17 (repetition of verb), 124ᵛ/4–5 and 125ʳ/5 (additions of *ant*).

[173] C ff. 5ᵛ/14 ('3e ne schulen, Ic segge, makie na ma uuz of feste biheastes') and 12ᵛ/17 (repetition of *blodi*).

[174] Adams 1991, p. 9, fn. 1, makes a similar point on variants in Langland: 'Certainly a London scribe, copying B for the local book trade, would be likely to replace a percentage of unfamiliar or archaic terms with more common ones, but the same consideration may have affected an author who, by the time of B's appearance, was very aware of himself as a Cornhill poet addressing local readers.'

[175] See Kane 1960, p. 115: 'The sole source of authority is the variants themselves, and among them, authority, that is, originality, will probably be determined most often by identification of the variant likeliest to have given rise to the others.'

[176] Cf. Langland's techniques of correction and revision in the C text of *Piers Plowman* as described in Kane and Donaldson 1975, pp. 125–7 ('All indications are that he revised or rewrote rather than restored his text', p. 126), and Russell and Kane 1997, p. 67: 'This [intimacy with the text and sensitivity to detail] is even more apparent in the additions probably or possibly expressions of an impulse to repair, as much as to revise. They are classified by the presence of archetypal error near or adjacent to the point of insertion in corresponding B, and thus presumably in the reviser's B copy. That he never systematically checked his B manuscript for errors of copying must appear from the number of scribal readings that survived his revision. Whether or not he had the means for such a check, and his use of the scribal copy might seem to imply that he did not, he seems to have read his text so to speak pen in hand, with variable degree of critical attention. A turn

This is not to say that no distinction at all can be made between authorial and non-authorial elements in A; the problem lies rather in drawing clear boundaries between them. Although *Ancrene Wisse* has come down to us as an anonymous work, and draws extensively on earlier sources, it is not in quite the same category as those Lollard works described by Anne Hudson which 'make one question the very concept of "original" text', anonymous compilations or works where the writer identifies himself only as *quidam fidelis*, or as a nameless 'pore precher'.[177] In its earliest form at least, it presents itself as the work of an individual cleric, addressing an immediate audience of anchoresses personally known to him; he exploits the common discourse of popular preaching with exceptional skill, and incorporates his diverse materials into an original and tightly-structured framework.[178] The distinctive qualities of the original version can be used to some extent to determine the origin of later revisions to the work; but most of the possible criteria offer an indication rather than a conclusive demonstration of authorial origin, and they cannot be applied to all the revisions in A.

In his discussion of the the C² modifications in C, Dobson used a variety of criteria to identify C² with the original author of *Ancrene Wisse*, including the use of the first-person pronoun in three of C²'s additions, the 'quality and character' of his additions and revisions and 'their relationship to those of Corpus', the 'precision, skill, intelligence, and understanding' of C²'s corrections, and his working method, correcting and revising directly from the C text rather than checking it against a better manuscript.[179]

The most powerful of these criteria is the use of the first person. It is true that the 'I' of medieval devotional literature can be less a personal 'I' than a persona to be assumed by any user of the work, and the first-person pronouns of the original version are usually

of language which he sensed to be not his own, or imperfect alliteration, or nonsense error that caught his eye would sharpen the critical attitude already implicit in the intent to revise, giving local application to general dissatisfaction. Quite often his reaction was to repair by rewriting, even to the extent of incorporating the scribal reading in the revised line or passage.'

[177] See Hudson 1977, p. 49. A similar point is made by Schnell 1999, p. 371, about the apparent lack of a unifying intentional element in some late-medieval German texts compiled for practical use: 'Zahlreichen Gebrauchstexten . . . liegt kein dominantes Konzept zugrunde, das alle Umformen durchdringt, sondern deren Redaktoren 'basteln' sich aus verschiedensten Texten einen neuen eigenen Text zurecht.'

[178] On the innovative reworking of earlier models of monastic and anchoritic legislation in *Ancrene Wisse*, see Millett 2003. [179] Dobson 1972, pp. xcvi–xcvii.

TEXTUAL INTRODUCTION

carried over even in the translations and rewritten forms of *Ancrene Wisse*. In some cases, however, the original 'I' does seem to reflect the voice of an individual, writing for (or, in the case of the two ascetics mentioned at the end of Part 6, about) people he knew personally.[180] The suggestion by John C. Hirsh that the original three anchoresses were a literary fiction[181] has not been taken up by other scholars; that they were more than a fiction is indicated by the circumstantial details about their situation supplied by the author, the early abridgement or removal of those details in forms of the work adapted for different audiences (see 4. 192 fn. and note), and the modification of the original instructions addressed to them as the size and circumstances of the group changed (see 4. 1076–1101). A recognition of this personal element is sometimes reflected in the variant readings of the later manuscript tradition. A distinctively authorial use of the first person in the Preface ('Nu, mine leoue sustren, þis boc Ich todeale on eahte "destinctiuns"') is converted in L and V into a passive construction; and the author's address to the original audience at the end of Part 1 has been replaced in S and T by a less personal transitional passage.[182] There are other cases where the Latin translator replaces a first-person by an impersonal construction,[183] and one passage, the account of the two ascetics at 6. 479–92, was seen in P and S as sufficiently autobiographical to require more thorough modification.[184] This does not, of course, mean that the 'I' used in a revised passage is necessarily to be identified with the 'I' of the basic text; there are a couple of instances in S where the first-person voice of the original author is tacitly conflated with that of a much later reviser.[185] But when the instance

---

[180] See, e.g., P. 10–12, P. 82–92, P. 93–4, 1. 450–1, 2. 1021–2, 2. 1027–30, 4. 192 fn., 4. 385–6, 4. 554–64, 4. 875–6, 4. 899–919 (note the addition in C), 4. 930–2, 4. 1563–4, 6. 432–6, 8. 1–7, 8. 33–4.

[181] See Hirsh 1988, pp. 44–5.

[182] See app. crit. for P. 157, and 1. 450–1 fn., app. crit., and note.

[183] e.g. L substitutes *dictum est* for 2. 819 *Ich seide*, 2. 1045 *we seiden*, and 4. 684–5 *Ich habbe . . . inempnet, clarificari potest* for 3. 421–2 'Ich hit wulle brihtin', and *que diuise seu fracte sunt* for 5. 587 'ant alle Ich habbe tobroken ham ow'.

[184] In the anecdote of the *loricatus*, the opening 'Ich wat swuch' is replaced in S by 'ieo ai oi parler de cel homme', and in P by 'A goode man telleþ þat he knew sum man'; and where the author describes his conversations with the *loricatus*, S replaces the authorial *me* (6. 483, 6. 486, 6. 488) by *soen confessour*, P by *his schrift-fader*. P has 'And also it was swich a womman' for 'Ich wat ec swuch wummon' (6. 491–2), S 'Ieo ai oi de aucune feme.'

[185] See 3. 183, where S retains the authorial *we* in a modified passage (Trethewey 1958, 224/24–30); and 6. 221, where a sentence added in S after *sunne* begins 'Par tel hontage e par tele peine cum ieo ai ci deuant tuche . . .' (referring back to 6. 98 ff.).

is early, the identification becomes more likely, especially when there is an explicit or implicit backwards reference to the original text, as in all three C² first-person additions,[186] and the addition in F after *ofte* at 5. 534.

Dobson's remaining criteria depend on relative rather than absolute distinctions between the work of the original author and that of his successors, and although they identify features consistent with authorial origin, they do not (as he noted) exclude other possibilities.

The case for identification is strongest for the C² revisions. Dahood has argued that the first-person additions 'could have been copied from another manuscript, and the others could be the work of an intelligent reader with access to a good exemplar.'[187] But Dobson's detailed analysis of the textual evidence indicates that C² normally preferred to work directly from the C text,[188] and it is hard to see why the first-person additions (which are very minor) should have been separately copied across. Dobson's more economical hypothesis remains the most plausible explanation; and if—as seems most likely—the revisions are in the author's own hand, it follows that not only the first-person additions but all the C² alterations must be authorial.

There is also a good case for attributing at least some (probably the majority) of the revisions in A to the original author. Some of them, again, are in the first person, and suggest a continuing personal relationship with the group of anchoresses addressed in earlier texts of the work;[189] some show evident similarities of style and tone with the original version; and some carry over or develop further the revisions made in C².

We cannot assume, however, that the text in A reflects a revised version made under the original author's supervision,[190] or that it contains only his modifications. The internal criteria for attribution discussed above can be applied to most of the longer additions, but not to some other types of variation and addition: minor alterations of wording and phrasing; brief glosses, explanations, qualifications, and other small-scale additions; longer additions with no distinctive

---

[186] See Dobson 1972, p. xcvi.
[187] Dahood 1984, p. 3.   [188] See p. liv above.
[189] e.g. 2. 208–10 (see note), 4. 1077–93. See also the discussion of the four extended additions shared by A and F, pp. xxxix–xl above.
[190] See pp. xli–xlii above.

stylistic features; and supplementary Latin quotations.[191] A few (such as the not wholly successful attempt to harmonize the pronoun-use of the original version at 5. 563–8,[192] and the addition to the powers of confession at 5. 593), are unlikely to have been by the original author; others, however, cannot be categorized with any certainty. For example, the Latin quotations added in A and other manuscripts to support the nine reasons for hastening to confession in 5. 361–408 were the common property of preachers on confession, and may have been added to the original version at different stages and by different people. The additions and revisions in other early manuscripts raise similar problems: in some the balance of evidence points towards the original author, in others away from him, but often there is not enough evidence available to make even a tentative judgement possible.

The point can be illustrated from a minor textual difficulty at 5. 306. Here the A text says that the 'circumstances' of sin have been mentioned only *as on urn*, 'in passing'. No surviving manuscript other than A has *as on urn*, and any competent textual critic checking the apparatus criticus at this point[193] would conclude that the original reading was the adverb *todreauetliche* 'in a scattered way', which is recorded in *MED* only from this passage. This would account for all the other surviving readings: F's *destinctement* translates it, A's *as on urn* paraphrases it, and a misreading of its *to*-prefix as a separate word would help to explain the homoeographic substitution of *to derfliche* 'too severely' in GV.[194] However, it looks as if the rarity of the original adverb made it problematic; the phrase replacing it in GV makes no sense in context, and the Latin translation and the later French translation omit it altogether. The status of the substitution in A is uncertain. It might be the responsibility of the original author, revising his own work (although this would be difficult to prove), of the A scribe (although the A

---

[191] A possible exception here is a small group of Scriptural annotations incorporated in Part 3 whose wording is influenced by the unacknowledged Latin source text the author is using, the Carthusian *Consuetudines*; see notes on 3. 504–5, 3. 511–12, 3. 513, 3. 538–9.

[192] See note on 5. 564.

[193] 5. 306 as on urn] A, todreauetliche T, todreauethliche C, todreuedliche N, destinctement F, to derfliche GV, *om*. LS. See also fn. 194 below.

[194] For this kind of error, see Kane 1960, pp. 132–3, on 'homœographs'. Mack (Mack and Zettersten 1963) transcribes the T reading as 'to dreauetliche', and Dobson (1972) the C reading as 'to dreauethliche'—although in both manuscripts (particularly T, where the handwriting is cramped) the space following the prefix is too small to constitute an unambiguous word-boundary, and I have given the scribes the benefit of the doubt.

scribe is not in the habit of making substitutions of this kind), or of an intermediate copyist or annotator. But whatever its origin, it is not, strictly speaking, erroneous; it is an appropriate replacement for an original choice of wording which had proved to be a source of difficulty. In cases like this, the the traditional editorial principle of *difficilior lectio potior* should perhaps be modified to *difficilior lectio prior*; the difference in the nature of the readings establishes the direction of textual change, but without necessarily requiring emendation. It is possible that at least some of the modifications in A to the original form of the work were introduced by people other than its author; but it could be argued that for many of its additions and revisions, the question of authorship is neither resolvable nor, for practical purposes, important.

In a textual tradition of this kind, the traditional aim of critical editing, the reconstruction of 'a single authorial intention',[195] becomes problematic; it is likely that what underlies the text of A is not a single authorial intention but a series of intentions, not all of them necessarily authorial. This edition, therefore, does not offer a 'critical text' of *Ancrene Wisse* in the traditional sense. Instead, it provides a corrected version of one historical form of the work, the text in A, removing mechanical errors and misunderstandings and supplying lacunae, but retaining other variations from the original version.

However, an edition for general scholarly use cannot limit itself to a corrected text of A; the edited text has to be contextualized within the broader historical development of *Ancrene Wisse*. The text in A is a relatively late and extensively modified form of the work; it lacks some material found in the original version and some probably authorial revisions in other manuscripts; and its sometimes unsystematic incorporation of the revisions it includes does not always make sense in isolation, creating apparent inconsistencies, discontinuities, or even contradictions.[196] In this edition, it is treated not as a separate and self-contained 'version' of *Ancrene Wisse*, but as a single stage in a multi-layered and sometimes multi-stranded process of revision; the edited text of A is used as a point of entry to the textual history of the work as a whole.

Following the precedent of some editions of medieval Latin works

---

[195] The phrase is used by Edwards (1995, p. 194) in a discussion of similar editorial problems.

[196] See pp. xli–xlii above, and Millett 1994, pp. 16–17.

TEXTUAL INTRODUCTION

with comparable textual traditions,[197] I have used a combination of typographical mark-up and footnotes to represent the process of textual change on the page: the reader is alerted to additions and alterations to the original version by the use of bold type in the edited text, and material from the earlier stages of the textual tradition not found, or found in altered form, in A is recorded in a series of footnotes separate from the apparatus criticus. The Textual Introduction provides an overview of the textual development of the work,[198] and the history and probable origin of individual readings and passages are discussed in detail in the Textual Commentary.

Although this edition does not share the aim of the traditional 'critical edition', it shares much of its methodology; the difference is in the way that the methodology is used. The editorial approach used here attempts to address the problems involved in editing a work with a 'dynamic' textual tradition. It draws on the principles of stemmatic editing to establish (as far as can be done in a textual tradition of this kind) the relationship of the manuscripts, and (much more extensively) on the techniques of 'deep editing' to establish the relationship of individual variants. It does not use these methods, however, to reconstruct a text representing 'a single authorial intention', whether first or final; and although it attempts, wherever possible, to distinguish between the contribution of the original author and that of his successors to the textual tradition of *Ancrene Wisse*, it does not treat the former as the only significant part of its textual history. Traditionally, the aim of textual criticism has been to establish the direction of textual change in order to reverse it.[199] In a 'dynamic' textual tradition, however, textual change can be regenerative as well as degenerative, and repairing the collateral damage caused by the process of change is only part of the editor's task. This edition also aims to trace and explain the continuing textual evolution of the work through time.

---

[197] See particularly Thomas 1965 (the early Dominican Constitutions), and d'Avray 2001 (model sermons).
[198] See pp. xxxvii–xlv above.
[199] Reynolds and Wilson (1974, p. 212) see the textual criticism of classical works as an attempt 'to reverse the process of transmission and restore the words of the ancients as closely as possible to their original form.'

EDITORIAL PROCEDURES AND CONVENTIONS

EDITED TEXT

The edited text is based on Cambridge, Corpus Christi College, MS 402 (A). Where the text has been emended, the manuscript reading is given in the apparatus criticus. Square brackets are used to enclose emendations, and material omitted (for whatever reason) in A which has been supplied from other manuscripts. Omission of words or letters from the edited text as a result of emendation is not indicated in the text, but is noted in the apparatus criticus.

The lacuna in A caused by the loss of two folios between f. 14 and f. 15 (2. 122–225) has been filled from other manuscripts, using C (as corrected by C²),[200] T (for a short omission in C), and F (for part of an addition surviving only in AF) as base manuscripts; the supplied text is indented from the left margin.

The spelling of A is retained for both Middle English and Latin, unless it seems anomalous in terms of the scribe's normal practice. Words or short passages incorporated into the text from other manuscripts are normally silently adapted to A's spelling-conventions; but where other Middle English manuscripts are being used as a base for the edited text, the spelling of the alternative base manuscript is retained.

Abbreviations are silently expanded, and capitalization, punctuation, and paragraphing modernized.[201] Word-division has been standardized, and in most cases modernized.[202] The accent-like hairlines sometimes used by the A scribe above vowels (see Ker in Tolkien 1962, p. xiii) are not reproduced.

Underlining is used to indicate rubrics in in A. Rubrics in manuscripts other than A are not normally recorded in the footnotes or apparatus criticus unless there is a corresponding rubric in A, although they may be discussed in the Textual Commentary (for a discussion of possibly authorial rubrics in C, F, and G not found in A, see Dobson 1972, pp. lvi–lxii).

---

[200] The text in C includes quite numerous minor abridgements, usually not affecting the sense; in this case only, I have modified the normal editorial policy of correcting only mechanical errors and misunderstandings to supply the omitted material.

[201] For a detailed study of the use of coloured initials and other division-markers in the early manuscripts of *Ancrene Wisse*, see Dahood 1988.

[202] The main exceptions are *forte*, which is treated as a single word, and *seolf*, which is always treated as a separate word (e.g. *him seolf*).

TEXTUAL INTRODUCTION lxiii

Bold type is used for alterations, additions, and revisions in A to the original version of *Ancrene Wisse*. It is used both for material unique to A and for additions and revisions also found in other manuscripts. It has not been used where it is uncertain whether a reading was a later addition or not (such readings are discussed in the Textual Commentary), or where the variation is minor and possibly casual. No typographical distinction is made between different chronological layers within this material, or between authorial and non-authorial elements; questions of chronology and origin are discussed generally in the Textual Introduction, and in detail in the Textual Commentary.

In some cases, the A text appears to incorporate marginal annotations not originally intended for inclusion in the main body of the work. Dobson comments on such incorporated annotations, 'The signs that a sentence (or more) included in the text was originally intended only as a marginal comment are its omission by some MSS, its variable placing, its failure to fit neatly into the text (and normally the actual disruption of the text) at any of the points found for it, and in the more common case of Latin citations the fact that, with one or two exceptions, they are not translated, paraphrased, or even referred to in the English text.'[203] In this edition, they have been left at the point at which they appear in the A text, but indicated by a smaller type size, unless they have been 'adopted' into the main text by subsequent rewriting and/or (in the case of Latin annotations) the provision of a Middle English translation.

Line-numbering is continuous within each part of the work, in fives; line-references are in the form P. 123 (Preface, line 123) or 2. 456 (Part 2, line 456). Individual paragraphs have also been numbered, for easier cross-reference from any future edition or translation,[204] but have not been used for cross-reference within the edition. Folio-references to the base manuscript are entered in the outer margin of the page. 'Morton numbers' (the pagination of James Morton's 1853 edition of *Ancrene Wisse*, used for cross-referencing in the EETS editions of *Ancrene Wisse* manuscripts) are also entered in the outer margin, prefixed by 'M.'; where they coincide with folio-numbers, they are entered immediately below them.[205]

[203] Introduction to unpublished edition of *Ancrene Wisse*.
[204] An annotated translation of *Ancrene Wisse*, to be published by the University of Exeter Press, is being prepared to accompany this edition.
[205] In the passage in Part 5 on the nine reasons for hastening to confession (5. 361–408), the different placing of the *Circumdederunt* addition in A and N means that the same 'Morton numbers' appear at more than one point.

FOOTNOTES

The footnotes function as a supplement to the apparatus criticus; they are used mainly to give more convenient access to material from the earlier stages of the textual development of *Ancrene Wisse* which is either not found, or found in altered form, in A. Normally only the more substantial variants (i.e. more than a few words long) are included; shorter variants are recorded only in the apparatus criticus, unless they significantly alter the meaning of a larger unit of text.

APPARATUS CRITICUS

The apparatus criticus is selective, making no attempt to reflect the full extent of variation in the textual tradition of *Ancrene Wisse*. Readers who need fuller information on the readings of the individual manuscripts, and on the textual modifications introduced in the later translations (LS) and reworked English versions (PR), should consult the diplomatic and facsimile editions listed under 'Manuscripts and Versions' above.

Normally only substantive variants are cited; variations in spelling, and variations in word-form which do not affect the sense, are not included unless the variant is ambiguous or helps to cast light on other manuscript readings. Variations between þe and þet (both as demonstrative adjective and as relative pronoun) are not recorded.

As a general rule, only those variants are cited which are shared by more than one manuscript, although single-manuscript variants may be cited where they are related to a preceding or following variant shared by more than one manuscript, or where they are of interest in themselves. Variants are cited more fully, however, at points of difficulty in the textual tradition, and in added passages where only one or two manuscripts are running alongside A. The alterations made by C^2 to C are recorded, except where they do no more than correct errors in C, or modify its spelling and punctuation; so are the alterations to adapt the work to a different audience found in two of the early manuscripts, G and T. There has been more selective citation of variants from the rewritten versions LPRS than from CFGHNTV, and the C^3 alterations to C have not normally been recorded. All departures from the base manuscript in the edited text are indicated, apart from self-corrections by the main scribe, where the reading before correction is not normally recorded.

Lemmata are from the A text unless otherwise indicated (A is specified only where it is the sole representative of a reading); where a different base manuscript is being used, this is noted where the manuscripts running change. If the word in a lemma occurs more than once in the line, the particular instance is identified by a superscript number. Longer lemmata precede any shorter ones they include, even if this involves repeating the same line-number before lemmata at two different points.

The form of a variant given in the apparatus criticus is that of the first manuscript listed; the readings of the French and Latin versions are not given separately where it is clear that they are translating one particular variant in the English. Variants are normally cited in alphabetical order of sigla; but this order may be departed from to group variants according to their distance from the lemma, to put the English form of a variant before the French and Latin, or to avoid citing a variant in an anomalous form. It should not be assumed that all manuscripts not cited support the reading of the lemma; fuller variants, however, are cited where the reading in A is not shared by the other manuscripts, has only minority support, or is otherwise problematic. Where supporting evidence for the A reading is given, any manuscript not cited is either temporarily not running or casts no light on the variants in question (e.g. where the French and Latin versions could be translating either of two Middle English synonyms).

As in the main text, abbreviations are silently expanded, and the original capitalization, punctuation, word-division, and paragraphing are modernized; where they are relevant to the reading, however, they are discussed in the Textual Commentary.

TYPOGRAPHICAL CONVENTIONS

Italic type is used to indicate Latin in the edited text, editorial comment in the footnotes and apparatus criticus.

<u>Underlining</u> indicates rubrication.

Bold type indicates alterations, additions, and revisions to the original text of *Ancrene Wisse* in the A text.

Small bold type indicates originally marginal annotations incorporated in the A text.

[ ] In the text, square brackets indicate emendations, and material from other manuscripts supplying omissions.

] In the apparatus criticus, a single square bracket follows the lemma.

⟨ ⟩ In the apparatus criticus, angle brackets enclose lost, illegible, or partially-legible letters; where the letters cannot be confidently supplied, the lacuna is indicated by an ellipsis ⟨. . .⟩ (regardless of the number of letters involved).

( ) In the apparatus criticus, parentheses enclosing ellipses (. . .) indicate intervening words not relevant to the reading in question; parentheses are also used to enclose surrounding or intervening words which are not part of the variant but are supplied to explain it, and editorial comments. Where a comment is entered in a sequence of sigla, it refers only to the text whose siglum immediately precedes it.

` ´ In the apparatus criticus, forward and reverse primes are sometimes used to indicate that letters or words have been interlined in a manuscript.

| In the apparatus criticus, | is used occasionally to indicate a line-break in a manuscript (e.g. to explain an accidental omission or repetition in A)

ABBREVIATIONS

add.	added
alt.	altered
conj.	conjecturally emended
cont.	continued (citation of Scriptural texts or prayers)
corr.	corrected (to reading of lemma)
del.	deleted (by any method)
expunct.	expuncted
interl.	interlined
marg.	added in margin
om.	omitted (referring back to reading of lemma)
prec.	preceded by
repl.	replaced by
sim.	similarly (referring back to immediately preceding reading)
suppl.	supplied (referring back to reading of lemma)
trs.	transposed
transl.	translating
v.r(r).	variant reading(s)

BIBLIOGRAPHY

1. ABBREVIATIONS AND SHORT TITLES

EETS	Early English Text Society
OS	= Original Series
SS	= Supplementary Series
ES	*English Studies*
JEGP	*Journal of English and Germanic Philology*
LALME	Angus McIntosh, M. L. Samuels, and Michael Benskin, *A Linguistic Atlas of Late Medieval English*, 4 vols (Aberdeen, 1986)
MÆ	*Medium Ævum*
MESN	*Medieval English Studies Newsletter*
MLR	*Modern Language Review*
NM	*Neuphilologische Mitteilungen*
PBA	*Proceedings of the British Academy*
RES	*Review of English Studies*
TLS	*Times Literary Supplement*

2. MANUSCRIPTS

Cambridge, Corpus Christi College
MS 402

Cambridge, Gonville and Caius College
MS 234/120

Cambridge, Magdalene College
MS Pepys 2498

Cambridge, Trinity College
MS 883 (R.14.7)
MS B. 1. 45

London, British Library
MS Cotton Cleopatra C. vi
MS Cotton Nero A. xiv
MS Cotton Titus D. xviii
MS Cotton Vitellius E. vii
MS Cotton Vitellius F. vii
MS Royal 7 C. x
MS Royal 8 C. i

Oxford, Bodleian Library
MS Bodley 90
MS Douce 180
MS Eng. poet. a. 1 (the 'Vernon manuscript')
MS Eng. th. c. 70 (the 'Lanhydrock fragment')
MS Laud misc. 201
MS Laud misc. 381
Oxford, Magdalen College
MS Latin 67
Oxford, Merton College
MS C. 1. 5 (Coxe 44)
Paris, Bibliothèque Nationale de France
MS fonds français 6276

3. EDITIONS AND SECONDARY WORKS

Ackerman, Robert W., and Roger Dahood (eds.), *Ancrene Riwle: Introduction and Part 1*, Medieval and Renaissance Texts and Studies 31 (Binghamton, NY, 1984)

Adams, Robert, 'Editing and the Limitations of the *Durior Lectio*', *Yearbook of Langland Studies* 5 (1991), 7–15

Allen, Hope Emily, 'Further Borrowings from "Ancren Riwle"', *MLR* 24 (1929), 1–15

——, 'The Ancren Riwle' (letter), *TLS*, 8 February 1936, 116

——, 'Wynkyn de Worde and a Second French Compilation from the "Ancren Riwle" with a Description of the First (Trinity Coll. Camb. MS. 883)', in Long 1940, pp. 182–219

d'Ardenne, S. R. T. O., and E. J. Dobson (eds.), *Seinte Katerine: Re-edited from MS Bodley 34 and the Other Manuscripts*, EETS ss 7 (1981)

d'Avray, D. L., *Medieval Marriage Sermons: Mass Communication in a Culture without Print* (Oxford, 2001)

Baugh, A. C. (ed.), *The English Text of the Ancrene Riwle: Edited from British Museum MS. Royal 8 C. 1*, EETS os 232 (1956)

Benson, Larry D. (ed.), *The Riverside Chaucer*, 3rd edn. (Oxford, 1988)

Bédier, Joseph, 'La Tradition manuscrite du *Lai de l'Ombre*; réflexions sur l'art d'éditer les anciens textes', *Romania* 54 (1928), 161–96, 321–56

Brewer, Charlotte, 'Authorial Vs. Scribal Writing in *Piers Plowman*', in Machan 1991, pp. 59–89

Cohen, Philip (ed.), *Texts and Textuality: Textual Instability, Theory, and Interpretation* (New York, 1997)

BIBLIOGRAPHY

Colledge, Eric [Edmund], '*The Recluse*: A Lollard Interpolated Version of the *Ancren Riwle*', *RES* 15 (1939), 1–15, 129–45

Coxe, Henricus O., *Catalogus Codicum MSS. qui in Collegiis Aulisque Oxoniensibus hodie adservantur*, 2 vols. (Oxford, 1852)

Dahood, Roger, '*Ancrene Wisse*, the Katherine Group, and the *Wohunge* Group', in Edwards 1984, pp. 1–33

——, 'The Use of Coloured Initials and Other Division Markers in Early Versions of *Ancrene Riwle*', in Kennedy, Waldron, and Wittig 1988, pp. 79–97

Davis, Norman, and C. L. Wrenn (eds.), *English and Medieval Studies Presented to J. R. R. Tolkien on the Occasion of his Seventieth Birthday* (London, 1962)

Day, Mabel (ed.), *The English Text of the Ancrene Riwle: Edited from Cotton MS. Nero A. XIV, on the Basis of a Transcript by J. A. Herbert*, EETS OS 225 (1952)

Diensberg, Bernhard, 'The English text of the *Ancrene Riwle* edited from Bodleian MS.Eng.Poet.a.1. (Vernon) by A. Zettersten and B. Diensberg', *MESN* 37 (1997), 6–20

Dobson, E. J., 'The Affiliations of the Manuscripts of *Ancrene Wisse*', in Davis and Wrenn 1962, pp. 128–63

——, 'The Date and Composition of *Ancrene Wisse*', British Academy Gollancz Lecture, 25 May 1966, *PBA* 52 (1966), 181–208

——, Review of Mack and Zettersten 1963, *MÆ* 36 (1967), 187–91

—— (ed.), *The English Text of the Ancrene Riwle: Edited from B.M. Cotton MS. Cleopatra C.vi*, EETS OS 267 (1972)

——, *The Origins of Ancrene Wisse* (Oxford, 1976)

Doyle, A. I., 'A Survey of the Origins and Circulation of Theological Writings in English in the 14th, 15th, and early 16th Centuries with Special Consideration of the Part of the Clergy therein', 2 vols. (unpublished Ph.D. thesis, Cambridge, 1954)

——, 'The Shaping of the Vernon and Simeon Manuscripts', in Rowland 1974, pp. 328–41; rev. repr. in Pearsall 1990, pp. 1–13

—— (ed.), *The Vernon Manuscript: A Facsimile of Bodleian Library, Oxford, MS Eng. Poet. a. 1* (Cambridge, 1987)

Edwards, A. S. G. (ed.), *Middle English Prose: A Critical Guide to Major Authors and Genres* (New Brunswick, NJ, 1984)

——, 'Middle English Literature', in Greetham 1995, pp. 184–203

—— (ed.), *A Companion to Middle English Prose* (Cambridge, 2004)

d'Evelyn, Charlotte (ed.), *The Latin Text of the Ancrene Riwle: Edited from Merton College MS. 44 and British Museum MS. Cotton Vitellius E.vii*, EETS OS 216 (1944)

Fisher, John H. (ed.), *The Tretyse of Loue*, EETS OS 223 (1951)

Franzen, Christine, 'The Tremulous Hand of Worcester and the Nero Scribe of the *Ancrene Wisse*', *MÆ* 72 (2003), 13–31

Graham, Timothy (ed.), *The Recovery of Old English: Anglo-Saxon Studies in the Sixteenth and Seventeenth Centuries* (Kalamazoo, MI, 2000)

Greetham, D. C. (ed.), *Scholarly Editing: A Guide to Research* (New York, 1995)

——, 'Reading in and around *Piers Plowman*', in Cohen 1997, pp. 25–57

——, *Theories of the Text* (Oxford, 1999)

Hanna, Ralph, *Pursuing History: Middle English Manuscripts and Their Texts* (Stanford, CA, 1996)

——, *The Index of Middle English Prose, Handlist XII: Manuscripts in Smaller Bodleian Collections* (Cambridge, 1997)

——, 'English Biblical Texts before Lollardy and their Fate', in Somerset, Havens, and Pitard 2003, pp. 141–53

——, and David Lawton (eds.), *The Siege of Jerusalem*, EETS OS 320 (2003)

Hasenfratz, Robert (ed.), *Ancrene Wisse*, TEAMS Middle English Texts (Kalamazoo, MI, 2000)

Herbert, J. A. (ed.), *The French Text of the Ancrene Riwle: Edited from British Museum MS. Cotton Vitellius F vii*, EETS OS 219 (1944)

Heuser, W., 'Die *Ancren Riwle*—Ein aus angelsächsischen Zeit überliefertes Denkmal', *Anglia* 30 (1907), 103–22

Hirsh, John C., *Hope Emily Allen: Medieval Scholarship and Feminism* (Norman, OK, 1988)

Hudson, Anne, 'Middle English', in Rigg 1977, pp. 34–57

——, *The Premature Reformation: Wycliffite Texts and Lollard History* (Oxford, 1988)

Imai, Mitsunori, and Hideki Watanabe (eds.), *Reading the Ancrene Riwle: Proceedings of the International Symposium Held on 25 January, 1997 at Osaka University* (Osaka, 2000)

James, Montague Rhodes, *The Western Manuscripts in the Library of Trinity College, Cambridge: A Descriptive Catalogue. 2: Containing An Account of the Manuscripts Standing in Class R* (Cambridge, 1901)

——, *A Descriptive Catalogue of the Manuscripts in the Library of Gonville and Caius College, Cambridge*, 2 vols. (Cambridge, 1907–8)

Kane, George (ed.), *Piers Plowman, The A Version: Will's Visions of Piers Plowman and Do-Well. An Edition in the Form of Trinity College Cambridge MS R. 3. 14, Corrected from Other Manuscripts, with Variant Readings* (London, 1960)

——, and E. Talbot Donaldson (eds.), *Piers Plowman, The B Version: Will's Visions of Piers Plowman, Do-Well, Do-Better and Do-Best. An Edition in the Form of Trinity College Cambridge MS B. 15. 17, Corrected and Restored from the Known Evidence, with Variant Readings* (London, 1975)

Kennedy, Edward Donald, Ronald Waldron, and Joseph S. Wittig (eds.), *Medieval English Studies Presented to George Kane* (Cambridge, 1988)

Ker, N. R., *Medieval Libraries of Great Britain: A List of Surviving Books*, 2nd edn. (London, 1964)

Kubouchi, Tadao, and Keiko Ikegami (eds.), *The Ancrene Wisse: A Four-Manuscript Parallel Text*, 2 vols. [vol. 1: *Preface and Parts 1–4*, vol. 2: *Parts 5–8 with Wordlists*], Studies in English Medieval Language and Literature 7, 11 (Frankfurt, 2003, 2005)

Laing, Margaret, *Catalogue of Sources for a Linguistic Atlas of Early Medieval English* (Cambridge, 1993)

——, 'Linguistic and textual relationships between the Corpus, Nero and Vernon manuscripts of *Ancrene Riwle*—a response', *MESN* 38 (1998), 4–16

——, and Angus McIntosh, 'The Language of *Ancrene Riwle*, the Katherine Group Texts and *þe Wohunge of ure Lauerd* in BL Cotton Titus D XVIII', *NM* 96 (1995), 235–63

Lee, Stuart, 'Oxford, Bodleian Library, MS Laud Misc. 381: William de l'Isle, Ælfric, and the *Ancrene Wisse*', in Graham 2000, pp. 207–42

Long, P. W. (ed.), *Essays and Studies in Honor of Carleton Brown* (New York, 1940)

Maas, Paul, *Textkritik* (Leipzig, 1927); 3rd edn. (1957), trans. Barbara Flower as *Textual Criticism* (Oxford, 1958)

Macaulay, G. C., 'The "Ancren Riwle"', *MLR* 9 (1914), 63–78, 145–60, 324–31, 463–74

McCarren, Vincent P., and Douglas Moffat (eds.), *A Guide to Editing Middle English* (Ann Arbor, 1998)

McGann, Jerome J., *A Critique of Modern Textual Criticism* (1983: rev. edn., Charlottesville, VA, 1992)

—— (ed.), *Textual Criticism and Literary Interpretation* (Chicago 1985)

Machan, Tim William (ed.), *Medieval Literature: Texts and Interpretation*, Medieval and Renaissance Texts and Studies 79 (Binghamton, NY, 1991)

Mack, Frances M., and Arne Zettersten (eds.), *The English Text of the Ancrene Riwle, Edited from Cotton MS. Titus D. xviii; together with the Lanhydrock Fragment, Bodleian MS. Eng. th. c. 70*, EETS os 252 (1963)

McKitterick, Rosamond, and Richard Beadle, *Catalogue of the Pepys Library at Magdalene College, Cambridge, vol. 5: Manuscripts. Part 1: Medieval* (Cambridge, 1992)

Madan, Falconer, and H. E. Craster, *A Summary Catalogue of Western Manuscripts in the Bodleian Library at Oxford*, vol. 2, part 1: nos. 1–3490 (Oxford, 1922)

Millett, Bella, 'The Audience of the Saints' Lives of the Katherine Group', in *Saints and Saints' Lives: Essays in Honour of D. H. Farmer*, *Reading Medieval Studies* 16, special issue (1990), 127–56

——, 'The Origins of *Ancrene Wisse*: New Answers, New Questions', *MÆ* 61 (1992), 206–28

——, '*Mouvance* and the Medieval Author: Re-Editing *Ancrene Wisse*', in Minnis 1994, pp. 9–20

——, *Ancrene Wisse, the Katherine Group, and the Wooing Group*, Annotated Bibliographies of Old and Middle English Literature 2 (Cambridge, 1996)

——, '*Ancrene Wisse* and the Conditions of Confession', *ES* 80 (1999), 193–215

——, '*Ancrene Wisse* and the Book of Hours' in Renevey and Whitehead 2000, pp. 21–40

——, Review of Imai and Watanabe 2000 in *JEGP* 101 (2002), 443–6

——, 'The Genre of *Ancrene Wisse*', in Wada 2003, pp. 29–44

——, 'The *Ancrene Wisse* Group', in Edwards 2004, pp. 1–17

——, and Jocelyn Wogan-Browne (eds.), *Medieval English Prose for Women* (1990: rev. edn., Oxford, 1992)

Minnis, A. J. (ed.), *Late-Medieval Religious Texts and their Transmission: Essays in Honour of A. I. Doyle*, York Manuscripts Conferences: Proceedings Series 3 (Cambridge, 1994)

Moffat, Douglas, with Vincent P. McCarren, 'A Bibliographical Essay on Editing Methods and Authorial and Scribal Intention', in McCarren and Moffat 1998, pp. 25–57

Morton, James (ed.), *The Ancren Riwle: A Treatise on the Rules and Duties of Monastic Life, Edited and Translated from a Semi-Saxon MS. of the Thirteenth Century*, Camden Society, first series 57 (London, 1853)

Napier, Arthur S. (ed.), 'A Fragment of the *Ancren Riwle*', *JEGP* 2 (1898), 199–202

——, 'The *Ancren Riwle*', *MLR* 4 (1909), 433–6

von Nolcken, Christina, 'The *Recluse* and its Readers: Some Observations on a Lollard Interpolated Version of *Ancrene Wisse*', in Wada 2003, pp. 175–96

Oliger, Livarius, 'Regulae tres reclusorum et eremitarum Angliae saec. XIII-XIV', *Antonianum* 3 (1928), 151–90, 299–320

Parkes, M. B., 'Book Provision and Libraries at the Medieval University of Oxford', *University of Rochester Library Bulletin* 30 (1987–8), 28–43; repr. in Parkes 1991, pp. 299–310

——, *Scribes, Scripts and Readers: Studies in the Communication, Presentation and Dissemination of Medieval Texts* (London, 1991)

Patterson, Lee, 'The Logic of Textual Criticism and the Way of Genius: The Kane-Donaldson *Piers Plowman* in Historical Perspective', in McGann 1985, pp. 55–91; rev. repr. in Patterson 1987, pp. 77–113

——, *Negotiating the Past: The Historical Understanding of Medieval Literature* (Madison, 1987)
Pearsall, Derek, 'Editing Medieval Texts: Some Developments and Some Problems', in McGann 1985, pp. 92–106
—— (ed.), *Studies in the Vernon Manuscript* (Cambridge, 1990)
——, 'Theory and Practice in Middle English Editing', *Text* 7 (1994), 107–26
Pulsiano, Phillip, 'William l'Isle and the Editing of Old English', in Graham 2000, pp. 173–206
Reiter, Eric H., 'The Reader as Author of the User-produced Manuscript: Reading and Rewriting Popular Latin Theology in the Late Middle Ages', *Viator* 27 (1996), 151–69
Renevey, Denis, and Christiania Whitehead (eds.), *Writing Religious Women: Female Spiritual and Textual Practices in Late Medieval England* (Cardiff, 2000)
Reynolds, L. D., and N. G. Wilson, *Scribes and Scholars: A Guide to the Transmission of Greek and Latin Literature*, 2nd edn. (Oxford, 1974)
Rigg, A. G. (ed.), *Editing Medieval Texts, English, French and Latin, Written in England: Papers Given at the Twelfth Annual Conference on Editorial Problems, University of Toronto, 5–6 November 1976* (New York, 1977)
Rowland, Beryl (ed.), *Chaucer and Middle English Studies in Honour of Rossell Hope Robbins* (London, 1974)
Russell, George, and George Kane (eds.), *Piers Plowman, The C Version: Will's Visions of Piers Plowman, Do-well, Do-better and Do-Best. An Edition in the Form of Huntington Library MS HM 143, Corrected and Restored from the Known Evidence, with Variant Readings* (London, 1997)
Salu, M. B. (trans.), *The Ancrene Riwle* (London, 1955)
Scahill, John, 'Introduction: Tracking the *Ancrene Wisse*', in Imai and Watanabe 2000, pp. 1–18
——, 'A Saner, Kinder Nero?' in Wada 2002, pp. 75–94
Schnell, Rüdiger, 'Konstanz und Metamorphosen eines Textes: Eine überlieferungs- und geschlechtergeschichtliche Studie zur volkssprachlichen Rezeption von Jacobus' de Voragine Ehepredigten', *Frühmittelalterliche Studien* 33 (1999), 319–95
Shepherd, Geoffrey (ed.), *Ancrene Wisse: Parts Six and Seven* (1959: rev. edn., Exeter Medieval English Texts, Exeter, 1985)
Smith, Thomas, *Catalogus Librorum Manuscriptorum Bibliothecae Cottonianae* (Oxford, 1696)
Somerset, Fiona, Jill C. Havens, and Derrick G. Pitard (eds.), *Lollards and their Influence in Late Medieval England* (Woodbridge, Suffolk, 2003)
Stanley, E. G., review of Davis and Wrenn 1962, *Archiv* 201 (1964), 130–2
Tarrant, R. J., 'Classical Latin Literature', in Greetham 1995, pp. 95–148
Thomas, A. H., *De oudste constituties van de Dominicanen: voorgeschiedenis,*

tekst, bronnen, ontstaan en ontwikkeling (*1215–1237*), Bibliothèque de la Revue d'Histoire Ecclésiastique 42 (Louvain, 1965)

Thompson, John J., 'Textual Instability and the Late Medieval Reputation of Some Middle English Religious Literature', *Text* 5 (1991), 175–94

Thompson, W. Meredith (ed.), *þe Wohunge of Ure Lauerd*, EETS OS 241 (1958)

Tolkien, J. R. R. (ed.), *The English Text of the Ancrene Riwle: Ancrene Wisse, Edited from MS. Corpus Christi College Cambridge 402*, introd. N. R. Ker, EETS OS 249 (1962)

Trethewey, W. H. (ed.), *The French Text of the Ancrene Riwle: Edited from Trinity College Cambridge MS. R. 14. 7, with Variants from Bibliothèque Nationale MS. F. fr. 6276 and MS. Bodley 90*, EETS OS 240 (1958)

Wada, Yoko, 'The Textual History of *Ancrene Wisse*: What the Latin Quotations Tell Us', in Imai and Watanabe 2000, pp. 19–32

—— (ed.), *A Book of Ancrene Wisse* (Osaka, 2002)

—— (ed.), *A Companion to Ancrene Wisse* (Cambridge, 2003)

Warner, George F., and Julius P. Gilson, *Catalogue of Western MSS in the Old Royal and King's Collections, British Museum*, 2 vols. (London, 1921)

Watson, Nicholas, '*Ancrene Wisse*, Religious Reform and the Late Middle Ages', in Wada 2003, pp. 197–226

——, and Jocelyn Wogan-Browne, 'The French of England: The *Compileison*, *Ancrene Wisse*, and the Idea of Anglo-Norman', in *Cultural Traffic in the Medieval Romance World, Journal of Romance Studies* 4.3, special issue, ed. Simon Gaunt and Julian Weiss (Winter 2004), 35–58

Webber, T., and A. G. Watson (eds.), *The Libraries of the Augustinian Canons*, Corpus of British Medieval Library Catalogues 6 (London, 1998)

White, Hugh (trans.), *Ancrene Wisse: Guide for Anchoresses*, Penguin Classics (London, 1993)

Wilson, R. M. (ed.), *The English Text of the Ancrene Riwle: Edited from Gonville and Caius College MS. 234/120*, introd. N. R. Ker, EETS OS 229 (1954)

Zettersten, Arne (ed.), *The English Text of the Ancrene Riwle: Edited from Magdalene College, Cambridge MS. Pepys 2498*, EETS OS 274 (1976)

—— and Bernhard Diensberg (eds.), *The English Text of the Ancrene Riwle: The 'Vernon' Text, Edited from Oxford, Bodleian Library MS Eng. poet. a. 1*, introd. H. L. Spencer, EETS OS 310 (2000)

Zumthor, Paul, *Essai de poétique médiévale* (Paris, 1972)

PREFACE

| I þe Feaderes ant i þe Sunes ant i þe Hali Gastes nome, her biginneð 'Ancrene Wisse'.

1. *Recti diligunt te. In Canticis: sponsa ad sponsum. Est rectum gramaticum, rectum geometricum, rectum theologicum; et sunt differencie totidem regularum. De recto theologico sermo nobis est, cuius regule due sunt: vna circa cordis directionem, altera uersatur circa exteriorum rectificationem.*

2. *Recti diligunt te.* 'Lauerd,' seið Godes spuse to hire deore[wu]rðe spus, 'þe rihte luuieð þe.' Þeo beoð rihte þe l[i]uieð efter riwle. Ant 3e, mine leoue sustren, habbe[ð] moni dei icrauet on me [e]fter ri[wl]e. Monie cunne riwlen beoð; ah twa beoð bimong alle þet Ich chulle speoken of þurh ower bone, wið Godes grace.

3. Þe an riwleð þe heorte, ant makeð efne ant smeðe wiðute cnost ant dolc of woh inwit ant of wrei3ende þe segge, 'Her þu sunegest', oþer 'þis nis nawt ibet 3et ase wel as hit ahte.' Þeos riwle is eauer inwið ant rihteð þe heorte.[1] *Et hec est caritas quam describit Apostolus, de corde puro et consciencia bona et fide non ficta.* Þeos riwle is chearite of schir heorte ant cleane inwit ant treowe bileaue. *Pretende, inquit Psalmista, misericordiam tuam scientibus te per fidem non fictam, et iusticiam tuam—id est, uite rectitudinem—hiis qui recto sunt corde—qui scilicet omnes uoluntates suas dirigunt ad regulam diuine uoluntatis. Isti dicuntur boni anto[no]masice: Psalmista: Benefac, Domine, bonis et rectis corde. Istis dicitur ut glorientur—testimonio uidelicet bone conscientie: Gloriamini, omnes recti corde, quos scilicet rectificauit | regula illa suprema rectificans omnia, de qua Augustinus: Nichil petendum preter regulam magisterii, et Apostolus: Omnes in eadem regula permaneamus.*

4. Þe oþer riwle is al wiðuten ant riwleð þe licome ant licomliche deden, þe teacheð al hu me schal beoren him wiðuten, hu eoten, drinken, werien, singen, slepen, wakien. *Et hec est exercitio corporis, que iuxta Apostolum modicum ualet; et est quasi regula recti mechanici quod geometri[c]o recto continetur.* Ant þeos riwle nis nawt bute forte serui

---

[1] C² adds in the margin, marked for insertion after *heorte*, '3ef þe con[s]cience—þet is, þe inwit of þi þoht ant of þin heorte—bereð witnesse i þe seolf te3eines þe seoluen þet tu art i sunne unscriuen ant þet tu misdest þet ant þet, ant hauest þet unþeaw ant þet, þulli conscience, þullic inwit is woh ant unefne ant cnosti ant dolki; ah þeos riwle efneð hire ant makeð hire smeðe ant softe'; similarly V, after *permaneamus* P. 26 (see app. crit.).

þe oþer. Þe oþer is as leafdi, þeos as hire þuften; for al þet me eauer deð of þe oðer wiðuten nis bute forte riwlin þe heorte wiðinnen.

5. Nu easki 3e hwet riwle 3e ancren schulen halden. 3e schulen alles weis, wið alle mihte ant strengðe, wel witen þe inre, ant te uttre for hire sake. Þe inre is eauer ilich, þe uttre is mislich; for euch schal halden þe uttre efter þet ha mei best wið hire serui þe inre. Nu þenne is hit swa þet alle ancren mahen wel halden an riwle *quantum ad puritatem cordis, circa quam uersatur tota religio*; þet is, alle mahen ant ahen halden a riwle onont purte of heorte, þet is cleane ant schir inwit[2] (*consciencia*) wiðuten weote of sunne þet ne beo þurh schrift ibet. Þis makeð þe leafdi riwle, þe riwleð ant rihteð ant smeðeð þe heorte ant te inwit of sunne; for nawt ne makeð hire woh[3] bute sunne ane. Rihten hire ant smeðin hire is of euch religiun ant of euch ordre þe go[d] ant al þe strengðe. Þeos riwle is imaket nawt of monnes fundles, ah is of Godes heaste; for-þi ha is eauer a[n] wiðute changunge, | ant alle ahen hire in an eauer to halden. Ah alle ne mahe nawt halden a riwle, ne ne þurue nawt ne ne ahe nawt halden on a wise þe uttre riwle, *quantum scilicet ad obseruantias corporales*: þet is, onont licomliche locunges efter þe uttre riwle, þet Ich þuften cleopede, ant is monnes fundles, for na þing elles istald bute to serui þe inre, þe[4] makeð feasten, wakien, calde ant hearde werien, swucche oþre heardschipes, þet moni fles mei þolien, moni ne mei nawt. For-þi mot þeos changin hire misliche efter euchanes manere ant efter hire euene.[5] For sum is strong, sum unstrong ant mei ful wel beo cwite ant paie Godd mid leasse. Sum is clergesse, sum nawt ant mot [t]e mare wurchen ant on oðer wise seggen hire bonen. Sum is ald ant eðelich ant is þe leasse dred of, sum is 3ung ant luuelich ant is neod betere warde. For-þi schal euch ancre habben þe uttre riwle efter hire schriftes read, ant hwet-se he bit ant hat hire in obedience þe cnaweð hire manere ant wat hire strengðe. He mei þe uttre riwle changin efter wisdom, as he sið þet te inre mahe beo best ihalden.

6. Nan ancre bi mi read ne schal makien professiun—þet is, bihaten ase heast—bute þreo þinges, þet beo[ð] obedience, chastete,

---

[2] After *inwit*, C[2] adds 'þet is, conscience þe ne beo weote ne witnesse of nan gret sunne inwið hire seoluen'; similarly F, after *sunne* P. 41.

[3] After *woh*, C[2] adds 'scraggi ant unefne'.

[4] C[2] replaces *þe* by 'þeos uttre riwle, þet is i þe ende of þis boc, þe eahtu[ð]e distincciun, þet is, þe leaste dale'.

[5] After *euene*, C[2] adds 'as hire meistre seið hire; for he bereð þeos riwle inwið his breoste, ant he efter þet sum is oðer sec oðer hal scal efter his wit changi þeos uttre riwle efter euchanes euene.'

ant stude-steaðeluestnesse (þet ha ne schal þet stude neauer mare changin bute for nede ane, as strengðe ant⁶ deaðes dred, obedience of hire bischop oðer of his herre).⁷ For hwa-se nimeð þing on hond ant bihat hit Godd as heast forte don hit, ha bint hire þer-to, ant sunegeð deadliche i þe bruche ʒef ha hit brekeð willes. Ʒef ha hit ne bihat nawt, | ha hit mei do þah ant leauen hwen ha wel wule— as of mete, of drunch, flesch forgan oðer fisch, alle oþer swucche þinges, of werunge, of liggunge, of Ures, of oþre beoden, segge swa monie oðer o swucche wise. Þeos ant þulliche oþre beoð alle i freo wil to don oðer to leten hwil me wule ant hwen me wule bute ha beon bihaten. Ah chearite, þet is luue, ant eadmodnesse ant þolemodnesse, treoweschipe ant haldunge of [alle] þe ten heastes, schrift ant penitence, þeos ant þulliche oþre, þe beoð summe of þe alde lahe, summe of þe neowe, ne beoð nawt monnes fundles ne riwle þet mon stalde, ah beoð Godes heastes, ant for-þi euch mon mot ham nede halden, ant ʒe ouer alle, for þeos riwl[i]ð þe heorte. Of hire riwlunge is al meast þet Ich write, bute i þe frumðe of þis boc ant i þe leaste ende. Þe þinges þet Ich write her of þe uttre riwle, ʒe ham haldeð alle, mine leoue sustren, ure Lauerd beo iþonket, ant schulen þurh his grace se lengre se betere. Ant þah nulle Ich nawt þet ʒe bihaten ham as heaste to halden; for as ofte as ʒe þrefter breken eni of ham, hit walde to swiðe hurten ower heorte ant makien ow swa offearet þet ʒe mahten sone—þet Godd forbeode ow!— fallen i desesperance, þet is, in an unhope ant an unbileaue forte beon iborhen. For-þi þet Ich write ow, mine leoue sustren, of uttre þinges i þe earste dale of ower boc of ower seruise, ant nomeliche i þe leaste, ʒe ne schule nawt bihaten hit, ah habbeð hit on heorte ant doð hit as þah ʒe hit hefden bihaten.

7. Ʒef ei unweote askeð ow of hwet ordre ʒe beon— | as summe doð, [ʒ]e telleð me, þe siheð þe gneat ant swolheð þe flehe— ondswerieð: of Sein Iames, þe wes Godes apostel ant for his muchele halinesse icleopet Godes broðer. Ʒef him þuncheð wunder ant sullich of swuch ondswere, easkið him hwet beo ordre, ant hwer he funde in Hali [W]rit religiun openluke[r] descriue[t] ant isutelet þen is i Sein Iames canonial epistel. He sei[ð hwet] is religiun, hwuch is riht ordre. *Religio munda et immaculata apud Deum et Patrem hec est: visitare pupillos et viduas in necessitate sua, et immaculatum se custodire ab hoc seculo*; þet is, 'Cleane religiun ant [wið]ute [w]em is iseon ant

---

⁶ After *ant*, C² adds in the margin 'as of fur oðer of oþer peril'.
⁷ After *herre*, C² adds 'Ʒe ne schulen, Ich segge, makie na ma uuz of feste biheastes.'

helpen [widewen ant feder]lese children, ant from þe [w]orld [w]iten
him cleane ant unwemmet.' Þus Sein Iame descriueð religiun ant
ordre. Þe leatere dale of his sahe limpeð to reclusen; for þer beoð
twa dalen, to twa manere þe beoð of religiuse. To eiðer limpeð his
dale, as ȝe mahen iheren. Gode religiuse beoð i þe world summe,
nomeliche prelaz ant treowe preachurs, þe habbeð þe earre dale of
þet Sein Iame seide; þet beoð, as he seið, þe gað to helpen
[wi]d[ewen ant fea]derlese children. Þe [saw]le is widewe þe haueð
forloren hire spus, þet is, Iesu Crist, wið eni heaued sunne. Þe is
alswa federles þe haueð þurh his sunne forloren þe Feader of
heouene. Gan iseon þulliche ant elnin ham ant helpen wið fode of
hali lare—þis is riht religiun, he seið, Sein Iame. Þe leatere dale of
his sahe limpeð to ower religiun, as Ich ear seide, þe witeð ow from
þe worlt ouer oþre religiuse cleane ant unwemmet. Þus þe apostle
Sein Iame, þe descriueð religiun, nowðer hwit ne blac ne nempneð
he in his ordre. Ah moni siheð þe gneat ant | swolheð þe flehe—þet
is, makeð muche strengðe þer-as is þe leaste. Pawel þe Earste Ancre,
Antonie ant Arsenie, Makarie ant te oþre,[8] neren ha religiuse ant of
Sein Iames ordre? Alswa Seinte Sare ant Seinte Si[n]cle[t]ice, ant
monie oþre swucche, wepmen ba ant wummen, wið hare greate
matten ant hare hearde heren; neren ha of god ordre? Ant hweðer
hwite oðer blake—as unwise ow easkið þe weneð þet ordre sitte i þe
curtel—Godd wat; noðeles ha weren wel baðe, nawt tah onont
claðes, ah as Godes spuse singeð bi hire seoluen, *Nigra sum set
formosa.* 'Ich am blac ant tah hwit', ha seið: unseowlich wiðuten,
schene wiðinnen. O þis wise ondswerieð to þe easkeres of ower
ordre, hweðer hwite oðer blake: seggeð ȝe beoð ba twa þurh þe grace
of Godd, ant of Sein Iames ordre[9] þet he wrat leatere: *Inmaculatum se
custodire ab hoc seculo*—þet is þet Ich seide ear, from þe worlt witen
him cleane ant unwemmet. Her-in is religiun, nawt i þe wide hod ne
i þe blake cape, ne i þe hwite rochet ne i þe greie cuuel. Þer-as monie
beoð igedderet togederes, þer for anrednesse me schal makie strengðe
of annesse of claðes, ant of oþerhwet of uttre þinges, þet te annesse
wiðuten bitacni þe annesse of a luue ant of a wil þet ha alle habbeð
imeane wiðinnen. Wið hare habit þet is an, þet euch haueð swuch as
oþer, ant alswa of oðerhwet, ha ȝeiȝeð þet ha habbeð alle togederes a
luue ant a wil euch alswuch as oþer (loke þet ha ne lihen!). Þus hit is
i cuuent. Ah hwer-se wummon liueð, oðer mon, bi him ane, hearmite

[8] After *oþre*, C² adds 'hali men sumhwile'.
[9] After *ordre*, C² adds 'ant of þe ilke dale'.

PREFACE 5

oðer ancre, of | þinges wiðuten hwer-of scandle ne cume nis nawt f. 4ʳ
muche strengðe. Hercne Michee: *Indicabo tibi, o homo, quid sit bonum
et quid Deus requirat a te: vtique facere iudicium et iusticiam et sollicite
ambulare cum Domino Deo tuo.* 'Ich chulle schawi þe, mon,' seið þe
145 hali Michee, Godes prophete, 'Ich chulle schawi þe soðliche hwet is
god, ant hwuch religiun ant hwuch ordre, hwuch halinesse Godd
easkeð of þe.' Low, þis; vnderstond hit. 'Do wel ant dem wac eauer
þe seoluen, ant wið dred ant wið luue ga mid Godd ti Lauerd.' þer-
as þeose þinges beoð, þer is riht religiun, þer is soð ordre; ant do al
150 þet oðer ant lete þis nis bute trichunge ant a fals gile. *Ve uobis, Scribe et
Pharisei, ypocrite, qui mundatis quod deforis est calicis et parapsidis, intus autem
pleni estis omni spursicia, similes sepulcris dealbatis.* Al þet gode religiuse
doð oþer werieð efter þe uttre riwle, al togedere is her-uore; al nis
bute ase tole to timbrin her-towart, al nis bute as þuften to serui þe
155 leafdi to riwlin þe heorte.

þis an boc is todealet in eahte leasse bokes.

8. Nv, mine leoue sustren, þis boc Ich todeale on eahte 'destinctiuns', þet ȝe cleopieð dalen; ant euch wiðute monglunge spekeð al bi
him seolf of sunderliche þinges, ant þah euchan riht falleð efter oðer, M. 14
160 ant is þe leatere eauer iteiet to þe earre.
þe earste dale spekeð al of ower seruise.
þe oðer is hu ȝe schulen þurh ower fif wittes witen ower heorte,
þet ordre ant religiun ant sawle lif is inne. I þis destinctiun aren
chapitres fiue, as fif stuchen efter [þe] fif wittes, þe witeð þe heorte
165 as wakemen hwer-se ha beoð treowe; ant spekeð of euch hwet
sunderlepes o rawe. |
þe þridde dale is of anes cunnes fuheles þe Dauið i þe Sawter f. 4ᵛ
eueneð him seolf to as he were ancre, ant hu þe cunde of þe ilke
fuheles beoð ancren iliche.
170 þe feorðe dale is of fleschliche fondunges ant gasteliche baðe, ant
confort aȝeines ham, ant of hare saluen.
þe fifte dale is of schrift.
þe seste dale is of penitence.
þe seoueðe, of schir heorte, hwi me ah ant hwi me schal Iesu Crist
175 luuien, ant hwet binimeð us his luue ant let us him to luuien.
þe eahtuðe dale is al of þe uttre riwle: earst of mete ant of drunch,
ant of oþre þinges þet falleð þer-abuten; þrefter of þe þinges þe ȝe
mahen underuon ant hwet þinges ȝe mahen witen oðer habben;

þrefter of ower claðes ant of swucche þinges as þer-abuten falleð; þrefter of ower werkes; of doddunge ant of blodletunge; of ower meidnes riwle; aleast hu ȝe ham schulen leofliche learen.

PART 1

Her biginneð þe earste boc, of Vres ant vreisuns þe gode beoð to seggen.

1. Hwen ȝe earst ariseð, blescið ow ant seggeð, *In nomine Patris et Filii et Spiritus Sancti, Amen,* ant biginneð anan *Veni, Creator Spiritus,* wið up-aheuene ehnen ant honden toward heouene, buhinde M. 16 o cneon forðward upo þe bedde, ant seggeð swa al þe ymne ut wið þe verset, *Emitte spiritum tuum,* ant te vreisun, *Deus, qui corda fidelium.* Her-efter, scheoiende ow ant claðinde ow seggeð Pater Noster ant Credo; *Iesu Criste, fili Dei viui, miserere nobis; qui de uirgine dignatus es nasci, miserere nobis.* Þis word seggeð eauer aþet ȝe beon al greiðe. (Þis word habbeð muchel on us, ant i muð ofte, euch time þet ȝe mahen, sitten ȝe oðer stonden.)

2. Hwen ȝe beoð al greiðe, spren|geð ow wið hali weater (þet ȝe f. 5ʳ schulen eauer habben), ant þenche[ð] o Godes flesch ant on his deorewurðe blod, þet is abuue þe hehe weoued, ant falleð adun þer-towart wið þeose gretunges:

Ave, principium nostre creationis.
Ave, precium nostre redemptionis.
Aue, viaticum nostre peregrinationis.
Ave, premium nostre expectationis.
Aue, solamen nostre sustentationis.

Tu esto nostrum gaudium
Qui es futurus premium;
Sit nostra in te gloria
Per cuncta semper secula.

Mane nobiscum, Domine,
Noctem obscuram remoue,
Omne delictum ablue,
Piam medelam tribue.

Gloria tibi, Domine,
Qui natus es de uirgine,
Cum Patre, et cetera.

(Alswa ȝe schule don hwen þe preost halt hit up ed te Measse, ant biuore þe *Confiteor* hwen ȝe schule beon ihuslet.) Efter þis, falleð o

cneon to ower crucifix wið þeose fif gretunges ine munegunge of 35
Godes fif wunden:

*Adoramus te, Christe, et benedicimus tibi quia per sanctam Crucem
redemisti mundum.*

*Tuam crucem adoramus, Domine; tuam gloriosam recolimus passio-
nem. Miserere nostri, qui passus es pro nobis.* 40

> *Salue, Crux sancta,*
> *Arbor digna,*
> *Cuius robur preciosum*
> *Mundi tulit talentum.*

Salue, Crux, que in corpore Christi dedicata es, et ex membris eius 45
tanquam margaritis ornata.

> *O Crux, lignum triumphale,*
> *Mundi uera salus, uale,*
> *Inter ligna nullum tale*
> *Fronde, flore, germine.* 50
>
> *Medicina Christiana,*
> *Salua sanas, egras sana;*

(ant wið þis word beateð on ower breoste)

> *Quod non ualet uis humana*
> *Sit in tuo nomine.* 55

Hwa-se ne con þeos fiue segge þe earste, *Adoramus te*, cneolinde fif
siðen. Ant blescið ow wið euchan of þeose gretunges, ant wið þeose
wordes, *Miserere nostri, qui passus es pro nobis*, beateð ower heorte, ant
cusseð þe eorðe, icruchet wið þe þume. Þrefter | wendeð ow to ure
Leafdi onlicnesse ant cneolið wið fif Auez; aleast to þe oþre ymagnes 60
ant to ower relikes luteð oþer cneolið, nomeliche to þe halhen þe ȝe
habbeð to þurh luue iturnd ower weofdes, swa muche þe reaðere ȝef
ei is ihalhet.

3. Þer-efter ananriht ure Leafdi Uhtsong seggeð o þis wise. Ȝef
hit is wercdei, falleð to þer eorðe, ȝef hit is halidei, buhinde sumdeal 65
duneward, seggeð Pater Noster ant Credo ba stille. Rihteð ow up
þrefter ant seggeð, *Domine, labia mea aperies*. Makieð on ower muð a
creoiz wið þe þume; ed *Deus, in adiutorium*, a large creoiz wið þe
þume ant wið þe twa fingres from buue þe forheaued dun to þe
breoste;[1] ant falleð to þe eorðe, ȝef hit is wercdei, wið *Gloria Patri*, 70

---

[1] After *breoste*, F has 'et en trauers et de lune espaule iesqal altre'.

PART I 9

oðer buheð duneward, ȝef hit [is] halidei, aþet *Sicut erat.* Þus ed
euch *Gloria Patri,* ant ed te biginnunge of þe *Venite,* ant i þe *Venite*
ed *Venite, adoremus,* ant ed te *Aue Maria,* ant hwer-se ȝe eauer hereð   M. 20
Maries nome inempnet, ant ed euch Pater Noster þet falle to ower
75 Ures, ant to þe Credo,[2] ant to þe collecte ed eauereuch Tide,[3] ant ed
te leatemeste vers of eauereuch ymne, ant ed te leaste vers wiðuten
an of þe salm *Benedicite omnia opera Domini, Domino:*[4] ed alle þes
ilke, ȝef hit is halidei, buheð sumdel dunewart; ȝef hit is wercdei,
falleð to þer eorðe. Ed te biginnunge of eauereuch Tide, wið *Deus, in*
80 *adiutorium,* makieð rode-taken as Ich ear tahte. Ed *Veni, creator*
buheð oðer cneolið efter þet te dei is. Wið *Memento, salutis auctor*
falleð eauer adun, ant ed tis word, *Nascendo formam sumpseris,* cusseð
þe eorðe; ant alswa i þe *Te Deum laudamus,* ed tis word, *Non horruisti*
uirginis uterum, ant ed te Messe i þe Muchele Credo, | ed *ex Maria*   f. 6ʳ
85 *uirgine, et homo factus est.*

4. Euchan segge hire Ures as ha haueð iwriten ham, ant euch
Tide sunderliche, ase forð as ȝe mahen, seggeð in his time, ear to
sone þen to leate ȝef ȝe ne mahen eauer halde þe time. Vhtsong bi
niht i winter, i sumer i þe dahunge. Þis winter schal biginnen ed te
90 Hali Rode Dei ine heruest, ant leasten aþet Easter. Prime in winter
earliche, i sumer bi forð marhen; *Pretiosa* þrefter (ȝef ȝe habbeð
neode for eani hihðe to speoken, ȝe muhe seggen hit biuoren, ant
efter Uhtsong anan ȝef hit swa neodeð). Non eauer efter mete, ant,
hwen ȝe slepeð, efter slep, hwil þet sumer leasteð, bute hwen ȝe
95 feasteð; i winter biuore mete hwen ȝe al ueasteð, þe Sunnedei þah
efter mete, for ȝe eoteð twien. Ed te an salm ȝe schulen stonden, ȝef
ȝe beoð eise, ant ed te oþer sitten; ant eauer wið *Gloria Patri* rungen   M. 22
up ant buhen. Hwa-se mei stonden al on ure Leafdi wurðschipe,
stonde o Godes halue. Ed alle þe seoue Tiden singeð Pater Noster
100 ant *Aue Maria* ba biuoren ant efter; *Fidelium anime* efter euch Tide
biuore þe Pater Noster. Ed þreo Tiden seggeð Credo wið Pater
Noster, biuoren Uhtsong ant efter Prime ant eft[er Complie.] From
ower Complie aþet efter *Pretiosa* haldeð silence.

5. Efter Euensong anan ower *Placebo* euche niht seggeð hwen ȝe
105 beoð eise, bute hit beo hali niht for feaste of nihe lesceuns þe cume
ine marhen. Biuore Cumplie oðer efter Uhtsong, *Dirige* wið þreo
salmes ant wið þreo lesceuns euche niht sundri; in aniuersaries of

---

[2] For *to þe Credo,* N has 'i ðe Crede et tis word, *natus ex Maria virgine*'.
[3] After *Tide,* N has 'ant to þe Letanie'.
[4] After *Domino,* N has 'et tisse uerse, *Benedicamus Patrem et Filium cum Sancto Spiritu.*'

ower leoueste freond, seggeð alle nihene. I stude of *Gloria* ed euch psalmes ende, *Requiem eternam dona eis, Domine, et lux perpetua luceat eis*. Ed *Placebo* sitteð | aþet *Magnificat;* alswa ed *Dirige* bute ed te lesceuns,[5] ant ed te *Miserere*, ant from *Laudate* al ut. *Requiescant in pace* i stude of *Benedicamus* seggeð on ende. Ine marhen oðer i niht, efter þe suffragies[6] of Uhtsong, seggeð Commendaciun; sittinde þe salmes, cneolinde þe ureisuns oðer stondinde. Ʒef ʒe þus doð euche niht bute ane Sunneniht, ʒe doð muche betere. In a-mel dei we seggeð ba *Placebo* ant *Dirige* efter þe mete graces, i twi-mel dei efter Non; ant ʒe alswa mote don.

6. Seoue Psalmes seggeð sittinde oðer cneolinde wið þe Letanie. Fiftene Psalmes seggeð o þis wise: þe earste fiue for ow seolf, ant for alle þe ow god doð oðer unnen; þe oþre fiue for þe peis of al Hali Chirche; þe þridde fiue for alle Cristene sawles. Efter þe forme fiue, *Kyrie eleison, Christe eleison, Kyrie eleison; Pater noster; Et ne nos; Saluos fac seruos tuos et ancillas tuas, Deus meus, sperantes in te. Oremus. Deus, cui proprium est.* Efter þe oþre fiue alswa: *Kyrie eleison, Christe eleison, Kyrie eleison; Pater noster; Et ne nos; Domine, fiat pax in uirtute tua, et abundancia in turribus tuis. Oremus. Ecclesie tue, quesumus, Domine, preces placatus.* Efter þe þridde fiue (þe ʒe schulen seggen wiðuten *Gloria Patri*), *Kyrie eleison* i.i.i.; *Pater noster; Et ne nos; A porta inferi erue, Domine, animas eorum. Oremus. Fidelium Deus omnium.* Seoue salmes, ant þus þeose fiftene, seggeð abuten under, for abute swuch time as me singeð Measse in alle religiuns, ant ure Lauerd þolede pine upo þe rode, ʒe ahen to beo nomeliche i beoden ant i bonen; ant alswa from Prime aþet mid-marhen, hwen preostes of þe worlt singeð hare meassen.[7]

7. [O] þis wise ʒe mahen, ʒef ʒe wulleð, seggen ower Pater Nostres. 'Almihti Godd, Feader, Sune, Hali Geast, as ʒe beoð

---

[5] After *lesceuns*, C² adds 'þear stonden.'

[6] Next to *suffragies*, C² adds in the margin 'þet beoð þe memoires of þe halhen'.

[7] After *meassen*, N has 'Vre leawede breþren siggeð þus hore Vres: vor Vhtsong ine werkedawes heihte and twenti Pater Nosteres, ine helidawes, forti; vor Euesonge, viftene; vor eueriche oþer Tide, seouene. Biuoren Uhtsong, Pater Noster and Credo, kneolinde to þer eorðe on werkedei, and buinde on halidei. And þenne schal siggen hwo-se con, *Domine, labia mea aperies; Deus, in adiutorium meum intende; Gloria Patri; Sicut erat; Alleluia*; and ine Leinten, *Laus tibi, Domine, / Rex eterne glorie*; efter þe laste, *Kirieleison, Christeleison, Kirieleison; Pater noster*; and efter þe *Amen, Per Dominum; Benedicamus Domino; Deo gratias*. And et alle þe oþre Tiden also biginnen and also enden; bute et Cumplie schal biginnen hwo-so con, *Conuerte nos, Deus salutaris*, and et alle þe oþre Tiden, *Deus in adiutorium* wiðvten *Domine, labia mea*. Ʒif ei of ou wule don þus, heo voleweð her, ase in oþre obseruaunces, muchel of vre ordre, and wel Ich hit reade.'

PART I

þreo | an Godd, alswa ȝe beoð an mihte, an wisdom, ant an luue; ant f. 7ʳ
þah is mihte iturnd to þe in Hali Writ nomeliche, þu deorewurðe
Feader, to þe wisdom, seli Sune, to þe luue, Hali Gast. Ȝef me,[8] an
140 almihti Godd, þrile i þreo hades, þes ilke þreo þinges: mihte forte
serui þe, wisdom forte cweme þe, luue ant wil to don hit; mihte þet
Ich mahe don, wisdom þet Ich cunne don, luue þet Ich wulle don aa
þet te is leouest. As þu art ful of euch god, alswa nis na god wone
þer-as þeose þreo beoð, mihte ant wisdom ant luue, iueiet togederes.
145 þet tu ȝetti me ham, Hali þrumnesse, i þe wurðschipe of þe', þreo
Pater Nostres, Credo. Verset: *Benedicamus Patrem et Filium cum
Sancto Spiritu; laudemus et superexaltemus eos in secula. Oremus.
Omnipotens sempiterne Deus, qui dedisti famulis tuis in confessione uere
fidei eterne [Trinitatis] gloriam agnoscere.* Alpha et ω, hwa-se hit haueð,
150 oðer [sum oþer] of þe Hali þrumnesse, segge þe wulle.

8. 'A, Iesu, þin are; Iesu, for mine sunnen ahonget o rode, for þe
ilke fif wunden þe þu on hire bleddest, heal mi blodi sawle of alle þe
sunnen þet ha is wið iwundet þurh mine fif wittes. I þe munegunge
of ham þet hit swa mote beon, deorewurðe Lauerd', fif Pater
155 Nostres. Verset: *Omnis terra adoret te [et psallat tibi;] et psalmum
dicat nomine tuo. Oremus. Iuste Iudex,* ȝef þu const, oþer of þe creoiz M. 28
sum oðer. *Deus, qui Unigeniti tui, Domini nostri Iesu Christi, pretioso
sanguine uexillum sancte Crucis*—þis is an of þe beste.

9. 'For þe seoue ȝiftes of þe Hali Gast, þet Ich ham mote habben,
160 ant for þe seoue Tiden þet Hali Chirche singeð, þet Ich deale in ham
slepe Ich oðer wakie, ant for þe seoue bonen i þe Pater Noster aȝein
þe seouen heaued ant deadliche sunnen, þet tu wite me wið ham ant
alle hare brokes, ant ȝeoue me þe seouene selie Eadinesses þe þu
hauest, Lauerd, bihaten þine icorene, | i þin eadi nome', seoue Pater f. 7ᵛ
165 Nostres. Verset: *Emitte spiritum tuum. Oremus. Deus, cui cor omne
patet. Ecclesie tue, quesumus, Domine. Exaudi, quesumus, Domine,
supplicum preces.*

10. 'For þe ten heastes þe Ich ibroken habbe, summe oðer alle,
ant me seoluen towart te (hwet-se beo of oðerhwet) untreoweliche
170 iteoheðet, i bote of þeose bruchen, forte sahtni me wið þe,
deorewurðe Lauerd', ten Pater Nostres. Verset: *Ego dixi, Domine,
miserere mei. Sana animam meam, quia peccaui tibi. Oremus. Deus, cui
proprium est misereri.*

11. '[I] þe wurðgunge, Iesu Crist, of þine tweof apostles, þet Ich
175 mote oueral folhin hare lare, þet Ich mote habben þurh hare bonen

[8] After *me*, C² adds in the margin 'Neomeð þe "þé" up.'

M. 30 þe tweolf bohes þe bloweð of chearite, as Seinte Pawel writeð,⁹ blisfule Lauerd', tweolf Pater Nostres. Verset: *Annuntiauerunt opera Dei, et facta eius intellexerunt. Oremus. Exaudi nos, Deus salutaris noster, et apostolorum tuorum nos tuere presidiis.*

12. H[a]lhen þe ȝe luuieð best, in heore wurðgunge seggeð oðer 180 leas oðer ma as ow bereð on heorte, ant þet uerset efterward wið hare collecte.

13. '[F]or alle þeo þe habbeð eani god ido me, iseid me oðer iunnen me, ant for alle þe ilke þe wurcheð þe six werkes of misericorde, mearciable Lauerd', six Pater Nostres. Verset: *Dispersit, dedit pauper-* 185 *ibus; iusticia eius manet. Oremus. Retribuere dignare, Domine.* Hwa-se wule, segge þe salm *Ad te leuaui* biuore þe Pater Nostres, ant *Kyrie eleison, Christe eleison, Kyrie eleison.*

14. 'For alle þe sawlen þe beoð forðfearen i þe bileaue of þe fowr Goddspelles, þe haldeð al Cristendom up o fowr halues, þet tu þe 190 f. 8ʳ fowr marheȝeuen | ȝeoue ham in heouene, milzfule Lauerd', fowr Pater Nostres. Ȝef ȝe seggeð nihene, as þer beoð nihene englene weoredes, þet Godd þurh his mearci hihi ham ut of pine to hare feolahredden, ȝe doð ȝet betere. Ant her alswa, [ȝef] ȝe wulleð, seggeð *De profundis* biuore þe Pater Nostres, ant *Kyrie eleison* iii. 195 Verset: *A porta inferi. Oremus. Fidelium.*

M. 32   15. Bi dei sum time o[ð]er bi niht gederið in ower heorte alle seke ant sarie, [þe wa þet pouere] þolieð, þe pinen þe prisuns habbeð þer ha liggeð wið irn heuie ifeðeret (nomeliche of þe Cristene þe beoð in heaðenesse, summe i prisun, summe in ase muche þeowdom as oxe is 200 oðer asse); habbeð reowðe of þeo þe beoð i stronge temptatiuns. Alle hare sares setteð in ower heorte ant sikeð to ure Lauerd, þet he neome reowðe of ham ant bihalde toward ham wið þe ehe of his are; ant ȝef ȝe habbeð hwile, seggeð þe salm *Leuaui oculos.*¹⁰ *Pater noster.* Verset: *Conuertere, Domine, usquequo? Et deprecabilis esto super seruos* 205 *tuos. Oremus. Pretende, Domine, famulis et famulabus.*

16. I þe Measse, hwen þe preost heueð up Godes licome, seggeð þis vers stondinde:

> *Ecce salus mundi, uerbum Patris, hostia uera,*
> *Viua caro, Deitas integra, uerus homo,*   210

ant þenne falleð adun wið þeose gretunges:

---

⁹ After *writeð*, C² adds in the margin *Ad Corinthios: Caritas patiens est, et cetera.*
¹⁰ After *oculos*, C² adds '*meos in montes*, ant swa al þe salm ut'.

PART I 13

*Ave, principium nostre creationis.
Aue, pretium nostre redemptionis.
Aue, viaticum nostre peregrinationis.*[11]
215 *Aue, premium nostre expectationis.
Aue, solamen nostre sustentationis.*

*Tu esto nostrum gaudium
Qui es futurus premium;
Sit nostra in te gloria*
220 *Per cuncta semper secula. Amen.*

Mane nobiscum, Domine.

Gloria tibi, Domine.

Set quis est locus in me quo ueniat in me Deus meus, quo Deus ueniat aut maneat in me, Deus qui fecit celum et terram? Itane, Domine, Deus meus,
225 *est quicquam in me quod capiat te?* | *Quis michi dabit ut uenias in cor* f. 8ᵛ
meum et inebries illud, et unum bonum meum amplectar, te? Qui[d] michi es? Miserere, ut loquar. Angusta est tibi domus anime mee, quo uenias ad eam; dilatetur abs te. Ruinosa est; refice eam. Habet que offendant oculos tuos, fateor et scio; set quis mundabit eam, aut cui alteri preter te
230 *clamabo? Ab ocultis meis munda me, Domine, et ab alienis parce famule tue. Miserere, miserere, miserere mei, Deus, secundum magnam,* ant swa al þe salm ut, wið *Gloria Patri; Christe, audi nos,* twien; *Kyrie eleison,* M. 34
Christe eleison, Kyrie eleison; Pater noster; Credo . . . carnis resurrectionem et uitam eternam, Amen. Saluam fac famulam tuam, Deus
235 *meus, sperantem in te. Doce me facere uoluntatem tuam, quia Deus meus es tu. Domine, exaudi orationem meam; et clamor meus ad te ueniat. Oremus. Concede, quesumus, omnipotens Deus, ut quem enigmatice et sub aliena spetie cernimus quo sacramentaliter cibamur in terris, fatie ad fatiem eum uideamus, eo sicuti est ueraciter et realiter frui mereamur, in*
240 *celis. Per eundem Dominum.*

17. Efter þe measse cos, hwen þe preost sacreð—þer forȝeoteð al þe world, þer beoð al ut of bodi, þer i sperclinde luue bicluppeð ower leofmon, þe into ower breostes bur is iliht of heouene, ant haldeð him heteueste aþet he habbe iȝettet ow al þet ȝe eauer easkið.

245 18. **Þis ureisun biuore þe muchele rode is of muche strengðe.**

Abute middei hwa-se mei (hwa-se ne mei þenne, o sum oðer time) þenche o Godes rode, ase muchel as ha eauer con mest oðer mei, ant

[11] After *peregrinationis*, N has *Aue solacium nostre tribulationis.*

of his derue pine, ant biginne þrefter þe ilke fif gretunges þe beoð iwriten þruppe;[12] ant | alswa cneolin to euchan, ant blescin as hit seið þer ant beate þe breoste, ant makie a þulli bone. *Adoramus te, Christe. Tuam Crucem. Salue, Crux que.* [*Salue, Crux sancta.*] *O Crux, lignum.*[13] Aris[e] þenne ant bigin[ne] þe antefne, *Salua nos, Christe Saluator, per uirtutem sancte Crucis*, wið þe rode-taken; ant segge stondinde þe salm *Iubilate*, wið *Gloria Patri;* ant þenne þe antefne segge eauer þus: *Salua nos, Christe Saluator, per uirtutem sancte Crucis*, ant blescin wið *Qui saluasti Petrum in mare, miserere nobis*, ant beate þe breoste, ant tenne falle adun ant segge, *Christe, audi nos; Iesu Christe, audi nos. Kyrie eleison, Christe eleison, Kyrie eleison. Pater noster. Et ne nos.* Verset: *Protector noster, aspice, Deus, et respice in faciem christi tui. Oremus. Deus, qui sanctam Crucem.*[14] Eft biginne *Adoramus* as ear, alle fiue; *Salua nos, Christe*, þe antefne as ear; þe salm *Ad te leuaui;* þe antefne [efter], al ut; ant tenne as ear to þe eorðe; *Christe, audi nos* twien. *Kyrie* iii. *Pater noster. Et ne nos.* Verset: *Protector noster*, as ear. *Oremus. Adesto, quesumus, Domine Deus noster, et quos sancte Crucis letari facis.*[15] Þridde chearre riht alswa, ant feorðe chearre ant fifte; nawiht ne changeð bute þe salmes ant te ureisuns. Þe forme salm, *Iubilate;* þe oþer, *Ad te leuaui;* þe þridde, *Qui confidunt;* þe feorðe, *Domine, non est exaltatum*; þe fifte, *Laudate Dominum in sanctis eius;* ant in euch beoð fif uers. Þe fif ureisuns beoð: *Deus, qui sanctam Crucem; Adesto, quesumus, Domine; Deus, qui pro nobis filium tuum; Deus, qui Unigeniti; Iuste iudex*, wið *O beata et intemerata*; ant hwa-se ne con þeos fif ureisuns, segge eauer an. Ant hwa-se þuncheð to long, leaue þe salmes.

19. 'Leafdi, seinte Marie, for þe ilke muchele blisse þet tu hefdest inwið þe i þet ilke time þet Iesu Godd, Godes sune, | efter þe engles gretunge nom flesch ant blod in þe ant of þe, underfeng mi gretunge wið þe ilke *Aue*, ant make me telle lutel of euch blisse utewið, ah froure me inwið, ant ernde me þeo of heouene. Ant ase wis as i þe ilke flesch þet he toc of þe nes neauer sunne, ne i þin, as me leueð,

---

[12] For *þe beoð iwriten þruppe*, V has 'in þe seuen and þritti vers abouen in þe selue columpne, *Aue, principium nostre creacionis, et cetera.*' F has after it *Adoramus te, Christe, et benedicimus.*

[13] For *O Crux, lignum*, N has *O Crux gloriosa, o Crux adoranda, o lignum preciosum et admirabile signum, per quod et diabolus est uictus et mundus Christi sanguine redemptus.*

[14] After *Crucem*, F has 'od cest oroison, *Deus, qui pro nobis Filium tuum*; ou ceste, *Deus, qui unigeniti filij tui*'.

[15] For *Adesto . . . facis*, N has *Perpetua nos, Domine, pace custodi quos per lignum sancte Crucis redimere dignatus es. Qui uiuis et regnas cum Deo Patre.*

PART I   15

efter þe ilke tacunge, hwet-se biuore were, clense mi sawle of
fleschliche sunnen.' Biginne þe Aue aþet *Dominus tecum*, as me
biginneð antefne, ant tenne þe salm, ant efter þe salm al ut fif
siðen, ant þus to euch salm. *Aue Maria, gratia plena, Dominus tecum;*
285 *Magnificat; Aue Maria* al ut fif siðen.

20. 'Leafdi, seinte Mari[e], for þe ilke muchele blisse þet tu
hefdest þa þu sehe þe ilke blisfule bearn iboren of þi cleane bodi
to moncunne heale, wiðuten eauereuch bruche, wið ihal meiðhad ant
meidenes menske, heal me, þet am þurh wil tobroken, as Ich drede,
290 hwet-se beo of dede; ant ȝef me in heoune seon þi blisfule leor, ant
bihalde lanhure meidenes menske, ȝef Ich nam wurðe forte beon
iblisset in hare ferredden.' *Aue Maria, gratia plena, Dominus tecum. Ad
Dominum cum tribularer.* Aue as ear, fi[f siðen].

21. 'Leafdi, seinte Marie, for þe ilke muchele blisse þet tu hefdest
295 þa þu sehe þi deore, deorewurðe sune efter his derue deað arisen to
blisful lif, his bodi seueualt brihtre þen þe sunne, ȝef me deien wið
him ant arisen in him, worltliche deien, gasteliche libben, dealen in
his pinen feolahliche in eorðe forte beon i blisse his feolahe in
heoune. For þe ilke muchele blisse þet tu hefdest, Leafdi, of his
300 blisful ariste efter þi muchele sorhe, efter mi sorhe þet Ich am in her   M. 40
lead me to þi blisse.' *Aue Maria, gratia | plena, Dominus tecum.*   f. 10ʳ
Retribue seruo tuo. Aue fif siðen.

22. 'Leafdi, seinte Marie, for þe ilke muchele blisse þet tu hefdest
þa þu sehe þi brihte, blisfule sune, þet te Giws wenden forte
305 aþrusmin[16] i þruh, se wurðliche ant se mihtiliche on Hali þursdei
stihe to his blisse, into his riche of heoune, ȝef me warpe wið him al
þe worlt under fet, ant stihen nu heorteliche, hwen Ich deie
gasteliche, o Domesdei al licomliche to heounliche blissen.' *Aue
Maria, gratia plena, Dominus tecum. In conuertendo.* Aue fif siðen.

310 23. 'Leafdi, seinte Marie, for þe ilke muchele blisse þet fulde
al[le] þe [oþere], þa he underueng þe into unimete blisse, ant wið his
blisfule earmes sette þe i trone, ant cwene crune [on] heaued, brihtre
þen þe sunne, heh heounliche cwen, underueng þeos gretunges of
me swa on eorðe þet Ich mote blisfulliche grete þe in heoune.' *Aue*
315 *Maria, gratia plena, Dominus tecum. Ad te leuaui.* Aue fif siðen.

24. Ant þenne þet uerset: *Spiritus sanctus superueniet in te, et uirtus
Altissimi obumbrabit tibi. Oremus. Gratiam tuam.* Antefne:

---

[16] After *aþrusmin*, N has 'ase anoþer deaðlich mon wiðute hope of ariste'; similarly P
(see app. crit.).

> *Ave, regina celorum,*
> *Aue, domina angelorum;*
> *Salue, radix sancta,*
> *Ex qua mundo lux est orta;*[17]
> *Vale, ualde decora,*
> *Et pro nobis semper Christum exora.*

Verset: *Egredietur uirga de radice Iesse, et flos de radice eius ascendet.* Oremus. *Deus, qui uirginalem aulam.* Antefne:

> *Gaude, Dei genitrix, uirgo inmaculata.*
> *Gaude, que gaudium ab angelo suscepisti.*
> *Gaude, que genuisti eterni luminis claritatem.*
> *Gaude, mater.*
> *Gaude, sancta Dei genitrix, uirgo.*
> *Tu sola mater innupta.*
> *Te laudat omnis filii tui creatura, genitricem lucis.*
> *Sis pro nobis pia interuentrix.*[18]

Verset: *Ecce, uirgo concipiet et pariet filium, et uocabitur nomen eius Emmanuel.* Oremus. *Deus, qui de beate Marie uirginis utero.* Antefne: *Gaude, uirgo; gaude, Dei genitrix; et gaude, gaudium, Maria, omnium fidelium. | Gaudeat Ecclesia, in tuis laudibus assidua; et, pia domina, gaudere fac nos tecum ante Dominum.* Verset: *Ecce, concipies in utero et paries filium; et uocabis nomen eius Iesum.* Oremus. *Deus, qui salutis eterne beate Marie uirginitate fecunda humano generi.* Antefne:

> *Alma Redemptoris mater, que peruia celi*
> *Porta manes et stella maris, succurre cadenti*
> *Surgere qui curat populo, tu que genuisti,*
> *Natura mirante, tuum sanctum genitorem,*
> *Uirgo prius ac posterius, Gabrielis ab ore*
> *Sumens illud 'Aue', peccatorum miserere.*

Her sitteð[19] þe Auez, fifti oðer hundret, oðer ma oþer leas efter þet me haueð hwile. On ende þet uerset *Ecce ancilla Domini; fiat michi secundum uerbum tuum.* Oremus. *O sancta uirgo uirginum.* Hwa-se wule mei stutten þruppe ananrihtes efter þe forme ureisun, *Gratiam tuam,* ant segge þenne hire tale of Auez efter þe leaste salm, *Ad te leuaui.*

---

[17] After *orta*, C² adds, *Aue, gloriosa, / Super omnes speciosa*; also in N and V.
[18] For *Gaude, que . . . interuentrix* (l. 327–33), F has 'tout hors, sicome vous lauez aillours'.
[19] After *sitteð*, C² replaces C's *Auez* by 'te seggen ower tale of Avez'.

PART I

Eauer biuore þe salm biginnen an Aue, aþet *Dominus tecum*, ant segge stondinde þe salm. Þe salmes beoð inumene efter þe fif leattres of ure Leafdis nome, hwa-se nimeð ȝeme;[20] ant al þis ilke ureisun, efter hire fif heste blisses, eorneð bi fiue. Tele i þe antefnes, ant tu schalt finden in ham gretunges fiue. Þe ureisuns þet Ich nabbe buten ane imearket beoð iwriten oueral wiðute þe leaste. Leoteð writen on a scrowe hwet-se ȝe ne kunnen.

25. Þus Ich biginne mine Auez oðerhwiles.[21] 'Leafdi, swete leafdi, swetest alre leafdi; Leafdi, leouest leafdi, lufsumest leafdi, *O pulcherrima mulierum;* Leafdi, seinte Marie, deorewurðe leafdi; Leafdi, cwen of heouene; Leafdi, cwen of are; Leafdi, do me are; Leafdi, meiden moder, meiden Godes moder, Iesu Cristes moder, meiden | of milce, moder of grace, f. 11r
O uirgo uirginum,

Maria, mater gratie,
Mater misericordie,
Tu nos ab hoste protege,
Et hora mortis suscipe.

Per tuum, Uirgo, filium,
Per patrem, [per] Paraclitum,
Assis presens ad obitum,
Nostrumque muni exitum.

Gloria tibi, Domine,
Qui natus es de Uirgine, et cetera,

ant fallen to þer eorðe ant cussen hire wið þis leaste uers, hwa-se is hal-iheafdet; ant tenne Auez tene ant tene togederes, þe teoheðe eauer þus forð: *Aue Maria, gratia plena, Dominus tecum; benedicta tu in mulieribus, et benedictus fructus uentris tui. Spiritus Sanctus superueniet in te, et uirtus Altissimi obumbrabit tibi; ideoque et quod nascetur ex te sanctum uocabitur filius Dei. Ecce ancilla Domini; fiat michi secundum uerbum tuum.* Ant cusse þe eorðe on ende, oðer degre oðer bench oþer sumhwet herres, ant biginnen, 'Leafdi, swete leafdi', as ear. Þe forme tene [of] þe fifti cneolinde up ant dun; þe oþre, cneolinde iriht up stille, buten ed te *Aue* ma[k]ie sum

---
[20] After ȝeme, N has 'of þisse worde "Maria", he mei ivinden þer-inne þe vorme vif lettres of ðeos biuoreseide psalmes.'
[21] For þus . . . oðerhwiles, F has the rubric 'Ici comence askunes Aueez.'

semblant wið þe [an] cneo a lutel; þe þridde tene adun upo þe elbohen riht to þer eorðe, þe feorðe, þe elbohen o degre oðer o bench, ant eauer to þe *Aue* lute wið þe heaued; þe fifte tene stondinde; ant eft biginne þe turn as i þe frumðe. 390

26. Al þet ȝe eauer seggeð of þulliche oþre bonen, as Pater Nostres ant Auez on ower ahne wise, salmes ant ureisuns, Ich am wel ipaiet. Euchan segge ase best bereð hire on heorte. Verseilunge of Sawter, redunge of Englisc oðer of Frensch, halie meditatiuns, ower cneolunges, hwen-se ȝe eauer mahen iȝemen, ear mete ant efter— 395 eauer se ȝe mare doð, se Godd ow eche forðre his deorewurðe grace. Ah lokið swa, Ich bidde ow, þet ȝe ne beon neauer idel, ah wurchen oðer reden, oþer beon i bonen, ant swa don eauer sumhwet þet god mahe of awakenin.

27. Þe Ures | of þe Hali Gast, ȝef ȝe ham wulleð seggen, seggeð 400 euch Tide of ham biuoren ure Leafdi Tide. Toward te preostes Tiden hercnið se forð se ȝe mahen, ah wið him ne schule ȝe nowðer uerseilin ne singen þet he hit mahe iheren.

28. Ower graces stondinde biuore mete ant efter as ha beoð iwriten ow, ant wið þe *Miserere* gað biuoren ower weoued, ant 405 endið þear þe graces. Bitweone mel þe drinken wule segge *Benedicite; Potum nostrum filius Dei benedicat; In nomine Patris*, ant blesci. Efterwart, *Adiutorium nostrum in nomine Domini. Qui fecit celum et terram. Sit nomen Domini benedictum. Ex hoc nunc et usque in seculum. Benedicamus Domino. Deo gratias.* 410

29. Hwen-se ȝe gað to ower bedd, i niht oðer in euen, falleð o cneon[22] ant þencheð i hwet ȝe habbeð i þe dei iwreaðet ure Lauerd, ant crieð him ȝeorne merci ant forȝeuenesse. Ȝef ȝe habbeð ei god idon, þonkið him of his ȝeoue, wiðute hwam we ne mahen ne wel don ne wel þenchen, ant seggeð *Miserere*, ant *Kyrie eleison, Christe* 415 *eleison, Kyrie eleison. Pater noster. Et ne nos.* Verset: *Saluas fac*[23] *ancillas tuas, Deus meus, sperantes in te. Oremus. Deus, cui proprium est;* ant stondinde, *Visita, Domine, habitationem istam;* ant aleast þenne, *Christus vincit* ✠, *Christus regnat* ✠, *Christus imperat* ✠, wið þreo creoiz wið þe þume upo þe forheaued, ant þenne, *Ecce Crucem Domini, fugite,* 420 *partes aduerse; vicit leo de tribu Iuda, radix Dauið, Alleluia.* A large creoiz, as ed *Deus, in adiutorium,* wið *Ecce Crucem Domini,* ant tenne fowr creoiz o fowr half wið þeose fowre efterwarde clauses,

---

[22] After *cneon*, N has 'to ðer eorðe'.
[23] For *Saluas fac*, CPT have *Saluos fac seruos tuos et*.

PART I

Crux ✠ *fugat omne malum; Crux* ✠ *est reparatio rerum;*
425 *Per Crucis hoc signum* ✠ *, fugiat procul omne malignum;*
Et, per idem signum ✠*, saluetur quodque benignum;*

| on ende, ow seolf ant o þe bedde baðe, *In nomine Patris et Filii.* I f. 12ʳ
bedd, se uorð se ȝe mahen, ne do ȝe ne ne þenchen na þing bute
slepen.

430 30. Þe ne con oþer Uhtsong, oðer ne mei hit seggen, segge for
Uhtsong þritti Pater Nostres, ant *Aue Maria* efter euch Pater Noster,
ant *Gloria Patri* efter euch Aue. Aleast, *Oremus*, hwa-se con: *Deus, cui
proprium est. Benedicamus Domino. Anime fidelium.* For Euensong,
twenti, for euch oðer Tide, segge fiftene, o þis ilke wise; bute þet ed
435 Uhtsong schal seggen earst hwa-se con, *Domine, labia mea aperies; Et
os meum; Deus, in adiutorium*; ant ed Complie, *Conuerte nos, Deus
salutaris; Deus, in adiutorium*; ed alle þe oþre Tiden, *Deus, in
adiutorium.*

31. Hwa-se is unheite, forkeorue of Uhtsong tene, of euch of þe
440 oþre fiue; þe haluendal of euchan ȝef ha is seccre. Hwa-se is ful
meoseise, of al beo ha cwite; neome hire secnesse nawt ane
þolemodliche, ah do swiðe gleadliche, ant al is hiren þet Hali Chirche
ret oðer singeð.

32. Þah ȝe ahen of Godd þenchen in euch time, meast þah in
445 ower Tiden, þet ower þohtes ne beon fleotinde þenne. Ȝef ȝe þurh
ȝemeles gluffeð of wordes, oðer misneomeð uers, neomeð owe[r]
Venie dun ed ter eorðe wið þe hond ane; al fallen adun for muche
misneomunge, ant schawið ofte i schrift ower ȝemeles her-abuten.

33. Þis is nu þe forme dale, þe haueð ispeken hiderto of ower   M. 48
450 seruise. Hwet-se beo nu þer-of, þeose riwlen her-efter, Ich walde ha
weren of alle as ha beoð of ow, þurh Godes grace, ihalden.[24]

---

[24] For *Ich walde . . . ihalden* (1. 450–1), T has 'muche ned is wel to loke (þat Godd ȝiue
ow grace), for hit spekes of þe fiue wardains of þe heorte'; similarly S.

PART 2

Her biginneð þe oþer dale, of þe heorte warde þurh þe fif wittes. |

1. *Omni custodia serua cor tuum, quia ex ipso uita procedit.* 'Wið alles cunnes warde, dohter,' seið Salomon, 'wite wel þin heorte; for sawle lif is in hire, ȝef ha is wel iloket.' Þe heorte wardeins beoð þe fif wittes: sihðe ant herunge, smechunge ant smeallunge, ant euch limes felunge. Ant we schulen speoken of alle. For hwa-se wit þeose wel, he deð Salomones bode: he wit wel his heorte ant his sawle heale. Þe heorte is a ful wilde beast, ant makeð moni liht lupe, as seint Gregoire seið: *Nichil corde fugatius*, 'Na þing ne etflið mon sonre þen his ahne heorte.' Dauið, Godes prophete, meande i sum time þet ha wes etsteart him: *Cor meum dereliquit me*: þet is, 'Min heorte is edflohe me.' Ant eft he blisseð him ant seið þet ha wes icumen ham: *Inuenit seruus tuus cor suum.* 'Lauerd,' he seið, 'min heorte is icumen aȝein eft, Ich hire habbe ifunden.' Hwen se hali mon ant se wis ant se war lette hire edstearten, sare mei anoðer of hire fluht carien. Ant hwer edbrec ha ut from Dauið, þe hali king, Godes prophete? Hwer? Godd wat, ed his ehþurl, þurh a sihðe þet he seh, þurh a bihaldunge, as ȝe schulen efter iheren.

2. For-þi, mine leoue sustren, þe leaste þet ȝe eauer mahen luuieð ower þurles. Alle beon ha lutle, þe parlurs least ant nearewest. Þe clað in ham beo twafald. Blac þet clað, þe cros hwit, wiðinnen ant wiðuten. Þet blake clað bitacneð þet ȝe beoð blake ant unwurð to þe world wiðuten, þet te soðe sunne[1] haueð utewið forculet ow, ant swa wið[u]ten as ȝe beoð unseowlich imaket ow þurh gleames | of his grace. Þe hwite cros limpeð to ow. For þreo crosses beoð, read ant blac ant hwit. Þe reade limpeð to þeo þe beoð for Godes luue wið hare blod-schedunge irudet ant ireadet, as þe martirs weren. Þe blake cros limpeð to þeo þe makieð i þe worlt hare penitence for ladliche sunnen. Þe hwite limpeð ariht to hwit meidenhad ant to cleannesse, þet is muche pine wel forte halden. Pine is ihwer þurh cros idon to understonden. Þus bitacneð hwit cros þe warde of hwit chastete, þet is muche pine wel to biwitene. Þe blake clað alswa, teke þe bitacnunge, deð leasse eil to þe ehnen, ant is þiccre aȝein þe wind

---

[1] After *sunne*, NST have 'þet is Iesu Crist', similarly P.

PART 2 21

35 ant wurse to seon þurh, ant halt his heow betere, for wind ant for
oðerhwet. Lokið þet te parlures beo on eauereuch half feaste ant wel
itachet, ant witeð þer ower ehnen, leaste þe heorte edfleo ant wende
ut as of Dauið, ant ower sawle seccli sone se heo is ute. Ich write
muchel for oþre þet nawiht ne rineð ow, mine leoue sustren, for
40 nabbe ȝe nawt te nome—ne ne schulen habben, þurh þe grace of
Godd—of totilde ancres,[2] ne of tollinde locunges ne lates þet summe
oðerhwiles—weilawei!—uncundeliche makieð; for aȝein cunde hit is,
ant unmeað sulli wunder, þet te deade dotie[3] ant wið cwike worltmen
wede þurh sunne.
45   3. 'Me, leoue sire,' seið sum, 'ant is hit nu se ouer-uuel forte totin M. 52
utwart?' Ȝe hit, leoue suster; for uuel þe þer kimeð of, hit is uuel ant
ouer-uuel to eauereuch ancre, nomeliche to þe ȝunge—ant to þe
alde, for-þi þet ha to þe ȝungre ȝeoueð uuel forbisne, ant scheld to
werien ham wið, for ȝef ei edwit ham, þenne seggeð ha anan, 'Me,
50 sire, þeo deð alswa þet is betere þen Ich am ant wat | betere þen Ich f. 13ᵛ
hwet ha haueð to donne.' Leoue ȝunge ancre, ofte a ful haher smið
smeoðeð a ful wac cnif. Þe wise folhe i wisdom, ant nawt i folie. An
ald ancre mei do wel þet te þu dest uuele; ah totin ut wiðuten uuel ne
mei ower nowðer. Nim nu ȝeme hwet uuel beo icumen of totunge.
55 Nawt an uuel ne twa, ah al þe wa þet nu is, ant eauer ȝete wes, ant
eauer schal iwurðen, al com of sihðe. Þet hit beo soð, lo her preoue.
  4. Lucifer, þurh þet he seh ant biheold on him seolf his ahne
feiernesse, leop into prude, ant bicom of engel eatelich deouel.
  5. Of Eue, ure alde moder, is iwriten on alre earst in hire sunne
60 inȝong of hire ehsihðe. *Vidit igitur mulier quod bonum esset lignum ad
uescendum, et pulcrum oculis aspectuque delectabile, et tulit de fructu eius
et comedit, deditque uiro suo;* þet is, 'Eue biheold o þe forboden
eappel, ant seh hine feier ant feng to delitin i þe bihaldunge, ant toc
hire lust þer-toward, ant nom ant et þrof, ant ȝef hire lauerd.' Low
65 hu Hali Writ spekeð, ant hu inwardliche hit teleð hu sunne bigon.
Þus eode [sihðe] biuoren ant makede wei to uuel lust, ant com þe
dede þrefter þet al moncun ifeleð.
  6. Þes eappel, leoue suster, bitacneð alle þe [þing] þet lust falleð to,
ant delit of sunne. Hwen þu bihaldest te mon, þu art in Eue point:

---

[2] 'Ich . . . sustren' (2. 38–9) is omitted in T, and 'for nabbe . . . ancres' (2. 39–41)
rewritten as a command, 'Loke þat ȝe ne hauen nawt te nome ne te wil of totinde anker';
similarly S and (with further modification) P.
[3] After *dotie*, C² adds in the margin 'þet is, ancre þet is deat ant as[e] deat ielet ant iput,
as i þr[uh], inwið hire ancre wahes. Sulli wunder is þet heo scal adotien ant wið cwike
worldmen weden þurh sunne.'

þu lokest o þe eappel. Hwa-se hefde iseid to Eue, þa ha weorp earst hire ehe þron, 'A, Eue, went te awei, þu warpest ehe o þi deað', hwet hefde ha iondsweret? 'Me, leoue sire, þu hauest woh! Hwer-of chalengest tu me? Þe eappel þet Ich loki on is forbode me to eotene, ant nawt to bihalden.' Þus walde Eue | inohreaðe habben iondsweret. O mine leoue sustren, as Eue haueð monie dehtren þe folhið hare moder, þe ondswerieð o þisse wise! 'Me, wenest tu', seið sum, 'þet Ich wulle leapen on him, þah Ich loki on him?' Godd wat, leoue suster, mare wunder ilomp. Eue þi moder leop efter hire ehnen, from þe ehe to þe eappel, from þe eappel i Parais dun to þer eorðe, from þe eorðe to helle. Þer ha lei i prisun fowr þusent ȝer ant mare, heo ant hire were ba, ant demde al hire ofsprung to leapen al efter hire to deað wiðuten ende. Biginnunge ant rote of al þis ilke reowðe wes a liht sihðe. Þus ofte, as me seið, 'Of lutel muchel waxeð.' Habbe þenne muche dred euch feble wummon, hwen þeo þe wes riht ta iwraht wið Godes honden wes þurh a sihðe biswiken ant ibroht [forð] into brad sunne þet al þe world ouerspreadde.

7. *Egressa est Dyna, filia Iacob, ut uideret mulieres alienigenas, et cetera.* A meiden [alswa], Dyna het, Iacobes dohter, as hit teleð i Genesy, eode ut to bihalden uncuðe wummen; ȝet ne seið hit nawt þet ha biheold wepmen. Ant hwet come, wenest tu, of þet bihaldunge? Ha leas hire meidenhad ant wes imaket hore. Þrefter of þet ilke weren trowðen tobrokene of hehe patriarches, ant a muchel burh forbearnd ant te king ant his sune ant te burhmen islein, þe wummen ilead forð, hire feader ant hire breðren, se noble princes as ha weren, utlahen imakede. Þus eode ut hire sihðe. Al þullich þe Hali Gast lette writen o boc forte warni wummen of hare fol ehnen. Ant nim þer-of ȝeme þet tis uuel of Dyna com nawt of þet ha seh Sichen, | Emores sune, þet ha sunegede wið, ah dude of þet ha lette him leggen ehnen on hire; for þet tet he dude hire wes i þe frumðe sare hire unþonkes.

8. Alswa Bersabee, þurh þet ha unwreah hire i Dauiðes sihðe, ha dude him sunegin on hire, se hali king as he wes, ant Godes prophete. Nu kimeð forð a feble mon, halt him þah ahelich ȝef he haueð a wid hod ant a loke cape, ant wule iseon ȝunge ancres, ant loki nede ase stan [hu] hire wlite him liki þe naueð nawt hire leor forbearnd i þe sunne, ant seið ha mei baldeliche iseon hali men—ȝe, swucche as he is for his wide sleuen! Me, surquide sire, ne herest tu þet Dauið, Godes ahne deorling, bi hwam he seolf seide, *Inueni uirum secundum cor meum* ('Ich habbe ifunden', quoð he, 'mon efter

min heorte')—þes, þe Godd seolf seide bi þis deorewurðe sahe king ant prophete icuret of alle, þes, þurh an ehe wurp to a wummon as ha wesch hire—lette ut his heorte ant forʒet him seoluen, swa þet he dude þreo utnume heaued ant deadliche sunnen: o Bersabee spusbruche, þe leafdi þet he lokede on; treisun ant monslaht on his treowe cniht Vrie, hire lauerd. Ant tu, a sunful mon, art se swiðe hardi to keasten cang ehnen upo ʒung wummon![4] ʒe, mine leoue sustren, ʒef ei is anewil to seon ow, ne wene ʒe þer neauer god, ah leueð him þe leasse. Nulle Ich þet nan iseo ow bute he habbe of ower meistre spetiale leaue; for alle þe þreo sunnen þet Ich spec of least, ant al þet uuel of Dina þet Ich spec of herre, al com nawt for-þi þet te wummen lokeden cangliche o wepmen, ah[5] [for heo vnwriʒen heom in monnes echsiððe, | ant duden hwar-þurch ha machten fallen in sunne. For-þi wes ihaten on Godes [halue in þe Alde] Laʒe þet put were iwriʒen eauer, ant ʒef ani were vnwriʒen ant beast feolle þer-in, he [þe unwreah þe put] hit schulde ʒelden. þis is a swiðe dredful word to wummon þet schaweð hire to wepmones echne. Heo is bitacned bi þeo þet vnwrið þe put. þe put is hire feire neb, hire hwite swire, hire lichte echnen, [hire] hond, ʒef ha halt forð in his echʒe-[sihðe]. ʒet beoð hire word put, bute ha beon þe bet iset. Al [þet] þe feaʒeð hire, hwet-se hit eauer beo, þurch hwat machte sonre fol [luue] awacnin—al vre Lauerd put cleopeð. þis put he hat þet beo ilided þet beast þrin ne falle ant druncni in sunne. Best is þe beastlich mon þet ne þenchet naut on God, ne ne noteð naut his wit as mon ach to donne, ach secheð for to fallen in þis put þet Ich spec of ʒef he hit open fint. Ach þe dom is ful strong to þeo þe þe put vnlideð; for heo | schal ʒelde þe best þet þrin bið ifallen. Ha is witi of his deað biforen vre Lauerd, ant schal for his saule ondsweren an Domesdei, ant ʒelde þe bestes lure hwenne ha naveð oðer ʒeld þenne hire seoluen. Strong ʒeld is her mid alle; ant Godes dom [is] ant his heste þet heo hit ʒelde allegate, for heo vnlidede þe put þet hit adrong inne. þu þet vnwrisd þis put, þu þet dest ani þing þet mon is þorch [þe] fleschliche ifonded, þach þu hit nute naut—dred þis dom swiðe. Ant ʒef he is ifonded swa þet he sunege deadliche on ani wise, þach hit ne beo naut wið þe bute wið wil

---

[4] After *wummon*, T has 'þis þet is nu seid limpes to wimmen; ah ase muche neod is wepman to wite wel his ehsihðe fra wimmenes sihðe', similarly S.
[5] After *ah*, two folios lost in A; C used as base MS, with material not in C supplied from T and F.

toward þe, oðer ȝef he secheð to fullen ed sum oðer þe fondunge [þe] þurch þe [ant et þe] awacnede, beo al siker of þe dom; þu schalt ȝelde þe best for þe puttes openunge, ant buten þu beo [iscriue] þer-of,[6] acorien his sunne. Hund wule in bluðelich hwar- se he fint open.

9. *Inpudicus oculus inpudici | cordis est nuncius. Augustinus.* Þet þe muð ne mei for scheome, þe licht echȝe spekeð hit, ant is as erende-beorere of þe lichte heorte. Ach nu is sum wummon þe nalde for nan þing wilni fulðe to mon, ant þach ne rochte [ha] neauer þach he þochte toward hire ant were of hire ifondet; [ach] [Sein] Austin deð ba [twa] þeos in [a cuple], wilnin ant habbe wil for to beon iwilned. *Non solum appetere sed et appeti uelle criminosum* [*est*]*:* 'Ȝirni mon oðer habbe wil [for] to beon iȝirned of mon ba is haued sunne.' *Oculi prima tela sunt adultere:* 'þe echnen beoð þe [arewen ant te forme armes] of Lecheries prickes.' Alswa ase men worreð mid þreo cunes wepnes, wið scheotung ant wið speres ord ant wið sweordes [egge], al richt wið þilke wepnen—þet is, wið schute of eche, wið spere [of] wund[i]n[de] word, wið sweord of deadlich hond[lunge]—werreð Lecherie, þe stinkinde hore, vpon þe lauedi Chastete, þet is Godes spuse. Earest scheot þe arewen of þe licht echnen, þe fleoð lichtliche | forð ase flaa þet is iuiðered ant stikeð i ðere heorte. Þer-efter schakeð hire spere ant neolachet vpon hire, ant mid schakinde word ȝeueð speres wunde. Sweordes dunt dunricht, þet is þe hondlunge; for sweord smit of nech ant ȝeueð deaðes dunt, ant [hit] is [soðes]—weilawei!—nech ido wið ham þe cumeð swa nech togederes þet ouðer hondli o[þ]er oðer ifele [oþer]. Hwa-se is wis ant seli, wið þe schute wite hire—[þet is], wite hire echnen; for al þet uvel þer-efter kimeð of þechne arewen. Ant nis ha [to] muche chang, oðer to folhardi, þe hald hire heued [baltliche] [forð] vt [i] þe opene carnel hwil me wið quarreus vtewið assailleð þe castel? Sikerliche vre fa, þe werreur of helle, he scheot (as Ich wene) ma quarreus to an ancre þenne to seouene-ant-[seoueti] lauedis i ðe worlde. Þe carneus of þe castel beoð hire hus-þurles.] [Ne tote ha nawt ut at ham, leste ho þe deoueles quarreus habbe amid te ehe ear ho least wene; for he asailȝes ai. Halde hire ehe inwið, for beo ho iblind earst, ho is eað-falle; ablinde þe heorte, ho is eað to ouercumen, and ibroht sone þurh sunne to grunde.][7] [*Bernardus:*

---

[6] After *þer-of*, N has 'ase mon seið, þu schalt acorien ðe rode; þet is'.
[7] 'Ne tote . . . grunde' (2. 179–83) omitted in C; T (f. 18va) used as base MS.

PART 2   25

Sicut mors per peccatum in orbem, ita per has fenestras [intrat] in
185   *mentem.* 'As deð com', seið Sein Bernard, 'into þe world þorch
sunne, asswa deað þurch þeos echþurles | haueð [inȝong] to þe   C f. 26ʳ
saule.' Lauerd Crist, as [a] mon walde steoke feste vh þurl [of his
hus] for-hwon [þet] he machte bisteoken deað þrute—[ȝe, deað of
fleschliche liue]—ant an ancre nule naut tunen hire eilþurl aȝein
190   þe deað of saule! Ant mid good richt muȝen ha beon ihaten
[eil]þurles, for ha habbeð idon muchel eil to moni ancre. [Al Hali
Writ is ful of warnunge of warde of echȝe.] *Dauid: Auerte oculos
meos ne uideant uanitatem.* 'Lauerd,' he seið, Dauid, 'went awei
min echnen from þe worldes dweole.' *Iob: Pepigi fedus cum oculis*
195   *meis, ne cogitarem [de] uirgine.* 'Ichabbe ifestned foreward', seið
Iob, 'mid min echnen, þet Ich ne misþenche.' Hu dele! [Hwet seið
he?] þencheð me mid echȝe? God hit wat, he seið wel; for efter þe
echȝe kimeð þe þocht, ant þer-efter þe dede. þet wiste wel   M. 64
Ieremie, þet mende [him ant seide] þus: [*Oculus meus depredatus*
200   *est animam meam.*] 'Weilawei!' he seið, 'min eche haueð irobbed al
min saule.' Wenne Godes prophete makede þulli mon of eche,
hwic man, wenest þu, beo icumen to moni mon [ant to moni
wummon], ant sorege, of heore echȝe? þe hwise askið [in his boc]
[h]weðer ani þing harmi mare wimmon | þenne deð hire echȝe. C f. 26ᵛ
205   *Oculo quid nequius? Totam faciem lacrimare faciet [quoniam] uidit.*
'Al þe leor', he seið, 'schal floȝen of teres for [þe ehe-]sichðe
ane.']⁸

10. [Ore pur ceo toutes les ouertures de toutes voz
fenestres, ausi come ci-deuant a la vewe de touz hommes
210   vnt esté closes, ausi soient ça enaprés. E si plus fermement
poient, plus fermement soient closes. Generale reule est:
toutes celes qe bien les closent, Dieu bien les garde; et
toutes celes qe | [moustrent sei meismes a vewe domme]   F f. 12ʳ
issi qil pecche [dedenz son queor] funt ensement [lomme]
215   pecchier ou od fol oil, ou od bouche, ou od main. Et [fet]
cel, od plus et multes tieles choses desauenantes et desna-
tureles a recluse sur toutes, lesqueux ne fuissent iames
avant venues si ele eust sa fenestre ferm estoppee. Et si
nule contredit ceste, ieo treis a testmoigne sa conscience
220   demeyne encontre lui, qele parmi sa fenestre demeine ad

---

⁸ After *ane*, an added passage in AF; the first part, before 'traisun' (2. 226), survives only in F. The parts of the text lost through fire damage have been conjecturally reconstructed by Dobson.

oil, ou bouche, ou main receu, et fole parole oueqe, tout fut ele adubbé et od feinte seinteté falsement coloree. A, tricheour traitre! 'Dieu, ieo nel faz a vous pur nul mal ne pur nule ordure', dit il, ou ele; et od cel meismes se soillent et coroucent les oilz Dampnedieu, qi regarde la]⁹ traisun inwið þe gale heorte. Nawt ane euch fleschlich hondlunge, ah ȝetten euch gal word is ladlich vilainie, ant Godes grome wurðe, þah hit ne weoxe forðre bitweone mon ant ancre. Nu, þurh riht Godes wrake, geað hit forðre ant forðre, ant bikimeð ofte, ant ear me least wene, into þet fule sunne. We hit habbeð—weilawei!—iherd of inohe. Ne leue na mon ancre þe let in monnes ehe to schawin hire seoluen. Ouer al þet ȝe habbeð iwriten in ower Riwle of þinges wiðuten, þis point, þis article of wel to beo bitunde Ich wulle beo best ihalden. To wummon þe wilneð hit, openið ow o Godes half; ȝef ha ne spekeð nawt þrof, leoteð swa iwurðen, bute ȝef ȝe dreden þet heo þrefter beo iscandlet. Of hire ahne suster haueð sum ibeon itemptet. In toward ower weoued ne beode ȝe na mon forte bihalden; ah ȝef his deuotiun bit hit ant haueð grant, draheð ow wel inward, ant te ueil adun toward ower breoste, ant sone doð þe clað aȝein ant festnið heteueste. Ȝef he lokeð toward bed oðer easkeð hwer ȝe liggeð, ondswerieð lihtliche, 'Sire, þer-of wel mei duhen', ant haldeð ow stille. Ȝef bisch[o]p kimeð to seon ow, hihið sone towart him; ah sweteliche bischeð him, ȝef he bit to seon ow, þet ȝe moten þer-onont halden ow towart him as ȝe habbeð idon, ant doð, to alle oþre. Ȝef he wule allegate habben a sihðe, lokið þet hit beo ful scheort, þe ueil anan adun, ant draheð ow behinden. An ancre wearnde eadmodliche Sein Martin hire sihðe, ant he þer-uore dude hire þe menske þet he neauer ne dude to nan oþer. Ant her-uore hire word is aþet cume þis dei iboren in Hali Chirche; | for as we redeð of hire, hwa-se wule hire windowes witen wel wið þe uuele, ha mot ec wið þe gode. Hwen-se ȝe moten to eani mon eawiht biteachen, þe hond ne cume nawt ut—ne ower ut ne his in. Ant ȝef hit mot cumen in, ne rine nowðer oþer. 'Heo is siker', seið Hali Writ, 'þe feor from grunen draheð hire; ant þeo þe luueð peril, i peril ha schal fallen.' *Qui caret laqueis securus est; et qui amat periculum incidet in illud.* Þe deofles grune is ofte itild þer me least

⁹ The lacuna in A ends at this point.

260 weneð. Nis nan þet nis dredful þet ha nis [sumchearre] ilecchet; for Godd nule wite nan þet is se folhardi þet ha ne wit wearliche wið him hire seoluen.

11. Þis is nu of þis wit inoh iseid ed tis chearre to warnin þen seli; M. 64 we schulen þah sone her-efter speoken her-of mare.

265 Spellunge ant smechunge beoð i muð baðe, as sihðe is i þe ehe; ah we schulen leten smechunge aþet we speoken of ower mete, ant speoken nu of spellunge, ant þrefter of herunge—of ba imeane sumchearre, as ha gað togederes.

12. On alre earst, hwen ȝe schulen to ower parlurs þurl, witeð ed 270 ower meiden hwa hit beo þet beo icumen, for swuch hit mei beon þet ȝe schule essunien ow. Hwen ȝe alles moten forð, crossið ful ȝeorne muð, ehnen, ant earen, ant te breoste mid al, ant gað forð mid Godes dred. To preost, on earst *Confiteor*, ant þrefter *Benedicite*, þet he ah to seggen. Hercnið hise wordes ant haldeð ow al stille, þet hwen he 275 parteð from ow, þet he ne cunne ower god ne ower uuel nowðer, ne ne cunne ow nowðer lastin ne preisin. Sum is se wel ilearet, oðer se wis iwordet, þet ha walde he wiste | hit þe sit ant spekeð toward hire, f. 16ʳ ant ȝelt him word aȝein word, ant forwurðeð meistre þe schulde beon ancre, ant leareð him þet is icumen hire forte learen; walde bi hire 280 tale beon sone wið wise icuððet ant icnawen. Icnawen ha is—for M. 66 þurh þet ilke þet ha weneð to beo wis ihalden, he understont þet ha is sot. For ha hunteð efter pris ant kecheð lastunge; for ed te alre leaste, hwen he is awei iwent, 'þeos ancre', he wule seggen, 'is of muche speche.' Eue heold i Parais long tale wið þe neddre; talde him 285 al þe lesceun þet Godd hefde ired hire ant Adam of þe eappel, ant swa þe feond þurh hire word understod ananriht hire wacnesse, ant ifond wei toward hire of hire forlorenesse. Vre Leafdi, seinte Marie, dude al on oþer wise. Ne talde ha þen engel na tale, ah easkede him scheortliche þing þet ha ne cuðe. Ȝe, mine leoue sustren, folhið ure 290 Leafdi, ant nawt te cakele Eue. For-þi ancre, hwet-se ha beo, hu muchel se ha eauer cunne, halde hire stille. Nabbe ha nawt henne cunde. Þe hen, hwen ha haueð ileid, ne con bute cakelin. Ah hwet biȝet ha þrof? Kimeð þe kaue ananriht ant reaueð hire hire eairen ant fret of þet schulde forð bringe cwike briddes. Al riht alswa þe caue 295 deouel bereð awei from cakelinde ancres ant forswolheð al þe god þet ha istreonet habbeð, þet schulde as briddes beoren ham up towart heouene, ȝef hit nere icakelet.[10] Þe wrecche poure peoddere, mare

---

[10] After *icakelet*, V has 'þe pedelere goþ criȝinde "Nelde!" and "Sope!"; þe riche marchaunt goþ forþ al stille.'

nurð he makeð to ȝeien his sape þen þe riche mercer al his deorewurðe ware, as is iseid her-efter. To sum gastelich mon þet ȝe beoð trusti upon—as ȝe mahe beon o | lut—god is þet ȝe easki read, ant salue þet he teache ow toȝeines fondunges; ant i schrift schawið him, ȝef he wule iheren, ower greaste ant ower ladlukeste sunnen, for-þi þet him areowe ow, ant þurh þe areownesse inwardluker crie Crist mearci for ow, ant habbe ow in his bonen. *Set multi ueniunt ad uos in uestimentis ouium, intrinsecus autem sunt lupi rapaces.* 'Ah witeð ow ant beoð warre,' he seið, ure Lauerd, 'for monie cumeð to ow ischrud mid lombes fleos, ant beoð wedde wulues.' Worltliche leueð lut, religiuse ȝet leas. Ne wilni ȝe nawt to muchel hare cuððunge. Eue wiðute dred spec wið þe neddre; vre Leafdi wes offearet of Gabrieles speche.

13. Vre Freres Prechurs ant ure Freres Meonurs beoð of swuch ordre þet al folc mahte wundrin ȝef ei of ham wende ehe 'towart te wude-lehe'. For-þi ed euch time þet eani of ham þurh chearite kimeð ow to learen ant to frourin i Godd, ȝef he is preost seggeð ear þen he parti, '*Mea culpa:* Ich schriue me to Godd almihti ant to þe þet Ich, as Ich drede, riht repentant neauer nes of mine greaste sunnen, þet Ich habbe ischawet to mine schrift-feaderes, ant tah min entente beo to beten ham her-inne, Ich hit do se poureliche, ant sunegi in oðre deihwamliche seoððen Ich wes nest ischriuen, ant þet wes þenne ant of þe', ant nempnin; 'Ich habbe þus isunget', ant segge o hwucche wise, as hit is iwriten ow in ower schriftes boc towart te ende þrof, ant aleast seggeð 'þis ant muche mare, *Confiteor*'; ant bide him underuo þe spetiale in his god, ant þonke | him of his inturn, ant bisech him aleast greten þe ant te, ant þet ha bidden for þe.

14. Wiðuten witnesse of wummon oðer of wepmon þe ow mahe iheren, ne speoke ȝe wið na mon ofte ne longe; ant tah hit beo of schrift, allegate i þe ilke hus oðer þer he mahe iseon toward ow sitte þe þridde, bute ȝef þe ilke þridde oþer stude trukie. Þis nis nawt for ow, leoue sustren, iseid, ne for oþre swucche; nawt for-þi þe treowe is ofte mistrowet, ant te saclese bilohen, **as Iosep i Genesy of þe gale leafdi**, for wone of witnesse. Me leueð þe uuele sone, ant te unwreaste bliðeliche liheð o þe gode. Sum unseli haueð, hwen ha seide ha schraf hire, ischriuen hire al to wundre. For-þi ahen þe gode habben eauer witnesse, for twa acheisuns nomeliche. Þe an is þet te ondfule ne mahe lihen on ham swa þet te witnesse ne pruuie ham

PART 2

false. Þe oÞer is forte ȝeouen Þe oÞre forbisne, ant reaui Þe uuele ancre Þe ilke unseli gile Þet Ich of seide.

340 **15.** Vt Þurh Þe chirche Þurl ne halde ȝe tale wið na mon, ah beoreð Þer-to wurðmunt for Þe hali sacrement Þet ȝe seoð Þer-Þurh, ant neomeð oðerhwile. To ower wummen, Þe huses Þurl; to oÞre, Þe parlur. Speoken[11] ne ahe ȝe bute ed tes twa Þurles.

16. Silence eauer ed te mete. Ȝef oðre religiuse—as ȝe witen—doð 345 hit, ȝe ahen ouer alle. Ȝef ei haueð deore gest, do hire meidnes as in hire stude to gleadien hire feire; ant heo schal habbe leaue forte unsperren hire Þurl eanes oðer twien, ant makie sines toward hire of a glead | chere. Summes curteisie is iturnt hire to uuel. Vnder semblant of god is ofte ihulet sunne. Ancre ant huses leafdi ah 350 muchel to beon bitweonen. Euche Fridei of Þe ȝer haldeð silence (bute hit beo duble feaste, ant tenne haldeð hit sum oðer dei i Þe wike); i Þe Aduenz ant i Þe Umbriwiken, Weodnesdei ant Fridei; i Þe Lenten, Þreo dahes, ant al Þe Swiing-wike aðet Non [on Easter] euen. To ower wummen ȝe mahen Þah seggen wið lut word hwet-se 355 ȝe wulleð. Ȝef eani god mon is of feorren icumen,[12] hercnið his speche ant ondswerieð wið lut word to his easkunges.

17. Muche fol were Þe mahte to his bihoue hweðer-se he walde grinden greot oÞer hweate, ȝef he grunde Þe greot ant lette Þe hweate. Hweate is hali speche, as Seint Anselme seið. Heo grint 360 greot Þe chafleð.[13] Þe twa cheken beoð Þe twa grindelstanes, Þe tunge is Þe cleappe. Lokið, leoue sustren, Þet ower cheken ne grinden neauer bute sawle fode, ne ower eare ne drinke neauer bute sawle heale—ant nawt ane ower eare, ah ower ehÞur[l], sperreð to aȝeines idel speche. To ow ne cume na tale ne tidinge of Þe 365 worlde.

Ȝe ne schule for na Þing wearien ne swerien, bute ȝef ȝe seggen 'witerliche' oðer 'sikerliche', oðer o sum swuch wise.

18. Ne preachi ȝe to na mon; ne mon ne easki ow cunsail ne ne telle ow. Readeð wummen ane. Seint Pawel forbeot wummen to 370 preachin: *Mulieres non permitto docere.* Na wepmon ne chastie ȝe, ne edwiten him his unÞeau bute he beo Þe ouer-cuðre. Halie al|de ancres hit mahe don summes weis, ah hit nis nawt siker Þing, ne ne limpeð nawt to ȝunge. Hit is hare meoster Þe beoð ouer oÞre iset ant habbeð ham to witene **as Hali Chirche larewes.** Ancre naueð forte

---

[11] After *Speoken*, N has 'buten uor neode'.
[12] *After icumen*, F has 'et vult en ces iours a vous parlier'.
[13] After *chafleð*, F has 'de terreines choses'.

[wite] [bute] hire ant hire meidnes. Halde euch [his] ahne meoster, ant nawt ne reaui oþres. Moni weneð to do wel þe deð al to wundre; for as Ich seide ear, vnder semblant of god is ofte ihulet sunne. þurh swuch chastiement haueð sum ancre arearet bitweonen hire ant hire preost oðer a falsinde luue oðer a muche weorre.

19. *Seneca: Ad summam uolo uos esse rariloquas, tuncque pauciloquas.* 'þet is þe ende of þe tale', seið Seneke þe wise; 'Ich chulle þet ȝe speoken seldene, ant þenne lutel.' Moni punt hire word forte leote ma ut, as me deð weater ed mulne. Swa duden Iobes freond þe weren icumen to frourin him: seten stille seoue niht, ah þa ha hefden alles bigunnen to speokene, þa ne cuðen ha neauer stutten hare cleappe. *Gregorius: Censura silencii nutritura est uerbi.* Swa hit is of monie, as Sein Gregoire seið: 'Silence is wordes fostrilt, ant bringeð forð chaffle.' On oðer half, as he seið, *Iuge silentium cogit celestia meditari,* 'Long silence ant wel iwist nedeð þe þohtes up towart heouene'. Alswa as ȝe mahe seon weater, hwen me punt hit ant stoppeð hit biuore wel, þet hit ne mahe duneward, þenne is hit inedd aȝein forte climben uppart, ant ȝe al þisses weis pundeð ower wordes, forstoppið ower þohtes, as ȝe wulleð þet ha climben ant | hehin toward heouene, ant nawt ne fallen duneward ant tofleoten ȝont te worlt, as deð muchel chaffle. Hwen ȝe nede moten, a lute wiht lowsið up ower muðes flod-ȝeten, as me deð ed mulne, ant leoteð adun sone. Ma sleað word þen sweord. *Mors et uita in manibus lingue;* 'Lif ant deað', seið Salomon, 'is i tunge honden.' *Qui custodit os suum custodit animam suam;* 'Hwa-se witeð wel his muð, he witeð', he seið, 'his sawle'. *Sicut urbs patens et absque murorum ambitu, sic, et cetera. Qui murum silencii non habet, patet inimici iaculis ciuitas mentis;* 'Hwa-se ne wiðhalt his wordes,' seið Salomon þe wise, 'he is as þe burh wiðute wal þet ferde mei in oueral.' Þe feond of helle mid his ferd wend þurh-ut te tutel þe is eauer open into þe heorte. I *Vitas Patrum* hit teleð þet an hali mon seide, þa me preisede ane breðren þet he hefde iherd of muche speche, *Boni utique sunt, set habitatio eorum non habet ianuam; quicumque uult intrat et asinum soluit.* 'Gode', quoð he, 'ha beoð, ah hare wununge naueð na ȝete', hare muð meaðeleð eauer; 'hwa-se eauer wule mei gan in ant leaden forð hare asse', þet is, hare unwise sawle. For-þi seið Sein Iame, *Si quis putat se religiosum esse, non refrenans linguam suam set seducens cor suum, huius uana est religio;* þet is, 'Ȝef eni weneð þet he beo religius, ant ne bridli nawt his tunge, his religiun is fals, he gileð his heorte.' He seið swiðe wel, 'ne bridleð nawt his tunge.' Bridel nis nawt ane i þe horses muð, ah sit

PART 2   31

415 sum upo þe ehnen, ant geaðabute þe earen, | for alle þreo is muche   f. 19ʳ
    neod þet ha beon ibridlet. Ah i þe muð sit tet irn, ant o þe lihte
    tunge, for þear is meast neod hald, hwen þe tunge is o rune ant ifole
    to eornen.
       20. Ofte we þencheð, hwen we foð on to speoken, forte speoke
420 lutel ant wel isette wordes; ah þe tunge is slubbri for ha wadeð i
    wete, ant slit lihtliche forð from lut word into monie, ant tenne, as
    Salomon seið, *In multiloquio non deerit peccatum.* Ne mei nawt muche
    speche, ne ginne hit neauer se wel, beo wiðute sunne; for from soð
    hit slit to fals, ut of god into sum uuel, from meosure into unimete,
425 ant of a drope waxeð into a muche flod þe adrencheð þe sawle; for
    wið þe fleotinde word tofleoteð þe heorte, swa þet longe þrefter ne   M. 76
    mei ha beon riht igederet togederes. *Et os nostrum tanto est Deo
    longinqum, quanto mundo proximum; tantoque minus exauditur in prece,
    quanto amplius inquinatur in locutione.* Þis beoð Seint Gregoires word
430 in his *Dyaloge*: 'Ase neh as ure muð is to worldlich speche, ase feor
    he is Godd hwen he spekeð toward him ant bit him eani bone.' For-
    þi is þet we ȝeiȝeð upon him ofte, ant he firseð him awei frommard
    ure steuene, ne nule nawt iheren hire, for ha stinkeð to him al of þe
    worldes meaðelunge ant of hire chafle. Hwa-se wule, þenne, þet
435 Godes eare beo neh hire tunge firsi hire from þe world. Elles ha mei
    longe ȝeiȝen ear Godd hire ihere; ant seið þurh Ysaie, *Cum
    extenderitis manus uestras, auertam oculos meos a uobis, et cum multi-
    plicaueritis orationes,* | *non exaudiam uos;* þet is, 'þah ȝe makien   f. 19ᵛ
    monifalde ower bonen toward me, ȝe þe pleieð wið þe world, nule
440 Ich ow nawt iheren, ah Ich wulle turne me awei hwen ȝe heoueð
    toward me hehe ower honden.'
       21. Vre deorewurðe Leafdi, seinte Marie, þe ah to alle wummen
    to beo forbisne, wes of se lutel speche þet nohwer in Hali Writ ne
    finde we þet ha spec bute fowr siðen; ah for se selt speche hire
445 wordes weren heuie ant hefden muche mihte. *Bernardus ad Mariam: In
    sempiterno Dei uerbo facti sumus omnes et ecce, morimur; in tuo breui responso
    refitiendi sumus ut ad uitam reuocemur. Responde uerbum et suscipe uerbum,
    profer tuum et concipe diuinum.* Hire forme wordes þet we redeð of weren
    þa ha ondswerede Gabriel þen engel; ant teo weren se mihtie þet wið
450 þet ha seide, *Ecce ancilla domini; fiat michi secundum uerbum tuum,* ed
    tis word Godes sune ant soð Godd bicom mon, ant te Lauerd þet al
    þe world ne mahte nawt bifon bitunde him inwið hire meidnes
    wombe. Hire oþre wordes weren þa ha com ant grette Elyzabeth hire
    mehe; ant hwet mihte wes icud ed þeose wordes? Hwet? þet a child

M. 78 bigon to pleien toӡeines ham—þet wes Sein Iuhan—in his moder 455
wombe. *Idem: Vox eius Iohannem exultare fecit in utero.* þet þridde time þet
ha spec wes ed te neoces; ant ter [þ]urh hire bisocne wes weater
iwent to wine. þe feorðe time wes þa ha hefde imist hire sune ant eft
him ifunde; ant hu muche wunder folhede þeose wordes? þet Godd
almihti beah to mon, **to Marie ant to Ioseph**, to a smið ant to a 460
f. 20ʳ wummon, ant folhede ham ase heoren hwider-se | ha walden.
Neomeð nu her ӡeme, ant leornið ӡeorne her-bi hu seltsene speche
haueð muche strengðe. *Vir linguosus non dirigetur in terra.* 'Feole
iwordet mon', seið þe Salmwruhte, 'ne schal neauer leaden riht lif on
eorðe.' For-þi he seið elleshwer, *Dixi: Custodiam uias meas ut non* 465
delinquam in lingua mea (y[þ]allage); ant is as þah he seide, 'Ich chulle
wite mine weies wið mi tunge warde; wite Ich wel mi tunge, Ich mei
wel halden þe wei toward heouene.' For as Ysaie seið, *Cultus iusticie*
silentium, 'þe tilunge of rihtwisnesse, þet is silence.' Silence tileð
hire, ant heo itilet bringeð forð sawles eche fode, for ha is 470
undeadlich, as Salomon witneð: *Iusticia inmortalis est.* For-þi feieð
Ysaie hope ant silence baðe togederes, ant seið in ham schal stonden
gastelich strengðe: *In silentio et spe erit fortitudo uestra*, þet is, 'I
silence ant in hope schal beon ower strengðe.' Neomeð ӡeme hu wel
he seið. For hwa-se is muche stille, ant halt silence longe, ha mei 475
hopien sikerliche þet, hwen ha speketh toward Godd, þet he hire
ihere; ha mei ec hopien þet ha schal singen, þurh hire silence,
sweteliche in heouene. þis is nu þe reisun of þe ueiunge, hwi Ysaie
ueieð hope ant silence ant cupleð ba togederes. Teke þet, he seið i þe
ilke auctorite þet i silence ant in hope schal beon ure strengðe i 480
Godes [seruise] toӡein þe deofles turnes ant his fondunges. Ah lokið
þurh hwet reisun. Hope is a swete spice inwið þe heorte, þet sweteð
M. 80 al þet bitter þet te bodi drinkeð. Ah hwa-se cheoweð spice, ha schal
tunen hire muð þet te swote breað ant te strengðe [þ]rof leaue
f. 20ᵛ wiðinnen; ah heo þe openeð hire muð wið muche meaðelunge, | ant 485
brekeð silence, ha spit hope al ut ant te swotnesse þrof mid
worltliche wordes, ant leoseð aӡein þe feond gastelich strengðe.
For hwet makeð us stronge i Godes seruise ant ine fondunges,
forte drehe derf, to wreastli stealewurðliche toӡein þe deofles
swenges, bute hope of heh mede? Hope halt te heorte hal, hwet-se 490
þe flesch drehe; as me seið, 'Ӡef hope nere, heorte tobreke.' A, Iesu,
þin are! Hu stont ham þe beoð þer-as alle wa ant weane is, wiðuten
hope of utcume, ant heorte ne mei bersten? For-þi, as ӡe wulleð
halden inwið ow hope, ant te swete breað of hire þe ӡeueð sawle

mihte, wið muð itunet cheoweð hire inwið ower heorte. Ne blawe ȝe
hire nawt ut wið meaðelinde muðes, wið ȝeoniende tuteles. *Non
habeatis linguam uel aures prurientes*; 'Lokið', seið Sein Ierome, 'þet ȝe
nabben ȝicchinde nowðer tunge ne earen', þet is to seggen, þet ow ne
luste nowðer speoken ne hercni worltlich speche.

22. Hiderto is iseid of ower silence, ant hu ower speche schal beo
seltsene. *Contrariorum eadem est disciplina;* of silence ant of speche nis
bute a lare, ant for-þi i writunge ha eorneð ba togederes. Nu we
schulen sumhwet speoken of ower herunge, aȝein uuel speche, þet ȝe
þer-toȝeines tunen ower earen, ant, ȝef ned is, spearren ower þurles.

23. For al uuel speche, mine leoue sustren, stoppið ower earen,
ant habbeð wleatunge of þe muð þe speoweð ut atter. *De omni uerbo
otioso, et cetera.* Vuel speche is þreofald: attri, ful, ant idel. Idel speche
is uuel, ful speche is wurse, attri is þe wurste. Idel is ant unnet al þet
god ne kimeð of, ant of þulli speche, seið ure Lauerd, schal euch
word beon irikenet, ant iȝeue reisun hwi þe an hit seide ant te oðer
hit lustne|de; ant þis is þah þet leaste uuel of þe þreo uueles. Hwet,
hu þenne schal me ȝelde reisun of þe wurse, hwet, hu of þe wurste,
þet is, of attri ant of ful speche?—nawt ane þet hit spekeð, ah þet hit
hercneð.

24. Ful speche is as of leccherie, ant of oðre fulðen þet
unweschene muðes speokeð oðerhwiles. þeose beoð alle ischrapede
ut of ancre riwle. þe swuch fulðe spit ut in eani ancre earen, me
schulde dutten his mu[ð] nawt wið scharpe sneateres, ah wið hearde
fustes.

25. Attri speche is heresie, þweartouer leasunge, bacbitunge, ant
fikelunge; þeos beoð þe wurste. Heresie, Godd haue þonc, ne rixleð
nawt in Englelond. Leasunge is se uuel þing þet Seint Austin seið
þet forte schilde þi feader from deað ne schuldest tu nawt lihen.
Godd seolf seið þet he is soð, ant hwet is mare aȝein soð þen is leas?
Diabolus mendax est et pater eius, 'þe deouel is leas ant leasunge
feader.' þe ilke, þenne, þe stureð hire tunge i leasunge, ha makeð of
hire tunge cradel to þe deofles bearn ant rockeð hit ȝeornliche as his
nurrice.

26. Bacbitunge ant fikelunge ant eggunge to don uuel ne beoð
nawt monnes speche, ah beoð þe deofles bleas ant his ahne steuene.
Ȝef ha ahen to beo feor alle worltliche men, hwet, hu ahen ancren
heatien ham, ant schunien þet ha ham ne iheren? 'Iheren', Ich segge;
for hwa-se speokeð ham, nis ha nawt ancre. *Salomon: Si mordet serpens
in silentio, nichil minus eo habet qui detrahit in occulto.* þe neddre, seið

Salomon, stingeð | al stille; ant þeo þe spekeð bihinden þet ha nalde biuoren nis nawiht betere. Herst tu hu Salomon eueneð bacbitere to stinginde neddre? Swa hit is, witerliche; ha is neddre cundel, ant bereð þeo þe uuel spekeð atter i þe tunge.

27. Þe fikelere blent mon, ant put him preon i þe ehe þet he wið fikeleð. *Gregorius: Adulator ei cum quo sermonem conserit quasi clauum in oculo figit.* Þe bacbitere cheoweð ofte monnes flesch i Fridei, ant beakeð wið his blake bile o cwike charoines, as þe þet is þes deofles corbin of helle. *Salomon: Noli esse in conuiuiis eorum, et cetera, qui conferunt carnes ad uescendum, et cetera.* Ʒef he walde pilewin ant toteoren wið his bile rotet stinkinde flesch, as is reauenes cunde, þet is, walde he seggen uuel bi nan oþer bute bi þeo þe rotieð ant stinkeð al i fulðe of hare sunne, hit were leasse wunder. Ah lihteð upo cwic flesch, tolimeð ant tolukeð hit, þet is, misseið bi swuch þet is cwic ine Godd; he is to ʒiuer reuen, ant to bald mid alle. On oðer half, neomeð nu ʒeme of hwucche twa meosters þes twa menestraws seruið hare lauerd, þe deouel of helle. Ful hit is to seggen, ah fulre forte beon hit, ant swa hit is allegate. *Ne uideatur hec moralitas minus decens, recolat in Esdra quod Melchia hedificauit portam stercoris. Melchia enim corus Domino interpretatur, filius Rechab, id est, mollis patris. Nam uentus aquilo dissipat pluuias, et faties tristis linguam detrahentem.* Ha beoð þes deofles gong-men, ant beoð aa in his gong-hus.[14] Þe fikeleres meoster is to hulie þe gong-þurl; þet he deð as ofte as he wið | his fikelunge ant wið his preisunge wrið mon his sunne, þet stinkeð na þing fulre; ant he hit huleð ant lideð swa þet he hit nawt ne stinkeð. Þe bacbitere unlideð hit ant openeð swa þet fulðe þet hit stinkeð wide. Þus ha beoð aa bisie i þis fule meoster, ant eiðer wið oþer striueð her-abuten. Þulliche men stinkeð of hare stinkinde meoster, ant bringeð euch stude o stench þet ha to nahið. Vre Lauerd schilde þet te breað of hare stinkinde þrote ne nahi ow neauer. Oþer spechen fuleð, ah þeose attrið baðe þe earen ant te heorte. Þet ʒe bet icnawen ham ʒef ei kimeð toward ow, low her hare molden.

28. Fikeleres beoð þreo cunnes. Þe forme beoð uuele inoh, þe oþre þah beoð wurse; þe þridde [ʒet] beoð wurst. *Ve illis qui ponunt puluillos, et cetera. Ve illis qui [dicunt] bonum malum et malum bonum, ponentes lucem tenebras et tenebras lucem (hoc scilicet detractatoribus et adulatoribus [con]uenit).* Þe forme, ʒef a mon is god, preiseð him biuoren him seolf, ant makeð him inohreaðe ʒet betere þen he beo, ant ʒef he seið

---

[14] After *gong-hus*, V has 'and makeþ of heore mouþ ladel for to drawen vp þat stinkinde drit, whon þe bacbytere speweþ oþures fulþe'; similarly F.

PART 2 35

wel oðer deð wel, heueð hit to hehe up wið ouerherunge. Þe oðer, ȝef a mon is uuel ant seið ant deð se muche mis þet hit beo se open
575 sunne þet he hit ne mahe nanes weis allunge wiðseggen, he þah biuore þe mon seolf makeð his uuel leasse. 'Nis hit nawt nu', he seið, 'se ouer-uuel as me hit makeð. Nart tu nawt i þis þing þe forme ne þe leaste; þu hauest monie feren. Let iwurðe, god-mon, ne geast tu nawt te ane; moni deð muche wurse.' Þe þridde cunne of fikelere is
580 wurst, as Ich seide, for he preiseð þe uuele ant his uuele dede, as þe þe seið to þe | cniht þe robbeð his poure men, 'A, sire, as þu dest f. 22ᵛ wel! For eauer me schal þene cheorl peolkin ant pilien, for he is as þe wiðin, þe spruteð ut þe betere þet me hine croppeð ofte.' *Laudatur peccator in desideriis anime sue, et iniquus benedicitur. Augustinus: Adulantium*
585 *lingue alligant hominem in peccatis.* Þus þes false fikeleres ablendeð þe ham her[c]nið, as Ich ear seide, ant wriheð hare fulðe þet ha hit ne mahe stinken; ant þet is hare muchel unselhðe, for ȝef ha hit stunken, ham walde wleatie þer-wið, ant eornen to schrift ant speowen hit ut þer, ant schunien hit þrefter.

590 29. *Clemens: Homicidarum tria esse genera dixit beatus Petrus, et eorum parem penam esse uoluit: qui corporaliter occidit, et qui detrahit fratri, et qui inuidet.* Bacbiteres, þe biteð bihinde bac oþre, beoð of twa maneres, ah þe leatere is wurse. Þe earre kimeð al openliche ant seið uuel bi anoþer, ant speoweð ut his atter se muchel se him eauer to muð M. 88
595 kimeð, ant culcheð al ut somet þet te attri heorte sent up to þe tunge. Ah þe leatere kimeð forð al on oþer wise, wurse feond þen þe oðer is, [ah] under freondes huckel. Warpeð adun þet heaued, feð on forte siken ear he eawt segge, ant makeð drupi chere. Bisampleð longe abuten, forte beo bet ileuet. Hwen hit alles kimeð forð, þenne is hit
600 ȝeolow atter. 'Weila,' ha seið, 'wa is me þet he oðer heo habbeð swuch word icaht. Inoh Ich wes abuten, ah ne healp me nawt to don her-of bote. Ȝare is þet Ich wiste þrof, ah þah þurh me ne schulde hit beon neauer mare iuppet; ah nu hit is þurh oþre swa wide ibroht forð þet Ich ne mei hit nawt wiðsaken. Vuel me seið þet hit is, | ant ȝet hit f. 23ʳ
605 is wurse. Sorhful Ich am ant sari þet Ich hit schal seggen. Ah for soðe swa hit is, ant þet is muchel sorhe, for i feole oðer þing he oðer heo is swiðe to herien, ah onont þis þing—wa is me þer-uore—ne mei ham na mon werien.' Þis beoð þe deofles neddren þe Salomon spekeð of. Vre Lauerd þurh his grace halde ower earen feor hare
610 attrie tungen, ne leue ow neauer stinken þet fule put þet ha unwreoð—as þe fikeleres wreoð ant hulieð, as Ich seide. Vnwreon hit to ham seoluen þeo þe hit to limpeð ant hulien hit to oþre, þet is

a muche þeaw, nawt to þeo þe hit schulden smeallen ant heatien þet fulðe.

30. Nv, mine leoue sustren, from al uuel speche, þet is þus þreouald, idel, ful, ant attri, haldeð feor ower eare. Me seið upon ancren þet euch meast haueð an ald cwene to feden hire earen, a meaðelilt þe meaðeleð hire alle þe talen of þe lond, a rikelot þe cakeleð al þet ha sið ant hereð; swa þet me seið i bisahe, 'From mulne ant from chepinge, from smiððe ant from ancre-hus me tidinge bringeð.' Wat Crist, þis is a sari sahe, þet ancre-hus, þet schulde beon anlukest stude of alle, schal beon ifeiet to þe ilke þreo studen þet meast is in of chaffle. Ah ase cwite as ȝe beoð of þullich, leoue sustren, weren alle oþre, ure Lauerd hit uðe.

31. Nv Ich habbe sunderlepes ispeken of þeos þreo limen, of ehe, of muð, of eare. Of eare is al þis leaste to ancre bihoue, for leflich þing nis hit nawt þet ancre beore swuch muð, ah muchel me mei dreden to swucche muðes sumcheare þet ha beie hire eare. Of sihðe, of speche, of hercnunge | is iseid sunderlepes of euchan o rawe. Cume we nu eft aȝein ant speoken of alle imeane.

32. *Zelatus sum Syon zelo magno. In propheta Zacharia.* Vnderstond, ancre, hwas spuse þu art, ant hu he is gelus of alle þine lates. *Ego sum deus zelotes. In Exodo.* 'Ich am', he seið bi him seolf, 'þe geluse godd.' *Zelatus sum, et cetera.* 'Ich am gelus of þe, Syon, mi leofmon, wið muche gelusie.' Þuhte him nawt inoh iseid þet he is gelus of þe, bute he seide þer-to, 'wið muche gelusie'. *Auris zeli audit omnia*, seið Salomon þe wise. *Vbi amor, ibi oculus.* Wite þe nu ful wel; his eare is eauer toward te, ant he hereð al. His ehe aa bihalt te ȝef þu makest ei semblant, eani luue lates toward unþeawes. *Zelatus sum Syon.* 'Syon', þet is 'schawere'. He cleopeð þe his schawere, swa his þet nan oþres. For-þi he seið *in Canticis, Ostende michi fatiem tuam.* 'Schaw þi neb to me', he seið, 'ant to nan oþer. Bihald me ȝef þu wult habbe briht sihðe wið þine heorte ehnen. Bihald inward, þer Ich am, ant ne sech þu me nawt wiðute þin heorte. Ich am wohere scheomeful, ne nule Ich nohwer bicluppe mi leofmon bute i stude dearne.' O þulli wise ure Lauerd spekeð to his spuse. Ne þunche hire neauer wunder, ȝef ha nis muchel ane, þah he hire schunie—ant swa ane þet ha putte euch worldlich þrung, ant euch nurð eorðlich, ut of hire heorte, for heo is Godes chambre. Nurð ne kimeð in heorte bute of sum þing þet me haueð oðer isehen oðer iherd, ismaht oðer ismeallet, ant utewið ifelet. Ant þet witeð to soðe, þet eauer se þes wittes beoð ma|re isprengde utward, se ha leasse wendeð inward. Eauer se

PART 2

recluse toteð mare utward, se ha haueð leasse leome of ure Lauerd inward, ant alswa of þe oþre. *Qui exteriori oculo negligenter utitur iusto*
655 *Dei iudicio interiori cecatur.* Lo hwet Sein Gregoire seið: 'Hwa-se ȝemelesliche wit hire uttre ehnen, þurh Godes rihtwise dom ha ablindeð i þe inre, þet ha ne mei iseo Godd mid gastelich sihðe', ne þurh swuch sihðe icnawen, ant þurh þe cnawleachunge ouer alle þing luuien. For efter þet me cnaweð his muchele godnesse, ant
660 efter þet me feleð his swote swetnesse, efter þet me luueð him mare oðer leasse.

33. For-þi, mine leoue sustren, beoð wiðute blinde, as wes þe hali Iacob, ant Tobie þe gode, ant Godd wule, as he ȝef ham, ȝeouen ow liht wiðinnen him to seon ant cnawen, ant þurh þe cnawlechunge ouer
665 alle þing him luuien. þenne schule ȝe iseon hu al þe world is nawt, hu hire froure is fals. þurh þet sihðe ȝe schule seon alle þe deofles wiheles, hu he biwrencheð wrecches. ȝe schulen iseon in ow seolf hwet beo ȝet to beten of ower ahne sunnen. ȝe schulen bihalde sumcheare toward te pine[n] of helle, þet ow uggi wið ham ant fleo þe swiðere
670 ham frommard. ȝe schulen gasteliche iseon þe blissen of heouene, þe ontenden ower heorte to hihin ham toward. ȝe schulen as i schawere iseon ure Leafdi wið hire meidnes, al þe englene weoret, al þe halhene hird, ant him ouer ham alle þe blisseð ham alle, ant is hare alre crune. þis sihðe, leoue sustren, schal frourin ow mare þen mahte ei worltlich
675 sihðe. Hali men witen wel þe habbeð | hit ifondet þet euch eorðlich gleadunge is unwurð her-toȝeines. *Manna absconditum est, et cetera; nomen nouum quod nemo scit nisi qui accipit.* 'Hit is a dearne healewi', seið Seint Iuhan Euuangeliste i þe Apocalipse; 'Hit is a dearne healewi þet na mon ne cnaweð þet naueð hit ismecchet.' þis smech ant tis
680 cnawunge kimeð of gastelich sihðe, of gastelich herunge, of gastelich speche, þet ha schulen habben þe forgað for Godes luue worldliche herunges, eorðliche spechen, fleschliche sihðen. *Videmus [nunc] quasi per speculum in enigmate.* Ant efter þet sihðe, þet is nu dosc her, ȝe schulen habbe þruppe þe brihte sihðe of Godes neb, þet alle
685 gleadunge is of, i þe blisse of heouene, muche biuore þe oþre. For þe rihtwise Godd hit haueð swa idemet þet euchanes mede þer ondswerie aȝein þe swinc ant aȝeines þe ennu þet ha her for his luue eadmodliche þolieð. For-þi hit is semlich þet ancren þeos twa marheȝeouen habben biuoren oþre, swiftnesse ant leome of a briht sihðe: swiftnes aȝeines
690 þet ha beoð nu swa bipinnet, leome of briht sihðe aȝeines þet ha her þeostrið nu ham seoluen, ne nulleð nowðer iseo mon ne of mon beon isehene. Alle þeo in heouene schule beon ase swifte as is nu monnes

þoht, as is þe sunne gleam þe smit from est into west, as þe ehe openeð. Ah ancres bisperret her schulen beo þer, ȝef ei mei, lihtre ba ant swiftre, ant i se wide schakeles (as me seið) pleien in heouene large lesewen þet te bodi schal beon hwer-se eauer þe gast wule in an hondhwile. þis is nu þe an marheȝeoue þet Ich seide ancren schulden habben biuoren oþre. þe oðer is of sihðe. *Gregorius:* [*Quid est*] *enim quod nesciunt ubi scientem omnia sciunt?* Alle þeo in heouene seoð i Godd alle þing, [ah] ancren schule brihtluker for hare blindfellunge her iseon ant understonde þer Godes dearne runes ant his derue domes, þe ne kepeð nu to witen of þinges wiðuten wið eare ne wið ehe.

34. For-þi, mine leoue sustren, ȝef ei mon bit to seon ow, easkið him hwet god þer-of mahte lihten; for moni uuel Ich iseo þrin, ant nane biheue. Ȝef he is meadles, leueð him þe wurse. Ȝef ei wurðeð swa awed þet he warpe hond forð toward te þurl-claðm, swiftliche ananriht schutteð al þet þurl to, ant leoteð him iwurðen. Alswa, sone se eauer eani feleð into ei luðer speche þet falle toward ful luue, sperreð þe þurl ananriht, ne ondswerie ȝe him nawiht, ah wendeð awei wið þis uers, þet he hit mahe iheren, *Declinate a me, maligni, et scrutabor mandata Dei mei;*[15] *Narrauerunt michi iniqui fabulationes, Domine, sed non ut lex tua;* ant gað biuoren ower weoued wið þe *Miserere.* Ne chastie ȝe na swuch mon neauer on oþer wise, for inwið þe chastiement he mahte ondswerie swa, ant blawen se liðeliche, þet sum sperke mahte acwikien. Na wohlech nis se culuert as o pleinte wise; as hwa-se þus seide, 'Ich nalde forte þolie deað þenche fulðe toward te' (**ant swereð deope aðes**), 'ah þah Ich hefde isworen hit, luuien Ich mot te. Hwa is wurse þen me? Moni slep hit binimeð me. Nu me is wa þet tu hit wast; ah forȝef me nu þet Ich habbe hit itald te. Þah Ich schule wurðe wod, ne | schalt tu neauer mare witen hu me stonde.' Ha hit forȝeueð him for he spekeð se feire. Speokeð þenne of oðerhwet; ah

> Eauer is þe ehe
> To þe wude-lehe,[16]

---

[15] After *mei*, F has 'ou od cestui'.
[16] *After wude-lehe*, C has
'Ant þe halte bucke
Climbeð þer-uppe.
Twa ant þreo,
Hu feole beoð þeo?
Þreo halpenes makeð a peni. Amen.'
and N 'þer-inne is þet Ich luuie.'

eauer is þe heorte i þe earre speche. ʒet hwen he is forðe, ha went in
hire þoht ofte swucche wordes, hwen ha schulde oðerhwet ʒeornliche
ʒemen. He eft secheð his point forte breoke foreward,[17] swereð he
mot nede,[18] ant swa waxeð þet wa se lengre se wurse;[19] for na
feondschipe nis se uuel as is fals freondschipe. Feond þe þuncheð
freond is sweoke ouer alle. For-þi, mine leoue sustren, ne ʒeoue ʒe to
swuch mon nan inʒong to speokene, for as Hali Writ seið, 'Hare
speche spreat ase cancre'; ah for alle ondsweres wendeð ow
frommard him, alswa as Ich seide þruppe. Sawuin ow seoluen ne
maten him betere ne mahe ʒe o nane wise.

35. Lokið nu hu propreliche þe leafdi i *Canticis*, Godes deore
spuse, leareð ow bi hire sahe hu ʒe schule seggen. *En dilectus meus
loquitur michi: Surge, propera, amica mea, et cetera.* 'Low!' ha seið,
'Hercne! Ich ihere mi leof speoken. He cleopeð me, Ich mot gan.'
Ant ʒe gan ananriht to ower deore leofmon, ant meaneð ow to his
earen þe luueliche cleopeð ow to him wið þes wordes: *Surge, propera,
amica mea, columba mea, formosa mea, et veni. Ostende mihi fatiem
tuam. Sonet uox tua in auribus meis.* Þet is, 'Aris up, hihe þe
heonewart, ant cum to me, mi leofmon, mi culure, mi feire, ant mi
schene spuse.' *Ostende michi faciem tuam.* 'Schaw to me þi leoue neb
ant ti lufsume leor. Went te from oþre.' *Sonet vox tua in auribus meis.*
'Sei hwa | haueð ido þe, hwa haueð ihurt mi deore, sing i mine earen.
For-þi þet tu ne wilnest bute to seo mi wlite, ne speoke bute to me,
þi steuene is me swete ant ti wlite schene.' *Vnde et subditur: Vox tua
dulcis et facies tua decora.* Þis beoð nu twa þinges þe beoð iluuet swiðe,
swete speche ant schene wlite, hwa-se ham haueð togederes.
Swucche cheoseð Iesu Crist to leofmon ant to spuse. ʒef þu wult
swuch beon, ne schaw þu na mon þi wlite, ne ne leote bliðeliche here
þi speche; ah turn ham ba to Iesu Crist, to þi deorewurðe spus, as he
bit þruppe, as þu wult þet ti speche þunche him swete ant ti wlite
schene, ant habben him to leofmon þet is þusent-fald schenre þen þe
sunne.

36. Hercnið nu ʒeornliche, mine leoue sustren, al anoðer speche,
ant frommard tis earre. Hercnið nu hu Iesu Crist speked as o
wreaððe, ant seið as o grim hoker ant o scarn to þe ancre þe schulde
beon his leofmon ant secheð þah gealunge utward ant froure wið ehe

---

[17] After *foreward,* V has 'þat he biheet þer-vppe'; similarly L.
[18] After *nede,* C has 'ant swa Ich habbe a-nede ernde dun in þe tun; þach hit reine arewen, Ich habbe a-nede erende.'
[19] After *wurse,* C has 'Lokede blind hors[e], ant wudemonnes echʒe orn al ut.'

oðer wið tunge. *In Canticis: Si ignoras te, o pulcra inter mulieres, egredere et abi post uestigia gregum tuorum, et pasce edos tuos iuxta tabernacula pastorum.* þis beoð þe wordes: 'ʒef þu ne cnawest te seolf, þu feier bimong wummen, wend ut ant ga efter gate heorden, ant lesewe þine tichnes bi heordemenne hulen of ris ant of leaues.' þis is a cruel word, a grim word mid alle, þet ure Lauerd seið as o grome ant o scarn to totinde ant to hercwile ant to speokele ancres. Hit is bileppet ant ihud, ah Ich hit wulle unualden. 'ʒef þu ne cnawest te seolf', he seið, ure Lauerd (**neomeð | nu gode ʒeme**): þet is, 'ʒef þu nast hwas spuse þu art, þet tu art cwen of heouene ʒef þu art me treowe as spuse ah to beonne, ʒef þu þis hauest forʒeten ant telest her-to lutel, wend ut ant ga', he seið. Hwider? Ut of þis hehschipe, of þis muchele menske, 'ant folhe heorde of geat', he seið. Hwet beoð heorde of geat? þet beoð flesches lustes, þe stinkeð ase geat doð biuoren ure Lauerd. ʒef þu hauest forʒete nu þi wurðfule leafdischipe, ga ant folhe þeos geat, folhe flesches lustes. Nu kimeð þrefter, 'ant lesewe þine tichnes'. [þeos tichnes beoð þine fif wittes. 'Lesewe þine tichnes':] þet is as [he] seide, 'Fed tine ehnen wið ut totunge, þi tunge wið chaflunge, þine earen wið spellunge,[20] þi nease wið smeallunge, þi flesch wið softe felunge.' þeose fif wittes he cleopeð tichnes; for alswa as of a ticchen þet haueð swete flesch kimeð a stinkinde gat oðer a ful bucke, al riht alswa of a ʒung swete locunge, oðer of a swote herunge, oðer of a softe felunge, waxeð a stincinde lust ant a ful sunne. Hweðer ei totilde ancre fondede eauer þis þe beakeð eauer utward as untohe brid i cage? Hweðer þe cat of helle cahte eauer towart hire, ant lahte wið cleaures hire heorte heued? ʒe, soðes, ant droh ut al þe bodi efter wið clokes of crokede ant kene fondunges, ant makede hire to leosen baðe Godd ant mon wið brad scheome ant sunne, ant bireafde hire ed an cleap þe eorðe ant ec þe heouene. Inoh sari lure! To wraðer heale beakede eauer swa ut ancre. *Egredere*, he seið o grome. 'Ga ut' as dude Dyna, Iacobes dohter, to [hinene hulen]; þet is to seggen, 'Leaf me ant mi cunfort, þet is inwið þi breoste, ant ga sech wiðuten þe worldes fra|kele froure, þe schal endin eauer i sar ant i sorhe. Tac þer-to ant leaf me hwen þe swa is leouere; for ne schalt tu nanes weis þes ilke twa cunforz, min ant te worldes, þe ioie of þe Hali Gast ant ec flesches froure, habbe togederes. Cheos nu an of þes twa, for þe oðer þu most leten. *O pulcra inter mulieres:* 'ʒef þu ne cnawest te seolf, þu

---

[20] For *spellunge*, TV have *hercninge* (similarly NS), followed in T by 'þi muð wið spellinge', in S by 'uostre bouche ou goustemenz'.

feier bimong wummen', seið ure Lauerd. 'Þu feier bimong wum-
800 men'—ӡe, nu her; do þer-to þet schalt, ant tu wel wulle, elleshwer
beo feier nawt ane bimong wummen ah bimong engles. 'Þu, mi
wurði spuse,' seið ure Lauerd, 'schalt tu folhin geat o feld?' (þet
beoð flesches lustes; feld is willes breade). 'Schalt tu o þis wise folhi
geat ӡont te feld?—þe schuldest i þin heorte bur biseche me cosses,
805 as mi leofmon þet seið to me i þet luue boc, *Osculetur me osculo oris
sui*'; þet is, 'Cusse me mi leofmon wið þe coss of his muð, muðene
swetest.' Þis coss, leoue sustren, is a swetnesse ant a delit of heorte
swa unimete swete þet euch worldes sauur is bitter þer-toӡeines. Ah
ure Lauerd wið þis coss ne cusseð na sawle þe luueð ei þing buten
810 him, ant te ilke þinges for him þe helpeð him to habben. Ant tu
þenne, Godes spuse, þet maht heren her-biuoren hu sweteliche þi
spus spekeð, ant cleopeð þe to him se luueliche, þrefter hu he went
te lof, ant spekeð swiðe grimliche ӡef þu ut wendest, hald te i ti
chambre. Ne fed tu nawt wiðuten þine gate tichnes, ah hald
815 wiðinnen þin hercnunge, þi speche, ant ti sihðe, ant tun feaste
hare ӡeten, muð ant ehe ant eare; for nawt ha beoð bilokene inwið
wah oðer wal þe þes ӡeten openið, bute aӡein Godes sonde, ant
liueneð of | sawle. *Omni custodia custodi cor tuum*: ouer alle þing,
þenne, as Salomon þe leareð ant Ich seide feor biuoren i þe frumðe
820 of þis dale, mine leoue sustren, witeð ower heorte. Þe heorte is wel
iloket ӡef muð ant ehe ant eare wisliche beon ilokene; for heo, as Ich
seide þer, beoð þe heorte wardeins, ant ӡef þe wardeins wendeð ut,
þe ham bið biwist uuele. Þis beoð nu þe þreo wittes þet Ich habbe
ispeken of; speoke we nu scheortliche of þe twa oþre. (Þah nis nawt
825 speche þe muðes wit, ah is smechunge, þah ba beon i muðe.)

37. Smeal of nease is þe feorðe of þe fif wittes. Of þis wit seið
Seint Austin, *De odoribus non satago nimis. Cum assunt, non respuo;
cum absunt, non requiro*. 'Of smealles', he seið, 'ne fondi Ich nawt
mucheles. Ӡef ha beoð neh, o Godes half; ӡef feor, me ne recche.' Vre
830 Lauerd þah þurh Ysaie þreateð ham wið helle stench þe habbeð delit
her i fleschliche smealles: *Erit pro suaui odore fetor*. Þer-toӡeines ha
schulen habben heouenliche smealles þe habbeð her of irnes swat,
oðer of heren þet ha beoreð, oðer of swati hettren, oðer of þicke eire
in hire hus ant muhlinde þinges, stench oðerhwiles ant strong breað i
835 nease.

38. Þer-of beoð iwarnet, mine leoue sustren, þet oðerhwile þe
feond makeð sum þing to stinken þet ӡe schulden notien, for-þi þet
he walde þet ӡe hit schulden schunien. Oþerhwile þe wiheleare of

sum dearne þing þet ȝe ne mahe nawt iseon, as dust of dearne sedes, makeð a swote smeal cumen as þah hit were of heouene, for ȝe schulden wenen þet Godd for ower hali lif sende ow his elne, | ant leote wel to ow seolf ant leapen into prude. Smeal þe kimeð o Godes half froureð þe heorte mare þen þe nease. Þeos ant oþre truiles, þet he bitruileð monie, schulen beon ibroht to nawt wið hali weater, ant wið þe hali rode-taken. Hwa-se þohte hu Godd seolf wes i þis wit ideruet, ha walde þe derf þrof þuldeliche þolien. I þe munt of Caluarie, þer ure Lauerd hongede, wes þe cwalm-stowe. Þer leien ofte licomes irotet buuen eorðe, ant stunken swiðe stronge; he, as he hongede, mahte habben hare breað, wið al his oðer wa, riht amidden his nease.

39. Alswa he wes ideruet in alle his oþre wittes. In his sihðe, þa he seh his deorewurðe moder teares, ant Sein Iuhanes Euuangeliste, ant te oðre Maries; ant þa he biheold hu his deore deciples fluhen alle from him ant leafden him ane. He weop him seolue þrien wið his feire ehnen. He þolede al þuldeliche þet me him blindfeallede. Hwen his ehnen weren þus i schendlac iblintfeallet, forte ȝeoue þe, ancre, þe brihte sihðe of heouene, þah þu þine ehnen, for his luue ant i munegunge þrof, blintfealli on eorðe to beoren him feolahreadden, nis na muche wunder.

40. Amid þe muð me gurde him sumcheare inohreaðe as me tobeot his cheken ant spitte him o scarne—ant an ancre is for a word ut of hire witte! Hwen he þolede þuldeliche þet te Giws dutten, as ha buffeteden him, his deorewurðe muð wið hare dreori fustes, ant tu, for þe luue of him ant for þin ahne muchele biheue, þi tutelinde muð dute wið þine lippen.

41. Teke þet,[21] he smahte galle on his tunge, forte | learen ancre þet ha ne grucchi neauer mare for na mete, ne for na drunch, ne beo hit swa unorne. Ȝef ha hit mei eoten, eote ant þonki Godd ȝeorne; ȝef ha ne mei nawt, beo sari þet ha mot sechen estfulre. Ah ear þen þet biddunge areare eani scandle, ear deie martir in hire meoseise. Deað me ah forte fleon ase forð as me mei wiðute sunne; ah me schal ear deien þen me do eani **heaued** sunne. Ant nis hit muche sunne to makien þet me segge, 'Estful is þeos ancre; muchel is þet ha bid'? Ȝet is wurse ȝef me seið þet ha is grucchilt ant fulitohe, dangerus ant erueð forte paien. Were ha imid te world, ha moste beo sumchearre ipaiet inohreaðe mid leasse ant mid wurse. Muchel hofles hit is cumen into ancre-hus, into Godes prisun, willes ant waldes, to stude

---

[21] After *þet*, F has 'entre touz les altres angoisses'.

PART 2   43

of meoseise, forte sechen eise þrin, ant meistrie, ant leafdischipe—
mare þen ha mahte habben inohreaðe ihaued i þe worlde. Þenc,
880 ancre, hwet tu sohtest þa þu forsoke þe world i þi biclusunge:
biwepen þine ahne ant oþres sunnen, ant forleosen alle þe blissen of
þis lif forte cluppen blisfulliche þi blisfule leofmon i þe eche lif of
heouene.
   42. *O, seið* [Ieremie], *quomodo obscuratum est aurum opti-*
885 *mum, et cetera.* 'O, weilawei, weilawei! Hu is gold iþeostret, hu
is feherest heow biturned ant forweolewet!' þe Apostle spekeð
to swucche grimliche, as o wreaðð̄e:[22] *Quis uos fascinauit, et
cetera, vt cum spiritu ceperitis, carne consummamini?* 'Me, hwuch
unseli gast haueð swa bimalscret ow þet ȝe i gast bigunnen
890 ant i flesch wulleð endin?' þe gastelich lif bigunnen i þe Hali
Gast beoð bicume|ne al fleschliche—lahinde, lihte ilatet, ane f. 29r
hwile lihte iwordet, anoðer luðere iwordet, estfule ant sar-
curne ant grucchildes, meanildes, ant ȝet (þet wurse is)
cursildes ant chidildes, bittre ant attrie wið heorte tobollen.
895 Bihofde nawt þet swuch were leafdi of castel; hoker ant hofles
þing is þet a smiret ancre—ant ancre biburiet, for hwet is
ancre-hus bute hire burinesse?—schal beo greattre ibollen,
leafdiluker leoten of, þen a leafdi of hames. Ȝef ha makeð hire
wrað aȝeines gult of sunne, ha [schal] sette[n] hire wordes swa
900 efne þet ha ne þunche ouersturet, ne nawt ilead ouer skile; ah
inwardliche ant soðliche, wiðuten hihðe ant hehschipe, in a
softe steuene. *Filia fatua in deminoratione erit.* Þis is Salomones sahe; þet hit limpe to ei of ow, Godd ne leue neauer.
'Cang dohter iwurð as mone i wonunge'; þrieð as þe cangun,
905 se lengre se wurse. Ȝe, as ȝe wulleð waxen ant nawt wenden
hindward, sikerliche ȝe moten rowen aȝein stream, wið
muchel swink breoken forð, gasteliche [earmes] stealewurðliche sturien—ant swa [we] moten alle, for alle we beoð i þis
stream, i þe worldes wode weater þe bereð adun monie. Sone
910 se we eauer wergið ant resteð us i slawðe, ure bat geað
hindward, ant we beoð þe cang dohter þe g[e]að woniende,
þe wlecche þe Godd speoweð (as is iwriten her-efter), þe
bigunnen i gast ant i flesch endið. Nai, nai! ah as Iob seið,
þe delueð efter golt-hord, eauer se he mare nahheð hit, se his
915 heortes gleadschipe makeð him mare lusti ant mare fersch to
diggin, ant deluen deoppre ant deoppre aðet he hit finde. |

   [22] After *wreaðð̄e*, F has 'sicome nous lisoms', V 'ac nout withouten serwe'.

f. 29ᵛ Ower [hord] nis nawt on eorðe; for-þi ne þurue 3e nawt deluen dunewardes, ah heouen uppart þe heorte. For þet is þe uprowunge a3ein þis worldes stream—[þa þe heorte walde lihten lihtliche adun mid te stream,] driuen hire a3einward to deluen þe golt-hord þet up is in heouene. Ant hwet is þet deluunge? 3eornful, sechinde þoht, hwer hit beo, hwuch hit beo, hu me hit mahe ifinden. þis is þe deluunge: beon bisiliche ant 3eornfulliche eauer her-abuten, wið anewil 3irnunge, wið heate of hungri heorte, waden up of unþeawes, creopen ut of flesch, breoken up ouer hire, astihen upon ow seolf wið heh þoht toward heouene—swa muchel þe neodeluker þet ower feble, tendre flesch heardes ne mei þolien. Nu, þenne, þer-a3ein 3eoueð Godd ower heorte i softnesse, i swetnesse, in alles cunnes meoknesse, ant softest eadmodnesse; nawt nu granin ant peonsin, þrefter hehi steuene, wreaðen hire unweneliche, sinetin hire wordes, wrenchen aweiward, wenden þe schuldre, keaste þe heaued, swa þet Godd heateð hire ant mon hire scarneð. Nai, nai; ripe wordes, lates ripe ant werkes bilimpeð to ancre. Hwen wordes beoð eadmodliche ant soðfestliche iseide, nawt fulitoheliche ne babanliche, þenne habbeð ha burðerne to beo riht understonden. Nu is þis al iseid þet 3e, efter Iesu Crist, þe me gurde ine muð ant galle 3ef to drinken, wið muðes sunne witen ow, ant þolieð sum derf i þet wit, as he wes þrin ideruet.

920

925

930

935

940

M. 108   43. In his eare he hefde, þe heouenliche Lauerd, al þe edwit ant te upbrud, al þe scarn ant al þe scheome þet eare mahte iheren; ant he
f. 30ʳ seið bi him seolf, us forte learen, *Et factus sum sicut | homo non audiens, et non habens in ore suo redargutiones.* 'Ich heold me', he seið, 'stille as dumbe ant deaf deð, þet naueð nan ondswere þah me him misdo oðer missegge.' þis is þi leofmonnes sahe; ant tu, seli ancre, þe art his leoue spuse, leorne hit 3eorne of him, þet tu hit cunne ant mahe soðliche seggen.

945

  44. Nv Ich habbe ispeken of ower fowr wittes, ant of Godes froure—hu he þurh hise froureð ow as ofte as 3e in ower feleð eani
M. 110 weane. Nu hercnið of þe fifte, þet is meast neod elne, for þe pine is meast þrin, þet is, i felunge—ant te licunge alswa, 3ef hit swa turneð.

950

  45. Þe fifte wit is felunge. þis ilke an wit is in alle þe oþre, ant 3ont al þe licome, ant for-þi hit is neod to habben best warde. Vre Lauerd wiste hit wel; ant for-þi he walde meast i þet wit þolien, al forte frourin us 3ef we þolieð wa þrin, ant forte wenden us frommard

955

PART 2

te licunge þet flesches lust easkeð, nomeliche i felunge mare þen in oþre. Vre Lauerd i þis wit nefde nawt in a stude, ah hefde oueral pine; nawt ane ȝond al his bodi, ah hefde ȝet inwið his seli sawle. In hire he felde þe stiche of sari sorhe ant sorhful, þet dude him sike sare. þis stiche wes þreouald, þe ase þreo speren smat him to þe heorte. þe an wes his modres wop ant te oþre Maries, þe flowen o teares; þe oðer, þet his ahne deore deciples ne lefden him namare ne ne heolden for Godd for-þi þet he ne healp him seolf in his muchele pine, ant fluhen alle from him ant leafden him as fremede. þe þridde wes þet muchele sar ant te ofþunchunge þet he hefde inwið him of hare forlorenesse þe drohen him to deaðe, þet he seh onont ham al his swinc forloren þet he swonc on eorðe. þeos ilke | þreo stichen weren in his sawle. In his licome euch lim, as Seint Austin seið, þolede sundri pine, ant deide ȝond al his bodi, as he ear ȝond al his bodi deaðes swat sweatte. Ant her seið Sein Beornard þet he ne weop nawt ane wið ehnen, ah dude as wið alle his limen. *Quasi, inquit, membris omnibus fleuisse uidetur.* For se ful of ango[i]sse wes þet ilke ned-swat þet lihte of his licome, aȝein þe angoisuse deað þet he schulde þolien, þet hit þuhte read blod. *Factus est sudor eius quasi gutte sanguinis decurrentis in terram.* On oðer half, swa largeliche ant swa swiðe fleaw þet ilke blodi swat of his blisfule bodi þet te streames urnen dun to þer eorðe. Swuch grure hefde his monliche flesch aȝein þe derue pinen þet hit schulde drehen; þet nes na feorlich wunder, for eauer se flesch is cwickre, se þe reopunge þrof ant te hurt is sarre. A lutel hurt i þe ehe derueð mare þen deð a muchel i þe hele, for þe flesch is deaddre. Euch monnes flesch is dead flesch aȝein þet wes Godes flesch, as þet te wes inumen of [þ]e tendre meiden, ant na þing neauer nes þrin þet hit adeadede, ah eauer wes iliche cwic of þet cwike Goddhead þe wunede þrinne. For-þi in his flesch wes þe pine sarre þen eauer eani mon in his flesch þolede. þet his flesch wes cwic ouer alle flesches, lo, hwuc an essample. A mon for uuel þet he haueð ne let him nawt blod o þe seke halue, ah deð o þe hale, to heale þe seke. Ah in al þe world þe wes o þe feure, nes bimong al moncun an hal dale ifunden þe mahte beon ilete blod bute Godes bodi ane, þe lette him blod o rode. Nawt o þe earm ane, ah dude o fif halue, forte healen moncun | of þe secnesse þet te fif wittes hefden awakenet. þus, lo, þe hale half ant te cwike dale droh þet uuele blod ut frommard te unhale, ant healde swa þe seke. þurh blod is in Hali Writ sunne bitacnet; þe reisuns hwi beoð efter sutelliche ischawet. Ah þer-of neomeð ȝeme, mine leoue sustren, þet ower deorewurðe spus, þe luuewurðe Lauerd, þe Healent of heouene, Iesu Godd, Godes sune, þe wealdent of al þe world, þa he wes þus ilete blod— understondeð þet dei hwuch wes his diete, i þe ilke blodletunge se baleful ant se bitter. þe ilke þet he bledde fore, ne brohten ha him to present ne win ne ale ne weater, ȝet þa he seide *Sicio*, ant meande as he bledde of þurst o þe rode, ah duden bitter galle. Hwer wes eauer iȝeuen to eani blodleten se poure pitance? Ant tah ne gruchede he nawt, ah underueng hit eadmodliche forte learen hise. Ant ȝet he dude mare us to forbisne: dude his deore muð þer-to ant smahte þrof, þah he hit notie ne mahte. Hwa is, þenne, efter þis—ant ancre hure ant hure—þe gruccheð ȝef ha naueð nawt oðer mete oðer drunch efter hire eise? Ant siker hwa-se gruccheð, ha offreð ȝet ure Lauerd þis luðere pitance, as duden þa þe Giws, ant is Giwes fere to beoden him in his þurst drunch of sur galle. His þurst nis bute ȝirnunge of ure sawle heale, ant grucchunge of bitter ant of sur heorte is him surre ant bittrure nu þen wes þa þe galle. Ant tu, his deore spuse, ne beo þu nawt Giwes make forte birlin him swa, ah ber him feolahreadden, ant drinc wið him bliðeliche al þet ti flesch þuncheð sur oðer bitter, þet is, pine ant wone ant | alle meoseises, ant he hit wule þe ȝelden, as his treowe fere, wið healewi of heouene.

46. Þvs wes Iesu Crist, þe almihti Godd, in alle his fif wittes derfliche ipinet; ant nomeliche i þis leaste, þet is, i felunge, for his flesch wes al cwic as is þe tendre ehe. Ant ȝe witen þis wit—þet is, flesches felunge—ouer alle þe oþre. Godes honden weren ineilet o rode; þurh þe ilke neiles Ich halsi ow, ancres (nawt ow, ah do oþre, for hit nis na neod, mine leoue sustren), haldeþ ower honden inwið ower þurles! Hondlunge oðer ei felunge bitweone mon ant ancre is þing swa uncumelich, ant dede se scheomelich, ant se naket sunne, to al þe world se eatelich ant se muche scandle, þet nis na neod to speoken ne writen þer-toȝeines, for al wiðute writunge þet ful[ðe] is to etscene. Godd hit wat as me were muche deale leouere þet Ich isehe ow alle þreo, mine leoue sustren, wummen me leouest, hongin on a gibet forte wiðbuhe sunne, þen Ich sehe an of ow ȝeouen anlepi cos eani mon on eorðe swa as Ich meane—Ich am stille of þet mare. Nawt ane monglin honden, ah putten hond utward bute hit beo for nede, is wohunge efter [Godes] grome ant tollunge of his eorre. Hire seolf bihalden hire ahne hwite honden deð hearm moni ancre þe haueð ham to feire, as þeo þe beoð foridlet; ha schulden schrapien euche dei þe eorðe up of hare put þet ha schulen rotien in. Godd hit wat, þet put deð muche god moni ancre; for as Salomon seið,

Memorare nouissima tua et in eternum non peccabis. Þeo þe haueð eauer hire deað as biuoren hire ehnen (þet te put munegeð), ʒef þet ha þencheð wel o þe dom of | Domesdei, þer þe engles schule cwakien, f. 32ʳ
1040 ant te eche ant te eateliche pinen of helle, ant oueral ant al o Iesu Cristes passiun, hu he wes ipinet (as is sumdeal iseid) in alle his fif wittes, lihtliche nule ha nawt folhi flesches licunge efter willes lust, ne drahen in toward hire nan heaued sunne wið hire fif wittes.

47. Þis is nu inoh iseid of þe fif wittes, þe beoð ase wardein[s]
1045 wiðuten of þe heorte, þet sawle lif is inne, as we seiden þruppe on earst þet Salomon seide: *Omni custodia custodi cor tuum, quoniam ex ipso uita procedit.* Nu beoð, Crist haue þonc, þe twa dalen ouercumen; ga we nu wið his help upo þe þridde.

PART 3

1. Mine leoue sustren, alswa as ȝe witeð wel ower wittes utewið, alswa ouer alle þing lokið þet ȝe beon inwið softe ant milde ant eadmode, swete ant swote iheortet, ant þolemode aȝein woh of word þet me seið ow, ant werc þet me misdeð ow, leste ȝe al leosen. Aȝein bittre ancres Dauið seið þis uers: *Similis factus sum pellicano solitudinis, et cetera.* 'Ich am', he seið, 'as pellican þe wuneð bi him ane.' Pellican is a fuhel se weamod ant se wreaðful þet hit sleað ofte o grome his ahne briddes hwen ha doð him teone; ant þenne sone þrefter hit wurð swiðe sari ant makeð swiðe muche man, ant smit him seolf wið his bile, þet he sloh ear his briddes wið, ant draheð blod of his breoste, ant wið þet blod acwikeð eft his briddes isleine. þis fuhel pellican is þe weamode ancre. Hire briddes beoð hire gode werkes, þet ha sleað ofte wið bile of scharp wreððe. | Ah hwen ha swa haueð idon, do as deð þe pellican: ofþunche hit swiðe sone, ant wið hire ahne bile beaki hire breoste—þet is, wið schrift of hire muð þet ha sunegede wið, ant sloh hire gode werkes, drahe þet blod of sunne ut of hire breoste, þet is, of þe heorte, þet sawle lif is inne; ant swa schulen eft acwikien hire isleine briddes, þet beoð hire gode werkes. Blod bitacneð sunne; for alswa as a mon bibled is grislich ant eatelich i monnes ehe, alswa is þe sunfule biuore Godes ehe. On oðer half, na mon ne mei iuggi wel blod ear hit beo icolet. Alswa is of sunne. Hwil þe heorte walleð inwið of wreaððe, nis þer na riht dom; oðer hwil þe lust is hat toward eani sunne, ne maht tu nawt te hwiles deme wel hwet hit is, ne hwet ter wule cumen of. Ah 'Let lust ouergan, ant hit te wule likin.' Let þet hate acolin, as deð þe wule iuggi blod, ant tu schalt demen ariht þe sunne ful ant ladlich þet te þuhte feier, ant vuel se muchel cumen þrof ȝef þu hit hefdest idon hwil þet hate leaste þet tu schalt deme wod te seolf þa þu þer-toward þohtest. þis is of euch sunne soð hwi blod hit bitacneð, ant nomeliche of wreaððe. *Impedit ira animum ne possit cernere uerum;* 'Wreaððe', hit seið, 'hwil hit least, ablindeð swa þe heorte þet ha ne mei soð icnawen.' *Maga quedam est, transformans naturam humanam.* Wreaððe is a forschuppilt, as me teleð i spelles, for ha reaueð mon his wit ant changeð al his chere, ant forschuppeð him from mon into beastes cunde. Wummon wrað is wuluene; mon, wulf oðer liun oðer unicorne.

Hwil þet eauer wreaððe is i wummone heorte, versaili, segge | hire

PART 3

Vres, Auez, Pater Nostres, ne deð ha bute þeoteð. Naueð ha bute, as þeo þet is iwent to wuluene i Godes ehnen, wuluene steuene in his lihte earen. *Ira furor breuis est*; 'Wreaððe is a wodschipe.' Wrað mon, nis he wod? Hu lokeð he? Hu spekeð he? Hu feareð his heorte inwið? Hwucche beoð utewið alle hise lates? He ne cnaweð na mon. Hu is he mon, þenne? *Est enim homo animal mansuetum natura*; 'Mon cundelich is milde.' Sone se he leoseð mildheortnesse he leoseð monnes cunde, ant wreaððe, þe forschuppilt, forschuppeð him into beast as Ich ear seide. Ant hwet ʒef eni ancre, Iesu Cristes spuse, is forschuppet into wuluene? Nis þet muche sorhe? Nis þer bute sone forwarpe þet ruhe fel abute þe heorte, ant wið softe sahtnesse makien hire smeðe ant softe as is cundeliche wummone hude; for wið þet wuluene fel na þing þet ha deð nis Gode licwurðe.

2. Lo her aʒeines wreaððe monie remedies, frouren a muche floc ant misliche boten.

ʒef me misseið þe, þench þet tu art eorðe. Ne totret me eorðe? Ne bispit me eorðe? Þah me dude swa bi þe, me dude þe eorðe rihte. ʒef þu berkest aʒein, þu art hundes cunnes; ʒef þu stingest aʒein,[1] þu art neddre cundel, ant nawt Cristes spuse. Þench, dude he swa *qui tanquam ouis ad occisionem ductus est et non aperuit os suum*? Efter alle þe schendfule pinen þet he þolede o þe longe Friniht, me ledde him ine marhen to hongin o wearitreo, ant driuen þurh his fowr limen irnene neiles; ah na mare þen a schep, as þe Hali Writ seið, cwich ne cweð he neauer.

3. | Þench ʒet on oþer half: hwet is word bute wind? To wac ha is istrengðet þet a windes puf, a word, mei afellen ant warpen into sunne. Ant hwa nule þunche wunder of ancre windfeallet? On oðer half ʒetten: ne schaweð ha þet ha is dust ant unstable þing þe wið a lute wordes wind is anan toblawen? Þe ilke puf of his muð, ʒef þu hit wurpe under þe, hit schulde beore þe uppart toward te blisse of heouene. Ah nu is muche wunder of ure muchele meadschipe. Vnderstondeð þis word. Seint Andrew mahte þolien þet te hearde rode heue him toward heouene, ant luueliche biclupte hire. Sein Lorenz alswa þolede þet te gridil heue him uppardes wið bearninde gleden. Seinte Stefne [þolede] te stanes þet me s[t]ende him [wið] ant underueng ham gleadliche, ant bed for ham þe ham senden him wið hommen ifalden. Ant we ne mahe nawt þolien þet te wind of a word beore us towart heouene, ah beoð wode aʒeines ham þe we

M. 122

f. 33ᵛ

---

[1] After *aʒein*, all manuscripts running except AR have variations on the reading 'wið attri wordes'; R has 'doing a wers ded for a wiked ded'.

schulden þonkin, as þe ilke þe seruið us of muche seruise, þah hit beo hare unþonkes. *Impius uiuit pio, uelit nolit.* Al þet te unwreaste ant te uuele deð for uuel, al is þe gode to god, al is his biheue, ant timbrunge toward blisse. Let him—ant þet gleadliche—breide þi crune. Þench hu þe hali mon i *Vitas Patrum* custe ant blescede þe oþres hond þe hefde him ihearmet, ant seide se inwardliche, cussinde hire 3eorne, 'Iblescet beo eauer þeos hond, for ha haueð itimbret me þe blissen of heouene.' Ant tu segge alswa bi hond þe misdeð þe, ant bi þe muð alswa þe ewt misseið þe. 'Iblescet beo þi muð,' sei, 'for þu makest lome þrof to | timbri mi crune. Wel me is for mi god, ant wa þah for þin uuel; for þu dest me freame ant hearmest te seoluen.' 3ef ei mon oðer wummon misseide oðer misdude ow, mine leoue sustren, swa 3e schulden seggen. Ah nu is muche wunder, 3ef we wel bihaldeð, hu Godes halhen þoleden wunden on hare bodi, ant we beoð wode 3ef a wind blawe a lutel toward us—ant te wind ne wundeð nawt bute þe eir ane. For nowðer ne mei þe wind—þet is, þet word þet me seið—ne wundi þe i þi flesch ne fule þi sawle, þah hit puffe upo þe, bute þe seolf hit makie. *Bernardus: Quid irritaris, quid inflammaris ad uerbi flatum, qui nec carnem uulnerat nec inquinat mentem?* Wel þu maht under3eoten þet ter wes lute fur of chearite, þet leiteð al of ure Lauerdes luue; lute fur wes þer [þrof] þet a puf acwencte, for þear-as muche fur is, hit waxeð wið winde.

4. A3ein misdede oðer missahe, lo her on ende þe beste remedie, ant cunneð þis essample. A mon þe leie i prisun [ant] ahte muche rancun, ne o nane wise ne schulde ut, bute hit were to hongin, ear he hefde his rancun fulleliche ipaiet—nalde he cunne god þonc a mon þe duste uppon him of peonehes a bigurdel forte reimin him wið ant lesen him of pine? Þah he wurpe hit ful hearde a3eines his heorte, al þe hur[t] were for3eten for þe gleadnesse. O þis ilke wise, we beoð alle i prisun her, ant ahen Godd greate deattes of sunne. For-þi we 3ei3eð to him i þe Pater Noster, *Et dimitte nobis debita nostra.* 'Lauerd,' we seggeð, 'for3ef us ure deattes, alswa as we for3eoueð ure deatturs.' Woh þet me deð us, oðer of word oðer of werc, þet is ur[e] rancun | þet we schule reimin us wið, ant cwitin ure deattes toward ure Lauerd, þet beoð ure sunnen; for wiðute cwitance, up of þis prisun nis nan inumen þet nis anan ahonget, oðer i Purgatoire oþer i þe pine of helle. Ant ure Lauerd seolf seið, *Dimittite et dimittetur uobis,* 'For3ef ant Ich for3eoue þe', as þah he seide, 'þu art endeattet toward me swiðe wið sunnen, ah wult tu god foreward? Al þet eauer ei mon misseið þe oþer misdeð þe Ich wulle neomen

PART 3   51

115 onward þe deatte þe þu ahest me.' Nu þenne, þah a word culle þe ful
hearde upo þe breoste, ant, as þe þuncheð on earst, hurte þin heorte,
þench as þe prisun walde þe þe oðer hurte sare wið þe bigurdel, ant
underueng hit gleadliche forte acwiti þe wið, ant þonke þe þe hit sent
te—þah Godd ne cunne him neauer þonc of his sonde. He hearmeð
120 him ant freameð þe, ȝef þu hit const þolien; for as Dauið seið swiðe
wel wið alle, Godd deð in his tresor þe unwreaste ant te uuele, forte
hure wið ham, as me deð wið gersum, þeo þe wel fehteð, *ponens in
thesauris abyssos* (*Glosa: crudeles, quibus donat milites suos*).
   5. Eft upon oðer half, pellican þis fuhel haueð anoðer cunde, þet
125 hit is aa leane. For-þi, as Ich seide, Dauið eueneð him þer-to in ancre
persone (in ancre steuene): *Similis factus sum pellicano solitudinis*, 'Ich
am pellican ilich þe wuneð bi him ane.' Ant ancre ah þus to seggen,
ant beon ilich pellican onond þet hit is leane. *Iudith clausa in cubiculo
ieiunabat omnibus diebus uite sue, et cetera*. Iudith, bitund inne, as hit
130 teleð in hire boc, leadde swiðe heard lif, feaste ant werede here.
Iudith | bitund inne bitacneð bitund ancre, þe ah to leaden heard lif,
as dude þe leafdi Iudith, efter hire euene—nawt ase swin ipund i sti
to feattin ant to greatin aȝein þe cul of þe axe.
   6. Twa cunnes ancren beoð þet ure Lauerd spekeð of ant seið i þe
135 Godspel of false ant of treowe, *Vulpes foueas habent, et uolucres celi
nidos;* þet is, 'Foxes habbeð hare holen, ant briddes of heouene
habbeð hare nestes.' Þe foxes beoð false ancres, ase fox is beast
falsest. Þeose habbeð, he seið, holen þe holieð inward eorðe wið
eorðliche unþeawes, ant draheð into hare hole al þet ha mahen
140 reopen ant rinnen. Þus beoð gederinde ancres of Godd i þe Godspel
to uoxes ieuenet. Fox ec is a frech beast ant freotewil mid alle; ant te
false ancre draheð into hire hole ant fret, ase fox deð, baðe ges ant
hennen. Habbeð efter þe uox a simple semblant sumchearre, ant
beoð þah ful of gile. Makieð ham oþre þen ha beoð ase uox, þe is
145 ypocrite; weneð forte gili Godd as ha bidweolieð simple men, ant
gilið meast ham seoluen. Gealstrið as þe uox deð, ant ȝelpeð of hare
god hwer-se ha durren ant mahen. Chafflið of idel, ant se swiðe
worltliche iwurðeð þet on ende hare nome stinkeð as fox þer he geað
forð; for ȝef ha doð uuele, me seið bi ham wurse.
150 7. Þeos eoden into ancre-hus as dude Saul into hole, nawt as
Dauið þe gode. Ba ha wenden into hole, Saul ant Dauið, as hit teleð i
Regum,[2] ah Saul wende þider in forte don his fulðe þrin, as deð
(bimong monie) sum unseli ancre: went into hole of ancre-hus to

f. 35ʳ
M. 128

[2] After *Regum*, C has 'wende in him for to clensen'.

bifule þet stude, ant don dearnluker þrin fleschliche fulðen | þen ha mahte ʒef ha were amidde þe worlde. For hwa haueð mare eise to don hire cweadschipes þen þe false ancre? Þus wende Saul into hole to bidon þet stude. Ah Dauið wende þider in ane forte huden him from Saul, þet him heatede ant sohte to sleanne. Swa deð þe gode ancre þe Saul, þet is, þe feond, heateð ant hunteð efter. Ha deð hire in to huden hire from hise kene clokes; ha hud hire in hire hole ba from worltliche men ant worltliche sunnen, ant for-þi ha is gasteliche Dauið, þet is, 'strong' toʒein þe feond ant hire leor 'lufsum' to ure Lauerdes ehnen—for swa muchel seið þis word 'Dauið' on Ebreische ledene. Þe false ancre is Saul, efter þet his nome seið: *Saul: abutens siue abusio.* For 'Saul' on Ebreisch is 'misnotunge'on Englisch, ant te false ancre misnoteð ancre nome ant al þet ha wurcheð. Þe gode ancre is Iudith, as we ear seiden, þet is bitund as heo wes ant, alswa as heo dude, feasteð, wakeð, swinkeð, ant wereð hearde. Ha is of þe briddes þet ure Lauerd spekeð of efter þe uoxes, þe wið hare lustes ne holieð nawt duneward ase doð þe uoxes, þet beoð false ancres, ah habbeð on heh ase brid of heouene iset hare nestes, þet is, hare reste. Treowe ancres beoð briddes icleopede for ha leaueð þe eorðe, þet is, þe luue of alle worltliche þinges, ant þurh ʒirnunge of heorte to heouenliche þinges fleoð uppart toward heouene. Ant tah ha fleon hehe wið heh lif ant hali, haldeð þah þe heaued lah þurh milde eadmodnesse, as brid fleonninde buheð þet heaued. Leoteð al noht wurð þet ha wel wurcheð, ant seggeð, as ure Lauerd learde | alle hise: *Cum omnia bene feceritis, dicite, Serui inutiles sumus.* 'Hwen ʒe al habbeð wel idon,' he seið, ure Lauerd, 'seggeð þet ʒe beoð unnete þrealles—fleoð hehe, ant haldeð þah þet heaued eauer lahe.' Þe wengen þe uppard beoreð ham, þet beoð gode þeawes, þet ha moten sturien into gode werkes as brid hwen hit fleo wule stureð hise wengen. Þe treowe ancres ʒetten þe we to briddes eueneð (nawt we þah ah deð Godd), ha spreadeð hare wengen ant makieð creoiz of ham seolf as brid deð hwen hit flið: þet is, i þoht of heorte ant i bitternesse of flesch beoreð Godes rode.

8. Þeo briddes fleoð wel þe habbeð lutel flesch, as þe pellican haueð, ant feole fiðeren. Þe struc[io]n for his muchele flesch, ant oþre swucche fuheles, makieð a semblant to fleon ant beateð þe wengen, ah þe uet eauer draheð to þer eorðe. Alswa fleschlich ancre þe liueð i flesches lustes ant folheð hire eise, þe heuinesse of hire flesch ant flesches unþeawes bineomeð hire hire fluht, ant tah ha makie semblant ant muche nurð wið wengen (**oþres, nawt hiren**),

PART 3

þet is, leote of as þah ha fluhe ant were an hali ancre, hwa-se ȝeorne
195 bihalt lahheð hire to bismere, for hire uet eauer, as doð þe struc[io]ns
(þet beoð hire lustes), draheð to þer eorðe. þeos ne beoð nawt ili[ch]
þe leane fuhel, pellican, ne ne fleoð nawt on heh, ah beoð eorð-
briddes ant nisteð on eorðe. Ah Godd cleopeð þe gode ancres briddes
of heouene, as Ich ear seide: *Vulpes foueas habent, et uolucres celi nidos,*
200 'Foxes habbeð hare holen, ant briddes of heouene habbeð hare
nestes.' Treowe ancres beoð ariht briddes of heouene, þe fleoð on
heh ant sitteð singinde murie o þe grene bohes (þet is, þencheð
uppart of þe | blisse of heouene, þe neauer ne faleweð ah is aa grene), f. 36ᵛ
ant sitteð o þis grene singinde murie (þet is, resteð ham i þulli þoht
205 ant, ase þeo þe singeð, habbeð murhðe of heorte). Brid tah oðerhwile
forte sechen his mete for þe flesches neode lihteð to þer eorðe. Ah
hwil hit sit on eorðe hit nis neauer siker, ah biwent him ofte ant
bilokeð him aa ȝeornliche abuten. Alswa þe gode ancre, ne fleo ha
neauer se hehe, ha mot lihten oðerhwiles dun to þer eorðe of hire
210 bodi, eoten, drinken, slepen, wurchen, speoken, heren of þet hire
neodeð to of eorðliche þinges. Ah þenne, as þe brid deð, ha mot wel
biseon hire, bilokin hire on euch half þet ha nohwer ne misneome, M. 134
leste ha beo icaht þurh sum of þe deofles grunen, oðer ihurt summes
weis þe hwil ha sit se lahe.
215 9. 'þeos briddes habbeð nestes', he seið, ure Lauerd, *volucres celi
nidos*. Nest is heard utewið of prikinde þornes, inwið nesche ant
softe. Swa schal ancre utewið þolien heard on hire flesch ant
prikiende pinen. Swa wisliche þah ha schal swenche þet flesch þet
ha mahe seggen wið þe Psalmwruhte, *Fortitudinem meam ad te
220 custodiam*, þet is, 'Ich chulle wite mi strengðe, Lauerd, to þine
bihoue.' For-þi beo flesches pine efter euchanes euene. Þet nest beo
heard wiðuten, ant softe ant swete þe heorte wiðinnen. Þeo þe beoð
of bitter oðer of heard heorte ant nesche to hare flesch, ha makieð
frommard hare nest, softe wiðuten ant þorni wiðinnen. Þis beoð þe
225 weamode ant te estfule ancres, bittre wiðinnen as þet swete schulde
beon, ant estfule wiðuten as þet hearde schulde beon. Þeos i þulli
nest mahen habben uuel rest hwen ha ham wel biþencheð; for leate
ha | schulen bringe forþ briddes of swuch nest, þet beoð gode werkes f. 37ʳ
þe fleon toward heouene. Iob cleopeð nest þe ancre-hus, ant seið as
230 he were ancre, *In nidulo meo moriar*, þet is, 'Ich chulle deien i mi
nest, beon ase dead þrin (for þet is ancres rihte), ant wunien aðet
deað þrin, þet Ich nulle neauer slakien, hwil þe sawle is i þe buc, to
drehen heard wiðuten, alswa as nest is, ant softe beo wiðinnen.'

10. Of dumbe beastes leorne wisdom ant lare. þe earn deð in his nest a deorewurðe ʒimstan, achate hatte, for nan attri þing ne mei þe stan nahhin, ne hwil he is i þe nest hearmin his briddes. Þis deorewurðe stan, þet is Iesu Crist, ase stan treowe ant ful of alle mihtes, ouer alle ʒimstanes; he is þe achate þet atter of sunne ne nahhede neauer. Do him i þi nest, þet is, i þin heorte; þench hwuch pine he þolede on his flesch wiðuten, hu swote he wes iheortet, hu softe wiðinnen, ant swa þu schalt driuen ut euch atter of þin heorte ant bitternesse of þi bodi. For i þulli þoht, ne beo hit neauer se bitter, pine þet tu þolie for þe luue of him þe droh mare for þe schal þunche þe swote. Þes stan, as Ich seide, afleieð attrie þinges. Habbe þu þes stan inwið þi breoste, þer Godes nest is, ne þearf þu noht dreden þe attri neddre of helle. Þine briddes, þet beoð þine gode werkes, beoð al sker of his atter.

11. Hwa-se ne mei þes ʒimstan habben ne halden i þe nest of hire heorte, lanhure i þe nest of hire ancre-hus habbe his iliche, þet is, þe crucifix. Bihalde ofte þron, ant cusse þe wunde studen i swote munegunge of þe soðe wunden þe he o þe soðe rode þuldeliche þolede. Se uorð se ha mei, beo Iudith: þet is, libben hearde, beon icnawen ofte to Godd his muchele godlec toward hire ant | hire fawtes toward him, þet ha him ʒelt hit uuele, crie him ʒeorne þrof mearci ant are, ant schriue hire ilome. Þenne is ha Iudith, þe sloh Oloferne, for 'Iudith' on Ebreisch is 'schrift' on Englisch, þet sleað gasteliche þen deouel of helle. *Iudith: confessio.* For-þi seið ancre to euch preost *Confiteor* on alre earst ant schriueð hire ofte, forte beo Iudith ant slean Oloferne, þet is, þe deofles strengðe; for ase muchel seið þis nome 'Oloferne' as 'stinkinde in helle.' *Secundum nominis ethimologiam: Olofernus, olens in inferno. Secundum interpretationem: infirmans uitulum saginatum.* On Ebreische ledene, 'Oloferne' is þe feond, þe makeð feble ant unstrong feat kealf ant to wilde—þet is, þet flesch, þe awildgeð sone se hit eauer featteð þurh eise ant þurh este. *Incrassatus est dilectus, et recalcitrauit*: 'Mi leof is ifeatte[d],' he seið, ure Lauerd, 'ant smit me wið his hele.' Sone se flesch haueð his wil, hit regibeð anan, ase feat meare ant idel. Þis featte kealf haueð þe feond strengðe to unstrengen ant buhen toward sunne; for swa muche seið þis nome 'Oloferne.' Ah ancre schal beo Iudith þurh heard lif ant þurh soð schrift, ant slean, as dude Iudith, þes uuele Oloferne. Temie ful wel hire flesch, sone se ha ifeleð þet hit awilgeð to swiðe, mid feasten, mid wecchen, wið here, wið [heui] swinc, wið hearde disceplines—wisliche þah ant wearliche. *Habete*, inquit, *sal in*

uobis. Item: In omni sacrifitio offeretis michi sal, þet is, 'In euch
sacrefise', he seið, ure Lauerd, 'offrið me salt eauer.' Veaste, wecche,
ant oþre swucche as Ich nempnede nu, beoð 'mi sacrefises.' Salt
bitacneð wisdom, for salt ȝeueð mete smech, ant wisdom ȝeueð sauur
al þet we wel wurcheð. Wiðute salt of wisdom, | þuncheð Godd
smechles alle ure deden. On oþer half, wiðute salt flesch gedereð
wurmes, stinkeð swiðe fule ant forroteð sone. Alswa wiðute wisdom
flesch as wurm forfret hire ant wasteð hire seoluen, forfeareð as þing
þe forroteð, ant sleað hire on ende. Ah þulli sacrefise stinkeð [to] ure
Lauerd.

12. Þah þe flesch beo ure fa, hit is us ihaten þet we halden hit up.
Wa we moten don hit, as hit is wel ofte wurðe, ah nawt fordon mid
alle; for hu wac se hit eauer beo, þenne is hit swa icuplet ant se feste
ifeiet to ure deorewurðe gast, Godes ahne furme, þet we mahten sone
slean þet an wið þet oþer. *Augustinus: Natura mentis humane que ad
ymaginem Dei creata est et sine peccato est solus Deus maior est*. Ant tis is
an of þe measte wundres on eorðe, þet te heste þing under Godd, þet
is monnes sawle as Seint Austin witneð, schal beo se feste ifeiet to
flesch, þet nis bute fen ant a ful eorðe, ant þurh þet ilke limunge
luuien hit se swiðe þet ha, forte cwemen hit in his fule cunde, geað ut
of hire hehe heouenliche cunde, ant forte paien hire wreaðeð hire
Schuppere, þe scheop hire efter him seolf, þet is king ant keiser of
eorðe ant of heouene. Wunder ouer wunder, ant hokerlich wunder,
þet se unimete lah þing—*fere nichil*, 'for-neh nawt', seið Seint
Austin—schal drahen into sunne se unimete heh þing ase sawle is,
þet Seint Awstin cleopeð *fere summum*, þet is, 'for-neh hest þing'
wiðute Godd [ane]. Ah Godd nalde nawt þet ha lupe i prude, ne
wilnede to climben ant feolle as dude Lucifer for he wes bute charge;
ant teide for-þi a clot of heui eorðe to hire, as me deð þe cubbel to þe
ku oþer to þe oþer | beast þet is to recchinde ant renginde abuten.
Þis is þet Iob seide: *Qui fecisti uentis—id est, spiritibus—pondus*.
'Lauerd,' he seið, 'þu hauest imaket foðer to feðerin wið þe sawlen',
þet is, þet heuie flesch þet draheð hire duneward. Ah þurh þe
hehschipe of hire hit schal wurðe ful liht, lihtre þen þe wind is ant
brihtre þen þe sunne, ȝef hit folheð hire her, ne ne draheð hire to
swiðe into hire lahe cunde. Leoue sustren, for his luue þet ha is ilich
to, beoreð hire menske; ne leote ȝe nawt þe lahe flesch meistrin hire
to swiðe. Ha is her in uncuððe, iput in a prisun, bitund in a cwalm-
hus, ne nis nawt edscene of hwuch dignete ha is, hu heh is hire
cunde, ne hwuch ha schal þunche ȝet in hire ahne riche. Þet flesch is

her ed hame, as eorðe þe is in eorðe, ant is for-þi cointe ant couer, as me seið þet 'curre is kene on his ahne mixne.' Ha haueð to muche meistrie—weilawei!—o monie. Ah ancre, as Ich habbe iseid, ah to beon al gastelich ȝef ha wule wel fleon, as brid þet haueð lutel flesch ant feole fiðeren. Nawt ane ȝet tis, ah teke þet ha temeð wel hire fulitohe flesch, ant strengeð ant deð menske þe wurðfule sawle—teke þis, ha mot ȝet, þurh hire forbisne ant þurh hire hali beoden, ȝeouen strengðe oþre, ant uphalden ham þet ha ne fallen i þe dunge of sunne. Ant for-þi Dauið, anan efter þet he haueð ieuenet ancre to pellican, he eueneð hire to niht-fuhel þe is under euesunges. *Similis factus sum pellicano solitudinis; factus sum sicut nicticorax in domicilio.*

13. Þe niht-fuhel i þe euesunges bitacneð recluses, þe wunieð for-þi under chirche euesunges þet ha understonden þet ha ahen to beon of se hali lif þet al Hali | Chirche—þet is, Cristene folc—leonie ant wreoðie upon ham, ant heo halden hire up wið hare lif-halinesse ant hare eadie bonen. For-þi is ancre 'ancre' icleopet, ant under chirche iancret as ancre under schipes bord forte halden þet schip, þet uþen ant stormes hit ne ouerwarpen. Alswa al Hali Chirche (þet is schip icleopet) schal ancrin o þe ancre, þet heo hit swa halde þet te deofles puffes, þet beoð temptatiuns, ne hit ouerwarpen. Euch ancre haueð þis o foreward, ba þurh nome of 'ancre' ant þurh þet ha wuneð under þe chirche, [as] to understiprin hire ȝef ha walde fallen. Ȝef ha brekeð foreward, loki hwam ha lihe, ant hu continuelement—for ha ne stu[t]eð neauer: ancre wununge ant hire nome ȝeieð eauer þis foreward ȝet hwen ha slepeð.

14. On oðer half, þe niht-fuhel flið bi niht ant biȝet i þeosternesse his fode. Alswa schal ancre fleon wið contemplatiun (þet is, wið heh þoht) ant wið hali bonen bi niht toward heouene, ant biȝeote bi niht hire sawle fode. Bi niht ah ancre to beon waker, ant bisiliche abuten gastelich biȝete. For-þi kimeð anan þrefter, *Vigilaui, et factus sum sicut passer solitarius in tecto.* 'Ich wes waker', seið Dauið in ancre persone, 'ant ilich spearewe under rof ane.' *Vigilaui,* 'Ich wes waker', for þet is ancre rihte, muchel forte wakien. Ecclesiasticus: *Vigilia honestatis tabefatiet carnes.* Na þing ne awealdeð wilde flesch, ne ne makeð hit tomre, þen muche wecche. Wecche is in Hali Writ i feole studen ipreiset. *Vigilate et orate ne intretis in temptationem.* 'Alswa as ȝe nulleð nawt fallen into fondunge,' he seið, ure Lauerd, 'wakieð ant ibiddeð ow'; þet schal don ow stonden. Eft he seið, *Beatus quem inuenerit uigilantem,* 'Eadi is þe ilke þet, hwen ure Lauerd kimeð, ifint wakiende'. Ant he him | seolf sumchearre *pernoctauit in oratione,*

PART 3

'wakede i beoden al niht', ant swa he tahte us wecche, nawt ane wið
355 his lare, ah dude wið his dede. Eahte þinges nomeliche leaðieð us to
wakien eauer i sum god ant beo wurchinde: (i) þis scheorte lif; (ii)
þis stronge wei; (iii) vre god, þet is se þunne; (iiii) vre sunnen, þe
beoð se monie; (v) deað, þet we beoð siker of, ant unsiker hwenne;
(vi) þet sterke dom of Domesdei, ant se nearow mid alle, þet euch
360 idel word bið þer ibroht forð, ant idele þohtes þe neren ear her
ibette. *Dominus in Euuangelio: De omni uerbo otioso, et cetera. Item: Et capilli de capite non peribunt, id est, cogitatio non euadet inpunita. Anselmus: Quid faties in illa die quando exigetur a te omne tempus impensum qualiter sit a te expensum, et usque ad minimam cogitationem?* Loke nu hwet beo of unwreaste willes
365 ant sunfule werkes. (vii) ʒet þe seoueðe þing þe munegeð us to
wakien, þet is þe sorhe of helle. þer bihald þreo þing: þe untaleliche
pinen, þe echnesse of euchan, þe unimete bitternesse. (viii) þe
eahtuðe þing: hu muchel is þe mede i þe blisse of heouene, world
buten ende. Hwa-se wakeð her wel ane hondhwile, hwa-se haueð
370 þeos eahte þing ofte in hire heorte, ha wule schaken of hire slep of
uuel slawðe. I þe stille niht, hwen me ne sið nawiht, **nowðer ne ne
hereð**, þet lette þe bone, þe heorte is ofte se schir; for na þing nis
witnesse of þing þet me þenne deð, bute Godes engel þe is i swuch M. 146
time bisiliche abuten to eggin us to gode, for þer nis nawt forloren as
375 is bi dei ofte. Hercnið nu, leoue sustren, hu hit is uuel to uppin, ant
hu god þing hit is to heolen goddede, ant fleo bi niht as niht-fuhel,
ant gederin bi þeostre—þet is, i priuite ant dearnliche—sawle fode.

15. *Oratio Hester | placuit regi Assuero*: þet is, Hesteres bone þe f. 40ʳ
cwen wes þe king Assuer licwurðe ant icweme. 'Hester' on Ebreisch,
380 þet is 'ihud' on Englisch, ant is to understonden þet bone ant oðer
goddede þet is idon on hudles is Assuer icweme, þet is, þe King of
heouene; for 'Assuer' on Ebreisch is 'eadi' on Englisch, þet is, ure
Lauerd þe is eadi ouer alle. Dauið spekeð to ancre þe wes iwunet in
hudles wel forte wurchen ant seoððen o sum wise uppeð hit ant
385 schaweð: *Vt quid auertis manum tuam, et dexteram tuam, de medio sinu tuo in finem?*—þet is, 'Hwi drahest tu ut þin hond, ant ʒet ti riht
hond, of midde þi bosum *in finem,* on ende?' Riht hond is god werc,
bosum is priuite; ant is as þah he seide, 'Þe riht hond þet tu heolde,
ancre, i þi bosum (þet is, þi gode werc þet tu hefdest idon priuement
390 as þing is dearne i bosum), hwi drahest tu hit ut *in finem,* on ende
(þet is, þet ti mede endi se sone, þi mede þet were endeles ʒef þi
goddede ihole were)? Hwi openest tu hit ant nimest se scheort mede,
hure þet is agan in an hondhwile?' *Amen, dico uobis, receperunt*

mercedem suam. 'Þu hauest iuppet þi god', he seið, ure Lauerd; 'witerliche þu hauest underuo þi mede.' Sein Gregoire awundreð him, ant seið þet men beoð wode þe trochið swa uuele: *Magna [uecordia] est grandia agere et laudibus inhiare; vnde celum mereri potest, nummum transitorii fauoris querit.* 'Muchel meadschipe hit is', he seið, 'don wel ant wilni word þrof, don hwer-þurh he buð þe kinedom of heouene ant sullen hit for a windes puf of wor[l]des hereword, of monnes herunge.' For-þi, mine leoue sustren, haldeð ower riht hond inwið ower bosum, leste mede endeles neome scheort ende. We redeð in Hali Writ þet Moyseses hond, Godes prophete, sone se he hefde idrahen hire ut of his | bosum, bisemde o þe spitel-uuel ant þuhte lepruse, þurh hwet is bitacnet þet goddede idrahe forð nis nawt ane forloren þurh þet uppinge, ah þuncheð ȝet eatelich biuore Godes ehe, as spitel-uuel is eatelich biuore monnes sihðe. Lo, a feorli god word þet te hali Iob seið: *Reposita est hec spes mea in sinu meo.* 'I mi bosum', he seið, 'is al min hope ihalden', as þah he seide, 'Hwet god se Ich do, were hit ut of bosum iuppet ant idrahe forð, al mine hope were edslopen. Ah for-þi þet Ich hit heole ant hude as i bosum, Ich hopie to mede.' For-þi ȝef ei deð eani god, ne drahe ha hit nawt utward ne ȝelpe nawiht þrof, for wið a lutel puf, wið a wordes wind, hit mei beon al toweauet.

16. Vre Lauerd i Iohel meaneð him swiðe of þeo þe forleoseð ant spilleð al hare god þurh wilnunge of hereword, ant seið þeos wordes: *Decorticauit ficum meam; nudans spoliauit eam et proiecit. Albi facti sunt rami eius.* 'Allas,' seið ure Lauerd, 'þeos þe schaweð hire god haueð bipilet mi fier, irend al þe rinde of, despuilet hire steort-naket ant iwarpen awei, ant te grene bohes beoð fordruhede ant forwurðen to drue hwite rondes.' Þis word is dosc, ah neomeð nu ȝeme hu Ich hit wulle brihtin. Fier is a cunnes treo þe bereð swete frut þet me cleopeð figes. Þenne is þe fier bipilet ant te rinde irend of hwen goddede is iuppet. Þenne is þe lif ut, þenne adeadeð þe treo, hwen þe rinde is awei; n[e] nowðer ne bereð hit frut ne [hit ne] greneð þrefter i lufsume leaues, ah druhieð þe bohes ant wurðeð hwite rondes, to na þing betere þen to fures fode. Þe boh hwen hit adeadeð, hit hwiteð utewið ant adruheð inwið, ant warpeð his rinde. Alswa goddede þe wule adeadin forwarpeð his rinde—þet is, unhuleð him. Þe rinde þe wrið | hit is þe treoes warde, ant wit hit i strengðe ant i cwicnesse. Alswa þe hulunge is þe goddedes lif ant halt hit i strengðe; ah hwen [þis] rinde is offe, þenne, as þe boh deð, hwiteð hit utewið þurh worltlich hereword, ant adruheð inwið ant

leoseð þe [wetnesse] of Godes grace, þe makede hit grene ant
435 licwurðe Godd to bihalden—for grene ouer alle heowes froureð
meast ehnen. Hwen hit is swa adruhet, þenne nis hit to nawt se god
as to þe fur of helle; for þe earste bipilunge, hwer-of al þis uuel is,
nis bute of prude. Ant nis þis muche reowðe þet te fier þe schulde
wið hire swete frut (þet is, goddede) fede Godd gasteliche, þe
440 Lauerd of heouene, schal adruhien rindeles þurh þet hit is unhulet,
ant wurðen buten ende helle fures fode? Ant nis ha to unseli þe wið
þe wurð of heouene buð hire helle? Vre Lauerd i þe Godspel seolf
eueneð heoueriche to gold-hord, þe hwa-se hit fint, as he seið, hudeð
hit: *Quem qui inuenit homo abscondit.* Golt-hord is goddede, þe is to
445 heouene ieuenet for me hit buð þer-wið; ant þis golt-hord, bute hit
beo þe betere ihud ant iholen, hit is forlore sone, for as Sein Gregoire
seið, *Depredari desiderat qui thesaurum puplice portat in uia*: þe bereð
tresor openliche i wei þet is al ful of reaueres ant of þeoues, him luste
leosen hit ant beon irobbet. Þis world nis bute a wei to heouene oðer
450 to helle, ant is al biset of hellene mucheres, þe robbið alle þe golt-
hordes þet ha mahen underȝeoten þet mon oðer wummon i þis wei   M. 152
openeð; for ase muchel wurð is as hwa-se seide, ant ȝeide as he eode,
'Ich beore golt-hord! Ich beore golt-hord! Lowr hit her—read gold,
hwit seoluer inoh, ant deorewurðe stanes!' A sapere þe ne bereð bute
455 sape ant nelden ȝeiȝeð hehe þet he bereð; a riche mercer geað forð al
stille. | Freinið hwet itidde of Ezechie, þe gode king, for-þi þet he   f. 41ᵛ
schawde þe celles of his aromaz, his muchele [tresor], his deorewurðe
[þinges]. Nis hit nawt for nawt iwriten i þe hali Godspel of þe þreo
kinges þe comen to offrin Iesu Crist þe deore þreo lakes, *Procidentes
460 adorauerunt eum, et apertis thesauris suis obtulerunt, et cetera*. Þet tet ha
walden offrin him, ha heolden eauer ihud aðet ha comen biuoren
him; þa earst ha unduden þe presenz þet ha beren. For-þi, mine
leoue sustren, bi niht, as þe niht-fuhel þet ancre is to ieuenet, beoð
ȝeorne sturiende. 'Niht' Ich cleopie priuite. Þis 'niht' ȝe mahen
465 habben euch time of þe dei, þet al þe god þet ȝe eauer doð beo idon
as bi niht ant bi þeosternesse, ut of monnes ehe, ut of monnes eare.
Þus i niht beoð fleonninde, ant sechinde ower sawle heouenliche
fode. Þenne ne beo ȝe nawt ane *pellicanus solitudinis*, ah beoð ec
nicticorax in domicilio.

470   17. *Vigilaui, et factus sum sicut passer solitarius in tecto*. Ȝet is ancre
ieuenet her to spearewe, þet is ane under rof as ancre. Spearewe is a
chiterinde brid; chitereð aa ant chirmeð. Ah for-þi þet moni ancre
haueð þet ilke unþeaw, Dauið ne eueneð hire nawt to spearewe þe

haueð fere, ah deð to spearewe ane. *Sicut passer solitarius*: 'Ich am', he seið bi ancre, 'as spearewe þet is ane', for swa ah ancre hire ane, in anlich stude as ha is, chirmin ant chiterin eauer hire bonen. Ant understondeð leofliche, mine leoue sustren, þet Ich write of anlich lif forte frourin ancren, ant ow ouer alle.

18. Hu god is to beon ane is ba i þe Alde Lahe ant i þe Neowe isutelet; for i baðe me ifint þet Godd his dearne runes ant heouenliche priuitez schawde his leoueste freond nawt i monne floc, ah dude þer ha weren ane bi ham seoluen. Ant heo ham seolf alswa, as ofte as ha walden þenchen schirliche of Godd ant makien cleane bonen, ant beon in heorte gasteliche ihehet toward heouene, aa me ifint þet ha fluhen monne sturbunge, ant wenden bi ham ane; ant þer Godd edeawde ham ant schawde him seolf to ham, ant ȝef ham hare bonen. For-þi þet Ich seide þet me ifint tis ba i þe Alde Testament ant ec i þe Neowe, Ich chulle of ba twa schawin forbisne.

19. *Egressus est Ysaac in agrum ad meditandum, quod ei fuisse creditur consuetudinarium.* Ysaac þe patriarche, forte þenche deopliche, sohte anlich stude ant wende bi him ane, as Genesys teleð; ant swa he imette wið þe eadi Rebecca, þet is, wið Godes grace. *Rebecca enim interpretatur multum dedit, et*

Quicquid habe[s] meriti, preuentrix gratia donat.

Alswa þe eadi Iacob, þa ure Lauerd schawde him his deorewurðe nebscheft ant ȝef him his blesceunge, ant wende his nome betere, he wes iflohe men ant wes him al ane—neauer-ȝete i monne floc ne cahte he swuch biȝete. Bi Moysen ant bi Helye, Godes deorewurðe freond, is sutel ant edscene hwuch baret ant hu dredful lif is eauer imong þrung, ant hu Godd his priuitez schaweð to þeo þe beoð priuement ham ane. Me schal, leoue sustren, þeose estoires tellen ow, for ha weren to longe to writen ham here; ant þenne schule ȝe al þis brihte understonden. *Set et Ieremias solus sedet.* Þe eadi Ieremie seið he sit ane, ant seið þe reisun for-hwi: *Quia comminatione tua replesti me*, vre Lauerd hefde ifullet him of his þreatunge. Godes þreatunge is wontreaðe ant weane i licome ant i sawle worlt buten ende. Þe were of þis þreatunge as he wes wel ifullet, nere þer nan empti stude i þe heorte to underfon fleschliche lahtren. For-þi he bed wealle of teares [to his ehnen]—*Quis dabit michi fontem lacrimarum?*—þet ha ne adruhede neauer, na mare þen wealle, forte biwepe slei folc (þet is, meast al þe world, þet is gasteliche islein mid deadliche sunnen), *Vt [lugeam] interfectos populi mei.* Ant to þis wop, lokið nu, he bit anlich stude (*Quis michi dabit diuersorium uiatorum in solitudine, ut, et cetera*), þe

PART 3

hali prophete, forte schawi witerliche þet hwa-se wule biwepen hire
515 ahne ant oþres sunnen, as ancre ah to donne, ant hwa-se wule ifinden
ed te nearewe Domesmon mearci ant are, a þing þet let him meast is
beowiste (þet is, wununge) bimong men, ant þet swiðest furðreð
hit, þet is anlich stude mon oþer wummon eiðer to beon ane. Ʒet
spekeð Ieremie of anlich [lif] mare: *Sedebit solitarius et tacebit.* 'Me
520 schal sitten', he seið, 'him ane ant beo stille.' Of þis stilnesse he
spekeð þer-biuoren lutel: *Bonum est prestolari cum silentio salutare dei; beatus qui portauerit iugum Domini ab adholescencia sua.* 'God
hit is i silence ikepen Godes grace, ant þet me beore Godes ʒeoc anan
from his ʒuheðe.' Ant þenne kimeð þrefter,[3] *Sedebit solitarius et*
525 *tacebit, quia leuabit se supra se*: hwa-se swa wule don, ha schal sitten
ane ant halden hire stille, ant swa heouen hire seolf buuen hire
seoluen—þet is, wið heh lif hehi toward heouene ouer hire cunde.
Teke þis, hwet oðer god cume of þis anliche sittunge þet Ieremie
spekeð of, ant of þis seli stilðe, kimeð anan efter: *Dabit percuscienti se*
530 *maxillam, et saturabitur obprobriis.* Ha wule, he seið, þe swa liueð
'aʒeines þe smitere beode forð þe cheke, ant beo þurhfullet wið
schentfule wordes'. Her beoð i þeos word twa eadi þeawes to noti   M. 158
swiðe ʒeorne þe limpeð ariht to ancre: þolemodnesse i þe earre half, i
þe leatere eadmodnesse of milde ant meoke heorte. For þolemod is
535 þe þuldeliche abereð woh þet me him deð; eadmod is þe þolie mei
þet | me him missegge. þeos þe Ich habbe inempnet her weren of þe   f. 43ʳ
Alde Testament; cume we nu to þe Neowe.

20. Sein Iuhan Baptiste, bi hwam ure Lauerd seide *Inter natos mulierum non surrexit maior Iohanne Baptista*, þet bimong wiues sunen ne
540 aras neauer herre, he kenneð us openliche bi his ahne dede þet anlich
stude is baðe, ant siker ant biheue. For þah þe engel Gabriel hefde
his burde ibocket, al were he ifullet of þe Hali Gast anan inwið his
moder wombe, al were he þurh miracle of bere[n]get iboren, ant in
his iborenesse unspende his feader tunge into prophecie, for al þis ne
545 durste he ʒet wunie bimong men, se dredful lif he seh þrin, þah hit
nere of nawt elles bute of speche ane. Ant for-þi hwet dude he? Ʒung
of ʒeres, fleh awei into wildernesse, leste wið speche sulde his
cleane lif. For swa is in his ymne:

Antra deserti teneris sub annis
550 *Ciuium turmas fugiens petisti,*
 Ne leui saltem maculare uitam
 Famine posses.

---

[3] After *þrefter*, C has 'þet Ich ear seide', S 'les moz deuant diz'.

He hefde, as hit þuncheð, iherd Ysaie, þe meande him ant seide, *Ve michi, quia homo pollutis labiis ego sum.* 'Wumme, wa is me,' he seið, þe hali prophete, 'for Ich am a mon of sulede lippen', ant seið þe acheisun hwer-uore: *Quia in medio populi polluta labia habentis ego habito.* 'Ant þet is for-þi', he seið, 'þet Ich wunie bimong men þe suleð hare lippen mid misliche spechen.' Lo hu Godes prophete seið he wes isulet þurh beowiste bimong monne. Swa hit is sikerliche: beo neauer se briht or (metal: gold, seoluer, irn, stel) þet hit ne schal drahe rust of anoþer þet is irustet, for-hwon þet ha longe liggen togedere. For-þi fleh Sein Iuhan þe feolahschipe of fule men, leste he were ifulet. Ah ȝet forte schawin us þet me ne mei þe uuele fleon bute me fleo þe gode, he fleh his hali cun, icoren of ure Lauerd, ant wende into anli stude ant wunede i þe wildernesse. Ant hwet biȝet he þer? He biȝet þet | he wes Godes baptiste. O, þe muchele hehnesse, þet he heold i fulluht under hise honden þe Lauerd of heouene, þe halt up al þe world wið his anes mihte. þer þe Hali Trinite ('**þrumnesse**' **on Englisch**) schawde hire al to him: þe Feader in his steuene, þe Hali Gast i culure heow, þe Sune in his honden. In anlich lif he biȝet þreo preminences: priuilegie of preachur, merite of martirdom, meidenes mede. þeos þreo manere men habbeð in heouene, wið ouerfullet mede, crune upo crune. Ant te eadi Iuhan, in anlich stude as he wes, alle þeose þreo estaȝ ofearnede him ane.

21. Vre leoue Leafdi, ne leadde ha anlich lif? Ne fond te engel hire in anli stude al ane? Nes ha nohwer ute, ah wes biloken feste. For swa we ifindeð: *Ingressus angelus ad eam dixit, Aue Maria, gratia plena, Dominus tecum, benedicta tu in mulieribus;* þet is, 'þe engel wende in to hire.' þenne wes heo inne in anli stude hire ane. Engel to mon i þrung ne eadewede neauer ofte. On oðer half, þurh þet nohwer in Hali Writ nis iwriten of hire speche bute fowr siðen, as is iseid þruppe, sutel prufunge hit is þet ha wes muchel ane þe heold swa silence.

22. Hwet seche Ich oþer? Of Godd ane were inoh forbisne to alle, þe wende him seolf into anli stude ant feaste þer-as he wes ane i wildernesse, forte schawin þer-bi þet bimong monne þrung ne mei nan makien riht penitence. þer in anli stude him hungrede, hit seið, ancre to froure þet is meoseise. þer he þolede þet te feond fondede him feole weis, ah he ouercom him, alswa forte schawin þet te feond fondeð muchel þeo þe leadeð anlich lif, for onde þet he haueð to ham, ah he is þer ouercumen; for ure Lauerd scolf þer stont | bi ham i fehte, ant bealdeð ham hu ha schulen stonden strongliche aȝein, ant

PART 3

ʒeueð ham of his strengðe. He, as Hali Writ seið, þet na nurð ne
þrung of folc ne mahte letten him of his beoden ne desturbin his god,
595 he þah noðeleatere, hwen he walde beon i beoden, he fleh nawt ane
oþre men, ah dude ʒet his halie deorewurðe apostles, ant wende ane
up on hulles, us to forbisne þet we schule turne bi us seolf ant
climben wið him on hulles: þet is, þenchen hehe ant leauen lahe
under us alle eorðliche þohtes hwiles we beoð i bonen. Pawel ant
600 Antonie, Hylariu[n] ant Benedict, Sincletice ant Sara, ant oþre
swucche monie, men ant wummen baðe, fondeden witerliche ant
underʒeten soðliche þe biʒete of anlich lif, as þeo þe duden wið
Godd al þet ha walden. Sein Ierome nu leate seið bi him seoluen,
Quotiens inter homines fui, min[us] homo recessi: 'As ofte as Ich eauer
605 wes', he seið, 'bimong men, Ich wende from ham leasse mon þen Ich
ear wes.' For-þi seið þe wise Ecclesiasticus, *Ne oblecteris in turbis,
assidua est enim commissio:* þet is, 'Ne þunche þe neauer god imong
monne floc, for þer is eauer sunne.' Ne seide þe steuene to Arsenie of
heouene, *Arseni, fuge homines et saluaberis,* 'Arseni, flih men ant tu
610 schalt beon iborhen'? Ant eft hit com ant seide, *Arseni, fuge, tace,
quiesce:* þet is, 'Arseni, flih, beo stille, ant wune studeuestliche i sum
stude ut of monne [floc].'

23. Nv ʒe habbeð iherd, mine leoue sustren, forbisne of þe Alde
Lahe ant ek of þe Neowe, hwi ʒe ahen anlich lif swiðe to luuien.
615 Efter þe forbisnes, hereð nu reisuns hwi me ah to fleo þe world, M. 164
eahte ed te leaste. Ich ham segge scheortliche; neomeð þe betere
ʒeme.

24. Þe forme is sikernesse. Ʒef a wod liun urne ʒont te strete,
nalde þe wise bitunen hire sone? Ant | Seinte Peter seið þet helle liun f. 44ᵛ
620 rengeð ant reccheð eauer abuten forte sechen inʒong sawle to
forswolhen, ant bid us beo wakere ant bisie in hali beoden leste he
us lecche. *Sobrii estote et uigilate in orationibus, quia aduersarius uester
diabolus, tanquam leo rugiens, circuit querens quem deuoret*—þis is
Seinte Petres word, þet Ich ear seide. For-þi beoð ancren wise þe
625 habbeð wel bitund ham aʒein helle liun forte beo þe sikerure.

25. Þe oþer reisun is: þe bere a deore licur, a deorewurðe wet as
basme is, in a feble uetles, healewi i bruchel gles, nalde ha gan ut of
þrung bute ha fol were? *Habemus thesaurum istum in uasis fictilibus, dicit
Apostolus.* Þis bruchele uetles, þet is wummone flesch, þah noðeleatere
630 þe basme, þe healewi is meidenhad þet is þrin, oðer, eft[er] meiðlure,
chaste cleannesse. Þis bruchele uetles bruchel [is] as is eani gles, for
beo hit eanes tobroken, ibet ne bið hit neauer, ne hal as hit wes ear,

na mare þene gles. Ah 3et hit brekeð mid leasse þen bruchel gles do, for gles ne tobrekeð nawt bute sum þing hit rine, ant hit onont meiðlure mei leosen his halnesse wið a stinkinde wil, swa uorð hit mei gan ant leaste se longe. Ah þis manere bruche mei beon ibet eft, ase hal allunge as hit wes eauer halest, þurh medecine of schrift ant bireowsunge. Nu þe preoue her-of. Sein Iuhan Euuangeliste, nefde he brud ibroht ham? Nefde he iþoht þa, 3ef Godd nefde ilet him, meiðhad to forleosen? Seoððen þah nes he meiden neauer þe unhalre, ah wes meiden bitaht meiden to witene: *Virginem uirgini commendauit*. Nu as Ich segge, þis deorewurðe healewi i bruchel uetles is meiðhad ant cleannesse in ower bruchele flesch, bruchelure þen eani gles, þet 3ef 3e weren i worldes þrung, wið a lutel hurlunge | 3e mahten al leosen, as þe wrecches i þe world þe hurlið togederes ant breokeð hare uetles ant cleannesse schedeð. For-þi ure Lauerd cleopeð þus: *In mundo pressuram, in me autem pacem habebitis.* 'Leaueð þe world ant cumeð to me, for þer 3e schulen beon i þrung, ah reste ant peis is in me.'

26. Þe þridde reisun of þe worldes fluht is þe bi3ete of heouene. Þe heouene is swiðe heh; hwa-se wule bi3eoten hit ant areachen þer-to, hire is lutel inoh forte warpen al þe world under hire fotes. For-þi alle þe halhen makeden of al þe world as a scheomel to hare uet to areache þe heouene. *Apocalypsis: Vidi mulierem amictam sole, et luna sub pedibus eius.* Þis is Sein Iuhanes word Euuangeliste i þe Apocalipse: 'Ich iseh a wummon ischrud mid te sunne, ant under hire uet þe mone.' Þe mone woneð ant waxeð ne nis neauer studeuest, ant bitacneð for-þi worltliche þinges, þe beoð as þe mone eauer i change. Þes mone mot te wummon halden under hire uet—þet is, worldliche þinges totreoden ant forhohien—þe wule heouene areachen ant beo þer ischrud mi[d] te soðe Sunne.

27. Þe feorðe reisun is preoue of noblesce ant of largesce. Noble men ant gentile ne beoreð nane packes, ne ne feareð itrusset wið trussews ne wið purses; hit is beggilde riht to beore bagge on bac, burgeise to beore purs, nawt Godes spuse, þe is leafdi of heouene. Trussen ant purses, baggen ant packes beoð worltliche þinges—alle eorðliche weolen ant worltliche rentes.

28. Þe fifte reisun is: noble men ant wummen makieð large relef; ah hwa mei makie largere þen þe oðer þeo þe seið wið Seinte Peter, *Ecce! nos reliquimus omnia et secuti sumus te*, 'Lauerd, forte folhi þe we habbeð al forleauet'? Nis þis large re|lef? Nis þis muche laue? Mine leoue sustren, kinge[s] ant keisers habbeð hare liueneð of ower large

relef þet ȝe ileauet habbeð. 'Lauerd, forte folhi þe', seið Seinte Peter, 'we habbeð al forleauet'; as þah he seide, 'We wulleð folhi þe i þe muchele genterise of þi largesce. Þu leafdest to oþre men alle richesces, ant makedest of al relef ant laue se large. We wulleð folhi þe; we wulleð don alswa, leauen al as þu dudest, folhi þe on eorðe i þet ant in oþerhwet, forte folhi [þe] ec into þe blisse of heouene, ant ȝet tear oueral folhi þe hwiderward-se þu eauer wendest, as nane ne mahen buten ane meidnes.' *Hii secuntur Agnum quocumque ierit, utroque scilicet pede, id est, integritate cordis et corporis.*

29. Þe seste reisun is, hwi ȝe habbeð þe world iflohen, familiarite (muche cu[ð]redden), forte beo priue wið ure Lauerd. For þus he seið bi Osee: *Ducam te in solitudinem et ibi loquar ad cor tuum.* 'Ich chulle leade þe', he seið to his leofmon, 'into anli stude, ant ter Ich chulle luueliche speoke to þin heorte, for me is lað preasse.' *Ego Dominus, et ciuitatem non ingredior.*

30. Þe seoueðe reisun is forte beo þe brihtre, ant brihtluker seon in heouene Godes brihte nebscheft for ȝe beoð iflohe þe world ant hudeð ow for hire her; ȝet ter-teken, þet ȝe beon swifte as þe sunne gleam, for ȝe beoð wið Iesu Crist bitund as i sepulcre, bibarret as he wes o þe deore rode, as is iseid þruppe.

31. Þe eahtuðe reisun is to habben cwic bone; ant lokið ȝeorne hwer-uore. Þe eadmode cwen Hester bitacneð ancre, for hire nome seið 'ihud' on Englische ledene. As me ret in hire boc, ha wes þe king Assuer ouer al icweme, ant þurh hire bone arudde of deað al hire folc, þe wes to deað idemet. | Þis nome 'Assuer' is ispealet 'eadi', as is ear iseid, ant bitacneð Godd, eadi ouer alle. He ȝetteð Hester þe cwen—þet is, þe treowe ancre þet is riht Hester, þet is, riht ihud— he hereð ant ȝetteð hire alle hire benen, ant sawueð þurh ham muche folc. Monie schulde beo forloren þe beoð þurh þe ancre benen iborhen, as weren þurh Hesteres, for-hwon þet ha beo Hester ant halde hire as heo dude, Mardochees dohter. 'Mardoche' is ispealet *amare conterens inpudentem*, þet is, 'bitterliche totreodinde þene scheomelese'. Scheomeles is þe mon þe seið eani untu oðer deð biuoren ancre. Ȝef eani þah swa do, ant heo breoke bitterliche his untohe word oðer his fol dede, totreode ham ananriht wið unwurð tellunge, þenne is ha Hester, Mardochees dohter, bitterliche breo- kinde þene scheomelese. Bitterluker ne betere ne mei ha him neauer breoken þen is itaht þruppe, wið *Narrauerunt michi*, oðer mid tis uers, *Declinate a me, maligni, et scrutabor mandata Dei mei;* ant wende

inward anan toward hire weouede ant halde hire ed hame, as Hester, 'þe ihudde'. Semei i *Regum* hefde deað ofseruet, ah he criede mearci, ant Salomon forȝef hit him; þah þurh swuch a foreward, þet he ed hame heolde him i Ierusalem, as he wunede, ant hudde him in his huse. Ȝef he ohwider wende ut, swuch wes þe foreward þet he were eft al ful ant to deað idemet. He þah brec foreward þurh his unselhðe: his þrealles edfluhen him ant edbreken him ut, ant he folhede ham ant wende ut efter ham—hwet wult tu mare? Wes sone forwreiet to þe king Salomon, ant for þe foreward tobroken wes fordemet to deaðe. Vnderstondeð ȝeorne þis, mine leoue sustren.

Semey bitacneð þe utwarde ancre, | nawt Hester þe ihudde. For 'Semey' seið *audiens*, þet is 'herinde' on ure ledene: þet is, þe recluse þe haueð asse earen, longe to here feor, þet is, hercninde efter utrunes. Semeis stude wes Ierusalem þet he schulde in huden him ȝef he walde libben. Þis word 'Ierusalem' spealeð 'sihðe of peis', ant bitacneð ancre-hus; for þrinne ne þearf ha seon bute peis ane. Ne beo neauer Semei (þet is, þe recluse) swa swiðe forgult toward te soðe Salomon (þet is, ure Lauerd), halde hire ed hame i Ierusalem, þet ha nawiht nute of þe worldes baret, Salomon ȝetteð hire bliðeliche his are. Ah ȝef ha entremeateð hire of þinges wiðuten mare þen ha þurfte, ant hire heorte beo utewið, þah a clot of eorðe, þet is, hire licome, beo inwið þe fowr wahes, ha is iwend wið Semei ut of Ierusalem, alswa as he dude efter his þrealles. Þeos þrealles beoð þe eðele fif wittes, þe schulden beon et hame ant seruin hare leafdi. Þenne ha seruið wel þe ancre, hare leafdi, hwen ha notieð ham wel in [hire] sawle neode: hwen þe ehe is o þe boc oþer o sum oðer god, þe eare to Godes word, þe muð in hali bonen. Ȝef ha wit ham uuele ant let ham þurh ȝemeles etfleon hire seruise, ant folhi ham utwart wið hire heorte—as hit bitimeð eauer meast, þet gan þe wittes ut, þe heorte geað ut efter—ha brekeð Salomon foreward, wið þe unseli Semey, ant is to deað idemet.

32. For-þi, mine leoue sustren, ne beo ȝe nawt Semey, ah beoð Hester þe ihudde, ant ȝe schule beon ihehet i þe blisse of heouene; for þe nome of Hester ne seið nawt ane *abscondita* (þet is, nawt ane 'ihud'), ah deð þer-teken *eleuata in populis* (þet is, 'i folc ihehet'), ant swa wes Hester, as hire no|me cwiddeð, ihehet to cwen of a poure meiden. I þis word 'Hester' beoð 'hudunge' ant 'hehnesse' ifeiet togederes; ant nawt ane 'hehnesse', ah 'hehnesse ouer folc', forte schawin witerliche þet teo þe hudeð ham ariht in hare ancre-hus, ha schulen beon in heouene ouer oþres cunnes folc wurðliche ihehet. Ba

PART 3

Hesteres nome ant hire hehunge pruuieð þet Ich segge. On oðer half, understondeð ʒe beoð i Ierusalem, ʒe beoð iflohe to chirche-grið, for nes ower nan þet nere sumchearre Godes þeof. Me weiteð ow, þet wite ʒe, ful ʒeorne wiðuten, as me deð þeoues þe beoð ibroke to chirche. Haldeð ow feaste inne—nawt te bodi ane, for þet is þe unwurðest, ah ower fif wittes, ant te heorte ouer al ant al þer þe sawle lif is, for beo ha bitrept utewið, nis þer bute leade forð toward te gealforke, þet is, þe wearitreo of helle. Beoð ofdred of euch mon, alswa as þe þeof is, leste he drahe ow utwart—þet is, biswike [o summe wise]—ant weiti forte warpen upon ow his cleches. Bisecheð ʒeornliche Godd, as þeof ibroke to chirche, þet he wite ant wardi ow wið alle þe ow weitið. Chiterið ower beoden aa, as spearewe deð ane—for þis [**word** 'ane'] is iseid of anlich lif, of anlich stude, þer me mei beon Hester, ihud ut of þe world, ant do betere þen i þrung euch gastelich biʒete. For-þi eueneð Dauið ancre to pellican, þet leat anlich lif, ant to spearewe ane.

33. Spearewe haueð ʒet a cunde þet is biheue ancre, þah me hit heatie, þet is, þe fallinde uuel; for muche neod is þet ancre of hali lif ant of heh habbe fallinde uuel. Þet uuel ne segge Ich nawt þet me swa nempneð, ah 'fallinde uuel' Ich cleopie licomes secnesse oðer temptatiuns of flesches fondunges, hwer-þurh hire þunche þet ha falle du|neward of hali hehnesse. Ha walde awilgin elles oðer to wel leoten of, ant swa to noht iwurðen. Þe flesch walde awilgin ant bicumen to fulitohen toward hire leafdi ʒef hit nere ibeaten, ant makie sec þe sawle ʒef secnesse hit ne temede. [Ʒef hare nowðer nere sec **wið uuel oðer wið sunne, þe licome ne þe gast**]—as hit timeð seldene—orhel walde awakenin, þet is þe measte dredfule secnesse of alle. Ʒef Godd fondeð ancre wið ei uuel utewið, oðer þe feond inwið wið gasteliche unþeawes—ase prude, wreaððe, onde— oðer wið flesches lustes, ha haueð þet fallinde uuel, þet me seið is spearewe uuel. Godd hit wule for-þi þet ha beo eauer eadmod, ant wið lah haldunge of hire seoluen falle to þer eorðe leste ha falle i prude.

34. Nv we hurteð, leoue sustren, to þe feorðe dale, þet Ich seide schulde beon of feole fondunges; for þer beoð uttre ant inre, ant eiðer moniualde. Salue Ich bihet to teachen toʒeines ham ant bote, ant hu hwa-se haueð ham mei gederin of þis dale cunfort ant froure toʒeines ham alle. Þet Ich þurh þe lare of þe Hali Gast mote halden foreward, he hit ʒetti me þurh ower bonen.

M. 176

f. 47^v

PART 4

1. Ne wene nan of heh lif þet ha ne beo itemptet. Mare beoð þe gode þe beoð iclumben hehe itemptet þen þe wake; ant þet is reisun, for se þe hul is herre, se þe wind is mare þron. Se þe hul is herre of hali lif ant of heh, se þe feondes puffes, þe windes of fondunges, beoð strengre þron ant mare. ʒef ei ancre is þe ne ueleð nane fondunges, swiðe drede i þet puint | þet ha beo ouermuchel ant ouerswiðe ifondet. For swa Sein Gregoire seið, *Tunc maxime inpugnaris cum te inpugnari non sentis.* Sec mon haueð twa estaz swiðe dredfule. þet an is hwen he ne feleð nawt his ahne secnesse, ant for-þi ne secheð nawt leche ne lechecreft, ne [ne] easkeð na mon read, ant asteorueð ferliche ear me least wene. þis is þe ancre þe nat nawt hwet is fondunge. To þeos spekeð þe engel i þe Apocalipse: *Dicis quia diues sum et nullius egeo, et nescis quia miser es et nudus et pauper et cecus*; 'þu seist þe nis neod na medecine, ah þu art blind iheortet, ne ne sist nawt hu þu art poure ant naket of halinesse ant gastelich wrecche.' þet oþer dredfule estat þet te seke haueð is al frommard þis: þet is, hwen he feleð se muchel angoise þet he ne mei þolien þet me hondli his sar ne þet me him heale. þis is sum ancre þe feleð se swiðe hire fondunges, ant is se sare ofdred, þet na gastelich cunfort ne mei hire gleadien ne makien to understonden þet ha mahe ant schule þurh ham þe betere beon iborhen. Ne teleð hit i þe Godspel þet te Hali Gast leadde ure Lauerd seolf into anlich stude to leaden anlich lif, forte beon itemptet of þe unwine of helle? *Ductus est Iesus in desertum a Spiritu ut temptaretur a diabolo.* Ah his temptatiun þe ne mahte sunegin wes ane wiðuten.

2. Understondeð þenne on alre earst, leoue sustren, þet twa cunne temptatiuns, twa cunne fondunges beoð, uttre ant inre, ant ba beoð feoleualde.

3. Vttre fondunge is hwer-of kimeð licunge oþer mislicunge wiðuten oðer wiðinnen. Mislicunge wiðuten: ase secnesse, meoseise, scheome, vnhap, ant euch licomlich derf þet te flesch eileð. Wiðinnen: heorte sar, grome, ant wreaððe alswa onont þet ha is pine.[1] Licunge wiðuten: licomes heale, mete, drunch, clað inoh, ant euch flesches | eise onont swucche þinges. Licunge wiðinnen: as sum fals gleadschipe, oðer of monne hereword, oðer ʒef me is iluuet mare

---

[1] After *pine*, V has 'þat is, sunnes ernynge'.

þen anoþer, mare iolhnet, mare idon god oðer menske. Þis dale of þis temptatiun þet is 'uttre' icleopet is swikelure þen þe oðer half. Ba beoð a temptaciun, ant eiðer wiðinnen ant wiðuten baðe of hire twa dalen; ah ha is 'uttre' icleopet for ha is eauer oðer i þing wiðuten oðer
40 of þing wiðuten, ant te uttre þing is þe fondunge. Þeos fondunge kimeð oðerwhile of Godd, of mon oðerhwiles. Of Godd: as of freondes deað, secnesse oðer on ham oðer o þe seoluen, pouerte, mishapnunge, ant oþre swucche; heale alswa ant eise. Of mon: as mislich woh, oðer of word oðer of werc, o þe oðer o þine; alswa
45 hereword oðer goddede. Þeos cumeð alswa of Godd, ah nawt, as doð þe oþre, wiðuten euch middel. Ah wið alle he fondeð mon hu he him drede ant luuie.

4. Inre fondunges beoð mislicbe unþeawes, oðer lust towart ham, oðer þohtes swikele þe þ[u]ncheð þah gode. Þeos inre fondunge
50 kimeð of þe feond, of þe world, of ure flesch oðerhwile.

5. To þe uttre temptatiun is neod patience (þet is, þolemodnesse); to þe inre is neod wisdom ant gasteliche strengðe.

6. We schulen nu speoken of þe uttre, ant teachen þeo þe habbeð hire hu ha mahen wið Godes grace ifinde remedie (þet is, elne)
55 aȝeines hire to frourin ham seoluen.

7. *Beatus uir qui suffert temptationem, quoniam cum probatus fuerit* M. 182 *accipiet coronam uite quam repromisit Deus diligentibus se.* Eadi is ant seli þe haueð i temptatiun þolemodnesse, for hwen ha is ipru[u]et, hit seið, ha schal beon icrunet mid te crune of lif þe Godd haueð
60 bihaten his leoue icorene. 'Hwen ha is ipruuet', hit seið. Wel is hit iseid; | for alswa pruueð Godd his leoue icorene as þe goltsmið f.49ʳ fondeð þet gold i þe fure. Þet false gold forwurðeð þrin, þet gode kimeð ut brihtre. Secnesse is a brune hat forte þolien, ah na þing ne clenseð gold as hit deð þe sawle. Secnesse þet Godd send—nawt þet
65 sum lecheð þurh hire ahne dusischipe[2]—deð þeose six þinges: (i) wescheð þe sunnen þe beoð ear iwrahte, (ii) wardeð toȝein þeo þe weren towardes, (iii) pruueð pacience, (iii[i]) halt in eadmodnesse, (v) muchleð þe mede, [(vi)] eueneð to martir þene þolemode. Þus is secnesse sawlene heale, salue of hire wunden, scheld þet ha ne kecche
70 ma, as Godd sið þet ha schulde ȝef secnesse hit ne lette. Secnesse makeð mon to understonden hwet he is, to cnawen him seoluen, ant, as god meister, beat forte leorni wel hu mihti is Godd, hu frakel is þe worldes blisse. Secnesse is þi goldsmið, þe i þe blisse of heouene

---

[2] After *dusischipe*, N (and, with some variation, P) have 'vor moni makeð hire sec þuruh hire fol herdischipe, auh þis miscwemeð God. Auh sicnesse ðet God sent'.

ouergulded þi crune; se þe secnesse is mare, se þe goldsmið is bisgre, ant se hit lengre least, se he brihteð hire swiðere. To beo martirs euening þurh a hwilinde wa, hwet is mare grace to þeo þe hefde ofearnet þe pinen of helle world abuten ende? Nalde me tellen him alre monne dusegest þe forseke a buffet for a speres wunde, a nelde pricchunge for an bihefdunge, a beatunge for an hongunge on helle wearitreo aa on ecnesse? Godd hit wat, leoue sustren, al þe wa of þis world, ieuenet to helle alre leaste pine, al nis bute bal-plohe, al nis nawt swa muchel as is a lutel deawes drope toȝeines þe brade sea ant alle worldes weattres. Þe mei þenne edstearten þet ilke grisliche wa, þe eateliche pinen, þurh secnesse þet agea[ð], þurh ei uuel þet her is, seliliche mei ha seggen.

8. On oðer half, leornið [her] moniualde frouren | aȝein þe uttre fondunge þe kimeð of monnes uuel—for þeos þe Ich habbe iseid of is of Godes sonde.

9. Hwa-se eauer misseið þe oðer misdeð þe, nim ȝeme ant understond þet he is þi vile (þe lorimers habbeþ), ant fileð al þi rust awei ant ti ruhe of sunne; for he fret him seoluen—weilawei!—as þe file deð, ah he makeð smeðe ant brihteð þi sawle.

10. On oðer wise, þench hwa-se eauer hearmeð þe oðer eni wa deð þe, scheome, grome, teone, he is Godes ȝerde; [Godd beateð þe mid him ant chastieð ase feader his leoue sune wið ȝerde.] For swa he seið [þet he deð] þurh Sein Iuhanes muð i þe Apocalipse: *Ego quos amo, arguo et castigo*. Ne beat he nan bute hwam-se he luueð ant halt for his dohter, na mare þen þu waldest beaten a fremede child, þah hit al gulte. Ah nawt ne leote he wel of þet is Godes ȝerde; for as þe feader, hwen he haueð inoh ibeaten his child ant haueð hit ituht wel, warpeð þe ȝerde i þe fur, for ha nis noht na mare, alswa þe Feder of heouene, hwen he haueð ibeaten wið an unwreast mon oþer an unwrest wummon his leoue child for his god, he warpeð þe ȝerde,[3] þet is, þe unwreste, into þe fur of helle. For-þi he seið elleshwer, *Michi uindictam, ego retribuam*, þet is, 'Min is þe wrake, Ich chulle ȝelden.' As þah he seide, 'Ne wreoke ȝe nawt ow seoluen, ne grucchi ȝe ne wearien hwen me gulteð wið ow, ah þencheð anan þet he is ower Feadres ȝerde, ant þet he wule ȝelden him ȝerde seruise.' Ant nis þet child fulitohen þet scratleð aȝein ant bit upo þe ȝerde? Þet deboneire child, hwen hit is ibeaten, ȝef þe feader hat hit, hit cusseð þe ȝerde; ant ȝe don alswa, mine leoue sustren, for swa hat ower

---

[3] All manuscripts running but AN have *Virga furoris mea, Assur*, either after ȝerde (C) or after *helle* (4. 104).

Feader, þet ȝe cussen—naw[t] wið muð, ah wið luue of heorte—þeo
þe he ow wið beateð. *Diligite inimicos | uestros, benefacite hiis qui* f. 50ʳ
oderunt uos, et orate pro persequentibus et calumpniantibus uos. Þis is
115 Godes heste, þet him is muchel leoure þen þet tu eote gruttene bred
oðer weredest hearde here: 'Luuieð ower uamen', he seið, 'ant doð
god', ȝef ȝe mahen, 'to þeo þet ow weorrið'; ȝef ȝe elles ne mahen,
'biddeð ȝeorne for þeo þet ow eni eil doð oðer misseggeð.' Ant te
Apostle leareð, 'Ne ȝelde ȝe neauer uuel for uuel', ah doð god eauer
120 aȝein uuel, as dude ure Lauerd seolf ant alle his hali halhen. Ȝef ȝe
þus haldeð Godes heaste, þenne beo ȝe his hende child ant cusseð þe
ȝerde þe he haueð ow wið iþorschen. Nu seið oþerh[w]ile sum, 'His
sawle (oðer hiren) Ich chulle wel luuien, his bodi o nane wise.' Ah
þet nis nawt to seggen. Þe sawle ant te licome nis bute a mon, ant ba
125 ham tit a dom. Wult tu dealen o twa þe Godd haueð to an isompnet?
He forbeot hit, ant seið, *Quod Deus coniunxit, homo non separet.* Ne
wurðe nan se wod þet he todeale þe þing þe Godd haueð iueiet.

11. Þencheð ȝet þisses weis. Þet child, ȝef hit spurneð o sum
þing oðer hurteð, me beat þet hit hurte on, ant þet child is wel
130 ipaiet, forȝeteð al his hurt, ant stilleð hise teares. For-þi frourið ow
seoluen; *letabitur iustus cum uiderit uindictam.* Godd schal o Domes- M. 188
dei don as þah he seide, 'Dohter, hurte þes þe? Dude he þe spurnen
i wreaððe, oðer in heorte sar, i scheome, oðer in eani teone? Loke,
dohter, loke!' **he seið**, 'hu he hit schal abuggen!' Ant þer ȝe schule
135 seon bunkin him wið þes deofles betles þet wa bið him þes liues. Ȝe
schulen beo wel ipaiet þrof, for ower wil ant Godes wil schal swa
beon iueiet þet ȝe schulen wullen al þet he eauer wule, ant he al þet
ȝe wulleð.

12. Ouer alle oþre þohtes, in alle ower passiuns | þencheð eauer f. 50ᵛ
140 inwardliche upo Godes pinen, þet te worldes wealdent walde for his
þrealles þolien swucche schendlakes: hokeres, buffez, spatlunge,
blindfeallunge, þornene crununge þet set him i þe heaued swa þet
te blodi strundes striken adun ant leaueden **dun to þer eorðe**; his
swete bodi ibunden naket to þe hearde piler, ant ibeate swa þet tet
145 deorewurðe blod ron on euche halue; þet attri drunch þet me him
ȝef þa him þurste o rode; hare heafde sturunge upon him þa heo on
hokerunge gredden se lude, 'Lo her þe healde oþre; lo hu he healeð
nu ant helpeð him seoluen!' Turneð þruppe þer Ich spcc hu hc wes
ipinet in alle his fif wittes, ant eueneð al ower wa, secnesse ant
150 oðerhwet, woh of word oðer of werc, ant al þet mon mei þolien, to
þet tet he þolede, ant ȝe schulen lihtliche iseon hu lutel hit reacheð,

nomeliche ȝef ȝe þencheð þet he wes al ladles, ant þet he droh al þis nawt for him seoluen, for he ne agulte neauer. Ȝef ȝe þolieð wa, ȝe habbeð wurse ofseruet, ant al þet ȝe þolieð al is for ow seoluen.

13. Gað nu þenne gleadluker bi strong wei ant bi swincful toward te muchele feaste of heouene, þer-as ower gleade freond ower cume ikepeð, þenne dusie worldes men gað bi grene wei toward te wearitreo ant te deað of helle. Betere is ga sec to heouene þen hal to helle, to murhðe wið meoseise þen to wa wið eise. *Salomon: Via impiorum complantata est lapidibus—id est, duris afflictionibus.* Nawt for-þi witerliche wrecche worltliche men buggeð deorre helle þen ȝe doð þe heouene. A þing to soðe wite ȝe: a mis word þet ȝe þolieð, a deies longunge, a secnesse of a stunde—ȝef me chapede ed ow an of þeos o Domesdei (þet is, þe mede þe | ariseð þrof), ȝe hit nalden sullen for al þe world of golde. For þet schal beon ower song biuoren ure Lauerd: *Letati sumus pro diebus quibus nos humiliasti, annis quibus uidimus mala*—þet is, wel is us for þe dahes þet tu lahedest us wið oðer monne wohes, ant wel is us nu, Lauerd, for þe ilke ȝeres þet we weren seke in, ant sehen sar ant sorhe. Euch worltlich wa, hit is Godes sonde. Heh monnes messager me schal hehliche underuon ant makien him glead chere, nomeliche ȝef he is priue wið his lauerd; ant hwa wes mare priue wið þe King of heouene hwil he her wunede þen wes þes sondesmon, þet is, worldes weane, þe ne com neauer from him aðet his liues ende? Þes messager, hwet teleð he ow? He froureð ow o þis wise: 'Godd, as he luuede me, he send me to his leoue freond. Mi cume ant mi wununge, þah hit þunche attri, hit is halwende. Nere þet þing grislich hwas schadewe ȝe ne mahte nawt [for grisl[e] bihalden? Ȝef þet ilke schadewe ȝet were se kene oðer se hat þet ȝe hit ne mahte nawt] wiðute[n] hurt felen, hwet walde ȝe seggen bi þet eisfule wiht þet hit of come? Wite ȝe to soðe þet al þe wa of þis world nis bute schadewe of þe wa of helle. Ich am þe schadewe', seið þes messager, þet is, worldes weane; 'nedlunge ȝe moten oðer underuo me oðer þet grisliche wa þet Ich am of schadewe. Hwa-se underueð me gleadliche ant makeð me feier chere, mi lauerd send hire word þet ha is cwite of þet þing þet Ich am of schadewe.' Þus speketh Godes messager. For-þi seið Sein Iame, *Omne gaudium existimate, fratres, cum in temptationes uarias incideritis*: alle blisse haldeð hit to fallen i misliche of þeose fondunges þe uttre beoð ihaten. Ant Seint Pawel, *Omnis disciplina in presenti uidetur esse non gaudii set meroris; postmodum uero fructum, et cetera*:

PART 4 73

alle þe ilke fondunges þe we beoð nu ibeaten wið þuncheð wop, nawt | wunne, ah ha wendeð efterward to weole ant to eche blisse.[4] f. 51ᵛ
14. Þe inre fondunge is twaualt, alswa as is þe uttre; for þe uttre M. 194
is in aduersite ant i prosperite, [ant þeos cundleð þe inre: aduersite
mislicunge, prosperite] licunge, þe limpeð to sunne (þis Ich segge
for-þi þet sum licunge is ant sum mislicunge þe ofearneð muche
mede, as licunge i Godes luue ant mislicunge for sunne). Nu, as Ich
segge, þe inre fondunge is twauald, fleschlich ant gastelich: fleschlich, as of leccherie, of glutunie, of slawðe; gastelich, as of prude,
of onde, ant of wreaððe [(wreaððe is inre fondunge, ah þet is þe
uttre fondunge þet cundleð þe wreaððe)], alswa of ȝiscunge. Þus

[4] After *blisse*, N has the following passage:
'Ȝe, mine leoue sustren, beoð þeo ancren þet Ich iknowe þet habbeð lest neode to uroure aȝean þeos temptaciuns, bute one of sicnesse; vor mid more eise ne mid more men[s]ke not Ich none ancre þet habbe al þet hire neod is þene ȝe þreo habbeð, ure Louerd beo hit iþoncked. Uor ȝe ne þencheþ nowiht of mete ne of cloð, ne to ou ne to ouwer meidenes. Euerich of ou haueð of one ureonde al þet hire is neod; ne þerf þet meiden sechen nouðer bread ne suuel fur þene et his halle. God hit wot, moni oþer wot lutel of þisse eise, auh beoð ful ofte iderued mid wone and mid scheome and mid teone. In hire hond ȝif þis cumeð, hit mei beon ham uroure. Ȝe muwen more dreden þe nesche dole þene þe herde of ðeos fondunges þet is 'uttre' ihoten; vor uein wolde þe hexte cwemen ou, ȝif he muhte mid olhnunge [MS oluhnunge] makien ou ful-itowen, ȝif ȝe [MS heo] nere þe hendure. Muche word is of ou, hu gentile wummen ȝe beoð, vor godleic and for ureoleic iȝirned of monie, and sustren of one ueder and of one moder, ine blostme of ower ȝuweðe uorheten alle wor[l]des blissen and bicomen ancren.
Al þis is strong temptaciun, and muhte sone binimen ou muchel of ower mede. *Popule meus, qui te beatificant, illi te decipiunt*. Þis is Godes word þuruh Isaie: hwo-se seið biuoren ou, 'Wel is þe moder þet ou iber, and te godre heale were ȝe euer iboren', heo biswikeð ou and is ower treitre. Þer-uppe is inouh iseid of figelunge. Þisses worldes figelunge, þet is plente of worldliche þinges. Hwonne ou ne wonteð nowiht, þeonne ueineð he mid ou, þenne beot he ou cos. Auh wo wurðe his cos, vor hit is Iudases cos þet he ou mide cusseð. Aȝean þeos fondunges beoð iwarre, leoue sustren. Hwat-se cume wiðuten to uonden ou, mid licunge oþer mid mislicunge, holdeð euer ower heorte in on wiðinnen, leste þe uttre uondunge kundlie þe inre.'
C has a shortened version of the first sentence of this passage: 'Ȝe, mine leoue sustren, beoð þe ancren þe habbeð least neod to frouren toȝein þis fondunge, bute anont sechnesse ane, þet Ich wat.' It omits the remainder of the first paragraph and the first sentence of the second; then runs (with minor variants from N) from *Popule meus* to *wiðinnen*, omitting the final clause of the paragraph.
T omits the beginning of the first paragraph in N (up to *ham uroure*), and has a shortened and rewritten version of the remainder: 'Mine leue childre, þe nesche dale is to drede swiðe as is te harde of þeose fondunges þat arn uttre ihaten; as is plente of mete oðer of clað, and of swiche þinges. Olhninge [MS olhtninge] oðer hereword mihte sone make sum of ow ful-itohen ȝif ȝe neren þe hendere. Muche word þat is of ow, hu gentille ȝe beon, ȝunge of ȝeres ȝulden ow and bicomen ancres, forsoken worldes blisses.' In the second paragraph, it runs (with minor variants) with N.
SLP reflect the version in T, although each rewrites it differently. A and V omit the passage altogether.

beoð þe inre fondunges þe seouen heaued sunnen, ant hare fule cundles.

15. Flesches fondunge mei beon ieuenet to fot-wunde; gastelich fondunge, þet is mare dred of, mei beon for þe peril icleopet breost- wunde. Ah us þuncheð greattre flesliche temptatiuns for-þi þet heo beoð eð-fele. Þe oþre þah we habben ham, ofte nute we hit nawt; ant beoð þah greate ant grisliche i Godes [briht] ehe, ant beoð muchel for-þi to drede þe mare. For þe oþre, þe me feleð wel, secheð leche ant salue; þe gasteliche hurtes ne þuncheð nawt sare, ne ne saluið ham wið schrift ne wið penitence, ant draheð to eche deað ear me least wene.

16. Hali men ant wummen beoð of alle fondunges swiðest ofte itemptet—ant ham to goder heale, for þurh þe feht toʒeines ham, ha biʒeoteð þe blisfule kempene crune. Lo þah hu ha meaneð ham i Ieremie: *Persecutores nostri uelociores aquilis celi; super montes persecuti sunt nos, in deserto insidiati sunt nobis.* Þet is, 'Vre wiðeriwines, swiftre þen earnes, upo þe hulles ha clumben efter us ant þer fuhten wið us; ant ʒet i þe wildernesse ha spieden us to sleanne.' Vre wiðeriwines beoð þreo: þe feond, þe worlt, ure ahne flesch, as Ich ear seide. Lihtliche ne mei me nawt oðerhwile icnawen hwuch | of þeos þreo him weorreð, for euch helpeð oþer—þah þe feond proprement eggeð to atternesse, as to prude, to ouerhohe, to onde, ant to wreaððe, ant to hare attri cundles, þe her-efter beoð inempnet; þe flesch sput proprement toward swetnesse, eise, ant softnesse; þe world bit mon ʒiscin worldes weole ant wurðschipe, ant oþre swucche giuegauen, þe bidweolieð cang men to luuien a schadewe. Þeos wiðeriwines, hit seið, folhið us on hulles, ant weitið i wildernesse hu ha us mahen hearmin. 'Hul': þet is heh lif, þer þe deofles asawz ofte beoð strengest. 'Wildernesse' is anlich lif of ancre wununge. For alswa as i wildernes beoð alle wilde beastes ant nulleð nawt þolien monne nahunge, ah fleoð hwen ha heom ihereð, alswa schulen ancres, ouer alle oþre wummen, beo wilde o þisse wise, ant þenne beoð ha ouer oþre leoue to ure Lauerd, ant swetest him þuncheð ham—for of all flesches is wilde deores flesch leouest ant swetest.

17. Bi þis wildernesse wende ure Lauerdes folc, as Exode teleð, toward te eadi lond of Ierusalem þet he ham hefde bihaten. Ant ʒe, mine leoue sustren, wendeð bi þe ilke wei toward te hehe Ierusalem, þe kinedom þet he haueð bihaten his icorene. Gað þah ful warliche, for i þis wildernesse beoð uuele beastes monie: liun of prude, neddre of attri onde, vnicorne of wreaððe, beore of dead slawðe, vox of

PART 4

ȝisceunge, suhe of ȝiuernesse, scorpiun wið þe teil of stinginde leccherie, þet is, galnesse. Her beoð nu o rawe itald þe seouen heaued sunnen.

245   18. Þe liun of prude haueð swiðe monie hwelpes, ant Ich chulle nempni summe. *Vana gloria*: þet is hwa-se let wel of ei þing þet ha deð oðer seið oðer haueð—wlite oðer wit, | god acointance oðer word mare þen anoþer, cun oðer meistrie, ant hire wil forðre. Ant hwet is wlite wurð her? Gold ring i suhe nease. Acointance i
250   religiun, wa deð hit ofte. Al is *uana gloria*, þe let eawiht wel of, ant walde habben word þrof, ant is wel ipaiet ȝef ha is ipreiset, mispaiet ȝef ha nis itald swuch as ha walde. Anoþer is *Indignatio*: þet is, þe þuncheð hokerlich of ei þing þet ha sið bi oðer oþer hereð, ant forhoheð chastiement, oþer ei lahres lare. Þe þridde hwelp is *Ypocresis*: þe makeð
255   hire betere þen ha is. Þe feorðe is *Presumtio*: þe nimeð mare on hond þen ha mei ouercumen, oðer entremeteð hire of þing þet to hire ne falleð, oðer is to ouer-trusti upo Godes grace, oðer on hire seoluen, to bald upon ei mon þet is fleschlich as heo is ant mei beon itemptet. Þe fifte hwelp hatte Inobedience (nawt ane þe
260   ne buheð, oðer grucchinde deð, oðer targeð to longe): þet child þe ne buheð ealdren, vnderling his prelat, paroschien his preost, meiden hire dame, euch lahre his herre. Þe seste is Loquacite. Þe fedeð þis hwelp þe is of muche speche, ȝelpeð, demeð oþre, liheð oðerwhile, gabbeð, upbreideð, chideð, fikeleð, stureð lahtre. Þe
265   seouede is Blasphemie: þis hwelpes nurrice is þe swereð greate aþes, oðer bitterliche curseð, oðer misseið bi Godd oðer bi his halhen for ei þing þet he þoleð, sið, oðer hereð. Þe eahtuðe is Inpatience: þis hwelp fet þe nis þolemod aȝein alle wohes ant in alle uueles. Þe niheðe is Contumace, ant þis fet hwa-se is anewil i þing þet ha haueð undernume
270   to donne, beo hit god, beo hit uuel, þet na wisure read ne mei bringen hire ut of hire riote. Þe teoheðe is *Contentio*: þet is, strif to ouercumen | þet te oþer þunche underneoðen awarpen ant crauant, ant heo meistre of þe mot, ant crenge ase champiun þe haueð biȝete þe place. I þis unþeaw is upbrud ant edwitunge of
275   al þet uuel þet ha mei bi þe oðer ofþenchen; ant eauer se hit biteð bittrure, se hire likeð betere, þah hit were of þing þe wes biuore ȝare amendet. Her-imong beoð oðerhwiles nawt ane bittre wordes, ah beoð fule, stinkinde, scheomelese, ant schentfule, sumchearre mid great sware, monie ant prude wordes,
280   wið warinesses ant bileasunges. Her-to falleð euenunge of ham seolf, of hare cun, of sahe oðer of dede (þis is among nunnen).

Ant gað wið swuch muð seoððen, ear schrift ham habbe iweschen, to herie Godd wið loftsong, oðer biddeð him priuee bonen. Me, þinges amansede! nuten ha þet hare song ant hare bonen to Godd stinkeð fulre to him ant to alle his halhen þen ei rotet dogge? Þe ealleofte hwelp is ifed wið supersticiuns, wið semblanz ant wið sines: as beoren on heh þet heaued, crenge wið swire, lokin o siden, bihalden on hokere, winche mid ehe, binde seode mid te muð, wið hond oðer wið heaued makie scuter signe, warpe schonke ouer schench, sitten oðer gan stif as ha istaket were, luue lokin on mon, speoken as an innocent ant wlispin for þen anes. Her-to falleð of ueil, of heaued-claðm of euch oðer claðto oue[r]gart acemunge oðer in heowunge oðer i pinchunge; gurdles, ant gurdunge o dameiseles wise;[5] scleater-unge mid smirles; fule fluðrunges, heowin her, litien leor, pinchen bruhen oðer bencin ham uppart wið wete fingres.

19. Monie oþre þer beoð, þe cumeð of weole, of wunne, of heh cun, of feier claðof wit, of wlite, of strengðe. Of heh [lif] waxeð | prude, ant of hali þeawes. Monie ma hwelpes þen Ich habbe inempnet haueð þe liun of prude; ah abute þeose studieð wel swiðe, for Ich ga lihtliche ouer, ne do bute nempni ham. Ah ʒe, eauerihwer-se Ich ga swiðere uorð, leaueð þer lengest, for þer Ich feðeri on a word tene oðer tweolue. Hwa-se eauer haueð eani unþeaw of þeo þe Ich her nempnede, oðer ham iliche, ha haueð prude sikerliche, hu-se eauer hire curtel beo ischapet oðer iheowet. Heo is þe liunes make þet Ich habbe ispeken of, ant fet [hise] wode hwelpes inwið hire breoste.

20. Þe neddre of attri onde haueð seoue[6] hwelpes. *Ingratitudo*: þis cundel bret hwa-se nis icnawen goddede, ah teleð lutel þrof oðer forʒet mid alle—goddede, Ich segge, nawt ane þet mon deð him, ah þet Godd deð him oðer haueð idon him—oðer him oðer hire, mare þen ha understont ʒef ha hire wel biþohte. Of þis unþeaw me nimeð to lutel ʒeme, ant is þah of alle an laðest Godd, ant meast aʒein his grace. Þe oðer cundel is *Rancor siue Odium*, þet is, heatunge oðer great heorte. Þe bret hit in breoste, al is attri to Godd þet he eauer wurcheð. Þe þridde cundel is Ofþunchunge of oþres god. Þe feorðe, Gleadschipe of his uuel.[7] Þe fifte, Wreiunge. Þe seste, Bacbitunge.

---

[5] After *wise*, PV have 'nebbes depeyntynge'; similarly L.
[6] For *seoue*, PLV have *þise*.
[7] After *uuel*, T has 'lahhen oðer gabben ʒif him mis times'; similarly NP, LV (after *god* 4. 316), G (after *feorðe* 4. 316), and C (after *Scarnunge* 4. 318).

PART 4

þe seoueðe, Upbrud oðer Scarnunge. þe eahtuðe is *Suspitio*: þet is, misortrowunge bi mon oðer bi wummon wiðuten witer
320 tacne, þenchen, 'þis semblant ha makeð, þis ha seið oðer deð, me forte gremien, hokerin oðer hearmin'—ant þet hwen þe oþer neauer þide[r]ward ne þencheð. Her-to falleð fals dom, þet Godd forbeot swiðe, as þenchen oðer seggen, 'ȝe, | ne f. 54ʳ luueð ha me nawt; her-of ha wreide me; lo, nu ha speokeð of
325 me, þe twa, þe þreo, oðer þe ma þe sitteð togederes; swuch ha is ant swuch, ant for uuel ha hit dude.' I þulli þoht we beoð ofte bichearret, for ofte is god þet þuncheð uuel; ant for-þi beoð al dei monnes domes false. Her-to limpeð alswa luðere neowe fundles ant leasunges ladliche þurh nið ant þurh onde.
330 Þe niheðe cundel is Sawunge of unsibsumnesse, of wreaððe, ant of descorde. Þeo þe saweð þis deofles sed, ha is of Godd amanset. Þe teoheðe is Luðer Stilðe, þe deofles silence, þet te an nule for onde speoken o þe oþer; ant þis spece is alswa cundel of wreaððe, for hare teames beoð imengt ofte toge-
335 deres. Hwer-as ei of þeos wes, þer wes þe cundel (oðer þe alde moder) of þe attri neddre of onde.

21. Þe vnicorne of wreaððe, þe bereð on his nease þe [h]orn þet he asneaseð wið al þet he areacheð, haueð six[8] hwelpes. Þe earste is Chast oðer Strif. Þe oðer is Wodschipe. **Bihald te ehnen ant te**
340 **neb hwen wod wreaððe is imunt; bihald hire contenemenz, loke on hire lates, hercne hu þe muð geað, ant tu maht demen hire wel ut of hire witte.** Þe þridde is Schentful Upbrud. Þe feorðe is Wariunge. Þe fifte is Dunt. Þe seste is wil þet him uuel M. 202 tidde, oðer on him seolf, oðer on his freond, oðer on his ahte. Þe
345 seoueðe hwelp is don for wreaððe mis, oðer leauen wel to don; forgan mete oðer drunch; wreoken hire wið teares ȝef ha elles ne mei, ant wið weariunges; hire heaued spillen o grome, oðer on oþer wise hearmin hire i sawle ant i bodi baðe—þeos is homicide, ant morðre of hire seoluen.

350 22. Þe beore of heui slawðe haueð þeose | hwelpes. *Torpor* is þe f. 54ᵛ forme: þet is, wlech heorte (**vnlust to eni þing**) þe schulde leitin al o lei i luue of ure Lauerd. Þe oþer is *Pusillanimitas*: þet is, to poure heorte ant to earh mid alle ei heh þing to underneomen in hope of Godes help ant i trust on his grace, nawt of hire strengðe. Þe þridde
355 is *Cordis Grauitas*. Þis haueð hwa-se wurcheð god, ant deð hit tah mid a dead ant mid an heui heorte. Þe feorðe is Ydelnesse—hwa-se

[8] For *six*, VL have *seuen*, P *þise*.

stut mid alle. þe fifte is Heorte Grucchunge. þe seste is a dead sorhe for lure of ei worltlich þing,⁹ oþer for eni unþonc, bute for sunne ane. þe seoueðe is ӡemelesschipe oðer to seggen oðer to don, oðer to biseon biuoren oðer to þenchen efter, oðer to miswiten eni þing þet ha haueð to ӡemen. þe eahtuðe is Unhope. þis leaste beore-hwelp is grimmest of alle, for hit tocheoweð ant tofret Godes milde milce ant his muchele mearci ant his unimete grace.

23. Þe vox of ӡisceunge haueð þeose hwelpes: Triccherie ant Gile, þeofðe, Reaflac, Wite ant Herrure Strengðe, False Witnesse oðer Að, Dearne Symonie, Gauel, Oker, Festschipe, Prinschipe of ӡeoue oðer of lane (**þis is icluht heorte, vnþeaw Gode laðest, þe ӡef us al him seoluen**), Monslaht oðerhwile. þis unþeaw is to uox for moni reisun ieuenet; twa Ich chulle seggen. Muche gile is i vox, ant swa is i ӡisceunge of worltlich biӡete. Anoðer: þe vox awurieð al a floc, þah he ne mahe buten an frechliche swolhen. Alswa ӡisceð a ӡiscere þet tet moni þusent mahten bi flutten, ah þah his heorte berste, ne mei he bruken on him seolf bute a monnes dale. Al þet mon wilneð mare, oðer wummon, þen ha mei | **rihtliche** leade þet lif bi, euch efter þet ha is, al is ӡisceunge ant rote of deadlich sunne. þet is riht religiun, þet euch efter his stat borhi ed tis frakele world se lutel se ha least mei of mete, of clað, of ahte, of alle hire þinges. Notið þet Ich segge, 'Euch efter his stat', for þet word is ifeðeret. Ӡe mote makien—þet wite ӡe—i moni word muche strengðe, þenchen longe þer-abuten, ant bi þet ilke an word understonden monie þe limpeð þer-to; for ӡef Ich schulde writen al, hwenne come Ich to ende?

24. Þe suhe of ӡiuernesse haueð gris þus inempnet. To Earliche hatte þet an, þet oþer To Esteliche, þet þridde To Frechliche; þet feorðe hatte To Muche, þet fifte To Ofte. I drunch mare þen i mete beoð þeos gris iferhet. Ich speoke scheortliche of ham, for nam Ich nawt ofdred, mine leoue sustren, leste ӡe ham feden.¹⁰

25. Þe scorpiun of leccherie (þet is, of galnesse) haueð swucche cundles þet in a welitohe muð hare summes nome ne sit nawt forte nempnin, for þe nome ane mahte hurten alle welitohene earen, ant sulen cleane heorten. þeo þah me mei nempnin wel hwas nomen me icnaweð wel, ant beoð, mare hearm is, to monie al to cuðe: Horedom, Eawbruche, Meiðlure, ant Incest (þet is bituhe sibbe fleschliche oðer gasteliche). þet is o feole idealet: ful wil to þet fulðe wið skiles

---

⁹ After *þing*, NP have 'oðer of freond', similarly T.
¹⁰ For *for . . . feden* (4. 385–6), G has 'þah seore Ich am adred þat to feole of ow esteliche ham feden.'

PART 4

ȝettunge;[11] helpen oþre þiderward; beo weote ant witnesse þrof; hunti þrefter wið wohunge, wið toggunge, oðer wið eni tollunge, wið gigge lahtre, hore ehe, eanie lihte lates, wið ȝeoue, wið tollinde word oðer wið luue speche, cos, vnhende grapunge (þet **mei beon** heaued sunne); luuie tide oðer stude | forte cumen i swuch keaft; ant oþre foreridles þe me mot nede forbuhen þe i þe muchele fulðe nule fenniliche fallen. As Seint Austin seið, *Omissis occasionibus que solent aditum aperire peccatis, potest consciencia esse incol[u]mis*; þet is, hwa-se wule hire inwit witen hal ant fere, ha mot fleon þe foreridles þe weren iwunet ofte to openin þe inȝong ant leoten in sunne. Ich ne dear nempnin þe uncundeliche cundles of þis deofles scorpiun, attri iteilet; ah sari mei ha beon þe, bute fere oðer wið, haueð swa ifed cundel of hire galnesse, þet Ich ne mei speoken of for scheome, ne ne dear for drede, leste sum leorni mare uuel þen ha con ant beo þrof itemptet. Ah þenche on hire ahne aweariede fundles in hire galnesse; for hu-se hit eauer is icwenct wakinde ant willes wið flesches licunge bute ane i wedlac, hit **geað to** deadlich sunne. I ȝuheðe me deð wundres. Culche hit i schrift ut utterliche as ha hit dude þe feleð hire schuldi, oðer ha is idemet þurh þet fule brune cwench to þet eche brune of helle. þe scorpiunes cundel þe ha bret in hire bosum, schake hit ut wið schrift ant wið deadbote slea. Ȝe þe of swucches nute nawt, ne þurue ȝe nawt wundrin ow ne þenchen hwet Ich meane, ah ȝeldeð graces Godd þet ȝe swuch uncleannesse nabbeð ifondet, ant habbeð reowðe of ham þe i swuch beoð ifallen.

26. Inoh is etscene hwi Ich habbe ieuenet prude to liun, onde to neddre, ant of þeo alle þe oþre, wiðute þis leaste—þet is, hwi galnesse beo to scorpiun ieuenet. Ah lo her þe skile þrof, sutel ant etscene.[12] Scorpiun is a cunnes wurm þe haueð neb, as me seið, | sumdeal ilich wummon, ant neddre is bihinden. Makeð feier semblant ant fikeð mid te heaueð, ant stingeð mid te teile. þis is leccherie; þis is þe deofles beast þet he leat to chepinge ant to euch gederunge ant chepeð forte sullen, ant biswikeð monie, þurh þet ha ne bihaldeð nawt bute þe feire neb oðer þet feire heaued. þet heaued is þe biginnunge of galnesse sunne, ant te licunge, hwil hit least, þe

---

[11] After ȝettunge, NT have (with minor variants) 'þet is, hwonne þe schil and te heorte ne wiðsiggeð nout, auh likeð wel and ȝirneð al ðet tet flescs to prokeð'; similarly P.
[12] All manuscripts running but A cite (with minor variants) *Salomon: Qui apprehendit mulierem quasi qui apprehendit scorpionem*, either after etscene (CN) or after teile (4. 424) (GLPSTV).

þuncheð swiðe swote. þe teil, þet is þe ende þrof, is sar ofþunchunge, ant stingeð her wið atter of bitter bireowsunge ant of deadbote. Ant seliliche mahen ha seggen þe þe teil swuch ifindeð, for þet atter ageað; ah ȝef hit ne suheð her, þe teil ant te attri ende is þe eche pine of helle. Ant nis he fol chapmon þe, hwen he wule buggen hors oðer oxe, ȝef he nule bihalden bute þet heaued ane? For-þi, hwen þe deouel beodeð forð þis beast, beot hit to sullen, ant bit ti sawle þeruore, he hut eauer þe teil ant schaweð forð þe heaued. Ah þu ga al abuten, ant schaw þe ende forð mid al, hu þe teil stingeð, ant swiðe flih þer-frommard ear þu beo iattret.

27. Þvs, mine leoue sustren, i þe wildernesse þer ȝe gað in wið Godes folc toward Ierusalemes lond, þet is, þe riche of heouene, beoð þulliche beastes, þulliche wurmes; ne nat Ich na sunne þet ne mei beon ilead oðer to an of ham seouene oðer to hare streones. Vnsteaðeluest bileaue aȝein Godes lare—nis hit **te spece** of prude, Inobedience? Her-to falleð sygaldren, false teolunges, lefunge o swefne, o nore, ant on alle wicchecreftes. Neomunge of husel in eani heaued sunne, oðer ei oþer sacrement—nis hit te spece of prude þet Ich cleopede *Presumptio*, ȝef me wat hwuch sunne hit is? | Ȝef me hit nat nawt, þenne is hit ȝemeles under accidie, þet Ich 'slawðe' cleopede. Þe ne warneð oðer of his uuel oðer of his biȝete, nis hit slaw ȝemeles oðer attri onde? Teoheði mis, edhalden cwide, fundles, oðer lane, **oðer þer-wið misfearen**, nis hit **spece of** ȝisceunge **ant anes cunnes** þeofðe? Edhalden oðres hure ouer his rihte terme—nis hit strong reaflac (**hwa-se ȝelden hit mei**), þe is under ȝisceunge? Ȝef me ȝemeð wurse ei þing ileanet oðer bitaht to witene þen he wene þe ah hit, nis hit oðer triccherie oðer ȝemeles of slawðe? Alswa is dusi heast oðer folliche ipliht trowðe, longe beon unbischpet, falsliche gan to schrift oðer to longe abiden, ne teache Pater Noster godchild ne Credo; þeos ant alle þulliche beoð ilead to slawðe, þet is þe feorðe moder of þe seoue sunnen. Þe dronc drunch oðer ei þing dude hwerþurh na child ne schulde beon on hire istreonet, oðer þet istreonede schulde forwurðen, nis þis strong monslaht of galnesse awakenet? Alle sunnen sunderliche bi hare nomeliche nomen ne mahte na mon rikenin, ah i þeo þe Ich habbe iseid alle oþre beoð bilokene. Ant nis, Ich wene, na mon þe ne mei understonden him of his sunne nomeliche under sum of þe ilke imeane þe beoð her iwritene.

28. Of þeose seoue beastes ant of hare streones i wildernesse of anlich lif is iseid her-to, þe alle þe forfearinde fondið to fordonne. Þe liun of prude sleað alle þe prude, alle þe beoð hehe ant ouerhohe

iheortet; þe attri neddre, þe ontfule ant te luðere iþonket;[13]
470 wreaðfule, þe vnicorne; alswa of þe oþre o rawe. To Godd ha
beoð isleine; ah | ha libbeð to þe feond, ant beoð al in his [hird] ant
seruið him in his curt, euch of þe meoster þe him to falleð.

29. Þe prude beoð his bemeres. Draheð wind inward [of] worltlich
hereword, ant eft wið idel ȝelp puffeð hit utward, as þe bemeres doð.
475 Makieð noise ant lud dream to schawin hare orhel; ah ȝef ha wel
þohten of Godes bemeres, of þe englene bemen þe schulen o fowr half
þe world biuore þe grurefule dom grisliche blawen, 'Ariseð, deade,
ariseð! Cumeð to Drihtines dom forte beon idemet', þear na prud
bemere ne schal beon iborhen—ȝef ha þohten þis wel, ha walden
480 inohreaðe i þe deofles seruise dimluker bemin. Of þeos bemeres seið
Ieremie, *Onager solitarius in desiderio anime sue attraxit uentum amoris
sui;* of þe wind drahinde in for luue of hereword seið as Ich seide.

30. Summe iuglurs beoð þe ne cunnen seruin of nan oþer gleo
bute makien cheres—wrenche þe muð mis, schulen wið ehnen. Of
485 þis meoster seruið þe unseli ontfule i þe deofles curt, to bringen o
lahtre hare ondfule lauerd. Ȝef ei seið wel oðer deð wel, ne mahen ha
nanes weis lokin þider wið riht ehe of god heorte, ah winkið o þet
half ant bihaldeð o luft ȝef þer is eawt to edwiten, oðer ladliche
þiderward schuleð mi[d] eiðer. Hwen ha ihereð þet god, skleatteð þe
490 earen adun; ah þe lu[s]t aȝein þet uuel is eauer wid open. Þenne he
wrencheð þe muð hwen he turneð god to uuel; ant ȝef hit is sumdel
uuel, þurh mare lastunge wrencheð hit to wurse. Þeos beoð
forecwidderes, hare ahne prophetes; þeos bodieð biuoren hu þe
eateliche deoflen schulen ȝet ageasten ham wið hare grennunge,
495 ant | hu ha schulen ham seolf grennin ant niuelin ant makien sur
semblant for þe muchele angoise i þe pine of helle. Ah for-þi ha beoð
þe leasse to meanen þet ha biuoren-hond leornið hare meoster to
makien grim chere.

31. Þe wreaðfule biuore þe feond skirmeð mid cniues, ant is his
500 cnif-warpere, ant pleieð mid sweordes; bereð ham bi þe scharp ord
upon his tunge. Sweord ant cnif eiðer beoð scharpe ant keoruinde
word þet he warpeð from him ant skirmeð toward oþre; ant he bodeð
hu þe deoflen schulen pleien wið him mid hare scharpe eawles,
skirmi wið him abuten ant dusten ase pilche-clut euch toward oðer,
505 ant wið helle sweordes asneasen him þurh-ut, þet beoð kene ant
eateliche ant keoruinde pinen.

[13] After *iþonket*, F has 'vers lour bienfesours'; T has 'þat beon malicius and liðere aȝain
oðere', similarly S.

32. þe slawe lið ant slepeð o þe deofles bearm, as his deore deorling; ant te deouel leið his tutel dun to his eare ant tuteleð him al þet he wule. For swa hit is sikerliche to hwam-se is idel of god: meaðeleð þe feond 3eorne, ant te idele underueð luueliche his lare. Idel ant 3emeles is þes deofles bearnes slep; ah he schal o Domesdei grimliche abreiden wið þe dredfule dream of þe englene bemen, ant in helle wontreaðe echeliche wakien. *Surgite, aiunt, mortui,*[14] *surgite et uenite ad iudicium Saluatoris.*

33. þe 3iscere is his eskibah. Feareð abuten esken, ant bisiliche stureð him to rukelin togederes muchele ant monie ruken; blaweð þrin ant blent him seolf, peaðereð ant makeð þrin figures of augrim, as þes rikeneres doð þe habbeð muche to rikenin. þis is al þe canges blisse; ant te feond bihalt tis gomen ant laheð þet he bersteð. Wel understont | euch wis mon þet gold ba ant seoluer, ant euch eorðlich ahte, nis bute eorðe ant esken, þe ablendeð euch mon þe ham in blaweð—þet is, þe bolheð him þurh ham in heorte prude. Ant al þet he rukeleð ant gedereð togederes ant ethalt of ei þing þet nis bute esken mare þen hit neodeð schal in helle wurðen him tadden ant neddren; ant ba, as Ysaie seið, schulen beon of wurmes his cuuertur ant his hwitel þe nalde þer-wið neodfule feden ne schruden. *Subter te sternetur tinea, et operimentum tuum uermis.*

34. þe 3iuere glutun is þe feondes manciple; ah he stikeð eauer i celer oðer i cuchene. His heorte is i þe dissches, his þoht al i þe neppes, his lif i þe tunne, his sawle i þe crohhe. Kimeð biuoren his lauerd bismuddet ant bismulret, a disch in his an hond, a scale in his oðer. Meaðeleð mis wordes, wigleð as fordrunke mon þe haueð imunt to fallen, bihalt his greate wombe, ant te deouel lahheð. þeose þreat[e]ð þus Godd þurh Ysaie: *Serui mei comedent et uos esurietis, et cetera.* 'Mine men schulen eoten ant ow schal eauer hungrin; ant 3e schule beon feo[ndes fo]de world buten ende.' *Quantum glorificauit se et in deliciis fuit, tantum date illi tormentum et luctum. In Apocalipsi: Contra unum poculum quod miscuit, miscete ei duo.* '3ef þe kealchecuppe wallinde bres to drinken, 3eot in his wide þrote þet he swelte inwið, a3ein an 3ef him twa': þullich is Godes dom a3ein 3iuere ant druncwile i þe Apocalipse.

35. þe lecchurs i þe deofles curt habbeð riht hare ahne nome; for i þes muchele curz þeo me cleopeð lecchurs þe habbeð swa forlore scheome þet heom nis nawiht of | scheome, ah secheð hu ha mahen

---

[14] After *mortui*, all manuscripts running but A have *qui iacetis in sepulcris.*

PART 4

545 meast vilainie wurchen.[15] Þe lecchur i þe deofles curt bifuleð him seoluen fulliche, ant his feolahes alle; stinkeð of þet fulðe, ant paieð wel his lauerd wið þet stinkinde breað betere þen he schulde wið eani swote rechles. Hu he stinke to Godd, i *Vitas Patrum* þe engel hit schawde þe heold his nease þa þer com þe prude lecchur ridinde, ant
550 nawt for þet rotede lich þet he healp þe hali earmite to biburien. Of alle oþre, þenne, habbeð þeos þe fuleste meoster i þe feondes curt, þe swa bidoð ham seoluen; ant he schal bidon ham, pinin ham wið eche stench i þe put of helle.

36. Nv 3e habbeð ane dale iherd, mine leoue sustren, of þeo þe me
555 cleopeð þe seoue moder-sunnen ant of hare teames, ant of hwucche meosters þes ilke men seruið i þe feondes curt þe habbeð iwiuet o þeose seouen haggen,[16] ant hwi ha beoð swiðe to heatien ant to schunien. 3e beoð ful feor from ham, ure Lauerd beo iþoncket; ah þet fule breað of þis leaste unþeaw—þet is, of leccherie—stinkeð se
560 swiðe feor, for þe feond hit saweð ant toblaweð oueral, þet Ich am sumdel ofdred leste hit leape sumchearre into ower heortes nease. Stench stiheð uppart; ant 3e beoð hehe iclumben, þer þe wind is   M. 218 muchel of stronge temptatiuns. Vre Lauerd 3eoue ow strengðe wel to wiðstonden!

565 37. Svm weneð þet ha schule stronglukest beon ifondet i þe forme tweofmoneð þet ha bigon ancre lif, ant i þe oþer þrefter. Ant hwen ha efter feole 3er feleð ham stronge, wundreð hire swiðe, ant is ofdred leste Godd habbe hire al forwarpen. Nai, nawt nis | hit swa. I f. 59ʳ þe forme 3eres nis bute bal-plohe **to monie men of ordre**. Ah
570 neomeð 3eme hu hit feareð bi a forbisne. Hwen a wis mon neowliche haueð wif ilead ham, he nimeð 3eme al softeliche of hire maneres; þah he seo bi hire þet him mispaieð, he let 3et iwurðen, makeð hire fei[er] chere, ant is umben euches weis þet ha him luuie inwardliche in hire heorte. Hwen he understont wel þet hire luue
575 is treoweliche toward him ifestnet, þenne mei he sikerliche chastien hire openliche of hire unþeawes, þet he ear forber as he ham nawt nuste. Makeð him swiðe sturne ant went te grimme toð to, forte fondin 3etten 3ef he mahte hire luue toward him unfestnin. Alest, hwen he understont þet ha is al wel ituht, ne for þing þet he deð hire
580 ne luueð him þe leasse, ah mare ant mare, 3ef ha mei, from deie to deie, þenne schaweð he hire þet he hire luueð sweteliche, ant deð al

---

[15] After *wurchen*, GLPTV have (with minor variants): *De continentibus dicitur: Hi sunt qui cum mulieribus non sunt coinquinati*.
[16] For 'þe habbeð . . . haggen' (4. 556–7), T has 'þus to maken baret'.

þet ha wule, as þeo þet he wel icnaweð. þenne is al þet wa iwurðe to wunne. ꒡ef Iesu Crist, ower spus, deð alswa bi ow, mine leoue sustren, ne þunche ow neauer wunder. I þe frumðe nis þer buten olhnunge forte drahen in luue; ah sone se he eauer understont þet he beo wel acointet, he wule forbeoren ow leasse. Efter þe spreoue on ende, þenne is þe muchele ioie. Al o þis ilke wise, þa he walde his folc leaden ut of þeowdom, ut of Pharaones hond, ut of Egypte, he dude for ham al þet ha walden, miracles feole ant feire; druhede þe Reade Sea ant makede ham freo wei þurh hire, ant þer ha eoden drufot, adrencte Pharaon ant hare fan alle. I þe desert forðre, þa he hefde | ilead ham feor i þe wildernesse, he lette ham þolien wa inoh—hunger, þurst, ant muche swinc, ant weorren muchele ant monie. On ende he ꒡ef ham reste, ant alle weole ant wunne, al hare heorte wil, ant flesches eise ant este, *terram fluentem lacte et melle*. Þus ure Lauerd speareð on earst þe ꒡unge ant te feble, ant draheð ham ut of þis world swoteliche ant wið liste. Sone se he sið ham heardin he let weorre awakenin, ant teacheð ham to fehten ant weane to þolien. On ende, efter long swinc, he ꒡eueð ham swote reste—her, Ich segge, i þis world, ear ha cumen to heouene. Ant þuncheð þenne swa god þe reste efter þe swinc, þe muchele eise efter þe muchele meoseise þuncheð se swote.

38. Nv beoð i þe Sawter, under þe twa temptatiuns þet Ich ear seide (þet beoð þe uttre ant te inre, þe temeð alle þe oþre), fowr dalen todealet þus: fondunge liht ant dearne, fondunge liht ant openlich, fondunge strong ant dearne, fondunge strong ant openlich; as is þer understonden, *Non timebis a timore nocturno, a sagitta uolante in die, a negotio perambulante in tenebris, ab incursu et demonio meridiano*. Of fondunge liht ant dearne seið Iob þeose wordes: *Lapides excauant aque, et all[u]uione paulatim terra consumitur*. Lutle dropen þurlið þe flint þe ofte falleð þron, ant lihte dearne fondunges þe me nis war of falsið a treowe heorte. Of þe lihte openliche, bi hwam he seið alswa, *Lucebit post eum semita*, nis nawt se muche dute. Of strong temptatiun þet is þah dearne is ec þet Iob meaneð: *Insidiati sunt michi | et preualuerunt, et non erat qui adiuuaret*, þet is, 'Mine fan weitið me wið triccherie ant wið treisun, ant ha strengden upo me, ant nes hwa me hulpe.' *Ysaias: Veniet malum super te et nescies ortum eius*. 'Wa schal cumen on þe ant tu ne schalt witen hweonne.' Of þe feorðe fondunge, þet is strong ant openlich, he makeð his man of his fan, þe hali Iob, ant seið, *Quasi rupto muro et aperta ianua irruerunt super me*,

þet is, 'Ha þreasten in upo me as þah þe wal were tobroken ant te
ȝeten opene.'

39. Þe forme ant te þridde fondunge of þeose fowre beoð al meast
under þe inre. Þe oþer ant te feorðe falleð under þe uttre, ant beoð al
meast fleschliche ant eð for-þi to felen; þe oþre twa beoð gasteliche,
of gasteliche unþeawes, ant beoð ihud ofte, ant dearne hwen ha
derueð meast, ant beoð muche for-þi þe mare to dreden. Moni þet
ne weneð nawt bret in hire breoste sum liunes hwelp, sum neddre
cundel, þe forfret þe sawle; of hwucche[17] Osee seið, *Alieni comederunt
robur eius et ipse nesciuit*, þet is, 'Vnholde forfreten þe strengðe of his
sawle ant he hit nawt nuste.' Ȝet is meast dred of hwen þe sweoke of
helle eggeð to a þing þet þuncheð swiðe god mid alle, ant is þah
sawle bone, ant wei to deadlich sunne. Swa he deð as ofte as he ne
mei wið open uuel cuðen his strengðe. 'Na,' he seið, 'ne mei Ich nawt
makien þeos to sungin þurh ȝiuernesse; ant Ich chulle as þe
wreastleare wrenchen hire þiderward as ha meast dreaieð, ant warpen
hire o þet half ant breiden ferliche adun ear ha least wene', ant eggeð
hire toward se muchel abstinence þet ha is þe unstrengre i Godes
seruise, ant to leaden se | heard lif, ant pinin swa þet licome, þet te
sawle asteorue. He bihalt anoþer þet he ne mei nanes weis makien
luðere iþoncket, se luueful ant se reowðful is hire heorte. 'Ich chulle
makien hire', he seið, 'to reowðful mid alle; Ich schal don hire se
muchel þet ha schal luuien ahte, þenchen leasse of Godd, ant leosen
hire fame.' Ant put þenne a þulli þonc in hire softe heorte: 'Seinte
Marie! Naueð þe mon, oðer þe wummon, meoseise? Ant na mon
nule don ham nawt. Me walde me ȝef Ich bede; ant swa Ich mahte
helpen ham ant don on ham ealmesse.' Bringeð hire on to gederin,
ant ȝeouen al earst to poure, forðre to oðer freond, aleast makien
feaste ant wurðen al worldlich, forschuppet of ancre to husewif of
halle. Godd wat, swuch feaste makeð sum hore. Weneð þet ha wel
do, as dusie ant adotede doð hire to understonden. Flatrið hire of
freolec; herieð ant heoueð up þe ealmesse þet ha deð, hu wide ha is
icnawen; ant heo let wel of, ant leapeð in orhel. Sum seið inohreaðe
þet ha gedereð hord, swa þet hire hus mei ant heo ba beon irobbet—
reowðe ouer reowðe! Þus þe traitre of helle makeð him treowe
readesmon; ne leue ȝe him neauer. Dauið cleopeð him *demonium
meridianum*, 'briht schininde deouel', ant Seinte Pawel *angelum lucis*,

---

[17] All manuscripts running but AF cite, with minor variations of reference, a further text, *Traxerunt me et ego non dolui, vulnerauerunt me et ego non sensi*, either after *hwucche* (LPTV) or after *nesciuit* (4. 631) (CN).

þet is, 'engel of liht', for swuch ofte he makeð him, ant schaweð him
to monie. Na sihðe þet ʒe seoð, ne i swefne ne waken, ne telle ʒe bute
dweole, for nis hit bute his gile. He haueð wise men of hali ant of heh
lif ofte swa bichearret; as þe þet he com to i wummone liche i þe
wildernesse, seide ha wes igan o dweole, [ant weop] as meoseise |
þing efter herbearhe; ant te oþer hali mon þet he makede ileuen þet
he wes engel, bi his feader þet he wes þe deouel, ant makede him to
slean his feader—swa ofte þer-biuoren he heafde iseid him eauer soð,
forte biswiken him sariliche on ende. Alswa of þe hali mon þet he
makede cumen ham forte dealen his feader feh to neodfule ant to
poure, se longe þet he deadliche sunegede o wummon, ant swa feol
into unhope, ant deide in heaued sunne. Of mon þe spekeð wið ow
þulliche talen hereð, hu ʒe schulen witen ow wið þes deofles wiltes
þet he ow ne bi[wrenche]. Sum of ow sumchearre he makede to
leuen þet hit were fikelunge ʒef ha speke feire ant ʒef ha eadmodliche
meande hire neode, ʒef ha þonckede mon of his goddede; ant wes
mare ouerhohe forte acwenchen chearite þen rihtwisnesse. Sum he is
umben to makien se swiðe fleon monne froure þet ha falleð i deadlich
sar, þet is accidie, oðer into deop þoht, swa þet ha dotie. Sum heateð
swa sunne þet ha haueð ouerhohe of oþre þe falleð þe schulde wepen
for hire, ant sare dreden for aswuch onont hire seoluen, ant seggen as
þe hali mon þe seac ant weop ant seide, þa me him talde þe fal of an
of his breðren, '*Ille hodie, ego cras*.' Weilawei, strongliche wes he
itemptet ear he swa feolle. As he feol to-dei, Ich mei', quoð he, 'alswa
fallen to-marhen.'

40. Nv, mine leoue sustren, monie temptatiuns Ich habbe ow
inempnet under þe seoue sunnen; nawt þah þe þusent-fald þet me is
wið itemptet. Ne mahte, Ich wene, ham na mon nomeliche nempnin;
ah i þeo þe beoð iseid alle beoð bilokene. Lut beoð i þis world, oðer
nan mid | alle, þet ne beo wið hare sum oðerhwile itemptet. He haueð
se monie buistes ful of his letuaires, þe luðere leche of helle, þe
forsakeð an, he beot anoðer forð ananriht, þe þridde, þe feorðe, ant
swa eauer forð aþet he cume o swuch þet me on ende underuo, ant
he þenne wið þet birleð him ilome. þencheð her of þe tale of his
ampoiles.

41. Hereð nu, as Ich bihet, aʒein alle fondunges moni cunne
froure, ant, wið Godes grace, þrefter þe salue.

42. Siker beo of fondunge hwa-se eauer stont in heh lif. Ant þis is
þe earste froure; for eauer se herre tur, se haueð mare windes. Ʒe
beoð tur ow seoluen, mine leoue sustren; ah ne drede ʒe nawt hwil ʒe

beoð se treoweliche ant se feste ilimet wið lim of anred luue, euch of
ow to oþer. For na deofles puf ne þurue ȝe dreden bute þet lim
falsi—þet is to seggen, bute luue bitweonen ow þurh þe feond wursi.
Sone se ei unlimeð hire, ha bið sone iswipt forð; bute ȝef þe oþre
halden hire, ha bið sone ikeast adun as þe lowse stan is from þe tures
cop, into þe deope dich of sum suti sunne.

43. Nv anoðer elne. Muchel ah to frourin ow hwen ȝe beoð
itemptet. Þe tur nis nawt asailet, ne castel ne cite, hwen ha beoð
iwunnen. Alswa þe helle weorrur ne asaileð nan wið fondunge þe he
haueð in his hond, ah deð þeo þe he naueð nawt. For-þi, leoue
sustren, hwa-se nis nawt asailet, ha mei sare beon ofdred leste ha beo
biwunnen.

44. Þe þridde cunfort is þet ure Lauerd seolf i þe Pater Noster
teacheð us to bidden, *Et ne nos inducas in temptationem*, | þet is,
'Lauerd Feader, ne suffre þu nawt þe feond þet he leade us allunge
into fondunge.' Lo, neomeð ȝeme: he nule nawt þet we bidden þet
we ne beon nawt ifondet, for þet is ure purgatoire, ure cleansing-fur,
ah þet we ne beon nawt allunge ibroht þrin wið consens of heorte,
wið skiles ȝettunge.

45. Þe feorðe froure is sikernesse of Godes help i þe fehtunge
aȝein, as Seinte Pawel witneð: *Fidelis est Deus, qui non sinit nos
temptari ultra quam pati possumus, set, et cetera.* 'Godd', he seið, 'is
treowe; nule he neauer suffrin þet te deouel tempti us ouer þet he sið
wel þet we mahen þolien.' Ah i þe temptatiun he haueð iset to þe
feond a mearke, as þah he seide, 'Tempte hire swa feor, ah ne schalt
tu gan na forðre', ant swa feor he ȝeueð hire strengðe to wiðstonden;
[ne] þe feond ne mei nawt forðre gan a pricke.[18]

46. Ant þis is þe fifte froure, þet he ne mei na þing don us bute
bi Godes leaue. Þet wes wel ischawet, as þe Godspel teleð, þa þe
deoflen þet ure Lauerd weorp ut of a mon bisohten ant seiden, *Si
eicitis nos hinc, mittite nos in porcos*, 'Ȝef þu heonne driuest us, do us i
þeos swin her', **þe eoden þer an heorde**. Ant he ȝettede ham—lo
hu ha ne mahten nawt fule swin swenchen wiðuten his leaue. Ant te
swin ananriht urnen an urn to þe sea to adrenchen ham seoluen.
Seinte Marie! swa he stonc to þe swin þet ham wes leoure to
adrenchen ham seoluen þen forte beoren him; ant an unseli sunful,

---

[18] After *pricke*, all manuscripts running but AF have (with minor verbal variants, and the omission of a clause in CN) *Gregorius: Diabolus, licet afflictionem iustorum semper appetat, tamen si a Deo potestatem non accipiat, ad temptacionis articulum non conualescit. Formidari igitur non debet qui nichil nisi permissus agere ualet.*

Godes ilicnesse, bereð him in his breoste ant ne nimeð neauer ʒeme. Al þet he dude Iob, eauer he nom leue þrof ed ure Lauerd. Þe tale i Dyaloge lokið þet ʒe cunnen, hu þe hali mon wes iwunet to seggen to þe deofles neddre, | *Si licenciam accepisti, ego non prohibeo*, 'Ʒef þu hauest leaue, do, sting ʒef þu maht', ant bead forð his cheke. Ah he nefde þa nan, bute [ane] to offearen him ʒef bileaue him trukede. Ant hwen Godd ʒeueð him leaue on his leoue children, hwi is hit bute for hare muchele biheue, þah hit ham greui sare?

47. Þe seste confort is þet ure Lauerd, hwen he þoleð þet we beon itemptet, he pleieð wið us as þe moder wið hire ʒunge deorling. Flið from him ant hut hire, ant let him sitten ane, ant lokin ʒeorne abuten, cleopien 'Dame! Dame!' ant wepen ane hwile; ant þenne wið spredde earmes leapeð lahhinde forð, cluppeð ant cusseð ant wipeð his ehnen. Swa ure Lauerd let us ane iwurðen oðerhwile, ant wiðdraheð his grace, his cunfort, ant his elne, þet we ne findeð swetnesse i na þing þet we wel doð, ne sauur of heorte; ant þah i þet ilke point ne luueð us ure Lauerd neauer þe leasse, ah deð hit for muche luue. Ant þet understod wel Dauið þa he seide, *Non me derelinquas usquequaque*; 'Allunge,' quoð he, 'Lauerd, ne leaf þu me nawt.' Lo hu he walde þet he leafde him, ah nawt allunge. Ant six acheisuns notið hwi Godd for ure god wiðdraheð him oðerhwiles. An is þet we ne pruden. Anoðer, þet we cnawen ure ahne feblesce, vre muchele unstrengðe ant ure wacnesse. Ant þis is a swiðe muche god, as Seint Gregoire seið. *Magna perfectio est sue inperfectionis cognitio*: þet is, muche godnesse hit is to cnawen wel his wrecchehead ant his wacnesse. *Ecclesiasticus: Intemptatus qualia scit?* 'Hwet wat', he seið, Salomon, 'þe þet is unfondet?' Ant Seint Austin bereð Seint Gregoire witnesse wið þeose wordes: | *Melior est animus cui propria est infirmitas nota quam qui scrutatur celorum fastigia et terrarum fundamenta*, 'Betere is þe þe truddeð ant ofsecheð wel ut his ahne feblesce þen þe þe meteð hu heh is þe heouene ant hu deop þe eorðe.' Hwen twa beoreð a burðerne ant te oþer leaueð hit, þenne mei þe þe up haldeð hit felen hu hit weieð. Alswa, leoue suster, hwil þet Godd wið þe bereð þi temptatiun, nast tu neauer hu heui hit is; ant for-þi ed sum chearre he leaueð þe ane, þet tu understonde þin ahne feblesce ant his help cleopie, ant ʒeie lude efter him ʒef he is to longe. Hald hit wel þe hwile up, ne derue hit te se sare. Hwa-se is siker of sucurs þet him schal cume sone, ant ʒelt tah up his castel to his wiðeriwines, swiðe he is to edwiten. Þencheð her of þe tale hu þe hali mon in his fondunge seh bi west toʒeines him se muche ferd of

775 deoflen, ant forleas for muche dred þe strengðe of his bileaue, aþet te oð[er] seide him, 'Bihald' (quoð he) 'bi esten. *Plures nobiscum sunt quam cum illis*, we habbeð ma þen heo beoð to help on ure halue.' M. 234 For[19] þe þridde þing, is þet tu neauer ne beo al siker; for sikernesse streoneð ӡemeles ant ouerhohe, ant ba þeose streonið inobedience. Þe
780 feorðe acheisun is hwi ure Lauerd hut him, þet tu seche him ӡeornluker, ant cleopie ant wepe efter him as deð þe lutel baban efter his moder. Þrefter is þe fifte: þet tu his ӡeincume underuo þe gleadluker. Þe seste: þet tu þrefter þe wisluker wite him hwen þu hauest icaht him ant festluker halde, ant segge wið his leofmon,
785 *Tenui eum nec dimittam*.[20] Þeose six reisuns beoð under þe seste froure þe ӡe mahen habben, mine leoue | sustren, aӡeines fondunge. f. 63ᵛ
48. Þe seoueðe confort is þet alle þe hali halhen weren wodeliche itemptet. Nim of þe heste on alre earst. To Seinte Peter seide ure Lauerd, *Ecce, Sathan expetiuit uos ut cribraret sicut triticum, et cetera*.
790 'Lo,' quoð he, 'Sathan is ӡeorne abuten forte ridli þe ut of mine icorene; ah Ich habbe for þe bisoht þet ti bileaue allunge ne trukie.' Seint Pawel hefde, as he teleð him seolf, flesches pricunge—*Datus est michi stimulus carnis mee*—ant bed ure Lauerd ӡeorne þet he dude hit from him; ant he nalde, ah seide, *Sufficit tibi gratia mea; virtus in*
795 *infirmitate perficitur*: þet is, 'Mi grace schal wite þe þet tu ne beo ouercumen; beo strong in unstrengðe, þet is muche mihte.' Alle þe oþre beoð icrunet þurh feht of fondunge. Seinte Sare, nes ha fulle þreottene ӡer itemptet of hire flesch? Ah for-þi þet ha wiste þet i þe muchele angoise aras þe muchele mede, nalde ha neauer eanes
800 bisechen ure Lauerd þet he allunge deliurede hire þrof, ah þis wes hire bone: *Domine, da michi uirtutem resistendi*, 'Lauerd, ӡef me strengðe forte wiðstonden.' Efter þreottene ӡer com þe acursede gast þe hefde hire itemptet, blac ase blamon, ant bigon to greden, M. 236 'Sare, þu hauest me ouercumen.' Ant heo him ondswerede, 'Þu
805 lihest,' quoð ha, 'ful þing; nawt Ich, ah haueð Iesu Crist, mi Lauerd.' Lo, þe sweoke, hu he walde makien hire aleast to leapen into prude; ah ha wes wel war þrof, ant turnde al þe meistrie to Godes strengðe. Sein Beneit, Seint Antonie, ant te oþre, wel ӡe witen hu ha weren itemptet, ant þurh þe temptatiuns ipru|uede to treowe champiuns, f. 64ʳ
810 ant swa wið rihte ofserueden kempene crune.

---

[19] LPTV add, with varying forms of reference to the Gloss on the Epistle to the Romans, *Contemptum nutrit resoluta securitas*, before *For* (V), after *siker* (4. 778) (L), or after *inobedience* (4. 779) (PT).
[20] After *dimittam*, F has 'Cest: Je lai pris et retenu; ieo ne li lerrai', similarly P.

49. Ant þis is þe eahtuðe elne: þet alswa as þe goltsmið cleanseð þet gold i þe fur, alswa deð Godd te sawle i fur of fondunge.

50. Þe niheðe confort is þet ȝef þe feond wið fondunge greueð þe sare, þu greuest him hwen þu edstondest hundret siðe sarre, for þreo reisuns nomeliche. Þe an is þet he forleoseð, as Origene seið, his strengðe forte temptin eauer mare þer-onuuen of swuch manere sunne. Þe oþer is þet he forðluker echeð his pine. Þe þridde, fret his heorte of sar grome ant of teone, þet he unþonc hise teð i þe temptatiun þet tu stondest aȝein muchleð þi mede, ant for pine þet he wende forte drahe þe toward, breideð þe crune of blisse, ant nawt ane an ne twa, ah ase feole siðen as þu ouerkimest him, ase feole crunen—þet is to seggen, ase feole mensken of mislíche murhðen. For swa Sein Beornard seið, *Quotiens uincis, totiens coronaberis*. Þe tale i *Vitas Patrum* witneð þis ilke, of þe deciple þe set biuoren his meistre, ant his meistre warð o slepe hwil þet he learde him, ant slepte aðet midniht. Þa he awakede, 'Art tu,' quoð he, 'ȝet her? Ga ant slep swiðe.' Þe hali mon, his meistre, warð eft o slep sone, as þe þe hefde þer-biuoren ibeon i muche wecche, ant seh a swiðe feier stude, ant iset forð a trone, ant þron seoue crunen. Ant com a steuene ant seide, 'Þis sege ant þeose crunen haueð þin deciple þis ilke niht of[earn]et.' Ant te hali mon abreaid ant cleopede him to him. 'Sei,' quoð he, 'hu stod te hwil þu as Ich slepte sete biuore me?' 'Ich þohte', quoð he, 'ofte þet | Ich walde awakenin þe, ant for þu sleptest swote, ne mah[te] Ich for reowðe. Ant þenne þohte Ich gan awei to slepen, for me luste, ant nalde bute leaue.' 'Hu ofte', quoð his meister, 'ouercome þu þi þoht þus?' 'Seoue siðen', seide he. Þa understod his meister wel hwet weren þe seoue crunen: seoue cunne blissen þet his deciple hefde in euch a chearre ofseruet þet he wiðseide þe feond ant ouercom him seoluen.

51. Al þus, leoue sustren, i wreastlunge of temptatiun ariseð þe biȝete. *Nemo coronabitur nisi qui legittime certauerit*: 'Ne schal nan beon icrunet', seið Seint Pawel, 'bute hwa-se strongliche ant treoweliche fehteð' aȝein þe world, aȝein him seolf, aȝein þe feond of helle. Þeo fehteð treoweliche þe, hu-se ha eauer beoð iweorret wið þeos þreo wiðeriwines, nomeliche of þe flesch, hwuch-se eauer þe lust beo, se hit meadluker is, wrinnið aȝein festluker, ant wiðseggeð þe grant þrof wið anewile heorte, ne prokie hit se swiðe. Þeo þe þus doð beoð Iesu Cristes feolahes, for ha doð as he dude honginde o rode: *Cum gustasset acetum, noluit bibere*, þet is, he smahte þet bittre drunch ant wiðdroh him anan, ant nalde hit nawt drinken þah he ofþurst were. Heo is þe swa deð wið Godd on his rode. Þah hire þurste i þe lust, ant te deouel beot hire his healewi to drinken, vnderstonde ant þenche þah þet ter is galle under;[21] ant tah hit beo a pine, betere is forte þolien þurst þen to beon iattret. 'Let lust ouergan, ant hit te wule eft likin.' Hwil þe ȝicchunge least, hit þuncheð god to gnuddin, ah þrefter me feleð hit bitterliche smeorten. Weilawei! ant moni an is for muchel heate se swiðe ofþurst mid alle þet hwil ha drinkeð þet drunch, ne beo hit ne se bitter ne | feleð ha hit neauer, ah gluccheð in ȝiuerliche, ne nimeð neauer ȝeme. Hwen hit is al ouer, spit ant schakeð þet heaued, feð on forte niuelin ant makien grim chere—ah to leate þenne. [Nawt for-þi, efter uuel god is penitence; þet is þe beste, þenne,] speowen hit anan ut wið schrift to þe preoste, for leaue hit inwið, hit wule deað breden. For-þi, mine leoue sustren, beoð biuoren warre; ant efter þe frouren þe beoð her iwritene, aȝein alle fondunges secheð þeose saluen.

52. Aȝein alle temptatiuns, ant nomeliche aȝein fleschliche, saluen beoð ant bote, under Godes grace. Halie meditatiuns, inwarde ant meadlese ant angoisuse bonen, hardi bileaue, redunge, veasten, wecchen, ant licomliche swinkes, oþres froure forte speoke toward i þe ilke stunde þet hire stont stronge, eadmodnesse, [þolemodnesse,] freolec of heorte, ant alle gode þeawes beoð armes i þis feht, ant anrednesse of luue ouer alle þe oþre. Þe his wepnen warpeð awei, him luste beon iwundet.

53. Hali meditatiuns beoð bicluppet in a uers þet wes ȝare itaht ow, mine leoue sustren:

Mors tua, mors Christi, nota culpe, gaudia celi,
Iudicii terror figantur mente fideli.

Þet is:

þench ofte wið sar of þine sunnen,
þench of helle wa, of heoueriches wunnen,
þench of þin ahne deað, of Godes deað o rode,
þe grimme dom of Domesdei mu[ne] ofte i mode,
þench hu fals is þe worlt, hwucche beoð hire meden,
þench hwet tu ahest Godd for his goddeden.

Euchan of þeose word walde a long hwile forte beo wel iopenet; ah ȝef Ich hihi forðward, demeori ȝe þe lengre. A word Ich segge. Efter

---

[21] After *under*, V has *Iob: Quis gustabit quod gustatum affert mortem?*

ower sunnen, hwen-se ʒe þencheð of helle wa ant of heoueriches wunnen, understondeð þet Godd walde o sum wise schawin ham to men i þis world bi worltliche pinen ant worltliche | wunnen, ant schaweð ham forð as schadewe—for na lickre ne beoð ha to þe **wunne of heouene ne to þe wa of helle þen is schadewe to þet þing þet hit is of schadewe.** ʒe beoð ouer þis worldes sea upo þe brugge of heouene. Lokið þet ʒe ne beon nawt þe hors eschif iliche þe schuncheð for a schadewe, ant falleð adun i þe weater of þe hehe brugge. To childene ha beoð þe fleoð a peinture þe þuncheð ham grislich ant grureful to bihalden. Wa ant wunne i þis world, al nis bute peintunge, al nis bute schadewe.

54. Nawt ane hali meditatiuns, as of ure Lauerd, ant of alle his werkes ant of alle his wordes, of þe deore Leafdi, ant of alle hali halhen, ah oþre þohtes sumchearre i meadlese fondunges habbeð iholpen—fowr cunne nomeliche **to þeo þe beoð of flesches fondunges meadlese asailet,**[22] dredfule, wunderfule, gleadfule, ant sorhfule, willes wiðute neod arearet i þe heorte. As þenchen hwet tu waldest don ʒef þu sehe openliche stonde biuore þe, ant ʒeoniende wide upo þe, þen deouel of helle, as he deð dearnliche i þe fondunge; ʒef me ʒeide 'Fur, fur!', þet te chirche bearnde; ʒef þu herdest burgurs breoke þine wahes—þeos ant oþre þulliche dredfule þohtes. Wunderfule ant gleadfule: as ʒef þu sehe Iesu Crist ant herdest him easki þe hwet te were leouest, efter þi saluatiun ant þine leoueste freond, of þing of þisse liue, ant beode þe cheosen wið þet tu wiðstode; ʒef þu sehe al witerliche heouene-ware ant helle-ware i þe temptatiun bihalde þe ane; ʒef me come ant talde þe þet mon þet te is leouest, þurh sum miracle, as þurh steuene of heouene, were icoren to Pape; | ant alle oþre swucche. Wunderfule ant sorhfule: as ʒef þu herdest seggen þet mon þet te is leouest were ferliche adrenct, islein, oþer imurðret,[23] þet tine sustren weren in hare hus forbearnde. þulliche þohtes ofte i fleschliche sawlen wrencheð ut sonre fleschliche temptatiuns þen sum of þe oþre earre.

55. Inwarde ant meadlese ant ancrefule bonen biwinneð sone sucurs ant help ed ure Lauerd aʒeines flesches fondunges; ne beon ha neauer se ancrefule ne se fulitohene, þe deouel of helle duteð ham swiðe, for teke þet ha draheð adun sucurs aʒein him, ant Godes hond of heouene, ha doð him twa hearmes, bindeð him ant bearneð. Lo her preoue of baðe. Publius, an hali mon, wes in his bonen, ant com

---

[22] For 'to þeo . . . asailet' (4. 902–3), CFNTV have 'to fleschliche asailet'; similarly S.
[23] After *imurðret*, C has 'ase he þet wrat þis boc'.

þe feond [buuen him] fleonninde bi þe lufte, ant schulde al on [hihðe] toward te west half of þe worlt þurh Iulienes heast þe empereur, ant warð ibunden heteueste wið þe hali monne[s] bonen, þe oftoken him as ha [st]uhen uppard toward heouene, þet he ne
930 mahte hider ne þider ten dahes fulle. Nabbe ȝe [þis] alswa of Ruffin þe deouel, Beliales broðer, in ower Englische boc of Seinte Margarete? Of þet oðer me redeð þet he gredde lude to Sein Bartholomew, þe muchel wes i benen, *Incendunt me orationes tue*, 'Bartholomew, wa me, þine beoden forbearneð me.'[24] Hwa-se mei þurh Godes ȝeoue i
935 beoden habbe teares, ha mei don wið Godd al þet ha eauer wule; for swa we redeð, *Oratio lenit, lacrima cogit; hec ungit, illa pungit.* Eadi bone softeð ant paieð ure Lauerd, ah teares doð him strengðe. Beoden smirieð him wið softe olhnunge, ah teares prikieð him ne ne ȝeoueð him neauer pes ear þen he ȝetti ham al þet ha easkið. | M. 246
940 Hwen me asa[i]leð burhes oðer castel, þeo wiðinnen healdeð f. 66ʳ scaldinde weater ut, ant werieð swa þe walles. Ant ȝe don alswa as ofte as þe feond asaileð ower castel ant te sawle burh: wið inwarde bonen warpeð ut upon him scaldinde teares, þet Dauið segge bi þe, *Contribulasti capita draconum in aquis*, 'þu hauest forscaldet te drake
945 heaued wið wallinde weater', þet is, wið hate teares. þear-as þis weater is, sikerliche þe feond flið leste he beo forscaldet. Eft anoþer: castel þe haueð dich abuten, ant weater beo i þe dich, þe castel is wel carles aȝeines his unwines. Castel is euch god mon þet te deouel weorreð; ah habbe ȝe deop dich of deop eadmodnesse, ant wete teares
950 þer-to, ȝe beoð strong castel. þe weorrur of helle mei longe asailin ow ant leosen his hwile. Eft me seið—ant soð hit is—þet a muche wind alið wið a lute rein, ant te sunne þrefter schineð þe schenre. Alswa a muche temptatiun—þet is, þe feondes bleas—afealleð wið a softe rein of ane lut teares, ant [te] soðe sunne[25] schineð þrefter
955 schenre to þe sawle. þus beoð teares gode wið inwarde bonen; ant ȝef ȝe understondeð, Ich habbe iseid of ham her fowr muchele efficaces for-hwi ha beoð to luuien. In alle ower neoden, sendeð cwicliche anan þes sonde toward h[e]ouene; for, as Salomon seið, *Oratio humiliantis se penetrat nubes, et cetera*, þet is, 'þe eadmodies bone
960 þurleð þe weolcne.' Ant ter seið Seint Austin, *Magna est uirtus pure [orationis], que ad Deum intrat, et mandata peragit ubi caro peruenire nequit*: O, muchel is þe mihte of schir ant cleane bone, þe flið up ant kimeð in biuoren almihti | Godd, ant deð þe ernde se wel þet Godd f. 67ʳ

---

[24] After *forbearneð me*, C has 'seide þe deouel'.
[25] *After sunne*, N has 'þet is, Iesu Crist'; similarly P.

haueð o liues boc iwriten al þet ha seið. As Sein Beornard witneð, edhalt hire wið him seolf, ant sent adun his engel to don al þet ha easkeð. Nule Ich her of bone segge na mare.

56. Hardi bileaue bringeð þe deouel o fluht ananrihtes. þet witneð Sein Iame: *Resistite diabolo et fugiet a uobis*, 'Edstont ane þe feond, ant he deð him o fluhte.' Edstond—þurh hwet strengðe? Seinte Peter teacheð: *Cui resistite fortes in fide*, 'Stondeð aȝein him wið stronge bileaue', beoð hardi of Godes help, ant witeð hu he is wac þe na strengðe naueð on us bute of us seoluen. Ne mei he bute schawin forð sumhwet of his eape-ware, ant olhnin oðer þreatin þet me bugge þrof. Hweðer-se he deð, scarnið him; lahheð þe alde eape lude to bismere þurh treowe bileaue, ant he halt him ischent ant deð him o fluht swiðe. *Sancti per fidem uicerunt regna*: þet is, þe hali halhen alle ouercomen þurh bileaue þe deofles rixlunge, þet nis bute sunne, for ne rixleð he i nan bute þurh sunne ane. Neomeð nu gode ȝeme hu alle þe seouene deadliche sunnen muhen beon afleiet þurh treowe bileaue—on earst, nu, of prude.

57. Hwa halt him muchel, as þe prude deð, hwen he bihalt hu lutel þe muchele Lauerd makede him inwið a poure meidenes breoste?

58. Hwa is ontful þe bihalt wið ehnen of bileaue hu Iesu Godd, nawt for his god ah for oþres god, dude ant seide ant þolede al þet he þolede? þe ontfule ne kepte nawt þet eani dealde of his god; ant Godd almihti ȝet efter al þet oþer lihte dun to helle | forte sechen feolahes, ant to deale wið ham þe god þet he hefde. Lo nu, hu frommard beoð ontfule ure Lauerd. þe ancre þe wearnde anoþer a cwaer to lane, f[e]or ha hefde heoneward hire bileaue ehe.

59. Hwa halt wreaððe þe bihalt þet Godd lihte on eorðe to makien þr[e]ofald sahte—bitweone mon ant mon, bitweone Godd ant mon, bitweone mon ant engel? Ant efter his ariste, þa he com ant schawde him, þis wes his gretunge to his deore deciples: *Pax uobis*, 'Sahtnesse beo bitweonen ow.' Neomeð nu ȝeorne ȝeme. Hwen leof freond went from oþer, þe leaste wordes þet he seið, þeo schulen beo best edhalden. Vre Lauerdes leaste wordes, þa he steah to heouene ant leafde his leoue freond in uncuðe þeode, weren of swote luue ant of sahtnesse: *Pacem relinquo uobis; pacem meam do uobis*, þet is, 'Sahtnesse Ich do imong ow; sahtnesse Ich leaue wið ow.' þis wes his druerie þet he leafde ant ȝef ham in his departunge. *In hoc cognoscetis quo[d] dicipuli mei sitis, si dilectionem ad inuicem habueritis*. Lokið nu ȝeorne for his deorewurðe luue hwuch a mearke he leide upon his

icorene þa he steah to heouene: *In hoc cognoscetis quod, et cetera.* 'Bi
þet ȝe schulen icnawen', quoð he, 'þet ȝe beoð mine deciples, ȝef
swete luue ant sahtnesse is eauer ow bitweonen.' Godd hit wite (ant
he hit wat), me were leouere þet ȝe weren alle o þe spitel-uuel þen ȝe
weren ontfule oðer feol iheortet; for Iesu is al luue, ant i luue he
resteð him ant haueð his wununge. *In pace factus est locus eius. Ibi
confregit potencias, arcum, scutum, gladium, et bellum.* þet is, i
sahtnesse is Godes stude, ant hwer-se sahte is ant luue, | þear he
bringeð to nawt al þes deofles strengðe. þer he brekeð his bohe, hit
seið, þet beoð dearne fondunges þet he scheot of feor, ant his sweord
baðe, þet beoð temptatiuns keoruinde of neh ant kene.

60. Neomeð nu ȝeorne ȝeme bi moni forbisne hu god is anrednesse of luue ant annesse of heorte. For nis þing under sunne þet me
is leouere, ne se leof þet ȝe habben.

61. Nute ȝe þer men fehteð i þes stronge ferdes, þe ilke þe haldeð
ham feaste togederes ne muhe beo descumfit o neauer nane wise?
Alswa hit is in gastelich feht aȝeines þe deouel. Al his entente is forte
tweamen heorten, forte bineomen luue þet halt men togederes; for
hwen luue alið, þenne beoð ha isundret, ant te deouel deð him
bitweonen ananriht ant sleað on euche halue.

62. Dumbe beastes habbeð þis ilke warschipe, þet hwen ha beoð
asailet of wulf oðer of liun, ha þrungeð togederes al þe floc feste, ant
makieð scheld of ham seolf, euch of heom to oþer, ant beoð þe hwile
sikere. Ȝef eani unseli went ut, hit is sone awuriet.

63. Þe þridde: þer an geað him ane in a slubbri wei, he slit ant
falleð sone. þer monie gað togederes, ant euch halt oþres hond, ȝef
eani feð to sliden, þe oðer hine breid up ear he ful falle. Ȝef ha
wergið, euchan halt him bi oþer. Fondunge is sliddrunge; þurh
wergunge beoð bitacnet þe unþeawes under Slawðe, þe beoð
[inempnet] þruppe. þis is þet Sein Gregoire seið: *Cum nos nobis
per orationis opem coniungimus, per lubricum incedentes quasi ad inuicem
manus teneamus, vt tanto quisque amplius roboretur quanto alteri
innititur.*

64. Alswa i strong wind ant swifte weattres þe me mot ouerwa-
den, of monie euch halt oðer; þe isundrede | is iswipt forð ant
forfeareð eauer.

65. To wel we witen hu þe wei of þis world is slubbri, hu þe wind
ant te stream of fondunge aren stronge. Muche neod is þet euch
halde wið bisie bonen ant wið luue oþres honden; for, as Salomon
seið, *Ve soli; quia cum ceciderit, non habet subleuantem,* 'Wa eauer þe

ane; for hwen he falleð, naueð he hwa him areare.' Nan nis ane þe haueð Godd to fere; ant þet is euch þet soð luue haueð in his heorte.

66. Þe seoueðe forbisne is þis, ʒef ʒe riht telleð. Dust ant greot, as ʒe seoð, for hit is isundret ant nan ne halt to oþer, a lutel windes puf todriueð hit al to nawt; þear hit is in a clot ilimet togederes, hit lið al stille.

67. An hondful of ʒerden beoð earueð to breoken hwil ha beoð togederes; euchan itweamet lihtliche bersteð.

68. A treo þe wule fallen, undersete hit wið anoþer, ant hit stont feste; tweam ham, ant ba falleð. Nu ʒe habbeð nihene.

69. Þus i þinges utewið neomeð forbisne hu god is annesse of luue ant sometreadnesse, þet halt þe gode somet þet nan ne mei forwurðen. Ant þis wule iwiss habben þe [i] rihte bileaue bihald ʒeorne ant understont Iesu Cristes deorewurðe wordes ant werkes, þe i luue weren alle ant i swetnesse. Ouer alle þing Ich walde þet ancren leorneden wel þis lesceunes lare; for monie—mare hearm is—beoð Samsones foxes, þe hefden þe neb euchan iwend frommard oþer, ant weren bi þe teiles iteiet togederes, as *Iudicum* teleð, ant in euchanes teil a blease bearninde. Of þeose foxes Ich spec feor þruppe, ah nawt o þisse wise. Neomeð gode ʒeme hwet þis beo to seggen. Me turneð þe neb bliðeliche towart þing þet me luueð, ant frommard | þing þet me heateð. Þeo þenne habbeð þe nebbes wrongwende, euch frommard oðer, hwen nan ne luueð oþer. Ah bi þe teiles ha beoð somet, ant beoreð þes deofles bleasen, þe brune of galnesse. On anoðer wise, 'teil' bitacneð 'ende'. In hare ende ha schulen beon ibunden togederes as weren Samsones foxes bi þe teiles, ant iset bleasen þrin—þet is, þet fur of helle.

70. Al þis is iseid, mine leoue sustren, þet ower leoue nebbes beon eauer iwent somet wið luueful semblant ant wið swote chere, þet ʒe beon aa wið annesse of an heorte ant of a wil ilimet togederes, as hit iwriten is bi ure Lauerdes deore deciples: *Multitudinis credentium erat cor unum et anima una.*

71. *Pax uobis:* þis wes Godes gretunge to his deore deciples, 'Grið beo bimong ow.' ʒe beoð þe ancren of Englond, swa feole togederes (twenti nuðe oðer ma—Godd i god ow mutli), þet meast grið is among, meast annesse ant anrednesse ant sometreadnesse of anred lif efter a riwle, swa þet alle teoð an, alle iturnt anesweis ant nan frommard oðer, efter þet word is. For-þi ʒe gað wel forð ant spedeð in ower wei; for euch is wiðward oþer in an manere of liflade, as þah ʒe weren an

cuuent of Lundene ant of Oxnefort, of Schreobsburi oðer of
Chester, þear-as alle beoð an wið an imeane manere, ant
wiðuten singularite, þet is anful frommardschipe, lah þing i
religiun, for hit towarpeð annesse ant manere imeane þet ah
to beon in ordre. Þis nu þenne, þet ȝe beoð alle as an cuuent,
is ower hehe fame; þis is Godd icweme; þis is nunan wide cuð,
swa þet ower cuuent biginneð to spreaden toward Englondes
ende. Ȝe beoð as þe moder-hus þet heo beoð of istreonet. | Ȝe f. 69ᵛ
beoð ase wealle; ȝef þe wealle woreð, þe strunden worið
alswa. A weila, ȝef ȝe worið ne bide Ich hit neauer. Ȝef ei is
imong ow þe geað i singularite, ant ne folheð nawt þe cuuent,
ah went ut of þe floc, þet is as in a cloistre þet Iesu is heh
priur ouer, went ut as a teowi schep ant meapeð hire ane into
breres teilac, into wulues muð, toward te þrote of helle—ȝef
ei swuch is imong ow, Godd turne hire into floc, wende hire
into cuuent, ant leue ow þe beoð þrin swa halden ow þrin þet
Godd, þe hehe priur, neome ow on ende þeonne up into þe
cloistre of heouene.

72. Hwil ȝe haldeð ow in an, offearen ow mei þe feond ȝef he
haueð leaue, ah hearmin nawt mid alle. Þet he wat ful wel, ant is for- M. 256
þi umben deies ant nihtes to unlimin ow wið wreaððe oðer wið luðer
onde, ant sent mon oþer wummon þe telle þe an bi þe oþer sum
suhinde sahe þet suster ne schulde nawt segge bi suster. Ower nan
Ich forbeode ow ne leue þe deofles sondesmon; ah lokið þet euch of
ow icnawe wel hwen he speketh i þe vuele monnes tunge. **Ant segge
ananrihtes,** 'Vre meistre haueð iwriten us as in heast to
halden þet we tellen him al þet euch of oþer hereð; ant for-
þi loke þe þet tu na þing ne telle me þet Ich ne muhe him
tellen, þe mei don þe amendement ant con swaliches don hit
þet Ich ant tu baðe, ȝef we beoð i þe soð, schule beon
unblamet.' Euch noðele[s] warni oþer, þurh ful siker sondesmon,
sweteliche ant lueliche as hire leoue suster, of þing þet ha
misnimeð, ȝef ha hit wat to soðe. Ant makie hwa-se bereð þet
word recordin hit ofte biuoren hire ear ha ga, hu ha wule seggen, þet |
ha ne segge hit oðerweis, ne cluti þer-to mare; for a lute clut mei f. 70ʳ
ladlechin swiðe a muchel hal pece. Þeo þe ed hire suster þis luue
salue underueð, þoncki hire ȝeorne, ant segge wið þe Salmwruhte,
*Corripiet me iustus in misericordia et increpabit me, oleum autem
peccatoris non inpinguet caput meum,* ant þrefter wið Salomon, *Meliora
sunt uulnera corripientis quam oscula blandientis.* 'Ȝef ha ne luuede me,

nalde ha nawt warni me i misericorde; leouere me beoð hire wunden þen fikiende cosses.' þus ondswerie eauer; ant ȝef hit is oðerweis þen þe oðer understont, sende hire word aȝein þrof luueliche ant softe, ant te oþer leue ananriht—for þet Ich chulle alswa, þet euch of ow l[eu]e oþer as hire seoluen. Ȝef þe feond bitweonen ow toblaweð eani wreaððe oþer great heorte—þet Iesu Crist forbeode!—ear ha beo iset wel, nawt ane to neomen Godes flesch ant his blod ne wurðe nan se witles, ah ȝet (**þet is leasse**) þet ha eanes ne bihalde þer-on, ne loki i ful wreaððe toward him þe lihte to mon in eorðe of heouene to makien þreouald sahte, as is iseid þruppe. Sende eiðer þenne oþer word þet ha haueð imaket hire, as þah ha were biuoren hire, eadmodliche Venie; ant þeo þe ear ofdraheð þus luue of hire suster, ant ofgeað sahte, ant nimeð þe gult toward hire þah þe oþer hit habbe mare, ha schal beo mi deorewurðe ant mi deore dohter. For ha is Godes dohter; he him seolf hit seið. *Beati pacifici, quoniam filii Dei uocabuntur.*

73. Þus prude ant onde ant wreaððe beoð ihwer afleiet hwer-se soð luue is ant treowe bileaue to Godes milde werkes ant luuefule wordes. Ga we nu forðre to þe oþre on a reawe.

74. | Hwa mei beo for scheome slummi, sloggi, ant slaw þe bihalt hu swiðe bisi ure Lauerd wes on eorðe?[26] *Pertransiit benefatiendo et sanando omnes.* Efter al þet oðer, bihaldeð hu he i þe euen of his lif swong o þe hearde rode. Oþre habbeð reste, fleoð liht, i chambre hudeð ham hwen ha beoð ilete blod on an earm-eðre; ant he, o Munt Caluaire, steah ȝet o rode herre, ne ne swong neauer mon se swiðe ne se sare as he dude þet ilke dei þet he bledde o fif half brokes of ful brade wunden ant deope, wiðuten þe eþren capitale þe bledden on his heaued under þe kene þornene crune, ant wiðuten þe ilke reowfule garces of þe luðere scurgunge ȝont al his leofliche lich, nawt ane o þe schonken. Toȝeines slawe ant sleperes is swiðe openliche his earliche ariste from deaðe to liue.

75. Aȝeines ȝisceunge is his muchele pouerte, þe weox eauer upon him se lengre se mare. For þa he wes iboren earst, þe þet wrahte þe eorðe ne fond nawt on eorðe swa muche place as his lutle licome mahte beon ileid upon. Swa nearow wes þet stude þet unneaðe his moder ant Iosep seten þrin; ant swa ha leiden him on heh up in a crecche, wið clutes biwrabbet, as þet Godspel seið: *Pannis eum inuoluit.* Þus feire he wes ischrud, þe heouenliche Schuppent þe

---

[26] After *eorðe*, all manuscripts running but ACFN have (with minor variants) *Exultauit ut gigas ad currendam uiam.*

schrudeð þe sunne. Her-efter þe poure [Leafdi] of heouene fostrede him ant fedde wið hire lutle milc as meiden deh to habben. Þis wes muche pouerte, ah mare com þrefter; for lanhure þe-ʒet he hefde fode as feol to him, ant i stude of in, his cradel herbearhede him. Seoððen, as he meande him, nefde he hwer he mahte his heaued huden: *Filius hominis non habet ubi capud suum reclinet.* Þus poure he wes of in, of mete he wes se neodful, þet þa he hefde i Ierusalem o Palm-Sunnedei al dei ipreachet, ant hit neolechede niht, he lokede abuten (hit seið i þe Godspel) ʒef ei walde cleopien him to mete oþer to herbearhe, ah nes þer nan; ant swa he wende ut of þe muchele burh into Bethanie, to Marie hus ant to Marthen. Þer-as he eode mid his deciples sumchearre, ha breken þe eares bi þe wei, ant gnuddeden þe curnles ut bitweonen hare honden ant eten for hunger, ant weren þer-uore swiðe icalenget. Ah alre meast pouerte com ʒet her-efter. For steort-naket he wes despuilet o þe rode; þa he meande him of þurst, weater ne mahte he habben; ʒet, þet meast wunder is, of al þe brade eorðe ne moste he habben a greot forte deien upon. Þe rode hefde a fot oðer lute mare, ant þet wes to his pine. Hwen þe worldes wealdent walde beo þus poure, unbileuet is he þe luueð to muchel ant ʒisceð worldes weole ant wunne.

76. Aʒein glutunie is his poure pitance þet he hefde o rode. Twa manere men habbeð neode to eote wel, swinkinde ant blodletene. Þe dei þet he wes baðe i sar swinc ant ilete blod, as Ich nest seide, nes his pitance o rode bute a spunge of galle. Loke nu, hwa gruccheð, ʒef ha þencheð wel her-on, [of] mistrum mel, of unsauuree metes, of poure pitance?

77. Of na mon ne of na wummon ne schule ʒe makie na man, ne pleainin ow of na wone, bute to sum treowe freond þet hit mei amendin, ant godin ham oðer ow; ant þet beo priueiliche iseid, as under seel of schrift, þet ʒe ne beon iblamet. Ʒef ʒe of ei þing habbeð wone, ant sum freond ʒeorne freini ow ʒef ʒe ei wone habbeð, ʒef ʒe hopieð god of him, ondswerieð o þis wise: 'Lauerd Godd forʒelde þe! Ich drede mare Ich habbe þen Ich were wurðe, ant leasse wone Ich þolie þen me neod were.' Ʒef he easkeð ʒeornluker, þonkið him ʒeorne, ant seggeð, 'Ich ne dear nawt lihen o me seoluen; wone Ich habbe, ase riht is. Hwuch ancre kimeð into ancre-hus to habben hire eise? Ah nu þu wult hit alles witen—vre Lauerd te forʒelde!—þis is nu an þing þet Ich hefde neode to.' Ant þus bid ure riwle, þet we schawin to gode freond as oþre

Godes poure doð hare meoseise wið milde eadmodnesse. Ne nawt ne schule we forsaken þe grace of Godes sonde, ah þonkin him ȝeorne leste he wreaðe him wið us ant wiðdrahe his large hond, ant þrefter wið to muche wone abeate ure prude. Ant nis hit muchel hofles hwen Godd beot his hond forð, puttinde hire aȝein, segge, 'Ne kepe Ich hit nawt; haue þe seolf. Ich wulle fondin ȝef Ich mei libben her-buten'? Þurh þis Ich habbe iherd of swuch þet nom uuel ende.

78. Aȝein leccherie is his iborenesse of þet cleane meiden, ant al his cleane lif þet he leadde on eorðe, ant alle þe hine fuleden.

79. Þus, lo, þe articles, þet beoð as þah me seide þe liðes of ure bileaue onont Godes monhead, hwa-se inwardliche bihalt ham, fehteð toȝein þe feond þe fondeð us wið þeose deadliche sunnen. For-þi seið Seinte Peter, *Christo in carne passo, et uos eadem cogitatione armemini.* 'Armið ow', he seið, 'wið þoht upo Iesu Crist, þe in ure flesch wes ipinet.' Ant Seinte Pawel: *Recogitate qualem aput semetipsum sustinuit contradictionem, ut | non fatig[emini].* 'Þencheð, þencheð,' seið Seinte Pawel, 'hwen ȝe wergið i feht aȝeines þe deouel, hu ure Lauerd seolf wiðseide his fleschliche wil, ant wiðseggeð ower.' *Nondum enim usque ad sanguinem restitistis;* 'ȝet nabbe ȝe nawt wiðstonden aþet te schedunge of ower blod', [as he dude of his for ow, aȝeines him seoluen, onont þet he mon wes of ure cunde. Ȝet ȝe habbeð þet ilke blod,] þe ilke blisfule bodi þet com of þe meiden ant deide o þe rode, niht ant dei bi ow. Nis bute a wah bitweonen; ant euche dei he kimeð forð ant schaweð him to ow fleschliche ant licomliche inwið þe Measse—biwrixlet þah on oþres lite, under breades furme, for in his ahne ure ehnen ne mahten nawt þe brihte sihðe þolien. Ah swa he schaweð him ow as þah he seide, 'Lowr, Ich her; hwet wulle ȝe? Seggeð me hwet were ow leof. Hwerto neodeð ow? Meaneð ower neode.' Ȝef þe feondes ferd—þet beoð his temptatiuns—asailið ow swiðe, ondswerieð him ant seggeð, *Metati sumus castra iuxta lapidem adiutorii. Porro Philistiim venerunt in Afech.* 'Ȝe, Lauerd, wunder is; we beoð iloget her bi þe þet art stan of help, tur of treowe sucurs, castel of strengðe, ant te deofles ferd is woddre upon us þen upon eani oþre.' Þis Ich neome of *Regum*, for þer hit teleð al þus þet Israel, Godes folc, com ant logede him bi þe stan of help, ant te Philistews comen into Afech. Philistews beoð unwihtes. 'Afech' on Ebreisch spealeð 'neowe wodschipe'. Swa hit is witerliche: hwen mon logeð him bi ure Lauerd, þenne on earst biginneð þe deouel to weden. Ah þer hit teleð þet Israel wende sone

PART 4

þe rug, ant weren fowr þusent i þe fluht sariliche isleine. Ne wende ȝe nawt te rug, mine leoue sustren, ah wiðstondeð þe feondes ferd amidde þe forheaued, as is iseid þruppe, wið stronge bileaue; ant, wið þe gode Iosaphath, sendeð beode sondesmon sone efter sucurs to þe | Prince of heouene. *In [Paralipomenon]: In nobis quidem non est tanta fortitudo ut possimus huic multitudini resistere que irruit super nos. Set cum ignoremus quid agere debeamus, hoc solum habemus residui, ut oculos nostros dirigamus ad te. Sequitur: Hec dicit [Dominus] uobis: Nolite timere, et ne paueatis hanc multitudinem. Non enim est uestra pugna, set Dei. Tantummodo confidenter state, et uidebitis auxilium Domini super uos. Credite in Domino Deo uestro, et securi eritis.* Þis is þet Englisch: 'In us nis nawt, deorewurðe Lauerd, swa muchel strengðe þet we mahen wiðstonden þe deofles ferd þe is se strong upon us. Ah hwen we swa beoð bisteaðet, swa stronge bistonden, þet we mid alle na read ne cunnen bi us seoluen, þis an we mahe don, heouen ehnen up to þe, mildfule Lauerd. Þu send us sucurs, þu todreaf ure fan, for to þe we lokið.' Þus, wið þe gode Iosaphath, hwen Godd kimeð biuoren ow ant freineð hwet ȝe wulleð, ant in euch time hwen ȝe neode habbeð, schawið hit swa sweteliche to his swote earen. Ȝef he sone ne hereð ow, ȝeieð luddre ant meadlesluker, ant þreatið þet ȝe wulleð ȝelden up þe castel bute he sende ow sonre help, ant hihi þe swiðere. Ah wite ȝe hu he ondswerede Iosaphath þe gode? Þus o þisse wise: *Nolite timere, et cetera.* Þus he onswereð ow hwen ȝe help cleopieð: 'Ne beo ȝe nawt offearede. Ne drede ȝe ham nawiht, þah ha beon stronge ant monie; þe feht is min, nawt ower. Sulement stondeð sikerliche, ant ȝe schulen [seon] mi sucurs. Habbeð ane to me trusti bileaue, ant ȝe beoð al sikere.'

80. Lokið nu hwuch help is hardi bileaue; for al þet help þe Godd bihat, þe strengðe to stonde wel, al is in hire ane. Hardi bileaue makeð stonden upriht, ant te unwiht nis nawt laðre. | For-þi þis is his word in Ysaie: *Incuruare ut transeamus.* 'Buh þe', he seið, 'duneward þet Ich mahe ouer þe.' Þeo buheð hire þe to hise fondunges buheð hire heorte; for hwil ha stont upriht, ne mei he nowðer upon hire rukin ne riden. Lo, þe treitre, hu he seið, *Incuruare ut transeamus.* 'Buh þe, let me leapen up; nule Ich þe nawt longe riden, ah Ich chulle wenden ouer.' He liheð, seið Sein Beornard; ne lef þu nawt þen traitre. *Non uult transire, set residere,* 'Nule he nawt wenden ouer, ah wule ful feaste sitten.' Sum wes þet lefde him, þohte he schulde sone adun, as he bihat eauer. 'Do,' he seið, 'þis enchearre, ant schrif þe þrof to-marhen. Buh þin heorte, let

me up, schec me wið schrift adun ȝef Ich alles walde ride þe longe.' Sum, as Ich seide, lefde him ant beah him; ant he leop up, ant rad hire baðe dei ant niht twenti ȝer fulle—þet is, ha dude a sunne i þe il[ke] niht þurh his procunge, ant þohte þet ha walde hire schriuen ine marhen, ant dude hit eft ant eft, ant fealh swa i uuel wune þet ha lei ant rotede þrin swa longe as Ich seide. Ant ȝef a miracle nere þe pufte adun þen deouel þe set on hire se feaste, ha hefde iturplet wið him, baðe hors ant lade, dun into helle grunde. For-þi, mine leoue sustren, haldeð ow efne upriht i treowe bileaue. Hardiliche ileueð þet al þe deofles strengðe mealteð þurh þe grace of þet hali sacrement, hest ouer oþre, þet ȝe seoð as ofte as þe preost measseð—þe meidene bearn, Iesu Godd, Godes sune, þe licomliche lihteð oðerhwiles to ower in, ant inwið ow eadmodliche nimeð his herbearhe. Deuleset, ha beoð to wake ant to unwreaste iheortet þe wið swilli gest hardiliche ne fehteð. Ȝe schulen bileaue habben þet al Hali Chirche deð, red, oþer singeð, ant alle hire sacremenz, strengeð ow gasteliche; ah nan ase forð ase | þis, for hit bringeð to noht al þes deofles wiheles. Nawt ane his strengðes ant his stronge turnes, ah deð his wiltfule crokes, his wrenchfule wicchecreftes, ant alle his ȝulunges; ase lease swefnes, false schawunges, dredfule offearunges, fikele ant sweokele reades, a[s] þah hit were o Godes half ant god forte donne. For þet is his unwrench, as Ich ear seide, þet hali men meast dredeð, þet haueð moni hali mon grimliche biȝulet. Hwen he ne mei nawt bringen to nan open vuel, he sput to a þing þet þuncheð god. 'Þu schuldest', he seið, 'beo mildre ant leoten iwurðe þi chast, nawt trubli þin heorte ant sturien into wreaððe.' Þis he seið for-þi þet tu ne schuldest nawt chastien for hire gult ne tuhte wel þi meiden, ant bringe þe into ȝemeles i stude of eadmodnesse. Eft riht þer-toȝeines: 'Ne let tu hire na gult toȝeues', he seið. 'Ȝef þu wult þet ha drede þe, hald hire nearowe. Rihtwisnesse', he seið, 'mot beo nede sturne.' Ant þus he liteð cruelte wið heow of rihtwisnesse. Me mei beon al to rihtwis[27] ('*Noli esse iustus nimis*', *in Ecclesiaste*); 'betere is wis liste þen luðer strengðe.' Hwen þu hauest longe iwaket ant schuldest gan to slepen, 'Nu is uertu,' he seið, 'wakien hwen hit greueð þe. Sei ȝet a Nocturne.' For-hwi deð he swa? For þet tu schuldest slepen eft hwen time were to wakien. Eft riht þer-toȝeines: ȝef þet [tu] maht wakien wel, he leið on þe an heuinesse, oþer deð i þi þoht, 'Wisdom is þinge best. Ich chulle ga nu to slepen, ant arise nunan ant don cwicluker þene nu þet Ich don nuðe schulde'—ant swa ofte

[27] After *rihtwis*, F has 'cest trop red en droiture'.

PART 4

inohreaðe ne dest tu hit i nowðer time. Of þis ilke materie Ich spec muchel þruppe. I þulliche temptatiuns nis nan se wis ne se war, bute Godd him warni, þet nis bigilet | ofte. Ah þis hehe sacrement, in hardi bileaue, ouer alle oðre þing unwrið hise wrenches ant brekeð
1325 hise strengðes. Iwis, leoue sustren, hwen ȝe neh ow feleð him, forhwon þet ȝe habben hardi bileaue, nulle ȝe bute lahhen him lude to bismere þet he is se muchel ald cang þe kimeð his pine to echen ant breiden ow crune. Sone se he sið ow hardi ant bald i Godes grace, his mihte mealteð ant he flið sone. Ah ȝef he mei underȝeoten þet ower
1330 bileaue falsi, swa þet ow þunche þet ȝe mahten beon allunge ilead forð ouer ȝef ȝe weren swiðe i þe ilke stude itemptet, þer-wið ȝe unstrengeð ant his mihte waxeð.

81. We redeð i *Regum* þet Ysboset lei ant slepte, ant sette a wummon ȝeteward þe windwede hweate. Ant come[n] Recabes
1335 sunen, Remon ant Banaa, ant funden þe wummon istunt of hire windwunge ant ifolen o slepe; ant wenden in ant slohen Ysboset þe unseli, þet lokede him se uuele. Þe bitacnunge her-of is muche neod to understonden. 'Ysboset' on Ebrew is 'mon bimeaset' on Englisch; ant nis he witerliche ameaset, ant ut of his witte, þe amidden his
1340 unwines leið him to slepen? Þe ȝeteward is wittes skile, þet ah to windwin hweate, schaden þe eilen ant te chef from þe cleane cornes (þet is, þurh bisi warschipe sundri god from uuel), don þe hweate i gerner, ant puffen eauer awei þe deofles chef, þet nis noht bute to helle smorðre. Ah þe bimeasede Ysboset, lo hu measeliche he dude:
1345 sette a wummon to ȝeteward, þet is, feble warde. Weila! as feole doð þus! Wummon is þe reisun, þet is, wittes skile, hwen hit unstrengeð þe schulde beo monlich, stealewurðe, ant kene in treowe bileaue. Þis ȝeteward lið to slepen sone se me biginneð consenti to sunne, leoten lust gan inward ant te delit | waxen. Hwen Recabes sunen, þet beoð
1350 helle bearnes, ifindeð swa unwaker ant swa nesche ȝeteward, ha gað in ant sleað Ysboset, þet is, þe bimeasede gast þe in a slepi ȝemeles forȝemeð him seoluen. Þet nis nawt to forȝeoten þet, as Hali Writ seið, 'Ha þurhstichden him dun into þe schere.' Her seið Sein Gregoire, *In i*[*n*]*guine ferire est uitam mentis carnis delectatione*
1355 *perforare.* Þe feond þurhsticheð þe schere hwen delit of leccherie þurleð þe heorte; ant þis nis bute i slep of ȝemeles ant of slawðe, as Sein Gregoire witneð. *Antiquus hostis, mox ut mentem otiosam inuenerit, ad eam sub quibusdam occasionibus locuturus uenit, et quedam ei de gestis preteritis ad memoriam reducit, [audita quondam uerba*
1360 *indecenter resonat]. Et infra: Putruerunt et deteriorate sunt cicatrices*

mee. Cicatrix [*quippe*] *est figura uulneris, set sanati. Cicatrix ergo ad putredinem redit quando peccati uulnus, quod per penitentiam sanatum est, in delectationem sui animum concutit.* þis is þet Englisch. Hwen þe alde unwine sið slepi ure skile, he draheð him anan toward hire ant feleð wið hire i speche. 'þenchest tu', he seið, 'hu þe spec oþer þeo of flesches galnesse?' Ant spekeð þus þe alde sweoke toward hire heorte wordes þet ha ȝare herde fulliche iseide, oðer sihðe þet ha seh, oðer hire ahne fulðen þet ha sumhwile wrahte. Al þis he put forð biuore þe heorte ehnen forte bifulen hire wið þoht of alde sunnen, hwen he ne mei wið neowe. Ant swa he bringeð ofte aȝein into þe adotede sawle þurh licunge þe ilke sunnen þe þurh reowðful sar weren ibet ȝare, swa þet heo mei wepen ant meanen sari man wið þe Salmwruhte, *Putruerunt, et cetera.* 'Weilawei! mine wunden, þe weren feire ihealet, gederið neowe wursum, ant foð on eft to rotien.' Ihealet wunde þenne biginneð to rotien hwen sunne þe wes ibet kimeð eft wið | licunge into munegunge, ant sleað þe unwarre sawle. *Gregorius: Ysboset inopinate morti nequaquam succumberet nisi ad ingressum mentis mulierem, id est, mollem custodiam, deputasset.* Al þis unlimp iwarð þurh þe ȝetewardes slep, þet nes war ant waker, ne nes nawt monlich, ah wes wummonlich, eð to ouerkeasten. Beo hit wummon, beo hit mon, þenne is al þe strengðe efter þe bileaue, ant efter þet me haueð trust to Godes help, þet is neh; bute bileaue trukie, as Ich ear buuen seide, heo unstrengeð þe unwiht ant deð him fleon ananriht. For-þi beoð eauer aȝein him hardi ase liun i treowe bileaue, nomeliche i þe fondunge þet Ysboset deide on, þet is galnesse.

82. Lo hu ȝe mahe cnawen þet he is earh ant unwreast hwen he smit þiderward. Nis he earh champiun þe skirmeð toward te uet, þe secheð se lahe on his kempe-ifere? Flesches lust is fotes wunde, as wes feor iseid þruppe. Ant þis is þe reisun: as ure fet beoreð us, alswa ure lustes beoreð us ofte to þing þet us luste efter. Nu þenne, þah þi va hurte þe o þe vet, þet is to seggen, fondeð wið flesches lustes, for se lah wunde ne dred tu nawt to sare, bute hit to swiðe swelle þurh skiles ȝettunge, wið to muchel delit up toward te heorte. Ah drinc þenne atterlaðe, ant drif þet swealm aȝeinward frommard te heorte; þet is to seggen, þench o þe attri pine þet Godd dronc o þe rode, ant te swealm schal setten.

83. Prude ant onde ant wreaððe, heorte sar for worltlich þing, dreori of longunge, ant ȝisceunge of ahte—þeose beoð heorte wunden, ant al þet of ham floweð, ant ȝeoueð deaðes dunt anan

PART 4

buten ha beon isaluet. Hwen þe feond smit þiderward, þenne is iwis to dreden, ant nawt for fot-wunden.

84. Prude salue is eadmodnesse; ondes, feolahlich luue; wreaðð̄es, þolemodnesse; accidies, redunge, misliche | werkes, gastelich froure; 1405 ȝisceunges, ouerhohe of eorðliche þinges; festschipes, freo heorte.

85. Nu of þe earste on alre earst[28] ([þet is to seggen, of eadmodnesse]). Ȝef þu wult beon eadmod, þench eauer hwet te wonteð of halinesse, ant of gasteliche þeawes. Þench hwet tu hauest of þe seolf. Þu art of twa dalen, of licome ant of sawle. In eiðer beoð 1410 twa þinges þe mahen muchel meokin þe ȝef þu ham wel bihaldest. I þe licome is fulðe ant unstrengðe. Ne kimeð of þet vetles swuch þing as þer is in? Of þi flesches fetles kimeð þer smeal of aromaz oðer of swote basme? Deale, drue spritlen beoreð win-berien, breres rose-blostmen! Þi flesch, hwet frut bereð hit in alle his openunges? Amid 1415 te menske of þi neb, þet is þe fehereste deal, bitweonen muðes smech ant neases smeal, ne berest tu as twa priue þurles? Nart tu icumen of ful slim? Nart tu fulðe fette? Ne bist tu wurme fode? *Philosophus: Sperma es fluidum, vas stercorum, esca uermium.* Nu a flehe mei eili þe, makie þe to blenchen—eaðe maht tu pruden! Bihald hali men þe 1420 weren sumhwile, hu ha feasten, hu ha wakeden, i hwuch passiun, i hwuch swinc ha weren, ant swa þu maht icnawen þin ahne wake unstrengðe. Ah wast tu hwet awildgeð monnes feble ehnen þet is hehe iclumben? Þet he bihalt duneward. Alswa, hwa-se bihalt to þeo þe beoð of lah lif, þet makeð him þunchen þet he is of heh lif. Ah 1425 bihald aa uppart toward heouenliche men þe clumben se hehe, þenne schalt tu seon hu lahe þu stondest. *Augustinus: Sicut incentiuum est elationis respectus inferioris, sic cautela est humilitatis consideratio superioris.* Feasten a seoueniht to weater ant to breade, þreo niht togederes wakien—hu walde hit unstrengen þi fleschliche strenge? Þus þeos 1430 twa þinges bihald i þi licome, | fulðe ant unstrengðe. I þi sawle, oþer twa, sunne ant ignorance (þet is, unwisdom ant unweotenesse); for ofte þet tu wenest god is uuel, ant sawle morðre. Bihald wið wet ehe þine scheome sunnen. Dred ȝet þi wake cunde, þet is eð-warpe; ant sei wið þe hali mon þe bigon to wepen ant seide, þa me talde him þet 1435 an of his feren wes wið a wummon i flesches fulðe ifallen, *Ille hodie, ego cras*, þet is, 'He to-dei, ant Ich to-marhen'—as þah he seide, 'Of as unstrong cunde Ich am as he wes, ant alswuch mei me ilimpen, bute ȝef Godd me halde.' Þus lo, þe hali mon, nefde he of þe oþres fal na wunderlich ouerhohe, [ah] biweop his unhap ant dredde þet

---

[28] After *earst*, C² inserts 'þet is, of edmotnesse'.

him a swuch mahte bitiden. O þis wise eadmodieð ant meokið ow
seoluen.

86. **Bernardus: Superbia est appetitus proprie excellencie; humilitas, contemptus eiusdem**—þet [is], alswa as prude is wilnunge of wurðschipe, riht alswa þer-to3eines eadmodnesse is forkeastunge of wurðschipe, ant luue of lutel hereword ant of lahnesse. þis þeaw is alre þeawene moder, ant streoneð ham alle. þe is umben wiðuten hire to gederin gode þeawes, he bereð dust i þe wind, as Sein Gregoire seið. *Qui sine humilitate uirtutes congregat quasi qui in uento puluerem portat.* þeos ane bið iborhen, þeos ane wiðbuheð þe deofles grunen of helle, as ure Lauerd schawde to Seint Antonie, þe seh al þe world ful of þe deofles tildunge. 'A, Lauerd,' quoð he, 'hwa mei wið þeose witen him þet he ne beo wið sum ilaht?' 'Ane þe þolemode,' quoð he, ure Lauerd. Swa sutil[29] þing is eadmodnesse, **ant swa gentilliche smeal** ant se smuhel, þet na grune ne mei hire edhalden. Ant lo, muche wunder: þah ha hire makie swa smeal ant se meoke, ha is þinge strengest, swa þet of hire is euch gastelich strengðe. Seint Cassio[d]re hit witneð: *Omnis fortitudo ex humilitate.* Ah Salo|mon seið þe reisun hwi: *Vbi humilitas, ibi sapientia.* þer-as eadmodnesse is, þer, he seið, is Iesu Crist, þet is his feader wisdom ant his feader strengðe. Nis na wunder, þenne, þah strengðe beo þer-as he is þurh his inwuniende grace.

87. þurh þe strengðe of eadmodnesse he weorp þe þurs of helle. þe 3ape wreastlere nimeð 3eme hwet turn his fere ne kunne nawt þet he wið wreastleð, for wið þet turn he mei him unmundlunge warpen. Alswa dude ure Lauerd, ant seh hu feole þe grimme wreastlere of helle breid up on his hupe ant weorp wið þe hanche-turn into galnesse, þe rixleð i þe lenden. Hef on heh monie ant wende abuten wið ham ant swong ham þurh prude dun into helle grunde. þohte ure Lauerd þe biheold al þis, 'Ich schal do þe a turn þet tu ne cuðest neauer, ne ne maht neauer cunnen, þe turn of eadmodnesse, þet is þe fallinde turn'; ant feol from heouene to eorðe, ant strahte him swa bi þe eorðe þet te feond wende þet he were al eorðlich, ant wes bilurd wið þet turn, ant is 3et euche dei of eadmode men ant wummen þe hine wel cunnen.

88. On oðer half, as Iob seið, he ne mei for prude 3et bute bihalden hehe: *Omne sublime uident oculi eius.* Hali men þe haldeð ham lutle, ant of lah lif, beoð ut of his sihðe. þe wilde bar ne mei nawt buhen him to smiten. Hwa-se falleð adun ant þurh meoke

---
[29] After *sutil*, C² adds 'ant smel'.

PART 4

eadmodnesse strecheð him bi þer eorðe, he is carles of his tuskes. Þis nis nawt toȝeines þet þet Ich habbe iseid ear, þet me schal stonden eauer toȝeines þe deouel; for þet stondinge is treowe trust of hardi bileaue upo Godes strengðe, þis fallunge is eadmod cnawunge of þin ahne wacnesse ant of þin unstrengðe. Ne nan ne mei stonde swa bute he þus falle, þet is, leote lutel tale ant unwurð ant eðelich eauer of him seoluen. Bihalde his blac ant nawt his hwit, | for hwit awilgeð þe ehe.

89. Eadmodnesse ne mei beon neauer ful preiset; for þet wes þe lesceun þet ure Lauerd inwardlukest learde his icorene, wið werc ba ant wið worde:[30] *Discite a me, quia mitis sum et humilis corde.* In hire he healdeð nawt ane dropemel, ah flowinde ȝeotteð weallen of his graces, as seið þe Salmiste: *Qui emittis fontes in conuallibus.* 'I þe dealen þu makest', he seið, 'weallen to springen.' Heorte tobollen ant ihouen ase hul ne edhalt na wete of grace. A bleddre ibollen of wind ne deueð nawt into þeose halwende weattres; ah a nelde prichunge warpeð al þe wind ut, an eðelich stiche oðer eche makeð to understonden hu lutel prude is wurð, hu egede is orhel.

90. Ondes salue, Ich seide, wes feolahlich luue, ant god unnunge ant god wil þer mihte of dede wonteð. Swa muchel strengðe haueð luue ant god wil þet hit makeð oþres god ure god ase wel as his þet hit wurcheð. Sulement luue [h]is god, beo wilcweme ant glead þrof; þus þu turnest hit to þe ant makest hit þin ahne. Sein Gregoire hit witneð: *Aliena bona si diligis, tua facis.* Ȝef þu hauest onde of oþres god, þu attrest te wið healewi, ant wundest te wið salue. Þi salue hit is, ȝef þu hit luuest, aȝein sawle hurtes; ant ti strengðe aȝein þe feond is al þe god þet oðer deð ȝef þu hit wel unnest. Witerliche, Ich leue, ne schulen flesches fondunges, na mare þen gasteliche, meistrin þe neauere ȝef þu art swote iheortet, eadmod, ant milde, ant luuest se inwardliche alle men ant wummen—ant nomeliche ancres, þine leoue sustren—þet tu art sari of hare uuel, ant of hare god glead as of þin ahne. Vnnen þet al þe luueð þe luuede ham ase þe, ant dude ham froure as þe. Ȝef þu hauest cnif oðer clað, oðer mete oþer drunch, scrowe oðer cwaer, hali monne froure, oðer ei oþer þing þet ham walde freamien, vnnen þet tu hefdest wonte þe seolf þrof, wið | þon þet heo hit hefden. Ȝef eani is þe naueð nawt þe heorte þus afeitet, wið sorhfule sikes ba bi dei ant bi niht grede on ure Lauerd, ne neauer grið ne ȝeoue him aðet he þurh his grace habbe hire swuch aturnet.

---

[30] After *worde*, F has 'dunt il dit en la Ewangeile'.

91. Salue of wreaðŏe, Ich seide, is þolemodnesse, þet haueð þreo steiren: heh, ant herre, ant alre hest ant nest te hehe heouene. Heh is þe steire ȝef þu þolest for þi gult; herre ȝef þu nauest gult; alre hest ȝef þu þolest for þi goddede. 'Nai!' seið sum ameaset þing, 'Ȝef Ich hefde gult þer-to, nalde Ich neauer meanen.' Art tu þet swa seist ut of þe seoluen? Is þe leouere to beon Iudase feolahe þen Iesu Cristes fere? Ba weren ahonget, ah Iudas for his gult; Iesu wiðute gult for his muchele godlec wes ahon o rode. Hweðeres fere wult tu beon?[31] Wið hweðer wult tu þolien? Of þis is þruppe iwriten muchel, hu he is þi file þe misseið oðer misdeð þe. 'Lime' is þe Frensch of 'file';[32] nis hit or[33] acurset þe iwurðeð swartre ant ruhre se hit is ifilet mare, ant rusteð þe swiðere þet me hit scureð hearde? Gold, seoluer, stel, irn, al is or. Gold ant seoluer cleansið ham of hare dros i þe fur; ȝef þu gederest dros þrin, þet is aȝein cunde. Þe chaliz þe wes þer-in imealt ant strongliche iweallet, ant seoððen þurh se moni dunt ant frotunge to Godes nep se swiðe feire afeitet—walde he, ȝef he cuðe speoken, awearien his cleansing-fur ant his wruhte honden? *Argentum reprobum uocate eos.* Al þis world is Godes smið to smeoðien his icorene. Wult tu þet Godd nabbe na fur in his smiððe, ne bealies ne homeres? Fur is scheome ant pine; þine bealies beoð þe þe misseggeð, þine homeres, þe þe hearmið. Þench of þis essample. Hwen dei of riht is iset, ne deð he scheome þe deme þe a þis half þe isette dei brekeð | þe triws ant wrekeð him o þe oðer on him seoluen? *Augustinus: Quid gloriatur impius si de ipso flagellum fatiat Pater meus?* Ant hwa nat þet Domesdei nis þe dei iset to don riht alle men? Hald þe triws þe hwiles, hwet woh se me deð þe. [Þe rihtwise Deme haueð iset te dei to loki riht bitweonen ow;] ne do þu nawt him scheome, forhohie wrake of his dom, ant neomen to þin ahne. Twa þinges beoð þet Godd haueð edhalden to him seoluen, þet beoð wurðschipe ant wrake, as Hali Writ witneð. *Gloriam meam alteri non dabo. Item: Michi vindictam, ego retribuam.* Hwa-se eauer on him seolf takeð owðer of þeos twa, he robbeð Godd ant reaueð. Deale! art tu se wrað wið mon oþer wið wummon þet tu wult forte wreoke þe reauin Godd mid strengðe?

---

[31] After *beon*, F has 'Judas ou Ihesu Crist'.
[32] 'Lime . . . file' (4. 1527) is in AGV only. C has 'Lime is þet þe þe file fret of þe iren'; C[2] alters the first part of the sentence ('Lime is þet þe') to 'Lime is þe Frencs of file', and modifies the second part to 'þe file fret of þe irn þe rust ant tet ragget ant makeð hit hwit ant smeðe.'
[33] In the margin opposite *or*, C[2] adds 'Golt, seluer, stel, irn, coper, mestling, breas, al is icleopet or.'

92. Accidies salue is gastelich gleadschipe ant froure of gleadful hope, þurh redunge,³⁴ þurh hali þoht, oðer of monnes muðe.³⁵ Ofte, leoue sustren, ȝe schulen uri leasse forte reden mare. Redunge is god bone. Redunge teacheð hu ant hwet me bidde, ant beode biȝet hit efter. Amidde þe redunge, hwen þe heorte likeð, kimeð up a deuotiun þet is wurð monie benen. For-þi seið Sein Ierome: *Ieronimus: Semper in manu tua sacra sit lectio; tenenti tibi librum sompnus subripiat, et cadentem faciem pagina sancta suscipiat.* 'Hali redunge beo eauer i þine honden; slep ga upo þe as þu lokest þron, ant te hali pagne ikepe þi fallinde neb.' Swa þu schalt reden ȝeornliche ant longe. Euch þing þah me mei ouerdon; best is eauer mete.

93. Aȝeines ȝisceunge, Ich walde þet oþre schuneden as ȝe doð gederunge. To muche freolec cundleð hire ofte. Freo iheortet ȝe schule beon; ancre of oþer freolec haueð ibeon oðerhwiles to freo of hire seoluen.³⁶

94. Galnesse kimeð of ȝiuernesse, ant of flesches eise; for, as Sein Gregoire seið, mete ant drunch ouer riht | temeð þreo teames, lihte wordes, lihte werkes, ant leccheries lustes. Vre Lauerd beo iþonket þe haueð of ȝiuernesse ihealet ow mid alle;³⁷ ah galnesse ne bið neauer allunge cleane acwenct of flesches fondunge. Ah þet understondeð wel, þet þreo degrez beoð þrin, as Seint Beornard witneð. þe forme is cogitatiun; þe oþer is affectiun; þe þridde is cunsence. Cogitatiuns beoð fleonninde þohtes, þe ne leasteð nawt, ant teo, as Sein Beornard seið, ne hurteð nawt te sawle; ah þah ha bispottið hire wið hare blake speckes swa þet nis ha nawt wurðe þet Iesu hire leofmon, þet is al feier,³⁸ bicluppe hire ne cusse hire ear ha beo iwesschen. Swuch fulðe, as hit kimeð lihtliche, lihtliche geað awei wið Venies, wið *Confiteor*,³⁹ wið alle goddeden. Affectiun is hwen þe þoht geað inward, ant delit kimeð up, ant te lust waxeð; þenne as wes spot ear upo þe hwite hude, þer waxeð wunde ant deopeð in toward te sawle efter þet te lust geað, ant te delit þrin, forðre ant forðre. þenne is neod to ȝeiȝen, *Sana me, Domine*;⁴⁰ 'A, Lauerd, heal me, for Ich am iwundet.' *Ruben, primogenitus meus, ne crescas*: 'Ruben, þu

---

[34] After *redunge*, F has 'de Seint Escripture'.
[35] For *of monnes muðe*, F has 'par bone parole de bouche'.
[36] After *hire seoluen*, C² adds 'þet is, in hire ahne bodi large towart lechur þurh hire gestninges'.
[37] For *mid alle*, N has 'mine leoue sustren'.
[38] After *feier*, F has 'sanz tecche'.
[39] After *Confiteor*, V has 'with psalmus, wiþ Pater Nosters'.
[40] *Sana me, Domine* is altered in N to *Sana, Domine, animam meam*.

reade þoht, þu blodi delit, ne waxe þu neauer.' Cunsense, þet is skiles ȝettunge, hwen þe delit i þe lust is igan se ouerforð þet ter nere nan wiðseggunge ȝef þer were eise to fulle þe dede. Þis is hwen þe heorte draheð to hire unlust as þing þe were amainet, ant feð on as to winkin, to leote þe feond iwurðen, ant leið hire seolf duneward. Buheð him as he bit, ant ȝeiȝeð 'Crauant! Crauant!' ase softe swohninde. Þenne is he kene þe wes ear curre; þenne leapeð he to þe stod ear feorren-to, ant bit deaðes bite o Godes deore spuse. Iwiss deaðes bite; for his teð beoð attrie, as of a | wed dogge. Dauið i þe Sawter cleopeð hine dogge: *Erue a framea, Deus, animam meam, et de manu canis unicam meam.*

95. For-þi, mi leoue suster, sone se þu eauer underȝetest þet tes dogge of helle cume snakerinde wið his blodi flehen of stinkinde þohtes, ne li þu nawt stille, ne ne site nowðer, to lokin hwet he wule don, ne hu feor he wule gan; ne sei þu nawt slepinde, 'Ame, dogge, ga her-ut, hwet wult tu nu her-inne?' Þis tolleð him inward. Ah nim anan þe rode steaf mid nempnunge i þi muð, mid te mearke i þin hond, mid þoht i þin heorte; ant hat him ut heterliche, þe fule cur-dogge, ant liðere to him luðerliche mid te hali rode steaf stronge bac-duntes. Þet is, rung up, sture þe. Hald up ehnen on heh ant honden toward heouene. Gred efter sucurs: *Deus, in adiutorium meum intende. Domine, ad adiuuandum. Veni, creator spiritus. Exurgat Deus et dissipentur inimici eius. Deus, in nomine tuo saluum me fac. Domine, quid multiplicati sunt? Ad te, Domine, leuaui animam meam. Ad te leuaui oculos meos. Leuaui oculos meos in montes.*[41] Ȝef þe ne kimeð sone help, gred luddre wið hat heorte, *Vsquequo, Domine, obliuisceris me, in finem? Usquequo auerteris faciem tuam a me?* ant swa al þe Salm ouer; Pater Noster, Credo, Aue Maria, wið halsinde bonen o þin ahne ledene. Smit smeortliche adun þe cneon to þer eorðe, ant breid up þe rode steaf ant sweng him o fowr half aȝein helle dogge— þet nis nawt elles bute blesce þe al abuten wið þe eadi rode taken. Spite him amid te beard to hoker ant to scarne þe flikereð swa wið þe ant fikeð dogge fahenunge. Hwen he for se liht wurð, for þe licunge of a lust ane hwile stucche, chapeð þi sawle, Godes deore bune, þet he bohte mid his blod, ant mid his deorewurðe deað o þe deore rode, aa bihald | hire wurð þet he paide for hire, ant dem þrefter hire pris ant beo on hire þe deorre. Ne sule þu neauer se eðeliche his fa, ant þin eiðer, his deorewurðe spuse, þet costnede him se deore. Makie

---

[41] After *montes*, N has 'alle þe salmes ouer; and', T 'Sai þe salmes al ouer'; similarly PS (see app. crit.).

PART 4

deofles hore of hire is reowðe ouer reowðe. To unwreast mid alle ha is þe mei wið toheouen up hire þreo fingres ouercumen hire fa ant ne luste for slawðe. Hef for-þi wið treowe ant hardi bileaue up þine þreo fingres, ant wið þe hali rode steaf, þet him is laðest cuggel, lei o þe dogge-deouel. Nempne ofte Iesu; cleope his passiunes help; halse bi his pine, bi his deorewurðe blod, bi his deað o rode; flih to his wunden. Muchel he luuede us þe lette makien swucche þurles in him forte huden us in. Creop in ham wið þi þoht—ne beoð ha al opene?—ant wið his deorewurðe blod biblod[g]e þin heorte. *Ingredere in petram, abscondere fossa humo.* 'Ga into þe stan,' seið þe prophete, 'ant hud te i þe doluen eorðe', þet is, i þe wunden of ure Lauerdes flesch, þe wes as idoluen wið þe dulle neiles, as he i þe Sawter longe uore seide: *Foderunt manus meas et pedes meos*, þet is, 'Ha duluen me baðe þe vet ant te honden.' Ne seide he nawt 'þurleden'; for efter þis leattre, as ure meistres seggeð, swa weren þe neiles dulle þet ha duluen his flesch ant tobreken þe ban mare þen þurleden, to pinin him sarre. He him seolf cleopeð þe toward teose wunden. *Columba mea, in foraminibus petre, in cauernis macerie*: 'Mi culure,' he seið, 'cum hud te i mine limen þurles, i þe hole of mi side.' Muche **luue he cudde to his leoue** culure, þet[42] he swuch hudles makede. Loke nu þet tu, þe he cleopeð 'culure', habbe culure cunde—þet is, wiðute galle—ant cum to him baldeliche, ant make scheld of his passiun; ant | sei wið Ieremie, *Dabis scutum cordis, laborem tuum*—þet is, 'þu schalt ȝeoue me, Lauerd, heorte scheld aȝein þe feond, þi swincfule pine.' Þet hit swincful wes, he schawde hit witerliche inoh þa he sweatte ase blodes swat-dropen þe runnen to þer eorðe. Me schal halden scheld i feht up abuuen heaued, oðer aȝein þe breoste, nawt ne drahen hit bihinden. Al riht swa, ȝef þu wult þet te rode scheld ant Godes stronge Passiun falsi þe deofles wepnen, ne dragse þu hit nawt efter þe, ah hef hit on heh buue þin heorte heaued, i þine breoste ehnen. Hald hit up toȝein þe feond; schaw hit him witerliche. Þe sihðe þrof ane bringeð him o fluhte, for ba him scheomeð þer-wið ant griseð ut of witte efter þe ilke time þet ure Lauerd þer-wið brohte swa to grunde his cointe couerschipe ant his prude strengðe. Ȝef þu þurh þi ȝemeles werest te earst wacliche, ant ȝeuest to þe feond inȝong to forð i þe frumðe, swa þet tu ne mahe nawt reculin him aȝeinward for þi muchele unstrengðe, ah art ibroht se ouerforð þet tu ne maht þis scheld halden o þin heorte, ne

---

[42] For 'Muche ... þet' (4. 1642), the majority of the manuscripts have 'Muche luueð [or 'luuede'] he þe culure þet'; see app. crit.

wrenchen hire þer-under frommard te deofles earowen, nim þe aleast
forð Sein Beneites salue—þah ne þearf hit nawt beon se ouer-strong
as his wes, þe of þe walewunge, rug ant side ant wombe, ron al o
gure-blode. Ah lanhure ȝef þe seolf hwen þe strongest stont a smeort
discepline, ant drif as he dude þet swete licunge into smeortunge. Ȝef
þu þus ne dest nawt, [ah] slepinde werest te, he wule gan to feor on
þe ear þu least wene, ant bringe þe of ful þoht into delit of ful lust;
ant swa he bringeð þe al ouer to skiles ȝettunge, þet is deadlich sunne
wiðuten þe dede—ant swa is ec þe delit of þet stin|kinde lust wiðute
grant of þe werc, se longe hit mei leasten. *Nunquam enim iudicanda
est delectatio esse morosa dum ratio reluctatur et negat assensum;*
þenne hit least to longe hwen þe skile ne fehteð na lengre þer-
toȝeines. For-þi, leoue suster, as ure Lauerd leareð, totred te neddre
heaued—þet is, þe biginnunge of his fondunge. *Beatus qui tenebit et
allidet paruulos suos ad petram.* 'Eadi is', seið Dauið, 'þe wiðhalt hire
on earst, ant tobrekeð [to] þe stan þe earste sturunges, hwen þe flesch
ariseð, hwil þet ha beoð ȝunge.' Vre Lauerd is icleopet stan for his
treownesse. *Et in Canticis: Capite nobis uulpes paruulas que destruunt
uineas.* 'Nim ant keche us, leofmon, anan þe ȝunge foxes', he seið,
ure Lauerd, 'þe strueð þe winȝardes'; **þet beoð þe earste pro-
cunges þe strueð** ure sawlen, þe mot muche tilunge to to beoren
win-berien. Þe deouel is beore cunnes, ant haueð asse cunde, for he
is bihinden strong ant i þe heaued feble, swa is beore ant asse, þet is, i
þe frumðe. Ne ȝef þu him neauer inȝong, ah tep him o þe sculle, for
he is as earh as beore þron, ant hihe him swa þeoneward, ant askur
him se scheomeliche sone se þu underȝetest him, [þet he halde him
him ischent, ant] þet him grise wið þe stude þet tu wunest inne, for
he is þinge prudest, ant him is scheome laðest.

96. Alswa, leoue suster, sone se þu eauer felest þet tin heorte wið
luue falle to eani þing eawt ouer mete, ananrihtes beo war of þe
neddre atter, ant totred his heaued. Þe cwene seide ful soð þe wið a
strea ontende alle hire wanes þet muchel kimeð of lutel. Ant nim nu
ȝeme hu hit feareð. Þe sperke þe wint up ne bringeð nawt ananriht
þe | hus al o leie, ah lið ant kecheð mare fur ant fostreð forð, ant
waxeð from leasse to mare, aðet al þe hus bleasie forð ear me least
wene. Ant te deouel blaweð to from þet hit earst cundleð, ant mutleð
his beali bleas eauer as hit waxeð. Vnderstond tis bi þe seolf. A sihðe
þet tu sist, oðer anlepi word þet tu misherest, ȝef hit eawt stureð þe,
cwench hit wið teares weater ant mid Iesu Cristes blod hwil hit nis
bute a sperke, ear þen hit waxe ant ontende þe swa þet tu hit ne

mahe cwenchen. For swa hit timeð ofte, ant hit is riht Godes dom, þet hwa ne deð hwen ha mei, ne schal ha hwen ha walde. *Ecclesiasticus: A scintilla una augetur ignis.*

97. Moni cunnes fondunge is i þis feorðe dale, misliche frouren ant monifalde saluen. Vre Lauerd ȝeoue ow grace þet ha ow moten helpen. Of alle þe oþre, þenne, is schrift þe biheueste. Of hit schal beon þe fifte dale, as Ich bihet þruppe; ant neomeð ȝeme hu euch an dale falleð into oþer, as Ich þear seide.

PART 5

1. Twa þinges neome[ð] ʒeme of schrift i þe biginnunge: þe earre, of hwuch mihte hit beo, þe oþer, hwuch hit schule beon. Þis beoð nu as twa limen, ant eiðer is todealet, þe earre o sixe, þe oþer o sixtene stucchen. Nu is þis of þe earre.

2. Schrift haueð monie mihtes, ah nulle Ich of alle seggen bute sixe, þreo aʒein þe deouel ant þreo on us seoluen. Schrift schent þen deouel, hackeð of his heaued, ant todreaueð his ferd. Schrift wescheð us of alle ure fulðen, ʒelt us alle ure luren, makeð us Godes children. Ei[ð]er haueð hise þreo. Pruuie we nu alle.

3. Þe earste þreo beoð alle ischawde i Iudithe deden. Iudith—þet is, schrift, as wes ʒare iseid—sloh Oloferne, þet is, þe feond of helle (turn þruppe þer we speken of fuhelene cunde þe beoð ieuenet to ancre). Ha hackede of his heaued ant seoððen com ant schawde hit to þe burh preostes. Þenne is þe feond ischend hwen me schaweð [i schrift] alle hise cweadschipes.[1] His heaued is ihacket of ant he islein i þe mon sone se he eauer is riht sari for his sunnen ant haueð schrift on heorte. Ah he nis nawt þe-ʒet ischend hwil his heaued is ihulet[2]— as dude on earst Iudith—ear hit beo ischawet: þet is, ear þe muð i schrift do ut þe heaued sunne, nawt te sunne ane ah al þe biginnunge þrof ant te foreridles þe brohten in þe sunne. Þet is þe deofles heaued, þet me schal totreoden anan as Ich ear seide. Þenne fli[ð] his ferd anan as dude Olofernes; his wiheles ant his wrenches þet he us wið asaileð doð ham alle o fluhte, ant te burh is arud þet ha hefden biset, þet is to seggen, þe sunfule is delifret. Iudas Macabeu, hwa stod aʒein him? Alswa i *Iudicum*, þet folc þa hit easkede efter Iosues deað hwa schulde beon hare dug ant leaden ham i ferde—*Quis erit dux noster?*[3]—ure Lauerd ham ondswerede, 'Iudas schal gan biuoren ow, ant Ich chulle ower faes lond biteachen in his honden.' Lokið nu ful ʒeorne hwet tis beo to seggen. 'Iosue' spealeð 'heale', ant 'Iudas' 'schrift', as 'Iudith'. Þenne is Iosue dead, hwen sawle heale is

---

[1] After *cweadschipes* (GNTV), *heorte* (5. 17) (PS), or *Iudith* (5. 18) (L), all manuscripts running except ACF have (with minor variants) *compuncte consciencie; vnde in cubiculo abscidit capud eius.*

[2] After *ihulet* (GPV), *ischawet* (5. 18) (T), or *seide* (5. 21) (LNS), all manuscripts running except ACF cite (with minor variants) Jud. 14: 15, *Una mulier Ebrea fecit confusionem in domo regis Nabugodonosor.*

[3] After *noster*, CGPTV cite (with minor variants) Judg. 1: 1, *Quis ascendet, et cetera.*

forloren þurh eani deadlich sunne. Þe sunfule seolf is þe unwihtes lond, þe is ure deadliche fa; ah þis lond ure Lauerd bihat to biteachen i Iudase honden, for-hwon þet he ga biuoren. Schrift, lo, is gun|fanuner, ant bereð þe banere biuoren al Godes ferd, þet beoð
35 gode þeawes. Schrift reaueð þe feond his lond, þet is, þe sunfule mon, ant al todriueð Chanaan, þe feondes ferd of helle. Iudas hit dude licomliche, ant schrift, þet [he] bitacneð, deð gasteliche þet ilke. Þis beoð nuðe þreo þing þet [schrift deð o þe deouel. Þe oðer þreo þing, þet] hit deð us seoluen, beoð þeose her-efter.
40 **4.** Schrift wescheð us of alle ure fulðen, for swa hit is iwriten: *Omnia in confessione lauantur* (Glosa super Confitebimur tibi, Deus, confitebimur). Ant þet wes bitacnet þa Iudith wesch hire, ant despulede hire of widewene schrud; þet wes merke of sorhe, ant sorhe nis bute of sunne. *Lauit corpus suum et exuit se uestimentis sue uiduetatis.* Schrift
45 eft al þet god þet we hefden forloren þurh heaued sunne bringeð al aȝein ant ȝelt al togederes. *Ioel: Reddam uobis annos quos comedit locusta, brucus, rubigo, et erugo.* Þis wes bitacnet þurh þet [Iudith] schrudde hire mid halidahne weden, ant feahede hire utewið, as schrift deð us inwið, wið alle þe feire urnemenz þe blisse bitacnið.
50 Ant ure Lauerd seið þurh Zacharie: *Erunt sicut fuerant antequam proieceram eos*; þet is, schrift schal makie þe mon al swuch as he wes biuore þet he sunegede, ase cleane ant ase feier ant ase riche of alle god þe limpeð to sawle. Þe þridde þing is þet schrift deð us seoluen þe frut of þes oþre twa, ant endeð ham baðe: þet is, makeð us Godes
55 children. Þis is bitacnet þer-bi þet Iudas i Genesy biwon of Iacob Beniamin. 'Beniamin' seið ase muchel ase 'sune of riht half'. 'Iudas', þet is 'schrift', alswa as is 'Iudith', for ba ha spealieð an on Ebreische ledene. Þes gasteliche Iudas biȝet of Iacob his feader—þet is, ure Lauerd—to beon his riht hondes sune ant bruken buten | ende þe
60 eritage of heouene.

5. Nu we habbeð iseid of hwuch mihte schrift is, hwucch efficaces hit haueð, ant inempnet sixe. Loki we nu ȝeornliche hwuch schrift schule beon þe beo of swuch strengðe; ant forte schawin hit bet, deale we nu þis lim o sixtene stucchen.

65 **6.** Schrift schal beo wreiful, bitter mid sorhe, ihal, naket, ofte imaket, hihful, eadmod, scheomeful, [dredful ant] hopeful, wis, soð, ant willes, ahne ant studeuest, biþoht biuore longe. Her beoð nu as þah hit weren sixtene stuchen þe beoð ifeiet to schrift, ant we of euchan sum word [schulen] sunderliche seggen.

70 **7.** Schrift schal beo wreiful. Mon schal wreien him i schrift, nawt

werien him ne seggen, 'Ich hit dude þurh oþre', 'Ich wes ined þer-to', 'þe feond hit makede me don.' þus Eue ant Adam wereden ham, Adam þurh Eue ant Eue þurh þe neddre. þe feond ne mei neden na mon to na sunne, þah he eggi þer-to; ah ful wel he let of hwen ei seið þet he makede him to sunegin, as þah he hefde strengðe þe naueð nan mid alle bute of us seoluen. Ah me ah to seggen, 'Min ahne unwrestlec hit dude, ant willes ant waldes Ich beah to þe deouel.' 3ef þu witest ei þing þi sunne bute þe seoluen, þu ne schriuest te nawt. 3ef þu seist þet tin unstrengðe ne mahte nawt elles, þu wrenchest þi sunne upo Godd, þe makede þe swuch þet tu (bi þin tale) wiðstonde ne mahtest. Wreie we þenne us seoluen; for lo hwet Seinte Pawel seið: *Si nos ipsos diiud[ic]aremus, non utique iudicaremur.* þet is, 3ef we wreieð wel her ant demeð her us seoluen, we schule beo cwite of wreiunge ed te muchele Dome, þear-|as Seint Anselme seið þeos dredfule wordes: *Hinc erunt accusancia peccata, illinc te[r]rens Iusticia; supra, iratus Iudex, subtra, patens horridum chaos inferni; intus, urens consciencia, foris, ardens mundus. Peccator sic deprehensus in quam partem se premet?* O þe an half o Domes[dei] schulen ure swarte sunnen strongliche bicleopien us óf ure sawle morðre; o þe oþer half stont Rihtwisnesse þet na reowðe is wið, dredful ant grislich ant grureful to bihalden; buuen us þe eorre Deme—for ase softe as he is her, ase heard he bið þer, ase milde as he is nu, ase sturne þenne, lomb her, liun þer, as þe prophete witneð: *Leo rugiet; quis non timebit?* 'þe liun schal greden', he seið; 'hwa ne mei beon offearet?' Her we cleopieð him lomb as ofte as we singeð *Agnus Dei, qui tollis peccata mundi.* Nu, as Ich seide, schule we seon buuen us þe ilke eorre Deme þet is ec witnesse ant wat alle ure gultes, bineoðen us 3eoniende þe wide þrote of helle, inwið us seoluen ure ahne conscience (þet is, ure inwit) forculiende hire seoluen wið þe fur of sunne, wiðuten us al þe world leitinde o swart lei up into þe skiwes. þe sari sunfule þus biset, hu schal him stonde þenne? To hwuch of þes fowre mei he him biwenden? Nis þer buten heren þet hearde word, þet wa word, þet grisliche word, grureful ouer alle: *Ite, maledicti, in ignem eternum qui paratus est diabolo et angelis eius.* 'Gað, 3e aweariede, ut of min ehsihðe into þet eche fur þet wes igreiðet to þe feond ant to his engles. 3e forbuhe monne dom þet Ich demde mon to, þet wes to libben i swinc ant i sar on eorðe, ant 3e schulen nu for-þi habben deofles dom, bearne wið him echeliche i þe fur of | helle.' Wið þis schulen þe forlorene warpen a swuch 3ur þet heouene ant eorðe mahen ba grimliche agrisen. For-þi Seint Austin leofliche us leareð: *Ascendat homo tribunal mentis sue, si illud cogitat quod oportet eum exiberi ante tribunal Christi. Assit accusatrix Cogitatio, testis Consciencia, carnifex Timor.* Þet is, þenche mon o Domesdei ant deme her him seoluen þus o þisse wise. Skile sitte as domesmon upo þe dom-seotel. Cume þrefter forð his þohtes Munegunge, wreie him ant bicleopie him of misliche sunnen: 'Beal ami, þis þu dudest þear, ant tis þear, ant tis þear, ant o þisse wise.' His Inwit beo icnawes þrof ant beore witnesse: 'Soð hit is, soð hit is, þis ant muchele mare.' Cume forð þrefter Fearlac þurh þe deme heast, þe heterliche hate, 'Tac, bind him heteueste, for he is deaðes wurðe. Bind him swa euch lim þet he haueð wið isuneget þet he ne mahe wið ham sunegi na mare.' Fearlac haueð ibunden him hwen he ne dear for fearlac sturie toward sunne. Ȝet nis nawt þe deme (þet is, Skile) ipaiet þah he beo ibunden ant halde him wið sunne, bute ȝef he abugge þe sunne þet he wrahte; ant cleopeð forð Pine ant Sorhe, ant hat þet Sorhe þersche inwið þe heorte wið sar bireowsunge, swa þet hire suhie, ant Pin[e] þe flesch utewið mid feasten ant wið oþre fleschliche sares. Hwa-se o þisse wise biuoren þe muchele Dom demeð her him seoluen, eadi he is ant seli, for as þe prophete seið, *Non iudicabit Deus bis in idipsum.* Nule nawt ure Lauerd þet a mon for a þing beo twien idemet. Hit nis nawt i Godes curt as i þe schire, þer-as þe þet nickeð wel mei beon iborhen, ant te ful þe is icnawen. Biuore Godd | is oþerweis. *Si tu accusas, Deus excusat, et vice uersa.* Ȝef þu wreiest te her, Godd wule werie þe þear, ant skerin mid alle ed te nearewe Dome, for-hwon þet tu deme þe as Ich itaht habbe.

8. Schrift schal beo bitter, aȝein þet te sunne þuhte sumchearre swete. Iudith, þe spealeð 'schrift', as Ich ofte habbe iseid, wes Merarihtes dohter; ant Iudas, þet is ec 'schrift', wiuede o Thamar. Merariht ant Thamar, ba ha spealieð an[4] on Ebreische ledene. Neomeð nu ȝeorne ȝeme of þe bitacnunge. Ich hit segge scheortliche. Bitter sar ant schrift, þet an mot cumen of þe oþer, as Iudith dude of Merariht. Ant ba beon somet ifeiet, as Iudas ant Thamar, for nowðer wiðuten oðer nis noht wurð, oðer lutel; Phares ant Zaram ne temið ha neaure. **Iudas streonede of Thamar Phares ant Zaram** (*Phares diuisio, Zaram oriens interpretatur*), **þe gasteliche bitacnið tweamunge from sunne, ant i þe heorte þrefter arisinde grace.** Fowr þinges, ȝef mon þencheð þet heaued sunne dude him, mahen makien him to sorhin ant bittrin his heorte. Lo, þis þe forme. Ȝef a mon hefde ilosed in a time of þe dei his feader ant his moder, his sustren

---

[4] *An* in A only; all other manuscripts running have *bitternesse*.

ant his breðren, ant al his cun ant alle his freond þet he eauer hefde weren astoruen ferliche, nalde he ouer alle men sorhful beon ant sari, as he eaðe mahte? Godd wat, he mei beon muche deale sorhfulre þet haueð wið deadlich sunne gasteliche islein Godd inwið his sawle; nawt ane forloren þe swete Feader of heouene ant Seinte Marie, his deorewurðe moder (oðer Hali Chirche, hwen he of hire naueð ne leasse ne mare), ant te engles of heouene ant alle hali halhen þe weren him ear | for freond, for breðren ant for sustren, as to him ha beoð deade. As onont him is, he haueð islein ham alle, ant haueð þear-as ha liuieð aa leaððe of ham alle, as Ieremie witneð: *Omnes amici eius spreuerunt eam; facti sunt ei inimici,* þet is, al þet him luuede ȝeieð spi him on, ant heatieð him alle. Ȝet mare: his children, sone se he sunegede deadliche, deiden alle clane—þet beoð his gode werkes, þe beoð forloren alle. Ȝet upon al þis ilke he is him seolf biwrixlet, ant bicumen of Godes child þe deofles bearn of helle, eatelich to seonne, as Godd seolf i þe Godspel seið, *Vos ex patre diabolo estis.* þenche euch of his estat þet he is oðer wes in, ant he mei seon hweruore he ah to siken sare. For-þi seið Ieremie, *Luctum unigeniti fac tibi, planctum amarum*; make bitter man as wif deð for hire child þe nefde bute him ane, ant sið hit biuoren hire fearliche asteoruen. Nu þe oþer þet Ich bihet. A mon þe were idemet, for a luðer morðre, to beo forbearnd al cwic oðer scheomeliche ahonget, hu walde his heorte stonden? Me, þu unseli sunful, þa þu þurh deadlich sunne murðredest Godes spuse (þet is, þi sawle), þa þu were idemet forte beon ahonget o bearninde wearitre[o] i þe eche lei of helle. þer þu makedest foreward mid te deouel of þi deað, ant seidest in Ysaie wið þe forlorene, *Pepigimus cum morte fedus, et cum inferno iniuimus pactum,* þet is, 'We habbeð treowðe ipliht deað, foreward ifeast mid helle.' For þis is þe feondes chaffere: he ȝeoue þe sunne, ant tu him þi sawle, ant ti bodi mid al, to weane ant to wontreaðe world abuten ende. Nu þe þridde scheortliche. þench, | a mon þe hefde al þe world o walde, ant hefde for his cweadschipe forloren al on a stunde, hu he walde murnin ant sari iwurðen. þenne ahest tu to beon hundret siðe sarure þe þurh an heaued sunne forlure þe riche of heouene, forlure ure Lauerd, þet is hundret siðen, ȝe, þusent siðen betere þen is al þe world, eorðe ba ant heouene. *Que enim conuentio Christi ad Belial?* Nu ȝet þe feorðe. Ȝef þe king hefde bitaht his deore sune to his an cniht to lokin, ant unþeode leadde forð þis child in his warde, swa þet tet child seolf weorrede upon his feader wið þet unþeode, nalde þe cniht beo sari ant scheomien ful sare? We beoð

190 alle Godes sunen, þe Kinges of heouene, þe haueð bitaht ure euchan engel i warde. Sari is he on his wise hwen unþeode leat us forð, hwen we ure gode Feader [weorrið] wið sunne. Beo we sari þet we eauer schulen wreaðen swuch feader, ant sweamen swuch wardein, þe wit ant wereð us eauer wið þe unseli gastes, for elles uuele us stode. Ah
195 we schuhteð him awei hwen we doð deadlich **sunne**,[5] ant heo leapeð þenne to sone se he us firseð. Halde we him neh us wið smeal of **gode**[6] werkes, ant us in his warde. [Wat] Crist, ure euchan to se g[ent]il wardein bereð to lutel menske, ant kunnen him to lutel þonc of his seruise. þeos ant monie reisuns beoð hwi mon mei beo
200 bitterliche sari for his sunnen, ant wepen ful sare; ant wel is him þe swa mei, for wop is sawle heale. Vre Lauerd deð toward us as me deð to uuel deattur—nimeð leasse þen we ahen him ant is þah wel ipaiet. We ahen him blod for blod, ant ure blod þah aȝein his blod þet he schedde for us were ful unefne change. Ah wast | tu hu me f. 85ᵛ
205 ȝeddeð, 'Me nimeð ed uuel dettur aten for hweate'? Ant ure Lauerd nimeð ed us ure teares aȝein his blod, ant is wilcweme. He weop o þe rode, o Lazre, o Ierusalem, for oðer monne sunnen; ȝef [we] wepeð for ure ahne, nis na muche wunder. 'Wepe we,' quoð þe hali mon i *Vitas Patrum*, þa me hefde longe on him iȝeiet efter sarmun. 'Leote
210 we', quoð he, 'teares leste ure ahne teares forseoðen us in helle.'

9. Schrift schal beon ihal: þet is, iseid al to a mon ut of childhade. M. 314 þe poure widewe hwen ha wule hire hus cleansin, ha gedereð al þe greaste on an heap on alre earst, ant schuueð hit ut þenne. þrefter kimeð eft aȝein ant heapeð eft togederes þet wes ear ileauet, ant
215 schuueð hit ut efter. þrefter o þe smeale dust, ȝef hit dusteð swiðe, ha flaskeð weater, ant swopeð ut efter al þet oðer. Alswa schal þe schriueð him efter þe greate schuuen ut te smealre. Ȝef dust of lihte þohtes windeð to swiðe up, flaski teares on ham; ne schulen ha nawt þenne ablende þe heorte ehnen. Hwa-se heleð eawiht, he naueð iseid
220 nawiht for-hwon he beo þe skerre, [ah] is ilich þe mon þe haueð on him monie deadliche wunden, ant schaweð þe leche alle ant let healen buten an, þet he deieð upon as he schulde on alle. He is ase men in a schip þe haueð monie þurles þer þe weater þreasteð in, ant heo dutteð alle buten an, þurh hwam ha druncnið alle clane. Me
225 teleð of þe hali mon þe lei on his deað-uuel ant wes lað to seggen a sunne of his childhad; ant his abbat bed him allegate seggen. Ant he ondswerede þet hit nere na neod, for-þi þet he wes lute child þa he

---

[5] For *sunne* (also LPSV), CFGT have *fulðe*, N *sunne and fulðe*.
[6] For *gode* (also LS), CGNV have *swote*, TS *swete*.

f. 86ʳ hit | wrahte. O least þah unneaðe þurh þe abbates ropunge he hit seide, ant deide þrefter sone. Efter his deað com a niht ant schawde him to his abbat i snaw-hwite schrudes as þe þet wes iborhen, ant 230 seide þet sikerliche ȝef he nefde þet ilke þing þet he dude i childhad i schrift utterliche iseid, he were idemet bimong þe forlorene. Alswa of anoþer þet wes for-neh fordemet for-þi þet he hefde enchearre ined a mon to drinken ant deide þrof unschriuen; alswa of þe leafdi, for-þi þet ha hefde ileanet to a wake a wummon an of hire weden. Ah hwa- 235
M. 316 se haueð ȝeorne isoht alle þe hurnen of his heorte ne ne con rungi mare ut, ȝef þer eawiht edluteð hit is, Ich hopie, i þe schrift ischuuen ut mid tet oþer,⁷ hwen þer ne lið na ȝemeles ant he walde fein mare ȝef he cuðe seggen.

10. Schrift schal beo naket: þet is, naketliche imaket, nawt 240 bisamplet feire ne hendeliche ismaket, ah schulen þe wordes beon ischa[p]et efter þe werkes. Þet is tacne of heatunge þet me tukeð to wundre þing þet me heateð swiðe. Ȝef þu heatest ti sunne, hwi spekest tu menskeliche þrof? Hwi hudest tu his fulðe? Spec hit scheome schendfulliche ant tuk hit al to wundre, alswa as þu wel 245 wult schende þen schucke. 'Sire,' ha seið, þe wummon, 'Ich habbe ihaued leofmon', oðer 'Ich habbe ibeon', ha seið, 'fol of me seoluen.' Þis nis nawt naket schrift. Biclute þu hit nawt. Do awei þe totagges!⁸ Vnwrih þe ant sei, 'Sire, Godes are! Ich am a ful stod-meare, a stinkinde hore!' Ȝef þi fa a ful nome ant cleope þi sunne fule. Make 250 hit i schrift steort-naket: þet is, ne hel þu nawiht of al þet lið þer-
f. 86ᵛ abuten. (Þah to fule me mei | seggen. Me ne þearf nawt nempnin þet fule dede bi his ahne fule nome, ne þe schend-fule limes bi hire ahne nome. Inoh is to seggen swa þet te hali schrift-feader witerliche understonde hweat tu wulle 255 meanen.)

11. Abute sunne liggeð six þing þet hit hulieð, o Latin 'circum-stances' (on Englisch 'totagges' mahe beon icleopede): persone, stude, time, manere, tale, cause.

12. Persone: þe dude þe sunne, oðer wið hwam me hit dude. 260 Unwreo ant segge, 'Sire, Ich am a wummon, ant schulde bi rihte beo mare scheomeful to habben ispeken as Ich spec, oðer idon as Ich dude; for-þi mi sunne is mare þen of a wepmon, for hit bicom me
M. 318 wurse. Ich am an ancre; a nunne; a wif iweddet; a meiden; a

---

⁷ *Augustinus: Si consciencia desit, pena satisfacit*, with minor variants, after *oþer* in PT, after *seggen* (5. 239) in CGLNV; not in AF.
⁸ After *totagges*, N has 'ðet beoð þe circumstaunces.'

265 wummon þet me lefde se wel; a wummon þe habbe ear ibeon ibearnd wið swuch þing ant ahte þe betere forte beon iwarnet. Sire, hit wes wið swuch mon'—ant nempni þenne: 'munek, preost, oðer clearc, ant of þet ordre; a weddet mon; a ladles þing; a wummon as Ich am.' þis is nu of persone.⁹

270 13. Alswa of þe stude: 'Sire, þus Ich pleide oðer spec i chirche; e[o]de o ring i chirch3ard; biheold hit oþer wreastlunge,¹⁰ ant oðre fol gomenes; spec þus oðer pleide biuoren worltliche men, biuoren [religiuse], in ancre-hus, ed oþer þurl þen Ich schulde, neh hali þing. Ich custe him þer; hondlede him i swuch stude, oðer me seoluen. I 275 chirche Ich þohte þus, biheold him ed te weouede.'¹¹

14. Of þe time alswa: 'Sire, Ich wes of swuch ealde þet Ich ahte wel to habben wisluker iwite me. Sire, Ich hit dude in Lenten; i feasten-dahes; in halidahes; hwen oþre weren ed chirche. Sire, Ich wes sone ouercumen, ant is þe sunne mare þen 3ef Ich hefde | ibeon f. 87ʳ 280 akeast wið strengðe ant feole swenges. Sire, Ich wes þe biginnunge hwi swuch þing hefde forð3ong, þurh þet Ich com i swuch stude ant i swuch time. Ich biþohte me ful wel, ear þen Ich hit eauer dude, hu uuele hit were idon, ant dude hit noðeleatere.'

15. Þe manere alswa seggen, þet is þe feorðe totagge: 'Sire, þis 285 sunne Ich dude þus, ant o þisse wise. Þus Ich leornede hit earst; þus Ich com earst þrin; þus Ich dude hit forðward, o þus feole wisen, þus fulliche, þus scheomeliche; þus Ich sohte delit, hu Ich meast mahte paien mi lustes brune', ant seggen al þe wise.

16. Tale is þe [fifte] totagge: [hu ofte hit is idon tellen al. 'Sire, M. 320 290 Ich habbe þis þus ofte idon, iwunet forte speoke þus, hercni þulli speche, þenchen swucche þohtes, for3eme þing ant for3eoten, lahhen, eoten, drinken leasse oðer mare þenne neode easkeð. Ich habbe ibeon þus ofte wrað seoððen Ich wes ischriuen nest, ant for þulli þing, ant þus longe hit leaste; þus ofte iseid leas, þus ofte þis 295 ant þis. Ich habbe idon þis to þus feole, ant o þus feole wisen.'

17. Cause is þe seste totagge.] Cause is hwi þu hit dudest, oðer hulpe oþre þer-to, oðer þurh hwet hit bigon. 'Sire, Ich hit dude for delit; for uuel luue; for bi3ete; for fearlac; for flatrunge. Sire, Ich hit dude for uuel, þah þer ne come nan of. Sire, mi lihte ondswere oðer 300 mine lihte lates tulden him earst upo me. Sire, of þis word com, oþer

---

⁹ After *persone*, T has 'O þis ilke wise weapmon cearche him seluen, and scheawe i schrift openli', similarly S.
¹⁰ After *wreastlunge*, T has 'oðer me seolf wrastlede', similarly S.
¹¹ After *weouede*, TS have 'as he offrede'.

of þis dede, wreaðða ant vuele wordes. Sire, þe acheisun is þis hwi þet uuel leasteð ȝet: þus wac wes min heorte.'

18. Euch efter þet he is segge his totagges, mon as limpeð to him, wummon þet hire rineð; for her nabbe Ich nan iseid bute forte munegin mon oðer wummon of þeo þe to ham falleð þurh þeo þe beoð her iseide as on urn. Þus of þeose six wriheles despoile þi sunne, ant make hit naket i þi schrift as Ieremie leareð: *Effunde sicut aquam cor tuum*, 'Sched ut ase weater þin heorte.' Ȝef eoile schet of a feat, ȝet ter wule leauen in sumhwet of þe licur; ȝef milc schet, þe heow leaueð; ȝef win sched, þe smeal leaueð; ah weater geað al somet ut. Alswa sched þin heorte—þet is, al þet uuel þet is i þin heorte. Ȝef þu ne dest nawt, lo hu grurefulliche Godd seolf þreateð þe þurh Naum þe prophete:[12] *Ostendam gentibus nuditatem tuam et regnis ignominiam tuam, et proitiam super te abhominationes tuas*. 'Þu naldest nawt unwreo þe to þe preost i schrifte; ant Ich schal schawin al naket to al folc þi cweadschipe, ant to alle kinedomes þine scheome sunnen—to þe kinedom of eorðe, to þe kinedom of helle, to þe kinedom of heouene—ant trussin al þi schendfulnesse o þin ahne necke, as me deð o þe þeof þe me leat to demen; ant swa wið al þe schendlac þu schalt, trusse ant al, torplin into helle.' O, seið Sein Beornard, *quid confusionis, quid ignominie erit quando dissipatis foliis et dispersis uniuersa nudabitur turpitudo, sanies apparebit*. 'O,' seið Sein Beornard, 'hwuch schendlac ant hwuch sorhe bið þer' **ed te Dome**, 'hwen alle þe leaues schule beon towarplet, ant al þet fulðe schaweð him, ant wringeð ut þet wursum' biuoren al þe wide worlt, eorðware ant heouenes—nawt ane of werkes, ah of idelnesses, of wordes ant of þohtes þe ne beoð ibet her, as Seint Anselme witneð: *Omne tempus impensum, requiretur a uobis qualiter sit expensum*. Euc tide ant time schal beo þer irikenet hu hit wes her ispenet. *Quando dissipatis foliis, et cetera*. 'Hwen alle þe leaues', he seið, Sein Beornard, 'schulen beon towarplet'. He biheold hu Adam ant Eue, þa ha hefden i þe frumðe isuneget, gedereden leaues ant makeden wriheles of ham to hare schentfule limen. Þus doð monie efter ham, *declinantes cor suum in uerba malicie, ad excusandas excusationes in peccatis*.

19. Schrift schal beon ofte imaket. For-þi is i þe Sawter, *Confitebimur tibi, Deus, confitebimur*. Ant ure Lauerd seolf seið to his deciples, *Eamus iterum in Iudeam*. 'Ga we eft', seide he, 'into Iudee.' 'Iudee' spealeð 'schrift'; ant swa we ifindeð þet he wende ofte ut of Galilee into Iudee. 'Galilee' spealeð 'hweol', forte learen us þet

---

[12] After *prophete*, all manuscripts running but A have *Ecce ego ad te, dicit Dominus*.

340 we of þe worldes turpelnesse ant of sunne hweol ofte gan to schrifte; for þis is þe sacrement, efter þe weofdes sacrement ant efter fulluht, þet te feond is laðest, as he haueð to hali men him seolf—sare his unþonckes—ibeon hit icnawen. Wule a web beon ed en chearre wið a weater wel ibleachet? A sol clað wel iweschen? Þu weschest þine
345 honden in anlepi dei twien oðer þrien, ant nult nawt þe sawle—Iesu Cristes spuse, þe eauer se ha is hwittre, se fulðe is senre upon hire, bute ha beo iwesschen—nult nawt to Godes cluppunge ofte umbe seoueniht wesschen hire eanes. *Confiteor*, hali weater, beoden, hali þohtes, blesceunges, cneolunges, euch god word, euch god werc,
350 wesscheð smeale sunnen þe me ne mei alle seggen; ah eauer is schrift þe heaued.

M. 324

20. Schrift schal beon on hihðe imaket: ȝef sunne timeð bi niht, anan oðer ine marhen; ȝef hit timeð bi dei, ear þen me slepe. Hwa durste slepen hwil his deadliche fa heolde an itohe sweord upon his
355 heaued? Þe neappið upon helle breord, ha torplið ofte al in ear ha least wenen. Hwa-se is ifallen amid te bearninde fur, nis he mare þen amead ȝef he lið [ant] biþencheð him hwenne he wule arisen? A wummon þe haueð ilosed hire nelde, oðer a sutere his eal, secheð hit ananriht ant towent euch strea aþet hit beo ifunden; ant Godd, þurh
360 sunne forloren, schal liggen unsoht seoue dahes fulle!

21. Nihe þinges | beoð þet ahten hihin to schrift. Þe pine þet okereð; for sunne is þe deofles feh, þet he ȝeueð to okere ant to gauel of pine, ant eauer se mon lið lengre in his sunne, se þe gauel waxeð of pine, i Purgatoire oðer her oðer in helle (*Ex usuris et iniquitate, et*
365 *cetera*[13]). Þe oðer þing is þe muchele ant te reowðfule lure þet he leoseð, þet na þing þet he deð nis Gode licwurðe (*Alieni comederunt robur eius*). Þe þridde is deað: þet he nat hweðer he schule þet ilke dei ferliche asteoruen (*Fili, ne tardes, et cetera*[14]). Þe feorðe is secnesse: þet he ne mei þenche wel bute ane of his uuel, ne speoken as he schulde,
370 bute granin for his eche, ant grunte mare for his stiche þen for his sunne (*Sanus confiteberis et viuens*). Þe fifte þing is muche scheome þet hit is efter val to liggen se longe, ant hure under þe schucke.[15] Þe

f. 88ᵛ
M. 326

---

[13] *Ex . . . et cetera* (5. 364–5) at this point in ANP, after *pine* (5. 363) in GLSTV; not in CF, but added in the margin of C by C³. C³GLNSTV complete the quotation, *redimet animas eorum*.

[14] *Fili . . . tardes* (5. 368), with varying forms of reference, at this point in all manuscripts but CF (added by C³ in the margin of C). LS complete the sentence, *conuerti ad Dominum, et ne differas de die in diem; subito enim veniet ira illius et in tempore vindicte disperdet te*. C³GNTV continue to *Dominum*, and add *Nescis enim*; T continues further, *quid pariat uentura dies*.

[15] After *schucke*, LNPST have *Surge qui dormis*; also added in the margin of C by C³.

seste is þe wunde, þet eauer wurseð on hond ant strengre is to healen (*Principiis obsta; [sero] medicina paratur / Cum mala per longas . . .*). þe seoueðe þing is uuel wune, þet Lazre bitacneð, þe stonc se longe he hefde ilein i þer eorðe; o hwam ure Lauerd weop, as þe Godspel teleð, ant risede, ant mengde him seoluen, ant ȝeide lude upon him. [þeose fowr þing he dude] ear he him arearde, forte schawin hu strong hit is to arisen of uuel wune þe roteð in his sunne. Seinte Marie! Lazre stonc of fowr dahes; hu stinkeð þe sunfule of fowr ȝer oðer of fiue? *Quam difficile surgit quem moles male consuetudinis premit.* 'O,' seið Seint Austin, 'hu [earueðliche] he ariseð þe under wune of sunne haueð ilein longe!' *Circumdederunt me canes multi.* 'Monie hundes', seið Dauið, 'habbeð biset me.' Hwen gredi hundes stondeð biuore þe bord, nis hit neod ȝerde? As ofte as eani lecheð toward te ant reaueð þe of þi mete, nult tu as ofte smiten? Elles ha walden kecchen of þe al þet tu hefdest. Ant tu alswa | þenne nim þe ȝerde of þi tunge, ant as ofte as þe dogge of helle kecheð ei god from þe, smit him ananriht mid te ȝerde of þi tunge i schrift, ant smit him se luðerliche þet him laði ant drede to snecchen eft toward te. þet dunt of alle duntes is him dunte laðest. þe hund þe fret leðer oðer awuri[e]ð ahte, me hit beat ananriht þet he understonde for-hwi he is ibeaten; þenne ne dear he nawt eft do þet ilke. Beat alswa mid ti tunge schrift þe hund of helle ananriht, ant he wule beon ofdred to do þe eft swuch þucke. Hwa is se fol þet he seið bi þe hund þet fret leðer, 'Abid aþet to-marhen, ne beat tu him nawt ȝetten'? Ah ananriht beat—beat, beat ananriht! Nis þing i þe world þet smeorteð him sarre þen deð swuch beatunge. Se me deoppre wadeð i þe feondes leiuen, se me kimeð up leatere. þe eahtuðe þing is þet Seint Gregoire seið: *Peccatum quod per penitenciam non diluitur mox suo pondere ad aliud trahit*; þet is, sunne þet nis sone ibet draheð anan anoðer, ant þet eft þe þridde, ant swa euchan cundleð mare ant wurse cundel þen þe seolue moder. þe niheðe reisun is, se he ear biginneð her to don his penitence, se he haueð to beten leasse i pine of Purgatoire. þis beoð nu nihe reisuns—ant monie ma þer beoð— hwi schrift ah to beon imaket aa on hihðe.

22. Schrift ah to beon eadmod, as þe puplicanes wes, nawt as þe Phariseus wes, þe talde his goddeden, ant schawde þet hale forð þa he schulde habben unw[r]ihen hise wunden; for-þi he wende unhealet, as ure Lauerd seolf teleð, ut of þe temple. Eadmodnesse

PART 5

is ilich þeose cointe hearloz,[16] hare gute-feastre, hare flowinde cweise þet ha putteð eauer forð, ant ȝef hit is eatelich, ha schawið hit ȝet eateluker i riche | monnes ehnen þet ha habben reowðe of ham ant ȝeouen ham god þe reaðere; hudeð hare hale clað ant doð on alre uuemest fiterokes al totorene. O þis ilke wise Eadmodnesse [eadiliche] bigileð ure Lauerd ant biȝet of his god wið seli truandise; hudeð eauer hire god, schaweð forð hire pouerte, put forð hire cancre, wepinde ant graninde biuore Godes ehnen; halseð meadlesliche on his derue passiun, on his deorewurðe blod, on his fif wunden, on his moder teares, o þe ilke tittes þet he seac, þe milc þet hine fedde, on alle his halhene luue, o þe deore druerie þet he haueð to his deore spuse (þet is, to cleane sawle **oðer to Hali Chirche**), on his deað o rode for hire to biȝeotene. Wið þis anewil ropunge halseð efter sum help to þe wrecche meoseise, to lechni wið þe seke, to healen hire cancre. Ant ure Lauerd, ihalset swa, ne mei for reowðe wearnen hire ne sweamen hire wið warne, nomeliche swa as he is se unimete large þet him nis na þing leouere þen þet he mahe ifinden acheisun forte ȝeouene. Ah hwa-se ȝelpeð of his god, as doð i schrift þeos prude, hwet neod is ham to helpe? Moni haueð a swuch manere to seggen hire sunnen þet hit is wurð a dearne ȝelp, ant hunteð efter hereword of mare halinesse.

23. Schrift ah to beon scheomeful. Bi þet te folc of Israel wende ut þurh þe Reade Sea, þet wes read ant bitter, is bitacnet þet we moten þurh rudi scheome þet is i soð schrift, ant þurh bitter penitence, passin to heouene. God riht is, wat Crist, þet us scheomie biuore mon þe forȝeten scheome þa we duden þe sunne biuore Godes sihðe. *Nam omnia nuda sunt et aperta oculis eius ad quem nobis sermo*: 'For al þet is naket', seið Seinte Pawel, 'ant o|pen to his ehnen wið hwam we schulen rikenin alle ure deden.' Scheome is þe measte deal, as Seint Austin seið, of ure penitence: *Verecundia pars est magna penitencie*. Ant Sein Bernard seið þet na deorewurðe ȝimstan ne deliteð swa muchel mon to bihalden as deð Godes ehe þe rude of monnes neb þe riht seið hise sunnen. Vnderstond wel þis word. Schrift is a sacrement, ant euch sacrement haueð an ilicnesse utewið of þet hit wurcheð inwið, as hit is i fulluht: þe wesschunge wiðuten bitacneð þe wesschunge of sawle wiðinnen. Alswa i schrift þe cwike rude of þe neb deð to understonden þet te sawle, þe wes bla ant nefde bute dead heow, haueð icaht cwic heow ant is irudet feire.

---

[16] After *hearloz*, F has 'mendianz et meseisez'.

(*Interior tamen penitencia non dicitur sacramentum, sed exterior uel puplica uel solempnis.*)

24. Schrift schal beo dredful, þet tu segge wið Ierome, *Quociens confessus sum, uideor michi non esse confessus*, 'As ofte as Ich am ischriuen, eauer me þuncheð me unschriuen'; for eauer is sum forȝeten of þe totagges. For-þi seið Seint Austin, *Ve laudabili hominum uite si remota misericordia discutias eam*: þet is, þe beste mon of al þe world, ȝef ure Lauerd demde him al efter rihtwisnesse ant nawt efter mearci, wa schulde him iwurðen. *Set misericordia superexaltat iudicium*: ah his mearci toward us weieð eauer mare þen þe rihte nearewe.

25. Schrift schal beon hopeful. Hwa-se seið as he con ant deð al þet he mei, Godd ne bit na mare. Ah hope ant dred schulen aa beon imengt togederes. þis forte bitacnin, wes i þe alde lahe ihaten þet te twa grindelstanes ne schulde na mon twinnin. þe neoðere, þe lið stille ant bereð heui charge, bitacneð fearlac, þe teieð mon from sunne | ant is iheueget her wið heard forte beo quite of heardre. þe vuere stan bitacneð hope, þe eorneð ant stureð hire i gode werkes eauer wið trust of muche mede. þeos twa na mon ne parti from oþer. For as Sein Gregoire seið, *Spes sine timore luxuriat in presumptionem, timor sine spe degenerat in desperationem*; dred wiðuten hope makeð mon untrusten, ant hope wiðute dred makeð ouertrusten. þeos twa unþeawes, vntrust ant ouertrust, beoð þe deofles tristen, þer þet wrecche beast seldene edstearteð. Triste is þer me sit mid te greahunz forte kepe þe heare, oðer tildeð þe nettes aȝein him. Toward an of þeos twa is al þet he sleateð; for þer beoð his greahunz, þer beoð his nettes. Vntrust ant ouertrust beoð of alle sunnen nest te ȝete of helle. Wið dred wiðuten hope—þet is, wið untrust—wes Caymes schrift ant Iudasen, for-hwi ha forferden. Wið hope wiðute dred—þet is, wið ouertrust—is þe unselies sahe þe seið i þe Sawter, *Secundum multitudinem ire sue non queret*: 'Nis nawt Godd', quoð h[e], 'se grim as ȝe him fore makieð.' 'Na,' he seið, Dauið, 'ȝeoi he'; ant seið þenne, *Propter quid irritauit impius Deum? Dixit enim in corde suo, Non requiret.* On alre earst he cleopeð þe ouer-trusti 'unbileuet'. þe unbileuet, wið hwon gremeð he Godd almihti? Wið þon þet he seið, 'Nule he nawt se nearowliche demen as ȝe seggeð.' Ȝeoi, siker, ah he wule. þus þeos twa unþeawes beoð to grimme robberes ieuenet, for þe an (þet is, ouertrust) reaueð Godd his rihte dom ant his rihtwisnesse, þe oðer (þet is, untrust) reaueð him his milce. Ant swa ha beoð umben to fordon Godd seolf; for

PART 5

Godd ne muhte nawt beon wiðuten rihtwisnesse, ne wiðuten milce. Nu þenne, | hwucche unþeawes beoð euening to þeose þe wulleð f. 91ʳ Godd acwellen on hare fule wise? ȝef þu art to trusti ant haldest Godd to nessche forte wreoke sunne, sunne likeð him bi þin tale. Ah
495 bihald hu he wrec in his hehengel þe þoht of a prude; hu he wrec in Adam þe bite of an eappel; hu he bisencte Sodome ant Gommorre, were ant wif ant wenchel, þe nomecuðe burhes, al a muche schire, dun into helle grunde, þer-as is nu þe Deade Sea þet nawiht cwikes nis inne; hu he i Noes flod al þe world adrencte, bute eahte i þe
500 arche; hu he in his ahne folc, Israel his deorling, grimliche awrec him M. 336 ase ofte as ha gulten—Dathan ant Abyron, Chore ant his feren, þe oþre alswa þe he sloh bi feole þusendes ofte for hare gruchunge ane. On oþer half loke, ȝef þu hauest untrust of his unimete milce, hu lihtliche ant hu sone Seinte Peter, efter þet he hefde forsaken him,
505 ant þet for a cwene wor[d], wes wið him isahtnet; [hu] þe þeof o rode, þe hefde aa iliued uuele, in a sterthwile [ofeode] ed him milce wið a feier speche. For-þi bitweone þeos twa, vntrust ant ouertrust, hope ant dred beon aa ifeiet togederes.

26. Schrift ȝet schal beo wis, ant to wis mon imaket, of uncuðe
510 sunnen, nawt to ȝunge preostes—ȝunge, Ich segge, of wit—ne to sotte alde. Bigin earst ed prude ant sech alle þe bohes þrof as ha beoð þruppe iwritene, hwuch falle to þe; þrefter alswa of onde; ant ga we swa duneward rawe bi rawe aþet to þe leaste, ant drah togedere al þe team under þe moder.

515 27. Schrift ah to beo soð. Ne lih þu nawt o þe seolf; for as Seint Austin seið, *Qui causa humilitatis de se mentitur fit quod prius ipse non fuit, id est, peccator*: þe seið leas on him seolf þurh | to muchel f. 91ᵛ eadmodnesse, he is imaket sunful þah he ear nere. Sein Gregoire seið þah, *Bonarum mentium est culpam agnoscere ubi culpa non est*: cunde of
520 god heorte is to beon offearet of sunne þer-as nan nis ofte, oðer weie swiðre his sunne sumchearre þen he þurfte. Weien hit to lutel is ase uuel oðer wurse; þe middel wei of meosure is eauer guldene. Drede we us eaure; for ofte we weneð forte don a lutel uuel ant doð a great sunne, ofte wel to donne ant doð al to cweade. Segge we eauer þenne
525 wið Seinte Anselme: *Etiam bonum nostrum [ita] est aliquo modo* M. 338 *corruptum ut possit non placere aut certe displicere Deo. Paulus: Scio quod non est in me—hoc est, in carne mea—bonum*. Na god in us nis of us; ure god is Godes. Ah sunne is of us, ant ure ahne. Godes god hwen Ich hit do, quoð he, Seint Anselme, swa o summe wise min
530 uuel hit forgneaieð, oþer Ich hit do ungleadliche, oþer to ear oðer to

leate, oðer leote wel þrof þah na mon hit nute, oþer walde þet ei hit wiste, oðer ʒemelesliche do hit oðer to unwisliche, to muchel oðer to lutel. Þus eauer sum uuel mongleð him wið mi god þet Godes grace ʒeueð me, þet hit mei lutel likin Godd, ant mislikin ofte.[17] Seinte Marie! hwen þe hali mon seide þus bi him seolf,[18] hu mahe we hit witerliche seggen bi us wrecches!

28. Schrift ah to beon willes: þet is, willeliche unfreinet, nawt idrahen of þe as þin unþonkes. Hwil þu const seggen eawt, sei al uneasket. Me ne schal easki nan bute for neode ane, for of þe easkunge mei uuel fallen bute hit beo þe wisre. On oðer half, moni mon abit forte schriuen him aðet te nede tippe; ah ofte him liheð þe wrench, þet he | ne mei hwen he wule þe nalde þa he mahte. Na mare cangschipe nis þen setten Godd tearme, as þah grace were his, **as he bere hire in his purs,**[19] to neomen upo grace þrin i þe tearme as he him seolf sette. Nai, beal ami, nai! Þe tearme is i Godes hond, nawt i þi bandun. Hwen Godd beot hit te, reach to ba þe honden; for wiðdrahe he his hond, þu maht þrefter lokin. Ʒef uuel oðer oþerhwet ned te to schrifte, lo hwet seið Seint Austin: *Coacta seruicia Deo non placent,* 'Seruises inedde ne cwemeð nawt ure Lauerd.' Þah noðeleatere betere is 'O!' Þene 'No!': *Nunquam sera penitencia si tamen uera,* 'Nis neauer to leate penitence þet is soðliche imaket', he seið eft him seoluen. Ah betere is as Dauið seið, *Refloruit caro mea et ex uoluntate mea confitebor ei:* þet is, 'Mi flesch is ifluret, bicumen al neowe, for Ich chulle schriue me ant herie Godd willes.' Wel seið he 'ifluret' to bitacnin wil-schrift; for þe eorðe al unnet, ant te treon alswa, openið ham ant bringeð forð misliche flures. *In Canticis: Flores apparuerunt in terra nostra.* Eadmodnesse, abstinence, culures unlaðnesse, ant oþre swucche uertuz beoð feire i Godes ehnen ant swote i Godes nease smeallinde flures. Of ham make his [herber] inwið þe seoluen, for his delices, he seið, beoð þer forte wunien. *Et delicie mee esse cum filiis hominum: in libro Prouerbiorum.*

29. Schrift ah to beon ahne. Na mon ne schal i schrift wreien bute him seoluen, ase forð as he mei. Þis Ich segge for-þi þet swuch auenture bitimeð to sum mon **oðer to sum wummon** þet **ha** ne mei nawt fulleliche wreien **hire** seoluen bute **ha** wreie oþre; ah bi nome noðeleatere ne nempni **ha** nawt þe ilke, þah þe schrift-feader

---

[17] After *ofte*, F has: 'Cest meismes dit seint Poul la desus. "Jeo sai qil ni ad en mei", ceo dit il, "nul bien", et par ceo entend il meismes ceo qe iai dit de la parole Seint Anselme.'

[18] For 'þe . . . seolf' (5. 535), F has 'ces seinz homs diseient issi par eus meismes', similarly PS.

[19] For 'as . . . purs' (5. 544) (in A only), L has *quasi in sua potestate esset.*

wite wel | toward hwam hit turne, ah 'a munk' oðer 'a preost', nawt
'Wilȝam' ne 'Water', þah þer beo nan oþer.

30. Schrift schal beo studeuest, to halde þe penitence ant leaue þe
sunne; þet tu segge to þe preost, 'Ich habbe studefestliche i þonc ant
in heorte þis sunne to forleten ant do þe penitence.' þe preost ne
schal nawt easki þe ȝef þu wult þeonneuorð forhate þi sunne; inoh is
þet tu segge þet tu hit hauest on heorte treoweliche to donne þurh
Godes grace, ant ȝef þu fallest eft þrin, þet tu wult ananriht arisen
þurh Godes help, ant cumen aȝein to schrifte. *Vade et amplius noli
peccare*: 'Ga,' quoð ure Lauerd **to a sunful wummon**,[20] 'ant haue
wil þet tu nult sungi na mare.' þus ne easkede he nan oðer
sikernesse.

31. Schrift ah to beon biþoht biuore longe. Of fif þinges wið þi
wit gedere þine sunnen: of alle þine ealdes, of childhad, of
ȝuheðehad, gedere al togederes; þrefter gedere þe studen þet tu in
wunedest, ant þench ȝeorne hwet tu dudest in euch stude sunderliche ant in euch ealde; þrefter sech al ut ant trude þine sunnen bi
þine fif wittes; þrefter, bi alle þine limen, i hwuch þu hauest isuneget
meast oðer oftest; aleast sunderliche bi dahes ant bi tiden.

32. Nu ȝe habbeð alle ihaued, as Ich understonde, þe sixtene
stuccchen þe Ich bihet to dealen; ant alle Ich habbe tobroken ham ow,
mine leoue sustren, as me deð to children þe mahten wið unbroke
bread deien on hunger. Ah me is, þet wite ȝe, moni crome edfallen;
secheð ham ant gederið, for ha beoð sawle fode.

33. þulli schrift, þet haueð þus þes sixtene stucchen, haueð þe
ilke muchele mihten þet Ich earst seide: þreo aȝein þe | deouel, þreo
on us seoluen, **ant þreo aȝeines þe world**, deorewurðe ouer gold or
ant ȝimmes of Ynde.

34. Mine leoue sustren, þis fifte dale, þe is of schrift, limpeð to
alle men iliche; for-þi ne wundri ȝe ow nawt þet Ich toward ow
nomeliche nabbe nawt ispeken i þis dale. Habbeð þah to ower bihoue
þis lutle leaste ende.

35. Of alle cuðe sunnen, as of prude, of great oðer of heh heorte,
of onde, of wreaððe, of slawðe, of ȝemeles, of idel word, of untohene
þohtes, of sum idel herunge, of sum fals gleadunge oðer of heui
murnunge, of ypocresie, of mete, of drunch to muchel oðer to lutel,
of gruchunge, of grim chere, of silences ibrokene, of sitten longe ed
þurl, of vres mis iseide, wiðute ȝeme of heorte oðer in untime, of

---

[20] For 'to . . . wummon' (5. 576), L has *adultere*, S 'a celui ke il garist e signefie le repentant'; not in other manuscripts.

sum fals word, of sware, of plohe, of ischake lahtre, of schede cromen
oðer ale, of leote þinges muhelin, rustin, oðer rotien, claðes
unseowet, bireinet, unwesschen, breoke nep oðer disch, oðer biseo
ȝemelesliche ei þing þet me wið feareð oðer ahte to ȝemen, of
keorfunge, of hurtunge þurh unbisehenesse, of alle þe þinges þe beoð
i þis riwle þe beoð misnumene—of alle þulliche þing schriue hire
euche wike eanes ed te leaste. For nan se lutel nis of þeos þet te
deouel naueð enbreuet on his rolle; ah schrift hit schrapeð of, ant
makeð him to leosen muchel of his hwile. Ah al þet schrift ne
schrapeð of, al he wule o Domesdei rede ful witerliche forte bicleopie
þe wið; a word ne schal þer wontin. Nu þenne, Ich reade, ȝeoueð
him to writen þet leaste þet ȝe eauer mahen, for na meoster nis him
leouere. Ant hwet-se he writ, beoð umben to schrapien hit of
cleanliche; wið na þing ne mahe ȝe matin him betere.

36. To euch | preost mei ancre schriuen hire of swucche utterliche
sunnen þe to alle bifalleð; ah ful trusti ha schal beon o þe preostes
godlec þet ha allunge schaweð to hu hire stonde abute flesches
temptatiuns, ȝef ha is swa ifondet, bute i deaðes dute. Þus, þah, me
þuncheð þet ha mei seggen: 'Sire, flesches fondunge þet Ich habbe,
oðer habbe ihaued, geað to uorð upo me þurh mi þeafunge. Ich am
ofdred leste Ich ga driuinde oðerhwiles to swiðe forðward mine fol
þohtes, ant fule umbe stunde, as þah Ich huntede efter licunge. Ich
mihte þurh Godes strengðe schaken ham ofte of me, ȝef Ich were
cwicliche ant stealewurðliche umben. Ich am offearet sare þet te delit
i þe þoht leaste to longe ofte, swa þet hit cume neh skiles ȝettunge.'
Ne dear Ich þet ha deopluker ne witerluker schriue hire to ȝung
preost her-abuten (**ant ȝet of þis inohreaðe him walde þunche
wunder**); ah to hire ahne schrift-feader, oðer to sum lif-hali mon, ȝef
ha mei him habben, culle al þe pot ut: þer speowe ut al þet wunder,
þer wið fule wordes þet fulðe efter þet hit is tuki al to wundre, swa
þet ha drede þet ha hurte his earen þet hercneð hire sunnen. Ȝef ei
ancre nat nawt of þulliche þinges, þonki ȝeorne Iesu Crist, ant halde
hire i drede; þe deouel nis nawt dead, þet wite ha, þah he slepe.

37. Lihte gultes beteð þus anan bi ow seoluen (ant þah seggeð
ham i schrift hwen ȝe þencheð ham on as ȝe speokeð mid preoste).
For þe leaste of alle, sone se ȝe underȝeoteð hit, falleð biuoren ower
weoued o cros to þer eorðe, ant seggeð, '*Mea culpa*, Ich gulte, mearci,
Lauerd.' Þe preost ne þearf for na gult, bute hit beo þe greattre,
leggen oþer schrift on ow þen þet lif þet ȝe leadeð efter þeos riwle.
Ah efter þe absolutiun he schal þus seg|gen: 'Al þet god þet tu eauer

⁶⁴⁵ dest, ant al þet vuel þet tu eauer þolest for þe luue of Iesu Crist inwið þine ancre wahes, al Ich engoini þe, al Ich legge upo þe i remissiun of þeose, ant i forȝeuenesse of alle þine sunnen.' Ant þenne sum lutles ihweat he mei leggen upon ow, as a salm oðer twa, Pater Nostres, Auez tene oðer tweolue; disceplines echi to ȝef him ⁶⁵⁰ swa þuncheð. Efter þe totagges þe beoð iwriten þruppe he schal þe sunne demen mare oðer leasse; a sunne ful forȝeuelich mei wurðe ful deadlich þurh sum uuel totagge þe lið þer-bisiden.

38. Efter schrift falleð to speoken of penitence, þet is deadbote; M. 348 ant swa we habbeð inȝong ut of þis fifte dale into þe seste.

PART 6

1. Al is penitence, ant strong penitence, þet ȝe eauer dreheð, mine leoue sustren. Al þet ȝe eauer doð of god, al þet ȝe þolieð, is ow martirdom i se derf ordre, for ȝe beoð niht ant dei upo Godes rode. Bliðe mahe ȝe beon þrof, for as Seinte Pawel seið, *Si compatimur, conregnabimus*; as ȝe scottið wið him of his pine on eorðe, [ant] ȝe schule scotti wið him of his blisse in heouene. Forþi seið Seinte Pawel, *Michi absit gloriari nisi in cruce Domini mei Iesu Christi*. Ant Hali Chirche singeð, *Nos opportet gloriari in cruce Domini nostri Iesu Christi*: 'Al ure blisse mot beon i Iesu Cristes rode.' Þis word nomeliche limpeð to recluses, hwas blisse ah to beon allunge i Godes rode; Ich chulle biginnen herre, ant lihten swa her-to. Neomeð nu gode ȝeme, for al meast is Sein Beornardes sentence.

2. Þreo manere men of Godes icorene liuieð on eorðe. Þe | ane mahe beon to gode pilegrimes ieuenet, þe oþre to deade, þe þridde to ihongede wið hare gode wil o Iesuse rode. Þe forme beoð gode, þe oþre beoð betere, þe þridde best of alle. To þe forme gredeð Seinte Peter inwardliche, *Obsecro uos, tanquam aduenas et peregrinos, ut abstineatis uos a carnalibus desideriis, que militant aduersus animam*. 'Ich halsi ow,' he seið, 'as elþeodie ant pilegrimes, þet ȝe wiðhalden ow from fleschliche lustes, þe weorrið aȝein þe sawle.' Þe gode pilegrim halt eauer his rihte wei forðward; þah he seo oðer here idele gomenes ant wundres bi þe weie, he ne edstont nawt as foles doð, ah halt forð his rute ant hiheð toward his giste. He ne bereð na gersum bute his speonse gnedeliche, ne claðes bute ane þeo þet him to neodeð. Þis beoð hali men þe, þah ha beon i þe world, ha beoð þrin as pilegrimes, ant gað wið god liflade toward te riche of heouene, ant seggeð wið þe Apostle, *Non habemus hic manentem ciuitatem, set futuram inquirimus*: þet is, 'Nabbe we na wununge her, ah we secheð oþer.' Beoð bi þe leaste þet ha mahen, ne ne haldeð na tale of na worltlich froure, þah ha beon i worltlich wei, as Ich seide of pilegrim, ah habbeð hare heorte eauer toward heouene—ant ahen wel to habben. For oðer pilegrimes gað [wið] muche swinc to sechen ane sontes banes, as Sein Iames oðer Sein Giles; ah þeo pilegrimes þe gað toward heouene, ha gað to beon isontet, ant to finden Godd seolf ant alle his hali halhen liuiende i blisse, ant schulen liuien wið him i

wunne buten ende. Ha ifindeð iwis Sein Iulienes in, þe weifearinde men ʒeornliche bisecheð.

3. Nv beoð þeose gode, ah ʒet beoð þe oþre betere; for allegate pilegrimes, as Ich ear seide, al gan | ha eauer forðward, ne bicumen burhmen i þe worldes burh, ham þuncheð sumchearre god of þet ha seoð bi weie, ant edstuteð sumdeal þah ha ne don mid alle; ant moni þing ham falleð to hwer-þurh ha beoð ilette, swa þet—mare hearm is—sum kimeð leate ham, sum neauer mare. Hwa is þenne skerre ant mare ut of þe world þen pilegrimes?—þet is to seggen, þen þeo men þe habbeð worltlich þing ant ne luuieð hit nawt, ah ʒeoueð hit as hit kimeð ham, ant gað untrusset lihte, as pilegrimes doð, toward heouene. Hwa beoð betere þene þeos? Godd wat, þeo beoð betere þe þe Apostle spekeð to ant seið in his epistle, *Mortui estis, et vita uestra abscondita est cum Christo in Deo. Cum autem apparuerit uita uestra, tunc et uos apparebitis cum ipso in gloria.* 'ʒe beoð deade, ant ower lif is ihud mid Criste. Hwen he, þet is ower lif, eadeaweð ant springeð as þe dahunge efter nihtes þeosternesse, ant ʒe schulen wið him springen, schenre þen þe sunne, into eche blisse.' þe nu beoð þus deade, hare liflade is herre. For pilegrim eileð monihwet; þe deade nis noht of þah he ligge unburiet ant rotie buuen eorðe. Preise him, laste him, do him scheome, sei him scheome—al him is iliche leof. þis is a seli deað, þet makeð cwic mon þus oðer cwic wummon ut of þe worlde. Ah sikerliche, hwa-se is þus dead in hire seoluen, Godd liueð in hire heorte; for þis is þet te Apostle seið: *Viuo ego— iam non ego, viuit autem in me Christus.* 'Ich liuie—nawt Ich, ah Crist liueð in me' **þurh his inwuniende grace**. Ant is as þah he seide, 'Worltlich speche, worltlich sihðe, ant euch worltlich þing ifindeð me deade; ah þet te limpeð to Crist, þet Ich seo ant here ant wurche i cwicnesse.' þus riht is euch religius dead to þe worlde, ant cwic þah to Criste.

4. þis is an heh steire; ah ʒet is þah | an herre. Ant hwa stod eauer þrin? Godd wat, þe þe seide, *Michi [autem] absit gloriari nisi in cruce Domini mei Iesu Christi, per [quem] michi mundus crucifixus est et ego mundo.* þis is þet Ich seide þruppe: 'Crist me schilde forte habben eani blisse i þis world bute i Iesu Cristes rode mi Lauerd, þurh hwam þe world is me unwurð, ant Ich am unwurð hire, as weari þe is ahonget.' A, Lauerd! hehe stod he þe spec o þisse wise; ant þis is ancre steire, þet ha þus segge, *Michi autem absit gloriari, et cetera*, 'I na þing ne blissi Ich me bute i Godes rode, þet Ich þolie nu wa ant am itald unwurð, as Godd wes o rode.' Lokið, leoue sustren, hu þis

steire is herre þen eani beo of þe oþre. þe pilegrim i þe wor[l]des
wei, þah he ga forðward toward te ham of heouene, he sið ant hereð
unnet, ant spekeð umbe hwile; wreaðeð him for wohes, ant moni
þing mei letten him of his iurnee. þe deade nis na mare of scheome
þen of menske, of heard þen of nesche, for he ne feleð nowðer; ant
for-þi ne ofearneð he nowðer wa ne wunne. Ah þe þe is o rode ant
haueð blisse þrof, he wendeð scheome to menske ant wa into wunne,
ant ofearneð for-þi hure ouer hure. þis beoð þeo þe neauer ne beoð
gleade iheortet bute hwen ha þolieð sum wa oðer sum scheome wið
Iesu on his rode; for þis is þe selhðe on eorðe, hwa-se mei for Godes
luue habben scheome ant teone. þus, lo, rihte ancres ne beoð nawt
ane pilegrimes, ne ȝet nawt ane deade, ah beoð of þeos þridde; for al
hare blisse is forte beon ahonget sariliche ant scheomeliche wið Iesu
on his rode. þeos mahe bliðe wið Hali Chirche singen, *Nos opportet
gloriari, et cetera*; þet is, as Ich seide ear, hwet-se beo of [oðre] (þe
habbeð hare blisse summe i flesches licunge, summe i worldes
dweole, summe in oþres uuel), 'We mote nede blissin us i Iesu
Cristes rode'—þet is, i scheome ant i wa þet he droh o rode. Moni
walde summes weis þolien flesches heardschipe, ah beon itald
unwurð ne scheome ne mahte he þolien. Ah he nis bute halflunge
upo Godes rode ȝef he nis igreiðet to þolien ham baðe.

5. *Vilitas et asperitas*, 'vilte ant asprete': þeos twa, scheome ant
pine, as Sein Beornard seið, beoð þe twa leaddre steolen þe beoð up
iriht to heouene; ant bitweone þeose steolen beoð of alle gode þeawes
þe tindes ifestnet bi hwucche me climbeð to þe blisse of heouene.
For-þi þet Dauið hefde þe twa steolen of þis leaddre, þah he king
were, he clomb uppard ant seide baldeliche to ure Lauerd, *Vide
humilitatem meam et laborem meum, et dimitte uniuersa delicta mea*.
'Bihald!' quoð he, 'ant sih min eadmodnesse ant mi swinc, ant forȝef
me mine sunnen, alle togederes.' Notið wel þes twa word þe Dauið
feieð somet, 'swinc' ant 'eadmodnesse'. Swinc i pine ant i wa, i sar
ant i sorhe; eadmodnesse aȝein woh of scheome þet mon dreheð þe
is itald unwurð. 'Ba þeos bihald in me', quoð Dauið, Godes deorling;
'Ich habbe þeos twa leaddre steolen.' *Dimitte uniuersa delicta mea*:
'Leaf', quoð he, 'bihinde me ant warp awei from me alle mine gultes,
þet Ich, ilihtet of hare heuinesse, lihtliche stihe up to heouene bi
þeos leaddre.'

6. þeose twa þinges—þet is, wa ant scheome ifeiet togederes—
beoð Helyes hweoles, þe weren furene, hit teleð, ant beren him up to
Parais, þer he liueð ȝetten. Fur is hat ant read. I þe heate is

understonden euch wa þet eileð flesch, scheome bi þe reade. Ah wel mei duhen; ha beoð her hweolinde ase hweoles, ouerturneð sone ne leasteð nane hwile. Þis ilke is ec bitacnet bi cherubines sweord |
120 biuore Paraise ʒeten, þe wes of lei ant hweolinde ant turninde
abuten. Ne kimeð nan into Parais bute þurh þis leitinde sweord, þe wes hat ant read, ant in Helyes furene hweoles—þet is, þurh sar ant þurh scheome, þe ouerturneð tidliche ant agað sone. Ant nes Godes rode wið his deorewurðe blod irudet ant ireadet forte schawin
125 on him seolf þet pine ant sorhe ant sar schulden wið scheome beon iheowet? Nis hit iwriten bi him, *Factus est obediens patri usque ad mortem—mortem autem crucis?* Þet is, 'He wes buhsum his feader nawt ane to deað, ah to deað o rode.' Þurh þet he seide earst, 'deað', is pine understonden; þurh þet he þrefter seið, 'deað o þe rode', is
130 schendlac bitacnet. For swuch wes Godes deað o þe deore rode, pinful ant schentful ouer alle oþre. Hwa-se eauer deieð ine Godd, ant o Godes rode, þeos twa ha mot þolien, scheome for him ant pine. Scheome Ich cleopie eauer her beon itald unwurð, ant beggin as an hearlot, ʒef neod is, hire liueneð, ant beon oþres beodesmon—as ʒe
135 beoð, leoue sustren, ant þolieð ofte danger, of swuch oðerhwile þe mahte beon ower þreal. Þis is þet eadi scheome þet Ich of talie. Pine ne trukeð ow nawt. I þeos ilke twa þing, þet al penitence is in, blissið ow ant gleadieð, for aʒein þeos twa ow beoð twafald blissen iʒarket: aʒein scheome, menske; aʒein pine, delit ant reste buten ende.
140 *Ysaias: In terra, inquit, sua duplicia possidebunt.* 'Ha schulen', seið Ysaie, 'in hare ahne lond wealden twauald blisse, aʒein twauald wa þet ha her dreheð.' 'In hare ahne lond', seið Ysaie; for alswa as þe vuele nabbeð na lot in heouene, ne þe gode nabbeð na lot in eorðe. *Super Epistolam Iacobi: Mali nichil habent in celo, boni uero nichil in terra.* 'In
145 hare ahne lond | ha schulen wealden blisse, twafald cunne mede aʒein twauald sorhe'—as þah he seide, 'Ne þunche ham na feorlich þah ha her þolien, as in uncuð lond ant in uncuð eard bituhhen unþeode, scheome ba ant sorhe; for swa deð moni gentil mon þe is uncuð in uncuððe.' Me mot ute swinken; ed hame me schal resten. Ant nis he
150 a cang cniht þe secheð reste i þe feht ant eise i þe place? *Milicia est vita hominis super terram*; al þis lif is a feht, as Iob witneð. Ah efter þis feht her, ʒef we wel fehteð, menske ant reste abit us ed hame in ure ahne lond, þet is heoueriche. Lokið nu hu witerliche ure Lauerd seolf hit witneð: *Cum sederit Filius Hominis in sede maiestatis sue,*
155 *sedebitis et uos iudicantes, et cetera. Bernardus: In sedibus quies inperturbata, in iudicio honoris eminencia commendatur.* 'Hwen Ich

sitte forte demen,' seið ure Lauerd, 'ȝe schulen sitten wið me, ant deme wið me al þe world þet schal beon idemet, kinges ant keisers, cnihtes ant clearkes.' I þe sete is reste ant eise bitacnet, aȝein þe swinc þet her is; i þe menske of þe dom þet ha schulen demen is hehschipe menskeful ouer alle understonden, aȝein scheome ant lahschipe þet ha her for Godes luue mildeliche þoleden.

7. Nis þer nu, þenne, bute þolien gleadliche, for bi Godd seolf is iwriten *quod per penam ignominiose passionis peruenit ad gloriam resurrectionis*: þet is, 'þurh schentful pine he com to gloire of blisful ariste.' Nis na selcuð, þenne, ȝef we wrecche sunfule þolien her pine, ȝef we wulleð o Domesdei blisfule arisen—ant þet we mahen þurh his grace, ȝef we us seolf wulleð. *Quoniam si complantati fuerimus similitudini mortis eius, simul et resurrectionis erimus*—Seinte Pawles sahe, þe seið se wel eauer. | 'Ȝef we beoð iimpet to þe ilicnesse of Godes dead, we schulen of his ariste': þet is to seggen, ȝef we libbeð i scheome ant i pine for his luue, i hwucche twa he deide, we schulen beon iliche his blisful ariste, ure bodi briht as his is, world buten ende, as Seinte Pawel witneð. *Saluatorem expectamus, qui reformabit corpus humilitatis nostre, configuratum corpori claritatis sue*. Let oþre acemin hare bodi þe eorneð biuoren-hond; abide we ure Healent, þe schal acemin ure efter his ahne. *Si compatimur, conregnabimus*: 'Ȝef we þolieð wið him, we schule blissin wið him.' Nis þis god foreward? Wat Crist, nis he nawt god feolahe ne treowe þe nule scottin i þe lure as eft i þe biȝete. *Glosa: Illis solis prodest sanguis Christi qui uoluptates deserunt et corpus affligunt*: 'Godd schedde his blod for alle, ah heom ane hit is wurð þe fleoð flesches licunge ant pinið ham seoluen.' Ant is þet eani wunder? Nis Godd ure heaued, ant we his limen alle? Ah nis euch lim sar wið sorhe of þe heaued? His lim þenne nis he nawt þe naueð eche under se sar akinde heaued. Hwen þe heaued sweat wel, þet lim þe ne swet nawt, nis hit uuel tacne? He þe is ure heaued sweatte blodes swat for ure secnesse, to turnen us of þet lond-uuel þet alle londes leien on, ant liggeð ȝette monie. Þe lim þe ne sweat nawt i swincful pine for his luue, deuleset hit leaueð in his secnesse, ant nis þer bute forkeoruen hit, þah hit þunche sar Godd, for 'betere is finger offe þen he ake eauer'. Cwemeð he nu wel Godd þe þus bilimeð him of him seolf þurh þet he nule sweaten? *Oportebat Christum pati, et sic intrare in gloriam suam*. Seinte Marie, mearci! 'Hit moste swa beon', hit seið, 'Crist þolie pi|ne ant passiun, ant swa habben inȝong into his riche.' Lo deale, hwet he seið—'swa habben inȝong into his riche', swa, ant nan oðerweis! Ant we wrecches

PART 6

sunfule wulleð wið eise stihen to heouene, þet is se hehe buuen us ant se swiðe muchel wurð; ant me ne mei nawt wiðuten swinc a lutel cote arearen, ne twa þwongede scheos habbe wiðute bune!
200 Oðer þeo beoð canges þe weneð wið lihtleapes buggen eche blisse, oðer þe hali halhen þe bohten hit se deore. Nes Seinte Peter ant Seinte Andrew þer-uore istraht o rode? Sein Lorenz, o þe gridil? Ant laðlese meidnes, þe tittes itoren of, tohwiðeret o hweoles, heafdes bicoruen? Ah ure sotschipe is sutel; ant heo weren ilich
205 þeose ȝape children þe habbeð [riche] feaderes, þe willes ant waldes toteoreð hare claðes forte habbe neowe. Vre alde curtel is þe flesch, þet we of Adam, ure alde feader, habbeð; þe neowe we schulen underuon of Godd, ure riche feader, i þe ariste of Domesdei, hwen ure flesch schal blikien schenre þen þe sunne, ȝef hit is totoren her
210 wið wontreaðe ant wið weane. Of þeo þe hare curtles toteoreð o þisse wise seið Ysaie, *Deferetur munus Domino exercituum a populo diuulso et dilacerato, a populo terribili.* 'A folc tolaimet ant totoren, a folc', he seið, 'fearlich, schal makien to ure Lauerd present of him seoluen.' 'Folc tolaimet ant totoren' wið strong liflade ant wið
215 heard he cleopeð 'folc [fearlich]', for þe feond is of swucche offruht ant offearet. For-þi þet Iob wes þullich, he meande him ant seide, *Pellem pro pelle, et uniuersa, et cetera*, þet is, 'He wule ȝeouen fel for fel', þe alde for þe neowe; as þah he seide, 'Ne geineð me nawt to asailin him; he is of þet totore folc, he tereð his | alde curtel, ant f. 98ᵛ
220 torendeð þe alde pilche of his deadliche fel for þe fel undeadlich M. 364 þet i þe neowe ariste schal schine seoueuald brihtre þen þe sunne.' Eise ant flesches este beoð þes deofles mearken. Hwen he sið þeos mearken i mon oðer i wummon, he wat þe castel is his, ant geað baldeliche in þer he sið iriht up swucche baneres, as me deð i
225 castel. I þet totore folc, he misseð his merken, ant sið in ham iriht up Godes banere, þet is heardschipe of lif, ant haueð muche dred þrof, as Ysaie witneð.

8. 'Me, leoue sire,' seið sum, 'ant is hit nu wisdom to don se wa him seoluen?' Ant tu ȝeld me ondswere: of tweie men, hweðer is
230 wisre? Ha beoð ba seke. Þe an forgeað al þet he luueð of metes ant of drunches, ant drinkeð bitter sabraz forte acourin heale. Þe oþer folheð al his wil, ant for[ð]eð his lustes aȝein his secnesse, ant leoseð his lif sone. Hweðer is wisre of þes twa? Hweðer is betere his ahne freond? Hweðer luueð him seolf mare? Ant hwa nis sec of sunne?
235 Godd for ure secnesse dronc attri drunch o rode, ant we nulleð nawt bittres biten for us seoluen. Nis þer nawiht þrof. Sikerliche, his

folhere mot wið pine of his flesch folhin his pine. Ne wene nan wið este stihen to **heouene**.[1]

9. 'Me, sire,' seið sum eft, 'wule Godd se wracfulliche wreoken upo sunne?' Ʒe, mon! For loke nu hu he hit heateð swiðe. Hu walde nu þe mon beate þet þing seolf, hwer-se he hit ifunde, þe for muchel heatunge beote þrof þe schadewe, ant al þet hefde þer-to eani licnesse? Godd, Feader almihti, hu beot he bitterliche his deorewurðe sune, Iesu, ure Lauerd, þet neauer nefde sunne, bute ane þet he ber flesch ilich ure, þet is ful of sunne, ant we | schulden beon ispearet, þe beoreð on us his sune deað? þe wepne þet sloh him, þet wes ure sunne; ant he, þe nefde nawt of sunne bute schadewe ane, wes i þe ilke schadewe se scheomeliche ituket, se sorhfulliche ipinet, þet ear hit come þer-to, for þe þreatunge ane þrof **swa him agras þer-aʒein þet** he bed his feader are: *Tristis est anima mea usque ad mortem. Pater mi, si possibile est, transeat a me calix iste.* 'Sare', quoð he, 'me grulleð aʒein mi muchele pine. Mi feader, ʒef hit mei beon, speare me ed tis time. þi wil, þah, ant nawt min, eauer beo iuorðet.' His deorewurðe feader for-þi ne forber him nawt, ah leide on him se luðerliche þet he bigon to greden wið reowðfule steuene, *Heloy, Heloy, lama zabatani?* 'Mi Godd, mi Godd, mi deorewurðe feader, hauest tu al forwarpe me, þin anlepi sune, þe beatest me se hearde?' For al þis ne lette he nawt, ah beot se swiðe longe, ant se swiðe grimliche, þet he stearf o rode. *Disciplina pacis nostre super eum,* seið Ysaie; þus ure beatunge feol on him, for he dude him seoluen bitweonen us ant his feader, þe þreatte us forte smiten, ase moder þet is reowðful deð hire bitweonen hire child ant te wraðe, sturne feader hwen he hit wule beaten. þus dude ure Lauerd Iesu Crist; ikepte on him deaðes dunt forte schilden us þer-wið—igracet beo his milce! Hwer-se muchel dunt is, hit bulteð aʒein upo þeo þe þer neh stondeð. Soðliche, hwa-se is neh him þe ikepte se heui dunt, hit wule bulten on him ne nule he him neauer meanen, for þet is þe preoue þet he stont neh him, ant liht is þe bultunge to þolien for his luue þe underueng se heui dunt us forte burhen from þe deofles botte i þe pine of helle.

10. Ʒet seið moni mon, 'Hweat | is Godd þe betere þah Ich pini me for his luue?' Leoue mon ant wummon, Godd þuncheð god of ure god. Vre god is ʒef we doð þet tet we ahen. Nim ʒeme of þis essample. A mon þe were feor ifearen, ant me come ant talde him þet his deore spuse se swiðe murnede efter him þet heo wiðuten him

---

[1] For *heouene* (in AL only), CFGNST have *þe steorren*.

delit nefde i na þing, ah were for þoht of his luue leane ant elheowet, M. 368
nalde him betere likin þen þet me seide him þet ha gleowde ant
gomnede ant wedde wið oþre men, ant liuede i delices? Alswa ure
Lauerd, þet is þe sawle spus, þet sið al þet ha deð þah he hehe sitte,
280 he is ful wel ipaiet þet ha murneð efter him, ant wule hihin toward
hire mucheles þe swiðere wið ȝeoue of his grace, oðer fecchen hire
allunge to him, to gloire ant to blisse þurhwuniende.

11. Ne grapi hire nan to softeliche, hire seoluen to bichearren. Ne
schal ha for hire lif witen hire al cleane, ne halden riht hire chastete,
285 wiðuten twa þinges, as Seint Ailred **þe abbat** wrat to his suster. þet
an is pinsunge i flesch wið feasten, wið wecchen, wið disceplines, wið
heard werunge, heard leohe, wið uuel, wið muchele swinkes. þe oþer
is heorte þeawes: deuotiun, reowfulnesse, **riht** luue, eadmodnesse,
ant uertuz oþre swucche. 'Me, sire,' þu ondswerest me, 'suleð Godd
290 his grace? Nis grace wil-ȝeoue?' Mine leoue sustren, þah cleannesse
of chastete ne beo nawt bune ed Godd, ah beo ȝeoue of grace,
vngraciuse stondeð þer-toȝeines, ant makieð ham unwurðe to halden
se heh þing, þe nulleð swinc þer-uore bliðeliche þolien. Bitweonen
delices ant eise ant flesches este, hwa wes eauer chaste? Hwa bredde
295 eauer inwið hire fur þet ha ne bearnde? Pot þe walleð swiðe, nule he
beon ouerleden, oðer cald weater iwarpe þrin, ant brondes |
wiðdrahene? þe wombe pot, þe walleð of metes, ant [mare] of f. 100ʳ
drunches, is se neh nehbur to þet fulitohe lim þet ha dealeð þer-
wið þe brune of hire heate. Ah monie—mare hearm is—beoð se
300 flesch-wise, ant swa ouerswiðe ofdred leste hare heaued ake, leste
hare licome febli to swiðe, ant witeð swa hare heale, þet te gast
unstrengeð ant secleð i sunne, ant þeo þe schulden ane lechnin hare
sawle, wið heorte bireowsunge ant flesches pinsunge, forwurðeð M. 370
fisitiens ant licomes leche. Dude swa Seinte Agace, þe ondserede
305 ant seide to ure Lauerdes sonde, þe brohte [salue] o Godes half to
healen hire tittes, *Medicinam carnalem corpori meo nunquam adhibui*,
þet is, 'Fleschlich medecine ne dude Ich me neaure'? Nabbe ȝe iherd
tellen of þe þreo hali men? Bute þe an wes iwunet for his calde mahe
to nutten hate speces, ant wes ornre of mete ant of drunch þen þe
310 tweien oþre: þah ha weren seke, ne nomen neauer ȝeme hweat wes
hal, hwet unhal to eoten ne to drinken, ah nomen eauer forðriht
hwet-se Godd ham sende, ne makeden neauer strengðe of gingiure
ne of zedual, ne of clowes de gilofre. A dei, as ha þreo weren ifolen o
slepe, ant lei bitweone þes twa þe þridde þet Ich seide, com þe Cwen
315 of heouene, ant twa meidnes wið hire. þe an as þah hit were ber a

letuaire, þe oþer of gold a sticcke. Vre Leafdi wið þe sticke nom ant dude i þe anes muð of þe letuaire, ant te meidnes eoden forðre to þe midleste. 'Nai,' quoð ure Leafdi, 'he is his ahne leche; ga ouer to þe þridde.' Stod an hali mon of feor biheold al þis ilke. Hwen sec mon haueð ed hond þing þet wule don him god, he hit mei wel notien; ah beon þrefter se ancreful, nomeliche religius, nis nawt Godd icweme. Godd ant his desciples speken of sawle lechecreft, | Ypocras ant Galien of licomes heale. Þe an þe wes best ilearet of Iesu Cristes lechecreft seið flesches wisdom is deað to þe sawle: *Prudencia carnis mors. Procul odoramus bellum*, as Iob seið; swa we dredeð flesches uuel ofte ear þen hit cume þet sawle uuel kimeð up, ant we þolieð sawle uuel forte edstearten flesches uuel, as þah hit were betere to þolien galnesses brune þen heaued-eche, oðer grucchunge of a mistohe wombe. Ant hweðer is betere i secnesse to beo Godes freo child þen i flesches heale to beo þreal under sunne? Ant þis ne segge Ich nawt swa þet wisdom ant meosure ne beon oueral iloket, þe moder is ant nurrice of alle gode þeawes. Ah we cleopieð ofte wisdom þet nis nan. For soð wisdom is don eauer sawle heale biuore flesches heale, ant, hwen he ne mei nawt ba somet halden, cheose ear licomes hurt þen, þurh to strong fondunge, sawle þrowunge. Nichodemus brohte to smirien ure Lauerd an hundret weies, hit seið, of mirre ant of aloes, þet beoð bittre speces, ant bitacnið bittre swinkes ant flesches pinsunges. Hundret is ful tale, ant noteð perfectiun, þet is, ful dede, forte schawin þet me schal fuldo flesches pine ase forð as eauer euene mei þolien. I þe weie is bitacnet meosure ant wisdom—þet euch mon wið wisdom weie hwet he mahe don, ne beo nawt se ouerswiðe i gast þet he forȝeme þe bodi, ne eft se tendre of his flesch þet hit iwurðe untohen ant makie þe gast þeowe. Nu is al þis meast iseid of bitternesse utewið. Of bitternesse inwið segge we nu sumhweat; for of þes twa bitternesses awakeneð swetnesse—her ȝet i þis world, nawt ane in heouene.

12. As Ich seide riht nu þet Nichodemus | brohte smirles to ure Lauerd, alswa þe þreo Maries bohten deorewurðe aromaz his bodi forte smirien. Neomeð nu gode ȝeme, mine leoue sustren. Þeos þreo Maries bitacnið þreo bitternesses, for þis nome 'Marie', as 'Meraht', ant 'Merariht' (þet Ich spec þruppe of), spealeð 'bitternesse'. Þe earste bitternesse is i sunne bireowsunge, ant i deadbote, hwen þe sunfule is iturnd earst to ure Lauerd. Ant þeos is understonden bi þe earste Marie, Marie Magdaleine, ant bi god rihte; for ha wið muche bireowsunge ant bitternesse of heorte leafde hire sunnen, ant

PART 6

turnde to ure Lauerd. Ah for-þi þet sum mahte þurh to muche bitternesse fallen into unhope, 'Magdaleine', þe spealeð 'tures hehnesse', is to 'Marie' ifeiet; þurh hwet is bitacnet hope of heh mearci ant of heouene blisse. Þe oðer bitternesse is i wreastlunge ant i wragelunge aȝeines fondunges. Ant þeos is bitacnet bi þe oðer Marie, Marie Iacobi, for 'Iacob' spealeð 'wreastlere'. Þis wreastlunge is ful bitter to monie þe beoð ful forð i þe wei toward heouene, for þe-ȝet i fondunges, þet beoð þe deofles swenges, waggið oðerhwiles, ant moten wreastlin aȝein wið strong wraglunge. For as Seint Austin seið, *Pharao contemptus surgit in scandalum.* Hwil eauer Israeles folc wes in Egypte under [Ph]araones hond, ne leadde he neauer ferd þron; ah þa hit fleah from him, þa wið al his strengðe wende he þrefter. For-þi is eauer bitter feht neod aȝein Pharaon—þet is, aȝein þe deouel. For ase seið Ezechiel, *Sanguinem fugies, et sanguis persequetur te*: flih sunne, ant sunne wule folhin eauer efter. Inoh is iseid þruppe hwi þe gode nis neauer sker of alle fondunges. Sone se he haueð þe an ouercumen, ikepe anan anoþer. Þe þridde bitternesse is i longunge | toward heouene[2] ant i þe ennu of þis world, hwen ei is se hehe þet he haueð heorte reste onont unþeawes weorre, ant is as in heouene ȝeten, ant þuncheð bitter alle worltliche þinges. Ant tis þridde bitternesse is understonden bi Marie Salomee, þe þridde Marie, for 'Salome' spealeð 'pes'; ant þeo ȝet þe habbeð pes ant reste of cleane inwit habbeð in hare heorte bitternesse of þis lif, þet edhalt ham from blisse þet ham longeð to, from Godd, þet ha luuieð. Þus lo, in euch stat rixleð bitternesse: earst i þe biginnunge, hwen me sahtneð wið Godd; i þe forðȝong of god lif; ant i þe leaste ende. Hwa is, þenne, o Godes half þe wilneð i þis world eise oðer este?

13. Ah neomeð nu ȝeme, mine leoue sustren, hu efter bitternesse kimeð swetnesse. Bitternesse buð hit; for, as þet Godspel teleð, þeose þreo Maries bohten swote smeallinde aromaz to smirien ure Lauerd. Þurh aromaz þe beoð swote is understonden swotnesse of deuot heorte. Þeos Maries hit buggeð; þet is, þurh bitternesse me kimeð to swotnesse. Bi þis nome 'Marie' nim eauer 'bitternesse'. Þurh Maries bone wes ed te neoces weater iwent to wine; þet is to understonden, þurh bone of bitternesse þet me dreheð for Godd, þe heorte þe wes weattri, smechles, ne ne felde na sauur of Godd, na mare þen i weater, schal beon iwent to wine, þet is, ifinden smech in him swete ouer alle wines. For-þi seið þe wise, *Vsque in tempus sustinebit paciens, et postea redditio iocunditatis*: 'þe þolemode þolie

---
[2] After *heouene*, F has 'en atente de cele grant ioie'.

bitter ane hwile; he schal sone þrefter habben ȝeld of blisse.' Ant Anna i Tobie seið bi ure Lauerd, *Qui post tempesta|tem tranquillum facit, et post lacrimationem et fletum, exultationem infundit*: þet is, 'Iblescet ibeo þu, Lauerd, þe makest stille efter storm, ant efter wopi weattres ȝeldest bliðe murhðes.' *Salomon: Esuriens etiam amarum pro dulci sumet.* Ȝef þu art ofhungret efter þet swete, þu most earst witerliche biten o þe bittre. *In Canticis: Ibo michi ad montem myrre, et ad colles turis.* 'Ich chulle,' ha seið, Godes deore spuse, 'gan to rechleses hul bi þe dun of myrre.' Lo hwuch is þe wei to rechleses swotnesse: bi myrre of bitternesse. Ant eft, i þet ilke luue boc: *Que est ista que ascendit per desertum sicut uirgula fumi ex aromatibus myrre ant thuris?* Aromaz me makeð of myrre ant of rechles; ah myrre he set biuoren, ant rechles kimeð efter: *Ex aromatibus myrre et thuris.* Nu meaneð hire sum þet ha ne mei habben na swotnesse of Godd ne swetnesse wiðinnen. Ne wundri ha hire nawiht, ȝef ha nis Marie; for ha hit mot buggen wið bitternesse wiðuten. Nawt wið euch bitternesse—for sum geað frommard Godd, as euch worltlich sar þet nis for sawle heale. For-þi i þe Godspel of þe þreo Maries is iwriten þisses weis: *Vt uenientes ungerent Iesum—non autem recedentes.* þeos Maries, hit seið, þeose bitternesses, weren cuminde to smirien ure Lauerd. þeo beoð cuminde to smirien ure Lauerd þe me þoleð for his luue, þe strecheð him toward us as þing þet ismired is, ant makeð him nesche ant softe to hondlin. Ant nes he him seolf reclus i Maries wombe? þeos twa þing limpeð to ancre, nearowðe ant bitternesse; for wombe is nearow wununge, þer ure Lauerd wes reclus, ant tis word 'Marie', as Ich ofte habbe iseid, spealeð 'bitternesse'. Ȝef ȝe þenne i nearow stude | þolieð bitternesse, ȝe beoð his feolahes, reclus as he wes i Marie wombe. Beo ȝe ibunden inwið fowr large wahes? Ant he in a nearow cader, ineilet o rode, i stanene þruh bicluset hetefeste. Marie wombe ant þis þruh weren his ancre-huses. I nowðer nes he worltlich mon, ah as ut of þe world, forte schawin ancren þet ha ne schulen wið þe world na þing habben imeane. 'Ȝe,' þu ondswerest me, 'ah he wende ut of ba.' Ȝe; went tu alswa of ba þine ancre-huses as he dude, wiðute bruche, ant leaf ham ba ihale. þet schal beon hwen þe gast went ut on ende, wiðuten bruche ant wem, of his twa huses. þet an is þe licome; þet oþer is þe uttre hus, þet is as þe uttre wah abute þe castel.

14. Al þet Ich habbe iseid of flesches pinsunge nis nawt for ow, mine leoue sustren, þe oðerhwile þolieð mare þen Ich walde, ah is for sum þet schal rede þis inohreaðe, þe grapeð hire to softe. Noðeles,

435 ȝunge impen me bigurd wið þornes leste beastes freoten ham hwil ha
beoð mearewe. Ȝe beoð ȝunge impen iset i Godes orchard. Þornes
beoð þe heardschipes þet Ich habbe ispeken of, ant ow is neoð þet ȝe
beon biset wið ham abuten, þet te beast of helle, hwen he snakereð
toward ow forte biten on ow, hurte him o þe scharpschipe ant
440 schunche aȝeinwardes. Wið alle þeose heardschipes, beoð gleade ant
wel ipaiet ȝef lutel word is of ow, ȝef ȝe beoð unwurðe; for þorn is
scharp ant unwurð. Wið þeose twa beoð bigurde. Ȝe ne ahen nawt to
unnen þet uuel word beo of ow. Scandle is heaued sunne; þet is,
þing swa iseid oðer idon³ þet me mei rihtliche turnen hit to
445 uuele, ant sunegin þrefter þer-þurh wið mis þoht, wið uuel |
word on hire, on oþre, ant sungin ec wið dede. Ah ȝe ahen
unnen þet na word ne beo of ow, ne mare þen of deade, ant beon
bliðe iheortet ȝef ȝe þolieð danger of Sluri þe cokes cneaue, þe
wescheð ant wipeð disches i cuchene; þenne beo ȝe dunes ihehet
450 toward heouene. For lo hu spekeð þe leafdi i þet swete luue boc,
Venit dilectus meus, saliens in montibus, transiliens colles. 'Mi leof kimeð
leapinde,' ha seið, 'o þe dunes, [ouerleapinde hulles.' Dunes bitacnið
þeo þe leadeð hest lif; hulles beoð þe lahre. Nu seið ha þet hire leof
leapeð o þe dunes;] þet is, totret ham, tofuleð ham, þoleð þet me
455 totreode ham, tuki ham al to wundre, schaweð in ham his ahne
troden þet me trudde him in ham, [ifinde] hu he wes totreden, as his
trode schaweð. Þis beoð þe hehe dunes, as munt of Muntgiw, dunes
of Armenie. Þe hulles, þe beoð lahre, þeo, as þe leafdi seið, hire
[leof] ouerleapeð, ne trust nawt se wel on ham, for hare feblesce ne
460 mahte nawt þolien swuch totreodunge. Ant he leapeð ouer ham,
forbereð ham ant forbuheð aþet ha waxen herre, from hulles to
dunes. His schadewe lanhure ouergeað ant wrið ham hwil he leapeð
ouer ham; þet is, sum ilicnesse he leið on ham of his lif on eorðe, as
þah hit were his schadewe. Ah þe dunes underuoð þe troden of him
465 seoluen, ant schaweð in hare lif hwuch his liflade wes, hu ant hwer he
eode, i hwuch vilte, i hwuch wa he leadde his lif on eorðe. Þulliche
dunes þe gode Pawel spek of,⁴ ant eadmodliche seide, *Deicimur
set non perimus, mortificationem Iesu in corpore nostro circumferentes, ut
et vita Iesu in corporibus nostris manifestetur.* 'Alle wa', quoð he, 'ant
470 alle scheome we þolieð, ah þet is ure selhðe, þet we beoren on ure
bodi Iesu Cristes deadlicnesse, þet hit suteli in us hwuch wes his lif

---
³ After *idon*, L has *occasionem prebens ruyne, hoc est*.
⁴ For 'þulliche . . . eadmodliche' (6. 466–7), CFNT have 'þullich dun wes þe gode Pawel, þe', similarly S.

on eorðe.' Godd hit wat, þe þus doð, ha pruuieð us hare luue toward ure Lauerd. | 'Luuest tu me? cuð hit!' For luue wule schawin him wið uttre werkes. *Gregorius: Probatio dilectionis exhibitio est operis.* Ne beo neauer þing se heard, **soð** luue lihteð hit ant softeð ant sweteð. *Amor omnia fatilia reddit.* Hweat þolieð men ant wummen for fals luue ant for ful luue, ant mare walden þolien? Ant hweat is mare wunder þet siker luue ant treowe ant ouer alle oþre swete ne mei meistrin us se forð as deð þe luue of sunne? Nawt for-þi Ich wat swuch þet bereð ba togederes heui brunie ant here, ibunden **hearde** wið irn, middel, þeh, ant earmes, mid brade þicke bondes, swa þet tet swat þrof is passiun to þolien. Feasteð, wakeð, swinkeð, ant, Crist hit wat, meaneð him þet hit ne greueð him nawt, ant bit me ofte teachen him sumhwet wið hwet he mahte his licome deruen. Al þet is bitter, for ure Lauerdes luue al him þuncheð swete. Deuleset, ʒet he wepeð to me [pinene] sarest, ant seið Godd forʒet him for-þi þet he ne sent him na muchel secnesse. Godd hit wat, þet makeð luue; for as he seið me ofte, for na þing þet Godd mahte don uuele bi him, þah he wið þe forlorene wurpe him into helle, ne mahte he neauer, him þuncheð, luuien him þe leasse. Ʒef ei mon eani swuch þing ortrowi bi him, he is mare mat þen þeof inume wið þeofðe. Ich wat ec swuch wummon, þet þoleð lutel leasse. Ah nis þer bute þoncki Godd i strengðe þet he ʒeueð ham, ant icnawen eadmodliche ure wacnesse. Luuie we hare god, ant swa hit is ure ahne; for as Sein Gregoire seið, of swa muchel strengðe is luue þet hit makeð oþres god wiðute swinc ure ahne, **as is iseid þruppe.** Nu, me þuncheð, we beoð icumen into þe seoueðe dale, þet is al of luue þe makeð schir heorte.

PART 7

1. | Seinte Pawel witneð þet alle uttre heardschipes, alle flesches pinsunges ant licomliche swinkes, al is ase nawt aȝeines luue, þe schireð ant brihteð þe heorte. *Exercitio corporis ad modicum ualet, pietas autem ualet ad omnia*: þet is, licomlich bisischipe is to lutel
5 wurð, ah swote ant schir heorte is god to alle þinges. *Si linguis hominum loquar et angelorum, et cetera; si tradidero corpus meum ita ut ardeam, et cetera; si distribuero omnes facultates meas in cibos pauperum, caritatem autem non habeam, nichil michi prodest.* 'Þah Ich cuðe', he seið, 'monne ledene ant englene, þah Ich dude o mi bodi alle pine ant
10 passiun þet bodi mahte þolien, þah Ich ȝeue poure al þet Ich hefde, ȝef Ich nefde luue þer-wið, to Godd ant to alle men in him ant for him, al were ispillet.' For as þe hali abbat Moyses seide, al þet wa ant al þet heard þet we þolieð o flesch, ant al þet god þet we eauer doð, alle swucche þinges ne beoð nawt bute as lomen to tilie wið þe
15 heorte. Ȝef þe axe ne kurue, ne spitelsteaf ne dulue, ne þe sulh ne erede, hwa kepte ham to halden? Alswa as na mon ne luueð lomen for ham seolf, ah deð for þe þinges þet me wurcheð wið ham, alswa na flesches derf nis to luuien bute for-þi, þet Godd te reaðere þiderward lok[eð] mid his grace, ant makeð þe heorte schir ant of
20 briht sihðe—þet nan ne mei habben wið monglunge of unþeawes, ne wið eorðlich luue of worltliche þinges, for þis mong woreð swa þe ehnen of þe heorte þet ha ne mei cnawen Godd ne gleadien of his sihðe. Schir heorte, as Seint Bernard seið, makieð twa þinges: þet tu al þet tu dest, do hit oðer for luue ane of Godd, oðer for oþres god
25 ant for his biheue. | Haue in al þet tu dest an of þes twa ententes— oðer ba togederes, for þe leatere falleð into þe earre. Haue eauer schir heorte þus, ant do al þet tu wult; haue wori heorte, al þe sit uuele. *Omnia munda mundis, coinquinatis uero nichil est mundum. Apostolus. Item. Augustinus: Habe caritatem, et fac quicquid uis (uoluntate uidelicet rationis).*
30 For-þi, mine leoue sustren, ouer alle þing beoð bisie to habben schir heorte. Hwet is schir heorte? Ich hit habbe iseid ear: þet is, þet ȝe na þing ne wilnin ne ne luuien bute Godd ane, ant te ilke þinges for Godd þe helpeð ow toward him—for Godd, Ich segge, luuien ham, ant nawt for ham seoluen—as is mete oðer clað, mon oðer wummon
35 þe ȝe beoð of igodet. For ase seið Seint Austin, ant speokeð þus to ure Lauerd, *minus te amat qui preter te aliquid amat quod non propter te*

amat: þet is, 'Lauerd, leasse ha luuieð þe þe luuieð eawt bute þe, bute ha luuien hit for þe.' Schirnesse of heorte is Godes luue ane. I þis is al þe strengðe of alle religiuns, þe ende of alle ordres. *Plenitudo legis est dilectio:* 'Luue fulleð þe lahe', seið Seinte Pawel. *Quicquid precipitur, in sola caritate solidatur:* alle Godes heastes, as Sein Gregoire seið, beoð i luue irotet. Luue ane schal beon ileid i Seinte Mihales weie. þeo þe meast luuieð schulen beo meast iblisset, nawt þeo þe leadeð heardest lif, for luue hit ouerweieð. Luue is heouene stiward for hire muchele freolec, for heo ne edhalt na þing, ah ȝeueð al þet ha haueð, ant ec hire seoluen—elles ne kepte Godd nawt of þet hiren were.

2. Godd haueð ofgan ure luue on alle cunne wise. He haueð muchel idon us, ant mare bihaten. Muchel ȝeoue ofdraheð luue. Me, al þe world he ȝef us in Adam, | ure alde feader; ant al þet is i þe world he weorp under ure fet, beastes ant fuheles, ear we weren forgulte. *Omnia subiecisti sub pedibus eius: oues et boues uniuersas, insuper et pecora campi, volucres celi, et pisces maris qui perambulant semitas maris.* Ant ȝet al þet is, as is þruppe iseid, serueð þe gode to sawle biheue. Ȝet te uuele seruið eorðe, sea, ant sunne. He dude ȝet mare: ȝef us nawt ane of his, ah dude al him seoluen. Se heh ȝeoue nes neauer iȝeuen to se lahe wrecches. *Apostolus: Christus dilexit Ecclesiam et dedit semetipsum pro ea.* Crist, seið Seinte Pawel, luuede swa his leofmon[1] þet he ȝef for hire þe pris of him seoluen. Neomeð nu gode ȝeme, mine leoue sustren, for-hwi me ah him to luuien. Earst, as a mon þe woheð, as a king þet luuede a **gentil poure** leafdi of feorrene londe, he sende his sonden biuoren, þet weren þe patriarches ant te prophe[te]s of þe Alde Testament, wið leattres isealet. On ende he com him seoluen, ant brohte þe Godspel as leattres iopenet; ant wrat wið his ahne blod saluz to his leofmon, luue gretunge forte wohin hire wið ant hire luue wealden. Her-to falleð a tale, a wrihe forbisne.

3. A leafdi wes mid hire fan biset al abuten, hire lond al destruet, ant heo al poure inwið an eorðene castel. A mihti kinges luue wes þah biturnd upon hire swa unimete swiðe þet he for wohlech sende hire his sonden, an efter oðer, ofte somet monie; sende hire beawbelez baðe feole ant feire, sucurs of liueneð, help of his hehe hird to halden hire castel. Heo underfeng al as on unrecheles, ant swa wes heard iheortet þet hire luue ne mahte he neauer beo þe neorre.

---

[1] After *leofmon*, F has 'cest Seinte Iglise'.

75 Hwet wult tu mare? He com him seolf on ende; schawde hire his
feire neb, as þe þe wes of alle men feherest to bihalden; spec se swiðe
swoteliche, ant wordes se murie | þet ha mahten deade arearen to
liue; wrahte feole wundres ant dude muchele meistries biuoren hire
ehsihðe; schawde hire his mihte; talde hire of his kinedom; bead to
80 makien hire cwen of al þet he ahte. Al þis ne heold nawt. Nes þis
hoker wunder?—for heo nes neauer wurðe forte beon his þuften. Ah
swa þurh his deboneirte luue hefde ouercumen him þet he seide on
ende: 'Dame, þu art iweorret, ant þine van beoð se stronge þet tu ne
maht nanes weis wiðute mi sucurs edfleon hare honden, þet ha ne
85 don þe to scheome deað **efter al þi weane**. Ich chulle, for þe luue of
þe, neome þet feht upo me, ant arudde þe of ham þe þi deað secheð.
Ich wat þah to soðe þet Ich schal bituhen ham neomen deaðes
wunde; ant Ich hit wulle heorteliche forte ofgan þin heorte. Nu,
þenne, biseche Ich þe, for þe luue þet Ich cuðe þe, þet tu luuie me
90 lanhure efter þe ilke dede dead, hwen þu naldest liues.' Þes king
dude al þus: arudde hire of alle hire van, ant wes him seolf to wundre
ituket ant islein on ende. Þurh miracle aras þah from deaðe to liue.
Nere þeos ilke leafdi of uueles cunnes cunde ȝef ha ouer alle þing ne
luuede him her-efter?

95 4. Þes king is Iesu, Godes Sune, þet al o þisse wise wohede ure
sawle, þe deoflen hefden biset. Ant he, as noble wohere, efter monie
messagers ant feole goddeden com to pruuien his luue, ant schawde
þurh cnihtschipe þet he wes luuewurðe, as weren sumhwile cnihtes
iwunet to donne. Dude him i turneiment, ant hefde for his leoues
100 luue his scheld i feht, as kene cniht, on euche half iþurlet. His
scheld, þe wreah his goddhead, wes his leoue licome, þet | wes
ispread o rode: brad as scheld buuen in his istrahte earmes, nearow
bineoðen, as þe an fot (efter monies wene) set upo þe oðer. Þet þis
scheld naueð siden is for bitacnunge þet his deciples, þe schulden
105 stonden bi him ant habben ibeon his siden, fluhen alle from him ant
leafden him as fremede, as þe Godspel seið: *Relicto eo omnes fugerunt.*
Þis scheld is iȝeuen us aȝein alle temptatiuns, as Ieremie witneð:
Dabis scutum cordis, laborem tuum.[2] Nawt ane þis scheld ne schilt us
from alle uueles, ah deð ȝet mare: cruneð us in heouene. *Scuto bone*
110 *uoluntatis*—'Lauerd,' he seið, Dauið, 'wið þe scheld of þi gode wil þu
hauest us icrunet.' 'Scheld', he seið, 'of god wil', for willes he þolede
al þet he þolede. Ysaias: *Oblatus est quia uoluit.* 'Me, lauerd,' þu

---

[2] After *tuum*, CFNPT have (with minor variations) *Et Psalmista: Scuto bone uoluntatis tue coronasti nos*, deleted in C by C[2], not in ALS.

seist, 'hwer-to? Ne mahte he wið leasse gref habben arud us?' ȝeoi, iwiss, ful lihtliche; ah he nalde. For-hwi? Forte bineomen us euch bitellunge aȝein him of ure luue þet he se deore bohte. Me buð lihtliche þing þet me luueð lutel. He bohte us wið his heorte blod—deorre pris nes neauer—forte ofdrahen of us ure luue toward him, þet costnede him se sare. I scheld beoð þreo þinges: þe treo, ant te leðer, ant te litunge. Alswa wes i þis scheld: þe treo of þe rode, þet leðer of Godes licome, þe litunge of þe reade blod þet heowede hire se feire. Eft þe þridde reisun: efter kene cnihtes deað, me hongeð hehe i chirche his scheld on his mungunge. Alswa is þis scheld—þet is, þe crucifix—i chirche iset i swuch stude þer me hit sonest seo, forte þenchen þer-bi o Iesu Cristes cnihtschipe þet he dude o rode. His leofmon bihalde þron hu he bohte hire luue: lette þurlin his scheld, openin his side to schawin hire his heorte, to schawin hire openliche hu inwardliche he luuede hire, ant to ofdrahen hire heorte.

5. Fowr heaued luuen me ifind i þis world: bitweone gode iferen; bitweone mon ant wummon; bi[tweone] wif ant hire child; bitweone licome ant sawle. Þe luue þet Iesu Crist haueð to his deore leofmon ouergeað þeos fowre, passeð ham alle.

6. Ne teleð me him god fere þe leið his wed i Giwerie to acwitin ut his fere? Godd almihti leide him seolf for us i Giwerie, ant dude his deorewurðe bodi to acwitin ut his leofmon of Giwene honden. Neauer fere ne dude swuch fordede for his fere.

7. Muche luue is ofte bitweone mon ant wummon. Ah þah ha were iweddet him, ha mahte iwurðen se unwreast, ant swa longe ha mahte forhorin hire wið oþre men, þet þah ha walde aȝein cumen, he ne kepte hire nawt. For-þi Crist luueð mare: for þah þe sawle, his spuse, forhori hire wið þe feond under heaued sunne feole ȝeres ant dahes, his mearci is hire eauer ȝarow hwen ha wule cumen ham ant leten þen deouel. Al þis he seið him seolf þurh Ieremie: *Si dimiserit uir uxorem suam, et cetera. Tu autem fornicata es cum multis amatoribus; tamen reuertere ad me, dicit Dominus.* Ȝet he ȝeiȝeð al dei, 'Þu þet hauest se unwreaste idon, biturn þe ant cum aȝein; welcume schalt tu beo me.' *Immo et occurrit prodigo uenienti.* Ȝet he eorneð, hit seið, aȝein hire ȝeincume ant warpeð earmes anan abuten hire swire. Hweat is mare milce? Ȝet her gleadfulre wunder: ne beo neauer his leof forhoret mid se monie deadliche sunnen, sone se ha kimeð to him aȝein, he makeð hire neowe meiden. For as Seint Austin seið, swa muchel is (bitweonen) bituhhen Godes neoleachunge ant monnes to wummon þet monnes neoleachunge makeð of meiden wif, ant

Godd makeð of wif meiden. *Restituit, | inquit Iob, in integrum.* Gode werkes ant treowe bileaue—þeose twa þinges beoð meiðhad i sawle.

8. Nu of þe þridde luue.[3] Child þet hefde swuch uuel þet him bihofde beað of blod ear hit were ihealet, muchel þe moder luuede hit þe walde þis beað him makien. Þis dude ure Lauerd us þe weren se seke of sunne, ant swa isulet þer-wið, þet na þing ne mahte healen us ne cleansin us bute his blod ane, for swa he hit walde. His luue makeð us beað þrof—iblescet beo he eaure! Þreo beaðes he greiðede to his deore leofmon forte weschen hire in ham se hwit ant se feier þet ha were wurðe to his cleane cluppunges. Þe earste beað is fulluht. Þe oðer beoð teares, inre oðer uttre, efter þe forme beað ȝef ha hire suleð. Þe þridde is Iesu Cristes blod, þet halheð ba þe oþre, as Sein Iuhan seið i þe Apocalipse: *Qui dilexit nos et lauit nos in sanguine suo.* Þet he luueð us mare þen eani moder hire child, he hit seið him seoluen þurh Ysaie, *Nunquid potest mater obliuisci filii uteri sui? Etsi illa obliuiscatur, ego non obliuiscar tui.* 'Mei moder', he seið, 'forȝeoten hire child? Ant þah heo do, Ich ne mei þe forȝeoten neauer.' Ant seið þe resun efter: *In manibus meis descripsi te.* 'Ich habbe', he seið, 'depeint te i mine honden.' Swa he dude mid read blod upo þe rode. Me cnut his gurdel to habben þoht of a þing; ah ure Lauerd, for he nalde neauer forȝeoten us, dude mearke of þurlunge in ure munegunge i ba twa his honden.

9. Nu þe feorðe luue. Þe sawle luueð þe licome swiðe mid alle, ant þet is etscene i þe twinnunge; for leoue freond beoð sari hwen ha schulen twinnin. Ah ure Lauerd willeliche totweamde his sawle from his bodi forte veien ure baðe togederes world buten ende i þe blisse of heo|uene.

10. Þus lo, Iesu Cristes luue toward his deore spuse—þet is, Hali Chirche oðer cleane sawle—passeð alle ant ouerkimeð þe fowr measte luuen þet me ifind on eorðe. Wið al þis luue ȝetten he woheð hire o þis wise.

11. 'Þi luue,' he seið, 'oðer hit is forte ȝeouen allunge, oðer hit is to sullen, oðer hit is to reauin ant to neomen wið strengðe.

12. 'Ȝef hit is forte ȝeouen, hwer maht tu biteon hit betere þen upo me? Nam Ich þinge feherest? Nam Ich kinge richest? Nam Ich hest icunnet? Nam Ich weolie wisest? Nam Ich monne hendest? Nam Ich þinge freoest?—for swa me seið bi large mon þe ne con nawt edhalden, þet he haueð þe honden, as mine beoð, iþurlet. Nam Ich alre þinge swotest ant swetest? Þus alle þe reisuns hwi me ah to

---

[3] After *luue*, T has 'þat is, bitwene wif and hire child'; similarly PS.

ӡeoue luue þu maht ifinden in me, nomeliche ӡef þu luuest chaste cleannesse; for nan ne mei luuie me bute ha hire halde (**ah ha is þreouald: i widewehad; i spushad; i meidenhad,** þe heste).

13. 'Ʒef þi luue nis nawt to ӡeouene, ah wult þet me bugge hire— buggen hire? [Hu?] Oðer wið oðer luue oðer wið sumhweat elles. Me suleð wel luue [for luue]; ant swa me ah to sulle luue, ant for na þing elles. Ʒef þin is swa to sullen, Ich habbe iboht hire wið luue ouer alle oþre, for of þe fowr measte luuen Ich habbe icud toward te þe measte of ham alle.

14. 'Ʒef þu seist þu nult nawt leote þron se liht chap, ah wult ӡette mare, nempne hweat hit schule beon. Sete feor o þi luue; þu ne schalt seggen se muchel þet Ich nule ӡeoue mare. Wult tu castles, kinedomes, wult tu wealden al þe world? Ich chulle do þe betere— makie þe wið al þis cwen of heoueriche. Þu schalt te seolf beo seoueuald brihtre þen þe sunne. Nan uuel ne schal | nahhi þe, [na þing ne schal sweame þe], na wunne ne schal wonti þe. Al þi wil schal beon iwraht in heouene ant ec in eorðe—ӡe, ant ӡet in helle. Ne schal neauer heorte þenchen [s]wuch selhðe þet Ich nule ӡeouen for þi luue unmeteliche, vneuenliche, unendeliche mare. Al Creasuse weole, **þe wes kinge richest**; Absalones schene wlite, þe as ofte as me euesede him, salde his euesunge—þe her þet he kearf of—for twa hundret sicles of seoluer iweiet; Asaeles swiftschipe, þe straf wið heortes of urn; Samsones strengðe, þe sloh a þusent of his fan al ed a time, ant ane bute fere; Cesares freolec; Alixandres hereword; Moysese heale—nalde a mon for an of þeos ӡeouen al þet he ahte? Ant alle somet aӡein mi bodi ne beoð nawt wurð a nelde.

15. 'Ʒef þu art se swiðe anewil, ant swa ut of þi wit þet tu, þurh nawt to leosen, forsakest swuch biӡete, wið alles cunnes selhðe, lo! Ich halde her heatel sweord upo þin heaued to dealen lif ant sawle, ant bisenchen ham ba into þe fur of helle, to beon [þer] deofles hore schentfulliche ant sorhfulliche world abuten ende. Ondswere nu ant were þe—ӡef þu const—aӡein me; oðer ӡette me þi luue þe Ich ӡirne se swiðe, nawt for min, ah for þin ahne muchele biheue.'

16. Lo þus ure Lauerd woheð. Nis ha to heard iheortet þet a þulli wohere ne mei to his luue turnen, ӡef ha wel þencheð þeose þreo þinges: hwet he is, ant hwet heo is, ant hu muchel is þe luue of se heh as he is toward se lah as heo is? For-þi seið þe salmwruhte, *Non est qui se abscondat a calore eius*—nis nan þet mahe edlutien þet ha ne mot him luuien. Þe soðe sunne i þe undertid wes for-þi istihen on heh o þe hehe rode, forte spreaden oueral hate luue gleames. Þus

neodful he wes—ant is aþet tes dei—to ontenden his luue [in] his
leoues heorte; ant seið i þe Godspel, *Ignem | ueni mittere in terram, et*
quid uolo nisi ut ardeat? 'Ich com to bringen', he seið, 'fur into
235 eorðe'—þet is, bearninde luue into eorðlich heorte—'ant hwet ȝirne
Ich elles bute þet hit bleasie?' Wlech luue is him lað, as he seið þurh
Sein Iuhan i þe Apocalipse: *Vtinam frigidus esses aut calidus! Set quia
tepidus es, incipiam te euomere de ore meo.* 'Ich walde', he seið to his
leofmon, 'þet tu were i mi luue oðer allunge cald oðer hat mid alle.
240 Ah for-þi þet tu art ase wlech bitweone twa, nowðer hat ne cald, þu
makest me to wleatien, ant Ich wulle speowe þe ut bute þu wurðe
hattre.'

17. Nu ȝe habbeð iherd, mine leoue sustren, hu ant for-hwi
Godd is swiðe to luuien. Forte ontenden ow wel, gederið wude þer-
245 to wið þe poure wummon of Sarepte, þe burh þe spealeð 'onten-
dunge'. *En, inquit, colligo duo ligna* (*Regum iii°*). 'Lauerd,' quoð ha to
Helye, þe hali prophete, 'lo, Ich gederi twa treon.' Þeos twa treon
bitacnið þet a treo þet stod upriht, ant þet oþer þe eode þwertouer, o
þe deore rode. Of þeos twa treon ȝe schulen ontende fur of luue
250 inwið ower heorte. Biseoð ofte towart ham; þencheð ȝef ȝe ne ahen
eaðe to luuien þe king of blisse, þe tospreat swa his earmes toward
ow, ant buheð as to beoden cos duneward his heaued. Sikerliche Ich
segge hit, ȝef þe soðe Helye, þet is, Godd almihti, ifint ow þeose twa
treon bisiliche gederin, he wule gestnin wið ow, ant monifalden in
255 ow his deorewurðe grace, as Helie dude hire liueneð ant gestnede wið
hire þet he ifond þe twa treon gederin i Sarepte.

18. Grickisch fur is imaket of reades monnes blod, ant þet ne mei
na þing bute migge ant sond ant eisil, as me seið, acwenchen. Þis
Grickisch fur is þe luue of Iesu ure Lauerd, ant ȝe hit schule makien
260 of reade | monnes blod, þet is, Iesu Crist ireadet wið his ahne blod o
þe deore rode—ant wes inread cundeliche alswa as me weneð. Þis
blod, for ow isched upo þe earre twa treon, schal makien ow
Sareptiens—þet is, ontende mid tis Grickisch fur, þet, as Salomon
seið, nane weattres (þet beoð worldliche tribulatiuns), nane tempta-
265 tiuns, nowðer inre ne uttre, ne mahen þis luue acwenchen. Nu nis
þenne on ende bute witen ow warliche wið al þet hit acwencheð: þet
beoð migge ant sond ant eisil, as Ich ear seide. Migge is stench of
sunne. O sond ne groweð na god, ant bitacneð idel. Idel akeldeð ant
acwencheð þis fur. Sturieð ow cwicliche aa i gode werkes, ant þet
270 schal heaten ow ant ontenden þis fur aȝein þe brune of sunne; for
alswa as þe an neil driueð ut þen oþer, alswa þe brune of Godes luue

driueð brune of ful luue ut of þe heorte. Þe þridde þing is eisil—þet is, sur heorte of nið oðer of onde. Vnderstondeð þis word: þa þe niðfule Giws offreden ure Lauerd þis sure present upo þe rode, þa seide he þet reowðfule word, *Consumatum est.* 'Neauer', quoð he, 'ear nu nes Ich ful pinet'—nawt þurh þet eisil, ah þurh hare ondfule nið, þet tet eisil bitacnede þet heo him duden drinken. Ant is ilich as þah a mon þet hefde longe iswunken, ant failede efter long swinc on ende of his hure. Alswa ure Lauerd mare þen twa ant þritti ʒer tilede efter hare luue, ant for al his sare swinc ne wilnede na þing bute luue to hure. Ah i þe ende of his lif, þet wes as i þe euentid, hwen me ʒelt wercmen hare deies hure, loke hu ha ʒulden him for piment of huni luue eisil of sur nið ant galle of bitter onde. 'O!' quoð ure Lauerd þa, '*consumatum est.* Al mi swinc on eorðe, al mi pine o rode | ne sweameð ne ne derueð me nawiht aʒein þis, þet Ich þus biteo al þet Ich idon habbe. Þis eisil þet ʒe beodeð me, þis sure hure, þurhfulleð mi pine.' Þis eisil of sur heorte ant of bitter þonc ouer alle oðre þing acwencheð Grickisch fur, þet is, þe luue of ure Lauerd; ant hwa-se hit bereð i breoste toward wummon oðer mon, ha is Giwes make. Ha offreð Godd þis eisil, ant þurhfulleð onont hire Iesues pine o rode. Me warpeð Grickisch fur upon his famen, ant swa me ouerkimeð ham. Ʒe schule don alswa hwen Godd areareð ow of ei va eani weorre. Hu ʒe hit schule warpen Salomon teacheð: *Si esurierit inimicus tuus, ciba illum; si sitierit, potum da illi. Sic enim carbones ardentes congeres super caput eius*—þet is, 'Ʒef þi fa hungreð, fed him; to his þurst ʒef him drunch.' Þet is to understonden, ʒef he efter þin hearm haueð hunger oðer þurst, ʒef him fode of þine beoden þet Godd do him are; ʒef him drunch of teares, wep for his sunnen. 'Þus þu schalt', seið Salomon, 'rukelin on his heaued bearninde gleden': þet is to seggen, þus þu schalt ontenden his heorte forte luuie þe— for 'heorte' is in Hali Writ bi 'heaued' understonden. O þulli wise wule Godd seggen ed te Dome, 'Hwi luuedest tu þe mon oðer þe wummon?' 'Sire, ha luueden me.' 'Ʒe,' he wule seggen, 'þu ʒulde þet tu ahtest. Her nabbe Ich þe nawt muches to ʒelden.' Ʒef þu maht ondswerien, '**Alle wa ha duden me, ne na luue ne ahte Ich ham,** ah, Sire, Ich luuede ham for þi luue', þet luue he ah þe, for hit wes iʒeuen him, ant he hit wule þe ʒelden.

19. Migge, as Ich seide, þet acwencheð Grickisch fur is stikinde flesches luue, þe acwencheð gastelich luue þet Grickisch fur bitacneð. Hweat flesch wes on eorðe se swete ant se hali as wes Iesu Cristes flesch? Ant þah he seide him seolf | to his deore deciples,

Nisi ego abiero, Paraclitus non veniet ad uos: þet is, 'Bute Ich parti from ow, þe Hali Gast—þet is, min ant mines Feaderes luue—ne mei nawt cumen to ow. Ah hwen Ich beo from ow, Ich chulle senden
315 him ow.' Hwen Iesu Cristes ahne deciples, hwil þet ha fleschliche luueden him neh ham, foreoden þe swetnesse of þe Hali Gast, ne ne mahte nawt habben baðe togederes, demeð ow seoluen: nis he wod oðer heo þe luueð to swiðe hire ahne flesch, oðer eani mon fleschliche, swa þet ha ʒirne to swiðe his sihðe oðer his speche? Ne
320 þunche hire neauer wunder ʒef hire wonti þe Hali Gastes froure. Cheose nu euchan of þes twa, eorðlich elne ant heouenlich, to hweðer ha wule halden, for þet oðer ha mot leten; for i þe tweire monglunge ne mei ha habben neauer mare schirnesse of heorte, þet is, as we seiden ear, þet god ant te strengðe of alle religiuns, ant in
325 euch ordre. Luue makeð hire schir, griðful, ant cleane. Luue haueð a meistrie biuoren alle oþre, for al þet ha rineð, al ha turneð to hire ant   M. 408 makeð al hire ahne. *Quemcumque locum calcauerit pes uester—pes videlicet amoris—uester erit.* Deore walde moni mon buggen a swuch þing þet al he rine [þer-wið] al were his ahne; ant ne seide
330 hit þruppe feor, ane þurh þet tu luuest þet god þet is in anoðer, wið þe rinunge of þi luue þu makest wiðuten oþer swinc his god þin ahne god, as Sein Gregoire witneð? Lokið nu hu muchel god þe ontfule leoseð. Streche þi luue to Iesu Crist, þu hauest him iwunnen. Rin him wið ase muche luue as þu hauest sum mon sumchearre, he is þin
335 to don wið al þet tu wilnest. Ah hwa luueð þing þet leaueð hit for leasse þen hit is wurð? Nis Godd betere uneuenlich þen al þet is i þe world? 'Chearite' is cherte of leof þing ant of deore. Vndeore he makeð Godd ant to un|wurð mid alle þet for ei worltlich [luue] of his   f. 110ᵛ luue leaskeð; for na þing ne con luuien riht bute he ane. Swa
340 ouerswiðe he luueð luue þet he makeð hire his euening. ʒet Ich dear segge mare: he makeð hire his meistre, ant deð al þet ha hat as þah he moste nede. Mei Ich pruuien þis? ʒe, witerliche, Ich, bi his ahne wordes; for þus he speketh to Moyses, þe monne meast him luuede, in *Numeri*: *Dimisi iuxta uerbum tuum. Non dicit preces*. 'Ich hefde',
345 quoð he, 'imunt to wreoke mine wreaððe i þis folc. Ah þu seist I ne schal nawt; þi word beo iforðet.' Me seið þet luue bindeð. Witerliche luue bint swa ure Lauerd þet he ne mei na þing don bute þurh luues leaue. Nu preoue her-of; for hit þuncheð wunder. *Ysaias: Domine, non est qui consurgat et teneat te.* 'Lauerd, þu wult smiten', seið Ysaie.
350 'Weilawei, þu maht wel; nis nan þet te halde.' As þah he seide, 'ʒef ei luuede þe riht, he mahte halden þe ant wearnen þe to smiten.' *In*

M. 410 *Genesy, ad Loth: Festina, et cetera. Non potero ibi quicquam facere donec egressus fueris illinc.* þet is, þa ure Lauerd walde bisenchen Sodome, þer Lot, his freond, wes inne, 'Hihe þe', quoð he, 'utward, for hwil þu art bimong ham, ne mei Ich nawt don ham.' Nes þis wið 355 luue ibunden? Hwet wult tu mare? Luue is his chamberleng, his conseiler, his spuse, þet he ne mei nawt heole wið, ah teleð al þet he þencheð. *In Genesy: Num celare potero Abraham que gesturus sum?* 'Mei Ich', quoð ure Lauerd, 'heolen Abraham þing þet Ich þenche to donne? Nai, o nane wise.' Nu con þes luuien þe þus spekeð ant þus 360 deð to alle þe him inwardliche leueð ant luuieð. þe blisse þet he ȝarkeð ham, as ha is uneuenlich to alle worldes blissen, alswa ha is untalelich to world|liche tungen. *Ysaias: Oculus non uidit, Deus, absque te que preparasti diligentibus te. Apostolus: Oculus non uidit, nec auris audiuit, et cetera.* Ȝe habbeð of þeos blissen iwriten elleshwer, mine leoue 365 sustren.

20. Þis luue is þe riwle þe riwleð þe heorte. *Confitebor tibi in directione* (id est, in regulatione) *cordis. Exprobratio malorum: Generatio que non direxit cor suum.* Þis is þe leafdi riwle. Alle þe oþre seruið hire, ant ane for hire sake me [ah] ham to luuien. Lutel strengðe Ich do of 370 ham, for-hwon þet þeos beo deorewurðliche ihalden. Habbeð ham þah scheortliche i þe eahtuðe dale.

PART 8

1. Biuoren on earst Ich seide þet ȝe ne schulden nawiht as i vu bihaten forte halden nan of þe uttre riwlen; þet ilke Ich segge ȝetten. Ne nane ne write Ich ham buten ow ane. Ich segge þis for-þi þet oþre ancren ne seggen nawt þet Ich þurh mi meistrie makie ham M. 412
5 neowe Riwle. Ne bidde Ich nawt þet ha halden ham; ah ȝe ȝet moten changin, hwen-se ȝe eauer wulleð, þeose for betere. Aȝein þinges þe beoð biuoren, of ham is lutel strengðe.

2. Of sihðe ant of speche, ant of þe oþre wittes, is inoh iseid. Nu is þis leaste dale, as Ich bihet on earst, todealet ant isundret o lutle
10 seoue stucchen.

3. Me let lease of þe þing þet me haueð ofte. For-þi ne schule ȝe beon bute as ure breðren[1] beoð ihuslet inwið tweolfmoneð fiftene siðen: (i) Midwinter Dei (ii) Tweofte Dei (iii) Condelmeasse Dei (iiii) a Sunnedei midwei bitweonen þet ant Easter, oðer Ure Leafdi
15 Dei ȝef he is neh þe Sunnedei, for þe hehnesse (v) Easter Dei (vi) þe þridde Sunnedei þrefter | (vii) Hali þursdei (viii) Witsunnedei f. 111ᵛ (ix) Midsumer Dei (x) Seinte Marie Dei Magdaleine (xi) þe Assumptiun (xii) þe Natiuite (xiii) Seinte Mihales Dei (xiiii) Alle Halhene Dei (xv) Seint Andrews Dei. Aȝein alle þeose beoð
20 cleanliche ischriuene ant neomeð disceplines—neauer þah of na mon bute of ow seoluen—ant forgað an dei ower pitance. Ȝef ewt ilimpeð mislische þet ȝe ne beon nawt ihuslet i þeose isette tearmes, beoð hit þe neste Sunnedei; oðer ȝef þe oþer terme is neh, abideð aþet tenne.

25 4. Ȝe schulen eoten from Easter aþet te Hali Rode Dei[2] þe leatere, þe is in heruest, euche dei twien bute þe Fridahes [ant Umbridahes, ȝongdahes ant uigilies. I þeos dahes] ne i þe Aduent ne schule ȝe nawt eoten hwit bute neode hit makie. Þe oþer half-ȝer feasten al, bute Sunnedahes ane, **hwen ȝe beoð in heale ant i ful strengðe;**
30 **ah riwle ne tweast nawt seke ne blodletene.**

5. Ȝe ne schulen nawt eoten flesch ne seim bute for muche

---

[1] For breðren, N has leawude breþren.
[2] After Dei, C² adds in the margin: 'þes riwle ant alle oðre beoð in owres scriftes read ant in oweres meistres breoste. He mei forkeoruen of ham oðer echi mare to ham efter þet God þurh his wit wisseð him te donne, efter hare biheue þet he haf[eð] to read⟨en⟩.'

secnesse, oðer hwa-se is ouer-feble.³ Potage eoteð bliðeliche, ant wunieð ow to lutel drunch. Noðeles, leoue sustren, ower mete ant ower drunch haueð iþuht me ofte leasse þen Ich walde. Ne feaste ȝe na dei to bread ne to weattre bute ȝe habben leaue.

6. Sum ancre makeð hire bord wið hire gest utewið. Þet is to muche freondschipe; for of alle ordres, þenne is hit uncundelukest ant meast aȝein ancre ordre þe is al dead to þe world. Me haueð iherd ofte þet deade speken wið cwike, ah þet ha eten wið cwike ne fond Ich ȝet neauer.

7. Ne makie ȝe nane gestnunges, ne ne tulle ȝe to þe ȝete nane uncuðe hearloz.⁴ Þah þer nere nan oðer uuel bute hare meadlese nurð, hit walde letten oðerhwile heouenliche þohtes. Ne limpeð nawt to ancre of oþer | monnes ealmesse to makien hire large. Nalde me lahhen a beggere lude to bismere þe leaðede men to feaste? Marie ant Marthe ba weren sustren, ah hare lif sundrede. Ȝe ancren beoð inumen ow to Marie dale, þe ure Lauerd seolf herede: *Maria optimam partem elegit.* 'Marthe, Marthe,' quoð he, 'þu art [i] muche baret. Marie haueð icore bet, ant ne schal hire na þing reauin hire dale.' Husewifschipe is Marthe dale. Marie dale is stilnesse ant reste of alle worldes noise, þet na þing ne lette hire to heren Godes steuene. Ant lokið hwet Godd seið, þet na þing ne schal ow reauin þis dale. [Marthe] haueð hire meoster; leoteð hire iwurðen. Ȝe sitten wið Marie stan-stille ed Godes fet, ant hercnið him ane. Marthe meoster is to feden poure ant schruden as hus-leafdi; Marie ne ah nawt to entremeatin þrof. Ȝef ei blameð hire, Godd seolf ihwer wereð hire, as Hali Writ witneð (*Contra Symonem: duo debitores, et cetera. Contra Martham: Maria optimam partem, et cetera. Contra apostolos, murmurantes, Vt quid perditio hec? Bonum, inquit, opus, et cetera*). On oðer half, nan ancre ne ah to neomen bute **meaðfulliche** þet hire to nedeð. Hwer-of, þenne, mei ha makien hire large? Ha schal libben bi ealmesse ase **meaðfulliche** as ha eauer mei, ant nawt gederin forte ȝeouen. Ha nis nawt husewif, ah is a chirch-ancre. Ȝef ha mei spearien eani poure schraden, sende ham al dearnliche ut of hire wanes. Vnder semblant of god is ofte ihulet sunne. Ant hu schulen þeose [riche] ancres þe

---

³ Instead of 'Ȝe . . . ouer-feble' (8. 31–2), F has: 'Solum la riule des chanoignes Seint Augustin, vous ne mangerez char ne seym, si grand maladie nel face ou grand fieblesce, fors trois iours en la symeyne, nen estee nen yuer, cest a sauer le dymeinge, le mardi, et le jeodi. Le iour de Noel poez vous mangier char quel iour qil auienge, fors sul le samadi si a tiel iour chiet. Solum la riule as freres ou de seint Benoit, ne deuez vous iames mangier char fors en grand maladie ou quant vous estes trop fieble.'

⁴ After *hearloz*, L has *pro nouis audiendis vel ad colloquendum cum eis.*

tilieð oðer habbeð rentes isette don to poure nehburs dearnliche hare ealmesse? Ne wilni ha nawt to habbe word of a large ancre, ne forte ȝeouen | muchel ne beo nan þe [grediure] forte habben mare. For- f. 112ᵛ hwon þet gredinesse beo rote **of þet gederunge**, of hire bitternesse
70 al beoð þe bohes bittre þe of hire spruteð. Bidden hit forte ȝeouen hit nis nawt ancre rihte. Of ancre curteisie, of ancre largesce is icumen ofte sunne ant scheome on ende.

8. Wummen ant children, **ant nomeliche ancre meidnes**, þe cumeð iswenchet for ow, þah ȝe spearien hit on ow, oðer borhin
75 oðer bidden hit, makieð ham to eotene **wið chearitable chere ant leaðieð to herbarhin**.

9. Na mon ne eote biuoren ow bute bi ower meistres leaue, general oðer spetial: [general] as of Freres Preachurs ant Meonurs, spetial of alle oþre. Ne leaðie ȝe nane oþre to
80 eoten ne to drinken bute alswa þurh his leaue. 'Liht is', me seið, 'leaue.'⁵ Nawiht ne ȝirne Ich þet me **for swucche boden** telle ow hende ancren. Ihwear þah ant eauer ȝemeð ow þet nan from ow þurh ower untuhtle ne parti wið scandle.⁶

10. Ed gode men⁷ neomeð al þet ow to nedeð; **ah þet lokið ow
85 wel**,⁸ þet ȝe ne kecchen þe nome of gederinde ancren. Of mon þet ȝe misleueð þurh his fol semblant oðer bi his wake wordes, nowðer ne neome ȝe ne leasse ne mare.⁹ Neode¹⁰ schal driuen ow forte bidden ei þing; þah eadmodliche schawið to **gode men ant wummen**¹¹ ower meoseise.

90   11. Ȝe, mine leoue sustren, bute ȝef neod ow driue ant ower meistre hit reade, ne schulen habbe na beast bute cat ane. Ancre þe haueð ahte þuncheð bet husewif ase Marthe wes, ne **lihtliche**¹² ne mei ha **nawt** beo Marie, **Marthe suster**, wið griðfullnesse | of f. 113ʳ

---

⁵ For 'Na . . . leaue' (8. 77–81), TCFN have (with minor variants) 'Na mon biforen ow, bute he haue nede, ne laðe ȝe to drinke'; C² alters C to 'Na mon ne laðe ȝe to swiðe to drinken, ne nane ne eoten biuoren ow bute bi ower meistres read ant bi his leaue.'
⁶ 'Ihwear . . . scandle' (8. 82–3) modifies an addition by C²: 'Ihwer þah ant euer ȝemið ow þet nan from ow ne parti wið scandle ne wrah ne mispaiet, ase forð as ȝe mahen wið riht wiðute sunne.' L has *Non ascultetis, karissime sorores, vel narretis aliquibus rumores tales quibus posset ⟨aliq⟩uo modo scandalum generari.*
⁷ For *gode men*, CFNT have *gode freont*, altered in C by C² to *treowe men*.
⁸ For 'ah . . . wel' (8. 84–5), CFNT have 'hwen ha beodeð hit ow. For nan bode ne neome ȝe naut wiðute sunne.'
⁹ After *mare*, CFNT have 'naut swa muche þet beo an rote of gingiure'.
¹⁰ Before *Neode*, CFNT have *muche*.
¹¹ For 'gode men ant wummen', CFNT have 'owre leoueste freont'.
¹² For *lihtliche*, CFNT have 'nanes weis', altered in C by C² to 'lihtliche oðer nanes weis'.

heorte; for þenne mot ha þenchen of þe kues foddre, of heorde-
monne hure, olhnin þe heiward, wearien hwen he punt hire, ant
ȝelden þah þe hearmes. Ladlich þing is hit, wat Crist, hwen me
makeð i tune man of ancre ahte. Nu þenne, ȝef eani mot nedlunge
habben hit, loki þet hit na mon ne eili ne ne hearmi, ne þet hire þoht
ne beo nawiht þron ifestnet. Ancre ne ah to habben na þing þet
utward drahe hire heorte.

12. Na chaffere ne driue ȝe. Ancre þet is chepilt—**þet is, buð
forte sullen efter biȝete**—ha chepeð hire sawle þe chapmon of
helle. **þing þah þet ha wurcheð ha mei þurh hire meistres
read for hire neode sullen.**[13] Hali men sumhwile liueden bi
hare honden.

13. Nawt, **deore dehtren**, ne wite ȝe in ower hus of oðer monne
þinges—ne ahte ne claðes, **ne boistes ne chartres, scoren ne
cyrograffes**, ne þe chirch-uestemenz ne þe calices—bute **neode
oðer** strengðe hit makie oðer muchel eie. Of swuch witunge is
muchel vuel ilumpen ofte-siðen.

14. Inwið ower wanes ne leote ȝe na mon slepen. Ȝef muchel neod
mid alle makeð breoken ower hus, hwil hit eauer is ibroken habbeð
þrinne wið ow a wummon of cleane lif deies ant nihtes.

15. For-þi þet **wepmen**[14] ne seoð ow ne ȝe ham, wel mei don of
ower clað beo hit hwit, beo hit blac, bute hit beo unorne, warm, ant
wel iwraht, felles wel itawet; ant habbeð ase monie as ow to neodeð to
bedde ant to rugge.

16. Nest flesch ne schal nan werien linnene clað bute hit beo of
hearde ant of greate heorden. Stamin habbe hwa-se wule; hwa-se
wule beo buten. Ȝe schulen in an hetter ant igurd liggen, swa
leoðeliche þah þet ȝe mahen honden put|ten þer-under. Nest
lich nan ne gurde hire wið na cunne gurdles bute þurh
schriftes leaue, ne beore nan irn ne here ne ilespiles felles, ne ne
beate hire þer-wið, ne wið scurge ileadet, wið holin ne wið breres, ne
biblodgi hire seolf, wiðute schriftes leaue. **Nohwer ne binetli hire,
ne ne beate biuoren, ne na keoruunge ne keorue, ne ne neome
ed eanes to luðere**[15] **disciplines, temptatiuns forte acwenchen;
ne for na bote aȝein cundeliche secnesses nan uncundelich
lechecreft ne leue ȝe ne ne fondin wiðuten ower meistres read,
leste ow stonde wurse.**

---

[13] After *sullen*, C² has 'þah swa dernliche as ha mei for mislicha monne wordes'.
[14] For *wepmen*, CFNT have 'nan mon'.   [15] For *luðere*, CFNT have *feole*.

17. Ower schon **i winter** beon **meoke**, greate, ant warme.[16] I sumer ȝe habbeð leaue bearuot gan ant sitten, **ant lihte scheos werien.**

18. Hosen wiðute vampez ligge in hwa-se likeð. **Ischeoed ne slepe ȝe nawt, ne nohwer bute i bedde.** Sum wummon inohreaðe wereð þe brech of here ful wel icnottet, þe streapeles dun to þe vet ilacet ful feaste; ah eauer is best þe swete ant te swote heorte. Me is leouere þet ȝe þolien wel an heard word þen an heard here.

19. Ȝef ȝe muhen beo wimpelles—ant ȝe wel wullen—beoð bi warme cappen, ant þer-uppon hwite oðer blake veiles. Ancren summe sungið in hare wimplunge na leasse þen leafdis. Ah þah seið sum þet hit limpeð to euch wummon cundeliche forte werien wimpel. Nai, wimpel ne heaued-claðnowðer ne nempneð Hali Writ, ah wriheles ane. *Ad Corinthios: Mulier uelet caput suum.* 'Wummon', seið þe Apostle, 'schal wr[ihe]n hire heaued.' 'Wrihen', he seið, nawt 'wimplin': wrihen ha schal hire scheome as Eue sunfule dohter, i mungunge of þe sunne þet schende us on earst alle, ant nawt drahe þe wriheles to tiffunge ant to prude. Eft wule þe Apostle þet wummon wreo i chirche hire neb ȝetten, leste uuel þoht arise þurh hire onsihðe: *et hoc est propter angelos.*[17] Hwi þenne, þu chirchancre iwimplet, openest[18] þi neb to wepmonnes ehe? Toȝeines þe [þe] sist men spekeð þe Apostle, ȝef þu þe ne hudest. Ah ȝef þet ei þing wriheð þi neb from monnes ehe, beo hit wah, beo hit claðiwel-itund windowe,[19] wel mei duhen ancre of oðer wimplunge. Toȝeines þe þe þus ne dest spekeð þe Apostle, nawt toȝeines oþre þet hare ahne wah wriheðwið euch monnes sihðe. Þer awakenið ofte wake þohtes of, ant werkes oðerhwiles.[20] Hwa-se wule beon isehen,[21] þah ha atiffi hire nis nawt muche wunder; ah to Godes ehnen ha is lufsumre þe is for þe luue of him untiffet wiðuten.

20. Ring ne broche ne habbe ȝe, ne gurdel imembret, ne glouen

---

[16] After *warme*, L has *prout necessitas requirit*.
[17] For '"Wrihen" . . . angelos' (8. 147–52), L has *velet, dice⟨. . .⟩ ⟨di⟩stingu⟨en⟩do de speci⟨fic⟩andis. Vnde velare debet anachorita caput, et faciem ne pateat ⟨as⟩pectibus hominum.*
[18] For *iwimplet, openest*, C² has 'al beo þu iwimplet, openest þah'.
[19] For *wel-itund windowe*, C² has 'þi parlures þurl'.
[20] For 'Ah . . . oðerhwiles' (8. 154–60), L has *et semper habeat pannum vel murum vel fenestram clausam contra aspiciencium intuitus ne forte ingruant scandala. Hoc non obseruatis.*
[21] After *isehen*, T has 'of alle þat hire cumen to'.

ne nan swuch þing þet ow ne deh to habben. A meoke surpliz ȝe mahen in hat sumer werien.

21. Eauer me is leouere se ȝe doð greattre werkes.

22. Ne makie ȝe nane purses forte freondin ow wið, bute to þeo þet ower meistre ȝeueð ow his leaue, ne huue ne blodbinde of seolc ne laz, buten leaue; ah schapieð ant seowið ant mendið chirche claðes[22] ant poure monne hettren. Na swuch þing ne schule ȝe ȝeouen wiðuten schriftes leaue,[23] na mare þen neomen þet ȝe ne seggen him fore—as of oðre þinges, kun oðer cuððe, hu ofte ȝe underuengen, hu longe ȝe edheolden. Tendre of cun ne limpeð nawt ancre beonne. A mon[24] wes of religiun, ant com to him efter help his fleschliche broðer, ant he tahte him to his þridde breðer, þe wes dead biburiet. þe ondswerede wundrinde, 'Nai,' (quoð he) 'nis he dead?' 'Ant Ich', quoð þe hali mon, | 'am dead gasteliche. Na fleschlich freond ne easki me fleschlich froure.' Amites ant parures worldliche leafdis mahen inoh wurchen; ant ȝef ȝe ham makieð, ne makie ȝe þrof na mustreisun. Veine gloire attreð alle gode þeawes ant alle gode werkes. Criblin ne schal nan of ow for luue ne for hure. Taueles ne forbeode Ich nawt, ȝef sum riueð surpliz oðer measse-kemese; oþre riuunges ne riue ha nawt, nomeliche ouer-egede, bute for muche neode.

23. Helpeð ow wið ower ahne swinc se forð se ȝe eauer mahen, to schruden ow seoluen ant feden ȝef neod is, ant þeo þe ow seruið.

24. As Sein Ierome leareð, ne beo ȝe neauer longe ne lihtliche of sum þing allunges idel,[25] for ananrihtes þe feond beot hire his werc þe i Godes werc ne swinkeð, ant tuteleð anan toward hire. For hwil he sið hire bisi, he[26] þencheð þus: 'For nawt Ich schulde nu cume neh hire; ne mei ha nawt iȝemen to lustni mi lare.' Of idelnesse awakeneð muchel flesches fondunge. *Iniquitas Sodome: saturitas panis et ocium*—þet is, Sodomes cwedschipe com of idelnesse ant of ful wombe. Irn þet lið stille gedereð sone rust; weater þe ne stureð nawt readliche stinkeð.

25. Ancre ne schal nawt forwurðe scolmeistre, ne turnen ancrehus to childrene scole. Hire meiden mei learen sum oðer[27] meiden

---

[22] For *chirche claðes*, L has *vestes proprias et ecclesias(t)icas*.
[23] After *schriftes leaue*, F has 'ou de vostre prelat'.
[24] Before *A mon*, L has *in Vitas Patrum*.
[25] For 'ne¹ ... idel' (8. 188–9), L has *Sem(per) aliquid boni facito ne diabolus inueniat oci(osas)*.   [26] After *he*, T has 'þe swike'.   [27] For *oðer*, CFN have *lute*.

PART 8

þet were pliht of to leornin **among wepmen oðer** bimong gromes, ah ancre ne ah to ʒemen bute Godd ane (**þah bi hire meistres read ha mei sum rihten ant helpen to learen**).

26. ʒe ne schulen senden leattres ne underuon leattres ne writen bute leaue.

27. ʒe schulen beon idoddet, **oðer ʒef ʒe wulleð ischauen**, fowr siðen i þe ʒer to lihtin ower heaued (**beo bi þe her ieueset | hwa-se swa is leouere**),[28] ant as ofte ileten blod, ant ʒef neod is oftre.[29] þe mei beo þer-buten, Ich hit mei wel þolien. Hwen ʒe beoð ilete blod, ʒe ne schule don na þing þe þreo dahes þet ow greueð, ah talkið to ower meidnes ant wið þeawfule talen schurteð ow togederes. ʒe mahen swa don ofte[30] hwen ow þuncheð heuie, oðer beoð for sum worltlich þing sare oðer seke—**þah euch worltlich froure is unwurðe to ancre**.

28. Swa wisliche witeð ow in ower blodletunge, ant haldeð ow i swuch reste, þet ʒe longe þrefter mahen i Godes seruise þe monluker swinken, ant alswa hwen ʒe feleð eani secnesse. Muchel sotschipe hit is leosen for an dei tene oðer tweolue.

29. Wesscheð ow hwer-se neod is as ofte as ʒe wulleð, **ant ower oþre þinges. Nes neauer fulðe Godd leof, þah pouerte ant unorneschipe beon him licwurðe**.

30. Vnderstondeð eauer of alle þeose þinges þet nan nis heast ne forbod þet beoð of þe uttre riwle, þet is lute strengðe of, for-hwon þet te inre beo wel iwist, as Ich seide i þe frumðe. þeos mei beon ichanget hwer-se eani neod oðer eani skile hit easkeð, efter þet ha best mei þe leafdi Riwle seruin as hire eadmode þuften—ah sikerliche wiðuten hire þe leafdi feareð to wundre.

31. Ancre þe naueð nawt neh honde hire fode, beoð bisie twa wummen, an eauer þe leaue ed hame, anoþer þe wende ut hwenne driueð neod; ant þeo beo ful unorne **wiðuten euch tiffunge, oðer a lutel þuftene** oðer of feier ealde. Bi þe wei as ha geað, ga singinde hire beoden, ne ne halde na tale wið mon ne wið wummon, ne sitte ne ne stonde, bute þet leaste þet ha eauer mei ear þen ha ham cume. Nohwider elles ne ga | heo bute þider as me send hire wiðute leaue,

---

[28] For 'beo . . . leouere' (8. 205–6), C² has 'hwa-se wule ieueset, ah ha ⟨mot⟩ te oftere weschen ant kemben hire heauet.'

[29] PT have 'fiftene siþes' for 'fowr siðen' (8. 204–5) and 'foure siþes' for 'as ofte' (8. 206).

[30] *Ofte* is altered in C by C² to *oftere*.

ne ne eote ha ne ne drinke ute. þe oþer beo eauer inne, ne wiðute þe
ʒeten ne ga wiðute leaue. Ba beon obedient to hare dame in alle þing   235
bute i sunne ane. Na þing nabben þet heo hit nute, ne underuo na
þing ne ne ʒeoue nowðer wiðuten hire leaue. Na mon ne leote[n] in,
ne þe ʒungre ne speoke wið na mon bute leaue. Ne ga ha nawt ut of
tune wiðute siker fere, **ʒef hit swa mei beon**, ne ne ligge ute. Ʒef
heo ne con o boke, segge bi Pater Nostres ant bi Auez hire Ures, ant   240
wurche þet me hat hire wiðute gruchunge. Habbe eauer hire earen
opene toward hire dame. Nowðer of þe wummen ne beore from hare
dame, ne ne bringe to hire, nane idele talen ne neowe tidinges, ne
bitweonen ham seolf ne singen ne ne speoken nane worldliche
spechen, ne lahhen swa ne pleien þet ei mon þet hit sehe mahte   245
hit to uuel turnen. Ouer alle þinges, leasunges ant luðere wordes
heatien. Hare her beo icoruen, hare heaued-claðsitte lahe. Eiðer
ligge ane. Hare cop beo hehe isticchet[31] ant bute broche. Na mon ne
seo ham unleppet ne open-heaued.[32] Lah locunge habben. Heo ne
schulen cussen na mon, ne cuð mon ne cunnesmon, ne for na cuððe   250
cluppen, ne weschen hare heaued, ne lokin feaste o na mon, ne
toggin wið ne pleien. Hare weden beon of swuch schape, ant al hare
aturn swuch, þet hit beo edscene hwer-to ha beoð iturnde. Hare lates
lokin warliche, þet nan ne mahe edwiten ham in hus ne ut of hus. On
alle wise forbeoren to wreaðen hare dame, ant as ofte as heo hit doð,   255
ear ha drinken oþer eoten makien | hare Venie o cneon dun biuoren
hire, ant seggen *Mea culpa*, ant underuon þe penitence þet ha leið
upon hire, lutinde hire lahe. Þe ancre þrefter neauer mare þet ilke
gult ne upbreide for na wreaððe, bute ʒef ha eftsone falle i þet ilke,
ah do hit allunge ut of hire heorte. Ʒef ei strif ariseð bitweone þe   260
wummen, þe ancre makie eiðer to makien oþer Venie o cneon to þer
eorðe, ant eiðer rihte up oþer, ant cussen on ende, ant te ancre legge
on eiðer sum penitence, mare upo þe ilke þe greatluker gulte. Þis is a
þing, witen ha wel, þet is Gode leouest, sahtnesse ant some, ant te
feond laðest; for-þi he is eauer umben to arearen sum leaððe. Nu sið   265
þe sweoke wel þet hwen fur is wel o brune ant me wule þet hit aga,
me sundreð þe brondes; ant he deð hond þet ilke. Luue is Iesu
Cristes fur, þet he wule þet bleasie aa i þin heorte; ant te deouel
blaweð forte puffen hit ut. Hwen his blawunge ne geineð nawt, he
bringeð up sum uuel word oðer sum oþer nohtunge hwer-þurh ha   270

---

[31] After *hehe isticchet*, F has 'pardeuant la poitrine'.
[32] After *open-heaued*, C² adds 'Inwið þe wanes ha muhe werie scapeloris hwan mantel ham heuegeð. Vte, gan imantlet, þe heaued ihudeket.'

PART 8

tohurten eiðer frommard oþer; ant te Hali Gastes fur cwencheð hwen þe brondes þurh wreaððe beoð isundret. For-þi halden ham i luue feaste togederes, ant ne beo ham nawt of hwen þe feond blawe, nomeliche ȝef monie beon iueiet somet ant wel wið luue ontende. þah þe ancre on hire meidnes for openliche gultes legge penitence, to þe preost noðeleater schriuen ham **hwen neod is**[33]—ah eauer þah wið leaue.

32. ȝef ha ne cunnen nawt þe mete graces, seggen in hare stude Pater Noster biuoren ant *Aue Maria*, ant efter mete alswa, ant a Credo mare, ant segge þus on ende: 'Feader, Sune, Hali Gast, [an] almihti Godd, ȝeoue ure dame his grace | se lengre se mare, ant leue hire ant us ba neomen god ende. Forȝelde alle þe us god doð, ant milci hare sawle; þe us god idon habbeð, hare sawle; ant alle Cristene sawles.'

33. Bitweone mel ne gru[s]e[l]i nawt, nowðer frut ne oðerhwet, ne drinken bute leaue; ant te leaue beo liht in al þet nis sunne. Ed te mete na word, oðer lut ant teo stille. Alswa, efter þe ancre Complie aþet Prime ne don na þing ne seggen hwer-þurh hire silence mahe beon isturbet.

34. Nan ancre seruant ne ahte bi rihte to easkin iset hure, bute mete ant [claðˇ] þet ha mei flutte bi, ant Godes milce. Ne misleue nan Godd, hwet-se tide of þe ancre, þet he hire trukie. þe meidnes wiðuten, ȝef ha seruið þe ancre alswa as ha ahen, hare hure schal beon þe hehe blisse of heouene. Hwa-se haueð ehe of hope toward se heh hure, gleadliche wule ha seruin ant lihtliche alle wa ant alle teone þolien. Wið eise ant wið este ne buð me nawt blisse.

35. Ȝe ancres ahen þis leaste [lutle] stucche reden to ower wummen euche wike eanes aþet ha hit cunnen. Ant muche neod is þet ȝe neomen to ham muche ȝeme, for ȝe mahen muchel beon þurh ham igodet—ant iwurset. On oðer half, ȝef þet ha sungið þurh ower ȝemeles, ȝe schule beo bicleopet þrof biuore þe hehe Deme. Ant for-þi as ow is muche neod, ant ham ȝet mare, ȝeornliche lereð ham to halden hare riwle, ba for ow ant for ham seolf, liðeliche ant luueliche; for swuch ah wummone lare[34] to beonne, luuelich ant liðe ant selthwenne sturne. Ba is riht þet ha ow dreden ant luuien, ant þah þet ter beo eauer mare of luue þen of drede; þenne schal hit wel fearen. Me schal healden eoli ant win ba i wunden efter Godes lare,

---

[33] For 'hwen neod is', CFNT have *ofte*.
[34] After *wummone lare*, T has 'of religiun'.

ah mare of softe eoli þen of | bitinde win—þet is, mare of liðe wordes þen of suhinde. For þer-of kimeð þinge best, þet is, luue eie. Lihtliche ant sweteliche forȝeoueð ham hare gultes hwen ha ham icnaweð ant bihateð bote.

36. Ase forð as ȝe mahen, of mete[35] ant of claðes, ant of oþre þinges þet neode of flesch easkeð, beoð large toward ham, þah ȝe nearowe beon ant hearde to ow seoluen. Swa deð þe wel blaweð: went te nearewe of þe horn to his ahne muð ant utward þet wide. Ant ȝe don alswa as ȝe wulleð þet ower beoden bemin wel ant dremen i Drihtines earen, nawt ane to ower ahnes ah to alle folkes heale—as ure Lauerd leue þurh þe grace of him seolf þet hit swa mote. Amen.

37. Hwen ower sustres meidnes cumeð to ow to froure, cumeð to ham to þe þurl earunder ant ouerunder eanes oðer twien ant gað aȝein sone to ower note gastelich, ne biuore Complie ne sitte ȝe nawt for ham ouer riht time, swa þet hare cume beo na lure of ower religiun ah gastelich biȝete. Ȝef þer is eani word iseid þet mahte hurten heorte, ne beo hit nawt iboren ut ne ibroht to oþer ancre þet is eð-hurte. To him hit schal beon iseid þe lokeð ham alle. Twa niht is inoh þet ei beo edhalden, ant þet beo ful seldene; ne for heom ne breoke silence ed te mete, ne for blodletunge, bute ȝef sum muche god oðer neod hit makie. þe ancre ne hire meiden ne plohien worldliche gomenes ed te þurle, ne ne ticki togederes; for ase seið Seint Beornard, vnwurðe þing is to euch gastelich mon, ant nomeliche to ancre, euch swuch fleschlich froure, ant hit binimeð gastelich, þet is, wiðute met utnume murhðe—ant þet is uuel change, as is iseid þruppe.

38. Of þis boc redeð hwen ȝe beoð eise euche dei leasse oðer mare. Ich hopie þet hit | schal beon ow, ȝef ȝe hit redeð ofte, swiðe biheue, þurh Godes muchele grace; elles Ich hefde uuele bitohe mi muchele hwile. Me were leouere, Godd hit wite, do me toward Rome þen forte biginnen hit eft forte donne. Ȝef ȝe findeð þet ȝe doð alswa as ȝe redeð, þonckið Godd ȝeorne. Ȝef ȝe ne doð nawt, biddeð Godes are, ant beoð umben þer-onuuen þet ȝe hit bet halden efter ower mihte.

39. Feader, Sune, Hali Gast, an almihti Godd, wite ow in his warde. He gleadie ow ant frouri ow, mine leoue sustren, ant for al þet

---

[35] Before *of mete*, N has 'of drunch and'; similarly T and (after *mete*) F.

345 ȝe for him dreheð ant dreaieð ne ȝeoue ow neauer leasse [hure] þen al togedere him seoluen. Beo he aa iheiet from world into worlde aa on ecnesse. Amen.

40. Ase ofte as ȝe habbeð ired eawiht her-on, greteð þe Leafdi wið an Aue for him þet swonc her-abuten.[36] **Inoh meaðful Ich am þe** 350 **bidde se lutel.**

Explicit.

Iþench o þi writere i þine beoden sumchearre, ne beo hit ne se lutel. Hit turneð þe to gode þet tu bidest for oþre.

[36] For 'þet swonc her-abuten', N has 'ðet makede þeos Riwle, and for him þet hire wrot and swonc her-abuten'.

APPARATUS CRITICUS

PREFACE

MSS running: ACFLNPSV   1–2 I¹. . . Wisse] *A only*   4 *before* rectum²] et NS   5 regule] *after* sunt 6 CL   6 exteriorum] exteriorem L(Ma)P, exteriorem corporis S   8 Recti . . . te] *om.* LSV   8–9 deorewurðe] deorewerðe (⟨pu⟩ *alt. to* we *by different hand*) A   9 liuieð] CFNP, luuieð AV   10 habbeð] habbeþ (⟨ð⟩ *alt. to* þ *by different hand*) A   on] *del.* C²   11 efter] after (⟨e⟩ *alt. to* a *by different hand*) A   riwle] ⟨pl⟩ *alt. to* wl *by different hand in* A   cunne] dyuers PV   bimong] among NP   12 wið] V, mid N, ant C (mid *interl.* C²)   13 makeð] le fet F, makeð hire N, makeþ it P, fet le quer S   ant smeðe] *om.* FP   13–14 cnost ant dolc] C, knotte and dolke N, knooste and doþe P, uene e (. . .) boce S, conuexo aut concauo L, spotte of fulþe V   14 woh inwit] N, vnriht inwit V, oblique (. . .) consciencie L, tote conscience S, ⟨þoncg inwið⟩ C (*corr.* C²), þou3th inwiþ P   ant of wrei3ende] N, seu accusantis L, and bywraieþ þe P, and of schewynge V, ⟨unwrest ant 3irninde⟩ C (*corr.* C²), e de enclinante a pecche S   16 *after* heorte] 3ef . . . softe (*see fn.*) *marg.* C², (*in text, after* permaneamus 26) Gif þi conscience, þat is, þin inwit of þi þou3t and of þin herte, bereþ witnesse in þi self a3eynes þi seluen, þat þou art in sunne unschryuen, and þat þou misdest þat and þat, and hast þat defaute, and þat, such conscience and such inwit is wouh and vneuene and hulli and dolki, ac þis rule eueneþ hire and makeþ hire euene and softe V   16–18 Et hec . . . bileaue] *om.* C   16 caritas] karitas illa FPV, illa L   18–26 Pretende . . . permaneamus] *not in* CF   19 *before* per] scilicet L, (*after* fidem) S   22 antonomasice] *conj. Dobson;* antomasice AV, antonomatice N, anthonomatice L (anachorite Ma), atthonomasice P   25 preter] N, nisi LPSV   regulam] regula LPS   26 *after* permaneamus] *see 16*   28 þe] heo C, car ele S   29 singen] liggen NPS   29–31 Et hec . . . continetur] LNP, *after* widinnen 33 SV, *not in* CF   29 exercitio] A(*alt. to* exercitatio *by different hand*)NPV, exercitatio LS   30 *before* modicum] ad LSV   31 *before* geometrico] sub LPSV   geometrico] LNSV, geometrio AP   forte] to CV   32 as²] L, is alse CNPSV   33 oðer] NSV, ordre CF, regulam L   35 *before* strengðe] mid alle N, ou tut uostre S   37 mei best] best mei CV   wið] and wiþ VS   41 inwit] ⟨inwið⟩ C (*corr.* C²), inwiþ and wiþoute P   *after* inwit] þet . . . seoluen (*see fn.*) *marg., marked for insertion before* þet C²   consciencia] A *only*   wiðuten . . . sunne] *del.* C²   weote] C, aparceuance F, wite NV, uice S, labe L, white P   *after* sunne] cest quant ele ne siet nen est testmoigne encontre sei meismes de nul grief pecchee dedenz soi meismes F   43 makeð] marreð C   hire] la conscience S, þe hert PL   woh] V, obliquat (*transl.* makeð woh) L, tort F, wrong P, ⟨þong⟩ C (*corr. to* woh, scraggi, ant unefne C²), torte e bozuse S, woc N   45 god] goð A   46 an] CFLNV, ant an (n *of* an *in different hand over erasure*) A, tut dis S   51 istald] establier (*for* establie) F, ʽnis' (...) istoʽl'd N, ⟨nis heo italt⟩ C (*corr.* C²), is clept V, nys it ymade P, est (...) trouee S   52 þe²] *alt. to* þeos ... dale C² (*see fn.*) swucche] A, ant swich CFNPSV   53 moni²] F, ant moni CLNSV   54 þeos] A, þeos riwle CFNV, ceste foreine reule S, þis vtter reule P   55 *after* euene] as ... euene (*see fn.*) *marg.* C²   *before* sum²] and PSV *after* sum²] is NFSV, beþ P   56–7 mot te] N, mot þe CV, moten A, hij moten þe P   58 eðelich] A, feble C, turpes L, leide F, *sim.* S, atelich NV, nouȝt louelich P   59 betere] V, þe betere CNP   habben] holde PLS   60 hire¹] *om.* NP   62 sið] seið (e *expunct. in darker ink*) A   64 beoð] beoþ (⟨ð⟩ *alt. to* þ *by different hand*) A   65 stude-steaðeluestnesse] N, stude-⟨staðel⟩uest⟨ninge⟩ C (*alt. to* studeuestnesse C²), þe stude þat heo woneþ inne V, to helde þe stede stille þere his bisschop hym doþe P   66 *after* ant] as ... peril (*see fn.*) *marg.* C²   67 his] hire NV   *after* herre] ȝe ... biheastes (*see fn.*) *interl.* C², Hoc ideo consulo L   68 bihat hit ... forte don hit] A, bihat hit (...) to donne N, *sim.* C, bihoteþ (...) to don hit V   69 *before* ȝef] and PV   71 *before* of²] and NLPSV   *before* alle] ant CFN   72 oþre] *om.* FNS   72–3 swa ... wise] *om.* CF   73 þulliche] swuche NV   76 alle þe ten] S, þe alde ten AC (*corr.* C²), ðe tene olde N, þe ten PFLV   77 þulliche] swuche NV   78–9 ne riwle ... stalde] *om.* CV   80 *after* alle] ⟨þinge⟩ C(*del.* C²)N   þeos riwlið] CFLP, þeos riwleð ANV, ceste reule (...) reule S   81 *before* Of¹] and NPS   88 an¹] *om.* NV an²] C (inte *add. before* an C²), in NFSV   92 hit hefden] *trs.* NV   94 ȝe] CV, alse ȝe NF, þe A   siheð] isihð N, seoþ V   95 of ... Iames] þet ȝe beoð of Seint Iames ordre NPS, *sim.* L   97 funde] A, finde C, ifinde N, fyndeþ PV   98 Writ] ⟨p⟩ *alt. to* w *by different hand in* A   openluker] NFLS, openlukest ACV   descriuet] descriueþ (⟨t⟩ *alt. to* þ *by different hand*) A   þen] NLS, ⟨þet⟩ C(*del.* C³)FV   99 seið hwet] seiþ what (⟨ð hþe⟩ *alt. to* þ hwa *by different hand*) A   *before* hwuch] ant CN   101 necessitate] L, tribulacione FNPSV   sua] A, eorum NSV, *om.* FLP   102 widute] ⟨wið⟩ *alt. to* wᵗ *by different hand in* A   wem is] PV, wem⟨e⟩s C (*corr.* C²), wem N(*corr. by different hand*)FS   wem] ⟨p⟩ *alt. to* w *by different hand in* A   *before* iseon] to gon and V, aler S   103 widewen ant federlese] wyducs and fa|lese (*alt. by different hand*) A   world] ⟨p⟩ *alt. to* w *by different hand in* A   witen] ⟨p⟩ *alt. to* w *by different hand in* A   104 him] hire V   descriueð] descriueþ (⟨ð⟩ *alt. to* þ *by different hand*) A   105 his] CN, þis VFLS   beoð] beoþ (⟨ð⟩ *alt. to* þ *by different hand*) A   106 þe ... religiuse] V(*om. of*)L, þe (...) religiun C(*corr.* C²)F, of men þet beoð of religiun NS   107 Gode religiuse] bones religiouses et bons religious F   109 seið] A, seide CNV   110 widewen ant feaderlese] wydewes and faderlese (*alt. by different hand*) A   sawle] sowle (⟨sap⟩ *alt. to sow by different hand*) A   113 *after* Gan] and NV   þulliche] swuche NV   117 þe] FV, *om.* CLNPS   117–18 nempneð he] vermail F   118 *before* in] ne grise religion ne bise S   siheð] isihð N, seoþ V   119 þe leaste] lutel NS   120 *after* oþre] hali men sumhwile *add.* C²   121 Sincletice] NPS, Sincletyse V, Synclitice F, Sicleclice A, Sinc⟨h⟩ete C (*corr. to* Sincletece C²), Sincletica L   122 ba] A, baðe CV (*before* wepmen), amedeus (*after* wummen) S, *om.* FLN   123 hweðer] wereþ V, userunt S   125 *after* curtel] oþer i þe kuuele NS, in þe couel oiþer (*before* in) P   127 unseowlich] nient veuables F, vnsemelich V, foul (. . .) and vnworði P   128 þe easkeres] þeo þet askeð ou NS   129 *before* hweðer] and NF   129–30 hweðer . . . ordre] *om.* C, þet ʒe beoð, as is iseit, of Sein Iames ordre *suppl.* C²   129 *after* hweðer] qil soit F, ʒe be VS   130 *after* ordre] ant . . . dale (*see fn.*) *add.* C²   131 seide ear] V, ear seide CNS   133 blake cape] chape close S   cape] *om.* CN   hwite] *om.* V   rochet] *om.* CN   *after* rochet] ne en blanc surpeliz S   134 togederes] en congregacion F   þer for] F, propter (unitatem) seruandam L, þer for⟨e⟩ C (*final e partly erased*), þerfore V, þereuore mid N, mes pur cco S   136 þet . . . habbeð] ke eus toz deiuent auer S, que habenda est L   138 ha ʒeiʒeð] C, il moustrent et crient F, heo criʒeþ V, clamat (. . .) et insinuat vnitas exteriorum L, dient il S, aʒeines N   139 euch] vchon VC   140 wummon . . . mon] mon ⟨ant mimmon⟩ C (*corr. to* mon oðer wummon C²), homme ou femme S, *sim.* L   him] ham C² (*corr. from* him C)SV   142 *after* Michee] þe prophete CFP, Godes prophete N, le seint prophete S   144–5 þe² . . . prophete] þe hali Michee C, li seint prophete Michee F, Michee le seint prophete Dampnedeu S   146 god] Godd A   *after* hwuch¹] is NS   *before* hwuch³] and NFSV   hwuch halinesse] *om.* C   147–8 wac . . . seoluen] F, ⟨as þe seolf⟩ C (*corr.* C²), feble euere þi seluen V, ðe suluen euer woc N, þat euere þi seluen be þe werst P, vus memes peccheour e cheitif S   149 soð] riht NP   150 trichunge] A, a⟨n⟩ tr⟨u⟩ch⟨unge⟩ C (*alt. to* a tri chi), a trukunge N, trufle V, treccherie P   *before* Ve] Matthei xxvj° (*for* xxiii) L, Seint Mathew seiþ P, et in Euangelio a Domino dicitur S, in Matheo V   150–2 Ve . . . dealbatis] LPSV (*after* heorte *155*), *not in* CFN   154 ase tole to] F, tol⟨e⟩ to C (*glossed* lome C²), ase a dole to N, a stole to P, une eschole S, to leten V   155 *after* heorte] *see 150–2*   156 þis . . . bokes] Coment ceste liure est parti F, *not in other MSS*   157 Ich todeale] is todelet VL   158 euch] V, vhan CP, chescune partie F, euerich dole N   160 earre] vorme N, first PV   161 al] *om.* FLPV   162 *after* oðer] dole VS   163 is] liþe PV   aren] A, beoð CNPV   164 þe¹] CFNPV, *om.* A   165 euch hwet] A, vhan ⟨wit⟩ CF, vche a wit V, eueriche wit N   167 of anes cunnes fuheles] N, dune maniere doyseaus FS, of one kunne foules V, de natura cuiusdam auis L, of fif cunnes fo⟨w⟩eles C, of al manere filþes P   170 fondunges] fondunge CS   173 dale] *om.* CPV

penitence] penaunce PV   174 *after* seoueðe] dole is NF   176–7 earst...
þrefter] *om.* C

PART 1

1–2 Her . . . seggen] A, Cest la premere partie, de vostre seruise F, *not in other MSS*   3 *from* Hwen] *MSS running:* ACFNPV   4 *after* Amen] and riseþ up V   5 up-aheuene] C, up-aheuinde N, *sim.* P *after* honden] iointes F   6 wið] mit CN   7 fidelium] *om.* FN   8 Her-efter] þer-efter NP   ow¹] *om.* CF   9 *after* Credo] and seoððen N, and þenne V   10 þis word] þeose wordes CP   aþet] A, ad C (*corr.* C²), vort N, til þat PV   al] *om.* CPV   13 wið] mid CN   14 *after* habben] en vostre celle F, mid ou N   þencheð] CFNPV, þenchen A   15 deorewurðe] *om.* CN   adun] A, a cneon CFNV   18–32 Ave . . . et cetera] *om.* F   20–1 Aue . . . sustentationis] *om.* V   21 Aue . . . sustentationis] A, Aue, gaudium nostre glorificacionis P, *om.* CN   31–2 natus . . . et cetera] A, natus C (es de uirgine, et cetera *add.* C²), natus es de uirgine N, natus est V, *cont. to end* P   35 ower] þe CP   37–55 et benedicimus . . . nomine] *om.* F   37 *after* Crucem] tuam NPV   52 sanas, egras] sanos, egros N   56 *before* Hwa-se] and PF *after* con] nout NV   earste] first PV   te] *om.* CFP   cneolinde] *after* siðen 57 NP   58 heorte] A, breoste NFPV, beoste (*corr. to* breoste C²) C   59 icruchet] icrucced C (*corr. to* icrucched C², icrucket C³), icreoiced NV, and croyce it P   60 aleast] afturward V, and after P ymagnes] A, imaines C, ymages V, onlicnesses N   61 ower] þe CV   64 Uhtsong] Matyns PV   *before* seggeð] ant A   65 buhinde] boweþ PF   66 *before* seggeð] ant C²FN   *before* Rihteð] and N, *sim.* P   67 ant seggeð] N, et comencez F, ed CPV mea aperies] mea C, *om.* V   *before* Makieð] ant CNP   68 wið¹] mid CN þe¹] oure VF   *before* ed] ant CNP   69 twa] þreo N   buue] A, abuue NV, *om.* CP   70 *after* breoste] et . . . altre F (*see fn.*)   *before* Gloria] þe VFN   71 is] NPV, bið C, *om.* A   *after* þus] doþ NFP   72 i þe Venite] *om.* CNP   73 *after* ed¹] tis word N   te] *om.* NP eauer] N, *om.* CFPV   74 ed] P, to CNV   falle] A, falleð CNPV ower] A, þe CFNPV   75 to þe Credo] i . . . virgine N (*see fn.*) Credo] Crede CNV   *after* Tide] ant to þe Letanie N   ed²] P, to CN, *om.* V   76 leatemeste] C, laste NPV   ed] interl. N, *om.* V   77 þe] V, þisse NF   omnia . . . Domino] omnia opera F, omnia C, *om.* P   *after* Domino] et . . . Spiritu N (*see fn.*)   ed] and et N, and V   79 Ed] and et NP   wið] et tisse worde N   80 *before* rode-taken] þe CV   ear] *om.* FP   *before* tahte] ou CF   *after* Ed] tis word N   81 Wið] and et tisse word N   83 laudamus] *om.* CN   84 i þe Muchele] *om.* NP

Credo] F, Crede CNPV   *after* ed] tisse worde NF   88 *before* time] rihte C²N   Vhtsong] Matyns PV   89 þis] þe C(*corr.* C²)P   90 aþet] C, vort N, vnto P, til V   91 bi forð marhen] C, by forþe mornes P, de grant iour F, bi forþ dayes V, biuordeies N   93 Uhtsong] Matyns PV   Non] naut C (*corr.* C²), and elles nou3th. Onon P   eauer] *om.* CP   *after* mete] and ine sumer N   95 al] C, alle V, *om.* FN þah] *om.* NV   96 te] *om.* FP   97 *before* eise] in PFV 97–8 rungen up] C, leuer sus F, arisen up N, ariseþ P, risen vp V 98 al] A, al þe time V, a toutes les Houres F, aa C, euer N 99 *before* Ed] and NP   singeð] A, seggeð CFNPV   101 Credo] Crede CP   *after* wið] þe PNV   102 Uhtsong] Matyns PV   efter¹] et CP   efter Complie] FNV, et Compelin CP, eft A   102–3 From . . . Complie] vrom þet N, *om.* PV   103 aþet efter] A, oðet (Preciosa beo iseid) C, efter NP, til þat V   104 ower] *om.* CF   seggeð] *before* ower FNP   hwen] 3ef CFP   105 *before* eise] in VF, on P   cume] A, comeð CNV   107 sundri] CV, seueral F, sunderliche N, *om.* P   in aniuersaries] ant 3ef hit bið ani munedai C, ine aniuersaries, þet is ine munedawes N   108 leoueste] A, leoue CFNV   alle nihene] touz les ix psalmes et les ix lessons F   *before* I] and NF   Gloria] A, Gloria Patri CFNPV   109 *before* Requiem] segeð CF, 3e schullen seie P 109–10 dona . . . eis] *om.* C (*suppl.* C²), etc. P   110 aþet] C, vort N, att P, til þat V   alswa] A, and also NCFV, and P   111 *after* lesceuns] þear stonden *add.* C²   112 *after* ende] *see* *115–17*   113 suffragies] C (*corr. from* suffrages), suffragijs FNV, suffrages P   *after* suffragies] þet . . . halhen (*see fn.*) *marg.* C²   115 ane] *after* Sunneniht CN, *om.* V   *before* betere] þe CF   115–17 In . . . don] A, *after* ende *112* V, *not in other MSS*   115 a-mel dei] a dai þat 3e fasteþ V   115–16 we seggeð] siggeþ V   116 ba] *om.* V   116–17 twi-mel dei] a day þat 3e eteþ twy3e V   119 *before* Fiftene] þe NP   earste] C, uormeste N, first PV 120 al] A *only*   122 Et ne nos] *om.* NPV   *after* nos] sed libera C 124 *after* est] misereri C, misereri semper et parcere, et cetera P, *cont. to end* N   125 Et ne nos] *om.* NPV   126 et . . . tuis] et cetera C (et . . . tuis *marg.* C²), *om.* P   127 quesumus] *om.* FN   quesumus . . . placatus] *om.* V   *after* placatus] et cetera C², admitte F, admitte, et cetera P, *cont. to end* N   128 Kyrie . . . i.i.i.] A, Kirieleyson C, Kyrieleison, Christeleison, Kyrieleison FNPV   128–9 Et ne nos] *om.* NPV 129–30 Deus omnium] Deus omnium conditor, et cetera P, Deus omnium conditor F, Deus V, *om.* C(et cetera *add.* C²)N   130 *after* fiftene] psalmes NF   abuten under] entour midi ou entour Tierce F   131 ant] *om.* C(*suppl.* C²)N   134 *after* meassen] Vre . . . reade (*see fn.*) N 135 O] on CPV, a N, ¶ (*directing letter* o *in margin*) A   136 *before* Sune] and NFPV   *before* Hali] and PFV, and soðfest N   137 *after* þreo] persones et F, persones in P   139 seli] of þine N   *before* Hali] of

APPARATUS CRITICUS

þe N   *after* me] Neomeð . . . up (*see fn.*) *marg.* C² 140 þrile i] auer en F, þeose V   142 aa] A, touz iours F, euere V, al CNP 144 iueiet] N, imenged C (*corr. to* ifeʒet C²), iioynet V, yfestned P 145 þrumnesse] C, þrumnesse Trinite N, Trinite VP   146 Verset] *om.* FN   147 eos in secula] AV *only*   148–9 famulis . . . agnoscere] *om.* FV   uere . . . agnoscere] *om.* C (et cetera *add.* C²) 149 Trinitatis] N, *om.* A   *after* agnoscere] *cont. to* regnas N 150 oðer sum oþer] N, ou ascun altre oroison F, al oðer sum ⟨oðer⟩ (*second* oðer *del.*) C, oðer AV   151 ahonget] anhonged N, honge⟨ð⟩ C (*corr. to* honged C²), was honged V, þou hongedest P   *before* rode] þe C(*del.* C²)FN   152–3 alle þe sunnen] of sun⟨ne⟩fule deden C (*corr. to* al þe blodi sunnen C²), alle þe wunden N   154 swa mote] *trs.* PV 155 Verset] *om.* FNP   *after* te] Deus CP   et¹ . . . tibi] FNV, *om.* AC 155–6 et² . . . tuo] *om.* CV   156–8 ʒef . . . beste] *om.* C   157 *after* Unigeniti] filij FNV   158 sanguine . . . Crucis] *om.* FN   þis . . . beste] *om.* N   160 deale] mote delen N, mote P   162 heaued ant] heaued NV, *om.* P   163 brokes] V, strunden C, suite e (. . .) issue F, bruchen N, braunches P   165 Verset] *om.* FP   *after* tuum] *cont. to* creabuntur P, *to* terre C²NV   cor omne] A, omne cor CFNPV 166 *after* patet] et cetera C²P, et F, *cont. to end* N   Ecclesie . . . Domine¹] *trs. with* Exaudi . . . preces *166–7* N   *after* Domine¹] preces placatus N, et cetera C²P, et F   167 *after* preces] et cetera P, *cont. to* peccatis F, *to end* N   170 me] N, *om.* CFPV   172 Sana . . . tibi] et cetera P, *om.* C   173 est] *om.* N   misereri] *om.* CFN   174 I] *om.* A   wurðgunge] A, wurchipe CNPV   175 þet Ich] V, and þet Ich NF, ant CP   mote habben] (*after* bonen) N, habbe (*after* bonen) CPV bonen] N, bone CFV, *sim.* P   176 writeð] FP, seið C, witneð N, witnesseþ V   *after* writeð] Ad . . . et cetera (*see fn.*) *marg.* C² 177 Verset] *om.* FNP   177–9 Annuntiauerunt . . . . presidiis] *om.* V   178 et . . . intellexerunt] et facta eius N, et cetera P, *om.* C (*suppl.* C²)   salutaris] *om.* FP   179 tuorum . . . presidiis] *cont. to end* N, tuorum C (et cetera *add.* C²), et cetera P   180 Halhen] Hlhen A best] mest C, best and mest N   wurðgunge] A, wurchipe CNPV   *after* seggeð] Pater Nosteres *add.* C²   183 For] ¶ or A   *before* iseid] oiþer PF   me²] *om.* CFP   iunnen] wolde P, iwilned V   184 me] N, *om.* CFPV   six] seuen P, *om.* F   misericorde] N, milce C, mercy PV 185 six] seue P   Verset] *om.* FNP   186 iusticia . . . manet] *om.* CPV *after* manet] in seculum seculi F, *sim.* N   Oremus] *om.* NP   Domine] *om.* CP   *after* Domine] Deus, omnibus F, *cont. to end* N   187 þe¹] þeos CN   188 Christe . . . eleison³] *om.* CV   189–96 For . . . Fidelium] *after* famulabus *206* PV   189 alle þe] hare alre CFV   190–1 þe fowr marheʒeuen] *glossed* .iiij. dotes C²   193 weoredes] C², ordes N, ordres V   194 feolahredden] N, feorredne C², felawschupe V   ʒef . . .

wulleð] *om.* N   3ef] C²FV, *om.* A   195 Nostres] F, noster CNV   ant
... iii.] Kirieleison, Christeleison, Kirieleison NP, and Kyrieleyson VF,
om. C   196 Verset] C, *om.* FNPV   *after* inferi] *cont. to end* N   *after*
Fidelium] Deus F, Deus omnium conditor P, *cont. to* famularumque N
197 oðer] oder A   gederið ... heorte] þencheð vpo (...) in oure heorte C
(*corr.* C²), þencheð and gedereð in owre heorte N   198 þe ... þolieð]
C², les poures qe soffrent le mal F, þet wa ant pouerte þolieð AN, þat wo
and pouert þat pore þoleð V, þe⟨o þet ...⟩ C (*del.* C²), *om.* P   pinen] pine
NV   þe³] come F   habbeð] V, þolieð ant habbeð A, þolieð C²N, doð CF
199 ifeðeret] A, ifeteret VN, fiergiez F, ibunden C   201 temptatiuns]
temptacioun P, fondunge C (*alt. to* fondunges C²)   201-2 Alle hare]
A, chescuns F, alle menne CNV   202 heorte] C, þouhte NFV
202-3 he neome] him neome C² (*corr. from* ⟨him nume⟩ C)   204 þe
salm] *om.* CF   *after* oculos] meos NP, meos in montes FV, meos ... ut (*see
fn.*) *add.* C²   *after* noster] et ne nos CF   205 Verset] C, *om.* FNPV
206 famulis et famulabus] famulis C(et cetera *add.* C²)V, misericordiam P,
cont. to end N   *after* famulabus] *see 189-96*   207 *from* I] *MSS
running:* ACFLNPV   211 wið] mid CN   gretunges] gretunge CN
214 *after* peregrinationis] Aue ... tribulationis (*see fn.*) N   216 Aue,
solamen ... sustentationis] A *only*   220 Amen] AL *only*   221 *after*
Domine] *cont. to* tribue NV   222 *after* Domine] *cont. to* uirgine L, *to*
secula V   223 *before* Set] dites cest F   Set] si NPV   223-31 quo²
... tue] et tout cel qe suit apres F   223 Deus²] *om.* CL
226 unum] CL(Me, R²)V, uinum L(Ma)NP   amplectar] amplector
NPV   Quid] CLPV, quis AN   227 tibi] AC *only*   230-1 famule
tue] C (seruo tuo *del. before* famule), seruo tuo uel famule tue L, seruo tuo
NV   231-40 Miserere¹ ... Dominum] *om.* F   231 *after* magnam]
misericordiam tuam LNPV   233 *before* Credo] Aue Maria and V
233-4 carnis resurrectionem] P, carnis C, *om.* NV   234 et ... Amen]
A *only*   Saluam] saluum LN   famulam tuam] CV, seruum tuum N,
seruum tuum uel ancillam tuam L   240 *after* Dominum] nostrum
Iesum Cristum, et cetera V, nostrum, et cetera P   242 i] is PV
244 heteueste] C, ueste NP, riht faste V   iʒettet] igranted NV   eauer] N,
om. CPV   easkið] A, wulleð CFNPV, *sim.* L   245-6 þis ... strengðe]
rubric Meditacions del passion nostre Seignour F, *not in other MSS*
247 *from* Abute] *MSS running:* ACFNPV   hwa-se ... þenne] *om.* CP
248 eauer] *om.* CP   249 derue] A, grieues F, harde V, deorewurðe
CN, *om.* P   pine] pinen NF   249-50 þe² ... þruppe] in ... et cetera
(*see fn.*) V   250 þruppe] ensiuant F   *after* þruppe] Adoramus ...
benedicimus (*see fn.*) F   cneolin] V, cneoli C, kneolinde N, kneleþ PF
blescin] CV, blesceð N, blisseþ ʒou PF   251 beate] C, beten V, beateð
NFP   þe] CV, ower NFP   makie] V, maken C, makieð NP, dites F
þulli] C, swuch NV   *after* Christe] *cont. to* tibi P, *to* mundum NV

APPARATUS CRITICUS

252 *after* Crucem] et cetera V, adoramus P, *cont. to* nobis N   *after* que] in corpore N, in corpore, et cetera V   Salue . . . sancta] CFNPV, *om.* A *after* sancta] *cont. to* Dominum N   252–3 O . . . lignum] O . . . redemptus (*see fn.*) N   253 *before* Arise] ant CP   Arise] C, aris A, ariseð NPV   biginne] C, bigin AV, biginneð NP   þe] þesne NF 254 Saluator . . . rode-taken] *om.* CN   segge] CV, siggeð NFP 255 þe¹] CV, þesne NFP   *after* Iubilate] *cont. to* terra F   *after* wið] te NV   Patri] P, *om.* CNV   256 segge] NV, seggeð (*before* þe antefne 255) CF, *om.* P   eauer] vt C, tout hors F   *after* Saluator] mundi C(*del.* C²)F   257 blescin] V, blescin hire C, blesceð ou NFP   wið] AP *only* mare] N, mari CFPV   258 beate] beateð C(*alt. from* beate)FNP, beten V   þe] on ower N, 3oure P   falle] fal C (*corr.* C²), valleð NP, fallen V   segge] seggeð C(*alt. from* segge)NP, siggen V   259 Iesu . . . nos] twie N, *om.* C (Criste audi nos *suppl.* C²)   260 Verset] NV, *om.* CFP   noster²] in te sperantium F   261 *after* Crucem] ascendisti FP, *cont. to end* NV, as ear A; od . . . tui (*see fn.*) *add. after* ascendisti F   *before* Eft] and NP   biginne] V, bigin C, biginneð NFP   262 *after* Adoramus] te, Christe FN   *before* ear²] 3e dude PV   263 efter] NFV, þenne (*before* þe antefne) C, as ear A   *before* to] falle C, valleð NF 264 Kyrie iii.] Kirielyson C, Kirieleison, Christeleison, Kyrieleison FNV Et ne nos] *om.* NV   265 *after* noster¹] aspice, Deus N, *sim.* V   as ear] *om.* CN   265–6 Adesto . . . facis] Perpetua . . . Patre (*see fn.*) N 266 *after* facis] *cont. to end* V   *before* þridde] þe NV   chearre] A, time CNV   *before* feorðe] þe CV   267 chearre] N, *om.* CV   *before* fifte] þe CNV   *after* fifte] cherre NF   changeð] C, changiez F, chaunge 3e N, chaungen V   268 *after* salm] is NF   270 ant] *om.* CFP   euch] V, euchan CP, euerichon N   *after* euch] of þise psalmes PF 271 quesumus] A *only*   Domine] *om.* CF   *after* Domine] Deus noster V, *cont. to* subsidiis N   272 filium tuum] filium C, *om.* FP *after* filium] *cont. to end* NV   *after* Unigeniti] filij tui CF, *cont. to end* V; *see also* 272–3   272–3 O . . . intemerata] *after* Unigeniti 272 N 274 leaue] lete N, so leten hij P   277 underfeng] C, vnderuong NPV 278 ah] C, and NFPV   279 ernde] CN, donez F, erne PV   þeo] celes ioie F, þe blisse C(þe *alt. to* þeo C²)NP, þe meede V   *before* of] lefdi *add.* C²   280 *after* sunne] in *add.* C²   282–4 Biginne . . . tecum] *om.* C 282 Biginne] V, dunqe comencez F, and bygynne P, *om.* N   aþet] A, uort N, to PV   282–3 as . . . antefne] FV, *om.* N, in stede of anteme P 283 ant tenne þe salm] FV, *om.* NP   ant² . . . ut] PV, *om.* FN 283–4 fif . . . tecum] AV *only*   285 *after* Magnificat] tout hors, et puis F, stonddinde N   *after* siðen] and eft þus N   286 Marie] CFNV, Mary P, Maria A   288 ihal] N, hal CV, holy P   meiðhad] A, medenhad CNPV   291 lanhure] A, hure and hure N, lowore V, *om.* CFP   nam] am C(*corr.* C²)V   wurðe] worþi VP   292 iblisset] A,

blissed P, iblesced NV, in blisse C(*corr.* C²)F   ferredden] C, veolauredden NP, cumpaignye V   gratia . . . tecum] *om.* CP   293 *after* tribularer] stondinde N   *after* Aue] Maria, tout hors F   fif siðen] CFNV, fiue A   295 deore] AV *only*   derue] C, swete deorewurðe N, deore V, *om.* P   297 in¹] wiþ PV   *before* gasteliche] and NF   300 *before* sorhe²] muchele CN   301 gratia . . . tecum] gratia uort Dominus tecum N, *om.* CP   302 seruo tuo] *om.* CF   *after* Aue] al out PF   303 ilke] *om.* CN   304 brihte] *om.* CP   *after* Giws] þrusschen and duden to deþe and P   305 aþrusmin] N, haue þrusmen him V, haue wrou3th wiþ him P, prisunen C, murdrir F   *after* aþrusmin] ase . . . ariste (*see fn.*) N, as wiþ anoþer man wiþouten hope of vp arisynge P   i þruh] þorw V, *om.* NP *before* se¹] iseie him N, sei3 him P   wurðliche] wurþilich PV   se mihtiliche] V, michteliche CF, so mildeliche N, semelich P   308 licomliche] bodilich PV   blissen] F, blisse CNPV   309 gratia . . . tecum] AV *only*   Aue] Aue Maria NFV, Aues P *before* fif] al vt NF   311 alle þe oþere] toutes les altres F, al þe oþure V, al þe eorðe AN, alle þeode C (*corr.* C²), al þe werlde P   he] þi swete blisfule sune N, þi derworþe sone V   into] A, in his NFPV, *om.* C (wið *suppl.* C²)   312 cwene] de royne F, cuwene C (*corr. to* cwenene C²), quenes P   *after* crune] sette þe *add.* C²   on] CNV, sur ta F, vpon þine P, of A   *after* heaued] mist F   315 Maria] *om.* C   gratia . . . tecum] V, gratia F, *om.* CNP   Aue] V, Auez NP, et puis Aue Maria, tout hors F, *om.* C   317 *after* tuam] Domine V, *cont. to* infunde P, *to end* N   320-3 Salue . . . exora] et dites tout hors F   321 *after* orta] Aue . . . speciosa (*see fn.*) C²(*marg.*)NV   324 de¹ . . . Iesse] *om.* F   et . . . ascendet] *om.* FPV   325 *after* aulam] *cont. to end* V   327-33 Gaude . . . interuentrix] tout . . . aillours (*see fn.*) F   333 *after* pia] perpetua *add.* C²   334-5 Ecce . . . Emmanuel] Ecce, in utero concipies et paries filium, et uocabis nomen eius Iesum C   335 uirginis utero] semper C   336-8 et . . . Dominum] tout hors F   338-9 concipies . . . paries] FP, virgo concipiet et pariet CV, uirgo concipiet N   339 et . . . Iesum] PV(*with* uocabitur *for* uocabis), *om.* CFN   340 beate . . . generi] A *only*   Antefne] et puis lantisme F, Antiphona CN, *om.* PV   341-6 que . . . miserere] tout hors F, *om.* P   347 sitteð] C, sunt a dire F, sigge𝛿 N, setteþ V, saiþ forþe P   *after* sitteð] te . . . Avez C² (*see fn.*)   þe] *om.* CN   *before* hundret] an NP   347-8 þet . . . hwile] V, 3e habbeð hwule N, ceo qe len ad en voluntee F, wil haldeð C (*alt. to* þet 3e wulleð C²)   348-9 fiat . . . tuum] *om.* CP   349 *after* uirginum] *cont. to* zabuli N, *to end* V   350 stutten] astunten N, stunten V   *after* tuam] quesumus, Domine N   351 segge] CV, siggen NF   352 aþet] A, oðet cume to C, uort N, to V   353 þe²] þeos NF   354 *after* 3eme] of . . . psalmes (*see fn.*) N, ⟨. . . M⟩aria F   þis . . . ureisun] C, þeos vreisuns NF, þeos ilke orisons V, þise fyue

APPARATUS CRITICUS

orisouns P   356 gretunges fiue] *trs.* NP   356–7 buten ane imearket] A, bute imerked N, but imarked one V, imarked bute an CF   357 *after* writen] hem PV   359–90 þus . . . frumðe] A, *after* awakenin 399 F, *not in other MSS*   359 þus . . . oðerhwiles] A, *rubric* Ici . . . Aueez (*see fn.*) F   369 *after* et] in F   371 per²] F, *om.* A   375 es . . . et cetera] *om.* F   376 hire] la terre F   wið . . . uers] *before* fallen F   377 hal-iheafdet] seine, die ceste F   378–80 plena . . . tui] tout hors F   385 of þe] de F, þe A   386 stille] en piez F makie] *conj.* Dobson; Marie A, face F   387 an] *conj.* Dobson; vn F, oðer A   þridde] terre (*for* terce) F   388 *after* feorðe] diseine F   þe elbohen²] *om.* F   389 lute] encliner F   391 *from* Al] *MSS running:* **ACFNPTV**   þulliche] swuche NTV   392 on . . . wise] *after* ureisuns F   salmes ant ureisuns] of salmes ant vreisuns *after* ipaiet 393 C (of *alt. to* Of C²)   393 ipaiet] apaied CV *after* ipaiet] *see 392* 394 of Englisc] Euangeiles F   395 iȝemen] C, ȝeme T, garder F, ihwulen NV   ear] biuore N, tofore V   396 eche] echeð C(*alt. to* echi C²)NT, enoiste F, helpeþ V   397 wurchen] wurcheð NF   398 reden] redeð NF   beon] beoð NF   don] doð NF   god] *alt. to* God' (= Godd) C²   399 awakenin] N, wacnen C (*alt. to* arisen C²), wakien T, awaken P, encresen V   *after* awakenin] *addition in F; see 359–90* 401 ure . . . Tide²] chescune Houre de nostre Dame aferant F   Tide²] PFT, tiden CNV   401–3 Toward . . . iheren] *om.* PT   401 te preostes] le prestre del iglise F   404 *after* graces] siggeþ P   ant efter] *om.* F   405 weoued] autere PT   406 þe¹] ouwer CF   407 *after* Benedicite] Dominus PV   *after* Patris] *cont. to end* FNPV blesci] blescin C, seignez le boire F, blesceð NT, *om.* V   408 Domini] *om.* CN   411 Hwen-se] C, hwon NPTV   ower] *om.* PT   412 *after* cneon] to ðer eorðe N   i¹] F, *om.* CNPTV   414 ȝeoue] ȝifte PV   we] NV, ȝe CFPT   ne²] N, noþing P, nouȝt V, *om.* CT   415 *after* Miserere] mei, Deus NP   ant] A *only*   416 Et ne nos] *om.* NV   Verset] A *only*   Saluas fac] NV, saluos fac seruos tuos et CPT 417 Deus . . . te] *om.* CP   est] *om.* NV   418 stondinde] sigge stondinde þesne vreisun N, stondynge seiþ þis P   *after* Visita] quesumus FN   *after* istam] *cont. to end* N   aleast þenne] *trs.* CN   420 upo] T, up buue N, vppe V, i CP   423 efterwarde] efter CN   427 ow seolf] N, on ou self CFPTV   o] *om.* N   þe] TV, oure CFNP   *after* Filii] et cetera P, *cont. to end* FNV   428 se . . . mahen] *om.* C   ne ne þenchen] *om.* CP   þenchen] þencheð NF   na þing] naut CP 430 þe] A, þe þe N, þe þat V, hwa-se CT, hij þat P   Uhtsong] Matyns PV   oðer . . . . seggen] *om.* CP   segge] he seie T, siggeþ hij P 431 Uhtsong] Matyns PV   432 *after* Aue] Maria CN   Oremus . . . con] T, hwa-se con Oremus CN, Oremus F, who-se con V, and an orisoun who-so can P   433 *after* est] misereri C, misereri semper N   Domino]

PART 1

Patrem et Filium C   *after* Domino] Deo gracias FNPV   *before* fidelium] omnium PV   *after* fidelium] requiescant in pace F, defunctorum P, *cont. to end* T   434 *after* twenti] Pater Nostres FT   bute þet] A, buten CTV, auh N, and P   435 *before* schal] he C, mon T   earst] C, first T, *om.* NPV   hwa-se con] *om.* PV   mea aperies] mea N, *om.* V   435–6 Et os meum] A, *cont. to end* F, *not in other MSS*   436–7 ant . . . . adiutorium] *after* adiutorium *438* NP, *om.* F   436 Deus²] *om.* PTV 437 salutaris] A *only*   Deus, in adiutorium] *om.* N   *before* ed] and NP 437–8 ed . . . adiutorium] *om.* CV   438 *after* adiutorium] *see 436–7* 439 unheite] CN, deheitee F, unheite oðer sec T, on hiȝþe V 439–40 of þe oþre] FV, oðer Tide CN, of þe oðre Tides T 440 of euchan] *om.* CP   440–1 hwa-se . . . cwite] *om.* C (al seke beoð al cwite *suppl.* C²)   441 *before* neome] and NP   hire] oure C 441–2 nawt . . . gleadliche] þolemodeliche ant gledliche C, in þolemodenesse and gladlich P   442–3 ant . . . singeð] *om.* C   443 ret oðer singeð] singes oðer redes TV   444 of Godd] F, *after* þenchen N, *after* Tiden C, in oure God V, þenne T   445 *before* ȝef] and NV 446 ȝemeles] ȝemeleaste N, ȝemeleshede P   gluffeð of] faillez des F, gliffen of T, forgluffeþ P   neomeð] takes TV   ower] owe A 447 *before* al] ant C (*sim.* P), oþer NFTV   adun] dun TV 448 ȝemeles] ȝemeleaste N, ȝemeleshede P   449 *from* þis] *MSS running:* ACFNPSTV   449–51 þis . . . ihalden] *om.* V   449 *after* dale] of þis booke PF, de cest escrit S   þe] don[t] S   haueð] Ich habbe NST   450 hwet-se . . . þer-of] *om.* ST   þeose riwlen] þis riwle T, Mes ceste reule S   450–1 Ich . . . ihalden] muche . . . . heorte (*see fn.*) T, vus est mout grant mester, mes duz enfaunz, a tenir e a garder e a ceo fere; vus doint Deu sa grace. Amen S   451 of alle] N, toutes F, þurch alle C (*alt. to* of alle oþre C²)

PART 2

1–2 Her . . . wittes] Ici comence la secunde partie, qi enseigne coment vous deuez par voz cink sens garder vostre queor FS(*with minor variants*), Incipit secunda pars huius operis: De obseruancia sensuum L (Ma *only*), *not in other MSS*   3 *from* Omni] *MSS running:* ACFLNPRSTV   serua] custodi PST   quia] quoniam CLS   4 dohter] *om.* PRSTV   seið Salomon] *om.* PT   *after* Salomon] ðe wise N   5 *after* þe²] monnes *add.* C², of man' (*after* wittes) R   6 sihðe] seiȝeynge PRV   ant¹] CN, *om.* FLPRSTV   smechunge] spekunge NP   ant²] *om.* LRSTV   ant³] *om.* ST   8 bode] heste CN   9 ful] *om.* LRST   liht] wilde NPV 10 ne] *om.* RV   etflið] flið CN   11 meande] meanede him TV   i] *om.* PRV   12 *before* is] mad lessee F, me ad deguerpi e S   13 wes]

APPARATUS CRITICUS

is CPS   15 wis] *trs. with* war ST   16 hire[1]] his hert RFS, cor L *after* edstearten] him CR, *sim.* S   sare] sory PV   17 from Dauið] *om.* LRST   king] *om.* FRS   Hwer] *om.* CLPRS   18 Godd wat] A, God hit wat CNPTV, en noun Dieu F, sachez le vus bien S, certe L, certeyn R ed his ehþurl] NPT, ed his eilþurl C (*corr.* C[2]), al ouerture de son oil F, in apertura oculi L, a la fenestre de soen oil S, at þe wyndoe of his iʒe R, at a lokynge V   20–1 þe leaste . . . lutle] fetes uos fenestres plus estreites ke vus porrez S   21 Alle] A, al C(*corr.* C[3])NT, tout F, and þat (heo) alle (ben) V   23 unwurð] vnworþi PV   to] P, towart CNTV, devers F, quant au S, quoad L   24 *after* sunne] þet is Iesu Crist NP(is *om.*)ST 25 wiðuten] wið ten *corr. by different hand* A   as] þat TS   unseowlich] CNT, nient vewables F, vnsemeliche V, desacesmees S   ow] *om.* CFS 26 *before* crosses] manere N, maneres de S   ant] *om.* FST   27–8 þe beoð (. . .) wið hare blod-schedunge] NV, þet beoð (. . .) wið haʒen blod C, suo sanguine L, þat hauen (. . .) wið hore blod schedynge T, ke ont (. . .) par espandre lour sanc eus memes S (BN; par *om.* Tr), qe unt (. . .) lour sang espandu F, þat scheden her bloode P   28 þe . . . weren] were þe martirs CF, *sim.* S   29 i . . . penitence] her penaunce in þe werlde PS, *sim.* L   ladliche] heore VF, lour ordz S   30 ariht] *om.* NLPS 32–3 þe . . . biwitene] *om.* ST   33 to biwitene] C, uorto witene NV alswa] *om.* PST   teke] NT, ⟨to⟩ echen C (*corr. to* techen C[2]), ensembliche od F, ouec S, to V   36 parlures] C(clað *add.* C[2])N, parlurs clað TSV, louerture del parler F   beo] beon NV   on eauereuch] TS, eauer on euche CF, *sim.* V, euer (. . .) on eueriche N   37 *after* witeð] wel TS, *sim.* PR   38 of] dude of PT, fist S, cor L 38–9 Ich . . . sustren] *om.* LPST   40–1 for . . . ancres] Loke . . . anker (*see fn.*) T, E si gardez ke vus neez pas le uolloir e le non de recluse aboutant S, þerfore ne beþ nouʒth outward (ne tellynge ne leiʒynge ne flikerynge) P 41 totilde] ⟨. . .⟩outeresces F, totinde CNTV, aboutant S   43 unmeað] unmete C, vnimete V   te . . . dotie] deade men ne dotieð C   *after* dotie] þet . . . sunne (*see fn.*) *marg.* C[2]   worltmen] A, worldes men NTV, werldeliche men P, *om.* C   44 wede] wedeð C   þurh] wið NT 45 Me] *om.* CP   *after* seið] forsan L   *after* sum] inouhreaðe N   ant] *om.* FLPS   totin] loken PT   46–7 for . . . ancre] ful vuel (. . .) to eauereuch anker is te vuel þat ter cumes of T, *sim.* S   47 *before* nomeliche] and NPS   48 ʒungre] F, ʒeunge CLNPSTV   50 þeo deð] hij done PST, senes (. . .) faciunt L   is] ben PST, habentur L 50–1 ant . . . donne] *om.* CL   50 wat] witen T, seuent S, cunnen P *after* Ich[2]] wot NT   51 ha haueð] ho ahen TS   52 folhe i] foleʒe ⟨his⟩ C (*corr.* C[2]), ouh to uolewen N, folowʒeþ P   *before* An] and NLS 53 te] A, at V, *om.* CNT   55 wa] euel RT, vuel and (. . .) wo N   þet . . . wes] þat euer was, and ʒut is P, quod fuit, est L   56 iwurðen] beon CP   *before* sihðe] a NT   lo] *om.* TV   *before* preoue] þe CNP

PART 2

59 Of] and of NF, e ausint S   alde] first RS, alre NLP   59–60 on . . . of] þe first þing þat brou3th hire to synne was P   in . . . in3ong] CT, peccatum in eam ingressum habuit L, en lentree de son pecchee F, in hire neowe in3ong N, of hire synne in3ong V, prist (. . .) entre en soen pecche S   60 igitur] *om.* CR   61 aspectuque] aspectu CL   62 biheold o] bihelde PR   63 *after* delitin] hire CP   64 ant nom] *om.* RV   66 sihðe] CFLNPRSTV, sunne A   67 dede] deað NST   ifeleð] now felyth' RT   68 suster] sustren N   68–9 alle . . . sunne] omne delectabile in quo est peccatum L   68 alle þe] CN, alle R, al þe V, al P, euch T   þing] CFNPRSTV, wa (*corr. in different hand*) A   70 weorp] cast PV   earst] *om.* NV   71 ehe] echnen CNV   72 Me] my PFV   þu . . . woh] what is þe V   74 inohreaðe] *om.* PV   75 sustren] suster TS   as] CTV, come F, hwat N, And so Ich drede me 3utt þat P   dehtren] sunes, 3ea, and dohtre T, *sim.* S, sones and dou3ttren boþe P, sones and doghteres R   76 Me] *om.* PR   77 on²] opon PRTV   78 ehnen] ehe TLS, eghe sight R   81 hire were] T, vir eius L, hire were⟨s⟩ (*last letter del.*) C, hire louerd N, hire spouse P, hire husband R, hire fere V, touz les seons F   ba] CV, boðe NT, also P, *om.* FLR   demde] CT, iuga F, tauhte N, dampned V, (sa progenie furunt) iugez e dampnez S   al] T, *om.* C, alle NFSV   83 waxeð] comeþ CPR   84 euch . . . wummon] *before* muche ST   wummon] mon and wummon NPRT, homo uel mulier L, *sim.* S   þeo] A, cele FS, illa L, heo CNTV, sche R, hij P   85 iwraht] imaked NP   honden] hand RFT   biswiken] bigylet NPR   86 forð] CFNTV, *om.* ALPRS   *before* brad] þe CV   ouerspreadde] N, ofspradde C (*corr., prob. by* C²), spred ouer P, ad (totum mundum) expandit L, ouerspredyth' RTV, coeure F, corre (*for* coure?) S   87 alienigenas] *om.* CR   88 alswa] NPTV, (*before* A) RS, as *del.* A   *before* Iacobes] was N, þat was PR   as] R, si com S, *not in other MSS*   89 *before* Genesy] þe CF   89–90 3et . . . wepmen] ant 3et . . . wepmen *after* meidenhad *91* C   90 wepmen] men PRV   *after* wepmen] auh deð wummen N, sed mulieres L, ac it were wymmen P, bot for to se wemen' R   come] A, com CLNPTV   91 *after* meidenhad] *see 89–90*   94 þe] and te NP   wummen] L, te wummen of þere buruh NP, wummon CSTV   hire¹ . . . breðren] pater et fratres Dyne L, her faders and her breþeren P   94–5 se . . . weren] *after* imakede *95* ST   95–6 Al þullich] C, al þus N, al swuch T, of al such þing V, ⟨. . .⟩tes celes choses F, et hec L, si com (. . .) le S, al þis R, þis and oþer P   96 wummen] men RT, les genz S   97 ehnen] si3th PRT   of¹ . . . com] þet com of Dina ne com NS   98 Sichen] Sichem NV   99 leggen] setten CT   101 *after* Bersabee] þat was Vrries wyf P, þe wyf of Vry RS   102 dude] makede N, make C (*corr. to* makede, *poss. by* C²)   103 *before* halt] ant CFNS, þat PR   ahelich] C, honeste F, hehlich T, heihliche N, holy PLRSV   104 loke cape] longe sleuen P   loke] long V   *after* ancres] ou ioefnes

noneines S, uel moniales L   104-5 loki nede ase stan] regardier en toutes manieres F, (ke sont) encloses ausi come pere S, *om.* LPR 105 hu] CFLNSTV, *om.* (*suppl. by different hand*) A   wlite] CT, veit F, hwite N, visage V, parleure S   leor] *om.* C, hude *suppl.* C² 106 *after* seið] þet NPS   107 for . . . sleuen] N, for (. . .) sleue CFV, propter (. . .) manticam (*for* manicam) L, for his wide and his lokene sleue T, for his wide hoode and his longe sleeue P, pur soen large chaperon e pur sa chape close S   surquide sire] surquiderie NV   108 Godes . . . deorling] CNV, lami Dieu esleu meismes F, Dei electus L, Godes prophete T, li seint prophete Dampnedeu S, Goddes prophete and (. . .) his derlynge P, kyng and prophet R   he seolf] F, he T, him seolf CV, God (. . .) hym self P, God sulf N, God RS, *om.* L   seide] seið NL   109 *before* Ich] þet is NR   *before* mon] enne NPRT   111 þes] CF, was V, þus TS, was þus N   ehe wurþ] CN, iet del oil F, ehe warp T, regard ke il getta S, si3th of his ei3e castynge P, ei3e siht V   to] opon PV   113 utnume] FNV, *om.* CLPST   heaued . . . sunnen] T, heaued sunnen ant deadliche N, heued dedlich sunnen V, deadliche heaued sunnen C, dedlich synnes PFS, capitalia peccata L   o Bersabee] CNPV, ou dame Bersabee S, cum Bersabee L, o Bersabees AT   115 a sunful mon] a wrecche sunful mon N, synful wrecches P, a foleherdy wrech' R   swiðe] CN, presumptuose L, foole(hardy) P, *om.* FSTV   116 cang] voz fols F, þin T, uostre S, 3oure P   ehnen] ehe TS   *before* 3ung] an CPT   wummon] wummen NR   *after* wummon] þis . . . sihðe (*see fn.*) T, ceo ke est ore ci dit, si afert a femmes; mes ausi grant mester est a homme de garder bien la regardure de soen oil come a feme S   117 anewil] N, swa anwil C, en volunte F, in wil V, ful willesful T, mout curius S   to] for to CN   þer] *om.* C(bi him *suppl. after* god C²)SV   118 leueð] T, ileueð N, tristeþ V, ⟨weneð⟩ (*corr.* C²) C   nan] no mon NS   119 meistre] mestresse F   spetiale] *before* meistre C, *after* leaue N, especiaument S, *om.* V   120 herre] A, er NFSTV   al²] *om.* NR   121 wummen lokeden] wimmon lokede CV cangliche] solement F, *om.* CR   122 *from* for] *MSS running:* **CFLNPRSTV** (*C used as base MS*)   for] R, for þat P, pur ceo qe F, þuruh þet NTV, par ceo ke S, ex eo quod L   monnes] monne NLS 123 in] into NT   sunne] sunnen NF   124 halue . . . Alde] NFTV, *sim.* PRS, *om.* C   eauer] *before* iwri3en FNSTV, *om.* PR   124-5 3ef . . . vnwri3en] C, 3if eni unwrie put were N, 3if eny vnwried þe put VFT(*with* vnhulede *for* vnwried), si acuns la descouerist S, if any man vncouered a pytte R, si quis aperuerit cisternam et non operuerit eam L, 3if any pytt were, what-so it were (. . .) and 3if any vnhiled it P   125 þe unwreah þc put] *add.* C², þet þene put unwreih *after* 3elden *126* N, þat vncouered þe pitt R, þat it vnhiled P, *not in other MSS*   126 dredful] dredlich NT wummon] FP, wummen NLV, wepmon and (. . .) wimmen T, hommes e (. . .) femmes S   126-7 þet . . . hire] FN, *sim.* P, þat schewen hem V,

PART 2

sim. LST   127 *before* schaweð] swiðe sone T, tost S   wepmones echne] hwa-se wile TS   Heo is] ȝe arn TS   127–8 þeo . . . put] FNV, aperientem cisternam et non operientem L, þe vnwrihene put TS, þe wreiȝeynge of þe pytt P   128 þe put²] þat TS   hire¹, ², ³] owre TS 129 echnen] C, eie NFSTV, lates P   *before* hire] and NS   hire] NFPV, owre TS, *om.* C   hond] NV, hondes PFST   ha] ȝe TS   *before* halt] ham TFS, hit V   halt forð] scheawen TS   in his echȝe-sihðe] *om.* ST   echȝe-sihðe] NV, siȝth P, echȝe C (*corr.* C²)   *before* ȝet] and NS 130 hire] owre TS   iset] C, biset NTV   þet] ⟨ȝet⟩ C(*corr.* C²)FNTV, *om.* PS   feaȝeð] falleð to NP, feleþ V   131 hire] ow TS   fol] S, ful NFTV   luue] FNSTV, ⟨lokig⟩ C (*for* loking, *corr.* C²)   132 awacnin] C, acwikien TV, of aquikien N, excrescere L, venir F, avenir S   put cleopeð] cleopeð put NPV, *sim.* T   hat] bit VT   *before* beo] it PV 133 þet (. . .) ne] C, lest PTV, leste eni N   þrin (. . .) falle] C, ualle þer-inne NPSTV   druncni] drenchen PV   134 mon¹] mon oðer wimmon TS, men and wemen R   on] of NT   135 ach¹] ouȝtte PFV   spec] V, speke NFPST   136 open fint] C, *trs.* FNPSTV   þeo] cele F, ham NPV, þa TS   136–7 þe² . . . vnlideð] C, qe descouere le puz F, þet unhelieð þene put N, þat vnlydeþ him þe put V, þat unliden ham þe put T, ke descouerent la fosse S, aperientem cisternam L, þat openen þe putt P 137 schal] schulen NPST   þrin] *before* ifallen NTV, *after* ifallen FP bið] C, is NPTV   ha is] ȝe arn TS   witi] C, gulti NP, schuldi T, culpable R, reus L, tenue F, cause VS   138 his¹] hore T, þe bestes N, hominis bestialis L, of sich bestly peple R   his²] hore TS   139 ha navet] ȝe ne hauen T, *sim.* S   oðer] *om.* ST   140 þenne] C, buten NPTV   hire] ow TS   mid] wiþ PT   is²] NLTV, *after* heste *141* PS, *om.* C(*corr.* C²)F 141 heo¹, ²] he TS   142 adrong] N, adreynt PV, druncnede T   þet¹] *om.* N, *expunct.* T   vnwrisd] V, unhelest NPT   þis] þe PT   þet³] (*alt. from* ⟨þurch⟩ þet) C, þurh hwat TV, par quey FS, per quod L, whar-þorouȝ þat P, hwar-of þet N   143 þorch þe] C (⟨þe⟩ *del., prob. by* C³), of þe N(*after* ifonded)PTV, *sim.* F, *om.* LS   145 *after* deadliche] þuruh þe NT(*after* wise)V   147 þe¹ . . . þe³] C² (*corr. from* ⟨hwer⟩-þurch þe ⟨dede⟩ C), þat of þe þurh þi dede TFV, *sim.* NPS   148–9 beo iscrive] C²(*corr. from* beo ⟨in schrifte⟩ C)FPV, schriue þe NT, *sim.* S   149 *after* þer-of] ase . . . is (*see fn.*) N   *before* acorien] þou schalt PT   his] hire T *before* Hund] vulgariter dicitur L, for men seien a bywoorde P   bluðelich] *om.* PRT   149–50 hwar-se . . . opene] ubi ostium inuenit apertum L, at open dure þer man him ne wernes T, *sim.* R   150 open] open⟨e⟩ (*final* e *erased*) C   151 nuncius] inimicus FP   Augustinus] *before* Inpudicus FL, *sim.* S   *before* þet] quia L, car S   153 wummon] man RST 154 mon] woman RST   ha] NV(*before* ne rochte), he R(*before* ne rochte)S, *om.* C(*corr.* C²)T   155 he] ho *alt. from* he T, sum woman R   hire¹] him T   hire²] him TR   ifondet] C, itempted NPRTV   ach] NFSTV, vnde L, ant nu C 156 Sein] FNPRSTV, beatus L, *om.* C (*corr.* C^2) deð] *before* Austin C, seiþ PR ba twa þeos] C (⟨twa⟩ *del.* C^3), amedeus cestes S, þeos two boðe NTV, þise two PF, hec L in a cuple] in a⟨ne⟩ C(*alt. to* in a cuple C^2)P, in one weie NTV, en vne voie F, en une ueie S 157 et] FLT, *om.* NPSV 158 est] FLNPRSTV, *om.* C 3irni] C, cuueiten NRTV, knowe P *after* oðer] ⟨to⟩ C (*del.* C^2) for to] NT, to C(*corr.* C^2)RPV i3irned] C, iwilned N, icuueitet TV, yknowe P, desired R 159 mon] NPTV, monne C (*corr.* C^2) ba] N, boþe PRTV is] beoð NFRS haued sunne] dedlich synne P, morteals pecchez F, *sim.* S, gret synnes R þe] CFS *only* 160 þe arewen . . . armes] NFTV, arewen of þe first Armes P, þe forme arewen CS forme] C, ereste NT, first P, *sim.* V prickes] C, pricches NT, pointes S, aprochement F, werkes V 161 men worreð] mon weorres TS, a man fi3tys R mid] N, wiþ PRTV cunes] T, kunne N, maner RV, manere of P ant] C *only* 162 speres ord] spers RL, spere P sweordes egge] gladijs L, swerdes and knyfes R, sweerd P egge] NTV, ech3e C 163 of wundinde] NFPSTV, wundunges C 164 hondlunge] NPTV, maner FS, hond C 164–5 Lecherie . . . hore] stynkynge leccherie PL, lechery R 165 lauedi] FSV, lefdi of N, lauedi⟨es⟩ C(*corr.* C^2)T 166 *before* scheot] heo NT, he PRV *after* scheot] ele FS 167 flaa] V, flan T, earewe NP 168 *before* schakeð] heo N, he PR hire^1] his PT mid] wið TV 169 *before* dunricht] is NT 171 *before* hit] certes F hit] FPSTV, tis N, *om.* C (*suppl.* C^2) soðes] T, soð NPV, issint S, dunqes F, *om.* C 172 oþer^1] oðer C (*corr.* C^2), *before* hondli NTV *before* ifele] ouhwar N, owðer TV oþer^2] NTV, *om.* C (*corr.* C^2) 173 þet is] NTV, cest a dire S, ⟨wið þis⟩ C (*corr.* C^2) *after* wite^2] wel NFP 174 Ant] *om.* FLPR ha] he PRS, *sim.* L to] NFLRSTV, *om.* C 175 baltliche] FLNRSTV, openlich P, ⟨bradliche⟩ C (*corr.* C^2) forð] NFPRSTV, *om.* C i] NFPRSTV, of C 178 seouene-antseoueti] *conj. Dobson,* seouene and seouenti NTV, seouene ant fifti C, tant seet F, an hundreþ P lauedis] men T 179 hire] þe TS hus-] huses NV, huse- T þurles] windohes T, doores and (. . .) wyndowes PS *from* Ne tote] *MSS running:* **FLNPSTV** (*T used as base MS*) 180 quarreus] quarrel F, telum L te ehe] þen eien NS 181 ai] efre NV 182 earst] *om.* FLV eað-falle] V, legiere a batre F, eð fallen N, legerement (. . .) abatuz S 182–3 to ouercumen] FS, ouercumen NPV 183 þurh] P, par FS, mid N, with V *from* Bernardus] *MSS running:* **CFLNPRSTV** (*C used as base MS*) 184 intrat] *om.* C (*corr.* C^2) in] ad FV 186 deað] *after* echþurles NRSTV, *sim.* F, *after vb.* P þeos echþurles] C, les ouertures del oil F, eieþurles NTV, les ouertures des fenestres des euz S, þe ei3e P, þe eghen R *before* in3ong] hire FNTV in3ong] V, ⟨angines⟩ C (*corr.* C^2), ingong NT to] C, into NPRTV 187 a mon] homo L, lem S, ⟨vh⟩ mon C(vh *corr. to* a C^2)P, men NFRTV

PART 2 183

walde steoke] uoudreit (...) ueroiller e barrer S, clauderet L, wolde scheten P, walden steken NTV, clorreient F, *v.r.* R þurl] NTV, hole R, ouerture F, fenestram L, wyndewes P, huis e (...) fenestre S   187–8 of his hus] *add.* C², of hire (*pl.*) hus R, *not in other MSS*   188 for-hwon þet] N, for-hwon C (*corr.* C²), for-hwi þat T, pur quei ke S, ȝif þat V, issi qe F, ut L, and P, and þey wyst þat R   he] *conj. Dobson*, heo CN, ha T, hij P, þey R, me VS   machte] VS, machten C(*corr.* C²)FNPT   bisteoken] N, steke TV, scheten PR   188–9 ȝe... liue] deað (...) liue NTV, Oil, la mort (...) vie F, la mort, di ge (...) vie S, mortem inquam corporalem L, of fleschlich lyf P (*after* deað¹), *om.* C   189 eilþurl] T, eiȝeþurl V, eiþurles N, ouertures F, fenestres de ses euz S, oculos L, eiȝen P, egh' sight' and (...) oþer wyttys R   190 þe] CFS *only   before* saule] helle and of N, ⟨helle⟩ (*del.*) T   ha] P, eiþurles NTV, les fenestres S   191 eilþurles] NTV, ⟨ech⟩þurles C (*corr.* C²), eyeþerlles L, pertuiz nuisables S, þirles of soule deþ P   idon] *after* eil TV   191–2 Al... ech3e] NLPRSTV, ⟨...⟩leine de gard⟨...⟩ F, *om.* C   192 is... warde] nus en garnit des regarz S, custodiam suadet L   of warnunge of warde] *conj. Dobson*, of warninge TN, de gard⟨...⟩ F, of wardynge V, techynge and warnynge of kepynge P, of wernyng of kepyng R   193 he] CS *only   awei*] *after* echnen TV   194 *after* dweole] and hire fantasme TN, e de fantosme S, and his vanyte V, and his vanitees P   Iob] and Iob seide NS   195 ne] L, nec P, ut ne NV, ut nec FST, ut non R   de] *om.* C (*corr.* C²) 195–6 seið Iob] FR, (*after* ifestned *195*) NTV, (*before* Ichabbe *195*) Iob seiþ PS   196 mid] N, with RSTV   196–7 Hwet... he¹] FNTSV, *sim.* L, *om.* C   197 ech3e] eien NLS   *before* wel] ful NPRS   199 him] NPSTV, *om.* C   ant seide] NFPSTV, *sim.* R, *om.* C   199–200 Oculus ... meam] FLNPRSTV, *om.* C   200 he seiþ] CFPS *only* 201 þulli] C, swuche NPRTV   *before* eche] hise PFRS   eche] eien NPS   202 *after* þu] þet C   beo] C, is NTV   icumen] *after* mon V, *after* wummon *203* N, *om.* T   202–3 ant... wummon] FTV, oþer to moni wummon N, seu mulieribus L, e meinte femme S, oiþer a womman P, and woman R, *om.* C   203 ant sorege] FT, seoruwe N, þe serwe V, e grant doel de mener S, to sorow (*vb.*) R, *om.* LP   ech3e] eien NLS   *after* hwise] man PRSV   in his boc] FNPTV, en Ecclesiastice S, Ecclesiastici xxxjº L(*after* ech3e)R, *om.* C   204 hweðer] weðer C (*corr.* C²) harmi] T, hermeð NPRV   wimmon] mon TS, a man R, þe man oiþer þe womman P   deð] FR, *om.* LNPSTV   hire] his TR   ech3e] eien NLP 205 nequius] nequicius C   faciet] facit NPTV   quoniam] F, ⟨quem⟩ C(*corr.* C²)V, quam PST   uidit] uidet ST   *after* uidit] in Ecclesiastico FTV   206 of] C, o NT, on V, þe P, (be wet) with R   teres] terres C þe ehe-sichðe] þech3e-sichðe C (*corr.* C²)   208–25 Ore... la] F *only* 213 moustrent... domme] *conj. Dobson, MS damaged*   214 dedenz... queor] *conj. Dobson, MS damaged*   lomme] *conj. Dobson, MS damaged*

215 fet] *conj. Dobson, MS damaged* 226–62 traisun . . . seoluen] AF *only* 228 Godes] nostre Seignour F 229 þurh riht] dreit par F 231 inohe] plusours F 236 ha ne spekeð] eles ne parlent F leoteð . . . iwurðen] tenez vous issi close F 237 heo . . . iscandlet] le prengent a mal F 240 adun] avalez auant F 241 heteueste] bien F 243 wel . . . duhen] ne te estuit chaler F 244 bischop] bischp A kimeð to seon] vult veer F 252 iboren] *om.* F 256 oþer] arere (*for* autre?) F 258 caret laqueis] cauet laqueos F 259 itild] telde F 260 sumchearre] ascune foiz F, *om.* A 262 wið him] ensemblement od Dieu *after* ha *261* F *after* seoluen] *addition in F; see 884–940* 263 *from* þis] *MSS running:* ACFLNPRSTV of þis wit] *after* inoh NV ed . . . chearre] *om.* CPR 265 Spellunge] smellunge C is] *om.* CP ehe] eien NP 266 *after* leten] of CP 267 spellunge] smellunge C ba] boþe PTV 270 meiden] maydens V, seruanz TS beo²] is CN 271 essunien] essuneien A *after* crossið] ow TS 272 *before* muð] ouwer CN ehnen (. . .) earen] A, *trs.* CFLNSTV 273 *before* Confiteor] siggeð NF, *sim.* PS *before* Benedicite] dites S 273–4 þet . . . seggen] qil vult dire F, (audiendi sunt sermones) loqui volentis L, Nekedent ceo deit il dire S, *om.* C 276 ne . . . nowðer] *om.* ST 277 hire] him NT, *sim.* S 278 forwurðeð] C, bicomeð NPTV meistre] mestresse FS 280 beon . . . icnawen¹] fayn be wys iknowen V, ben yholden wyse P beon sone] F, sone beon C(*after* wise)N (*after* tale), sone (. . .) beo T *before* wise] þe CFNST 282–3 alre leaste] leste C, laste NV 283 awei] *om.* CV, *after* iwent N 284 *before* talde] and NFPR 286 wacnesse] vnstablenesse V, febylnes and hire vnstabilnes R, feblesse and her brotylnesse of fallynge P, infirmitatem et pronitatem ad lapsum L 289 3e (. . .) folhið] E uus ausint (. . .) ensuiez S, imitanda est L, folow þerfore R, þerfore vche man and womman folowe P sustren] frend T 290 cakele] cakelinde T, cakelinge R 290–300 For-þi . . . lut] *om.* C 291 Nabbe ha] N, *sim.* LS, nabbe T, nabbe 3e VF, *sim.* PR 292 ileid] ouum posuerit L, leide an eye PR Ah] FT, and NLRSV 293 kaue] A, chaue F, coue N, knaue V, 3eape T, le fiz sa mere S, garcio L, keme P, on R 294 fret of] A, fret of þat heo V, *sim.* T, comedit de quo (deberet) L, deuoert tutz dunt ele F, fret al þat of hwat heo N, les maniut dont ele S, etiþ hem of wich sche R, þat sche (. . .) of P Al riht] A, tout FS, ri3th PT, ant riht N, *om.* LRV caue] A, chawe denfer, (le) F, luðere coue N, knaue V, luðere T, soudiuanz S, *om.* LPR 296 as briddes] come plais volanz F 297 icakelet] vt cakeled T, hors fauelez S *after* icakelet] þe . . . stille V (*see fn.*) wrecche poure] wreche NFLPSTV, pore R peoddere] pedelere VR(*corr. by different hand from* peddie), sauoner FS, smigmarius L 298 nurð] A, murþe V, noise NPRT þe] a NP 299 as . . . her-efter] *om.* LNPR 300 as . . . lut] *om.* PST 302 3ef . . . iheren] si vous

volez qe si il voille oir F, si vus uolez sauer S, *om.* L   303 areownesse] V, reowenesse CT, bireounesse N   304 inwardluker] CTV, inwardliche NFLPS   in his bonen] ine munde and in his bonen N, e vus recoille (e vus eit) en ses prieres S, in mynde in her byddynges P, in memoria L   306 warre] CT, iwarre N, war PV   307 *after* beoð] wiðinnen TS, vderneþen P   wedde] T, wode NV, madde C, rauisshande P   308 Worltliche] CT, seculers FS, worldliche men NPV   leueð lut] CSTV, *sim.* P, poi se donnent garde F, ileueð hit N   309 cuððunge] kuþlechunge N, cuþreden V   309–10 Eue . . . speche] *om.* C, þe . . . speche *om.*, *suppl. in different hand* N   310 offearet] ofdred N, adradde P   311–26 Vre . . . þe²] AF *only*   313 te wudelehe] le cour del boes F   320 deihwamliche] mortelement F 321 of þe] a celui F   nempnin] le nomer F   325 in his god] en Dieu F 327 *from* Wiðuten] *MSS running:* ACFLNPSTV   wummon] V, *trs. with* wepmon CLNST   wepmon] N, mon CTV   329 þer] þat TSV 330 bute . . . trukie] NT(*with* stunde *for* stude), ne soit qe altre lui faille icelui tierz F, oþer þe stude fayle V, bute ʒef ʒe him nabben C, si tercius possit haberi L, *om.* S   oþer] *corr. by different hand to* owðer A 331 leoue sustren] *om.* T   332–3 as . . . leafdi] A *only* 333 þe uuele] A, þet uuel CNPTV, le mal FS, malum L 334 unseli] mal⟨uois⟩ homme F, vnseli ancre T, mesauentureuse femme religious recluse ou autre S   335 *after* schraf hire] a lui F   ischriuen hire] la confessa F   ahen] N, ouʒten V, ach CFST, schulde P 336 *before* habben] to NT   eauer] *om.* LT   340 þurh] of NP *before* tale] no PNTV   341 wurðmunt] wurðschipe NV 342 wummen] NV, wimon C, meignee F, seruanz TS, seruaunt P *after* wummen] parlez F, deuez vus parler S   *before* þe¹] at PF, to N, par S   oþre] PT, þe oðre CFSV, þeo oþre men ant wummen N   *before* þe²] vers F, to N, at P, par S   343 parlur] CF, parloures PT, parlurs þurle N, la fenestre du parlour S, parlurs hole V   Speoken . . . þurles] *om.* C   *after* Speoken] buten uor neode N   344 *after* Silence] tenez F, deuez uus (. . .) tenir S, est (. . .) seruandum L, (*after* eauer) holdeþ P *before* ʒef] vor NPS   344–5 ʒef . . . alle] *om.* C   344 witen] wel wuteð N, witen wel V   344–5 doð hit] *before* as *344* FN 345 meidnes] FV, meiden CN, seruanz T, seruaunt PS   as] *om.* CPST 346 hire²] him T   feire] uere N, *om.* C (*but see* unsperren *347*)   forte] to NT   347 unsperren] P, gladien hire fere ant for to ondsweren ed C, openen NTV   þurl] windohe TV   hire²] him T   348–50 Summes . . . bitweonen] *om.* C   349 huses leafdi] husebond oðer husewif T, homme espus e femme espusee S   351 bute] bute ʒif NP   i] of CS 352 Aduenz] FST, Aduent CNPV   Umbriwiken] Umbridawes N, Ymbrynge dayes P, Vmbridei C   353 *after* dahes] in þe week P, *sim.* S   Swiing-wike] A, Sueiʒeng-week P, Swi⟨ʒen⟩-wike C (*alt. to* Swiwike C³), Swihende-wike T, Swið-wike N, Passion Wike V, Symeyne penouse FS   aðet] C, uort N, ai til T, riht to V   353–4 on ... euen] CP, of Ester euen NFTV, ant from Non efter mete aðet euen *expunct. and corr.* A   354 wummen] V, wimmon C, meignee F, meiden N, seruanz TS, seruaunt P   355 *before* 3ef] and NP   *after* icumen] et ... parlier (*see fn.*) F   356 wið] mid CN   easkunges] FT, askunge NSV 357 *from* Muche] *MSS running:* ACFLNPRSTV   were] FL, he were CNP, wer he RV, ho were T, serreit cil ou cele S   his] hire T   he] ha T, il ou ele S   358 greot¹] CNTV, secche terre F, chaf R, bren S   *after* hweate] *see 359*   he] heo T, il ou ele S   grunde ... greot] greot grunde CT   greot²] CNT, gret V, terre F, grauel P, paleas L, chaf R, bren S lette] A, leafde CNT, leue V   359 Hweate² ... speche] *after* hweate *358* V   Heo] NT, he CPV, celui F, ceus ou celes S   360 greot] CN, grot T, gret V, la terre F, grauel P, paleas L, bren S   *after* chafleð] de terreines choses F, of ydel speche and werldelich P   þe twa cheken] les dous genciues F, les deus leures de uostre bouche S, maxillis L, þe ouer party and þe neðer party of þe mouþ R   þe¹] *om.* CV   grindelstanes] grind⟨el⟩stanes C(el *erased*)PTV, grinstones N, gryndyng-stonys R 361 þe cleappe] le batuel F, li kliket ou li cloket du molin S, batellum molendini L   leoue sustren] *om.* T   cheken] genciues F, leueres S, maxille L, mouthes R   362 eare] C, earen NFLSTV   drinke] CTV, beiuent FS, hauriant L, hercnen N   neauer²] *om.* CLV   363 eare] TV, earen CFLNS   ehþurl] T, ehþurh A, echþurles CN, ⟨le⟩s ouertures de voz oilz F, fenestre L, le oil du pertuis de uostre fenestre S, eȝesiht V 363–4 sperreð to] T, isperret to V, spareð (*before* ower) C, tuneð N 366 *before* wearien] ne NT   368–79 Ne preachi ... weorre] *om.* RST   368 *before* mon²] no NFV   368–9 ne⁴ ... ane] *om.* C 371 edwiten] A, edwiteð CFNV   *before* his] of NV   unþeaw] N, unðeawes CF, maneres V   372 nis ... ne¹] *om.* C   374 as ... larewes] A *only*   forte] A, to CNV   375 wite bute] *conj. Tolkien;* witene buten N, gardier fors F, lokin buten CV, loken bute *add. in different hand* (bute *over erasure*) A   *after* hire¹] ane *expunct.* A, seluen C, *not in other MSS*   euch] V, vhan C, euerich N   his] CNV, hire A 377 seide ear] A, *trs.* CNV   379 falsinde] fals PF 382 þenne] *om.* CP   *before* Moni] auh NL   383 *after* ed] ter NT   mulne] mulne-cluse N, milne-cluses T   *before* Swa] and NP 384 frourin] comfort RV   384–5 hefden ... bigunnen] bigunne CLRS, haueden T   384 alles] *om.* FLPRS   385 ne] *om.* PRV stutten ... cleappe] desistere L, lynne P   stutten] C, astunten N, stunten TRV, cessir F, refrener S   cleappe] NV, kliker S, cleppen C, lange F, tonges R   386 of] S, i CFNTV   390 seon] iseon CN 391 *after* mahe] renne RF, issir S   393 hehin] hien NV 394 tofleoten] CNV, flete R, flowen T, descurrent F, uoisent S, fluat L,

fleiʒen P   *before* te] al TV   395–6 Hwen . . . sone] *om.* CP
395 *after* moten] speken NR   lowsið up] letes up T, lifte vp R, haucez S, eleuande sunt L   396 flod-ʒeten] flodeʒate RST   *after* ed] ter NR
398 *before* Qui] Gregorius FNT, e Seint Gregorie dit (. . .) S
398–9 Qui . . . suam] *om.* N   399 *after* witeð²] wel PV
402 wiðhalt] halt CP   þe²] A, a PRV, *not in other MSS*   burh] cyte RV   403 þet] þer-ase NS   404 þurh-ut] A, þurch CNTV
405 ane breðren] men V, diuerse men of gode conuersacion R, a man þat lyued holy lif P   407 quoð] seide CR   409 eauer] *om.* CPR
hare²] þe PT   412 bridli] T, bridleð CNPRV   413 *before* he¹] et FS   414 *before* Bridel] vor NS   415 sum] *om.* RST
419 *before* Ofte] vor NP   foð on] begyn RTV   420 ha] it PV
421 into] to CV   422 deerit] deest NR   423 ginne] C, aginne N, begynne RTV   424 sum] *om.* NSV   425 into] *om.* CFNPS   þe¹] ant CP   426 tofleoteð] fleoteð CR   427 ha] it PR
428 tantoque] tanto LN   429 *before* inquinatur] co *interl. in* A
431 he²] we NPST   him¹] Godd TS   bit] bidden TS   433 ne] ant CT   *after* nule] he NP   iheren] heren CP   to] *om.* CV   434 ant . . . chafle] *om.* STV   435 hire¹] his T   436 ant] A, ach CFNV, as TS, *om.* L   *before* seið] he NFST   439 pleieð] NV, pleideð CF, moten T, fauelez e ianglez S   442 deorewurðe] *om.* PRTV   wummen] men RT, genz S   443 to] *om.* CNV   444 se] þe CNV
445–8 Bernardus . . . diuinum] *after* engel 449 R, *not in* CFN
448 *after* diuinum] *see 456*   449 Gabriel] *after* engel FNP   *after* engel] *see 445–8*   449–50 wið þet] mid tet N, whan þat P, wen RV
452 inwið] in CPR   hire] þe NFRS   453 *before* þa] *see 456*
454 *after* mihte] wenest tu N, or me dites S   *after* Hwet²] *see 456*
456 Idem . . . utero] S, *after* diuinum *448* V, *before* þa *453* P, *after* Hwet² *454* T, *not in* CFLNR   Idem] *om.* PST   Iohannem] *after* fecit ST
456–7 þet ha spec] *repeated* A   457 þurh] þurh A   458 hefde imist] misde CPR   459 ifunde] ivond N, troua FS, fonde P
460 *after* beah] him NP   to² . . . Ioseph] Ioseph and Mary (*after* wummon *461*) R, *not in other MSS*   462 Neomeð] takiþ RV   nu her] nu CP, her V, *om.* LR   *before* ʒeme] ʒeorne T, good VS   ʒeme] hede RV ʒeorne] *om.* CLRS   seltsene] seeld P, seldene VR   463 Vir . . . terra] *after* eorðe *465* SV   464 ne] *om.* RV   465 *after* eorðe] *see 463*
466 ypallage] CFRTV, ywallage A, *not in* LNPS   ant] *om.* FLRS
469 þet] *om.* FPR   471 undeadlich] undeaðlich CN   feieð] seið CST, coupleþ, seiþ V   472 in] þet in NFR   473 uestra] nostra SV
474 silence (. . .) hope] *trs.* CS   ower] vre VS   *before* Neomeð] ore S *after* Neomeð] ore F   475 longe] *before* silence NRS, diuturnum L
477 ihere] orra F, wule iheren N   478 nu] *om.* SV   479 ba] A, boðe NTV, *om.* CFP   Teke] to eke þilke C, ouesqe ceo F

481 seruise] C(*corr. from* strengðe)FNSTV, strengðe A   to3ein] a3ein NP
482 inwið] wiðinne NR   483 ha] he PRT, celui S   484 hire] his PRT   swote] swete RV, spece T, *om.* S   þrof] ƥrof A   485 heo] T, þeo CFN, he P, celi S, þulke V   hire] his P   486 swotnesse] N, swetnesse CTV   489 forte . . . derf] vt sustineat aduersa et L, *after* stronge CFNSTV   derf] hard T, e duranz S   to3ein] a3ein NPV
491 drehe] N, drei3eð CTV   seið] seiþ in Englisch V, uulgariter dicitur L tobreke] NT, breke V, ⟨breke atwa⟩ C (*corr. to* toburste C³), tobrast P
494 swete] swote CN   *before* sawle] þe CNST   496 muðes] muðe CNS   tuteles] bochers S, *om.* F   497 habeatis] habetis PV, habebitis S
498 earen] ere PST   502 ba] A, *erasure* (*2 letters*) C, boðe NV, *om.* PST   504 spearren] sparen (*corr. to* speren C³) C, tunen NV, weren T þurles] A, echþurles CNT, fenestres FS, sihtes of oure lokynges V
505 For] urom NLV   speche] speches C³T, paroles FS
506–7 De . . . et cetera] LV, *after* of¹ *509* P, *after* irikenet *510* R, *after* lustnede *511* ST, *not in* CFN   507 ant] *om.* LN   508 *after* attri] speche NRS   509 *after* of¹] *see 506–7*   euch] euerich NV   510 *after* irikenet] *see 506–7*   511 *after* lustnede] *see 506–7*   Hwet] *om.* CF
512 of¹ . . . hu] *om.* ST   516–7 þeose . . . riwle] *om.* LN
518 muð] mud A   *after* nawt] soulement S   wið¹] mid CN   sneateres] T, sneates C, paroles F, wordes NV, responses S, reprehensione L   *after* sneateres] solement F   518–9 hearde fustes] greate neue duntes T, gros coups de poins ou de pieres S   521 þe wurste] peiores F, þe wurse T
524 leas] lesyng RT, leas and leasunge N   525 *after* deouel] hit seið CNV, dit il F, he seis T, *sim.* S   leas] mencongier F, a lier R   leasunge] C, leasunges NFRSTV   527 cradel] cader C   bearn] childe RV his] AR *only*   529 ne beoð] nis TS, is R   530 beoð] is TSV
531 feor] feor from CNTV   ahen²] a3en to (*after* ancren) CNT
532 iheren¹ . . . segge] hereren (*for* heren ne?) seggen C, oient ne dient F *after* Iheren²] hom TS   536 nis] nis ha C, heo nis N
537 witerliche] sikerliche NV   ha] he TS   538 þeo] þa T, toz iceus S   uuel spekeð] spekeð vuel bihinden NS   spekeð] speken TS *after* tunge] *see 540–1*   539 *before* mon] þene NP   preon] CNV, pryk PT, prikes R, broche F, aguilon S   ehe] eien NR   540–1 Gregorius . . . figit] *after* tunge *538* F, *not in* CNP   541 *after* figit] *see 543–4*   i] CN, on RTV, ⟨su⟩r F, au S, opon P   Fridei] Uridawes NLV   beakeð] pekkiþ RV, pykeþ P   wið] mid CN   542 charoines] careyne VS
543–4 Salomon . . . et cetera] L, *after* figit *541* RTV, *before* On *549* S, *not in* CFNP   544 3ef he walde] A, si isti vellent L, 3et walde he CNTV, wolde he 3utt P, wold he R, encore qil vousist F, mes onkore si il uoudroit S pilewin] C, pileken (*trs. with* totoeren) N, pekken V, pike RT
544–5 rotet stinkinde] *trs.* RTV   545 walde he] sil vousist FS, 3if he nolde N, si nollent L   546 sunne] sunnen NTV   547 tolukeð]

PART 2

A, teoreð C, teticreð N(*trs. with* tolimeð)TV   548 *after* Godd] *see 552–5*
549 *before* On] *see 543–4*   On oðer] anoðer NV   nu] *om.* SV
550 *after* twa²] manere CV   551 seggen] nempnen TS   fulre] fulre hit is NR, ȝutt it is fouler P, plus est uile et orde S   552–5 Ne . . . detrahentem] A, *after* Godd *548* P, *before* þe fikeleres *556* S(*to patris only*)TV, Neemie iij°. c: Melchias edificauit portam sterquilinij, et cetera L, *not in* CFNR   552 recolat] V, recolatur ST, *om.* P
553 Melchia¹] V, Melchias PT, Micheas S   Melchia²] V, Melchias T, Micheas S   corus] T, chorus P, thorus S, coram V   555 gong-men] gonge-fermers PV   556 *after* gong-hus] and . . . fulþe V (*see fn.*), *sim.* F (*with* ceux detractors parlent daltrui ordure *for* þe bacbytere (. . .) fulþe) *before* þe fikeleres] *see 552–5*   gong-þurl] gange-hus oðer þe þurl TS *before* þet] and NR   557 wrið] hyleþ PT, heleð and wrihð N
558 mon his] mannes PTV   559 unlideð] unheleð and unwrihð N, vnhileþ R   560 aa] C, euere PRV, *om.* LNT   561 þulliche] swuche NV   562 stinkinde] fule TS   stench] stinke RV
563 nahið] cumeð NR   564 spechen fuleð] speke foule V, owre speches fulen T   fuleð] sulleð C, suillent F, soileð and fuleð N, soillent e ensalissent S   565 bet] F, ðe bet N, þe beter V, sone TS, *om.* C icnawen] cnawen T, muȝe cnawen C, *sim.* P   567 forme] first PRV
568 ȝet] CFNTV, þah A, *om.* LPRS   wurst] alre wurste NP
568–71 Ve . . . conuenit] LPST, Ve (. . .) puluillos, et cetera R, *after* ouerherunge *573* V, *not in* CFN   569 dicunt] LNPST, dant A
570 scilicet] A, similiter V, solis ST, de. P, *om.* L   detractatoribus] A, detractoribus LPSTV   et adulatoribus] *om.* ST   571 conuenit] LPSTV, peruenit A   forme] first PV, *sim.* R   572 inohreaðe] *om.* PRV   ȝet] *om.* FPS   573 *after* ouerherunge] *see 568–71*   *after* oðer²] is NLP, is þis R   574 mis] yuel PRTV   576 he seið] CFNT(*after* makeð *577*)V, and seiþ þat it (*before* Nis) P, seiþ it R, dicens L, font les losengeours S   577 *after* makeð] *see 576*   *after* nawt] te ane A   i þis þing] *om.* CRS   þis] repeated A   forme] first PRV   578 *before* þe leaste] þou ne schalt nouȝth be P, eris L   *after* leaste] ne serrez FS   Let . . . god-mon] lete God yworþe P, let God alon, man R   god-mon] CT, prodhom FS, gode mon NV, bone homo L   579 cunne of] F, cunne C, cunnes VT, genus L, maner R, cumeð efter and N, *om.* PS   fikelere] *om.* LP   580 *before* seide] er NFS   he] ha C   dede] deden CNS   þe²] he PV   581 as] CV, come F, hwat N, *om.* LPRST   582 *after* wel] *see 583–4*   peolkin] A, polkin C, pilken NT, peler S, pluke RV, plumer F, deplumare L   583 spruteð ut] springeþ out V, springeþ and spredeþ R   hine] N, him CV, it PRT   croppeð ofte] *trs.* CFNS   ofte] oftere CFS   583–4 Laudatur . . . benedicitur] LSV, *after* wel *582* RT, *not in* CNP   584–5 Augustinus . . . peccatis] *not in* CN
585 hominem] homines RST   þes] þe CNP   *before* þe] þeo CN

586 hercnið] her|nið A   wriheð] hilen PRT   586–7 ha . . . mahe] it ne may nou3th P, hit ne mowe V   587 is hare] A, lour est F, est (. . .) a lour oes S, est (. . .) eis L, is CNPTV   588 *before* eornen] swa CFNTV   590–2 Clemens . . . inuidet] *not in* CFN   590 tria] LV, duo PRST esse] sunt RST   dixit] dicit PST   beatus] A *only*   591 uoluit] uolumus ST   593 earre] C, uorme N, first PRTV, primer FS, primi L   594 speoweð] seiþ P, spekiþ R   se muchel se] all þat RT   eauer] *om.* PRT   595 up] *om.* CT   597 ah] CFNSTV, ant AR, *om.* L adun] dun CRT   *before* feð] and NR   feð on] CN, bigynneþ PRT, he ginneþ V   598–9 Bisampleð . . . abuten] CNT, veit tastant et fesant amberloges F, par amberloges e par essamples longement uet entur roitant S, prologum premittunt et a longe inchoant L, makeþ a longe prolong tofore al aboute (. . .) And hij maken many ensamples P, *om.* V   599 bet] C, þe bet V, ðe betere NPT   hit alles] hit al T, tout FS, totum (fecerint) L 600 Weila] weylaway PRV, weilawei and wolawo N   ha] CFNV, he PRT, cestui S   601 ne healp] ne halp hit CT, hit ne halp V   602 her-of] A, her-on CNT, en ceo F, þer-of V   603 beon] *before* iuppet CN mare] NV, *om.* CFLRST   þurh oþre] *after* wide T, *om.* PR 604 þet¹] *om.* NV   hit¹] *before* ne CN   605 *before* wurse] wel PRV   Ah] ant CP   606 feole] many RT   607 swiðe] muche CV onont] non in L, nout for N   607–8 ne . . . mon] 'for' ne mei nan mon hit C   608 ham] him VLS   þis] CN, þese PRTV   609 feor] A, from CFNRSTV   610 *before* ne] ant CN   611 wreoð ant hulieð] le couerent F, hulen T   seide] er seide NST, *trs.* F   616 haldeð] haues T, eez S   eare] A, earen CFLNSTV   617 an ald cwene] an ald cheorl oðer cwene T, un ueillard ou une ueille S, auum (R², V¹; auem Me(e *over erasure*)Ma) L   618 a meaðelilt] N, a maðelere T, vne iangleresse F, un fauelor ou un [*for* une] faueleresse S, *om.* CV   hire] ham TS, *om.* CFL   rikelot] NST, rigelot F, rikelotam L, kikelot C (*glossed* piot C³), tellere V   619 cakeleð] cakeleð hire N, li iargone F, lour iargoille S ant] oþer NS   621 tidinge] tiðinge N, tiðindes T   Wat Crist] Dieu le siet F, God wot V   sahe] tale N, conte S   623 in] *om.* CV   þullich] C, cele chose F, þulliche þinges T, celes choses S, swuche N, suche wordes V   624 *before* leoue] myne VF   leoue sustren] *om.* ST 626 *before* of¹] ant CN   *before* of²] ant CLNS   626–7 leflich . . . nawt] legerement nel porreit lem pas crere S   626 leflich] T, creable F, leoflich C(*glossed* comeliche C³)N, louelich V   627 þing] *om.* CTV 628 eare] earen CNSV   629 *before* of²] and NS   hercnunge] heringe TNV   630 speoken] speke we C, parlerom FS   631 In . . . Zacharia] V, in propheta C, in Zacharia propheta F, en Zacharie le prophete S, in Zacharia T, (*before* Zelatus) Zacharie viij°. a L, *om.* NP 632 *before* Ego] *see 633*   633 In Exodo] CFNTV, sicut in Exodo legitur S, (*before* Ego *632*) Exodi xx. a L, *om.* P   635 wið] of CF

635–6 þuhte . . . gelusie] *om.* FNS   637 Wite þe] CF, custodiat (. . .) anima (. . .) se L, wite ðu NT, ceo sachez vus S, wyte ȝee P, wite V   nu] CFV, *om.* LNPST   638 he] *om.* CF   aa] euer NV   ei] *om.* ST   639 *before* eani] oðer NLST   Syon²] *om.* FPV   640 *after* schawere²] ant CNS   642 to me] me (*after* Schaw *641*) CFP   643 ne] *om.* PV   644 ne] *om.* NPV   644–5 nule Ich] A, *trs.* CNPSTV, ieo ne ⟨. . .⟩ F   645 bicluppe] cluppe CPV   þulli] swuche NV   646 *after* hire] þeonne N   *before* wunder] donc S   648 þrung] þing NT(*corr. to* þring), choses S   nurð] C, noise F, murhðe NTV, ioie S   649 Nurð] C, noise FNRST, murþe V   650 ant] oðer CFS   651 *after* witeð] ȝe TS   653 leome] brihtnesse V, gostely brightnes R, luue NP   654 oþre] oðre wittes N, autres quatre sens S   655 cecatur] excecatur RST   656 hire] his RT   rihtwise] richte CR   ha] he PRT   657 ablindeð] blindeð CT, is blynd R   i] *om.* CFP   inre] inre eien N, euz denzeins S   ha] he PRST   660 swote] swete NV, muchele CFST, *om.* P   swetnesse] swotnesse N   662 *from* For-þi] *MSS running:* ACFLNRSTV   sustren] childre TS   663 Iacob] CFLV, Isaac NRST   664 cnawen] icnowen NV   665 *before* þenne] and NS iseon] se RT   is nawt] nis nawt wurð T, rien ne uaut S, is noght or lytyl worth R   665–6 hu . . . fals] hu fals is hire froure T, *sim.* S   666 *before* þurh] and NFS   667 *after* biwrencheð] and bicherreð NS   669 pinen] *conj.* Dobson; pine ACNTV, peine F, penas L, peynes R, peines S   ow uggi wið] T, ou grise wið C, ou agruwie aȝean N, ȝe ben aferd of V   670 ham frommard] V, *trs.* CNT   670–1 þe ontenden] C, qi esprendrunt F, que incendat L, þat hit teende V, uorto ontenden N, to ontende T, pur fere (. . .) entendre S   671 heorte] heorten CST   672 iseon] se RT   *before* al¹] and NS   weoret] A, rute C, uerd NT, compaignie FS, exercitum L   *before* al²] ant CLNS, and also R   673 him] God VL, nostre Seignur S   blisseð] CT, enioist F, blesceð NV, signe e beneit S, benedicentem L   674 sustren] childre T   675 *before* witen] hit CFLST   677 scit] sit L(Me)SV   677–8 Hit . . . Apocalipse] *om.* RST   680 *before* of³] and NFS   682 herunges] herunge NR   *before* eorðliche] and NS   spechen] speche CR   *before* fleschliche] and NLRS   682–3 Videmus . . . enigmate] ALV, *after* oþre *685* ST, *not in* CFNR   682 Videmus] videamus AV   nunc] LST, enim AV   685 gleadunge] gledschipe C, glednesse NV, godnesse T, beautez (. . .) e (. . .) bountez S   þe²] *om.* NT *after* oþre] *see 682–3*   686 hit haueð] S, haueþ hit V, haueð CFLNT ondswerie] schal onswerien NV   688 þolieð] N, soefre F, þoleþ V, þoleden TS, þolede C   *from* For-þi] *MSS running:* ACFLNSTV semlich] riht ant somlich N, bien resons e droiz S   689 *before* swiftnesse] cest a sauoir F, þet is N   689–90 swiftnes . . . sihðe] *om.* LST   689 aȝeines] aȝein CV   690 nu] F, her N, *om.* CV

bipinnet] C, encloseez F, bipenned N, bituyned V   690–1 her (. . .) nu]
nu her (*before* þeostrið) CT, *sim*. S   691 mon (. . .) mon] men (. . .)
men TLSV   693 *before* as²] and NS   694 *after* openeð] and tuneð
NS   ba] baðe T, beon NV   695 as me seið] *after* heouene N
heouene] N(*dat*.)T, heouenes CFS, celorum L   *before* large] ine heouene
is N   696 lesewen] T, pascuis L, communes S, lesewe CN, pasture F
697 *after* hondhwile] *see 698–9*   schulden] schulen NV   698 oðer]
oðer morhȝiue NLS   698–9 Gregorius . . . sciunt] V, *after* hondhwile
697 T, *after* þing 700 LS, *not in* CFN   698 Quid est enim] T, quid
enim (. . .) erit S, quid est L, enim AV   700 *after* þing] *see 698–9*   ah]
CFNSTV, ant A   701 derue] derue *alt. to* derfe C, derne NFSTV
702 eare] earen CN   ehe] echnen CN   703 sustren] childre T
704 iseo] N, seo CTV   705 *before* meadles] ful T, mult S   *before* ȝef]
and NS   706 awed] A, wod CT, wod and so awed N, forsanez ou si
osez S, mad V   te þurl-clað] FNTV, þe þurch þe clað C, le drapel du
pertuis (. . .) ou uers vus S   707 al þet] þe CST   him] hire T
707–8 Alswa . . . se] NT, alswa, se sone se C, ausi tost come FS, als soone
as PV   708 eauer] *om.* CNP   feleð] feolleð C, comence F, biginneþ V,
ualleð NT, motist ou fauele S, hereþ P   falle] falles TV   709 sperreð]
tuneð CN   þe] ȝor VS   *before* ne] ant CN   ne . . . nawiht] wiðuten euch
onswere TS   710 *after* awei] et partiez diloeke F   he] ha T
710–11 Declinate . . . mei] FPSTV, *not in* CN   711 *after* mei] ou od
cestui F   712 Domine] *after* tua T, *not in other MSS*   gað] goð forð
N, alez vus en S   714 swa] *before* ondswerie CF   blawen] parler FS
liðeliche] N, sotilment S, lihtliche C, beel e (. . .) doucement F, liðerliche T,
luþerliche V   715 as] V, as is CFNST, que fit L   717 ant . . .
aðes] A *only*   hit] *om.* CL   719 *after* forȝef] hit CFNS   habbe hit]
V, *trs.* CNT   720 schule] CF, schulde NLSTV   mare] A, amplius L,
eft CT, altrefeez FS, more eft NV   721 hit] *after* forȝeueð PV   *before*
Speokeð] ant CLNP   Speokeð] C, parlent F, spekeð NV, diuertit (. . .)
verbotenus L, spekeþ (. . .) wiþ hym P, spekes TS   724 *after* wude-
lehe] Ant . . . Amen (*see fn.*) C, þer-inne is þet Ich luuie N   725 i] to
CF   ȝet] and ȝet N, et L, and þan P, e souent S   ha went] si entrent S,
wenden T, (swich þouȝttes) wil lasten P   726 þoht] hert PLV
727 *after* foreward] þat he biheet þer-vppe V, *sim.* L   swereð] ant swereð
CN   728 *after* nede] ant . . . erende (*see fn.*) C   *after* wurse] Lokede . . .
ut (*see fn.*) C   730 alle] touz altres FS   sustren] childre TS
731 *before* swuch] nan CNSTV   732 *after* ow] ant wencheð N, e
destornez S   733 *before* seide] auant F, er N, isci par deuant S
þruppe] A *only*   ne] ant CFN   734 maten] maten and ouercomen N,
ouercomen V   him] hem VS   735 *from* Lokið] *MSS running*:
ACFGLNPRSTV   737 et cetera] *om.* FP   738 ihere] N, here
CGPTV   739 leofmon] spuse and leofmon N, spouse P   742 þe]

PART 2

om. CV 743 heonewart] A, toward me G, þeoneward CFNSV, þeðenward T, a mundanis et terrenis L *before* mi³] ant C ant²] *om.* CNST mi⁴] *om.* C 744 Ostende... tuam] *om.* CP 746 ido] GT, do V, rien fait F, misdon N, ihurt C *after* ihurt] te NV, vus S earen] eare TS 748 Vnde et subditur] hwar-fore he seið C 751 cheoseð] luues TS 753 turn] tun N, tuin T, estouez (estonez Tr) S ham] S, *om.* CFGNTV ba] boðe NTV 755 habben] haue P, habbe V, eez F, si com vus uolez auer S *after* is] an CN 757 mine ... sustren] *om.* ST sustren] freonð G speche] wise GV 758 earre] vorme N, furste V, primere S 760 utward] A, *before* gealunge CFGNTV, *om.* S 762 tuos] *om.* LT 763 ne] *om.* PRV *after* cnawest] nout GPRTV 764 gate heorden] les pastours des ch⟨...⟩ F, þe stepis of þi flokes R, les traces des chieures S 766 mid] wið CT 768 ihud] bihud CGN *after* unualden] *see 769* *after* cnawest] naut CNV 769 neomeð... 3eme] A, *after* unualden *768* CFGNSTV 770 nast] A, nast naut CFGNPTV 772 her-to] þer-of CP þis] his T, mine N 773 þis] his T, mine N heorde] heorden NLT, pastours F, les traces S, þe stepes R he seið] *om.* CG 773–4 Hwet... geat] *om.* GLP heorde] heorden N, pastours F, traces S 777–8 þeos.... tichnes] CFGLNT, *sim.* P, *om.* ASV 778 he] CFGNSTV, Ich A 779 spellunge] CG, oiant cuntant F, herunge N, hercninge TV, escutemenz S *after* spellunge] þi muð wið spellinge T, uostre bouche ou goustemenz S 783 swote] G, sweote N, swete TV 784 totilde] N, auouteresce F, totinde CGTV, aboutant S 786 cahte] A, clachte CGTV, clauerede N lahte] cauhte NV *before* cleaures] his CNV, her PT, ses FS 787 *after* soðes] 3e, he haueð C clokes] crokes CGV 789–90 ant²... heouene] *om.* LN 790 eauer] *om.* CG 792 to hinene hulen] to himmere heile, hire to wraðer heale A, to himmere heale C, a malhoure de soen F, sei a mal eure S, to wraðer heale TN, *sim.* V, to uwelleer hele G, *om.* LP 793 þi] þe CGN *before* sech] and TS 794 endin eauer] *trs.* GT 795 swa is] *trs.* CV 796 ec] V, þe CFGS, *om.* NLT 797 an] *om.* CS þe oðer] þet on VS 798 *after* cnawest] nout NV 799–800 seið... wummen] *om.* FGT þu... wummen] *om.* V 800 *after* wummen] auh bimong engles N 800-1 3e... wummen] *om.* ST 800 3e... þer-to] CV, veir, mettet od tout ore ici F, ge do nu her-to þer-to G, þu meiht don þer-to N, etiam nunc hic; adde, etiam L þet] F, þu NV ant ... wulle] siker N ant] gif G 802 wurðli] A, wurðliche CG, honorable F, wurði TV, deorewurðe N, chere digne S, cara L 804 þe] þu NV 805 þet] *om.* CV 806 Cusse] boisez F, cus CN, cusse (*imper.*) P þe] FRS, *om.* GNPTV his] þi CNP 807 leoue sustren] leoue frend G, wite 3e wel TS 808 swete] swote GV, swote and swete N þer-to3eines] þer-a3eines NP 809 þis] *corr. from* his C, his

APPARATUS CRITICUS

NRS   ne] *om.* RV   816 ehe] eien N, oculorum L   eare] eren CN, aurium L   817 wah oðer] þauh our N, þe oþer V   818 liueneð] lif C, ceo qe partient al salut et a la vie F   *after* Omni] igitur FNTV 819–20 ant... sustren] *om.* C   819 ant] as V, e sicom S   feor] *om.* FS   820 mine... sustren] *om.* T   sustren] frend G   *after* witeð] wel NFSTV   820–1 þe... iloket] *om.* ST   821 ehe] eien NLV eare] earen NLV   ilokene] iloked CG   822 þer] GTV, ear CFN, isci en auant S   823 þe ham] þe hous PT, heo CV, þe heorte NL   biwist] wist G, iwust V, yloked P, loked T   824 *from* speoke] *MSS running:* **ACFLNPRSTV**   825 speche] V, spellunge NPT, smellunge C   ah is] V, ah T, ase CFNS   ba beon] FS, ha beon C, heo beoþ V, heo beon beoðe N, þa beon baðe T   829 o Godes half] ne forho3e Ich ham nocht C, ieo ne les refuse pas F   3ef[2]] ant þach ha beon C, and 3if heo beoð NS, and 3if it be P   me... recche] naut I ne reche C, ieo ne les quer pas F recche] PT, reccheð NV   831 ha] 3e TS   832 of irnes] C, irnes T, of iren N (*after* swat) V   833 ha] 3e TS   þicke] CFL, wicke NSTV 834 ant... þinges] *om.* LN   *before* muhlinde] of CF   muhlinde] V, mulede T, musies FS   836 *before* þer-of] auh NLS   iwarnet] iwar NPV   mine... sustren] *om.* ST   840 swote] swete PV   were] come VS   842 to] þer-of ant of C, of NFS, of to T   843 truiles] C, trufles NTV   844 bitruileð] bitrufleð NT   monie] monie men N, meintes genz S   *after* monie] wið CTV, mide N   *before* hali] þe CF 846 ha] he T   I] ALV *only*   848 licomes] bodies PV   stronge] fule CP   *after* he[1]] *see 849*   849 hare] þet CFS   wið... wa] *after* he[1] *848* C, *after* nease *850* FS   wið] T, mid CN, wiðouten V   riht] A, al C, *not in other MSS*   850 *after* nease] *see 849*   851 *after* Alswa] as A 852 seh] isech CN   Iuhanes] Iohan CV   *before* Euuangeliste] þe CFRSV Euuangeliste] Euuuangeliste A   853 hu] *interl.* C, *om.* PST   *after* deciples] þat PST   855 þuldeliche] mildeliche CV   857 þe] *om.* CNP   858 þrof] A, her-of NV, de ceste F, de son bendement S, eius L, *om.* T   feolahreadden] felawschipp PV   859 na] nout NV 860 gurde] smot V, smiten PT   861 *after* spitte] on CTV   a] V, an CT, o N, un seul petit S, leui L   865 dute] ne uolez (...) clore e estoper S, claudere (...) recusat L   866 *after* þet] entre touz les altres angoisses F   ancre] ancren NV, vs P, *sim.* LR   867 ha] he T, we P, *sim.* LR   mare] ANT *only*   868 swa] neuer so NV   *before* 3ef[2]] ant NS   869 ha[1,2]] he T   870 scandle] scheonde CT   deie] heo ouh forto deien N, *sim.* P   *before* Deað] noðeles N, e nekedent S, licet enim L 871 ah forte] T, ach to CP, ou3te forte V, mot N   872 me] *om.* FNS do... sunne] grefment peccher S   heaued sunne] V, crimen (...) mortale L, sunne CFNT   873 *before* 3et] and NS   874 grucchilt] N, grucinde CV, grucchere T   875 imid] A, amidde NTV, aa mid C sumchearre] *om.* CL   876 ipaiet] apaied PV   inohreaðe] FST, *om.*

CLNPV   hit is] A, is CFS, is þet NTV   879 ha] he T   inohreaðe]
om. CLV   i] i | i A   þenc] þene (. . .) þenc N, cogita igitur L
880 sohtest] þouhtes and souhtes N, pensastes S, (hij) þenchen P
881 oþres] oðre monnes N, oþer mennes PT   882 cluppen] bicluppen
NV   884–940 O . . . ideruet] AF(*after* seoluen 262)V(*at end of text of
AW*) *only*   884 O] A *only*   seið Ieremie] *after* optimum V   *before*
Ieremie] li prophete F   Ieremie] FV, Sein Ierome A   *after* obscuratum]
est sol, mutatum V   885 et cetera] A *only*   O, weilawei] *om*. V
before gold] tres bon F   886 ant] en F   887 as . . . wreaððe] *om*. F
after wreaððe] sicome nous lisoms F, ac nout withouten serwe V
888 carne consummamini] carnem consummatis V   Me] Cest a dire F,
O, he seiþ V   889 bimalscret] fete (*followed by erasure*) F, begylet V
889–90 3e (. . .) bigunnen ant] vous quauez (. . .) comence F
889 bigunnen] biginnen V   890 before þe] vous F   bigunnen]
biginnen V   891 *after* fleschliche] al fleschliche iwurðen A   lihte
ilatet] de legiere porture F, liht chere V   891–2 ane hwile] oþerwhile V
892–3 estfule . . . meanildes] hei3-hertet, scornynge, grucchinge, and
ianglinge V, ⟨. . .⟩ouses a p⟨. . .⟩ F   893 ant²] *om*. V
894 cursildes ant childildes] ⟨. . .⟩oisantes et tencouses F, cursinges and
chidynges V   895 *before* Bihofde] hit V   swuch] celes F   were]
fuissent F   leafdi] dames F   ant] an V   hofles] hauenles V
896 is¹] F, *om*. V   ant] an VF   biburiet] iburiet V   897 *before* schal]
ant heo A   ibollen] of herte V   898 leoten of] contenir sei F   leafdi]
grande dame F   hames] terres F   makeð] make V   899 ha . . .
setten] VF, 3ef ha setteð A   900 þunche] beo V   902 steuene]
speche V   deminoratione] diminucione V   þis] þat V   903 limpe]
falle V   904 iwurð] iworðen V   *before* wonunge] þe V   905 3e,
as] vous ausi come F, 3if V   907 breoken forð] efforcier vous auant F,
bereþ forþ V   *after* forð] ant A   earmes] braz F, armus V, earmões A
908 sturien] mouer F, steeren V   we¹] *conj*. Dobson; 3e AFV   we beoð]
estes F, þat beoþ V   909–10 Sone se] as sone as V   910–11 se . . .
beoð] *lacuna* F   910 we] 3e V   eauer] *om*. V   us] ou V   ure] oure V
911 we] 3e V   cang] fole F   geað] veit F, geþ V, gað A
912 wlecche þe] terres (*for* te(t)ves?) de F   speoweð] spekeþ of V
913 bigunnen] biginneþ V   ah] *om*. V   914 he mare] innore me V
915 heortes . . . lusti] herte is more glad þer-of V   916 aðet] til þat V
917 Ower] ure V   hord] tresor F, heorte A, lord V   on] en F, in V
919 uprowynge] vpdrawynge V   919–20 þa . . . stream] *conj*. Dobson;
quant le queor uoldreit aual eisiement aualer od le corant F, *om*. AV
923 ifinden] finden V   924 bisiliche] semblement F
924–5 anewil 3irnunge] a wil 3erninge V, volunte desirante F
926 astihen] and stei3en V   927–8 neodoluker] nedfoloker V
928 ower] vr V   929 *before* Godd] to V   softnesse] suef⟨. . .⟩ F,

soþnesse V   929-31 i² . . . nu] *lacuna* F   930 alles cunnes] alle maner V   930-1 ant . . . eadmodnesse] *om.* V   931 nu] to V   ant peonsin] ne wonen V   hehi] with hei3 V   932 unweneliche] desmesureement F, vncomeliche V   sinetin] smyten V   933 wenden] schrokken with V   keaste] wrenchen V   934 heateð] loþeþ V   hire scarneð] la vous escharnia F   ripe] angri V   935 lates ripe] angri leetes V   ant] ne V   *before* werkes] angri V   bilimpeð] falleþ not V 936 eadmodliche] mekeliche V   soðfestliche] suefment F   iseide] assises F, isette V   936-7 nawt . . . babanliche] *om.* V   937 babanliche] bobincousement F   þenne] nient F   burðerne] strengþe V   riht] bien F, wel (*before* to) V   938 þet 3e, efter] qe nous aprist F, Now V 939 ine] i þe V   galle] fol (*for* fel) F   *before* 3ef] li F   *after* wið] cest F witen] gardez F, witeþ V   940 derf] pyne V   ideruet] ipynet V 941 *from* In] *MSS running:* ACFLNPRSTV   eare] earen NL   *before* te] al NF   942 *before* al¹] and NS   eare] earen NT   945 *before* stille] al NS   946 þi] oure PST   leofmonnes] Lauerdes TS   947 leoue] deore CT   spuse] espouse e sa chambrere S, seruant T   950 froure] CS, foure NTV, quatre sens F   hise] his wittes NS   ower] C, les voz F, owres T, ouren V, ouwer wittes NS   951 weane] CN, orne T, meschance S, defalte F, wonte V   *after* fifte] sen FS   952 i] *om.* CF 953 oþre] oðre wittes NLS   954 licome] body RV   955 wiste] sout S, custodiuit L   þolien] þolien wa N, soffrir e peines endurer S   al] AV *only*   957 lust] lustes NS   *before* nomeliche] ant NS   959 al] *om.* LNV   hefde] *om.* CF   inwið] C, inwið in TV, wiðinnen in N, par dedenz en F, in P, en S   960 felde] F, hefde CNSTV   962 oþre] oðres NV   flowen] fluwen C, deculerent F, floweden T, fleoweden and melten al N, totes decorrurent (. . .) e fondirent S   963 þet] was þet N, wes (his . . . deciples) þet C   964 *after* heolden] him NSTV 965 him²] *om.* CT   *after* þridde] stiche NS   966 ofþunchunge] forþinchinge TV   967 drohen] duden CPV   969 euch lim] *om.* C 970 *before* þolede] he CN   971 ne] *om.* RT   972 *before* ehnen] his NRS   as] *om.* CFNR   973 angoisse] angosse A   978 dun] adun NP   979 þet²] and þet NPS, and R, nec L   980 *before* flesch] þet NRV   þe . . . ant] *om.* CLPR   reopunge] T, adesance F, rippynge V, pine N, blesceure S   þrof] *after* hurt CR, *om.* FLPS   981 derueð] greues RV   deð] *om.* CPR   982 dead flesch] dead CL, morte e flestrie S, dedlich V   983 þe] þe A   984 adeadede] muhte adeaden NT, *sim.* LS   986 wes] were CNT   988 *before* ne] he CFNTV   hale] hole half NFLPS, harme þat is hole R   989 seke] sike half NFPS Ah] and VP   þe² . . . feure] *om.* CP   *after* feure] and o ðe herebarde N bimong] among NV   991 *before* rode] þe CN   *before* Nawt] ant NS 993 lo] N(*before* þus)TV, nu C, *om.* FLPS   ant . . . dale] *om.* LPV, e la uiue S   994 unhale] partie malade FS, partem non sanam L   þe seke]

PART 2

cele partie F, ðe sike half N   before in] see 995   995 sunne bitacnet] trs. (before in 994) NPST   reisuns] reisun CLV   efter] her-efter CN 996 þer-of] NV, her-of CFST, here P   mine . . . sustren] om. T 997 Godd] om. NV   998 al] A only   999 þet dei] after diete NS 1000 ha] interl. A, om. FST   to] na TSV   1001 ne¹] noiþer PV meande] mende him NFSV   1002 of þurst] C, de soif (before as) FS, ofþurst NT, aþurst V   duden] boden VS   1003 blodleten] blodleten mon TS, blodletunge NPV   1006 notie] after mahte CT 1006–7 ant . . . hure²] om. V   1008 eise] wille CS   ha] he T 1009 þa] om. CLPV   1012 bittrure] bittere C, bitture N, bittre T þa] om. CP   1013 spuse] seruante T, espouses e (. . .) anceles S 1014 ti] AV only   1015 meoseises] meoseise CNS   1016 þe] after 3elden CNTV   his] he is NS   1019 after 3e] donqe F, ideo L, pur ceo S   1020 oþre] oðre wittes NS   1021 before rode] þe CFNS   1021–2 nawt . . . sustren] om. LST   1021 do] om. CF 1023 before Hondlunge] vor NLS   1024 uncumelich] AV, uncundelich CFNST   before to] and NF   1026 fulðe] CNTV, ful | A 1028 þreo] CFNV, om. ST   mine . . . sustren] FNV, om. CST wummen me leouest] CFNV, om. ST   1029 wiðbuhe] wiðhuhe TS   sehe] isec3e CN   1030 before eani] to NT   1031 monglin] monglinde NV   hond] FT, honden CLNSV   1032 Godes] CFNTV, om. (suppl. by different hand) A   of] after TV   his eorre] his vuel N, synne V   1033 before moni] to NT   1034 haueð] N, habbeð CFTV   1035 schulen] schulien A, schule C, schulden NTV 1036 before moni] to NT   1037 tua] om. PT   1038 þet²] V, om. CNT   ha] he T   1040 oueral . . . o] NT, sur toutes choses de F, super omnia L, of al C, also of V, de (. . .) ausint S   1042 ha] he T licunge] licunges CFLS   efter . . . lust] om. LV   willes] A, wittes CNT, des sens F, de ses cinc sens S   lust] luste C, lustes NS   1043 hire¹] him T   hire²] hise T   1044 wardeins] CFLNSTV, wardein A 1046 þet] þer NS   custodi] serua CN   1046–7 quoniam . . . procedit] et cetera N, om. V   1047–8 beoð (. . .) ouercumen] auom (. . .) passee F, transiuimus L   1047 Crist haue þonc] NT, Crist aþonc C, Dieu merci FS, God be þonked V, Dei gracia L   after dalen] de ceste liure F   1048 his] CV, Godes NFLST   þe] repeated A

PART 3

1 from Mine] MSS running: ACFLNPRSTV   2 inwið] wiðinnen CN
3 woh of] word of C, om. N   4 seið ow] seið on ou mis N, misseiþ ou
V, uus mesdit S   ant] of TV   al leosen] V, aleosen C, al uorleosen NT
5 after Dauið] le psalmistre F   6 before pellican] þe CFPS

APPARATUS CRITICUS

7 *before* fuhel] leane N hit] he RV o] uor NPV, fo R 9 hit] N (*interl.*) T, he RV, *om.* C 10 he] hit N 11 acwikeð] a cwikeð N, he quikeþ V, *sim.* R 13 ha²] he T 13-14 swa haueð] *trs.* CV 15 ahne] *om.* CLS beaki] bete V, bate S hire¹] to T hire²] his T 16 ha] he T 17 hire] his T 18 hire²] *om.* CL gode] *om.* FNT 20 ehe²] R, si3th P, echnen CFLNTV 21 iuggi wel] *trs.* CPR icolet] cold NPR 24 *before* hit²] eft CP, *sim.* L 26 ariht] þa riht TLS þuhte] NV, þuhte ear CT, *sim.* FSL 27 vuel se muchel] swa muchel ufel CN 28 wod te seolf] þe seolf wod CN 35 Wummon wrað] wommone wraþþe V, ire de femme S *before* wulf] is CN 36 wummone] mones T 37 Auez] *after* Pater Nostres LNS ha²] he T 38 *after* iwent] fra mon TS wuluene¹] wulf TLS, woluen kynde P ehnen] brihte ehne T, clere ueue S wuluene²] wulues TS 40 *after* inwið] him CNS 42-3 cundelich] A, cundeliche CNTV 43 *before* Sone] auh NS mildheortnesse] mildeschipe CP 44 þe forschuppilt] *om.* LV 45 spuse] seruant T, *sim.* S 46 wuluene] wulf TF 47 forwarpe] A, awarpe C, vorworpen NT, casten awey V 48 *after* hude] oðer wepmonnes T, *sim.* S 49 *before* wuluene] ruhe T, uelue S wuluene] wolues TFSV ha] he T 50 *from* Lo] *MSS running:* ACFGLNPRSTV 52 misseið þe] myssaien þe oiþer misdone þe P, *sim.* RS 54 *after* a3ein²] wið atterne wordes C, wið attri wordes TV, *sim.* N, od venimouses paroles F, *sim.* S, verbis venenatis L, wið attri bordes G, wiþ attry woord P, doing a wers ded for a wiked ded R 55 spuse] seruant RT, *sim.* S 56 est] *om.* LT 58 *before* marhen] erne G *after* wearitreo] de la croiz F 59 irnene] irene NV a shep] a lombe P, a shep' . . . eiþer a lambe R 59-60 cwich ne . . . neauer] GTV, quic ne cweð he neauer an word C, ne cweð he neuer a word N, ne quei3tte he P, he made no (. . .) noise ny crie R, rien ne respondi F, ne sona il mot ne ne tinta ne sa bouche nem oueri S, nec (. . .) clamauit L 61 ha] he G 63 ancre] a mon G 64 ha¹·²] he G 65 wordes wind] V, word (*alt. to* wordes C³) wind C, vord of wind G, wind of a word NT 66 þe¹] þine vet NR, feete P te blisse of] *om.* PR 71 þolede] *conj.* Dobson; soffri ke S, þet ACGNTV, qi F, quod L þet . . . wið] CFGLNSTV, whan men stoneden hym P, þet me sende him A 73 wið . . . ifalden] C(ho⟨mm⟩en *alt. to* honden C³)GNV, od genoilz pliez F, ou iarrez ploiez S, genibus flexis L, wiþ folden honden (. . .) and knelande P, (þat þreu3 on him) so fele stones V *after* ifalden] þet is, cneolinde N 76 hare] *om.* C(*corr.* C³)GTV 77 ant te uuele] NSTV, ant | ant eke to uuele *after* uuel C, and and te uuele *after* deð G, *om.* FL *before* his] to NV 78 þi] þe GV, ðe ane NP 79 Vitas] Vitis LR 79-80 þe oþres] his PLST 82 blissen] blisse CFLS *before* hond] þe CN 83 alswa] *om.* CS 84 *before* lome] me NST 85 freame] god NTV 86 misseide oðer misdude] misseið oðer misdeð

PART 3

NF   86–7 mine . . . sustren] *om.* T   89 blawe] blaweð CGNV   90 eir] eare N, eares TS   92 upo] on NT   þe seolf] T, þi seolf GNV, seolf C   94 underӡeoten] understonden NV   95 þrof] CGNT, of V, *om.* A   a puf] a litel wynde PR, une petite bouffe S   96 waxeð] wile waxe TS   97 her on ende] her-anonden CGN   98 *after* cunneð] wel NS   ant] CFGNSTV, *sim.* LPR, oðer A   99 ne[1]] TFS, þet CL, and NV, *om.* G   to] for to CN   101 *before* of] ful CFNPV, *sim.* S   a bigurdel] T, *after* him[1] CFGNSV, *sim.* LP   103 hurt] hurd A   105 ӡeiӡeð] crie PV   106 *after* forӡeoueð] to C(*interl.*)GNTV   108 ure] ura A   110 þis] FG(*interl.*)SV, his CNT   *before* nis[2]] he CN   i Purgatoire] in fur of Purgatorie C, in pena purgatoria L   111 Dimittite] dimitte CNV   112 Ich . . . þe] GTV, Ichulle forӡiue ðe NFPS, hit schal beo forӡeoue þe C, *sim.* R   113 toward] to PR   sunnen] sunne GSV   116 hurte] G, hurteð CNTV   118 þe[2]] him GN   sent] VS, sende CFGNT   121 wið] mid CN   123 donat] domat N, *alt. to* domat L(Me)   124 *from* Eft] *MSS running:* ACFLNPRSTV   *before* pellican] þe NRS   þis fuhel] is a fuel ðet NST, est auis L   125 aa] C, euer NRTV   *before* seide] er NS   125–6 in . . . persone] *om.* C   126 in . . . steuene] CTV, ant in (. . .) stefne N, et dit ausi come de bouche de recluse F, e en sa uoiz S solitudinis] et cetera CP, *om.* T   129 et cetera] *om.* CFPSV 131 ah to] ouhte NV   132 efter hire euene] after hire strengþe V, apres la semblance de lui F, en sa persone S, secundum possibilitatem suam L *before* nawt] and NPS   ipund] iput V, *sim.* P   133 to[1]] for to CN ant to greatin] *om.* FPV   to[2]] forte N   135 *before* Vulpes] Mathei vj⁰ V, Matthei viij⁰ L(xiij⁰ Me)R   137 *before* false] ðe NST   ancres] men and wymmen P, men R   138 *before* eorðe] ter NV   wið] mid CN 139 hole] holes NT   al] V, *before* into CFNST, *sim.* P   140 reopen ant rinnen] ropin ant rinnen C, ⟨. . .⟩chacer F, repen and rinen T, repen and renden P, arepen and arechen N, cacchen V, coillier e auoir S, rapere L 141 ec] *after* is CN, *om.* STV   freotewil] frete wole V, fret swuðe wel N mid] wið CT   143 *before* Habbeð] and NP, e si S, iterum L   Habbeð] haþ PT   sumchearre] of chere V, une simple chere S   144 beoð] is PT   145 *before* weneð] and NS   146 Gealstrið] N, galstres T, galieð C, vuchent F, glauereþ V, breent e crient S, ululat L   þe] *om.* CT hare] his T   147 *before* god] ahne TS   ant[1]] oðer TS   147–8 se . . . iwurðeð] so swiþe worldliche iwordet V, si seculers paroles parolent S 148 hare] his T   149 ha] he T   ham] him T   152 *after* Regum] wende 'in' him for to clensen C   153 to] V, for to CNPT 155 mahte] CFNTV, mahten APS   were] NFTV, weren AP 156 cweadschipes] queadschipe CV   157 bidon] bifuile T, fuylen V, make foule P, defoule R   158 *before* Swa] and NS   159 þe[1]] A (*corr. from* þes), þet C, quam L, *om.* FNTV, car S   *after* feond] qe la F

APPARATUS CRITICUS

after efter] hire NFT, *sim.* S   160 ba] C, boðe NTV   162 hire] his T   164 *after* ledene] ase strong toӡein þe ueond N   164–5 Saul . . . abusio] *om.* F   165 Ebreisch] Ebreu CV   168 hearde] dure vesture F, asperam vestem L, here N, la dure here S   171 on heh] up C, up an heih N   brid] C, briddes NFSTV   hare¹] hire C   nestes] ST, nest CFLNV   hare²] hire C   172 *after* eorðe] world V   173 alle] *om.* CLST   worltliche] V, eorðeliche CNT   174 uppart] up CT 177 learde] leareð CLSV, biddeþ P   178 al] V, *after* habbeð *179* CN, *om.* PT   179 he] *om.* CP   183 we¹] God C   euenið] *before* to CFNS   183–4 nawt . . . Godd] *om.* C   188 feole] monie NT strucion] C, strucoin A, ostrice T, ostryk P, steorc N, storken V 189 a] *om.* CTP   190 uet] PTV, pez S, pedes L, fette N, gresse F, heaued C   draheð to] NV, draӡeð towart C, drahen upo T (*sim.* R), les tret a F (*sim.* S), ben on P, non eleuantur a L   193 nurð] C, noise NFS, dyn' RT, murþe V   oþres . . . hiren] nient seons mes altrur F, *not in other MSS*   195 uet] CTV, pedes L, pez S, uette N, gresse F   strucions] struciones C, strucoins A, strorkes N, storkens V, ostrices T 196 draheð to] TV, treient a F, beoð (. . .) idraӡe towart C, draweð hire to N, lour treinent (. . .) a S, tendunt ad L   ilich] ilihc A   197 fuhel] AV *only*   198 *before* eorðe] þe CN   ancres] *om.* CFT   203 of¹] to CT   aa] A, ai T, eauer CNRV   207 on eorðe] V, on þeorðe CN, ter-on T   hit nis] V, hit ne bið C, nis hit NT   siker] careles T, sanz doel ne sanz tristour S   biwent] biturneþ V, turnes T   208 aa] C, ai T, euer NV   ha] he T   209 ha] he T   hire] his T   210 slepen (. . .) speoken] *trs.* RS   *after* heren] nime T, *sim.* S   hire] him T   211 ha] he T   212 hire¹,²] him T   ha] he T   213 ha] he T   sum] summe N, sunne V, pecche de acun S   þe] þeos CV   214 þe] *om.* CTV   ha] he T   215 *after* celi] habent NS, (*after* nidos *216*) L 216 *after* nidos] *see 215*   of] and PST   217 on] C, in NTV   hire] his T   218 ha] he T   þet¹] hire CFV, *sim.* S   219 ha] he T 223 oðer] and TLS   226 þulli] swuche NV   227 *before* leate] to NST   229 þe fleon] A, qe volent F, ut (. . .) volant L, þat fleoþ V, to fleon CT, vorte vleon N, pur uoler S   231–2 aðet deað] FS, uort heo deie N, ase deað C, aðet dead T, as ded V   234 *after* beastes] and of dumbe fueles N   236 þis] þat PT   238 *before* atter] þe CT 239 hwuch] what PR   240 pine] pinen NV   *before* hu¹] and NRS swote] C, swete NPTV   *before* hu²] and NPS   242 þulli] C, swuche NV   243 þet . . . þolie] to þolien TS   þolie] þolest NP   droh] suffered RV   244 swote] C, swete NTV   245 inwið] wiðinnen CN breoste] heorte NP, piz (enz) quer S   247 sker] siker V, securi L, quites e assueres S   248 habben] habben ai T, *sim.* FS   hire] his T 249 lanhure] A, hure and hure N, lonh hire V, saltem L, þenne T, donc au meins S   hire] his T   250 *before* Bihalde] ant CNS   swote] C, swete

NTV   251 þuldeliche] T, pacienter L, mildeliche CNV, humblement
FS   252 libben] NV, libbe CFLST   beon] N, beo CFLSTV
253 *before* his] of CN   254 him²... hit] hit ʒelt him CN, hit him ʒeld
T, hath ʒolden him V   *before* crie] and NP   255 ha] he T
256 Ebreisch] T, Ebrew CNPV   257 *before* confessio] interpretatur T,
sim. S   263 þet] A, fat calf ant to wilde CFNSTV (to *om*. ST)
264 eauer] *om*. CT   264–5 þurh¹ ... este] A, par eise et par delices F,
þurch este ant þurch eise CNT, þorw ese VS, þorouʒ mete oiþer þorouʒ
dry(n)k oiþer þorouʒ eise P   265 *after* dilectus] meus LNPT
ifeatted] ifeatteð A   266 *before* flesch] ðet NPV   267–8 haueð...
strengðe] FLS, haueð (*corr. from* haueðes) strengðe C, haueð ðe ueondes
strencðe NV, haues te feond vnstrengðet T   268 to unstrengen] *om*.
TV   buhen] A, forte makien buwen N, and buhet TV, ant bringen C
270 þurh] *om*. NTV   271 *before* Temie] and NS   ful] *om*. CV   hire]
his T   ha] he T   ifeleð] N, feleð CTV   awilgeð] awildeþ P, wildes T
272 wecchen] N, waken V, wakunge CT   wið¹] mid CN   heui] CNTV,
peisant F, heard A, dur S, duro L   274 michi] LNS(*after* sal), *om*.
CFPTV   275 *before* wecche] ant CF   276 mi] nu CFT
278 wel] A *only*   280 *before* stinkeð] and NS   281 hire¹,²] him T
before forfeareð] and NS   282 hire] him T   þulli] swuch NV   to]
CNSTV, deuant F, coram L, opon P, *om*. A   285 wel ofte] *trs*. NV,
ofte CF, wel TS, *om*. L   287 we] he C (*corr. to* ʒe, *prob. by* C²)
288–9 Augustinus ... maior est] LPTV, *marg. opposite* Seint Awstin 299 C,
before Wunder¹ 296 S, *not in* FN   290 under] NRV, efter CFLSPT
after Godd] self TS, hym self P   291 witneð] witnesseþ VP, seis RS
292 *before* flesch] ðe NPR   a] FT, *om*. CNPSV   *from* ant²] *MSS
running*: ACFHLNPRSTV   294 hire²] þe flesch V, þis fleisch H
296 eorðe (...) heouene] FHV, *trs*. CLNPST   *before* Wunder¹] *see* 288–9
wunder²] wundres T, alle wundres N   297 for-neh] wel-neih NH
297–8 seið ... Austin] ase Seint Austin seið N, *sim*. S   298 sawle is]
trs. CN   299 Seint Awstin] *see* 288–9   for-neh] wel-neih NH
300 ane] CFHLNTV, memes F, *om*. A   i] into HNP   301 feolle]
fallen NT   bute] wiþoute HPTV   303 ku] HTV, vasche FS, reoðer
C, swine N, animali indomito, simie L   þe] T, an C, *om*. FSV
304 seide] seiþ HP   305 sawlen] ST, saule CFNV
307 hehschipe] heuischipe NV   *before* lihtre] ʒe NP, voire S
308 ne¹] HT, ant CFNSV   310 *before* ne] and NS
311 uncuððe] vncouþ þede P, vncuþþe ⟨...⟩ H   312 ne] nec L,
ant HNV, þat TS, it P, *om*. CF   313 þunche] iwurðen NST   ʒet] *om*.
NS   315 curre] CFHV, coc NLPST   mixne] mixne 'id est dunchul'
H, dunge hylle P   316 *before* iseid] ear CHS   ah²] ouʒte VH
317 wel] *om*. LT   318 feole] monie NT   ha] he T   hire] his T
319 *before* fulitohe] ahne TS   þe] hire CN   320 ha] he T   hire¹]

his T   hire²] hise T   321 strengðe oþre] C, *trs.* N, strengþe to oþere HTV   323 eueneð] likneþ PR   hire] him T   euesunges] PRT, euesunge CFNSV   325 euesunges] FT, euesinge CHNSV 326 euesunges] FT, euesunge CNSV   ahen] ouhten VH 327 Cristene folc] al cristen folc N, totus fidelis populus L 327–8 leonie . . . upon] apreigne (*transl.* leornie?) de S, imitetur L 328 hire] hem VS   334 o] A, on C, en FS, a HNV, *om.* T   ha] he T   335 *from* þe chirche] *MSS running:* ACFHLNPRSV   as] CFHNS, and V, *om.* A   337 stuteð] *conj.* Dobson; stut C, studeð N, stunteþ HV, defaut S, stureð A, fuie F   ʒeieð] crieþ HV   340 his] hire CP   *before* Alswa] and NS   343 *from* et] *MSS running:* ACFLNPRSV   344 *after* tecto] Vigilaui ANV   345 *before* spearewe] þe CP   347 ne ne] N, ne CV   348–9 i feole studen] wel muchel C, multum L, en meint liu mout S   351 *before* þet] and NS 352 Eadi] blissed PRV   352–3 þet . . . wakiende] A, whome þe Lorde shall' fynd wakyng when he comes R, *sim.* S   352 hwen . . . kimeð] ure Louerd hwon he cumeð NFV   354 wecche] to wake RV 355 dede] deden NS   *from* Eahte] *MSS running:* ACFGLNPRSV 355–69 Eahte . . . ende] *Points numbered throughout only in* A (*in Roman numerals, above line*) *and* R (*in words*); *indicated by paragraph-marks in* V 357 wei] lif CF   359 mid] wiþ VP   *after* alle] *see 361–4* 360 ear her] A, her CL, ear GFNSV   361–4 Dominus . . . cogitationem] L, *marg. at foot of page* C, *after* alle *359* N (Anselmus . . . cogitationem *om.*), *after* werkes *365* GPSV, *not in* FR   361–2 capilli (. . .) peribunt] GLPV, capillus (. . .) peribit CNS   362 capite] P, capite vestro CGNV, *trs.* L, capite nostro S   363 sit] fuerit GS 364 et] etiam LS   *after* nu] þenne G, *sim.* FPS   365 *after* werkes] *see 361–4*   seoueðe] seste CGN   366 þer bihald] FNV, isci (. . .) regardez S, vbi (tria) videnda sunt L, þere (þise þinges ben) P, þet bihalt CG   367 *after* pinen] ðet no tunge ne mei tellen N   echnesse] egednesse C, encresynge V, orouʒ PS   *after* euchan] ðet lesteð wiðuten ende NP(ðet *om.*)S   367–8 þe³ . . . i þe] þe muchele reounesse of þe lure of þe muchele C   370 hire¹,²] his G   heorte] mynde PR   ha] he G   371 I] *om.* CV   sið] seið CP   371–2 nowðer . . . hereð] AFLR *only*   372 lette] letteþ hym P, myʒte lett hym (of his bedys) R 373 þing] A, opus L, god CFGNPRSV   Godes engel] God one and his engel N, le angele Deu e nostre Sire memes S   375 nu] *om.* CGL leoue] V, mine leoue CFGNS, *om.* L   sustren] frend G   uppin] uppen and ʒelpen of goddede N, sei auanter de aucun bien S   378 *from* Oratio] *MSS running:* ACFLNPRSV   379 icweme] queme CV Ebreisch] N, Ebreu CPRV   382 Ebreisch] N, Ebreu CFPV 384 *from* uppeð] *MSS running:* ACFLNPRSTV   uppeð] C, uppede N, telleþ V, ʒelpes T   388 þe] A, þi CFNST   391 se] *om.* CV

392 ihole were] *trs.* NV   393 hondhwile] schort hwile TV 396 trochiö] C, faillent F, treoweð N, ianglent S, mangen T, scheweþ heore dedes V   397 uecordia] CFT, uerecundia ALNPSV   potest] A, potuit CFLNPSTV   398 nummum] nimium FPT   he seið] seiþ Gregori P, Seynt Gregory seis R   399 *before* don²] ant CP   don²] to do PRT   he] me NS   400 worldes] CSTV, wordes ALN, *om.* F 401 herunge] preisinge PRV   sustren] men C   haldeð] habbeð CF 404 bisemde . . . ant] *om.* FLRS   404-5 ant . . . lepruse] *om.* P 406 eatelich] laðliche TR   407 sihðe] ech3e CF   408 seið] seide NT   410 *before* bosum] mine NSV   412 ha] *om.* TV 415 *after* Iohel] le prophete FS   418 hire] his T   *before* haueð] ha NFV, he T   420 *before* fordruhede] al NS   421 drue hwite] *trs.* GV   nu] A *only*   *before* 3eme] gode NT   422 wulle] wulle ou N, vus uoil S   424 goddede] goode dedes PV   425 ne¹] no A   ne bereð hit] hit ne bereð CNPT   ne hit ne] CGNPV, ne ne T, ne A 427 rondes] *om.* FLS   428 utewið] wiðuten CN   inwið] wiðinnen CN   430 wrið] hileþ PT   432 þis] GFNTV, le (escorce) en S, his C, þe A   as (. . .) deð] is (. . .) ded GV 434 wetnesse] GFV, þetnesse C, hwitnesse T, swetnesse ALN, douce uie S   makede] maked G, makeþ VF   435 ouer] of CG heowes] þinges GS   436 *before* ehnen] þe GV   437 bipilunge] pilunge CPV   438 þis] hit CN   441 ha] he G   to] *om.* CLNP 442 hire] him G   seolf] *after* Lauerd NFST   443 *after* heoueriche] þat is derne V   fint] iuint NT   444 hit] *before* hudeð *443* C, *om.* GNT 447 puplice . . . uia] N, puplice in uia portat C(uia *corr. from* uiam)FGPRTV(*with* viam *for* via), in via publice portat LS 448 *before* wei] þe CPRS   al] *om.* CPRS   reaueres . . . þeoues] þeoues and of robbares and of reauares N, þeefes and roberes R 453 Ich² . . . golthord] *om.* CGV   455 nelden] anguilles (*for* aguilles?) FS   3ei3eð] cri3eþ V, crieþ out on P   *before* a] ant CNPS 456 Freinið] herknet GFP, nota L   itidde] bitidde TV   457 tresor] GFNSTV, þinges A   *before* his³] and NFS   458 þinges] GFNPSTV, tresor A   459 deore] deorewurðe NT   459-60 Procidentes . . . obtulerunt] T, *to* apertis N, *to* thesauris G, apertis thesauris suis R, *cont. to* munera FLV, *to* mirram SP   461 *before* heolden] hit NF 462 *before* eauer] hit P   *before* þa] and VS   presenz] present GNLV 463 sustren] frend G   þe] *om.* CG   þet . . . ieuenet] *om.* G   466 ut² . . . eare] *om.* ST   ut²] ant C, and ut N   eare] earen NV   470 *from* Vigilaui] *MSS running:* ACFLNPRSTV   471 her] *om.* CF 472 aa] C, ai T, euer NV   Ah] and NV   473 hire] him T 474 *after* solitarius] in tecto FN   475 bi] en noun de F, en la persone de S   *after* ancre] beo VF   hire ane] *after* stude *476* ST   476 as ha is] *before* in ST   bonen] beoden CV   477 leofliche] N, amyablement

F, wel VS, 3eornliche T, *om.* CL   sustren] childre T   479 *before* is¹] hit NPR, ceo F   ba] A, baðe CNPRTV   481 leoueste] leoue NV monne] monie CV   483 schirliche] sikerliche C, sincere L   484 aa] ant NV   485 ifint] fint CTV   486 edeawde . . . ant¹] *om.* CP   edeawde ham] F, visitede ham NST, cunforted hem V, eos beatificauit L   ant¹ . . . to ham] *om.* NV   487 ifint] fint CT   ba] A, baðe CNTV   488 ec] *om.* CF   ba twa] N, baðe C, baðe twa TV   491 bi him ane] into þe feeld P, *sim.* R   492 swa] þere PR   imette] mett PRTV   wið²] *om.* FLNP   494 habes] R, habet ACLNPSTV   496 wende] turned PV, turne N   499 edscene] sene C, isene V   501 priuement] prieueliche TV   502 ha weren] hit were N, serroit S   ham] *om.* FT   *before* here] nu TS   503 brihte] V, brihtliche NT *before* þe] *see 504*   504 seið he] V, seis þat he TF, he seið C, *om.* LP; (*before* þe *503*) hit seið ðet N, dit il ke S   504–5 Quia . . . me] *after* þreatunge¹ *505* PT, *om.* F   504 Quia] quid ST   505 *after* þreatunge¹] *see 504–5*   506 weane] weone T, wone V, defalte F, defectus L   508 lahtren] lahtre TS   *after* lahtren] *see 509* 509 to his ehnen] CFNTV, assez enz (*for* a ses euz) S, *om.* AL   Quis . . . lacrimarum] CT, *after* lahtren *508* V, *after* wealle *510* N, *om.* F   ha] is echnen C   510 adruhede] adru3eden CN, druyeden TV, seccheient F, sechisent S, siccetur L   *after* wealle] *see 509*   *before* forte] *see 511–12 after* folc] *see 511–12*   511 sunnen] NTV, sunne CFLPS 511–12 Vt . . . mei] S,   *before* forte *510* N(*prec. by* Quis . . . lacrimarum; *see 509*)V, *after* folc *510* CPT, *om.* F   512 lugeam] NPSTV, lugeant A wop] weping CP   *after* nu] hu NV, *sim.* S   513 Quis . . . . solitudine] L, *after* prophete *514* NSTV, *om.* CFP   michi dabit] S (michi *interl.* Tr), *trs.* LNTV   ut, et cetera] LT, et cetera V, *om.* NS   514 *after* prophete] *see 513*   hire] hise T   515 oþres] oðre monnes NP, oðre T, aliena L   sunnen] *after* ahne CPS   516 him] hit TV 517 beowiste] A, beowust N, beust T, iwist C, biknowen V, de estre mout S, pressura (hominum) L, *om.* F   þet is, wununge] A *only* 518 to] A *only*   519 lif] liue NFLTV, stude A, liu S (lui Tr), stude (. . .) ant of lif C   522 beatus . . . sua] AL, *after* 3uheðe *524* TV, *sim.* P, *after* cunde *527* S, *not in* CFN   523–4 ant . . . 3uheðe] *om.* C 524 *after* 3uheðe] *see 522*   *after* þrefter] þet Ich ear seide C, les moz deuant diz S   525 ha] he T   526 hire¹, ², ³] him T   527 hire] his T *after* cunde] *see 522*   528 cume] F, kimeð CLNSTV   530 Ha] he T   531 þe²] hire CN   534 *after* ant] of N(*interl.*)T 535 him deð] *trs.* NT   *before* eadmod] and NS   537 *after* Neowe] *see 538–9*   538 *before* Baptiste] þe CPR   seide] seið NL 538–9 Inter . . . Baptista] CLPT, *after* Neowe *537* NV, *after* lif *548* S, *not in* FR   539 þet] *om.* CV   bimong] among NPR   540 herre] P, greignur S, betere CFNRTV   kenneð] A, docet L, porte temoign F,

PART 3

kende T, learede C, enseigna F, teihte NV 541 baðe, ant] S, baðe CNTV, et F 542 before al] ant CNS 543 before al] ant C(*interl.*)NS, and þeiȝ P berenget] *conj.* Diensberg; bereget A, barain ȝe T, barain N, bareyne V, femme baraigne FS, sterili L 545 he[1]] hæ A (ha *partly alt. to* he) *after* he[1]] nouȝth PT ȝet] L, *before* for CS, *before* ne *544* FNPTV bimong] among NV, amonges P seh] isech CN 546 nawt] N, na þing TV 547 sulde] A, soillast FS, fulde NV, schulde (. . .) forfulen C, schulde (. . .) fuilen T, schulde haue filed P, sholde be defiled R 548 *after* lif] *see 538–9* is] hit is NV 549–50 Antra . . . petisti] *om.* C 549–52 teneris . . . posses] et cetera F 550–2 Ciuium . . . posses] et cetera LN, *om.* V 554 pollutis] NLTV, pollutus CFPRS Wumme . . . me] NT, alas mei alas F, wo me, wo me V, wumme C, wo is me P, wo to me R, helas S 555 of] A, wið CTV, mid N sulede] T, suilede N, fulede CV, foule P, filed R 557 bimong] among NRV, amonges P 558 suleð] V, suileð N, fuleð C, fuilen T, foulen P, *v.r.* (filed) R *after* seið] ðet NR 559 isulet] ifuled CT, filed R beowiste] beouste N, bewiste T, þe wonyng R, cohabitatione L, (for he) wes C, (pur) estre F, (par) soen estre S, knowynge V bimong] T, among CNRV *after* beo] it RV 560 or] ACTV *only* metal . . . stel] N(*om.* metal)LPRSTV, *not in* CF 561 anoþer] F, un autre metal S, alio metallo L, an CNTV for-hwon] for-hwi CT 563 Ah] ant NRS 566 O] A *only* 568 Trinite] RPV, þrumnesse CNT 568–9 þrumnesse on Englisch] A *only* 570 honden] honde PT 571 lif] stude NST 572 *after* martirdom] ant CNPRV 573 ouerfullet] A, ouerfulle CNTV crune upo crune] aureolam super auream L, special crownes in heuen þat are called aureals bysid her essencial med R 575 *after* Leafdi] seinte Marie TS 577 ifindeð] finden TV 577–8 Aue . . . mulieribus] Aue (. . .) tecum NPSV(Maria *om.*), Aue (. . .) plena, et cetera F, Aue, gratia plena CL, Aue Maria, et cetera T 579 wes heo] *trs.* CN 580 eadewede] A, *alt. to* adaiede ha him C, scheawude him NT, apered R On] an CN 581–2 is iseid] Ich seide CF 582 hit is] C, is NTV 584 Ich] we NS Of] A, o NT, on CV, en FS, in L 585 into] to CT 586 bimong] among CNR 588 froure] T, remedium L, frouren CN, cunforten V, conforter F, reconforter S *before* meoseise] in CFSTV 589 ah] NS, ant CFLRTV he] *om.* CV 592 *before* fehte] þe CFNTV 593 nurð] C, muruhðe ne noise N, noise PTV 594 him] *om.* RT beoden] bonen CT 596 deorewurðe] *om.* CN apostles] deciples NR 599 bonen] beoden NV 600 Hilariun] N, Hyllarion FS, Hylarun T, Hylarium A, Yllarium C, Hillarius L, Hillarij V, Hillari R 601 swucche monie] *trs.* CV 604 minus] CFNRSTV, minor ALP 605 bimong] among NRV 606 wes] were TV 607 est enim] *trs.* FSV 608 monne floc] muche folc CSV, folk P   608–9 to . . . heouene] C, a Arsene del (*for* de ciel?) F, of heuene to Arseinie NV, *sim.* PRST, bono Arsenio L 609 *after* saluaberis] þat is PF   610 hit] þat vois P, la uoiz S, vox L   611 *before* beo] ant CNP   612 ut . . . floc] T (*with* monnes *for* monne), ut (. . .) sihðe N, hors de la compaignie e hors de la presse des genz S, extra tumultum hominum L, ut of monne A, from monne C, hors des gent F, out of peple V, out of men P, from þe peple R 613 sustren] childre T   614 ek] *om.* PST   615 *from* hereð] *MSS running*: **ACFGNPRSTV**   to] T, for to N, *om.* CGV 619 bitunen hire] schete his dores P, shyd þe dore R, sperren his dores V *after* hire] inne NT   *before* helle] þe CN   620 to] A, for to CNTV 621 forswolhen] swoleȝen CTV   *before* beo] te GN   622 lecche] kecche NV   625 *before* helle] þe CN   þe sikerure] þe sikere C, sikere G, *sim.* LS   626 oþer] secund RV   *after* reisun] *see 628*   a deore . . . wet] G, a derworþe licur, a derworþe weet V, *sim.* N, vn cler liquor et precious F, an deorewurðe licur C, *sim.* LRS, a deorewurðe wet T 627 feble] brotil PR   ha] he CRST   628 ha] he CST, *sim.* L, be R   *before* Habemus] *see 628–9*   Habemus . . . fictilibus] LRST,   *after* reisun *626* P, *after* flesch *629* GNV, *after* cleannesse *631* C, *not in* F 628–9 dicit Apostolus] A; (*before* Habemus *628*) Apostolus GTV, of þisse bruchele uetles ðe Apostle seið N, þe Apostle seiþ P, mes si com li seint apostle Seint Poel dit (. . .) S, Sed Corinthiorum iiij° dicitur L, Seynt Poul seys, 2 Corinthiorum 4 R; *not in* CF   629 wummone] monnes GT *after* flesch] *see 628*   þah noðeleatere] *om.* CN   630 þe¹ . . . healewi] þe halewi C, li balme F   *before* is] þet CN   meidenhad] maidhað G, maihod T   efter] CGNTV, eft A   meiðlure] meidenlure T, meidene lure C, maydenhodes lure V   631 *after* cleannesse] *see 628*   bruchel is as is] *conj.*; adeo fragile est ut L, est freinant ausi come F, bruchel as is ACG, bruchel as TV, bruchelure þene beo N, est plus frelle (. . .) ke ne soit S 632 tobroken] ybroken PRV   *after* neauer] ibet AGV   wes ear] A, *trs.* CGNT, euer was V   633 mid] wiþ PT   634 tobrekeð] brekeð CPRT   ant] auh N, but R, mes S, tamen L   635 meiðlure] meidenlure TV, meiðhad C, meydenhod R, pucellage S   halnesse] holinesse NLV   637 allunge] *om.* CF   eauer] ear G, eauer ear TS, *om.* C   638 *before* bireowsunge] þurch CGNTV, par FS   her-of] þer-of CG   Euuangeliste] Euuangeliste A   640 meiðhad] meidenhod NPTV   642 segge] ai dit FS, dixi L   643 meiðhad] meidenhod NTV   644 hurlunge] GNV, þurlung C, truiller F, hurtlinge T, blesceure S, lesione L   645 leosen] uorleosen NT   647 þus] us CLV, nous (. . .) issi F   648 *from* for] *MSS running*: **ACGLNPRSTV** 651 hit] hire CN   652 hire¹] him GT   warpen] cast PV   hire²] his GT   654 areache] reache CV   Apocalypsis] T (*alt. from* Apostolus), Apocalypsis xij° L, *sim.* R, in Apocalipsi S, Apolis C, Apostolicus G, þe

PART 3

Apostle seið N, Apostolus V   luna] lunam LP   655 Euuangeliste] Euuuangeliste A   656 *after* iseh] he seið NS   ischrud] cloþed PR mid] with RT   *after* under] *see 657*   657 þe mone¹] *before* under *656* CNPR   woneð (. . .) waxeð] *trs.* NLS, *sim.* R   ne] T, ant CGNRV 659 wummon] mon G   660 hire] his G   þet is] PT, ceo est a dire S, *om.* CGNV   661 mid] CNT, mið A(*partly alt. from* mid)G, wið VR 663 nane] CGPT, nanes A, nout NRV   664 trussews] N, trusses CGTV   beggilde] beggares NRV   665 *before* nawt] ant CNSV 669 þe (. . .) þeo] he (. . .) heo TV   671 forleauet] bileaued NG   Nis . . . relef] *om.* ST   laue] A, loue C, leaowe G, loaue N, leue V 672 sustren] freonð G   kinges] CGLNV, kinge A   liueneð] G, bileoue CN, lyflode V   674 forleauet] bileaued CGN   þe²] þi CGV 676 laue] A, leaue CT, leoue G, loaue N, leuen V   We] þe C, þat G 677 we] þe C   678 þe] CGLNTV, *om.* A   679 ȝet tear] A, þer ȝet CGNTV   680 ane meidnes] *trs.* PST   681 scilicet] *om.* CPT, *after* pede S   684 muche cuðredden] AGTV, þet is CN   cuðredden] cudþradden G, cuðredne T, cunredden A, felaweschupe V   685 solitudinem] solitudine GN   686 *after* seið] ure Louerd NP 689 seon] iseon CN   692 *before* bibarret] and NS   694 to] for to CNP   bone] bonen PST   *after* ant] ore S   *after* lokið] nu N 695 *before* bitacneð] þet CGLNT   697 ouer al] A, of alle þinges C, ouer alle GNT, pre ceteris L, ouur alle oþere V, sour totes autres femmes S arudde] harudde C, he aredde N, heo sauede V, sche red P   699 ear iseid] *trs.* CTV   701 ȝetteð] grauntep PV   703 for-hwon] for-hwi TV   704 heo] Hester NL   is ispealet] ispeleð G, speleð NP 705 inpudentem] inprudentem NP   706 *after* mon] oðer þeo wummon N   untu] C, untuhðe T, untoweschipe N, foul word V, uncuþe G, (any þing) bot good P   708 totreode] *conj. Tolkien;* to trede NV, totreoden AG, to treoden T, ha ach to treoden C   710 mei] me CN(*alt. to* mei)   him] T, ham CGNV   712 ant] *om.* CGV   715 a] *om.* CN   715–16 ed hame] *after* him CNP   717 ohwider] ouȝwher V, owðer T   719 edfluhen] N, fluwen CGRTV   720 ant wende] ALNS, wende CGTV   wende] *interl. above* brec (*not del.*) A   *before* Wes] he NP   721 tobroken] C, ibroken GNTV   *before* wes] he NP 722 fordemet] idemet CN   sustren] frenð G   723 ancre] religius G For] *om.* GV   724 recluse] T, ancre CNV, religius G 725 hercninde] A, hercnið C, herinde GT, audiens L, axinde N, pur oier S, to heren V   726 utrunes] tiðinges N, typinges of worldliche þinges V, tinðendes wiðuten T   stude] *om.* CN   *before* Ierusalem] i GNSTV 728 ancre-hus] religius G   ha] he G   seon] iseon GN   729 recluse] religius G   730 ha] he G   731 þe] *om.* CGV   *before* Salomon] and NL   ȝetteð] ȝiueþ PV   732 ha¹, ²] he G   hire] him G 733 hire¹] his G   734 fowr] fif GV   736 eðele] NT, atele V, outwarde R, *om.* CGLPS   737 þe ancre] *om.* G   wel²] A, alle wel N, alle CGSTV   738 hire] CGNTV, hare A   739 in] to CN   740 folhi] folehin GNV   741 bitimeð] biualleð GN   744 *from* For-þi] *MSS running:* ACLNPRSTV   750 togederes] togedere CT   ouer] of CN   752 Ba] boðe NT   754 *before* 3e¹] ðet NV   *before* 3e²] and tet N   755 nes] A, nis CLNSTV   nere] T, nes CN, nis V   757 te] i TS   760 þet is] A *only*   ofdred] ofdredde and offeared N, feard T   761 *after* biswike] ou CNV   761–2 o summe wise] CLNTV, ou par aucun sodiuant tourn ou par aucune gile S, wið sunne A   762 cleches] C, crokes N, clokes TV   763 3eornliche] 3eorne CNV   764 aa] A, ai T, euere NV, *om.* C   deð] V, þe deð C, ðeð [*for* deð] ðet is NS, þat is T   765 word 'ane'] nomen 'solitarius' L, an word A, ane CNTV, *sim.* S   769 *before* biheue] swuðe NS   *after* biheue] to CNTV   770 *before* is²] hit CV   773 temptatiuns] temptaciun NLST   775 *after* of] hire suluen NC³   776 leafdi] lauerd T   777–8 3ef . . . gast] 3ef (. . .) temede. 3ef hare nouðer nere sech C, 3ef (. . .) temede wið uuel oðer wið sunne. þe licome ne þe gast, 3ef hare nowðer nere sec A, nisi infirmitas eam domaret morbo uel peccato. Si nec corpus nec spiritus infirmarentur L, 3ef (. . .) temede with euel oþur with sunne. Hit was euel forboden þe bodi ne þe soule 3if þer neiþer neore sek V, 3if (. . .) temede, þe licome wið uuel ni þe gast wið sunne. 3if hare nowðer nere sek T, *sim.* N, si il ne fust mis souz pie e chastiez e batu par dehors, e li esperiz ausint par dedenz. Se li un ne li autres ne fust malades S   784 *after* falle¹] dun NS   784–5 leste . . . prude] L, leste ho prude TV, *sim.* S, leste heo beo prud N, *om.* C   786 sustren] childre T   788 to3eines] a3ein C, a3eines V

PART 4

1 *from* Ne wene] *MSS running:* ACLNPSTV   3 se¹ . . . þron] *om.* ST   6 *after* drede] hire NV   10 ne ne] NPT, ne (. . .) ne C, ne (. . .) he V, ne A   13 et nudus] *om.* PT, *after* cecus S   14 þe] þet C, ðet te NV   neod na] T, *trs.* CNPSV   ne ne] ant ne ne C, and ne NP   15 gastelich] N, a gostlich V, gasteliche CLST   16 estat] stat CV   20 *after* makien] hire NT   mahe ant schule] NLV, may PST, muchte ant schulde C, mahen ant schulen A   21 *before* Ne teleð] *see 23–4*   23 unwine] feont CPV   23–4 Ductus . . . diabolo] *before* Ne teleð *21* V, *om.* N   24 his] þis TS   sunegin] ruine him T, li (. . .) greuer S   26 sustren] childre T   29 *before* Vttre] þe CP   31 licomlich] licomes CT   32 *before* Wiðinnen] mislikunge NS   32–3 alswa . . . is pine] V, also (. . .) is N, alswa (. . .) is ipinet T, *sim.* S, for þat he is pyned in his body P, ant swich C, *om.* L   32 ha] he T   33 *after* pine] þat

is, sunnes ernynge V   *before* drunch] ant CSV   *before* claðˇ] ant CNSTV, oiþer P   38 hire] þise TS   40 wiðuten] wiðinnen NST fondunge²] fondunges NP   41 of mon oðerhwiles] V (*interl.*), oðerhwile of mon CNT, *om.* P   42 freondes] de ami S, amici L oðer¹] *om.* CN   ham] þine frend T, de ami S   43 mishapnunge] mishap CNP   44 mislich woh] NT(mislich *interl.*), quelibet iniuria L, muchel wouȝ V, mislicunge CP, desplesance, tort S   46 euch middel] *om.* CP   49 þohtes swikele] *trs.* NP   þuncheðˇ] CNV, semen T, resemblent S, apparentes L, þencheðˇ A, (men) þenchen (þat hij ben) P fondunge] vondunges NPSV   50 *after* feond] ant CS, oþer N   *after* world] ant CNP, ou S   ure] þe CSV   53 uttre] uttre vondunge N, temptacions foreines S   54 wið] þurch CP   57 is] is he N, he is P(*after* seli *58*)V   58 *after* seli] *see 57*   ha] he CPTV   ipruuet] ipruet A   59 ha] he CPTV   60 ha] he TV   62 *before* þet³] and NP   *after* gode] gold NPS   63 brune] brennynge PV   na þing] T, nan fur CSV, *sim.* L, noþing (ne clenseþ fire þe gold) P   64 *before* gold] þe CP   hit] sekenesse PLV   65 lecheðˇ] keccheðˇ NV   *after* dusischipe] vor . . . sent N (*see fn.*), for many maken hem seek for here fole hardischippes and þorouȝ vncunnynge, and swiche sekenesse ne quemeþ nouȝt God P   65–8 *Roman numerals in A only*   66 beoðˇ] C, weren NTV   67 iiii] iii A   68 vi] *om.* A   69 sawlene] CT, soule NLPSV   heale] leche NT   *before* salue] and NP   70 sið] A, prouidet L, seið CNPSTV   71 *before* to²] and NPS   72 þe] *om.* CTV   75 To beo] A, beo CTV, vorte beon N, to PL 76 hwilinde] wilninde NV, þat þou haste here and takes it wiþ good wille P   hefde] CV, hefden NLST, haddest P   77 ofearnet] deserued V, deserued and oferned P   abuten] N, aa buten C, wiþouten PV 78 dusegest] maddest PV   79 pricchunge] A, pricunge CNPTV *before* beatunge] lute TS   80 aa on ecnesse] A, ai wiðuten ende T, euer withouten ende V, world abuten ende N, sanz fin S, eternaliter L, *om.* CP 81 ieuenet] NLST, is ieuenet A, efneðˇ CV   82 is] *om.* NP   toȝeines] aȝean NP   83 alle] T, al þe CNPV   84 *before* þe] and NP eateliche] hetelich PL   pinen] pine TLPS   *after* þurh¹] a PT   ageaðˇ] agead A   85 seliliche] NV, feliciter L, selili T, sely P, richeliche C ha] he T   86 her] CNPSTV, *om.* A   90 þi . . . habbeðˇ] T, þi file CN, þe fyle þat lokyers habbeþ V, lima lorimarij L, uostre lime ausi com lorimers ke ont lour limes pur limer e pour oster le roill de entour le feer e le ascer S, þe file þat þise lorymers han þat hij filen þe yrne wiþ and maken it briȝth P   *after* fileðˇ] *see 91*   þi²] þe PSV   91 awei] *after* fileðˇ 90 CNP ti] þe VS   for] A, and N, *not in other MSS*   93 oðer²] ant CT 94 *before* teone] oþer NPS   94–5 Godd . . . ȝerde] CLNPTV, *sim.* S, *om.* A   95 *after* feader] deðˇ NPTV, *sim.* S   sune] C, filium L, child NPSTV   96 þet he deðˇ] CNPTV, *om.* AS   98 dohter] V, *om.* C, childe NT, fiz (. . .) ou (. . .) filie S, filium L 99 al gulte] TS, al (. . .) agylte P, agulte CNV, delinqueret L 102–3 an unwrest] *om.* NPT 103 *before* for] for his gulte and T, pur sa deserte ou S *after* ӡerde] i þe fur TS; virga furoris mei, Assur C, (*after* helle *104*) LPTV, *sim.* S 104 *after* unwreste] mon NPSTV *after* helle] *see after* ӡerde *103* 105 *after* uindictam] et CLNPSTV wrake] wreche NPV *after* wrake] ant CNPSTV *after* Ich] hit CP *after* chulle] hit V 106–7 grucchi ӡe] N, gucceþ P, gruchen CTV 107 *after* ӡe] nout NP gulteð] agulteð NV 109 scratleð] A, schindleð C, schrepeð N, cracchen P, gratine S, scrattes T, crasseþ V, rebellat L upo] o CT 111 sustren] childre T hat] biddeþ PTV ower] vr VLS 112 nawt] nawd A 115 eote] A, (ӡe) eten P, ete NTV 116 weredest] A, (ӡe) wered P, werie NT, were V 117 *before* ӡef²] ant CNPS 118 eil] vuel NPV *after* Ant] as CLNPSTV 119 ӡe] *om.* NT doð] S, ӡeldeþ P, *not in other MSS* god eauer] *trs.* NP 121 child] C, children NLPSTV ant] A, þe CLNPSTV 122 iþorschen] ibeten PV oþerwhile] oþerhile A 123 *before* his] ant C, auh NPST his] þe CT 124 licome] body PV 125 dealen] todealen NT to an] ATV *only* 129 þet¹] TV, þet þing NLPS, *sim.* C wel] *om.* CLPT 130 *before* forӡeteð] ant CNPS 131 *after* schal] *see 132* 132 don] *after* schal *131* NP Dohter] sune T 133 oðer²] *om.* TV eani] *om.* CN 134 dohter] sune T he seið] A *only* 135 seon] iseon NV bunkin] buncin C, bunsen NV, berien T, tormenter e pener S, verberari L, beten P *before* ӡe] ant CLNPSTV 136 beo wel] *trs.* CTV 136–7 swa beon] *trs.* CNPV 137 he¹] God CL 140 for] of CV 141 schendlakes] schenschipes PV spatlunge] spatlunges CPS 143 striken] A, streamden T, *sim.* P, strenden C, urnen NV ant leaueden] *om.* LPS leaueden] A, laueden V, leafden CT, bileaueden N dun . . . eorðe] A, in terram L, *not in other MSS before* his] and PLS 144 hearde] *om.* PST *after* ibeate] þer T, *sim.* S 145 *after* ron] adun NP, *sim.* S 152 droh] suffred PV 153 *before* ӡef] ӡe TV 154 ofseruet] deserued PT al²] hit CP 155 þenne] *om.* CLP 157 ikepeð] kepeð CPT 159–60 Salomon . . . afflictionibus] A, *after* heouene *162* LNPSTV, *om.* C 161 witerliche] *om.* NP þe] *om.* CNPT 162 *after* heouene] *see 159–60* 164 þet is . . . þrof] *om.* C 165 al . . . golde] VT, al (. . .) on golde C, toto mundo aureo L, al þe worldes golde N, plein cest mond comble de or esmerez S, an hundreþ þousande werldes of gold P 167 *after* us¹] mi Louerd NP, beaus sire Deus S 169 hit] *om.* NP 171 *before* nomeliche] and NPS 173 weane] wo PV 175 *after* Godd] he seið NS send] sende CL 177 *after* þing] sulf N, *sim.* P 178–9 for . . . nawt] CLNSTV, *sim.* P, *om.* A 178 grisle] *conj.;* grisung C, grislich NT, fere V, *v.r.* P 179 ӡe . . . nawt] NV, ӡe ne machten hit C, ӡe ne mihten

PART 4   211

hit nawt T, ȝe ne miȝth nouȝth (...) hit P   wiðuten] wið uter A   180 wiht]
A, þing CLNPSTV   to soðe] forsoþe PV   181 *before* schadewe] an
CNPT   of] aȝean NV   182 weane] wo PV   nedlunge] nedelich PV
185 hire] him T   ha] he T   186 *before* For-þi] and NS
189 *after* Pawel] seið CNSTV, *sim.* L   191 wop] wouh NV
192 *before* nawt] ant CNPST   eche] *om.* CP   *after* blisse] *see fn.*
194 i] *om.* CLPV   194–5 ant þeos... prosperite] CTV, *sim.* NPS, *om.* A
198 segge] seide TLS   199 *before* of[3]] and NSV   200 *before* of[1]] ant
CN   200–1 wreaððe is .... wreaððe] CNTV, *sim.* LS, *om.* AP
201 alswa] as C, also as N   ȝiscunge] coueitise PV   þus] þise PV
206 temptatiuns] fondunge C, fondinges T   for-þi þet] for CT, for þat P
208 briht] CNSTV, *om.* ALP   ehe] ehnen CLNP   209 secheð] C, me
secheð NT, si quiert len S, queritur L   210 ne[1]] þet TS   ne ne] mon ne
TS   211 ant] ach CV   213 *before* wummen] holi NS   214 itemptet]
ifonded CP   þurh] A, in CLNPSTV   toȝeines] aȝeines N, aȝein P   215 i]
bi NS   217 *before* swiftre] beo C(*expunct. by main scribe*)NPST
218 *before* earnes] þe NV   219 ha spieden] *trs.* ST   spieden] aspieden N,
spyen P, weiteden C   220 *after* worlt] and NLS   222 euch] V, euhan
CPT, euerichon N   proprement] A, propreliche CTV, kundeliche N, *om.* P
after eggeð] us NP, *sim.* S   224 beoð] *after* þe NP   sput] put NPT
225 proprement] A, propremen N, propreliche CTV   *before* þe] and NS
226 wurðschipe] wunne and wurschipe N, wunne T   227 hit] he NP
228 *after* weitið] us NPT, *sim.* S   us mahen] *trs.* CP   229–35 Hul...
swetest] *om.* C   231 *before* wildernes] þe PV   alle] *om.* LP   232 ihereð]
N, heren PTV   *after* ihereð] oþer iseoð NS   233 wummen] men T
234 leoue] leouest NV   235 flesch] fleschs AN   236 *from* Bi] *MSS
running:* ACGLNPSTV   Bi] i NPST   237 lond of] burch of G, terram
promissionis et L, terre de promission, ce est a S   238 sustren] frend G,
childre T   239 *after* kinedom] of heuen PSTV   *before* icorene] leue
TV, *sim.* S   241 dead] heui GP   242 stinginde] GP, stinkinde
CNSTV   245 *from* þe] *MSS running:* ACGLNPTV   swiðe] *om.*
CLP   monie] feole CPT   246 ha] he GT   247–50 oðer seið...
ofte] ALPV *only*   247 *before* wlite] oþur V, utpote L   wlite] beute V
god] A, familiari L, *om.* PV   248 word] P, worþ V, fama L
249 Ant] ac VL   wlite] hujusmodi pulcritudo L, luyte V
249–50 Acointance i religiun] and queynte religius V, cognatio (sepe
dampnum infert) religiosa L, *v.r.* P   250 Al ... of] A *only*
251 ha] he T   252 ha[1,2]] he T   *after* Anoþer] hweolp NP, catulus
superbie L   253 oðer] oðre CGNV   hereð] ihereð CN   254 is
Ypocresis] *trs.* (*before* þe þridde) PT   255 hire] him T   ha] he T
256 ha] he T   *after* ouercumen] *see 257–9*   hire[1, 2]] him T
257–9 oðer is ... itemptet] uel nimis confidit de Dei misericordia uel
nimis confidit de homine aut de se, nimis confidens in aliquo homine carnali

qui temptari potest L, oþur is to ouer-trust vppon Godes merci, and to bold touward mon and vppon hire seluen V, oiþer is to ouer-trosty of Goddes mercy oiþer to bolde toward hym, oiþer to trosti opon hym seluen P (*after* ouercumen *256*), *not in other MSS* 259–60 nawt . . . buheð] A *only* 260 oðer¹ . . . longe] A, oþur grucchinde idon oþur tariende V, factum cum murmure seu tarditate L, *not in other MSS* 261 *before* ealdren] his CNT 262 meiden . . . dame] *om.* T euch lahre] *trs.* GT Loquacite] PT, Loquacitas CGNV 267 Inpatience] Inpaciencia CG 268 *before* fet] heo CG 269 ha] he T 270 to] for to GNP 271 hire¹] him T hire²] his T *before* riote] fol T 271–96 þe teoheðe . . . fingres] ALPV *only* 272 underneoðen awarpen] A, vnderneoþen V, inferior, prostratus L, *v.r.* P 274 biʒete] A, ygeten PV 276 were] A, be PV 279 sumchearre] A, oþurhwile V, and sum tyme P wordes] A, þretes VL, *om.* P 280 warinesses ant bileasunges] schome bilesynges V, mendacia, diffamancia L, *om.* P 281 þis . . . nunnen] A *only* 282 ham habbe] *trs.*V, *v.r.* P 284 Me . . . amansede] awaried, and a wood þing VL, *v.r.* P 284–5 nuten . . . Godd] for her mouþ PV, os talis L 285 to him . . . halhen] to God and to alle halewen V, coram Deo et omnibus sanctis L, tofore God P 286 þe . . . ifed] V, vndecimus est catulus nutus superbie et iste nutritur L, semblaunce is anoþer whelp P wið supersticiuns] A *only* 289 binde . . . muð] A, bende wiþ þe mouþ, maken mowe P, maken mouwe with þe mouþ V, cachinnare L 289–90 makie . . . signe] A, derisorium signum facere L, maken mony a scorn (. . .) and oþure schrewede signes V, scornen (. . .), sueteliche singen P 290 warpe . . . schench] A, tibiam super tibiam iacere L, werpen legge ouer oþer P, casten leg ouer oþur V 291 as¹ . . . were] A, as he weore isteken V, as hij weren stichen P, *om.* L 292 Her-to falleð] L, her-to V, alle þise and many mo P of heauedclað] of hext cloþ V, *om.* LP of³] A, and V, uel L 293 to . . . oðer¹] subtilitas in gestu L ouergart] V, ouegart A, ouer girt P acemunge] A, semynge V, as meninge P 294 gurdles ant] V, gurdlesant A, girdels P, *om.* L *after* wise] nebbes depeyntynge PV, fucatione L 294–5 scleaterunge mid smirles] A, wiþ smeres sclaterynge V, wiþ synneres claustringe P, *om.* L 295 fule fluðrunges] A, oiþer foule flitterynge P, oþur oþer foul floþeringe V, uel huiusmodi L heowin her] A, tinctura capillorum L, tenture of hire her V, teyntoure of here beiʒes P litien leor] A, and lowe slihtynge V, liteinge P, uel lexiue L 296 pinchen] A, whinering PV, decapillatione L fingres] A, strikynges PV, strictione L 297 *before* of²] ant CN 298 lif] CGLNTV, cun A 301–3 Ah . . . tweolue] *om.* C 302 eauerihwer-se] A, euerihwar hwar-se NTV, eauerihwer hwer G swiðere . . . lengest] swiðe (. . .) lengest TG, swuðest (. . .) lengure N, swiþest (. . . .) lengest V, citius (. . .) diucius L 303 feðeri . . . word] GT, feþri on, awurðeð N, feo þer on a word V,

PART 4   213

tango uerbum unum, sunt L, v.r. P   before Hwa-se] ach CP   eauer] om.
GNP   304 her] V, ear CGLNT   nempnede] habbe (...) inempned
G, sim. P   ha] he T   305 hire] his T   Heo] he T   306 liunes]
leunnesse C, leonissa, leonis L   hise] CT, his GNV, þe lyoun P, hire A
307 hire] his T   breoste] heorte CP   308 seoue] ACGNT, þise PLV
hwelpes] A, whelpes cundles V, cundles CGNPT   309 nis icnawen] T,
nule icnawen C, nis icnowen of G, sim. NP, ne con iknowen V
310 after forʒet] it PV   mid] wiþ PT   311 oðer[1] ... hire] om.
LPT   312 ha[1,2]] he T   understont] understonde CN   hire] him T
313 to] om. GP   after laðest] to PV   315 he] TV, ha CG, heo N, hij
P   316 after god] lauʒhwen oþur gabben ʒif hit is mis wiþ him V,
ridere uel deridere alterius infortunium L, lachʒen oðer gabbin ʒef him mis
timeð C(after Scarnunge 318)G(preceded by is, after feorðe 316)T(after uuel
317), lauhwen oþer gabben ʒif him mis biueolle N (after uuel 317), lihend
oiþer gabbende opon hym ʒif hym mystyde P (after uuel 317)
316 after feorðe] is GNP; see also 315   317 after uuel] see 315
after fifte] is NP   318 after Scarnunge] see 315   318-33 þe
eahtuðe ... oþer] ALV only   319 misortrowunge] mis ouurtrouwynge
V, mali L   witer] A, siker V   321 gremien] greuen V   hokerin]
hokereþ V   hearmin] harmeþ V   322 þiderward] þideward A
325 þe twa ... ma] A, þe two oþur þe þreo V, tribus L   326 þoht] L,
þouʒtes V   327 bichearret] bigylet V   328 monnes] A, humanum
L, mony V   limpeð] L, beoþ V   329 neowe fundles] A, adinuentiones
L, fondynges V   þurh[1,2]] A, for V   onde] A, envye V, odio L
330 before cundel] nedder V   330-1 of[1] ... ant] om. L   330 of[1]]
A, om. V   331 þeo] A, þulke V   332 Stilðe] A, stilleschupe V
333 onde] A, wraþþe V, odio L   o] A, vppon V   333-5 ant ...
togederes] A only   335 oðer þe] o þer þe GN   337 horn]
GNPTV, þorn AC, cornu seu spinam L   338 six] CGNT, seuen VL,
þise P   earste] C, uormeste N, first PTV   339-42 Bihald ... witte]
ALPV only   342 wel] L, wel-neih V   343 is[3]] ANP only
344-9 þe seoueðe ... seoluen] ALPV only   347 hire heaued spillen o
grome] A, pullen on wraþþe hire heued V, toteren her here for tene P, om. L
349 hire] A, him V   351 vnlust ... þing] cui non placet bonum L,
(after þet is) vnlust to eny good V, wo þat haþ P; not in other MSS
353 earh] herde NT   mid] wiþ PT   354 on] V, of CGNPT   of] on
CV   hire] his T   357 stut] C, stunt GNT, wiþstont V   is[2]] om. CV
358 after þing] oþer of freond NP, oðer frend T   360 biseon] seon GV
efter] om. PV   to[2]] C, om. GNPTV   361 ha] he T   366 Dearne]
A, a derne G, þat doð P, om. CLNTV   before Prinschipe] see 367-8
367-8 þis is ... seoluen] cor tenax siue tenacita[tem], que maxime displicet
Deo qui se ipsum totum dedit nobis L, þat vnþeuh God loþest V (before
Prinschipe 366), not in other MSS   368 þis unþeaw is] þeos unþeawes

beoþ NV, þise vnþewes is P 369 reisun] G, þing C, reisuns NPTV *before* vox] ðe NPV 371 swolhen] forswoleȝen CN, *sim*. G 372 tet] *om*. NPT 374 rihtliche] A, gnedeliche CGNT, neodiliche V, scarslich P, *om*. L þet¹] hire CN euch] vhan CP 375 ha] he GT 376 euch] uhan CP ed] of GP se¹] als P, as V se²] as PV ha] N, he CGPTV least] euer NTV 377 hire] worldliche NL 378 Euch] uhan CP *after* ifeðeret] þet is, icharged N 382 *after* ȝiuernesse] þet is glutunie N, is glotonye P gris] pigges NP þus] þus þet beoð C, þat þus beod G 383 Esteliche] hastilich PV 385–6 for . . . feden] þah . . . feden G (*see fn.*) 386 leste] T, þet CNV 390 sulen] C, fulen GNTV þah] A, þat G, ac (*before* þeo) P, *om*. CLNTV nomen] nome CT 391 icnaweð] N, cnaweð CGPTV 392 Eawbruche] spousebreche PTV Meiðlure] A, meidlure C, meidelure N, maidenlure GTV ant] *om*. LPTV bituhe] bitwixen PT 394 *after* ȝettunge] þet is (. . .) al ðet tet fleschs to prokeð (*see fn.*) N, þet is (. . .) þet flesch hire to prokieð T, *sim*. P 396 *before* eanie] wið CGPTV, mid N, cum L ȝeoue] ȝift PV 397 *before* cos] wiþ PL *before* vnhende] wiþ PL mei beon] A, is CGLTV, *sim*. N 398 keaft] A, kefte N, caft T, caf V, cast G, *om*. C 399 nede] A *only* 401 incolumis] incolimis A 402 hire] his T hal ant fere] clene and feir N, al clene P ha] he T 403 weren] A, beoð CGNTV, *sim*. L 405 ha] he T 406 þet (. . .) of] þat (. . .) þar-of GLTV 407 beo þrof] A, *trs*. CGNTV, ben (ytempted) þere-of P 408 þenche] A, euchan þenche C, þenche euch GNTV, *sim*. L on] V, of CGNT fundles] cundles NP 410 geað to] A, is CGLNTV 410–11 I . . . wundres] *after* schuldi *412* G 411 ut] *after* hit¹ NT feleð] ifeleð GNT 412 *after* schuldi] *see 410–11* 413 brune] A, fur CGNTV, *sim*. P 414 wið² . . . slea] A, slea wið dedbote CG, slea hit mid dedbote NV, swa wið deadbote T 414–18 ȝe . . . ifallen] A *only* 420 þeo] A *only* 421 galnesse] leccherie PV 422 *after* etscene] Salomon: Qui apprehendit mulierem quasi qui apprehendit scorpionem CN(*with* seið *after* Salomon), (*after* teile *424*) GTV(*with* seið *after* Salomon), *sim*. LPS 423 ilich] alse C, iliche ase N 424 mid¹, ²] wið CP *after* teile] *see* *422* 426 *after* chepeð] hit NPT, hire V 427 þe feire neb oðer] A *only* 428 *after* hwil] þat GN 429 swote] swete NPTV 430 after ofþunchunge] þer-of CNV her] hire CV 435 þis] his PST *before* beot] and NP 437 *from* þe ende] *MSS running:* ACFGLNPSTV mid al] ðer-mide NV stingeð] stinkeð C, stinkeð uel stingeð G 439 sustren] frend G þer] þet CG 440 Ierusalemes lond] la seinte terre de Ierusalem F, Ierusalem L, Ierusalem, þat is toward þe holy londe P, la terre de promission S 441 þulliche¹] sulliche G, swuche NV þulliche²] swuche NV 442 oðer¹] *om*. CNP seouene] seoluen GT *before* hare] an of C,

PART 4 215

aucune de S, aliquod L   443 Vnsteaðeluest] vnstedfast PV   Godes lare] A, hali lare CGNPTV, sacram doctrinam L, la prise del Seint Escripture F, Seinte Escripture S   te spece] A, *sim*. S, *not in other MSS*   444 sygaldren] sigaldrie CP   444–5 o swefne, o nore] o nore, on swefne CG, en esternues, en songes F, on ore, o swefnes T, *sim*. N, sor pie ou sour songes S, on sweuenes VL, o fals sweuenes P   on] AS *only* 447 cleopede] clepe VF   Presumptio] presumciun CGNT   *before* 3ef²] and NP   448 hit¹] *om*. NST   448–9 Ich (...) cleopede] ieo appele F, is (...) iclepet VS   slawðe cleopede] *trs*. NT   449 þe] þe þat GN uuel] lure CL   biȝete] lure NST, lere P   450 Teoheði] typing PV mis] amys PV   451 oðer² ... misfearen] A *only*   hit] P, þis CFGNSTV   spece of] A *only*   451–2 ant ... cunnes] A, oþer NP, *not in other MSS*   452 hwa-se ... mei] A *only*   455 ah hit] *trs*. GN   oðer¹] *om*. CN   457 godchild] *before* Pater Noster GN 458 Credo] Crede CPV   þulliche] swuche NTV   459 sunnen] pecchez mortels F, heaued sunnen N   460 *after* þet] þe CT   462 nomeliche] oune VF, owune nomeliche N   463 *before* oþre] ðe NT bilokene] ilokene CT   464 sunne] sunnen CGNV   465 imeane] CN, þat I mene G, *om*. FLPTV   467 her-to] A, hiderto CGNTV forfearinde] G, forðfarinde CNTV, passanz F   468 ouerhohe] AC, dedeignanz (de quer) F, for hehe G, ouer-heie NTV, (de) trop haut (quer) S, elatos (corde) L   469 *after* iþonket] vers lour bienfesours F, þat ... oðere (*see fn*.) T, ou ki mal quer portent uers les autres S   471 hird] CGNT, meignee F, seruice S, excercitu L, warde V, hond A   473 of] CFGNPSTV, *sim*. L, wið A   474 hereword] worschupe V, *sim*. P bemeres] GS, bemere CFLPTV, demare N   475 orhel] pompose melodie F, gle P, craft V   476 of¹] on CP   479 iborhen] ysaued PV   *after* iborhen] *see 513–14*   482 *after* seið] Ieremie NF 484 *before* wrenche] and NP   schulen] schuldi T, stulleli P, staren V *before* ehnen] þe CGPTV, hore N   487 þider] þiderwart CGN 489 mid] NTV, wið C, mið A   skleatteð] stoppen PV   490 lust] GN, auditus L, oreilles S, luft ACV, senestre F, luf T, loue P   491 *after* muð] mis CGLNV   492 lastunge] leasinge TS   494 eateliche] atterluche TS   deoflen] deouel CN   schulen] schal CN   hare] his CN *before* grennunge] grimme CN   499 mid] wiþ PTV   500 *before* bereð] and NFP   502 he¹] ho T   him] hire T   he²] heo CNT 503 him] hire T, ham NP, *om*. V   504 *before* skirmi] and NPV   him] hire T, ham NPV   *after* ase] an CGNSTV   505 asneasen] snesen CT him] AFS, hire T, ham NPV, *om*. CG   506 eateliche] atheliche C, pardurablement (*transl*. echeliche?) F, atterliche T   ant] *om*. GV 508 eare] earen GN, arm C   509 *after* he] euer GNV 511 þes ... bearnes] al filz del diable et a la fille F   bearnes] bermes N, barme PT, *sim*. S   513 echeliche] ateliche CN, ferfulliche V, wonderlich P 513–14 Surgite . . . Saluatoris] *om.* F, *after* iborhen 479 S 513 aiunt] A *only* *after* mortui] qui iacetis in sepulcris CGLNPSTV 515 his] þes feondes NV eskibah] eskebach C, eskebah G, askebaðie N, askebaþi V, askebaðe T, cendre S, haþ swich a bay P, despit enfant F, *v.r.* L *after* eskibah] and lið euer i þen asken N, *sim.* P 516 *after* rukelin] ham C, hem to P, la ceindre (. . .) a F *before* blaweð] and NP 517 peaðereð] A, paðereð CGN, piþeriþ V, puðeres T, poþereþ P, trestourne (. . .) de fusiaus F, portereit S, se in eis balneat, eos palpat et planat L 518 al] *om.* GLV 519 bersteð] tobersteð CN 520 euch wis mon] þis euch mon G, euerich wis mon þis N *after* mon] and wummon TS ba] boðe N(*after* seoluer)TV eorðlich] worldlich GLTV 521 *after* ant] ahte A ablendeð] LV, ablent CFGN, ablente P, blinden T 524 hit] hire T him] hire T 525 ba] boðe NTV his] hire T 526 his] hire T þer-wið] VL, her-wið CFT, her NS 528 ʒiuere] *om.* CLP feondes] deofles CV ah] uor N, e S, *om.* LPT 529 *before* celer] ðe NP *before* cuchene] ðe NP *after* þoht] is PV 530 neppes] nepp CN, cuppe V *after* sawle] is PV *after* Kimeð] forð NS 531 bismuddet] GT, bismuðeled C, bismitted N, bismottet V, bismoked P, esmite F, soille S, perfusus L bismulret] A, bismurlet T, bismorlet V, bismured G, bismeored C, bismeoruwed N, bismered P, enbue F, enoint S, fedatus L *after* hond] and NFS 532 *before* wigleð] and NS 534 þreateð (. . .) Godd] God þreates T, (*before* þeose 533) CN þreateð] þreatið A 535 *after* men] he seið NS, *sim.* F 536 feondes fode] CFGNPTV, feode A buten] abuten NT, wiþouten PV 537 illi] ei CLNV tormentum (. . .) luctum] *trs.* CN 538–9 kealche-cuppe] GT, keache-cuppe C, gulche-cuppe N, (ʒif þou þe) kelche þe cuppe V, gloton PS, *v.rr.* FL 540 ʒiuere] glutuns T, gredi glotouns V 545 *after* wurchen] De continentibus . . . coinquinati (*see fn.*) GLPTV 548 stinke] A, stinkeð CGNTV, (þise lecchours) stynken P *after* Patrum] hit telleð NP 549 schawde] telleð G 550 lich] cors PV biburien] N, burien GPTV 551 *before* oþre] þe CGNTV 552 *before* pinin] ant CGLNSTV eche] *om.* CT 553 stench . . . put] pine and stench i þe put G, stunche i ðe pine N 554 *from* Nu] *MSS running:* ACFGLNTV sustren] freond G 555 moder-sunnen] pecchez mortels, meres des altres F, criminalibus peccatis L 556 þes ilke] A, þe ilke GNTV, swiche C feondes] deofles NV 556–7 þe habbeð . . . haggen] þus to maken baret T 560 feor, for] FL, fule, for N, fer V, for CGT 563 *before* strengðe] wit and N, grace and V 565 *from* Svm] *MSS running:* ACFLNPTV forme] first PV 567 *before* stronge] se CFLNTV 568 ofdred] adred NP *before* forwarpen] uorʒiten and N, *sim.* PT forwarpen] forsaken PV nawt nis hit] nis hit nout NV 569 *after* nis] hit CNP to . . . ordre] A *only* 570 a wis mon] A, þe wise mon C, þe mon TV, a

PART 4

mon NP, hom F, vir L 572 bi hire] *om.* CF mispaieð] A, mispaie NTV, *sim.* C *after* let] hire CV *before* makeð] and NL 573 feier] CTV, feire (cheres) N, feire A 574 *before* Hwen] and NP hire] þe CNT 577 went] turneþ PV 578 he] ha CFT 579 wel ituht] *trs.* TV 582 wel] AL *only* icnaweð] N, cnaweð CTV 585–6 he beo] ȝe ben V, estis L 586 *after* acointet] mid ou N 591 *before* adrencte] ant CFPTV adrencte] drenhde CV 593 *before* þurst] and NPV 595 terram . . . melle] A *only* 597 swoteliche] sweteliche NV 598 weane] wa CPV to] uorte NV 599 swote] C, swete NPTV 602 swote] A, swete CNPTV 603 ear] earest CNT, furst V 605 todealet þus] *trs.* CNTV, *sim.* P 607 þer] her NT, here-inne P *before* understonden] to CNV 610 excauant] excauent CNPV alluuione] alliuione A 614 *after* dute] *see 617–18 after* Of] *see 617–18 before* strong] *see 618–19* 616 adiuuaret] A, ferret auxilium CFLNPTV *after* adiuuaret] *see 617–18 before* Mine] *see 618–19* weitið] P, waiteden CFTV, awaiteden N 617 ha] A *only* strengden] strencðeden NV, strengþen P 617–18 Ysaias . . . eius] CN (Ysaias *om.*), *after* dute *614* T, *after* Of (*taken with* dute) *614* P, *after* adiuuaret *616* V, *sim.* L, *not in* F 618–19 wa . . . hweonne] (*before* Mine *616, with* nymen *for* cumen *on*) V, (*before* strong *614*) Ysaye seiþ: yuel come vpe þe, and þou wost nouȝt his wexynge P, *not in other MSS* 619 *after* hweonne] þis euel V 620–1 þe hali Iob] V, Iob xxx° L, *not in other MSS* 622 þreasten] wresten NT 623 ȝeten] ȝate PV 625 oþer] secounde PV al] aa C, euer N 630–1 of . . . nesciuit] F, of hwich Osee seið: Alieni (. . .) nesciuit. Et alibi: Traxerunt (. . .) nesciui C (*see fn.*), *sim.* N (*with* Salomon *for* Osee), of whiche Osee seiþ: Traxerunt (. . .) sensi. Item Osee: Alieni (. . .) nesciuit V, de hijs Prouerbiorum xxiij°: Traxerunt (. . .) sensi. Osee vij°: Alieni (. . .) nesciuit L, of swuche seið Salomon: Traxerunt (. . .) sensi. Osee: Alieni (. . .) nesciuit T, as Salamon seiþ: Traxerunt (. . .) sentiui (. . .) Osee seiþ: Alieni (. . .) nesciuit P 630 hwucche] swuche NT 632 sweoke] fende PV 636 ȝiuernesse] glotonye PV ant] ac PT 637 *after* wreastleare] deð NV dreaieð] C, draheð TV, *sim.* P, dredeð N 640 to leaden] V, la fet mener F, lede CLP, let NT þet[1]] hire NV 641 asteorue] V, steorue C, asterueþ PT, steorueð N 642 reowðful] rewful CPT 643 he seið] AP(*before* Ich *642*)T(*before* makien), he þencheð (*before* makien) CNV, (*after* makien) F, (*before* Ich *642*) L reowðful] rewful CPT 644 *before* þenchen] and NFV 645 a þulli] a swuc N, such a V 648 on ham] A *only before* Bringeð] and NP 649 al earst] T, alre earst CN, al comencement F, furst VL to[1]] þe CN 650–1 forschuppet . . . halle] *after* hore *651* PT 650 forschuppet] forschepeþ PLTV 651 halle] helle NPT *after* hore] *see 650–1* 652 *after* dusie] men NT adotede] dotede TV 655 irobbet] A, ibroken CNT, brisee F, tobroken V, perfodi (et ipsa) periclitari L 656 reowðe ... reowðe] A *only* þus] L, þus lo CTV, lo þus N, veez ore coment F 658 *after* meridianum] þet is CFNP *before* angelum] cleopeð hine NP, seiþ V 660 waken] C, in wakene V, wakiinde NFLT 662 lif] *after* hali NT 663 o dweole] T, adweleð CNV ant weop] CFLNPTV, *om.* A 665 *before* bi] and NP, *sim.* L 670 wið] od F, toward T 671 wiltes] C, wieles NTV, wrenches P 672 biwrenche] CNT, begyle V, bichearre A, circumueniat L sumchearre] *after* makede CFN 673 leuen] A, wenen CFLNTV 676 umben] abuten NPV 679 for²] of CN 680 seac] F, set CNT, sedens L him talde] A, talde him CNT, tolde V 680–1 þe fal ... breðren] ðet on of his breðren was iuallen NF 681 *before* Ille] in heaued sunne N 686 na mon] A, no mouþ VF, os aliquod L, muð T, wið muðe C, mid none muðe N 687 bilokene] ilokene CT 699 anred] ancre CN euch] euchan CTV, euerichon N 703 sone ikeast] A, *trs.* CNTV 705 *before* Muchel] þat TLV frourin] confort PV 706 þe] þet CT, que F 709 beon ofdred] ofdreden C, dreden N 712 in temptationem] et cetera CV 713 þe feond þet he] ðet te feond NP allunge] *om.* FT 714 we] 3e CN 715 we] 3e CN *before* ure²] and NP 717 *before* wið] and NSP 719 witneð] seið CNP 720 pati] A *only* set] A *only* et cetera] APT *only* 721 suffrin] T, þolien CNV, *om.* P 722 þolien] sufferen VP to] *om.* CV 723 hire] A, us CNPV, *om.* LT, *v.r.* F 725 ne¹] CFLTV, and NP, *om.* A *after* pricke] Gregorius ... ualet (*see fn.*) TCN (ad ... conualescit *om.* CN), *sim.* LPV, *not in* AF 726 froure] confort PV he] diabolus L, þe fende P 727 *before* þet] and NP 728 weorp] cast PV 729 eicitis] eicis FLPT mittite] mitte FLNPT heonne] *after* us NP 730 þe ... heorde] A *only* 3ettede] graunted PV 731 wiðuten ... leaue] L, *after* nawt CFNPTV 732 an urn] T, a vn cours F, adun C, faste V, *om.* LNP to adrenchen] ant adrenhden CLNP 736 *before* ed] ear TFV, *sim.* P, ec N 739 sting] stink NV 740 *after* nan] leaue N, my3th P, pouwer V ane] NPTV, soulement F, an C, *om.* AL offearen] offren C, enticen (þer-to) P 741 3eueð] 3ef CPT leoue] dere PV 745 him¹,²] hit C 751 us ure Lauerd] T, he us CP, he us, ure leoue ueder NV, *sim.* FL 754 hu he walde] A, wel he walde C, (Veez) bien. Voleit F, he wolde wel N, what he wolde VL, whan he wolde PT 755 notið] beoð N, þere beþ P 756 *before* vre²] and NPV, *sim.* L 757 ant ... wacnesse] *om.* LPV swiðe] *om.* CT 759 hit] *om.* CP wrecchehead] T, wrechedome CN, wrecchednesse V 760 scit] sit FPV 761 þe] *om.* CTV 764 *before* Betere] þet is CFNPTV þe¹] þeo T *after* truddeð] wel NT his] hire T 765 *after* deop] is NPV 766 leaueð] leaue CT 769 leaueð] let NP 770 3eie] crien PV

PART 4 219

771 *before* Hwa-se] vor NP   773 edwiten] A, witen CTV, blamen NP
774 to3eines] a3an N, a3eins P   775 forleas] les PV   his] *om.* CTV
776 oðer seide] CFNT, (his) felawe seide P, oðre seiden A, (on þat) oþur syde V, *sim.* L   778 *before* For] dicitur, Epistola ad Romanos: Contemptum nutrit resoluta securitas V, (*after* siker) sicut dicitur in glossa Epistole ad Romanos: Contemptum (. . .) securitas L, (*after* inobedience 779) super Epistolam ad Romanos: Contemptum (. . .) securitas P(*with* contentum *for* contemptum)T   For] *om.* LNP   þing] anchesun NL   is] Ich segge C   *after* is] he seiþ N   neauer ne beo] A, ne beo neauer CNTV, *sim.* P   779 *after* inobedience] *see 778*   781 baban] CN, babe V, barn T, childe P   782 *after* fifte] anchesun NL   783 *after* seste] anchesun NL   *before* þet] is NLP   784 *before* festluker] te NT
785 *after* dimittam] Cest: Je lai pris (. . .) deshoremes F (*see fn.*), I schal holde þe my lef and I ne schal nou3th lete þe P   786 froure] urouren N, cunfortes V   fondunge] A, fondunges CFNPTV   788 on] AT *only*   789 et cetera] *om.* CLPT   790 quoð] seide CP   he] ure Louerd NP   791 for þe] *after* bisoht NP   allunge] *after* trukie CNV
794 *before* virtus] nam FLNP   798 itemptet] ifonded CT
802 forte] to CV   803 ase] as an CNTV   804 me] *after* ouercumen NP   *after* ondswerede] and seide NP   805 Crist] *om.* CPV
806 to] *om.* NV   807 war] iwar NV   808 *after* Beneit] ant CNT
809 temptatiuns] temptation V, fondinge CP   to] *om.* PV   811 elne] kunfort NV   812 *before* fur²] ðe NPTV   815 seið] telleþ PV
817 *before* fret] is þet he N, þat he TF, he P   820 forte] *om.* CT
821 ane] *om.* CPV   824 witneð] witnesseþ PV, bereð witnesse N
825 hwil þet] A, wið þet CTV, mit tet ðet N   827 þe²] he CV
829 trone] crune CF   831 ofearnet] CNT, iernet V, erned P, ofsaruet (*alt. from* ofearnet) A   him] his disciple V, *sim.* L, his grome P
832 hwil . . . slepte] T, þeo hwule Ich slepte ant tu N, *sim.* LV   as Ich slepte] *after* me CF   833 awakenin] T, awakien CNV, (to hane) waked P   ant] ach CL   834 mahte] mah| A   836 his meister] he CN   837 understod] understond A   wel] *om.* CF   838 in] V, on T, ed CN   euch a chearre| A, euch chere T, euchere C, eueriche cherre N, vche tyme V   840 temptatiun] temptaciuns TL   843 feond] P, enemy F, unwicht CNT, deuel V, diabolum L   844 ha] he T   eauer] *before* ha TV   wið] of CFN   846 meadluker] meaðluker T, unmeðluker N   847 anewile] an wille of TV   prokie] prikk PV
849 *before* rode] þe NP   851 Heo] he T   hire] him T   852 hire] him T   853 *after* under] Iob . . . mortem (*see fn.*) V   853–4 a pine] of win C, swete ane hwule N   854 forte] to PTV   855 eft] *om.* NT   856 þuncheð] is PV   gnuddin] A, gnudden T, gnidden V, gniden N, grinden C, rudden P, grauer et frotier F, scalpere L
858 ha] he T   ne²] neuer NV   859 ha] he T   gluccheð]

gulcheð N, glutten P ne] and ne N, and V 861–2 Nawt... þenne] CFLNV, *sim*. P, *om*. AT 862 *before* efter] for C speowen] schawen C, scheuh V 863 deað] *after* breden *864* NP 867 *from* A3ein¹] *MSS running:* ACFLNPSTV 868 bote] boten CNV 869 *before* hardi] and NP 870 licomliche] bodilich PV 871 þolemodnesse] CFLNSTV, *om*. AP 873 þe¹] *om*. TV his wepnen] *after* warpeð T, *after* awei PV his] hire T 874 him] hire T 875 a uers] þise uers TL 877 Christi] L, Domini CFNPSTV 880 of þine] of heorte o þine N, of þyne schome V sunnen] synne V 881 *after* þench] ofte C, ec N *before* of²] and NS wunnen] wunne CSV 882 *after* þench] ek N of¹˒²] on PTV *before* of²] and NS Godes] nostre seignour FS 883 þe grimme... Domesdei] *after* mode N mune] *conj*., mung V, munneð A, nim CNT, remenbrez FS, cogita L ofte] ofte | ofte A mode] heorte C 884 þe] þes NPV hire] his NP meden] mede PLST 885 goddeden] goddede TS, gode dede P 886 *after* walde] habben NP, *sim*. C 889 wunnen] wunne CNSV 890 i] of TS *after* ant¹] bi TS, *sim*. F 891 schaweð] V, ostendit (...) ac exhibit L, schawede CFNPST 891–3 to... schadewe] V (*preceded by* ne), for alle werldlich ioyes þat euer wore and now ben and euer schulle ben vntil Domesday nys bot a schadewe to þe lest ioye of heuene, ne alle þe werldelich pynes ne ben bot a schadewe to þe lest pyne of helle P, *not in other MSS* 894 hors eschif] chiual eschieu F, hors restif V, scheunchinde hors C, skerre hors T, horse þet is scheouh N, hors þat (...) is eschu P, equus vmbratilis L 895 adun] dun CT i] into NPT weater] foueam uel aquam L, þe pytt P 896 brugge] brinke CT ha beoð] ho is T, est cil S, is he P peinture] peintinge C, þe peyntyng on a wal P 900 þe] oure PST *after* alle²] his NP hali] AP *only* 901 oþre] oþres A sumchearre] sumwhile PV 902 cunne] manere PV 902–3 to... asailet] a ceus ke furunt e ki ore sunt charnelement assaliz e entemptez S, to fleschliche asaillet CFNTV, a3ein fleschlich temptaciouns P, *v.r.* L 903 *before* dredfule] cest a sauoir FS *before* gleadfule] ant CNSV 904 arearet i] excitantur in L, surdent en F, reare i T, *sim*. P, leuez S þe] þi TS þenchen] þench TS 905 3eoniende] A, 3eonen CNTV, abeier FS, hyare L 907 3eide] A, seide CT, creast FS, remde lude N, cri3eþ V, clamaretur L 908 burgurs] A, þeoues NTV, *om*. C 910 *before* þine] of CF 911 of²] on CV, en F beode] offrist F, offerret L, bede C(o expunct.) NTV, commaundast S, badde P 912 al witerliche] A, *trs*. CN(*with* soðliche *for* witerliche)PTV, *sim*. FS *before* helle-ware] al NFS 914 is] were NT 917 islein] A *only* *after* imurðret] ase he þet wrat þis boc C *before* þet] oðer CN sustren] breðre TS 918 þulliche] swuche NPV 919 sum] A, summe CFLNSTV oþre] A *only* 923 *before* draheð] tost S *after* draheð] sone NF *after*

PART 4 221

adun] sone V *after* sucurs] sone CV   926 buuen him] CNT, abouen
him V, ouer him P, *sim.* FLS, *om.* A   926-7 al on hihŏe] sei hastier F
927 hihŏe] NTV, sichŏe C, festinatione L, *om.* A   928 monnes]
monne A   bonen] A, beoden CNPTV   929 stuhen] T, steih3en V,
stei3en P, tu3en C, clumben N, monterent FS, ascendebant L, fluhen A
930 þis] CFLNTV, *om.* A   932 *after* oðer] deouel NS
934 beoden] P, bonen CNT, preyeres V   *after* me²] seide þe deouel C
935 ha¹⁻ ²] il F   937 bone] bonen N, preyers V   938 softe] A,
douz F, softe and swete T, douce e (. . .) squeue S, swote C, swete NV
ne] ant CNPV   939 pes] peis ne reste T, rest P   940 asaileð]
asaleð A   burhes] vrbs L, burg S   castel] LS, castles CFNTV   þeo] þeo
ðet beoð N, qui (. . .) sunt L   946 forscaldet] scaldet T, yscoldet P
948 *after* mon] oðer wummon T, *sim.* S   deouel] feont CN
951 *before* his] al NFP, tost S   Eft] often PLV   þet] ALS, *not in
other MSS*   953 afealleð] falles TV   954 of . . . teares] CNTV, of
ane lut wordes teares A, des lerms FS, lacrimarum L   te] NT, þe CVP,
om. A   *after* sunne] þet is, Iesu Crist N, Ihesus Crist P   958 sonde]
sonden CLN   heouene] houene A   959 humiliantis] humilitatis PT
se] *om.* NPT   960 est] *om.* CFPTV   961 orationis] CFLNPSTV,
conscientie A   962 *after* O] dit il F, (*after* is) he seið N, (*after* mihte) fet
il S   *before* cleane] of NT   964 haueð] C(*alt. by main scribe from*
hat)PV, hat N, bides T, comande FS   iwriten] A, writen CNPTV, escrire
FS   As] ant CN   968 þe feond] A, a3ein him CFTV, a3ean þe
ueonde N, a3ein þe deue[l] PS   970 him] *om.* PT   972 us¹] vous
FS   us seoluen] vous meismes FS   *after* schawin] ðe N, a vus S
973 eape-ware] NTV, aped ware P, merces simiacas L, a3en ware C, menuz
merz F, aucune sotie ou aucun pecche S   976 halhen] halhen al|hen A
977 þe] þeos CV   981 *from* Hwa] *MSS running:* ACFGLNPSTV
Hwa] hwa-se CG   983 breoste] wombe CNP   984 Hwa (. . .) þe]
A, ki F, [h]wa-se G, ho (. . .) þat V, ki ke (. . .) ke S, quis (. . .) si L   Godd]
Crist FN, Crist, uerai Deu S, Christus (Iesus) Dominus L   985-6 al . . .
þolede] *om.* GT   987 þet oþer] þet he þolede N   989 þe ancre]
fere G   989-90 a cwaer] a þing G, ses biens S   990 feor] CF, ful
ueor N, for ATV   ha] he G   hire] his G   992 þreofald] þrofald A
993 *before* bitweone] and PFS   995 Sahtnesse] pes and sau3tnisse P,
pees V   3eorne] gode NS   996-7 þeo . . . edhalden] A, ceux serrunt
meuz retenuz F, þeo beoð best athalden G, þulke beoþ best to halden V, he
wule þet beon best edhalden C, *sim.* NS, wiln best beo wiðhalden T, volunt
melius (. . .) retineri L, þat men best athold P   1000 *before* sahtnesse²]
and NP   sahtnesse] my pes P, myn oune pees V   1002 quod] quoð A
sitis] estis LSV   1004 to] into CN   quod, et cetera] A, quod discipuli,
et cetera F, et cetera GV, *om.* CNT   1005 icnawen] knowe PT
1006 ow bitweonen] *trs.* NT   1008 Iesu is] A, Iesu Crist CG, Ihesu

Crist quest F, Iesu Crist is NPTV, Deu est S, Christus (. . .) est L
1009 him] *om.* TV   1011 sahtnesse] pes and sau3tnes P, pees V
sahte] G, sahtnesse TCN, pes PV   1012 hit] he CGNV
1015 3eorne] gode NS   1018 *after* 3e] nou3 wel P, wel V
1019 neauer] *om.* CN   1020 a3eines] T, a3ein CGNV
1021 tweamen] C, twinnen GTV, unuestnen N, departen P
1024 *after* habbeð] 3et TS   1026 euch] V, euchan CT, euerichon N
1027 *before* 3ef] and NP, mes S   1028 *after* þridde] uorbisne NFS
slubbri] sliddrie N, slider P   1030 ful] A, fulliche V, allunge N,
omnino L, fule GT, en la bouue S, *om.* CF   1031 halt] A, wreoðeð
CGN, weorþeþ V, leones T   1032 beoð¹] is GT   1033 inempnet]
CFGLNTV, itemptet A   1035 teneamus] N, tenemus CFGLPSTV
1037 Alswa] riht so V, iterum L, le quart essample est S   *before* swifte] in
CFGNTV   1038 oðer] oðeres hont CN, *sim.* P   *before* is] he CN,
sim. P   *before* iswipt] sone NL, *sim.* P   1041 fondunge] fondinges TS
1042 *after* halde] wið oðer C, mid oðer N   1043 *after* Wa] is CFGNPV
þe] him ðet is N, *sim.* P, þat is T   1044 areare] arereþ P, reareð C
ane²] A, him ane CGNTV   1045 soð luue haueð] A, luue haues T,
haueð soð luue CGNV   his] hire T, *om.* C   1046 þe seoueðe
forbisne] le quint essample S, a forbisen P, iterum L   1050 earueð]
uuele CV   1051 *before* euchan] ach CNS   itweamet] A, totwimed C,
itwinned GTV, todealed N   lihtliche] lichtluker CN   bersteð] tobersteð
CN   1052 *before* A treo] le sime essample S, iterum L   undersete] me
underset CN, *sim.* G, men vndersetten P   wið] mid CN
1053 tweam] C, totwin GTV, 3if men twynnen P, todel N   ham] ham
atwa C, eiðer urom oðer NS   1054 i] of CF   *after* neomeð] nu CN
1055 sometreadnesse] A, somedrednesse N, sum drednesse V, somenrednesse T, somednesse CG   1056 þis] ðe þet N, icest amur S   habben]
ane T   þe] cele qi F, alle (. . .) þe G, *om.* NS   i] CFG, *om.* ALNSTV
before bihald] he N, pur iceo S   1056–8 bihald . . . weren] beoð G
1056 bihald] regarde F, regardez S, considera L   1057 3eorne] souent
par le oil de fei S   understont] entent F, entendez S, intellige L
deorewurðe] *after* werkes T, cheres (oueres) S   1058 alle þing] al CNT
ancren] we G   1063 þis] hit GV   1064 towart] to CP   *before*
þing¹] te NT   *before* þing²] þe CN   1065 wrongwende] NGT, wrong
wende ACV, trestournees F, destornez S, auersas L   euch] euch an CV,
euerihon N   1067 beoreð] A, habbeð in ham CGNTV, la ount F, ont
en les cues S, in eis L   *before* þe] þet is NF, *sim.* S   1071 mine . . .
sustren] *om.* C   sustren] frend G, childre T   1072 swote] swete NTV
1073 an] *om.* CFGLS   a] *om.* C   1074 iwriten is] *trs.* NTV
1076–1101 Pax . . . heouene] A *only*   1102 haldeð] habbeð NV
1103–4 is for-þi] C, for-þi he is GNTV   1105 þe telle] A, ðet telleð NT, to
tellen CGV, que cunte FS, ut narret L   þe an . . . oþer] T, to þe on bi þat oðer

V, *sim.* S, lune a laltre F, of þe an to þe oðer C, ou bi þat oþer G, to þe and bi ðe, oðer N, tibi de te L 1106 suhinde] T, suwinde N, hundes C, bitter G, vnhende V, maluoise FS, displicens L sahe] tale GV segge] tellen ne seien T, conter S bi suster] A, bi þe suster CN, bi þat oþer GFV, bi oþer TLS 1106–7 Ower . . . ow] F, ower al (. . .) ow G, for-þi Ich forbeode ow C, Ich forbeode ou þet non of ou N, Ich forbede þat owre nan T, inhibeo ne aliqua vestrum L, ieo vus prie (. . .) ke nul de vus S 1107 leue] leue ȝe naut CG euch] euchan TC, euerich N 1108 icnawe] cnawe CV 1108–14 Ant . . . unblamet] A *only* 1114 noðeles] noðele A 1115 hire (. . .) suster] his (. . .) freond G, hire (. . .) suster oðer broðer T ha] he G 1116 ha] he G hwa-se] so þeo þet N, swa þat T 1117 hire] him G ha[1,2]] he G, il ou ele F *after* ga] ut CN 1118 ha] he G 1119 þeo] þe ilke GV hire] his G suster] freond G 1119–20 luue salue] warninge C 1120 hire] him G 1123 ha] he G, he oðer ho T 1124 ha] he G, ho (*pl.*) T i misericorde] in mine gulte C, in so gret charite V hire] his G, hare T 1125 fikiende] N, fikelinde GTV, þat is fykel P, lufferes C, del losengeour FS, adulantis L ondswerie] A, ondsweređ CGNV, onsweren T, deuez (. . .) respondre S, respondeas L, respoun ieo F 1126 hire] him G 1128 leue] CFLNTV, luuie AG hire seoluen] him seoluen G toblaweð] bloweð NTV 1131 ah . . . leasse] A, ach C, mes S, mes ensement F, ne o none weis N, nec solum hoc, immo L, *om.* GTV ha] he GT ne] *om.* GNTV i] A, wið CGTV, mid N, od F, cum L 1132 ful] A *only* in] on NTV 1133 eiðer þenne] V, *trs.* CNT, eiðer G 1134 ha[1]] he G 1135 ear] *om.* CGL of hire suster] of hire suster oðer of hire broðer T, of oðer N, *om.* G 1136 toward] upon CN hire] him G hit] *om.* CTV 1137 *before* mare] þe C ha[1,2]] he G dohter] T, suster NFV, broþer G 1138 dohter] chilð C hit seið] N, *trs.* CGTV 1142 on a reawe] areawe NV, o rawe T 1144 swiðe] *om.* CGLP *after* eorðe] Exultauit vt gigas ad currendam uiam PGTV (*with* suam *after* uiam), Exultauit, inquit Dauid, (. . .) viam S, Psalmista: Exultauit (. . .) currendam, et cetera L (*with* uiam *after* currendam MaV[1]), *not in* ACFN 1144–5 Pertransiit . . . omnes] Et in Euangelio dicitur: Pertransiit (. . .) omnes S, et Actum x°: Pertransijt (. . .) omnes L, Pertransijt (. . .) omnes, et cetera VG(*with* Pertransisiit *for* Pertransiit), Pertransiit (. . .) sanando, et cetera T, Pertransiuit bene faciendo P, *not in* CFN 1145 *before* Efter] and NP bihaldeð] regardez S, *not in other MSS* euen] endynge PST 1146 Oþre] oþer men NP, autre genz S *before* fleoð] and GNS 1147 *after* o] ðe NPV 1148 *before* Caluaire] þe C, of NFPS, on V ȝet] *om.* GV 1150 wiðuten] wið TS eþren] eddre TS on] upon T, of VLS 1152 scurgunge] GL, schurginges T, schurgen CFNV lich] licome NT 1153 þe] his CGNS Toȝeines] toȝein CV, aȝean NP 1155 ȝisceunge] coueitise PV 1156 se[1] . . . mare] mare ant mare CN, lengere more and more P   he] ha T   þe] he CTV   1157 licome] bodi GPV   1158 upon] P, on CGNTV   1159 þrin] upon C, þereopon P   1160 biwrabbet] biwrabled N, biwrappet V, iwarbbet T 1162 Leafdi] CFGLNTV, meiden A, v.r. P   1164 lanhure þe-ȝet] A, lanhure get GV, hure and hure ȝet N, þa ȝette hure T, ȝet C 1167 huden]   before   his   CGN(with   resten   for   huden)V 1172 Marthen] G, Marthe CNTV   1174 curnles] cornes CN weren] A, weren ȝet CFGNT, ȝutt hij weren PV, adhuc tamen (. . . calumpniabantur) L   1176–7 of þurst] ofþurst A   1177 meast] mare T, greignour F, maius L   is] wes CN   1178 greot] V, grot CGNT, bleste F, aliquid L, fote of erþe P   1179 a fot] vn pee de largesce F, a foote of brede V, spacium pedis L   to] eke uorto echen N, more to P   1180 is he] P, trs. CGNV   he] ho T   1181 ȝisceð] wusscheþ V, wisscheþ of P   1183 after swinkinde] men NP 1184 baðe] om. CF   nest] er NV   1185 gruccheð] grucche NT 1186 ha] he GT   her-on] þer-on T, þere-opon P   of] CFGLNSTV, om. A   mistrum mel] defalte de repast F, poi a manger ou a boiuere S, om. P   mistrum] CG, mistrum oðer leane N, a symple V, mistime T, om. L of²] ou FS, seu L   of³] ou de F, ou S, aut L   1188–1209 Of¹. . . ende] A only   1209 of] þof A   1210 after iborenesse] on eorðe NP al] om. ST   1213 Godes monhead] monnes. God wat C, Godes monheade. God wot N   1214 before deadliche] seoue CFGLNST 1215 uos] nos CFS   1216 upo] of PV   1217 after Pawel] seið NFSTV   1218 fatigemini] CFGST, fatiget AP, fatigetis NV, fatigaremini L (fatigemini Ma, fatis with general mark of abbreviation over s V¹)   1219 hwen] hwen-se CT   wergið] weorreð NV, alez F, gon and fiȝtten P   1220 after ant] ge GF   1222–4 as . . . blod] CFGL(om. aȝeines him seoluen)NP(om. aȝeines . . . blod)S(om. aȝeines . . . cunde)TV, om. A   1225 after Nis] þer GN   bute a wah] nawt G 1227 biwrixlet] biturnd GV, biwrien N, couert FS, tectum et velatum L 1227–8 on oþres lite] F, on oðeres liche CT, an oþer liche G, in oðres like N, also V, om. LS   1228 ahne] forme demeine FS, owune heowe N, ahne liche T   1229 þolien] iþolien CN   before ow] to TV 1230 Lowr] loo PV   1239 Ebreisch] Ebru PV   1241 deouel] deoflen CLNV   wende] wenden CFN   1242 fluht] uihte NFP 1243 nawt] neauer CN   sustren] freonð G   1244 is iseid] iseide T, Ich seide C, I seide V   1245 beode sondesmon] T, beoden sondesmon V, boden sondesmen G, beoden to sondesmon C, beoden uor sondesmon N, oreison uostre messager S, sondes many P, message F, nuncium L 1246 in Paralipomenon] CT, in libro (. . .) Paralipomenon S, Paralipomenorum xx° L, in parabolis AFGNV, om. P   1247 huic] hinc SV 1248 cum] om. GV   ignoremus] ignoramus LNPS   residui] residuum CN   1249 Dominus] CFGLNPSTV, Deus A   uobis] om. NS

PART 4 225

1250 enim est] *trs.* LNT 1252 Domini] Dei GS 1253 þet] an C, on N 1254 we mahen] mei GFV 1255 swa beoð] G, *trs.* CNPV 1257 ehnen up] up eien and honden N, vp oure ei3en PV þe] þet C mildfule] milsfule NPTV *after* Lauerd] ant seggen C 1260 hit] F, ow V, *om.* CGLNT 1261 swote] swete NTV 1262 3e wulleð] we wil PT *after* bute] 3if NP ow] N, *om.* CFGLPTV 1263 ondswerede] ondswereð CV, onswered G 1266 *before* nawt] ant CNPS 1267 seon] stonden sikerliche (*del.*) A, seon CGT, ise V, haben N 1273 þeo] þilke G, he T hire] him GT 1274 fondunges] L, fondinge CFGNSTV hire] his GT ha] he G 1275 hire] him G *before* rukin] ne CGNT 1276 *after* þe¹] he seið NPS *before* let] and NPS, quasi diceret L þe²] A *only* 1277 *after* liheð] þe traitre CS 1278 nawt þen traitre] him naut CPS, him nawt, þe traitre GV 1279 *before* wule] he CP 1280 *before* þohte] and NV 1281 *after* heorte] to me TS *before* let] and PST 1282 schec (. . .) adun] schend N, honisez S þe] to CNV 1283–6 Sum . . . ant eft] *om.* T, a ki ele crut e par ceo chai en le pecche de luxurie S 1283 *before* seide] ear CN he leop up] lette him up CN, and lete hym lepe up P *before* rad] he CN 1284 hire] him G twenti 3er fulle] twenti ger and mare G, fulle twenti 3er and more N 1285 ilke] N, il| A, *not in other MSS* hire schriuen] *trs.* CNV 1286 uuel] A, ful FGNV, orde FS, fulle P, *om.* L ha] he GT 1287 *before* seide] ear GNV 1288 pufte] abati F, put V, geta S, depulit L hire] him G ha] he GT 1290 sustren] freond G efne] euer efne N, tot dis S 1292 *before* oþre] alle NS 1294 Deuleset] Crist hit wat C, God hit wat GV 1295 swilli] A, þullich CGT, swuche N, such a V gest] CG, (cum adiutorio talis) hospitis L, goste NT, blessed gost V, (encontre le) maligne spirit S 1296 al] A, al þet CGNTV 1297 deð] *om.* NS oþer] ant NS strengeð] strencðeð NTV 1298 ase¹] A, se CGNTV 1299 *after* deð] alswa CFGNTV, *sim.* S 1300 wiltfule] G, widfule CG, gros F, wihtfule N, wilfule TV, uoluntifs e (. . .) uiolens S *before* his¹] and NS 3ulunges] C, bulunges G, deceuances F, deceptiones L, 3issunges NT, couetises S, olnynges and (. . .) 3ellynges V, tiliynges P 1301 ase] and alle T, alle P schawunges] schriuinges TS dredfule] dredliche CG offearunges] offrunges C, offrendes TS 1302 reades] redles CV as þah] CFLNSV, as þat G, ah þah A 1303 unwrench] an wrench TV, une de ses deceites S 1304 þet haueð] CF, þet he haueð AGNV, þat he haueð wið T, paront il (. . .) ad S, per quam (decepit) L, þe fende haþ (. . .) þere-þorou3 P mon] men CV bi3ulet] ibuled G, bigulet T, bigiled V 1305 sput] G, sprut C, eggeð NTV a] *om.* GV 1308 meiden] suget G, seruanz TS 1309 bringe] bringeð NT, bringed G *after* Eft] he seið N, *sim.* S 1310 hire] him G, *om.* ST ha] he G, ho (*pl.*) T 1311 hire] him G, ham T   *before* nearowe] ful TS   1313 *after* rihtwis] cest . . . droiture (*see fn.*) F   Noli . . . Ecclesiaste] A *only*   wis] wiþ V, par S 1314 *before* luðer] wið GV, par S   1315 *after* ʒet] he seið N, *sim*. S 1316 tu] ha G, he V   schuldest] shulde GV   1317 þet tu] CGN, þet A, þu TV   1320 þene nu] *om*. CF, þenne G   nuðe] A, nu GNTV, *om*. C   1321 nowðer] *om*. ST   1322 temptatiuns] fondinge C, temptatiun T   1323 him] ham N, hire T   ofte] oðerhwile CN 1325 sustren] freond G   1329 he[1]] *om*. TV   1330 þunche] þuncheð CGT   mahten] mahen CV   1331 forð] A *only*   stude] TV, stunde CFGLNS   1332 unstrengeð] unstrencðeð NTV   1333 lei ant] lei CV, *om*. LST   1334 comen] comer A   1337 *before* muche] ful CF   1338 Ebrew] Ebreisch CGNT   1339 he] ho T   his[1, 2]] hire T   1340 unwines] CN, fon GT, enemys V, wiþerwynnes P him] hire T   1341 ant te] ant te | ant te A   1345 warde] wardein NS   Weila] A, weilawei CGNTV   1346 unstrengeð] unstrencðeð NPTV   1347 *before* stealewurðe] and NS   1348 *before* leoten] and NS   leoten] A, let CFGLNSTV   1349 *before* lust] þe CGNPV waxen] wexeþ PGV   1350 ha A, il FS, *not in other MSS* 1351 slepi ʒemeles] slepi scheomeles C, slepe gemeles GSV, sompno necgligentie L   1352 him] hire T   1353 *before* seið[1]] hit CG   into þe] A, i þe CGTV, into N   1354 inguine] iguine A delectatione] dileccione CGV, dileccionis P   1359–60 audita . . . resonat] CFGLNPTV, *om*. A   1359 quondam] quedam GLNV, quadam P   1361 quippe] CFGLPSTV, quidem A 1363 delectationem] dilectionem FP   1364 slepi] C, dormante F, slepen GNSTV   ure skile] *before* slepi CNT   1365 þe . . . þeo] þu speke þo G, þu spek oðer ʒer TS   1366 *from* sweoke] *MSS running*: ACFGLNPSV   1367 ʒare herde] A, *trs*. CGNV   ha[2]] he G 1368 hire] his G   1369 hire] him G, cor L   1372 heo] he G 1373 Putruerunt] *cont. to* corrupte G, *to* sunt L, *to* mee FPS   1374 foð on] gynneþ P, biginneþ V   1377 inopinate morti] L, inopinata morte CFGNSV, inopinata mortem P   1379 unlimp] vnhap PV   iwarð] A, is CG, is icomen N, ke auint a Ysbosech e ke uus auient, auient S, comeþ P nes (. . .) ne nes] A, nis (. . .) ne nis CGNV, *sim*. FLS   1380 wes] A, is CFGNPSV, *sim*. L   1381 al] NV, a CG, touz iours F, tote ueirs S 1382 *before* is] a CG, euer NV, touz iours F   1383 ear buuen] A, er abouen VG, her-buuen C, la sus F, her-biuoren N   unstrengeð] unstrencðeð NV   1385 on] upon CN   1392 vet] foot VL 1395 swealm] swel N, swellynge P   1396 pine] pinen GLNV   dronc] suffrede N, soffri S   1397 swealm] swel N, swellyng P   1398 ant[1]] *om*. FLPSV   ant[2]] *om*. LPS   1400 wunden] wounde VL 1403 feolahlich luue] felaschipus loue V, felauʒschipp P   *after* wreaðões] salue NP   1404 *after* redunge] ant C[2]N, de F   froure] froures CN,

PART 4 227

cunfortes V 1406–7 þet... eadmodnesse] *conj.;* þet is, of edmotnesse C², þet is to seggen (*before* Nu) A 1407 hwet] hwenne C(*corr.* C²)FV 1409 licome] body PV *before* In] and NP 1411 þe] ðine NPS 1415 *after* deal] de vostre corps F, de vus S 1417 *after* slim] *see 1417–18* fette] C(oðer vetles *add.* C²)G, (mid fulðe) al ifulled N, uessel V bist tu] schalt tu beon NV, artow P 1417–18 Philosophus... uermium] PS, *after* slim *1417* CGV, *after* pruden *1419* LN, *om.* F 1417 Philosophus] sicut enim dicit sapiens S, *om.* P 1418 fluidum] fetidum GS 1419 makie] AC(*alt.* to ant makie C²)G, and makien NFLPSV pruden] beon prut NP *after* pruden] *see 1417–18* 1423 *after* duneward] *see 1426–7* *from* Alswa] MSS *running:* ACFGLNPSTV *before* Alswa] *see 1426–7* 1424 *before* Ah] *see 1426–7* 1426 seon] iseon GN 1426–7 Augustinus: Sicut... superioris] A, *before* Alswa *1423* GLNSTV, *before* Ah *1424* C, *between* duneward *1423* and Ah *1424* (*intervening sentence om.*) P, *om.* F 1426 Augustinus] *om.* S 1428 weater (...) breade] T, *trs.* CFGLNPSV 1429 unstrengen] unstrencðen NPTV strenge] A, strengðe CGTV, strenðe N 1432 þet] *expunct.* N *before* god] þet beo NF, beo V, ke est S god] godd A 1433 wake] feble PV 1435 feren] felawes V, *sim.* P flesches] flesliche NT 1436 *before* ego] et ST ant] AST, *sim.* P, *not in other MSS* 1437 mei me] V, *trs.* CGNT ilimpen] C, bilimpen G, limpen T, bitiden N, bifallen V 1438–9 nefde (...) na wunderlich ouerhohe] nefde (...) not ful gret wonder VS, non mirabatur contempnendo L 1438 he] A *only* 1439 ah] CFGLNSTV, ant A 1440 a swuch] A, alswuch NTV, (*after* mahte) CG, autiel F, autel cas S, casum consimilem L 1442–3 Bernardus... eiusdem] *after* lahnesse *1445* CFS(*from* Superbia *only*) 1442 Bernardus] sicome dit Seint Bernard FS, Bernard seiþ P 1443 þet] A *only* is¹] *conj.* White 1445 *after* lahnesse] *see 1442–3* 1446 *before* þis] *see 1448–9* þeawene] vertues N, *sim.* P *after* alle] *see 1448–9* 1448 seið] ST, witneð CGN, witnesseþ V, testmoigne F *after* seið] qui sine humilitate, et cetera CV *before* Qui] Gregorius CTV 1448–9 Qui... portat] *before* þis *1446* C, *after* alle *1446* GPV 1453 þolemode] A, þolemode man P, edmode CGNT, meoke V he] *om.* GNV *after* sutil] ant smel *add.* C² 1454 ant¹... smuhel] A, ant swa smuhel C(smuwel *corr.* by C²)GT, so smel N, si greelle S, si soef F, so strong V gentilliche] A *only* 1455 hire makie] *trs.* NV 1456 *after* is] þauh NF, *sim.* L 1457 Cassiodre] Cassioðre A 1458 *after* humilitas] ibi humilitas A 1461 þurh... grace] A, per inhabitantem graciam L, þurch grace inwuniende CN(*with* inne wuniinde *for* inwuniende)TV, wid grace inwuniinde G, dedenz manant pur sa grace F, (oue nostre Seignur) en abite par sa grace S 1462 þurs] T, wurse CGN, deuel V 1463 fere] felawe PT kunne] can PTV

1464 warpen] casten TV 1465 ant seh] C, he seh GNSTV, vidit L 1469 biheold al þis] A, al þis biheolt CGNV, al biheld T 1474 hine] A, hit CT, cel torn S, huiusmodi insultum L 1479 he] *om.* CGV 1480 toʒeines] agein GN þet þet] þat GN 1483 *after* þin] achne CN 1484 ant eðelich] *om.* FNV 1485 *before* his[1]] euer NS 1486 ehe] echnen CN 1487 beon neauer] C, *trs.* GNTV 1488 icorene] disciples VS ba] boðe (*before* wið) NT 1489 *after* worde] dunt il dit en la Ewangeile F hire] him T 1490 flowinde ʒeotteð] *trs.* N, flowynde stremed V, flowinde wattres T 1491 graces] CL, grace FGNPSTV Salmiste] A, spalmustre C, psalmistre F, salmwurhte GNT, psalmworþe V 1492 he seið] *after* dealen CFNS 1493 *after* ihouen] on heih NV *before* grace] Godes NS, his T 1494 prichunge A, prechunge G, pricunge CNTV 1495 *before* an] also N, *sim.* S 1497 *before* Ich] as VFL wes] is G(*before* Ich)FLPSV feolahlich] felawschipe V, felahschipes T, felawschipes and P 1498 wonteð] faileð GP 1500 his] CFLT, autri S, oþere mennes P, is AGNV 1501 *before* þus] and NSV 1502 witneð] witnesses TV 1506 fondunges] fondunge NS 1507 *before* eadmod] and NS 1508–9 ant[2] . . . sustren] *om.* G 1508 *before* þine] baðe þine breðre and T 1513 þe seolf] *after* þrof GPT, *om.* N 1515 grede] grete T, ploure S 1516 aðet] til þat T, til V hire] him seluen T 1518 is] wes CGNT 1521 ameaset] bikimet *marg.* C[2] 1522 nalde Ich] *trs.* NT 1523 þe seoluen] þine witte NST 1524 Ba] C, baþe GNTV *after* gult[1]] and NPS Iesu] Jhesu Crist FPS, Christus L 1525 *after* beon] Judas ou Ihesu Crist *add.* F 1526–7 hu . . . file[1]] hu he is þin lime C, en uostre liure F 1527 *after* misseið] þe NPT Lime . . . file] GV, lime is 'þet' þe þe file fret of þe iren C, *alt. to* Lime . . smeðe (*see fn.*) C[2], *om.* FLNPST 1528 *after* or] Golt . . . or (*see fn.*) *marg.* C[2] iwurðeð] is TV *before* swartre] þe GNV ifilet mare] *trs.* GNV ifilet] ilimed C (ifilet *interl.* C[2]) 1529 hearde] hardere CFS 1529–30 Gold . . . or] or e argent, fer e ascer S, *not in* FNP; *for* C[2], *see 1528* 1530–1 þu gederest] þey gedere VS 1531 *after* cunde] *see 1534–5* þer-in] i ðe fur LN(*after* imealt) 1533 nep] neb CN(*corr. to* biheue *by different hand*) 1534–5 Argentum . . . eos] LPST, *after* cunde *1531* GNV, *not in* CF 1535 smið] ACGT, smiððe N, smiþe P, smiþie V, forge FS, officina L 1536 smiððe] smiðe G, smiðie TV 1537 þe[2]] *after* misseggeð C(*interl.*)NT 1538 *after* hearmið] *see 1540–1* *after* essample] *see 1540–1* 1539 þe deme] A, þe demare GNV, to þe domesmon T, þat demes P, *om.* C 1540 wrekeð] awrekeð GNV on him seoluen] of him suluen N, him seoluen C, or þat day come V 1540-1 Augustinus . . . meus] L, *after* hearmið *1538* PST, *after* essample *1538* GNV, *not in* CF 1540 Augustinus] *om.* GP, *interl. in paler ink* N 1541 fatiat] facit

GPSV   *after* nat] wel NS   1542 nis þe] is NP   dei iset] isette dei GV   1543-4 þe rihtwise . . . ow] CFGLNSTV, *om.* A 1543 Deme] CT, demere GNV   te dei] GFST, diem L, enne dei N, þulke day V, todei C   1544 loki] don TS   nawt him] *trs.* GT 1546 haueð edhalden] haldes TS   1547 wrake] wreche NP 1547-8 Gloriam . . . retribuam] *after* reaueð *1549* N, *after* strengðe *1551* C; *quotations trs.* P   1548 *before* ego] et FGLNSTV   1549 *after* reaueð] *see 1547-8*   1550 mid] C, wið GPT, his N, *sim.* S 1551 *after* strengðe] *see 1547-8*   1552 Accidies] sloupe P, *sim.* V 1553 *after* redunge] de Seint Escripture F   of monnes muðe] par bone parole de bouche F   1554 sustren] frend G, childre T 1555 bidde] schal bidden NT   1558 Ieronimus] A *only* 1558-9 Semper . . . suscipiat] *after* neb *1561* F(*prec.* cest le Latin de cest)S   1559 beo eauer] *trs.* CP   1560 honden] honde PST 1561 *after* neb] *see 1558-9*   1562 þah mei] *trs.* NV 1563 ʒisceunge] coueitise PV   1565-6 of hire seoluen] CNT, de lecheresse sei meismes F, of lecherie GV   1566 *after* seoluen] þet . . . gestninges (*see fn.*) *add.* C[2] *over erasure of 6-7 words in* C   1567 as] as A   1569 *after* wordes] and NST   1570 mid alle] mine leoue sustren N   1572 þrin] *om.* G, en ceste pecche F, en charnal temptacion S, carnalis (. . .) concupiscencie L, of fleschlich fondynges P   1574 teo] A, þeos CGNV, þase T, ces F, iceste S   1576 swa] *after* hire CG   nis ha] *trs.* CN   1577 *after* feier] sanz tecche F   1578 kimeð] harmes T, soille S   1579 *after* Confiteor] wiþ psalmus, wiþ Pater Nosters V 1580 *before* delit] ðe NPST   1583 Sana . . . Domine] *alt. to* Sana, Domine, animam meam N   1586 nere] nis CN   1587 to . . . dede] to þe fole dede T, a fere la folie S   þis] þat GTV   1588 hire] him T amainet] G, amaset CNPTV, tresuasee F, infatuatam L   1589 *after* winkin] and NLV   hire] him T   1590 *before* Buheð] and NL   softe] A *only*   1591 curre] C(*alt. to* cuard C[3])GTV, couard F, eruh N, timidus L, pourus S   1593 wed] A, wod GNTV, mad C   1596 mi leoue suster] mine leue sustre TV, mine leoue frend GS   þu] ge G   tes] þe CPST   1597 cume] kumeð NPTV   1599 *before* slepinde] sicome F, quasi L   Ame] a V, a vus S, *om.* FL   1601 *before* mid[2]] and NS   1604 rung] rys V, arise P   ant honden] and ehnen G, *om.* CF 1605 Gred] ʒei TG   1606 spiritus] *om.* GN   1607 inimici eius] *om.* CP   saluum me fac] saluum, et cetera C, *om.* GL, *cont. to* iudica me S 1608 sunt] *om.* GP   animam meam] animam, et cetera C, animam F, *om.* GNV   1608-9 Ad . . . meos[1]] *om.* NS   1609 oculos meos[1]] et cetera C, *om.* G   meos in montes] meos T, et cetera C, *om.* FGN   *after* montes] alle ðe salmes ouer; and N, Sai þe salmes al ouer T, Si la temptacion ne se departe donc tantost de vus, dites iceus saumes devant dites e dites les tot outre oue *Gloria Patri* S, Saieþ þise psalmes, and P

1610 gred] 3ei TG, cri V, crieþ P   1611 Usquequo . . . me] AV *only*
1613 *before* Smit] and NPS   þe] þine NSV   1614 *before* helle] þene
NP   1616 him] lennemi F, le mastin S   1618 ane hwile stucche]
one hondhwule NT, one luyte hwile V   bune] G, bugging CT, achat FS,
mercem L, spuse NP, loue V   1619 *after* bohte] se deore C
1620 aa] A, a CGT, A! F, A! A! L, euer N, (regardez) bien S, he (bihalt) V,
om. P   1621 *before* his] to PT   1622 *before* Makie] to TV, vorte N
1623 reowðe²] reowðes TS   ha] he G   1624 wið toheouen] uorto
hebben NT, heuen V   hire¹] his V   hire²] his G   1628 pine] pinen
GLNSTV   1629 *after* wunden] *see 1630–1*   us] vous FS
1630 us] vous FS   1630–1 Creop . . . heorte] *after* wunden *1629* F
Creop . . . opene] *after* wunden *1629* N   1630 ne beoð ha] ðet beoð N,
heo beoþ V   al] euere V, totes oures S   1631 biblodge] biblodege
GTV, ensanglantez FS, fac sanguinolentum L, biblod|de A, biblodgede C
before Ingredere] Ysaie ij° L, Ysaye V   1632 abscondere] absconde CP
before seið] he NT   1633 doluen] deoluen A   1634 dulle] dulte
NV   *after* neiles] de fer F   1635 uore] biforen GNTV   1636 me
(. . .) þe] mine NP   baðe] A *only*   te] mine NP   1638 dulle] dulte
GNV   1639 him sarre] his licome TS   1640 *before* Columba]
veni N   *before* in¹] veni et abscondere S   cauernis] cauerna CFL,
cauernas GN   1641 *after* seið] ure Lourd N   mine . . . þurles] þe
þurles of mine limes GNT   1641–2 i². . . side] *om.* ST (*see also 1643*)
1642 luue . . . to] A, luuede he NP, luued he G, luueð he CFLSTV   his
leoue culure] þe culure CFGNTV, þat culuer P, teu columb S, columbam L
1643 *after* makede] i þe hole of his side (*see also 1641–2*) TS
1648 swat-dropen] A, swotes dropen N, dropen CFGLSTV   *after*
runnen] adun NST   1649 *before* heaued] his TSV   1650 hit] *om.*
CFGT   swa] V, alswa CGNT   1652 dragse] A, dra3e CT, drah
GNV   1655 scheomeð (. . .) griseð] S, *trs.* CFGLNTV
1657 werest] NST, weredest CFG, keptest V, defendisti L
1658 to¹] A *only*   mahe] A, macht CGNV   1659 nawt] AT *only*
1660 o] i TS   1661 nim] nin NV   aleast] alre earst C, on earst TS
1664 gure-blode] red blod GV   1665 drif] A, drach CGNTV, trahiez
FS, extrahe L, (to) drawe out P   1666 ah] CFGNSTV, si L, 3if P,
om. A   feor] A, forð CGNT, auant FS, fer forþ V   1668 þe] N, vus
S, *om.* CFGTV   1670–1 Nunquam . . . assensum] *after* þer-to3eines
1672–3 LNS, *om.* F   1672 þenne . . . longe] A *only*   1673 *after*
þer-to3eines] *see 1670–1*   suster] frend G   1675 hire] him GT
1676 to] *om.* A   *after* sturunges] beoð A   1678 destruunt] L,
demoliuntur G(destruunt vineas *marg.*)FNSTV   1679 *after* us] *see
1679–80*   *after* foxes] *see 1680–1*   1679–80 he . . . Lauerd] *after* us
1679 F, *sim.* S, *after* win3ardes *1680* N   1680 strueð] sturieð NV
after win3ardes] *see 1679–80*   1680–1 þet . . . procunges] A, *after* foxes

PART 4

1679 FGNSTV(*om*. þet beoð), *om.* C   1681 þe strueð] A, þet beoð CFGLNPSTV   1683 bihinden strong] burðen-stronge bihinde T, fort a fes porter par derere S   i... feble] GV, feble i þe heaued CFLNT, leþi bifore PS   swa . . . asse] GTV, *after* frumðe *1684* CFN, *om.* LPS 1684 *after* frumðe] *see 1683*   1686–7 þet... ant] CFGLNSTV, *om.* A 1688 þinge] þing PST   1689 suster] freond G   1690 eani þing] A, ani mon CFNTV, nule femme S, ani fleschlich luue G, alicuius amorem L   1692 ontende] A, tende CGV, brouhte o brune NT, brou3th (. . .) on brennyng P   1696 mutleð] mudleð C, mucheleð NGV, muccles T   1699 teares weater] teares waterie G, teares of watere N, eueuses lermes S   1699–1700 nis bute] is T, seit S 1700 þe] *om.* STV   1701 timeð] biualleð N, falleþ V   1702 ha[1,3]] CF, he GNPTV   ne schal ha] C, ne shal GF, he ne schal NPT, *sim.* V 1702–3 Ecclesiasticus . . . ignis] A *only*   1704 *from* Moni] *MSS running:* ACFLNTV   1706 hit] hire NV   1707 euch an] euch T, euerich N   1708 dale] *om.* T   þear] er NLTV

PART 5

1 *from* Twa] *MSS running:* ACFGLNPTV   neomeð] neomed A   earre] uorme N, furste V, premere F, primum L   4 earre] uorme N, furste V, premer F, primo L   5 *from* Schrift] *MSS running:* ACFGLNPSTV 7 *before* hackeð] and NP   7–8 Schrift . . . children] *om.* C   8 fulðen] sunnes TS   *before* makeð] and NP, e apres S   9 Eiðer] Eider A 10 earste] firste TV   deden] dede CFT   13 ancre] recluses F, anachoritis L   14–15 i schrift] CFGLNTV, *om.* A   15 *after* cweadschipes] compuncte consciencie; vnde in cubiculo abscidit capud eius GN(*with* eius *after* cubiculo)T(vnde *om.*, abscidunt *for* abscidit)V; (*after* heorte *17*) sicome dit li seint en la glose sur le Liuere Iudith: Conpuncta, inquit, consciencia in . . . capud Olofernis S, compuncte sciencie in cubiculo abscidit caput P; (*after* Iudith *18*) vnde . . . eius L   16 eauer is] N, *trs.* CGV   17 *after* heorte] *see 15*   ihulet] ihud NT   *after* ihulet] Iudith: una mulier Ebrea fecit confusionem in domo regis Nabugodonosor GV, Vagao: vna . . . ebria, id est, Iudif, fecit in . . . Nabugodonosor P; (*after* ischawet *18*) Vagao: vna . . . Hebrea, id est Iudith, fecit . . . Nabugodonosor T; (*after* seide *21*) una . . . Nabugodonosor NS(*with* inquit *after* una), Iudith xiiij°: Vagao: vna . . . Hebrea, id est Iudith, fecit . . . Nabugodonosor L 18 *after* Iudith] *see 15*   *after* ischawet] *see 17*   19 heaued sunne] heued sunen V, pecchez capitals F, teste (. . .) ceo sunt les set morteus pecchez ke sunt appelez capitaus S, heued P   21 *after* seide] *see 17* flið] CFGLPTV, flih AN   22 dude Olofernes] fist lost Holoferne F, dude Oloferne V, dude Iudit Olofernes N, Iudif dude Oloferne P   wiheles

APPARATUS CRITICUS

(...) wrenches] *trs.* PT   27 *after* noster] j° Iudicum: Iudas ascendet, et cetera C, In Iudicum: Iudas ascendet T, Isto iudicio Iudas ascendet, et cetera GV(*with* ascendit *for* ascendet), Iudas ascendit, et cetera P   ham] A *only*   ondswerede] onswerede and seide NS, seide P   31 seolf] him self TV   33 honden] hond GT   36 todriueð] todreaueð NT   37 licomliche] bodilich PV   þet he bitacneð] GNTV, þet hit bitacneð A, ec ⟨...⟩ bitacneð þet ⟨...⟩ C (*erasures prob. by main scribe*)   38 nuðe] A, nu CGNV   þing] þring A   38–9 schrift... þet] CFGLNST, *om.* A   39 *before* beoð] þet A   *after* her-efter] *see 41–2*   40 fulðen] pecchez F, sunnes and (...) fulðes TS   *after* fulðen] *see 41–2*   *after* iwriten] *see 41–2*   41–2 Glosa... confitebimur²] NT, Glosa: Confitebimur... confitebimur CP, Glosa super Psalmum, Confitebimur... confitebimur F, (*after* herefter *39*) Glosa super Confitebimur G, Psalmus: Confitebimur... confitebimur tibi V, (*after* fulðen *40*) Glosa... confitebimur² L, (*after* iwriten *40*) la glose sour Confitebimur... confitebimur, en un saume du Sauter, Confessio est euacuacio a malis S   42 þet] N, þeos CFGLPTV   44 uiduetatis] A(e *corr.* to i *in different ink*)F, uiduitatis CGNSPT   45–6 al aʒein] N, hit al aʒein GV, aʒein ham CT, ariere a lostel F   47 *before* brucus] et PT   Iudith] Dauið A   48 mid] wiþ PT   feahede] feirede V, fairehede T, makede (...) ueir N   50 Erunt] erant CGNV   fuerant] fuerunt PS   53 *before* sawle] þe CNTV   is] *after* seoluen ST   *before* us] to CGNV   56 half] hond GV   57 is²] *om.* NT   58 þes] þe GV   *before* ure] of CFGSTV   62 Loki we] veez vous F, *sim.* S   66 dredful ant] CFGNV, dredful TL, *sim.* S, *om.* A   68 *after* we] *see 69*   69 schulen] (*after* we *68*) NT, wiln C³G, *om.* ACV   70 him] him suluen NV   *before* nawt] and NLS   72 *before* don] te GNTV   Eue (...) Adam] *trs.* PSV   73 ant] *om.* FLV   74 to na sunne] CT, to synne P, te sunegin G, ad peccandum L, to don sunne NV, de fere nul pecche S   let of] is ipaied NV   76 of] þuruh NP   77 unwrestlec] C, vnwrastele`i´c T, unwrestlich G, unwrestschipe N, wrecchednesse V, maluoiste F, iniquitas L   80 upo] A, o CGNPTV   81 þenne] ASV(*after* seoluen) *only*   82 nos ipsos] nosmetipsos PS   diiudicaremus] diiudaremus (*corr. by different hand*) A   iudicaremur] diiudicaremur LV   83 her²] wel GPV   85 terrens] terens A   86 subtra] subtus FNS   88 Domesdei] CFGNPTV, domes A   91 eorre] harde TV   Deme] demare NPV   94 *after* schal] þer CGNSTV   96 *before* seide] er VS   þe] þis CFT   97 Deme] demare NV   99 forculiende] N, fortuliinde (*or* forculiinde) G, forswiðande T, forblaket V, brennande P, ardant F, forcweðinde C, nus remordant e ardant S   102 biwenden] bitornen V, turnen P   103 þet wa word] *om.* GN   104 qui paratus] S, qui preparatus PT, quod paratum CFGLV   106 monne] CF, mine GLNPSTV   108 *before* deofles] ðes N, þe P   109 ʒur] cry PV   110 ba] baðe TNV   111 cogitat] cogitet PT   114 domesmon] A, deme C(*corr. to* domesman C³)GTV, demare N   115 dom-seotel] dom-stol NV   þohtes Munegunge] A, þocht, þochtes mungunge CG(*with* þonc *for* þocht)NTV, pensee qi remenbrance F, mauueis pensers S, cogitatio L, þou3th P   116 þis] þus GLPV   117 beo icnawes] A, beo icnawe (*alt. from* icnawes) C, beo icnawen GNV, beo (. . .) cnawe T, biknoweþ P 123 þah] þat T, *sim.* S   125 hat] bides TV   126 swa . . . suhie] *om.* CL   127 Pine] CGPTV, peine FS, pini A, pinie N, flagellet L feasten] fastinge TV   131 *before* i²] hit is GNV, est S   þer-as] as GTV   132 te ful] dampnari L, celui fou F, dampnez e penduz e afolez S, þe fool V   134 *after* skerin] þe TV   135 for-hwon] for-hwi TV 139 an] A, bitternesse CFGLNSTV   143–4 ne . . . neaure] ne timeð ham neauer T, nichil producunt L, nymeþ here P   144–6 Iudas . . . grace] A *only*   148 *after* þis] is NTV   149–50 sustren (. . .) breðren] *trs.* LNPS   151 astoruen] asteoruen A   152 Godd wat] P, Godd hit wat C(hit *del.* C³)GNTV   muche deale] A, muche C, mult F, unliche GNV, incomparabiliter L, vnimeteliche T, wel P, mil atant S 154 his] þe CF   155 moder] *om.* C   oðer] od F, and PS 156 leasse (. . .) mare] A, *trs.* CFGNSTV   ant¹] and alle N, alle P 157 freond (. . .) breðren (. . .) sustren] A, breðren (. . .) freont (. . .) sustren CFGV, breþren (. . .) sustren (. . .) ureond NT, *sim.* LS   as] ach CT 159 þear-as . . . aa] her as he liues aa T, tant com il uist en pecche S   aa] euer NV   160 eam] eum PS   *before* facti] et GLPS   166 his] þis C(*alt. to* his C³)FG   seon] iseon GN   168 nefde] CF, naued GNTV 169 asteoruen] FGV, astoruen CLNT   172 Me] and VS   173 þet is] *om.* CF   174 weairtreo] wearitre A   lei] pine NV   177 *before* deað] to C, wid G   178 3eoue] C (*alt. to* 3eouet C³) LT, 3iueð NGPV 179 *after* tu] 3iuest N, donez F, 3iuc T   *before* mid al] to CTV, to do G 180 abuten] N, buten CGT, withouten V   181 al²] hit al TS, hit V 185 ba] boðe NT   186 Belial] bellum PV   *after* king] of þe londe PS 187 to¹] *om.* GNPTV   þis child] his sune T, li fiz le rei S   189 þe] þis PF   190 ure euchan] *conj.*, ure euch an AG, ure vch an an C, ure euerichon enne N, vchon of his childer an P, us euchan an T, vche of vs an V 192 weorrið] NCFLSTV, weorþed G, wreaðeð A   193 schulen wreaðen] A, schulde wraððe CGNTV, deuiom couroucier F, auoms coruce S, offendimus L   194 unseli] A, unseinede C, maluois F, unsegene GNTV, inuisibilibus L, malignes (. . .) ke nostre oil ne puet ueer S 195 schuhteð] C, shughet (*corr. from* shulenget) G, schuncheð N, fesom eschiu F, en ostoms S, abigimus L, schutten TV, putten P   sunne] LPSV, fulðe CFGT, sunne and fulðe N   196 *before* sone] so GN 197 gode] LS, swote CGNV, swete T, douces F   us] do we us N, *sim.* P   Wat] wac A   197–8 se gentil] CGNTV, *sim.* P, segil A 199 *after* monie] ma C, oðre NFLPS   200 sunnen] sunne TS   him]

ALN *only* 201 heale] leche TV 204 þet . . . us] *om.* PST 206 aȝein] for PSTV wilcweme] wel ipaied NPV 207 *after* rode] and NS we] CFGNST, *om.* A (*interl. in different hand*) 208 na] nawt GNV 210 ure ahne] ure ehne T, de nos euz S 211 mon] femme F 213 earst] first PV ut þenne] A, *trs.* CGNTV 214 eft aȝein] A, *trs.* CGNTV 216 þe] cele F 217 him] hire T *after* greate] sunnen VS *before* ȝef] and NS 218 *before* ne] and NS 220 skerre] readre GV ah] NLTV, as AC(*corr. to* ac C³)G, *om.* F, *v.r.* S 221 *after* let] alle NT 223 men] mon TLSV monie] feole CGV þurles] holes PV 224 heo dutteð] he duttes TS, *sim.* L druncnið] drenchen V, myȝth drenchen P, adrencheð N 225 þe¹] an PSV 227 nere] C, nes GNPTV 228 hit¹] hit | hit A 228–9 he hit seide] NL, þet he hit seide AFGTV, þet hit seide C, il reconeut e le dit S 229 *before* com] he NV 231 *after* nefde] *see 232* 232 utterliche] *om.* CST iseid] *after* nefde *231* CNT bimong] imong C, among NV 233 fordemet] idemed NT 234 deide] was TS þe] one NPSV 235 hefde ileanet] lenede CP a wummon . . . weden] *after* ileanet FPS a wummon] *after* ileanet CN 236 his] hire T ne ne] T, ant ne CGN, *sim.* V 237 *after* edluteð] forȝeten C 238 *after* oþer] Augustinus: Si consciencia desit, pena satisfacit CP(Augustinus *om.*)T, (*after* seggen *239*) GLN(Augustinus *after* quotation)V ne] *om.* TV he] ho T 239 he] ho T *after* seggen] *see 238* 240 schal] LP, ȝet schal CFGNV, schal ȝet T 242 ischapet] ischapen (n *alt. from* d) C, taillez F, asises e dites S, iset and iseid i schrift T, ischawet ANV, iswawed G, exponi L, *v.r.* P tukeð] tuke GT 243 *after* swiðe] *see 252–6* 246 schucke] fende PV *after* schucke] *see 252–6* 248 *before* Biclute] ne NP *after* totagges] ðet beoð þe circumstances N 249 *after* are] and tin NP 251 hit] A, þi sunne CFGLSTV i schrift] A *only* 252–6 þah . . . meanen] FLNT, *sim.* PS, *after* swiðe *243* GV, *after* schucke *246* C 253–4 ne . . . nome] *om.* NV 254 *before* is] hit NPV hali] A *only* 258 on . . . icleopede] *om.* FLS 261 a] *om.* CF bi] C, wiþ PGTV, mid N 263 *before* for-þi] ant CFGNSTV *before* mare] þe GP wepmon] man PV bicom] bicomeþ PG 265 lefde] F, leueð CGLPSTV, ileueð N 266 þing] sunne TS 268 a ladles þing] a sunful wretche V, lede chose a FS, *om.* P 269 *after* persone] o . . . openli T (*see fn.*), *sim.* S 270 þe] *om.* GT pleide (. . .) spec] *trs.* GV 271 eode] eede A *after* wreastlunge] oðer me seolf wrastlede T, *sim.* S ant oðre] ou altres F, uel alios L, oðer C, autres S 273 religiuse] CFGLNPSTV, recluse A ed . . . schulde] *om.* GPV þurl] loco L 275 *after* weouede] as he offrede TS 280 strengðe] FNP, stronge CGLSTV 285 earst] first PV 289 þe fifte] CFGLNSTV, þe feorðe A, anoþer P 289–96 hu . . . totagge] CFGLNTV, *sim.* PS, *om.* A 290 þulli] CT, swulli G, swuche NV 291 swucche] GNV, þulli T,

PART 5

þus fele P, hwiche C   for3eme] for3emed PN   293 nest] last PTV
294 þulli] swuche NV, þis TS   iseid] CTV, I seide GFLNS   295 to
þus ... wisen] TF, *sim.* S, to þus feole ant þus feole siðen C, þus ofte to þus feole and o þus feole wise GV, þus feole siðen and o þus feole wisen and to þus feole N, tot et tot modis L   296 Cause ... totagge] *om.* GP
297 oþre] V, oðer CFL, *om.* GNPST   þurh hwet] GV, hwer-þurch C, þuruh hwon N, þorouh wham PFLST   298 flatrunge] fluttunge TS
298–9 Sire ... of] *after* me *300* ST   299 nan] uuel CL, non vuel NFV
300 *after* me] *see 298–9*   300–1 com ... dede] C, oðer of þis dede com TF, *sim.* LS, com oþer, of þis dede AGN, coome mo. And of þis deede V
303 Euch] vchan CT   he] ho T   his] hire T, ðe NV   306 iseide] *before* þus CGNTV   as on urn] A, todreuedliche N, todreauetliche T, todreauethliche C, destinctement F, to derfliche GV, *om.* LS
307 sunne] sunnen VF   309 in] *om.* TV   313 *after* prophete] Ecce .. Dominus (*see fn.*) CFGLNPSTV   316 cweadschipe] cweadschipes NP   317 *before* to[2, 3] and NS, *sim.* P   317–18 helle (...) heouene] *trs.* NPS   318 schendfulnesse] schendfullec GV
320 trusse ant al] G, trussin C, toute troisse F, trussen, and al NV, trussen and 'al' T, trusse e traine S, wiþ al togeder P, *om.* L   320–1 seið ... Beornard] he seið, seint Beornard NV, he seið GT, seið he C, ceo dit F, fet il S   323 ed te Dome] A *only*   325 eorðware] A, eorðe ware CNT, eorþe boþe V   328 uobis] T, nobis CFLNSV   sit expensum] *trs.* GV tide ant time] *trs.* CFS   331 i þe frumðe] *om.* GV   333 *before* þus] and NS   336 seolf] hym seluen (*after* seið) PV   seið] CGL, seide NPTV   340 þe] þeos GV   342 te feond] P, þe deouel NT, diabolus L, lui diables S, him CFGV   343 ed en] N, an CGT
344 wel[2]] CF, hwit GNSTV, bene (lotus) et mundus L   345 þe] C, þi GFLNPSTV   346 *before* fulðe] ðe NV   senre] schenre CN
348 beoden] beode TS   351 *after* heaued] of alle NP, *sim.* S
352 timeð] bitimeð N, cumeð TG, come P   353 oðer] *om.* FPST timeð] bitimeð N, kimed G, come P   355 ha torplið] FG, torpleð (*pl.*) P, he tur[p]leð CNTV, *sim.* S, precipitatur L   355–6 ha[2] (...) wenen] G, hij (...) wene P, ele (...) se doune garde F, he (...) wene CNSTV, putet L   357 he[1, 2]] ho T   lið ant biþencheð] GLNT, *sim.* S, gist sei purpensant F, lið biþencheð ACV   him] hire T   360 seoue] viij F, octo L   *after* fulle] *see 383–401*   361 hihin to] hihen GFL   *before* þe pine] þe furste is V, *sim.* S   362 okere (...) gauel] LS, *trs.* CFGNTV(*om.* gauel)   363 *after* pine] *see 364–5*   364–5 Ex usuris ... et cetera] NP, *after* pine *363* GLSTV, *not in* C(*marg.* C[3])F   et cetera] P, *cont. to* eorum LNSTV, *sim.* G   365 *after* is] *see 366*   *before* þe[2]] *see* 366–7] reowðfule] dreadfule GV   366 *after* licwurðe] ne icweme N, ne hym ne quemeþ P   *before* Alieni] Ieremias GNV, þat Ieremie seis (*after* is *365*) TS, Osee vij° L   366–7 Alieni ... eius] *before* þe[2] *365* T, *not in*

APPARATUS CRITICUS

C(*marg*. C³)F   368 *before* Fili] Ecclesiasticus GNPTV, *sim*. LS   Fili ... et cetera] *not in* C(*marg*. C³)F   et cetera] *cont. to* disperdet te LS, Fili, ne tardes conuerti ad Dominum; nescis enim, et cetera GNV, *sim*. T (*with* tardas *for* tardas, *cont. to* quid pariat uentura dies), Filij, ne tardas qui ad Dominum vestrum, et cetera P   *after* feorðe] þing NS   371 sunne] sunnen NPST   *before* Sanus] Ecclesiasticus GNPTV, *sim*. LS   Sanus... viuens] *not in* C(*add. in margin* C³)F   372 se] to GV, *om*. PST   *after* schucke] Surge qui dormis LNPS(*cont. to* Christus)T, *marg*. C³ 373 *after* seste] þing NSV   374 Principiis ... paratur] *not in* C(*add. in margin* C³)F   sero] *om*. A   Cum ... longas] A *only* 375 þing] *om*. PT   377 mengde] mende CV   378 þeose ... dude] CFGLNTV, *sim*. PS, *om*. A   arearde] N, rearde CGTV   379 *after* sunne] *see 381*   381 *before* Quam] Augustinus LV   Quam ... premit] *after* sunne *379* S   382 *after* O] Deus CFGNTV   earueðliche] N, earmliche ACGT, arewelich P, haruliche V   383–400 Circumdederunt ... beatunge] GV, *after* fulle *360* FLNPST, *not in* C   385–7 As ... smiten] *om*. ST   386 reaueð (...) of] A, reveþ VG, binimeð N 388 *after* tu] do GNV   þenne] *om*. LPV   389 dogge] hund NP *before* mid] on þe snoute P, sour la kaboche S   390 of þi tunge i schrift] A, of 3oure tunge P, of tunge schrift GFLNTV, de la confession de uostre langue S   391 ant drede] A *only*   toward] A, to GNTV 393 awurieð] awurið A   hit] A, him GPTV, hine N   394 for-hwi] A, for hwuch þing GNTV   *before* þenne] and NP   395 *after* tunge] i GFLNSTV   396 ofdred] A, offered G, afered NV, feard T   Hwa is se] hwa-se is GV   397 he] ho T   aþet] til PTV   399 þe] V, þis GFNST   sarre þen] A, sare as him GF, so sore ase him NSTV 400–1 Se ... leatere] GV, *after* moder *405* CLNPST, *not in* F 403 sone] nout N, nou3t sone P   405 *after* moder] *see 400–1 after* is] þis NS   he] me NV, a man P   406 to beten] *after* leasse NV, *sim*. P   *before* pine] þe NV   407 þis] þise PTV   408 hwi] NP, for-hwi CGTV   409 *before* nawt] and NPS   *after* as²] *see 410* 410 wes] T, *after* as² *409* NS, *not in* CFGPV   411 unwrihen] unwihen AC (*corr.* C³)   413 *before* hare²] and NS   416 clað] cloðes NP 417 fiterokes] C, viterokes N, fiteruches G, fiteres T, viteres V, drapeaus F, de pouere dras S   417–18 eadiliche] CGT, eadiliche (...) and edmodliche N, seintement F, feliciter L, sutilment S, eþelyche V, eadmodliche A   418 bi3et] geteþ P, deeþ geten V 421 on¹,²] bi NP   derue] GT, tresgreue F, deore CV, deorewurðe N, digne (passion) dure S, *om*. LP   422 on] bi NP   o] bi NP   teares] tittes GV   424 oðer ... Chirche] A *only*   425 ropunge halseð] A, halsung ropeð CGT, *sim*. NV   halseð] ropeð CGT, weopeð and gret N, cri3eþ V, crie (*pres. 3 sg.*) S, aiez F, clamate L   426 lechni] lechen VT 427 *after* healen] mide N, wiþ V   ure ... mei] vre Lauerd ihalseð swa þet

PART 5

he ne mei C, nostre Seign⟨our⟩ ne puit F, halseð ure Louerd so, and he ne mei N 432 hunteð] FS, huntung CGLNTV 434 ah to] schal PT 437 penitence] penance PV God . . . is] *after* Crist C, *sim.* N 438 *before* scheome] þe PT 439 sihðe] ech3e C, ei3en P 442 penitence] penaunce PV pars] *after* magna GST magna] maxima PT 445 *before* monnes] þe GV, þe sunefule T, *sim.* S 446 ant . . . sacrement] þet NP ilicnesse] liknesse PV 448 *before* sawle] ðe NT 449 of] i GV bla] CGV, bloc N, liuida L, blac and bla T, *sim.* S 451–2 Interior . . . solempnis] A *only* 453 Ierome] Ieronimo L, Seint Ierome CFGSTV, Ieremie NP 458 al þe] T, al þisse N, þis CFGSV 461 rihte nearewe] NT, *trs.* CGV 462 schal beon] beo G *before* beon] for-þi GFT, *sim.* C as] al þet NT 462–3 al þet] alse G, as P 463 aa] euer NPV 464 wes (. . .) ihaten] wes ihaten (*after* lahe) CGTV, *sim.* P, (*before* i) N 470 presumptionem] presumpcione PV 471 desperationem] presumpcionem G (*corr. in MS*), presumpcione P 473 tristen] tristren GNT 474–5 Triste . . . him] *om.* FL 474 Triste] tristre GT, stristre N 475 tildeð] tilleþ V, tillen (*inf.*) N 478 3ete] 3ates TS 479 for-hwi] A, for-þi CFGLNSTV 482 Godd] *after* he[1] CNT he[1]] CFGNPTV, ha A fore] *om.* CT 486 *before* þet] he seið CFGTV, he seið mid tet N 487 siker] sikerliche NTV 487–8 beoð . . . ieuenet] A, arn euenet to grimme robberes T, depredatoribus comparantur L, sunt comparez a robeours S, beoð to grimme robberes CGV, robben God to gretlich P, sunt dous robeours F, beoð two grimme robbares N 491 nawt] *om.* TV 495 wrec in[1]] A, wrec on CGT, wreek him on V, awrec him of N þe þoht] *conj.* Dance; le pensir F, þe þohte ACG, þet þohte NTV, pur ceo ke il pensa S, *om.* L of a prude] CGNV, dun orgoil F, of prude T, orgoil S, superbiam L wrec in[2]] awrec him of N, wreek him on V 498 Deade] Reade NT 500 grimliche] L, hu grimliche he CFNTV, hu grimliche G, *om.* S awrec him] N, wrec him CTV, wrec G 501 gulten] agulten NV 505 word] worð A hu] CFGLNSTV, o A 506 aa] euer NV ofeode] CG, ouereode T, hefde ANV 508 aa] euer NV 512 ga we] A, ga CFGLPSTV 513 aþet to] T, til þet C, a to G, uorto kume to N, til þow come to V 515–16 as . . . seið] N, Seint Austin seið TS, as seið Seint Austin GC(seið *repeated*)FLV 516 de se] AL *only* 517 þe . . . leas] þe þet lihð N, he þat lei3eþ P 521 his] hire T he] hire T 522 guldene] þe beste VFS 524 eauer] *om.* PT 525 ita] CFGNPTV, *om.* AL 528 sunne] ure sunne N, oure synnes P 529 he] *om.* CG 530 forgneaieð] forgnaweð NV ear] earliche CTV 533 sum uuel] meum malum L, sum yuel of myne P 534 *after* ofte] Cest . . . Anselme (*see fn.*) F 535 þe . . . seolf] ces . . . meismes (*see fn.*) F, les seinz hommes come Seint Poel e Seint Anselme diseient issi de eus memes S, swich holy men seiden þus by hem seluen P 537 unfreinet] moustree F, reuelata L *before* nawt] and NPS 540 hit] TPS, ha GV, þe askunge CFN 542 he¹ . . . mahte] ho-se nule whon he may, he schal not whon he wolde V, *sim.* P, e ke ne ueut quant il puet, il ne fra quant il uoudra S 543 cangschipe] madschipe TV 544 as . . . purs] A, quasi in sua potestate esset L, *not in other MSS* 546 *before* nawt] and NSTV 547 þrefter lokin] A, loke þrefter CV, loken eafter GNT, loke eft þere after P oþerhwet] A, oþer þing CGNTV 550 O þene No] C(*with* oa *for* O)GT, ascune foiz qe iammes F, þo þene no, betere is er þen to lete N, tunc quam numquam L, (confession) tardiue ke nule S, late þan neuer PV sera] PS, sera est CGLNTV, est sera F *after* tamen] est GV 555 unnet] vnneð C, se adonne F 556–7 In Canticis . . . nostra] C, Cantici ij°: flores . . . terra L, (*after* flures *559*) In Canticis . . . nostra GNTV, *sim.* S, *not in* F 557 *before* abstinence] and NST 559 *after* flures] *see 556–7* herber] erber C, herebere G, erber F, herbarium L, herbearhe A, herboruwe N, herberhe T, herborwe V, ostel S 560 *before* Et delicie] *see 561* 561 in . . . Prouerbiorum] A, Prouerbiorum viij° L (*before* Et delicie *560*), in libro Sapiencie GCFNP(*before* Et delicie *560*)TV 563–4 swuch aventure] C, swuch cas, swuch auenture GFTV, *sim.* NS 564 oðer . . . wummon] AST *only* ha] A, he CFGNSTV, *sim.* L, many P 565 hire seoluen] A, him seoluen CGLNTV, hem P ha] A, he CFGNSTV, hij P 566 ha] CF, he GNTV, il ne ele S, hij P þe ilke] celui F, illum L, na mon T, nul homme ne nule femme S, hem P 567 a munk oðer] bimong oþre G, entre altres F, *om.* L 568 Wil3am ne Water] Robert ne William P, Robert ne Water S 569 penitence] penaunce PV 570 i þonc ant] i þoht and T, iþoht GV 571 to forleten] C, forto leten G, to leten P, uorte bileauen N, to leaue TV 574 fallest eft] N, rechiuet F, renchiecez autre foiz S, (te) residiuare (contingat) L, fallest CGTV, (I) falle P 575 amplius noli] *trs.* FGLPSV 576 to . . . wummon] A, adultere L, a . . . repentant (*see fn.*) S, *not in other MSS* 579 to] forte GNT 580 wit] A, þocht CGNTV ealdes] elde NFV 581 *before* þe] alle TF 587 *after* bihet] 3ou P, *sim.* FS 588 sustren] freond G 589 on] of CN edfallen] tofallen GT 592 mihten] maht TV earst] ear CT *before* þreo²] and NVS 593 ant . . . world] A *only* gold or] C (or *corr. from* hort), mine dor F, or ou (. . .) argent S, golthord GTV, thesauro auri L, alle goldhordes N 595 sustren] frend G, childre T 596 ow¹] *om.* GNV 599 cuðe] CT, kudde and kuðe N, cunne GFLV, si vus e[n] sentez coupable S oðer of heh] *om.* PT 602 of mete, of drunch] mete, drynk P, of mete ant of drunh CGNV, *sim.* F, of mete oðer of drunch TL 603 silences] F, silence CGLNPTV *before* longe] to NPV 606 of] oþer NV rustin, oðer rotien] *om.* GP rotien] uorrotien NTV 607 broeke] broken GNPT 608–9 of (. . .)

PART 5

of¹] LT, of (...) oðer CFGV, oþer of (...) oþer of N   610 þulliche] swuche NTV   schriue hire] schriueþ 30w ow PST   611 after lutel] þing NPST   617 umben] abuten TV   to] for to GN   618 before wið] for TV   620 to] N, om. CGTV   621 godlec] godnesse NV schaweð] N, schawi CGTV   622 temptatiuns] CN, fondunge GV, fondynges PT   623 fondunge] fondunges CLP   624 þeafunge] feblete N, feblesse P   628 umben] abuten TV   þet] leste NC 631 preost] preostes NPV   631–2 ant ... wunder] A, and 3it of þis hem wolde þunche muche wonder V, not in other MSS   634 þer] om. TV   tuki ... wundre] om. TV   636 þulliche] swuche NV 638 anan] T, ananricht GNPV, anan rich C   639 mid] wið TV 648 ihweat] A, hwet CGNTV   upon] A, on CGNTV   649 after Pater Nostres] oðer CS, and V   tene] before Auez NL   echi] eche CGT, eke V, echen N, aioindre F, augere L, om. S   651 sunne] sunnen GV ful] om. FN   wurðe] beon NS   654 we] ge GF

PART 6

1 from Al] MSS running: ACFLNPSTV   penitence¹] penaunce V penitence²] penaunce PV   2 mine ... sustren] om. T   Al¹] and N, e tut S   before al²] and NS   5 before conregnabimus] et FNS   3e] we PS   wið] mid CN   6 ant] CFT, also N, ausi S, so V, om. AP   3e] we PS   wið] mid N   7 mei] CFL, nostri NPSTV   8 before Hali] al PL   singeð] seiþ PL, dit e chante S   from Nos] MSS running: ACFGLNPSTV   opportet gloriari] autem gloriari oportet GLPS 9 after biisse] and ure gladinge TS, sim. P   10–11 þis ... rode] om. C   10 recluses] T, ancren NV, men of religiun G   11 before herre] of NT   12 her-to] þer-to CN   14 men] A, of men TV, de genz S, hominum L, om. CFGNP   15 gode] Godes GV, om. LS   þe oþre] þat oþer PV, aliud L   to³] interl. C, om. STV   16 Iesuse] CFG, Iesu Cristes NSTV, Christi L, (on rode) (...) wiþ Ihesu Crist P 17 before best] beoð GNPSV   18 after inwardliche] and seið NFS 18–19 ut abstineatis] abstinere FLS   21 fleschliche] flessches PT 24 rute] waie PV, richte wei GL   25 gnedeliche] scarslich PV 27 riche] richesce F, blisse PV, glorie S   30 after oþer] þat is to comen PF   ne ne] ant ne CG, and V   31 after seide] er NS   pilegrim] pilegrimes NL   33 wið] PT, mid GNV, ou S, cum L, in C, en F, om. A 36 him] V, nostre Seignur S, ham CFGNPT, ipsis L   36–7 i wunne] om. PV   37 before buten] world C, en siecle F, euer NV   ifindeð] finden PTV   38 3eornliche] T, 3eorne CGNV, om. P 42 edstuteð] A, stutteð C, etstondeð NGPTV   44 before sum²] and NPSV   45–6 þet ... þing] om. F   47 doð] AV only

APPARATUS CRITICUS

49 to] of GLPV   51 et] *om.* PT   ipso] S, Domino C, eo FGLNPV, ea T   52 *before* Criste] Ihesu FS   eadeaweð] edeawet C, apparra FS, deweð GV, daweð N, adaies T, diescet L, *om.* P   54 nu] *om.* GPV   56 buuen] abouen PV   57 laste] lak PV   sei him scheome] *om.* GPS   58 þus] *om.* CPV   cwic²] *om.* NS   59 Ah] and PV   hire] him GT   60 hire] his GT   61 *before* Crist] Ihesu FS   62 þurh... grace] A *only*   63 ifindeð] finded G, hit fyndeð V, I finde (ded in me) PS   65 riht] A, *after* is V, *after* euch CF(droit)L(vere)T, *om.* GN, *v.rr.* PS *after* religius] mon and wummon N   þah] AV *only*   66 to] A, in CFGLNPSTV   *before* Criste] Ihesu FS   67 ah] ant CV   Ant] mes F, ac P   68 þe¹] N, he CGPTV   *after* seide] þus PST   autem] CFGLNPSTV, *om.* A   69 mei] nostri LNPST   quem] LNPSV, quam AFGT   70 Crist] Deu FS   schilde] ischilde GNV   74 ancre] reliuses G   ha] he G   autem] *om.* NT   75 Godes] mon seignour Ihesu Crist F, Iesu Crist S, Christi L   nu] A *only*   76 leoue sustren] leoue frend G, nu ȝeorne TS   77 þe³] *om.* CV   worldes] wordes A   79 wohes] weohes A   82 þe¹] he GPTV   83 menske] gomen TS   84 ofearneð] ofserues TGV   86 *after* Iesu] Crist FST   87 ancres] religiuse G   89 *after* Iesu] Crist FS   91 *after* gloriari] *cont. to* cruce GV, *to* Christi FN   oðre] CFGLNSTV, ordre A, hem P   93 oþres uuel] oþer vuel V, oþer wickednesse P, autres choses S   nede] *om.* GV   us] AN *only*   95 heardschipe] herdschipes NPSTV   ah] and GN   96 he¹] ho T   he²] ho T, celes F   97 Godes] Ihesu F, Iesu Crist S, Christi L   he] ho T, eles F   ham] *om.* PV   99–100 up iriht] A, *trs.* T, upricht CGNV   100 *before* heouene] þe NT   *before* steolen] two PFLS   steolen] *om.* P   102 þe] þeos GLNPST   106 alle togederes] alle (*before* mine) PST   112 ilihtet] beo ilihted NPSV   *before* lihtliche] and VS, þat Ich may P   114 þeose] þeos ilke CFGTV   þet is] *om.* LNPSV   115 hit teleð] *om.* LPST   116 ȝetten] A, ȝet CGNTV   I] bi NP   117–18 Ah ... duhen] T, ah (...) don CNV, ah (...) buhien G, mes il est ⟨...⟩ chaler F, e bien estre puet S, sed (rota,) licet (profundetur) L, ac P   118 *before* hweoles] þe CT   *before* ne] and NPV   121–2 þurh... is] *om.* PST   123 þurh] CF, *om.* GLNPST   tidliche] A, tytliche V, cwicliche C, sone G, lihtliche NFPST, *om.* L   125 schulden] P, schule CGNTV   126 him] him sulf NP   patri] *om.* GSV   127 *before* his] to CNPT   128 seide] seið CLNP   earst] first PV   129 seið] seide TV   þe] AS *only*   130 þe deore] A *only*   131 alle oþre] LNPS, oðre CFGTV   132 ha] A, he CGLNPTV   133 her] *om.* FLPST   134 hire] A, his CGNTV   beodesmon] beodesmen CGV   135 sustren] breþren G, childre T   þolieð] suffre PV   136 þis] þat GNV   talie] spekie T, speke V   137 trukeð] truke GV   ilke] *om.* PT   138 blissen] NL, blisse CFGTV, gladnesse and blis P, glorie S   139 *before* aȝein²] and

PART 6 241

NS buten] wiðuten NPV 142 *after* dreheð] *see 144* In... Ysaie] *om*. NP *after* Ysaie] *see 144* 143 þe] þe | þe A 144 Super... terra] *after* dreheð *142* NP, *after* Ysaie *142* T, *after* blisse *145* C, *after* sorhe *148* S Super... Iacobi] sicome dit la glose sur la Pistle seint Jake F uero] *om*. NS 145 *after* blisse] *see 144* 148 *after* sorhe] *see 144 after* mon] and wummon T 149 uncuððe] uncuðe þeode CP *before* ed] and NLPST ed... resten] to resten ed hame C, at home rest PLST 154 witneð] witnesseþ PTV 155 et cetera] ALV *only* 157 *after* sitte] en le siege de ma maiestee F 160 her is] *trs*. NPT 162 luue] nome CFG þoleden] CT, þolieð GFLNSV 166 selcuð] wonder PV 3ef] þei3 PV pine] pinen CLN 167 blisfule] blisfulliche CNP 168 fuerimus] sumus V, simus P 169 simul] similiter C, similes GV 171 *after* schulen] beon iimped to þe iliknesse N, *sim*. S, ben lyche P 173 buten] wiðuten NPTV 174 witneð] witnesseþ PTV 177 *before* conregnabimus] et CFLT 180 eft] *om*. GLPSV 183 Ah] and NST 185 *from* heaued[1]] *MSS running:* ACFGLNPST 186 *before* He] hwen TS 187 blodes] blodi GP 189 deuleset] God hit wat GN 190 þah... Godd] *om*. F Godd] *del*. C[3], *om*. GLP 193 sic] ita FGS 195–6 Lo... riche] *om*. PST 196–7 wrecches sunfule] G, wrecche sunefule CNT, wrecched synful P, cheitifs peccheours FS, miseri peccatores L 199 ne] A, ne naut CGNPT bune] buggunge NP 200 þeo] A, we CFGLNPST wið lihtleapes] N, wið licht lepes C, wið lichteleapes G, wið lihte scheapes T, wiþ li3th chep P, a legier marchee F, *sim*. S, vili precio L 202 *before* Sein] and NS 203 itoren] ikoruen NP *before* tohwiðeret] and NPS 204 *before* heafdes] and NP, *sim*. S 205 þeose 3ape] wis 3ep P, sages e queintes S riche] CFGLNPST, 3ape A 208 riche] rihtc TS 209 3ef hit] 3if þat hit T, 3if þat P, uor-þi þet hit N, þet hit C, þat GF 210 curtles] kurtel NFP 213 makien] *after* Lauerd PT 215 fearlich] T, fearlac A, ferlich GN, hydous F, espontable S, terribilem L, feorlich C, wonderful P 216 *before* For-þi] and NS meande him] A, mened hym Iob P, mende of him CFGNST, de Iob (...) conqueritur L 217 *after* uniuersa] *cont. to* habet G, *to* sua FS 219 *before* he[1]] uor NPST he[2]] G, þe C, þet NPT, qi FS, qui L 220 þe[1]] his CS fel[2]] *om*. PST *after* fel[2]] is AN 223 *after* wat] þat GN, *sim*. P, hwet C his] *om*. CP 225 totore] P, itorene CGNT, esleu (*transl*. icorene?) F 226 up] *om*. CG banere] baneres GP haueð] ase C(*corr*. C[3])G 227 witneð] *om*. C 229 him] hire T 231 *before* heale] his NS 232 forðeð] GT, parfet F, paremplit S, forðeð AC(*partially erased*), fedeð N 233 his[1]] A, þe CGNT 234 *after* hwa] est qe F, is þet ðet N, est ceo ke S 235 secnesse] sunnes TS 236 *before* Nis] ne mei hit nout so beon N 238 heouene] AL, þe steorren CFGNST 239 *after*

APPARATUS CRITICUS

wreoken] him NP 240 mon] sire F, homme S, homo L, mon oðer wummon NP 241 þe¹] a NP 243 licnesse] ilicnesse GN 244 Iesu] CG, Ihesu Crist FLNPST 245 ure] ure vlessche NLS 247 wes] is TS sunne] sunnen NP, *sim.* L þe] *om.* PST 248 *before* wes] he N, e nekedent (fu) il S, and he P *before* se²] and NPS 249–50 swa . . . þet] AL, *not in other MSS* 252 *after* he] ure Louerd N muchele] A *only* 253 me] *om.* CGT 255 luðerliche] A, bitterliche CGNPT, amerement F, amerement e (. . .) asprement S, amare L greden] ʒeien TG reowöfule] reoufule CGP 257 þe] CT, vus S, þattow P, quem L me] *om.* LPT 258 swiðe¹] A *only* swiðe²] *om.* CS 259 nostre] mee PST 260 on] upon NP seoluen] *om.* PT 262 reowöful] reouful CPT wraðe, sturne] *trs.* T, *sim.* S 265 þer] *om.* CP 266 se] L, þe CFNPT, eni G (*om.* heui) 267 ne] and NPS 269 se] NLP, þe CFGST dunt] duntes NPS 271–2 pini me] NLS, pine CGPT, soefre peine F 272 ant] oðer NF 276 elheowet] A, eliheowed CG, helhewet T, vuele iheowed N, male colouree F, *sim.* S, pallida L 280 murneð] N, murni CGPT *before* wule] he NP 281 mucheles] muche CP 282 þurhwuniende] buten ende N, wiþouten ende P 283 *before* to¹] to nesche ne PST 284 al] AL, *not in other MSS* 285 þe abbat] AL, *not in other MSS* 288 *after* reowfulnesse] merci, pite of heorte N riht] AL, *not in other MSS* 289 uertuz . . . swucche] C, oþer swucche vertuz GNPT 290 wil-ʒeoue] wil geuene G, wel to ʒiuen TS, to ʒiuen P sustren] frend G, childre T 291 beo (. . .) bune] ematur L bune] C, bunie N, luue G, bimeded T, by meded P, deseruie FS beo ʒeoue] largiatur L ʒeoue of grace] ʒeouen of grace N, *sim.* P, ʒiuen grace T, grace donee S 293 swinc] swynken PT, peines e angoisses S 295 swiðe] LN, eauer C, *not in other MSS* he] GN, hit CTP 296 iwarpe] casten C, *sim.* P ant] oþer GLPST 297 mare] CFGNPT, e plus souent S, *om.* AL 299 *after* monie] ancren N 301 hare²] his CG 302 unstrengeð] unstrenc|deð N, vnstrengþes P secleð] secneð NT ane] *om.* FP 303 pinsunge] pinunge NP forwurðeð] bicomen PT 304 leche] leches PFLST 305 *before* salue] hire NS salue] CFGLNS, sonde (*corr. in different hand*) A o Godes half] *om.* NP 306 adhibui] exhibui FN 307 *after* medicine] sche seide PS me neaure] neauer to mi bodi TS 309 of²] *om.* CPT 310 þah] GT, þe þach CFL, þeo, þah N, kar ia seit iceo S, (and þe oþer to,) þeiʒ P *after* nomen] ha GN, *sim.* S 311 *after* hwet] wes GNP 312 *after* makeden] ha GNPT 313 clowes] clou CN 315 as . . . were] *after* ber LNPS 316 of gold] *after* sticcke NP 319 *before* biheold] and NFLPS *before* Hwen] naþeles PS 320 ed] on CG hit mei] *trs.* NT 321 ancreful] A, angerful CT, angresful N, estful G, angri and desirand gretlich P, angoissous F, plein dennui pur le desir S, multum sollicitari L

PART 6

nomeliche religius] and ancre ful nomilche, uor swuch religiun N, *om.*
ST   322 *before* Ypocras] and NP   324 lechecreft] deciples NL   *after* seið] þet CFGNPST   to] FP, of CGNST   325 *before* Procul] Iob P, et Iob xxxi[x]⁰ L   odoramus] adoramus CN, adorabimus S   331 oueral] eauer wel G, tut dis S, eauer (...) oueral T, semper (...) in omnibus L, euere (...) in boþe parties P   334 he] A, me CFGN, mon T, homme S, quis L, men P   ba] A, baðe CGNPT   cheose] cheosen CGN   336 hit seið] ceo dit la Euangeile F, *sim.* S, *om.* LP   338 pinsunges] T, pincunge GP, pinunges C, pinunge N, peines F, trauails e penance S, afflictiones L   342 i gast] igast ACT, en esperit F, al espirit entendant S, spiritualis L, agast G, agest N   343 þeowe] plorer F, languir S   344–5 segge... sumhweat] *before* Of² *344* NPS   344 nu] her CGST   346 *before* nawt] and NS   347 to] uorte smurien mide N, *sim.* PS   348 þe] *om.* CGT   bohten] FL, brochten CGNPST   349 mine... sustren] *om.* LPST   sustren] frend G   350 Meraht] L, Maracht C, Marach F, Marah G, Mararaht N, Marath PT   351 Merariht] LN, Merarit C, Mararith G, Mariath P, Marith T, *om.* F   353 understonden] to understonden GN   354 wið] L, in CFNST, þorou3 P, *om.* G   355 *before* bitternesse] ine muchele NS   356 ure Lauerd] God PL   359 mearci] mede PST   360 fondunges] fondunge CG   361 Marie, Marie] Marie CLP   362 þe²] *om.* CG   363 þe-3et i] þeo 3et i C, ceaux vnqore par F, illi adhuc in L, þa-3et te T, þe-3et N, adonc onkore S, þe G   364 wreastlin] wresten CGN   366 Pharaones] hParaones A   370 folhin (...) efter] uoluwen efter þe N, folowe þe P, vous siwera F, uus pursuira S, foleȝen him efter C   371 hwi] L, hu CFGNT   sker] CF, siker GLNPST   372 þe an ouercumen] ouercumen þat an GN   373 i¹] *om.* PST   *after* heouene] en atente de cele grant ioie F   ennu] ende TS, endynge P   374 weorre] *om.* GP   377 ant... pes] *om.* GS   378 edhalt] wiþholdeþ PT   379 ha luuieð] ham luuieð G, ham luues TS   380 euch] eueriche NP   381 þe¹] *om.* CNT   383 *before* 3eme] her GFN, good PS, 3eorne T, (attendite) diligenter L   sustren] frenð G, childre T   384 swetnesse] swotnesse CGN   385 bohten] brou3tten PS   swote] swete PT   386 beoð] is PT   swote] swete PT   swotnesse] swetnesse PT   387 *before* Maries] þreo NS   buggeð] bou3tten PST   388 swotnesse] swetnisse PT   389–92 to²... is] *om.* C   391 smechles] smelles T, par sauour S, sapore L   Godd] FT, goð G, god N, bien S, eorum qui Dei sunt L   392 to] into PT   *before* ifinden] schal NT   394 *before* þe] þet is CFGNPT   þe... þolie] þolemodelich þoly PT, soffrez (...) paciaument S   395 *before* he] and PST   he schal (...) habben] þou schalt (...) haue P, vus auerez S   396 Anna... Lauerd] Tobie seiþ P, seint Thobie dit S   398 ibeo] A, beo CGNPT   402 gan] A, *after* chulle CGNPT   404 swotnesse] swetnesse PT   406–7 Aromaz...

APPARATUS CRITICUS

thuris] *om.* CPST   406 me makeð] he maked GF   ah] L, and GFN
407 Ex . . . thuris] *om.*   GL   408 na] nan (*after* swotnesse) CN
swotnesse] swetnesse PT   409 swetnesse] swotnesse C   410 euch]
eueriche NP   413 non . . . recedentes] *om.* G   414 *before* Maries]
þreo NS   *before* þeose] þet is N, ceo sunt FS, þat spelleþ (bitternesse) P
415 þeo . . . Lauerd] *om.* FP   416 þe strecheð him] lui font entendre
sei S   is] *before* ismered GNP   417 makeð him] machieð him G, lui
font S   *from* Ant] *MSS running:* ACFLNPST   418 Maries] ðe
meidenes N, a maydens P   419 for] *om.* FS   420 Ich (. . .) habbe
iseid] A, is (. . .) iseid CFLNT   423 cader] cradel PT   424 þis]
his CF   425 *before* I] and NS   as] A, wes C, was ase NFLST   þe]
om. CT   427 3e¹] CN, vnquore F, 3if TS, forte L, now (þou may
answere) P   *after* me] and seist N, and saie P   ba] boðe NPT
429 ba] boðe NT   ihale] hole PT   430 *before* wem] wiðute NS   his]
þise TFS   433 mine . . . sustren] *om.* T, *v.rr.* PS   þe . . . walde] *om.*
PST   is] *om.* ST   435 *after* hwil] þet CNT   437 *before* ispeken]
deuant S, supra L   438 snakereð] NT, smakereð C, veit snequerant F,
vous gueitent S, (mordere vos) nitens L, (wil) snacche P   440 þeose
heardschipes] L, þis herdschipe CFNST, wo þat 3ou comeþ P
440–1 ant . . . ipaiet] et contente L, e ne faces force S, *not in other MSS*
442 bigurde] igurde CN, gurde T   443–7 uuel . . . þet] *om.* ST
443–6 þet is . . . dede] AL *only*   443 þet²] scandalum L
444 *after* idon] occasionem prebens ruyne, hoc est L   445 þrefter]
A *only   before* wið²] uel L   446 on hire, on oþre] de aliquo L   ant
(. . .) ec] uel L   447 ant] mes S, sed L   448 bliðe iheortet] T,
bliðe in heorte CF, bliðe on heorte N   449 ant wipeð] A *only   before*
cuchene] ðe NT   450 toward] versus L (ad Ma), up to þe CFN, sus en
S, to þe T   swete] *om.* PST   451 *before* kimeð] *see 452*   452 ha
seið] A, *before* leapinde CFNST, *before* kimeð *451* P, *om.* L
452–4 ouerleapinde . . . dunes] CFNPST, *om.* AL   454 o] CFN, i
TS, ouer P   *before* tofuleð] and NS   tofuleð] N, þe fuleð C, defules T
455 totreode] C, totret NT   *before* tuki] and NST   456 *before* ifinde]
ant CNT, *sim.* F   ifinde] N, ifinden A, finde CT   457 munt] CNS,
munz TF   *before* dunes²] ant þe NS   458 þe beoð] arn þe TS
459 leof] CFLS, seolf ANT, *om.* P   *before* ouerleapeð] he AP   for] pur
FS, pre L   459–60 ne mahte nawt] ne purreient pas F, non possent L,
ne muhte heo nout N, eus ne porrient pas S   459 ne] CPT, ne ne A,
uor ne NLS   460 *before* he] þereuore NPS   461 *before* forbereð]
and NP   462 lanhure] CF, hure and hure N, hure T, ci S, forsan L
465 schaweð] CNT, mustre il S, moustrent F, ostendunt L
466–7 þulliche . . . of] L (*om.* gode), þullich dun wes þe gode Pawel
CFNPT, vn de ces granz monz (. . .), si fu seint Poel S   466 þulliche]
þullich C, swuch N, swich a PT   467 ant] AL, þe CFNST

PART 6 245

eadmodliche] AL *only* 471 deadlicnesse] mortification F, deaðlicnesse N, deþ liknesse P, la semblance de la mort S, similitudinem mortis L 472 þe] C, ceaux qe F, þeo þet N, he þat T, cil ke S, qui L, þat P doð] dos TLPS ha] he PST pruuieð] preoues TLPS us] A *only* hare] his PT, quam habet L 474 *after* operis] *see 475–6* 475 after heard] þet NFST soð] AL *only after* luue] ne NFST *before* Amor] item P, idem S 475–6 Amor . . . reddit] *after* operis *474* FPST 476 fatilia reddit] *trs.* FN þolieð . . . wummen] þoleþ man and womman PST 476–7 ant . . . luue] *om.* NP 477 for] *om.* LST Ant²] *om.* PST 478 *after* oþre] luuen NL swete] *om.* N 479 of sunne] L, fause e orde de pecche S, sunne NT, summe C, a ascuns F, þat is fals P 480 hearde] AL *only* 481 þeh] þauh N, nepurquant F 483 *before* meaneð] he CFNPST 483–5 ant . . . swete] *after* secnesse *487* F 483 me] his schrift-fader PS 484–5 Al . . . swete] L, *after* secnesse *487* CNPST 486 me] his schrift-fader P, lui S pinene sarest] *conj.;* wiuene sarest AT, monne sarest CN, plorant angoissousement F, mout tendrement S, *om.* LP forȝet] CT, haueð (. . .) uorȝiten N, lad oblie F, obliuioni tradidit L, had forȝeten PS 487 *after* secnesse] *see 483–5, 484–5* 488 me] a soen confessour S, *om.* P 490–1 ȝef . . . þeofðe] *om.* LPS 490 eani] eut CT 491 *before* þeof] ðe NT ec] *om.* CFST 492 wummon] wimmen TF þoleð] þolied C, þolien TF i] C, of N, *om.* T, *v.r.* P 493 *before* strengðe] his NS, þe TF, þat P 494 *before* Luuie] and NS ure ahne] LP, uren CFNTS *after* ure ahne] god NP, *sim.* S 496 as . . . þruppe] AL *only before* we] þet NF

PART 7

1 *from* Seinte] *MSS running*: ACFLNPST *after* heardschipes] and NPS 2 ant] *om.* CS *before* licomliche] alle NP 3 Exercitio] CN, exercitatio FLPST 6 et cetera] LP, infra CF, item T, *om.* N 7 et cetera] L, infra CF, item PT, *om.* N 9 *before* þah] and NPS alle pine] A, al þe pine CFPST, alle þe pinen N 10 *before* þah] and NPS 14 nawt] A *only* 15 þe¹] AC *only* spitelsteaf] spade NP sulh] plouȝ PT 19 lokeð] CLP, loki ANT, gardereit S makeð] CFLP, makie NT, fereit S 21 mong] loue PST woreð] N, empeire F, weorreð CLT, ablindeþ PS 22 ha (. . .) mei] ho (. . .) muhen TS cnawen] P, icnawen CNT 23 makieð] FS, makeð CP, makes T, facit L 25 twa] *om.* CFL 26 togederes] *om.* PST earre] A, forme CNT, primere FS, primum L, first P 27 wori heorte] CN, le queor soille F, cor turbidum L, weari herte T, le quer non cler e la entente corompue S, wleche hert P *before* al] ant CFNPT *after* uuele] *see 28* 28 Apostolus] (*after* uuele *27*) sicome dit Seint Poul FS Item] *om.* FP 30 For-þi . . . sustren] for T

to] uorte NP   34 oðer¹] A, ant CFNT, *om*. LS   *before* mon] ant CFN
35 seið] *after* Austin NPT   37 ha luuieð (...) luuieð] N, ha luueð (...)
luueð C, he louep (...) louep PFST   38 ha luuien] N, ha luuie C, he
luue TFS, loue P   hit] *om*. P   39 *before* þe²] and NPS   45 hire]
his PT   heo] he P   edhalt] wiþholdep PT   46 ha] he P   hire]
hym P   nawt of] *trs*. CT   50 ure alde feader] A, primo parente nostro
L, ure fader CFNPST   55 *before* sawle] þe NP   seruið] C, serueð
NP, serues T, sert FS, seruit L   ȝet²] *before* He NP, *om*. CFT
57 wrecches] wrecch|ces A   59 *after* leofmon] cest Seinte Iglise F
60 mine... sustren] *om*. T   61 a¹] *om*. CT   a²] N, *om*. CPT   gentil
poure] AL *only*   62 he] and NP   63 prophetes] prophes A
69 inwið] wiðinnen NP   71 *before* ofte] and NST   72 *before*
sucurs] and NP   *before* help] and NS   hehe] *om*. FL   73 *before* Heo]
and PFS   as on unrecheles] C , as an unrecheles (e *expunct. after* s *of*
recheles*) T, ase on unrecheleas þing N, as reccheles P, ausi come rien ne lui
fust F, quasi non curans L, ausi nonchalereuse S   75 *before* schawde]
and NPS   76 þe¹] he PT   *before* spec] and NP   77 swoteliche]
A, swetelich CNPT   *before* deade] þe CNPS   80 ne heold nawt] A,
ne halp nawt CNPT, rien ne valut F, (de hoc toto) non curauit L, ne tint ele
a rien S   81 hoker wunder] wunderlich hoker N, escharnissable
merueille F, derisibile mirandum L, trop grant merueille S   82 þurh]
om. PST   *before* luue] wiþ PST   85 efter al þi weane] AL *only*
86 þet] þis CFNPT   arudde] so rede PT, *sim*. S   90 þe... dead]
CF, talis facti mortem L, þen ilke deade deaðe NT, after my deþ PS   þes]
þe TS   91 arudde] redd PT   alle] *om*. PST   92 *before* islein]
siðen T, þan PS   þah] *after* miracle CN   95 *after* Iesu] Crist NLPS
99 to] for to CNT   100 His²] þis NL   101 leoue] *om*. PST
102 *before* nearow] and NP   103 efter monies wene] CF, after monnes
wene T, as by mannes wene P, efter þet me weneð N, sicut putant homines
L, ausi com nus quidom S   set] CN, iset T, sist F, seit S, posito L
104 naueð] ne had PF   *before* siden] none NP   105 alle] *om*. PST
108 *after* tuum] et Psalmista: Scuto... nos (*see fn.*) C(*del.* C²)F(et *om*.)NT,
sim. P   109 *before* cruneð] hit NPS   110 *after* uoluntatis] *cont. to*
tue N, *to* coronasti T, *to* nos FLPS   111 us] *after* icrunet NP
112 uoluit] uoluit ipse F, ipse uoluit S   113 *after* us] fram helle PT, de
la mort de enfern S   114 bineomen] bitaken PT   euch] euerich NP
116 wið] mid CN   heorte] precioso L, precius S, *om*. PT
117 ofdrahen] drawen PT   118 sare] CP, deore NFLST   *from* I
scheld] *MSS running:* ACFGLNPST   ant] *om*. GLP   119 wes i þis]
auoit en ceste F, auoit Iesu Crist en soen S, wes Ihesus Cristes P
120 þe²] his GPS   121 Eft... reisun] an oþer half G, icist escu
si est en Seinte Eglise en haut pendu, e ne mie sanz reson. Car S, also P,
om. L   122 hehe] *om*. PST   126 *before* to²] and NS

127 openliche] *om.* GL   128 iferen] felawes PT   129 bitweone²]
bi| A   130 deore] *om.* PST   131 þeos] alle þise PFS, ham alle N
132 fere] feolawe NP   134 of Giwene honden] N, of þe Iewen honden
P, in Gywene honden C, i Giwerie honden G, of Giwene hond T (Giwene
corr. from Giwriene), des mains des diables F, de la Gieuerie de enfern S,
om. L   135 ne dude] *after* fordede CT   his fere] oðer C, anoþer P,
autre S   138 aȝein cumen] *trs.* NP   141 hwen] hwen-se CGN
ham] to him NS   143 cetera] infra CFG   143-4 multis
amatoribus] *trs.* GLS   144 ȝeiȝeð] A, crie F, clamat L, seið CGNPT
145 unwreaste] unwresteliche NP, unwrestli T   148 her] CGT, her is
N, is (*after* wunder) P, veez ici F, nunc audi L, poez vus ci oer S
149 leof] leofmon NP   mid] wiþ PT   *before* to] *see 150*
150 aȝein] *before* to *149* NPT   151 (bitweonen) bituhhen] C,
bitwenen GNPT   Godes neoleachunge] coniugium Dei et anime L,
knowleching of (. . .) God and his lemman P   neoleachunge] CNT,
nehunge G, renouelure F, conisance S   152 neoleachunge] CNT,
nehunge G, renouelure F, coniugium L, knowleching P, conoissance S
wif] femme despucelee F, coruumptam L, femme corompue S   153 wif]
la depucelee F, corrupta L, femme corompue S   in integrum] gentes in
integrum CF, gen's integre P, genus integrum ST   154 meiðhad] A,
maidhod G, meidehod N, maidenhad CPT   155 *after* luue] þat . . .
child (*see fn.*) T, *sim.* PS   157 him] *before* þis¹ GN, hit CT
158 se] *om.* PST   *before* healen] ⟨ne⟩ C(*del.* C³)GT   160 makeð] A,
maked G, makede CFLNST, *v.r.* P   162 to] *om.* CNT   cluppunges]
cluppinge GPS   164 suleð] fuleð NT, yfiled P   *after* þridde] beð
NFST   halheð] NT, sanctifia F, dona uertuz a S, healed G, halðeð CP
ba] boðe NPT   þe] þeos CGN   166 luueð] luuede GL   *after*
moder] deð NPT, *sim.* FGS   hire] þe P, *om.* CGT   171 i] inwiþ PT
mid] wiþ PT   172 to] uorte NP   173-4 in . . . munegunge] *om.*
GN   175 *before* þe¹] of CFGNPST   licome] bodi NP
177 totweamde] totwinnede GT   182 ȝetten] ȝet NPT
185 to¹] forto NP   187 þinge] NT, de toute rien F, omnium
rerum L, þing CG, kyng P, homme ke onkes fust S   kinge] king CFGP
188 weolie wisest] CGN, peritorum sapientissimus L, de touz le plus sage
F, wisest P, li plus sages S, weore wisest T   189 þinge freoest] CGT,
le plus franc et le plus larges F, monne ureoest N, hominum liberalissimus
L, man freest P, li plus larges hom e li plus franc S   190 he] *om.* GP
191 swotest ant] *om.* CPT   192 ifinden] finde PT   193 hire
halde] T, *trs.* CN, holden hem clene P, hire habbe GF, *sim.* S   193-4 ah
. . . heste] AL *only*   þe heste] que precellit L   196 buggen hire? Hu?]
CFG, buggen hire A, quomodo potest emi L, do seie hwu N, dites coment
vus la uolez doner S, hu T   197 for luue] CFGLNPST, *om.* A
198 *after* þin] luue NLS   hire] hit CG   203 schalt seggen] maht

nempne T, may (. . .) nempny P, *sim.* S *after* 3eoue] þe GLNPST 204 *before* kinedomes] wultu GP 205 *before* makie] Ich chulle NFPS 206–7 na ... þe¹] CFG(*after* þe² 207)NP(*with* scheme *for* sweame)ST, *om.* A 207 *after* þe²] *see* 206–7 208 ec] A *only* 209 swuch] CGNT, hwuch A *after* 3eouen] þe PST 210 unmeteliche] unimeteliche GNT Creasuse] A, Cressuse CT, Cressus P, Cres. F, du riche rei Cresi S, Crisis L, Cresoles G, Kresules N 211 þe ... richest] AL *only* 212 me] N, he CGPT 213 iweiet] A *only* 216 ahte] hadd PT 217 alle somet] al somen T, al þis GP, alle þeos þinges somed NLS bodi] bode N, ofre F ne beoð] nis GPT 218 anewil] wode PST 220 to dealen] CGNT, to todelen P, todealen A 221 ba] boþe PT þer] CGLNST, la F, þe P, *om.* A 222 abuten] A, buten CGT, wiðuten NP 224 muchele] *om.* FP biheue] goode PT 227–8 se heh] se hech king C, si grant rei et (. . .) si haut S, tam nobilis (. . .) tam alti L, so hei3e þinge P 229 mahe] mahte GP 232 in] CFGLNST, ant A 234 he seið] CT, *before* to GFNPS 235 heorte] heorten NP 236 luue] hert PST 240 hat (. . .) cald] FP, *trs.* CGNST 241 *after* bute] 3if NP 243 *from* Nu] *MSS running:* ACFNPST 244 *before* Forte] and NS 246 Regum iiiᵒ] A, (*before* En) in Regum FT, en le Liuere des Reis S, 3 Regum xvijᵒ L, *not in other MSS* 251 tospreat] tospradde CF, spredde P, spreades T his earmes] *after* ow 252 CFN, *sim.* T 252 *after* ow] *see 251* 253 Godd almihti] ure Lauerd Godd almihti TS, oure Lorde P twa] *om.* CFPT 254 gederin] C, gederinde NPT 255 hire] þe poure wummone N, paupercula L, þe pouere womman in Sarept P, la femme de Sarepte S 256 gederin] C, gederinde NPT 257 *after* þet] feu F, ignem L 259 Iesu ure Lauerd] C, ure Louerde NF, Ihesu Crist PL, Iesu Crist ure Lauerd T, *sim.* S 260 wið] mid CN 261 deore] seinte S, *om.* LNP 262 earre] C, auantdiz F, predicta L, herde N, *om.* ST 263 ontende] C, alumeez F, accensas L, enbrasez S, ontendet T, ontenden ʼouʼ (ou *interl. in paler ink*) N, tendyng fyre P tis] *om.* PST 266 hit] ceu feu S, *sim.* F 267 as ... seide] *om.* NP 273 oðer] and NP 277 bitacnede] bitacnes TS duden] T, makeden N, bude C, offrirent F, optulerunt L, donerent S 278 þet] *om.* LT *before* long] his NFS long] sore NT 284 consumatum] A, consummatum CFLNPST *before* al²] and NP 289 wummon (. . .) mon] CF, *trs.* LNST 292 *before* 3e] and NS 293 *after* teacheð] ou NS 296 drunch] C, drincken N, drinke T 298 drunch] drynk PT sunnen] sunne TFPS 300 forte] to PT 303 *before* ha] uor NLPS 305–6 Alle ... ah] A, omne malum mihi fecit nec eum diligere tenebar, sed L, *not in other MSS* 306 ham] hym PL 312 Bute] bute 3if NP 318 *after* mon] oðer wummon TS 319 his (. . .) his] hire (. . .) hire (. . .) oðer his T 320 3ef] C, þauh NT 321 þes twa] A *only* ant] ou F, uel L *before*

PART 7

heouenlich] of NT 322 þe tweire] A, duorum L, þeos tweire CFNST 325 *before* griðful] and NFS 326 *after* oþre] þinges NS 329 þerwið] CT, þere-mide N, to A 330 hit] A, *sim.* L, Ich CFNST 331 his] hire T 332 god[1]] *om.* LPST 333 *before* þu] and NS 334 *after* mon] oðer wummon T, *sim.* S 336 *before* leasse] wel TS 337 is] L, þet is CFNPST 338 luue] CFLNST, þing A, *sim.* P 338–9 of (...) leaskeð] A, de (...) diminuit L, menuse S, trukeð C, trukie N, guerpist F, manges T 341 meistre] mestresse F, magistram L hat] biddeþ PT 342 Ich[2]] CN(*after* 3e)T, *om.* FLPS 345 i] L, o CFNST, of P 347 don] *after* mei CNT 349 þu wult smiten] A, percutere vis L, wult þu smiten CFNPST 350 *before* nis] uor NLS halde] holdeþ PFT 352 quicquam facere] *trs.* NS 353 egressus fueris] egrediaris T, ingrediaris LS illinc] FN, illuc CLS, illic P 354 wes inne] wunede C, wunede inne N 357 heole wið] wiþhele PT ah] ant CFN *after* teleð] hire NPST 358 *from* que] *MSS running:* AC[3]FLNPST (*missing text in C supplied by C[3]*) 360 *before* o] cweð he N, fet il S, he seide P, quasi diceret L 361 inwardliche] treuuelike C[3]ST leueð... luuieð] A, *sim.* N (*with* ileueð *for* leueð), louen and leuen C[3]S, *sim.* L, luues and leues T, louen PF 362 *after* alswa] as A 364 Apostolus] et Apostolus FPT, et Apostolus ad Corinthios C[3], et Corinthiorum ij° L, e Seint Poel dit S *after* audiuit] *cont. to* ascendit P, *to* diligentibus te FS 364–5 et cetera] *om.* C[3]FST 365 3e... elleshwer] *om.* C[3]P 365–6 mine... sustren] *om.* C[3]LPST 368 *after* directione] cordis C[3]L id... regulatione] *om.* F, *after* cordis S Exprobratio malorum] *om.* FS Exprobratio] exprobacione C[3]PT 369 *after* suum] *cont. to* creditus N, *to* cum eo [*for* Deo] P, *to* spiritus eius C[3]FT *from* þis] *MSS running:* AFLNPST 370 me ah] mon ah TF, *sim.* N, deuez vuz S, me hat A, precipiuntur L do] A, makie NT 371 ihalden] A, iwust N, ykept P, iloket T

PART 8

1 *from* Biuoren] *MSS running:* AFLNT 2 riwlen] riwle TF 4 þurh mi meistrie] per presumptionem L 5 Riwle] riwlen NF ah] A, and NFLT 3et] *om.* FL 11 leasse] A, lesse deinte N, te lasse T *from* ne] *MSS running:* AFLNP(*with heavily-abridged text*)T 12 as... beoð] *om.* FLP *before* breðren] leawude N 13 *from* Midwinter] *MSS running:* AFL(V[1](*fragmentary*) *only*)NPT 13–19 Midwinter... Andrews Dei] *items numbered in AFT only, above the line in A* 15 he] N, it PT 18 *from* þe Natiuite] *MSS running:* ACFLNPT *after* Natiuite] beate Marie L, of hir P 19 *before* A3ein] and NL þeose] T, þeos (*corr.* C[2]) C, þeos dawes NFP, festiuitates predictas L

APPARATUS CRITICUS

20 neomeð] takeþ PT   22 isette] iseide TL   25 *after* Dei] þes . . . read⟨en⟩ (*see fn.*) *marg.* C²   26 þe²] *om.* CNPT   26–7 ant . . . dahes] CFNT, *sim.* LP, *om.* A   28 nawt eoten] L, *sim.* P, ʽeten' nout N, eote nan CFT   feasten] A, vesteð CT, iuneretz F, ӡe schulen uesten NP, ieiunare habetis L   29–30 hwen . . . blodletene] A, ⟨. . .⟩ infirmitatem aute⟨m⟩ et fleobotomiam a ieiunio excus⟨. . .⟩ pacientes L, *not in other MSS* 31–2 3e . . . ouer-feble] Solum . . . fieble (*see fn.*) F   31 nawt] numquam L, *not in other MSS*   for] A, i CNT(*interl.*)   33–4 Noðeles . . . walde] *om.* T   34 haueð iþuht] semble F   35 ne] T, ant CFNP   36 gest] CF, gestes TNP, *sim.* L   37 uncundelukest] N, uncumelukest CT, mest (. . .) vncomelich P, plus mescheant F, non conuenit L   38 al] *om.* LT   41 þe ӡete] owre ӡate TF, vos L   42 *after* hearloz] pro . . . eis (*see fn.*) L   42–3 meadlese nurð] A, demesuree noise F, meaðlese nowse T, meðlease muð N, medlaseschipe C 43 letten oðerhwile] *trs.* CP   45 lude] AN, *not in other MSS* 46 ba] boðe NT   sundrede] sundreð CF   46–7 beoð inumen ow] C, estes pris F, habbeð inumen ou NT, elegistis L, han chosen P   48 i] CFNT, *om.* A   53 Marthe] CFNT, Marie A   56 entremeatin] A, intermittere L, entremetin hire NCT, se (. . .) entremettre F   *before* ӡef] and NP   57 *after* Writ] *see* 57–9   57–9 Contra Symonem . . . opus, et cetera] AL, contra Symonem . . . opus operata est in ⟨me⟩ *marg. after* Writ 57 C², *not in other MSS*   60 meaðfulliche] A, gnedeliche C(*corr.* C²)NT, escharsement F, *v.r.* L   hire to] *trs.* C(*corr.* C²)T 62 meaðfulliche] A, naruliche C(*corr.* C²)NT, estreitement F 63 nawt] N, nan CT   64 schraden] schiue T, victum L, uesture F 65 riche] CFNT, chirch A   67 ne wilni ha nawt] A, ne wilni naut C, ne wilnen nout N, ne wilne nan T, ne desirrez pas F, non concupiscatis L 68 grediure] N, plus coueitouse F, gredire T, gredure C, gnedure A 68–9 For-hwon . . . beo] A, beo gredinesse CN(*with* ðeo *for* beo)T, si couoitise est F, quia (ex radice) auaricie L   69 of þet gederunge] A *only* 73 Wummen] wepmen T   ant² . . . meidnes] AC²(*interl. in* C *after* for ow 74)L *only*   ant nomeliche] seu ipse L   74 cumeð iswenchet] A, beoð iswunken CT, sunt (. . .) travaillez F, habbeð iswunken N, aliquid (. . .) operentur L   74–5 oðer . . . hit] AC² *only*   75–6 wið . . . herbarhin] AC², *sim.* L, *not in other MSS*   76 herbarhin] herberhe C² 77–81 Na . . . leaue] L, na . . . drinke (*see fn.*) TC(biforen ow *om.*; *alt.* C² *to* Na . . . leaue (*see fn.*))FN(*with* bute ӡif *for* bute)   78 general oðer spetial] AL *only*   general²] *conj. Salu*   78–9 as . . . oþre¹] A *only* 79 nane oþre] aliquam L   80 his] *om.* L   80–1 me seið] quia dicitur *before* Liht L   81 for . . . boden] A *only*   82–3 Ihwear . . . scandle] AC², Non . . . generari L (*see fn.*), *not in other MSS*   83 þurh . . . untuhtle] A *only*   *after* scandle] ne wrah . . . sunne (*see fn.*) C² 84 gode men] A, gode freont C(*alt. to* treowe men C²)FNT   84–5 ah

... wel] C², hwen ... nede (*see fn.*) CFNT 86 þurh ... wordes] AC², per verba sua ⟨ina⟩nia vel aliquem gestum inordinatum L, *not in other MSS* 87 ne²] *om.* CNT leasse (...) mare] *trs.* FL *after* mare] naut ... gingiure (*see fn.*) C(*del.* C²)FNT *before* Neode] muche C(*del.* C²)FNT 88–9 gode ... wummen] C², bonis et ⟨ho⟩nestis L, owre leoueste freont C(*del.* C²)FNT(*with* leue *for* leoueste) 90 mine ... sustren] *om.* T bute ... driue] AC², nisi summa necessitate vrgente L, *not in other MSS* 90–1 ant ... reade] AL *only* 92 lihtliche] A, for nanes weis C (lihtliche oðer *add. after* for C²), ne nanes weies TFN 93 nawt] A *only* Marthe suster] AC² *only* griðfullnesse] A, griðfulnesse CNT 96 hit] A *only* 97 Nu þenne] A, nu þah CT(þenne *del.*, *repl.* þah *interl.*), mes nepurquant F, þauh N, verumptamen L 101 þet is chepilt] *om.* L chepilt] chapmon T 101–2 þet² ... biʒete] AC²L *only* 101 þet is, buð] þe buð C², emens L 103–4 þing ... sullen] AC², si quid tamen man⟨ibus ...⟩ L, *not in other MSS* 103 *after* mei] wel C² 104 *after* sullen] þah ... wordes (*see fn.*) C² 104–5 Hali ... honden] A *only* 106 deore dehtren] A *only* 107–8 ne³ ... cyrograffes] A *only* 108 ne¹] A, nient F, nawt T, ne nout ne vnderuo ʒe N 108–9 neode oðer] AC²L, *not in other MSS* 110 vuel] *interl. in paler ink* N, *om.* T 111 mon] wepmon T 113 *before* wummon] honeste F cleane] bone (...) et honeste L 114 wepmen] A, nan mon CFNT seoð] A, sið C, veit F, isihð N, seo T ham] T, him C, nenne mon NF 115 clað] cloðes NP 118 *before* linnene] nan CFNP linnene clað] NP, linnene CT 119 *before* hwase²] ant CFN 120–3 swa ... leaue] AL(*fragmentary*) *only* 123 ne beore] ne bere ʒe N, nec induatis L, ne were T, ne wereþ P 124 hire] ou N(*interl. in paler ink*)P, *sim.* L *before* ileadet] ileðered ne N, (cum stragulis) nodulatis vel L 125 *after* leaue] *see 130* 125–6 Nohwer ... keorue] A *only* 127 luðere] A, feole CFNT 127–9 temptatiuns ... read] A *only* 130 leste ... wurse] A, ne forte deterius inde contingat L (*after* leaue *125*), *not in other MSS* 131 i winter] ALP *only* meoke] A *only* *after* warme] prout necessitas requirit L 132–3 ant ... werien] A, *sim.* L, *not in other MSS* 134–5 Ischeoed ... bedde] A, *sim.* L, *not in other MSS* 137–9 ah ... here] A, *sim.* L, *not in other MSS* 140 ʒef ... wimpelles] *om.* T ant ... wullen] AC² *only* 141 cappen] huueles qe len appele kappes F ant ... veiles] *om.* T hwite ... veiles] A, ⟨... si⟩ue nigro L, blake ueilles C(oder hwite oðer *add.* C² *before* blake)FN 141–7 Ancren ... heaued] AC²L(*fragmentary*)V(*from* werien *144 only*), *not in other MSS* 142–3 Ah ... sum] A, sum seið C² 144 *from* werien] *MSS running:* ACFLNPTV 145 ane] V, of heuet C² 146 wrihen] C²V, wreon A 147–52 Wrihen¹ ... angelos] AC²V, velet ... hominum (*see fn.*) L, *not in other MSS* 148 Eue sunfule] A, sunfule Eue C²V 149 on earst] A,

APPARATUS CRITICUS

erst C², furst V   150 þe Apostle] V, Seinte Pauel C²   152–4 Hwi
... Apostle] AC² *only*   153 iwimplet, openest] al .. þah (*see fn.*) C²
154 þe²] C, *om.* A   sist] isist C²   þe Apostle] Seinte Pauel C²   ʒef ...
hudest] A *only*   154–7 Ah ... wimplunge] AC², et ... clausam (*see fn.*
to oðerhwiles *160*) L, *not in other MSS*   156 wel-itund windowe] A, fenestram clausam L, þi parlures þurl C²   157–60 Toʒeines ...
oðerhwiles] A, contra ... obseruatis (*see fn.*) L, *not in other MSS*
160 *after* isehen] of alle þat hire cumen to T   nawt] nan CT
163 *from* Ring] *MSS running:* ACFLNPT   164–5 A ... werien] A, in estate vti poteritis superpelliciis si libeat L, *not in other MSS*
166 Eauer ... werkes] *om.* L   doð] A, don CNPT   167–70 Ne ...hettren] *om.* T   167–8 bute ... leaue] AC² *only*   168 ne huue] A, nec tenas L, *not in other MSS*   168–9 blodbinde ... laz] laqueos de serico nec similia L   168 blodbinde] A, blodbinden CN, bendes F
169 ne ... leaue] AC², *sim.* L, *not in other MSS*   170 chirche claðes] vestes proprias et ecclesias⟨t⟩icas L   *after* claðes] *see 220–5*   swuch] AC² *only*   171 *after* leaue] ou de vostre prelat F   171–82 na ... werkes]
AL(*fragmentary; text from* A *mon 174 onwards*) *only*   174 *before* A mon] in Vitas Patrum L   178 *before* Na] ergo L   181 *before* Veine] quia L   182–5 Criblin ... neode] A *only*   186 ow] A *only*   eauer] A *only*   187 ant¹ ... is] AC², *sim.* L, *not in other MSS*   188 *from* As]
MSS running: ACFLNPTV   188–9 As ... idel] Ocium ... oci⟨osas⟩ (*see fn.*) L   longe ... allunges] AV, allunge C², *not in other MSS*
191 *after* he²] þe swike T   192 iʒemen] C, ʒeme T, attendre (de) F, ihwulen NV   192–3 Of ... fondunge] multa enim mala fec⟨it ...⟩ L
193 fondunge] fondinges TV   196 *after* stinkeð] *see 202–3*
197 *from* Ancre] *MSS running:* ACFLNPT   198–201 Hire ... learen] *om.* T   198 oðer] A, lute CFN   199 pliht] dute CN, doute F   among ... oðer] A *only*   200–1 þah ... learen] AC², *sim.* L, *not in other MSS*   202–3 ʒe ... leaue] *after* stinkeð *196* CF
202 ne writen] *om.* CLP   204 oðer ... ischauen] AC²(*after* heaued *205*), et ⟨...⟩ si libeat L, *not in other MSS*   204–5 fowr siðen] (*after* ʒer *205*) fiftene siþes PT   205 *after* ʒer] *see 204–5*   to ... heaued] *om.* PT
after heaued] *see 204*   205–6 beo ... leouere] A, hwa-se ... heauet (*see fn.*) C², vel ⟨... sup⟩ra aures tondi ⟨...⟩ v⟨olu⟩erit L, *not in other MSS*
206 as ofte] foure siþes PT   206–7 ant² ... blod] *om.* C   206 ʒef ... oftre] AC², *sim.* L, oftere ʒif neod is NT, *sim.* FP   þe] A, hwo-so NT
207 þer-buten] A, þer-wiðuten N, wiðuten T   *before* ilete] ⟨al greiðe⟩ A (*del., poss. by A scribe*)   208 na þing] *after* dahes CFT   þe] A, les F, þeo N, *om.* C(þeo *suppl.* C²)PT, per L   þet ... greueð] þet ou greue N, vnde grauari poteritis L   209 meidnes] seruanz T, seruaunt P
210 ofte] *alt. to* oftere C²   211 sare] A, sari CNT   211–12 þah ... ancre] A *only*   217–18 ant ... þinges] A *only*   218–19 Nes ...

PART 8 253

licwurðe] A, *sim.* L, *not in other MSS* 218 pouerte] paupertas voluntaria L 219 unorneschipe] inornatus exterius L 220–5 Vnderstondeð . . . þuften] AC²(*after* claðes *170*), *sim.* L, *not in other MSS* 220 eauer] A, sane L, *not in* C² þet] *before* of C² nan nis] A, nis nan C² 221 *before* heast] simpliciter L þet¹] AL, for alle ha C² 222 for-hwon . . . iwist] C², bene tamen regulam interio⟨rem⟩ custodiatur L 222–3 as . . . frumðe] *om.* L 223 þeos] A, ant C² hwer-se] A, hwer-se euer C² 223–4 oðer . . . skile] *om.* L 224–5 efter . . . þuften A, efter þet ha mei ase þuften best seruin þe leafdi Riwle C², *om.* L 225–6 ah . . . wundre] A, verumptamen sine hiis exterioribus con⟨t⟩ingit quoque interiorem periclitari L, *not in other MSS* 228 eauer þe leaue] A, þe eauer leaue CF, þat leaue euer T, ðet bileaue euer N 229 driueð neod] A, *trs.* CFT, hwon hit is nede N ful . . . tiffunge] A, non (. . .) exquisite ornata L, ful unorne CNT, bien ledes F *before* wiðuten] *see 229–30* 229–30 oðer . . . ealde] *before* wiðuten *229* L oðer . . . þuftene] AC², siue iuuenis L, *not in other MSS* 230 *before* Bi] and NP singinde] N, segginde CFT, bidden P 232 ne ne] N, ne CT eauer] A *only* 234 ne ne] A, ne CFNT 235 ȝeten] A, ȝete CFNT *after* ga] ha CN Ba] boðe NT 236 *after* nabben] heo CN heo] hore dame N 237 leoten in] CT, leten heo in N, lessent entrer F, introducat L, leote ȝe in A 238 þe ȝungre] *om.* C speoke] speoken C wið . . . bute] wiðute C mon] wepmon T ha] A *only* 239 ȝef . . . beon] A *only* 241 þet] ant do hwat C 242 of þe wummen] N, des dous femmes F, illarum L, of þe familiers T, of þe seruauntz P, *om.* C 242–3 ne . . . hire] ne beore ne bringe to heore dame C, referat domine sue L, ne bere P 243 nane] *om.* CT 246 leasunges] leasing CN 247 hare² . . . lahe] *om.* T *after* lahe] *see 249* 248–9 Hare . . . openheaued] *om.* T 248 cop] C, cotes F, hesmel N *after* isticchet] pardeuant la poitrine F ant bute] A, wiðute CF, al wiðute N 249 unleppet] C, unweawed N *after* open-heaued] Inwið . . . ihudeket (*see fn.*) C² Lah . . . habben] vt nec nimium respiciant (*after* lahe *247*) L 251 ne¹ . . . heaued] *om.* T 252 toggin] toggle T 254 mahe edwiten] puisse reproecer F, edwite NT, wite C (*alt. to* etwite C²) 256 dun] T, adun CN *after* dun] to þer eorðe N 258 hire¹] N, ham CFLT þrefter] *after* mare NT 259 upbreide] upbeide (*for* upbreide) hire N, lour reprocce F falle] fallen CF 260–1 þe wummen] ham utewið T 261 *after* eiðer] of ham NF 264 *from* sahtnesse] *MSS running:* ACFNPT 266 aga] A, ga ut CNT 267 hond þet ilke] A, þet ilke C, meismes ceste chose F, onond þet ilke N (*also interl. in different hand before* onond), hond to þat ilke T 268 þin] A, owre T, ure CFN 269 *before* Hwen] and NF 270 uuel] A, luðer CN, maluoise F, *om.* T sum² . . . nohtunge] ascune altre chose qe rien ne vaut F, sum oðerhwat T 271 tohurten] N, tohurren C(*alt. by*

APPARATUS CRITICUS

C from tohutren)T, seuerent L   275 meidnes] seruanz T
276 hwen neod is] A, ofte CFNT   279 biuoren . . . Maria] and
Aue Maria biuoren mete N   ant²] AN *only*   a] AC *only*   280 *before*
Hali] ant CFN   an] CFNT, *om.* A   282 ba] C, boðe NT   *before*
Forȝelde] and NF   þe] ceaux et celes F   283 sawle¹] soulen NF
before þe] and T   hare sawle] *om.* CF   sawle²] soulen N   284 sawles]
saule CT   285 gruseli] *conj. Tolkien;* gru`ch´esi A (ch *with general mark
of abbreviation, add. in different hand over erasure*), gruselie N, gruuesi C,
gruse T, manguent F   *after* gruseli] ȝe ANT   286 al þet] toutes
choses la ou F, alle þeo þinges þer N   291 claðÌ] CNT, a uestir F,
hure A   292 þe meidnes] þeo þat arn T   294 hehe] A, eche
CFNT   296 ant] A, ne CFNT   297 leaste lutle] CFT, lutle laste
N, leaste A   298 wummen] seruanz T   muche] god TN(god *add. in
different hand over erasure*)   299 beon] *after* ham *300* NT
300 *after* ham] *see* 299   *after* iwurset] par vostre necgligence F   ȝef
þet] A (*corr. from* þurh þet), ȝef CNT   301 Deme] T, demare N, dom
CF   Ant] AN *only*   303 riwle] riuwlen CN   ba] C, boðe NT
304 *after* lare] of religiun T   305 Ba] C (*alt. to* baþe C³), boðe NT
ant þah] A, ach CNT, fors F, þat P   306 eauer mare] T, *trs.* CN
307 ba] C, baðe TN   308 mare²] N, ma CT   312 *before* of mete]
of drunch and NT(*with* baðe *before* of)   *after* mete] et des boires F
317 earen] eare TF   ahnes] A, anes C(*corr.* C³)N, anres T
319 Amen] AFN *only*   320–35 Hwen . . . þruppe] A *only*
336 *from* Of] *MSS running:* ACFNPST   338 muchele¹] A *only*
mi muchele] A, muche CT, mon F, muchel of mine N, mout de (tens) ke
ieo ai mis entour ceo S   339 Godd hit wite] A, God hit wot N, Deu le
set CFT   do] A, to do CT, uorto don N   340 hit (. . .) forte donne]
ceste liure faire F   343 *before* Hali] and NFS   345 dreheð ant
dreaieð] C, soffrez et faites F, drieð and suffreð N, drehen oðer drehden T,
auez suffert ou ore suffrez S   hure] CFNPST, *om.* A   346 aa¹] A, ai
T, eauer CN   348 habbeð ired] readeð NP   her-on] A, þron C, en
ceste riule F, o þisse boc NST, it P   þe] ure TFS   349 *after* Aue]
Marie NS   þet swonc her-abuten] ðet makede . . . her-abuten (*see fn.*) N
her-abuten] entour ceste Riule F, entour cest escrit S   349–50 Inoh . . .
lutel] AC²N *only*   351 Explicit] AC(*del.* C²), *not in other MSS*
352–3 Iþench . . . oþre] A *only*